The Making of the American Essay

Also by John D'Agata

Halls of Fame

About a Mountain

The Lifespan of a Fact

A New History of the Essay:

The Lost Origins of the Essay

The Making of the American Essay

The Next American Essay

THE
Making of
the American
Essay

Edited and introduced by
JOHN D'AGATA

Graywolf Press

Permission acknowledgments begin on page 797

This publication is made possible, in part, by the voters of Minnesota through a Minnesota State Arts Board Operating Support grant, thanks to a legislative appropriation from the arts and cultural heritage fund, and through a grant from the Wells Fargo Foundation Minnesota. Significant support has also been provided by Target, the McKnight Foundation, Amazon.com, and other generous contributions from foundations, corporations, and individuals. To these organizations and individuals we offer our heartfelt thanks.

Published by Graywolf Press
250 Third Avenue North, Suite 600
Minneapolis, Minnesota 55401

www.graywolfpress.org

Published in the United States of America
Printed in Canada

ISBN 978-1-55597-734-4

2 4 6 8 9 7 5 3 1
First Graywolf Printing, 2016

Library of Congress Control Number: 2015953595

Cover design: Christa Schoenbrodt, Studio Haus

Make it plain.
WHITMAN

—◦—

Make it new.
POUND

—◦|◦—

Make it sweet again.
ASHBERY

—◆—

Contents

To the Reader

One summer evening, in 1908, the hay in the fields around Folsom, New Mexico, was cut and waiting for baling. The town's two hundred residents had gone to bed that night after a light rain cleared just in time for the sunset. But by midnight, when everyone was asleep, heavier clouds settled over the mountains above the town, and soon more than twenty inches of rain began to fall. Streams of it poured down the mountains all night, rushing into the fields, gathering up the hay, and carrying it to a trestle that spanned a nearby creek. The hay clumped and clogged around the railroad bridge's beams, and for a while the debris managed to chock off the surging water, but as the rain continued to fall, and as the pressure began to swell, the accidental dam of iron, mud, and hay burst onto the town, killing people in their sleep, drowning the town's livestock, crushing almost every permanent building along the way. The next morning, while surveying the flood's damage, a local cowboy noticed the bones of a very large animal protruding from the creek. The flood had washed away so much of the creekbed that previously hidden layers of earth were now exposed—ancient, secret, long-lost layers, suggesting that the animal the cowboy came upon was not only very old but probably extinct. As he inspected the bones more closely, the cowboy noticed an arrowhead lodged between two ribs, but he couldn't figure out how an arrow had killed such an animal before it was even thought that humans lived in America. The cowboy's discovery was considered so

1

incredible, in fact, that it took over a decade before any archaeologists would come to examine it. Yet by the time they did, arrowheads in nearby Clovis, New Mexico, were found in bones determined to be even older still. And quickly thereafter, artifacts were discovered in Texas, Wisconsin, Pennsylvania, and Virginia that pushed back the date for human presence in America to 14,000 B.C.E.—long preceding the Neolithic Revolution, that cultural explosion in the ancient Near East that led to the domestication of animals, the cultivation of land, the development of towns, and the beginning of civilization. What this means, say most archaeologists today, is that whatever the earliest occupants of the Americas achieved they achieved in isolation, negating the long-held belief that their only real achievement was in emigrating from the Old World with inherited skills. Indeed, the first occupants of the Americas constructed their world from scratch. They lived collectively on massive farms that they developed after clear-cutting huge tracts of land. They developed cities that held hundreds of thousands of people. They maintained an estimated twenty-five thousand miles of complex highway systems, dozens of written languages, giant athletic arenas, stone towers, observatories, libraries, schools. They created a 365-day calendar that was more accurate than any other calendar in the world. They developed the concept of zero. They perfected mummification. And in the most striking example of their independent innovations, they also invented the wheel—yet they only found a use for it as a novelty in children's toys. The obvious lesson here is that we ought to pay tribute to the talents and ambitions of America's earliest occupants, those pioneering humans who frequently fall victim to the dreamy racist stereotype of the gentle noble savage, peacefully living in unison with an uncorrupted Earth. But I have to admit that the lesson that interests me more about our earliest American ancestors is that we all apparently have a need to shape the world around us, to build it into something new, to make it into what we want. The best illustration of this comes from a creation story from Northern California. In the my-thologies of the Cahto, who live in the Pacific Coast Ranges, the world is made by two gods who spend their time design-ing mountains, trees, animals, and people, only to see them wiped away by a devastating flood. The flood doesn't come as a punishment, or a warning, or even as a lesson, but instead it seems to come because floods will sometimes come—leaving us with nothing but the opportunity to rebuild. So that's what the Cahto do. But before they reconstruct the world they lost in their creation story, the Cahto make a point of lingering on the details of the flood's devastation, noting how it methodically disassembled the world around them by eras-ing each part of it, piece by piece by piece: the mountains, trees, birds, people, weather, dirt, and light. What we're left with, momentarily, is just the shell of what had been there, the physical shape of nothingness, an emblem of the ineffable that we're nevertheless allowed to see and smell and touch. The Cahto want us to palpably know what nothing really means, because the meaning behind "Creation" is creativity itself, the power and the pleasure of making. What we all have is a world, the Cahto seem to say, but what we do with it is create. To my ear, this is the predicament of every essay too, situated as essays always are between chance and contrivance, between the given and the made. The world provides non-fiction, and humans provide the rest. The essays in this anthology have an appetite for the rest—for what else nonfiction can do. They are essays with a penchant for making new things, regardless of expectation, regardless of consequence. Let floods come, let dreams come, let something unexpected overtake us and make us new. The world, we all know, is already a nonfiction.

Let the essay be what we make of it.

The Making of the American Essay

✦

Creation

Water went they say. Land was not they say. Water only then, mountains were not, they say. Stones were not they say. Fish were not they say. Deer were not they say. Grizzlies were not they say. Panthers were not they say. Wolves were not they say. People were washed away they say. Grizzlies were washed away they say. Panthers were washed away they say. Deer were washed away they say. Coyotes were not then they say. Ravens were not they say. Herons were not they say. Woodpeckers were not they say. Then wrens were not they say. Then hummingbirds were not they say. Then otters were not they say. Then jack rabbits, grey squirrels were not they say. Then long-eared mice were not they say. Then wind was not they say. Then snow was not they say. Then rain was not they say. Then it didn't thunder they say. Then trees were not when it didn't thunder they say. It didn't lighten they say. Then clouds were not they say. Fog was not they say. It didn't appear they say. Stars were not they say. It was very dark.

—Anonymous, Cahto Indian, 1000 C.E.

1630

Early in the seventeenth century, when a group of Europeans decided to remake their world, the first thing they did was gather up ingredients. These included 20,000 biscuits, 600 salted codfish, 200 dried ox tongues, 320 chickens, 140 cows, 130 sheep, and about 60 horses. They packed 10,000 gallons of ale and 3,000 gallons of water. They filled barrels and crates with hammers and spoons, shovels and skillets and pitchforks and axes and cauldrons and muskets and candles and clothes. Among them was a handful of clergy, a pair of midwives, and an eighteen-year-old writer who was fluent in Greek, Latin, Hebrew, and French, and who had read nearly everything in English literature at the time. And now, three months after leaving her home in England, Anne Bradstreet is clinging to the wet seat of a boat being rowed away from the ship that carried her across the Atlantic Ocean. They've all come to America because the Reformation in England was not re-formed enough for them, and they want to build a world in which they can worship their own god without the inter-ference of a pope or priests or rituals that they think are bordering on the ungodly. And so now they've arrived, in the blazing heat of the summer, and at the shore of a town that was founded a year earlier by three hundred people whom they had paid to clear forests, build homes, and plant fields that could be ready for them to harvest upon arrival. Behind Bradstreet's rowboat is a fleet of twelve ships that are filled to the brim with eight hundred affluent people, ready to disembark and start making this world theirs. However, as they row closer to the shore of New Salem, the immigrants see a landscape devoid of any houses—let alone chimneys, shops, hedgerows, streets. Wandering around the shore are half as many people as they'd originally sent over, and they are sweaty with famine, piercingly skeletal, dazed, frightened, and hanging on with desperation to the edge of the new continent. Bradstreet and the other settlers don't even bother unpacking. They return to their ships, sail a few miles south, and try to start their own town in a place they call "New Towne." Within a year, however, Anne Bradstreet moves again with her family . . . And then again . . . And then again . . . In a ten-year period, Bradstreet will help settle five new towns, raise eight young children, fight off tuberculosis, and somehow still manage to produce more essays, aphorisms, poems, and letters than any other English writer of her time—either male or female, from either the New World or the Old. "A prosperous state makes a secure Christian," she once wrote, "but adversity makes him consider." If there's one thing American history can teach us about the essay, it's that sometimes the best intentions are undermined by better experiments.

For My Dear Son
Simon Bradstreet

Parents perpetuate their lives in their posterity and their manners; in their imitation children do naturally rather follow the failings than the virtues of their predecessors, but I am persuaded better things of you. You once desired me to leave something for you in writing that you might look upon, when you should see me no more; I could think of nothing more fit for you nor of more ease to myself than these short meditations following. Such as they are, I bequeath to you; small legacies are accepted by true friends, much more by dutiful children. I have avoided encroaching upon others' conceptions because I would leave you nothing but mine own, though in value they fall short of all in this kind; yet I presume they will be better prized by you for the author's sake. The Lord bless you with grace here and crown you with glory hereafter, that I may meet you with rejoicing at that great day of appearing, which is the continual prayer of your affectionate mother, A. B.

—◆—

There is no new thing under the sun: there is nothing that can be said or done that has not been said or done before.

—◆—

There is no object that we see, no action that we do, no good that we enjoy, no evil that we feel or fear, but we may make some spiritual advantage of. And he that makes such improvement is wise as well as pious.

—◆—

Many can speak well, but few can do well. We are better scholars in the theory than the practice.

—◆—

Youth is the time of getting, middle age of improving and old age of spending; a negligent youth is usually attended by an ignorant middle age, and both by an empty old age. He that hath nothing to feed on but vanity and lies must needs lie down in the bed of sorrow.

—◆—

A ship that bears much sail and little or no ballast is easily overset, and that man whose head hath great abilities and his heart little or no grace is in danger of foundering.

—◆—

It is reported of the peacock that, priding himself in his gay feathers, he ruffles them up, but spying his black feet, he soon lets fall his plumes; so he that glories in his gifts and adornings should look upon his corruptions, and that will damp his high thoughts.

—◆—

Downy beds make drowsy persons, but hard lodging keeps the eyes open; a prosperous state makes a secure Christian, but adversity makes him consider.

—◆—

Sweet words are like honey: a little may refresh, but too much gluts the stomach.

—◆—

Diverse children have their different natures: some are like flesh which nothing but salt will keep from putrefaction, some again like tender fruits that are best preserved with sugar. Those parents are wise that can fit their nurture according to their nature.

—◆—

Authority without wisdom is like a heavy axe without an edge: fitter to bruise than polish.

—❦—

If we had no winter, the spring would not be so pleasant; if we did not sometimes taste of adversity, prosperity would not be so welcome.

—❦—

Few men are so humble as not to be proud of their abilities, and nothing will abase them more than this: what hast thou, but what thou hast received? Come, give an account of thy stewardship.

—❦—

Corn, till it have past through the mill and been ground to powder, is not fit for bread. God so deals with his servants: he grinds them with grief and pain till they turn to dust, and then are they fit manchet for his mansion.

—❦—

Lightning doth usually precede thunder, and storms rain, and strokes do not often fall till after threatening.

—❦—

Fire hath its force abated by water, not by wind, and anger must be allayed by cold words and not by blustering threats.

—❦—

All weak and diseased bodies have hourly mementos of their mortality, but the soundest of men, have likewise their nightly monitor by the emblem of death, which is their sleep (for so is death often called), and not only their death, but their grave is lively represented before their eyes by beholding their bed, the morning may mind them of the resurrection, and the sun approaching of the appearing of the Sun of righteousness, at whose coming they shall all rise out of their beds, the long night shall fly away, and the day of eternity shall never end. Seeing these things must be, what manner of persons ought we to be, in all good conversation?

1682

So when exactly does the American essay begin to experiment? On February 10, 1676, a band of fifteen hundred Indians from the Wampanoag tribe attacked the village of Lancaster, a tiny outpost in the middle of Massachusetts that consisted of fifty-five families. Nearly a quarter of the town's residents were killed in the raid, and another twenty-four were taken captive as slaves. Among those who were taken was Mary Rowlandson, the thirty-nine-year-old wife of Lancaster's minister and the mother of three children, who were kidnapped as well. Because she was related to a town leader, Rowlandson was eventually ransomed back to her family, but not before being marched for three snowy months through the wilderness of the new and foreign world. "The portion of some is to have their afflictions by drops, now one drop and then another," Rowlandson later wrote about her experience. "But the dregs of the cup, the wine of astonishment, like a sweeping rain that leaveth no food, did the Lord prepare to be my portion." Rowlandson eventually published her reflections on that experience in a book that became wildly popular throughout New England. It is filled with what we might expect from a white Christian settler in seventeenth-century America: nearly every ordeal that Rowlandson describes is adroitly paired with a biblical passage revealing the religious significance in the brutality of her experience. "I have learned to look beyond present and smaller troubles," she writes, "and to be quieted under them."

And no doubt this is what made her book so popular, for in keeping with Puritan teaching, the book enacts a repudiation of the "vanity of the world," an acceptance of Rowlandson's role as "a vessel of the Lord," who guides her, magically, "through the wilderness . . . into safety." Indeed, the Puritan spiritual leader Increase Mather wrote a preface to the book in which he emphasizes more than anything else the text's miraculous ability to turn deeply personal experiences into relevant Puritan teachings—or, as Mather puts it, how "to talk of God's acts, and to speak of and publish His wonderful works." According to Mather, Rowlandson made the personal public, in other words. But not just public: she made it conveniently useful propaganda too. Orthodox spiritual leaders like Increase Mather taught their New World congregants that the Indians were the instruments of Satan, which meant that the kidnappings that proliferated in seventeenth-century New England were not the predictable outcome of white infringement on native lands but rather proof of God's efforts to test his children's faith. In the title he imposed on Rowlandson's book, Mather made this idea explicit:

The Sovereignty and Goodness of God, Together with the Faithfulness of His Promises Displayed: Being a Narrative of the Captivity and Restoration of Mrs. Mary Rowlandson, Commended by Her to All Who Desire to Know the Lord's Doings to, and Dealings with, Her

The title Rowlandson herself originally gave to the book emphasizes an entirely different intention:

> A True History of the Captivity and Restoration of Mrs. Mary Rowlandson, a Minister's Wife in New-England: Wherein Is Set Forth the Cruel and Inhumane Usage She Underwent amongst the Heathens for Eleven Weeks Time, and Her Deliverance from Them

Hers is a title that emphasizes experience over knowing. By foregrounding herself not only as the protagonist in the book but as a woman in the world—"Mrs. Mary Rowlandson, a Minister's Wife in New-England"—by detailing her affliction—"Cruel and Inhumane Usage"—by specifying a time frame—"Eleven Weeks Time"—and perhaps most important by acknowledging her antagonists before she does her savior—"the Heathens . . . and Her Deliverance from Them"—Rowlandson creates a concrete framework through which her captivity can be embodied, felt, and embraced as more than merely an existential threat. Indeed, her "deliverance" is even recast here as a grammatically dependent clause, thus resetting the terms by which she wants her story read: yes, Rowlandson rediscovers her faith while she is being held captive, but not before she has to watch her own child starve, not before she steals food from a child to save herself, not before she realizes, with heartbreaking clarity, that she doesn't miss her husband, that the heathens are not all bad, that sometimes they are kind, that maybe the war is wrong. "I can remember the time,"

Rowlandson writes in her book, "when I used to sleep quietly without workings in my thoughts, whole nights together, but now it is other ways with me." This other voice that occasionally emerges from the book is quiet, hesitant, and tinged with skepticism, and when it's set against the confidence that's exhibited elsewhere, a troubling and pervasive dissonance is exposed, a kind of rupture that we can imagine Rowlandson tumbling through in the book, trapped within that rift between knowing how to deflect a difficult personal experience with elegantly abstract Christian exegesis, and not knowing how to do anything at all but open up her eyes with resignation to the world. I think this is the first great essay that America produced.

The Narrative of the Captivity

The First Remove

Now away we must go with those barbarous creatures, with our bodies wounded and bleeding, and our hearts no less than our bodies. About a mile we went that night, up upon a hill within sight of the town, where they intended to lodge. There was hard by a vacant house (deserted by the English before, for fear of the Indians). I asked them whether I might not lodge in the house that night to which they answered, What will you love English men still? This was the dolefullest night that ever my eyes saw. Oh the roaring, and singing and dancing, and yelling of those black creatures in the night, which made the place a lively resemblance of hell. And as miserable was the waste that was there made, of horses, cattle, sheep, swine, calves, lambs, roasting pigs, and fowl (which they had plundered in the town) some roasting, some lying and burning, and some boiling to feed our merciless enemies; who were joyful enough though we were disconsolate. To add to the dolefulness of the former day, and the dismalness of the present night: my thoughts ran upon my losses and sad bereaved condition. All was gone, my husband gone (at least separated from me, he being in the Bay; and to add to my grief, the Indians told me they would kill him as he came homeward) my children gone, my relations and friends gone, our house and home and all our comforts within doors, and without, all was gone (except my life) and I knew not but the next moment that might go too. There remained nothing to me but one poor wounded babe, and it seemed at present worse than death that it was in such a pitiful condition, bespeaking compassion, and I had no refreshing for it, nor suitable things to revive it. Little do many think what is the savageness and brutishness of this barbarous enemy, aye even those that seem to profess more than others among them, when the English have fallen into their hands.

Those seven that were killed at Lancaster the summer before upon a Sabbath day, and the one that was afterward killed upon a week day, were slain and mangled in a barbarous manner, by One-eyed John, and Marlborough's praying Indians, which Captain Mosely brought to Boston, as the Indians told me.

The Second Remove

But now, the next morning, I must turn my back upon the town, and travel with them into the vast and desolate wilderness, I knew not whither. It is not my tongue, or pen can express the sorrows of my heart, and bitterness of my spirit, that I had at this departure: but God was with me, in a wonderful manner, carrying me along, and bearing up my spirit, that it did not quite fail. One of the Indians carried my poor wounded babe upon a horse, it went moaning all along, I shall die, I shall die. I went on foot after it, with sorrow that cannot be expressed. At length I took it off the horse, and carried it in my arms till my strength failed, and I fell down with it: Then they set me upon a horse with my wounded child in my lap, and there being no furniture upon the horse's back, as we were going down a steep hill, we both fell over the horse's head, at which they like inhuman creatures laughed, and rejoiced to see it, though I thought we should there have ended our days, as overcome with so many difficulties. But the Lord renewed my strength still, and carried me along, that I might see more of his power; yea, so much that I could never have thought of, had I not experienced it.

After this it quickly began to snow, and when night came on, they stopped: and now down I must sit in the snow, by a little fire, and a few boughs behind me, with my sick child in my lap; and calling much for water, being now (through the wound) fallen into a violent fever. My own wound also growing so stiff, that I could scarce sit down or rise up; yet so it must be, that I must sit all this cold winter night upon the cold snowy ground, with my sick child in my arms, looking that every hour would be the last of its life; and having no Christian friend near me, either to comfort or help me. Oh, I may see the wonderful power of God, that my spirit did not utterly sink under my affliction: still the Lord upheld me with his gracious and merciful spirit, and we were both alive to see the light of the next morning.

The Third Remove

The morning being come, they prepared to go on their way. One of the Indians got up upon a horse, and they set me up behind him, with my poor sick babe in my lap. A very wearisome and tedious day I had of it; what with my own wound, and my child's being so exceeding sick, and in a lamentable condition with her wound. It may be easily judged what a poor feeble condition we were in, there being not the least crumb of refreshing that came within either of our mouths, from Wednesday night to Saturday night, except only a little cold water. This day in the afternoon, about an hour by sun, we came to the place where they intended, *viz.* an Indian town called Wenimesset, northward of Quabaug. When we were come, Oh the number of pagans (now merciless enemies) that there came about me, that I may say as David, Psalms 27.13, *I had fainted, unless I had believed,* etc. The next day was the Sabbath: I then remembered how careless I had been of God's holy time, how many Sabbaths I had lost and misspent, and how evilly I had walked in God's sight; which lay so close unto my spirit, that it was easy for me to see how righteous it was with God to cut off the thread of my life, and cast me out of his presence forever. Yet the Lord still showed mercy to me, and upheld me; and as he wounded me with one hand, so he healed me with the other. This day there came to me one Robert Pepper (a man belonging to Roxbury) who was taken in Captain Beers his fight, and had been now a considerable time with the Indians; and up with them almost as far as Albany, to see King Philip, as he told me, and was now very lately come into these parts. Hearing, I say, that I was in this Indian town, he obtained leave to come and see me. He told me, he himself was wounded in the leg at Captain Beers his fight; and was not able some time to go, but as they carried him, and as he took oaken leaves and laid to his wound, and through the blessing of God he was able to travel again. Then I took oaken leaves and laid to my side, and with the blessing of God it cured me also; yet before the cure was wrought, I may say, as it is in Psalms 38.5–6, *My wounds stink and are corrupt, I am bowed down greatly, I go mourning all the day long.* I sat much alone with a poor wounded child in my lap, which moaned night and day, having nothing to revive the body, or cheer the spirits of her, but instead of that, sometimes one Indian would come and tell me in one hour, that your master will knock your child in the head, and then a second, and then a third, your master will quickly knock your child in the head.

This was the comfort I had from them, miserable comforters are ye all, as he said. Thus nine days I sat upon my knees, with my babe in my lap, till my flesh was raw again; my child being even ready to depart this sorrowful world, they bade me carry it out to another wigwam (I suppose because they would not be troubled with such spectacles) whither I went with a very heavy heart, and down I sat with the picture of death in my lap. About two hours in the night, my sweet babe like a lamb departed this life, on Feb. 18, 1675, it being about six years, and five months old. It was nine days from the first wounding, in this miserable condition, without any refreshing of one nature or other, except a little cold water. I cannot, but take notice, how at another time I could not bear to be in the room where any dead person was, but now the case is changed; I must and could lie down by my dead babe, side by side all the night after. I have thought since of the wonderful goodness of God to me, in preserving me in the use of my reason and senses, in that distressed time, that I did not use wicked and violent means to end my own miserable life. In the morning, when they understood that my child was dead they sent for me home to my master's wigwam: (by my master in this writing, must be understood Quinnapin, who was a sagamore, and married King Philip's wife's sister; not that he first took me, but I was sold to him by another Narragansett Indian, who took me when first I came out of the garrison). I went to take up my dead child in my arms to carry it with me, but they bid me let it alone: there was no resisting, but go I must and leave it. When I had been at my master's wigwam, I took the first opportunity I could get, to go look after my dead child: when I came I asked them what they had done with it? Then they told me it was upon the hill: then they went and showed me where it was, where I saw the ground was newly digged, and there they told me they had buried it: there I left that child in the wilderness, and must commit it, and myself also in this wilderness condition, to Him who is above all. God having taken away this dear child, I went to see my daughter Mary, who was at this same Indian town, at a wigwam not very far off, though we had little liberty or opportunity to see one another. She was about ten years old, and taken from the door at first by a Praying Indian and afterward sold for a gun. When I came in sight, she would fall a-weeping; at which they were provoked, and would not let me come near her, but bade me begone; which was a heart-cutting word to me. I had one child dead, another in the wilderness, I knew not where, the third they would not let me come near to:

Me (as he said) *have ye bereaved of my children, Joseph is not, and Simeon is not, and ye will take Benjamin also, all these things are against me.* I could not sit still in this condition, but kept walking from place to another. And as I was going along, my heart was even overwhelmed with the thoughts of my condition, and that I should have children, and a nation which I knew not ruled over them. Whereupon I earnestly entreated the Lord, that He would consider my low estate, and show me a token for good, and if it were His blessed will, some sign and hope of some relief. And indeed quickly the Lord answered, in some measure, my poor prayers; for as I was going up and down mourning and lamenting my condition, my son came to me, and asked me how I did; I had not seen him before, since the destruction of the town, and I knew not where he was, till I was informed by himself, that he was amongst a smaller parcel of Indians, whose place was about six miles off; with tears in his eyes, he asked me whether his sister Sarah was dead; and told me he had seen his sister Mary; and prayed me, that I would not be troubled in reference to himself. The occasion of his coming to see me at this time, was this: there was, as I said, about six miles from us, a small plantation of Indians, where it seems he had been during his captivity: and at this time, there were some forces of the Indians gathered out of our company, and some also from them (among whom was my son's master) to go to assault and burn Medfield: In this time of the absence of his master, his dame brought him to see me. I took this to be some gracious answer to my earnest and unfeigned desire. The next day, viz, to this, the Indians returned from Medfield, all the company, for those that belonged to the other small company, came through the town that now we were at. But before they came to us, Oh! the outrageous roaring and whooping that there was: They began their din about a mile before they came to us. By their noise and whooping they signified how many they had destroyed (which was at that time twenty-three). Those that were with us at home, were gathered together as soon as they heard the whooping, and every time that the other went over their number, these at home gave a shout, that the very earth rung again: and thus they continued till those that had been upon the expedition were come up to the sagamore's wigwam; and then, Oh, the hideous insulting and triumphing that there was over some Englishmen's scalps that they had taken (as their manner is) and brought with them. I cannot but take notice of the wonderful mercy of God to me in those afflictions, in sending me a Bible. One of the Indians that came from Medfield fight, had brought some plunder, came to me, and asked me, if I would have a Bible, he had got one in his basket. I was glad of it, and asked him, whether he thought the Indians would let me read? He answered, Yes: So I took the Bible, and in that melancholy time, it came into my mind to read first the 28th Chapter of Deuteronomy, which I did, and when I had read it, my dark heart wrought on this manner, That there was no mercy for me, that the blessings were gone, and the curses come in their room, and that I had lost my opportunity. But the Lord helped me still to go on reading till I came to Chapter 30 the seven first verses, where I found, there was mercy promised again, if we would return to him by repentance; and though we were scattered from one end of the earth to the other, yet the Lord would gather us together, and turn all those curses upon our enemies. I do not desire to live to forget this scripture, and what comfort it was to me.

Now the Indians began to talk of removing from this place, some one way, and some another. There were now besides myself nine English captives in this place (all of them children, except one woman). I got an opportunity to go and take my leave of them; they being to go one way, and I another, I asked them whether they were earnest with God for deliverance, they told me they did as they were able, and it was some comfort to me, that the Lord stirred up children to look to Him. The woman *viz.* Goodwife Joslin told me, she should never see me again, and that she could find in her heart to run away; I wished her not to run away by any means, for we were near thirty miles from any English town, and she very big with child, and had but one week to reckon; and another child in her arms, two years old, and bad rivers there were to go over, and we were feeble, with our poor and coarse entertainment. I had my Bible with me, I pulled it out, and asked her whether she would read; we opened the Bible and lighted on Psalm 27, in which Psalm we especially took notice of that, *ver. ult., Wait on the Lord, Be of good courage, and he shall strengthen thine heart, wait I say on the Lord.*

The Fourth Remove

And now I must part with that little company I had. Here I parted from my daughter Mary (whom I never saw again till I saw her in Dorchester, returned from captivity), and from four little cousins and neighbors, some of which I never saw afterward: the Lord only knows the end of them. Amongst them also was that poor woman before mentioned, who came to a sad end, as some of the company told me in my travel: she having much grief upon her spirit, about her miserable condition, being so near her time, she would be often asking the Indians to let her go home; they not being willing to that, and yet vexed with her importunity, gathered a great company together about her, and stripped her naked, and set her in the midst of them; and when they had sung and danced about her (in their hellish manner) as long as they pleased, they knocked her on head, and the child in her arms with her: when they had done that they made a fire and put them both into it, and told the other children that were with them that if they attempted to go home, they would serve them in like manner: the children said, she did not shed one tear, but prayed all the while. But to return to my own journey; we travelled about half a day or little more, and came to a desolate place in the wilderness, where there were no wigwams or inhabitants before; we came about the middle of the afternoon to this place, cold and wet, and snowy, and hungry, and weary, and no refreshing, for man, but the cold ground to sit on, and our poor Indian cheer.

Heart-aching thoughts here I had about my poor children, who were scattered up and down among the wild beasts of the forest: my head was light and dizzy (either through hunger or hard lodging, or trouble or all together) my knees feeble, my body raw by sitting double night and day, that I cannot express to man the affliction that lay upon my spirit, but the Lord helped me at that time to express it to himself. I opened my Bible to read, and the Lord brought that precious scripture to me, Jeremiah 31 16 *Thus saith the Lord, refrain thy voice from weeping, and thine eyes from tears, for thy work shall be rewarded, and they shall come again from the land of the enemy.* This was a sweet cordial to me, when I was ready to faint, many and many a time have I sat down and wept sweetly over this scripture. At this place we continued about four days.

The Fifth Remove

The occasion (as I thought) of their moving at this time, was, the English army, it being near and following them: for they went, as if they had gone for their lives, for some considerable way, and then they made a stop, and chose some of their stoutest men, and sent them back to hold the English army in play whilst the rest escaped: and then, like Jehu, they marched on furiously, with their old, and with their young: some carried their old decrepit mothers, some carried one, and some another. Four of them carried a great Indian upon a bier; but going through a thick wood with him, they were hindered, and could make no haste; whereupon they took him upon their backs, and carried him, one at a time, till they came to Baquag River. Upon a Friday, a little after noon we came to this river. When all the company was come up, and were gathered together, I thought to count the number of them, but they were so many, and being somewhat in motion, it was beyond my skill. In this travel, because of my wound, I was somewhat favored in my load; I carried only my knitting work and two quarts of parched meal: being very faint I asked my mistress to give me one spoonful of the meal, but she would not give me a taste. They quickly fell to cutting dry trees, to make rafts to carry them over the river: and soon my turn came to go over: by the advantage of some brush which they had laid upon the raft to sit upon, I did not wet my foot (which many of themselves at the other end were mid-leg deep) which cannot but be acknowledged as a favor of God to my weakened body, it being a very cold time. I was not before acquainted with such kind of doings or dangers. *When thou passeth through the waters I will be with thee, and through the rivers they shall not overflow thee,* Isaiah 43.2. A certain number of us got over the river that night, but it was the night after the Sabbath before all the company was got over. On the Saturday they boiled an old horse's leg which they had got, and so we drank of the broth, as soon as they thought it was ready, and when it was almost all gone, they filled it up again.

The first week of my being among them, I hardly ate anything; the second week, I found my stomach grow very faint for want of something; and yet it was very hard to get down their filthy trash: but the third week, though I could think how formerly my stomach would turn against this or that, and I could starve and die before I could eat such things, yet they were sweet and savory to my taste. I was at this time knitting a pair of white cotton stockings for my mistress; and had not yet wrought upon a Sabbath day; when the Sabbath came they bade me go to work. I told them it was the Sabbath day, and desired them to let me rest, and told them I would do as much more tomorrow; to which they answered me, they would break my face. And here I cannot but take notice of the strange providence of God in preserving the heathen: they were many hundreds, old and young, some sick, and some lame, many had papooses at their backs, the greatest number at this time with us were squaws, and they travelled with all they had, bag and baggage, and yet they got over this river aforesaid; and on Monday they set their wigwams on fire, and away they went: on that very day came the English army after them to this river, and saw the smoke of their wigwams, and yet this river put a stop to them. God did not give them courage or activity to go over after us; we were not ready for so great a mercy as victory and deliverance; if we had been, God would have found out a way for the English to have passed this river, as well as for the Indians with their squaws and children, and all their luggage. *Oh, that my people had hearkened to me, and Israel had walked in my ways, I should soon have subdued their enemies, and turned my hand against their adversaries,* Psalms 81.13–14.

The Sixth Remove

On Monday (as I said) they set their wigwams on fire, and went away. It was a cold morning, and before us there was a great brook with ice on it; some waded through it, up to the knees and higher, but others went till they came to a beaver dam, and I amongst them, where through the good providence of God, I did not wet my foot. I went along that day mourning and lamenting, leaving farther my own country, and travelling into the vast and howling wilderness, and I understood something of Lot's wife's temptation, when she looked back: we came that day to a great swamp, by the side of which we took up our lodging that night. When I came to the brow of the hill, that looked toward the swamp, I thought we had been come to a great Indian town (though there were none but our own company). The Indians were as thick as the trees: it seemed as if there had been a thousand hatchets going at once: if one looked before one, there was nothing but Indians, and behind one, nothing but Indians, and so on either hand, I myself in the midst, and no Christian soul near me, and yet how hath the Lord preserved me in safety! Oh the experience that I have had of the goodness of God, to me and mine!

The Seventh Remove

After a restless and hungry night there, we had a wearisome time of it the next day. The swamp by which we lay, was, as it were, a deep dungeon, and an exceeding high and steep hill before it. Before I got to the top of the hill, I thought my heart and legs, and all would have broken, and failed me.

What through faintness and soreness of body, it was a grievous day of travel to me. As we went along, I saw a place where English cattle had been: that was comfort to me, such as it was: quickly after that we came to an English path, which so took with me, that I thought I could have freely lain down and died. That day, a little after noon, we came to Squakeag, where the Indians quickly spread themselves over the deserted English fields, gleaning what they could find; some picked up ears of wheat that were crickled down, some found ears of Indian corn, some found ground nuts, and others sheaves of wheat that were frozen together in the shock, and went to threshing of them out. Myself got two ears of Indian corn, and whilst I did but turn my back, one of them was stolen from me, which much troubled me. There came an Indian to them at that time, with a basket of horse liver. I asked him to give me a piece: What, says he, can you eat horse liver? I told him, I would try, if he would give a piece, which he did, and I laid it on the coals to roast; but before it was half ready they got half of it away from me, so that I was fain to take the rest and eat it as it was, with the blood about my mouth, and yet a savory bit it was to me: *for to the hungry soul, every bitter thing is sweet.* A solemn sight methought it was, to see fields of wheat and Indian corn forsaken and spoiled: and the remainders of them to be food for our merciless enemies. That night we had a mess of wheat for our supper.

The Eighth Remove

On the morrow morning we must go over the river, *i.e.* Connecticut, to meet with King Philip; two canoes full, they had carried over, the next turn I myself was to go; but as my foot was upon the canoe to step in, there was a sudden outcry among them, and I must step back; and instead of going over the river, I must go four or five miles up the river farther northward. Some of the Indians ran one way, and some another. The cause of this rout was, as I thought, their espying some English scouts, who were thereabout. In this travel up the river, about noon the company made a stop, and sat down; some to eat, and others to rest them. As I sat amongst them, musing of things past, my son Joseph unexpectedly came to me: we asked of each other's welfare, bemoaning our doleful condition, and the change that had come upon us. We had husband and father, and children, and sisters, and friends, and relations, and house, and home, and many comforts of this life: but now we may say, as Job, *Naked came I out of my mother's womb, and naked shall I return: the Lord gave, and the Lord hath taken away, blessed be the name of the Lord.* I asked him whether he would read; he told me he earnestly desired it. I gave him my Bible, and he lighted upon that comfortable scripture, Psalms 118.17–18, *I shall not die but live, and declare the works of the Lord: the Lord hath chastened me sore, yet he hath not given me over to death.* Look here, mother (says he), did you read this? And here I may take occasion to mention one principal ground of my setting forth these lines: even as the psalmist says, To declare the works of the Lord, and His wonderful power in carrying us along, preserving us in the wilderness, while under the enemy's hand, and returning of us in safety again, and His goodness in bringing to my hand so many comfortable and suitable scriptures in my distress. But to return, we travelled on till night; and in the morning, we must go over the river to Philip's crew. When I was in the canoe, I could not but be amazed at the numerous crew of pagans that were on the bank on the other side. When I came ashore, they gathered all about me, I sitting alone in the midst: I observed they asked one another questions, and laughed, and rejoiced over their gains and victories. Then my heart began to fail: and I fell a-weeping, which was the first time to my remembrance, that I wept before them. Although I had met with so much affliction, and my heart was many times ready to break, yet could I not shed one tear in their sight: but rather had been all this while in a maze, and like one astonished: but now I may say as Psalms 137.1, *By the rivers of Babylon, there we sat down: yea, we wept when we remembered Zion.* There one of them asked me, why I wept, I could hardly tell what to say: yet I answered, they would kill me. No, said he, none will hurt you. Then came one of them and gave me two spoonfuls of meal to comfort me, and another gave me half a pint of peas; which was more worth than many bushels at another time. Then I went to see King Philip, he bade me come in and sit down, and asked me whether I would smoke (a usual compliment nowadays amongst saints and sinners) but this no way suited me. For though I had formerly used tobacco, yet I had left it ever since I was first taken. It seems to be a bait, the devil lays to make men lose their precious time: I remember with shame, how formerly, when I had taken two or three pipes, I was presently ready for another, such a bewitching thing it is: but I thank God, he has now given me power over it; surely there are many who may be better employed than to lie sucking a stinking tobacco pipe.

Now the Indians gather their forces to go against Northampton: overnight one went about yelling and hooting to give notice of the design. Whereupon they fell to boiling of ground nuts, and parching of corn (as many as had it) for their provision: and in the morning away they went. During my abode in this place, Philip spake to me to make a shirt for his boy, which I did, for which he gave me a shilling: I offered the money to my master, but he bade me keep it: and with it I bought a piece of horse flesh. Afterwards he asked me to make a cap for his boy, for which he invited me to dinner. I went, and he gave me a pancake, about as big as two fingers; it was made of parched wheat, beaten, and fried in bear's grease, but I thought I never tasted pleasanter meat in my life. There was a squaw who spake to me to make a shirt for her sannup, for which she gave me a piece of bear. Another asked me to knit a pair of stockings, for which she gave me a quart of peas: I boiled my peas and bear together, and invited my master and mistress to dinner, but the proud gossip, because I served them both in one dish, would eat nothing, except one bit that he gave her upon the point of his knife. Hearing that my son was come to this place, I went to see him, and found him lying flat upon the ground: I asked him how he could sleep so? He answered me, that he was not asleep, but at prayer; and lay so, that they might not observe what he was doing. I pray God he may remember these things now he is returned in safety. At this place (the sun now getting higher) what with the beams and heat of the sun, and the smoke of the wigwams, I thought I should have been blind. I could scarce discern one wigwam from another. There was here one Mary Thurston of Medfield, who seeing how it was with me, lent me a hat to wear: but as soon as I was gone, the squaw (who owned that Mary Thurston) came running after me, and got it away again. Here was the squaw that gave me one spoonful of meal. I put it in my pocket to keep it safe: yet notwithstanding somebody stole it, but put five Indian corns in the room of it: which corns were the greatest provisions I had in my travel for one day.

The Indians returning from Northampton, brought with them some horses, and sheep, and other things which they had taken: I desired them, that they would carry me to Albany, upon one of those horses, and sell me for powder: for so they had sometimes discoursed. I was utterly hopeless of getting home on foot, the way that I came. I could hardly bear to think of the many weary steps I had taken, to come to this place.

The Ninth Remove

But instead of going either to Albany or homeward, we must go five miles up the river, and then go over it. Here we abode a while. Here lived a sorry Indian, who spoke to me to make him a shirt. When I had done it, he would pay me nothing. But he living by the riverside, where I often went to fetch water, I would often be putting of him in mind, and calling for my pay: at last he told me if I would make another shirt, for a papoose not yet born, he would give me a knife, which he did when I had done it. I carried the knife in, and my master asked me to give it him, and I was not a little glad that I had anything that they would accept of, and be pleased with. When we were at this place, my master's maid came home, she had been gone three weeks into the Narragansett country, to fetch corn, where they had stored up some in the ground: she brought home about a peck and half of corn. This was about the time that their great captain, Naananto, was killed in the Narragansett country. My son being now about a mile from me, I asked liberty to go and see him, they bade me go, and away I went: but quickly lost myself, travelling over hills and through swamps, and could not find the way to him. And I cannot but admire at the wonderful power and goodness of God to me, in that, though I was gone from home, and met with all sorts of Indians, and those I had no knowledge of, and there being no Christian soul near me; yet not one of them offered the least imaginable miscarriage to me. I turned homeward again, and met with my master, he showed me the way to my son: when I came to him I found him not well: and withall he had a boil on his side, which much troubled him: we bemoaned one another a while, as the Lord helped us, and then I returned again. When I was returned, I found myself as unsatisfied as I was before. I went up and down mourning and lamenting: and my spirit was ready to sink, with the thoughts of my poor children: my son was ill, and I could not but think of his mournful looks, and no Christian friend was near him, to do any office of love for him, either for soul or body. And my poor girl, I knew not where she was, nor whether she was sick, or well, or alive, or dead. I repaired under these thoughts to my Bible (my great comfort in that time) and that scripture came to my hand, *Cast thy burden upon the Lord, and He shall sustain thee* (Ps. 55.22).

But I was fain to go and look after something to satisfy my hunger, and going among the wigwams, I went into one, and there found a squaw who showed herself very kind to me, and gave me a piece of bear. I put it into my pocket, and came home, but could not find an opportunity to broil it, for fear they would get it from me, and there it lay all that day and night in my stinking pocket. In the morning I went to the same squaw, who had a kettle of ground nuts boiling: I asked her to let me boil my piece of bear in her kettle, which she did, and gave me some ground nuts to eat with it: and I cannot but think how pleasant it was to me. I have sometime seen bear baked very handsomely among the English, and some like it, but the thought that it was bear, made me tremble: but now that was savory to me that one would think was enough to turn the stomach of a brute creature.

One bitter cold day, I could find no room to sit down before the fire: I went out, and could not tell what to do, but I went into another wigwam, where they were also sitting around the fire, but the squaw laid a skin for me, and bade me sit down, and gave me some ground nuts, and bade me come again: and told me they would buy me, if they were able, and yet these were strangers to me that I never saw before.

The Tenth Remove

That day a small part of the company removed about three-quarters of a mile, intending further the next day. When they came to the place where they intended to lodge, and had pitched their wigwams, being hungry I went again back to the place we were before at, to get something to eat: being encouraged by the squaw's kindness, who bade me come again; when I was there, there came an Indian to look after me, who when he had found me, kicked me all along: I went home and found venison roasting that night, but they would not give me one bit of it. Sometimes I met with favor, and sometimes with nothing but frowns.

The Eleventh Remove

The next day in the morning they took their travel, intending a day's journey up the river. I took my load at my back, and quickly we came to wade over the river: and passed over tiresome and wearisome hills. One hill was so steep that I was fain to creep up upon my knees, and to hold by the twigs and bushes to keep myself from falling backward. My head also was so light, that I usually reeled as I went; but I hope all these wearisome steps that I have taken, are but a forewarning to me of the heavenly rest. *I know, O Lord, that thy judgments are right, and that thou in faithfulness hast afflicted me* (Ps. 119.75).

The Twelfth Remove

It was upon a Sabbath day morning, that they prepared for their travel. This morning I asked my master whether he would sell me to my husband; he answered me Nux, which did much rejoice my spirit. My mistress, before we went, was gone to the burial of a papoose, and returning, she found me sitting and reading in my Bible; she snatched it hastily out of my hand, and threw it out of doors; I ran out and caught it up, and put it into my pocket, and never let her see it afterward. Then they packed up their things to be gone, and gave me my load: I complained it was too heavy, whereupon she gave me a slap in the face, and bade me go; I lifted up my heart to God, hoping the redemption was not far off: and the rather because their insolence grew worse and worse.

But the thoughts of my going homeward (for so we bent our course) much cheered my spirit, and made my burden seem light, and almost nothing at all. But (to my amazement and great perplexity) the scale was soon turned: for when we had gone a little way, on a sudden my mistress gives out, she would go no further, but turn back again, and said, I must go back again with her, and she called her sannup, and would have had him gone back also, but he would not, but said, he would go on, and come to us again in three days. My spirit was upon this, I confess, very impatient, and almost outrageous. I thought I could as well have died as went back: I cannot declare the trouble that I was in about it; but yet back again I must go. As soon as I had an opportunity, I took my Bible to read, and that quieting scripture came to my hand, Psalms 46.10, *Be still, and know that I am God.* Which stilled my spirit for the present: but a sore time of trial, I concluded, I had to go through. My master being gone, who seemed to me the best friend that I had of an Indian, both in cold and hunger, and quickly so it proved. Down I sat, with my heart as full as it could hold, and yet so hungry that I could not sit neither: but going out to see what I could find, and walking among the trees, I found six acorns, and two chestnuts, which were some refreshment to me. Toward night I gathered some sticks for my own comfort, that I might not lie a-cold: but when

we came to lie down they bade me to go out, and lie somewhere else, for
they had company (they said) come in more than their own: I told them, I
could not tell where to go, they bade me go look; I told them, if I went to
another wigwam they would be angry, and send me home again. Then one
of the company drew his sword, and told me he would run me through if
I did not go presently. Then was I fain to stoop to this rude fellow, and to
go out in the night, I knew not whither. Mine eyes have seen that fellow
afterward walking up and down Boston, under the appearance of a friendly
Indian, and several others of the like cut. I went to one wigwam, and they
told me they had no room. Then I went to another, and they said the same;
at last an old Indian bade me to come to him, and his squaw gave me some
ground nuts; she gave me also something to lay under my head, and a good
fire we had: and through the good providence of God, I had a comfortable
lodging that night. In the morning, another Indian bade me come at night,
and he would give me six ground nuts, which I did. We were at this place
and time about two miles from Connecticut River. We went in the morning to gather ground nuts, to the river, and went back again that night. I
went with a good load at my back (for they when they went, though but a
little way, would carry all their trumpery with them). I told them the skin
was off my back, but I had no other comforting answer from them than
this, That it would be no matter if my head were off too.

The Thirteenth Remove

Instead of going toward the Bay, which was that I desired, I must go with
them five or six miles down the river into a mighty thicket of brush: where
we abode almost a fortnight. Here one asked me to make a shirt for her
papoose, for which she gave me a mess of broth, which was thickened with
meal made of the bark of a tree, and to make it the better, she had put into
it about a handful of peas, and a few roasted ground nuts. I had not seen
my son a pretty while, and here was an Indian of whom I made inquiry
after him, and asked him when he saw him: he answered me, that such a
time his master roasted him, and that himself did eat a piece of him, as big
as his two fingers, and that he was very good meat: but the Lord upheld
my spirit, under this discouragement; and I considered their horrible ad-
dictedness to lying, and that there is not one of them that makes the least
conscience of speaking of truth. In this place, on a cold night, as I lay by the

fire, I removed a stick that kept the heat from me, a squaw moved it down again, at which I looked up, and she threw a handful of ashes in my eyes: I thought I should have been quite blinded, and have never seen more: but lying down, the water run out of my eyes, and carried the dirt with it, that by the morning, I recovered my sight again. Yet upon this, and the like occasions, I hope it is not too much to say with Job, *Have pity upon me, have pity upon me, O ye my friends, for the hand of the Lord has touched me.* And here I cannot but remember how many times sitting in their wigwams, and musing on things past, I should suddenly leap up and run out, as if I had been at home, forgetting where I was, and what my condition was: but when I was without, and saw nothing but wilderness, and woods, and a company of barbarous heathens, my mind quickly returned to me, which made me think of that, spoken concerning Samson, who said, *I will go out and shake myself as at other times, but he wist not that the Lord was departed from him.* About this time I began to think that all my hopes of restoration would come to nothing. I thought of the English army, and hoped for their coming, and being taken by them, but that failed. I hoped to be carried to Albany, as the Indians had discoursed before, but that failed also. I thought of being sold to my husband, as my master spake, but instead of that, my master himself was gone, and I left behind, so that my spirit was now quite ready to sink. I asked them to let me go out and pick up some sticks, that I might get alone, and pour out my heart unto the Lord. Then also I took my Bible to read, but I found no comfort here neither, which many times I was wont to find: so easy a thing it is with God to dry up the streams of scripture comfort from us. Yet I can say, that in all my sorrows and afflictions, God did not leave me to have my impatience work toward himself, as if his ways were unrighteous. But I knew that he laid upon me less than I deserved. Afterward, before this doleful time ended with me, I was turning the leaves of my Bible, and the Lord brought to me some scriptures, which did a little revive me, as that Isaiah 55.8, *For my thoughts are not your thoughts, neither are your ways my ways, saith the Lord.* And also that, Psalms 37.5, *Commit thy way unto the Lord, trust also in him, and he shall bring it to pass.* About this time they came yelping from Hadley, where they had killed three Englishmen, and brought one captive with them, *viz.* Thomas Read. They all gathered about the poor man, asking him many questions. I desired also to go and see him; and when I came, he was crying bitterly, supposing they would quickly kill him. Whereupon I asked one of them, whether they intended to kill him; he answered me, they would not: he being a little cheered with that, I asked him about the welfare of my husband, he told me he saw him such a time in the Bay, and he was well, but very melancholy. By which I certainly understood (though I suspected it before) that whatsoever the Indians told me respecting him was vanity and lies. Some of them told me, he was dead, and they had killed him: some said he was married again, and that the governor wished him to marry; and told him he should have his choice, and that all persuaded I was dead. So like were these barbarous creatures to him who was a liar from the beginning.

As I was sitting once in the wigwam here, Philip's maid came in with the child in her arms, and asked me to give her a piece of my apron, to make a flap for it. I told her I would not: then my mistress bade me give it, but still I said no: the maid told me if I would not give her a piece, she would tear a piece off it: I told her I would tear her coat then, with that my mistress rises up, and take up a stick big enough to have killed me, and struck at me with it, but I stepped out, and she struck the stick into the mat of the wigwam. But while she was pulling of it out, I ran to the maid and gave her all my apron, and so that storm went over.

Hearing that my son was come to this place, I went to see him, and told him his father was well, but very melancholy: he told me he was as much grieved for his father as for himself; I wondered at his speech, for I thought I had enough upon my spirit in reference to myself, to make me mindless of my husband and everyone else: they being safe among their friends. He told me also, that a while before, his master (together with other Indians) were going to the French for powder; but by the way the Mohawks met with them, and killed four of their company which made the rest turn back again, for which I desired that myself and he may bless the Lord; for it might have been worse with him, had he been sold to the French, than it proved to be in his remaining with the Indians.

I went to see an English youth in this place, one John Gilbert of Springfield. I found him lying without doors, upon the ground; I asked him how he did? He told me he was very sick of a flux, with eating so much blood: they had turned him out of the wigwam, and with him an Indian papoose, almost dead (whose parents had been killed), in a bitter cold day, without fire or clothes: the young man himself had nothing on, but his shirt and waistcoat. This sight was enough to melt a heart of flint. There they lay quivering in the cold, the youth round like a dog; the papoose stretched out with his eyes and nose and mouth full of dirt, and yet alive, and groaning. I advised John to go and get to some fire: he told me he could not stand, but I persuaded him still, lest he should lie there and die: and with much ado I got him to a fire, and went myself home. As soon as I was got home, his master's daughter came after me, to know what I had done with the Englishman, I told her I had got him to a fire in such a place. Now had I need to pray Paul's prayer, 2 Thessalonians 3.2, *That we may be delivered from unreasonable and wicked men.* For her satisfaction I went along with her, and brought her to him; but before I got home again, it was noised about, that I was running away and getting the English youth, along with me; that as soon as I came in, they began to rant and domineer: asking me where I had been, and what I had been doing? and saying they would knock him on the head: I told them, I had been seeing the English youth, and that I would not run away, they told me I lied, and taking up a hatchet, they came to me, and said they would knock me down if I stirred out again; and so confined me to the wigwam. Now may I say with David, 2 Samuel 24.14, *I am in a great strait.* If I keep in, I must die with hunger, and if I go out, I must be knocked in the head. This distressed condition held that day, and half the next; and then the Lord remembered me, whose mercies are great. Then came an Indian to me with a pair of stockings that were too big for him, and he would have me ravel them out, and knit them fit for him. I showed myself willing, and bade him ask my mistress if I might go along with him a little way; she said yes, I might, but I was not a little refreshed with that news, that I had my liberty again. Then I went along with him, and he gave me some roasted ground nuts, which did again revive my feeble stomach.

Being got out of her sight, I had time and liberty again to look into my Bible: which was my guide by day, and my pillow by night. Now that comfortable scripture presented itself to me, Isaiah 54.7, *For a small moment have I forsaken thee, but with great mercies will I gather thee.* Thus the Lord carried me along from one time to another, and made good to me this precious promise, and many others. Then my son came to see me, and I asked his master to let him stay a while with me, that I might comb his head, and look over him, for he was almost overcome with lice. He told me, when I had done, that he was very hungry, but I had nothing to relieve him; but bid him go into the wigwams as he went along, and see if he could get anything among them. Which he did, and it seems tarried a little too long; for his master was angry with him, and beat him, and then sold him. Then he came running to tell me he had a new master, and that he had given him some ground nuts already. Then I went along with him to his new master who told me he loved him: and he should not want. So his master carried him away, and I never saw him afterward, till I saw him at Pascataqua in Portsmouth.

That night they bade me go out of the wigwam again: my mistress's papoose was sick, and it died that night, and there was one benefit in it, that there was more room. I went to a wigwam, and they bade me come in, and gave me a skin to lie upon, and a mess of venison and ground nuts, which was a choice dish among them. On the morrow they buried the papoose, and afterward, both morning and evening, there came a company to mourn and howl with her: though I confess, I could not much condole with them. Many sorrowful days I had in this place: often getting alone; *Like a crane, or a swallow, so did I chatter: I did mourn as a dove, mine eyes ail with looking upward. Oh, Lord, I am oppressed; undertake for me* (Isa. 38.14). I could tell the Lord as Hezekiah, verse 3. *Remember now O Lord, I beseech thee, how I have walked before thee in truth.* Now had I time to examine all my ways: my conscience did not accuse me of unrighteousness toward one or other: yet I saw how in my walk with God I had been a careless creature. As David said, *Against thee, thee only have I sinned:* and I might say with the poor publican, *God be merciful unto me a sinner.* On the Sabbath days, I could look upon the sun and think how people were going to the house of God, to have their souls refreshed; and then home, and their bodies also: but I was destitute of both; and might say as the poor prodigal, *he would fain have filled his belly with the husks that the swine did eat, and no man gave unto him* (Luke 15.16). For I must say with him, *Father I have sinned against heaven, and in thy sight,* verse 21. I remembered how on the night before and after the Sabbath, when my family was about me, and relations and neighbors with us, we could pray and sing, and then refresh our bodies with the good creatures of God; and then have a comfortable bed to lie down on: but instead of all this, I had only a little swill for the body, and then, like a swine, must lie down on the ground. I cannot express to man the sorrow that lay upon my spirit, the Lord knows it. Yet that comfortable scripture would often come to my mind, *For a small moment have I forsaken thee, but with great mercies will I gather thee.*

The Fourteenth Remove

Now must we pack up and be gone from this thicket, bending our course toward the Bay towns, I having nothing to eat by the way this day, but a few crumbs of cake, that an Indian gave my girl the same day we were taken. She gave it me, and I put it in my pocket; there it lay, till it was so moldy (for want of good baking) that one could not tell what it was made of; it fell all to crumbs, and grew so dry and hard, that it was like little flints; and this refreshed me many times, when I was ready to faint. It was in my thoughts when I put it into my mouth, that if ever I returned, I would tell the world what a blessing the Lord gave to such mean food. As we went along, they killed a deer, with a young one in her, they gave me a piece of the fawn, and it was so young and tender, that one might eat the bones as well as the flesh, and yet I thought it very good. When night came on we sat down; it rained, but they quickly got up a bark wigwam, where I lay dry that night. I looked out in the morning, and many of them had lain in the rain all night, I saw by their reeking. Thus the Lord dealt mercifully with me many times, and I fared better than many of them. In the morning they took the blood of the deer, and put it into the paunch, and so boiled it; I could eat nothing of that, though they ate it sweetly. And yet they were so nice in other things, that when I had fetched water, and had put the dish I dipped the water with, into the kettle of water which I brought, they would say, they would knock me down; for they said, it was a sluttish trick.

The Fifteenth Remove

We went on our travel. I having got one handful of ground nuts, for my support that day, they gave me my load, and I went on cheerfully (with the thoughts of going homeward) having my burden more on my back than my spirit: we came to Baquag River again that day, near which we abode a few days. Sometimes one of them would give me a pipe, another a little tobacco, another a little salt: which I would change for a little victuals. I cannot but think what a wolfish appetite persons have in a starving condition: for many times when they gave me that which was hot, I was so greedy, that I should burn my mouth, that it would trouble me hours after, and yet I should quickly do the same again. And after I was thoroughly hungry, I was never again satisfied. For though sometimes it fell out, that I got enough, and did eat till I could eat no more, yet I was as unsatisfied as I was when I began. And now could I see that scripture verified (there being many scriptures which we do not take notice of, or understand till we are afflicted), Micah 6.14, *Thou shalt eat and not be satisfied.* Now I might see more than ever before, the miseries that sin hath brought upon us: many times I should be ready to run out against the heathen, but the scripture would quiet me again, Amos 3.6, *Shall there be evil in the city, and the Lord hath not done it?* The Lord help me to make a right improvement of His word, and that I might learn that great lesson, Micah 6.8–9, *He hath showed thee (O Man) what is good, and what doth the Lord require of thee, but to do justly, and love mercy, and walk humbly with thy God? Hear ye the rod, and who hath appointed it.*

The Sixteenth Remove

We began this remove with wading over Baquag River: the water was up to the knees, and the stream very swift, and so cold that I thought it would have cut me in sunder. I was so weak and feeble, that I reeled as I went along, and thought there I must end my days at last, after my bearing and getting through so many difficulties; the Indians stood laughing to see me staggering along: but in my distress the Lord gave me experience of the truth, and goodness of that promise, Isaiah 43.2, *When thou passest through the waters, I will be with thee, and through the rivers, they shall not overflow thee.* Then I sat down to put on my stockings and shoes, with the tears running down mine eyes, and many sorrowful thoughts in my heart, but I got up to go along with them. Quickly there came up to us an Indian, who informed them, that I must go to Wachusett to my master, for there was a letter come from the Council to the sagamores, about redeeming the captives, and that there would be another in fourteen days, and that I must be there ready. My heart was so heavy before that I could scarce speak or go in the path; and yet now so light, that I could run. My strength seemed to come again, and recruit my feeble knees, and aching heart: yet it pleased them to go but one mile that night, and there we stayed two days. In that time came a company of Indians to us, near thirty, all on horseback. My heart skipped within me, thinking they had been Englishmen at the first sight of them, for they were dressed in English apparel, with hats, white neckcloths, and sashes about their waists, and ribbons upon their shoulders:

but when they came near, there was a vast difference between the lovely faces of Christians, and foul looks of these heathens, which much damped my spirit again.

The Seventeenth Remove

A comfortable remove it was to me, because of my hopes. They gave me a pack, and along we went cheerfully; but quickly my will proved more than my strength; having little or no refreshing my strength failed me, and my spirits were almost quite gone. Now may I say with David, Psalms 109.22–24, *I am poor and needy, and my heart is wounded within me. I am gone like the shadow when it declineth: I am tossed up and down like the locust; my knees are weak through fasting, and my flesh faileth of fatness.* At night we came to an Indian town, and the Indians sat down by a wigwam discoursing, but I was almost spent, and could scarce speak. I laid down my load, and went into the wigwam, and there sat an Indian boiling of horse's feet (they being wont to eat the flesh first, and when the feet were old and dried, and they had nothing else, they would cut off the feet and use them). I asked him to give me a little of his broth, or water they were boiling in; he took a dish, and gave me one spoonful of samp, and bid me take as much of the broth as I would. Then I put some of the hot water to the samp, and drank it up, and my spirit came again. He gave me also a piece of the ruff or ridding of the small guts, and I broiled it on the coals; and now may I say with Jonathan, *See, I pray you, how mine eyes have been enlightened, because I tasted a little of this honey,* 1 Samuel 14.29. Now is my spirit revived again; though means be never so inconsiderable, yet if the Lord bestow his blessing upon them, they shall refresh both soul and body.

The Eighteenth Remove

We took up our packs and along we went, but a wearisome day I had of it. As we went along I saw an Englishman stripped naked, and lying dead upon the ground, but knew not who it was. Then we came to another Indian town, where we stayed all night. In this town there were four English children, captives; and one of them my own sister's. I went to see how she did, and she was well, considering her captive condition. I would have tarried that night with her, but they that owned her would not suffer it. Then I went into another wigwam, where they were boiling corn and beans, which was a lovely sight to see, but I could not get a taste thereof. Then I went to another wigwam, where there were two of the English children; the squaw was boiling horse's feet; then she cut me off a little piece, and gave one of the English children a piece also. Being very hungry I had quickly eaten up mine, but the child could not bite it, it was so tough and sinewy, but lay sucking, gnawing, chewing and slobbering of it in the mouth and hand, then I took it of the child, and eat it myself, and savory it was to my taste. Then I may say as Job 6.7, *The things that my soul refused to touch, are as my sorrowful meat.* Thus the Lord made that pleasant refreshing, which another time would have been an abomination. Then I went home to my mistress's wigwam; and they told me I disgraced my master with begging, and if I did so any more, they would knock me in the head: I told them, they had as good knock me in the head as starve me to death.

The Nineteenth Remove

They said, when we went out, that we must travel to Wachusett this day. But a bitter weary day I had of it, traveling now three days together, without resting any day between. At last, after many weary steps, I saw Wachusett hills, but many miles off. Then we came to a great swamp, through which we travelled, up to the knees in mud and water, which was heavy going to one tired before. Being almost spent, I thought I should have sunk down at last, and never gotten out; but I may say, as in Psalms 94.18, *When my foot slipped, thy mercy, O Lord, held me up.* Going along, having indeed my life, but little spirit, Philip, who was in the company, came up and took me by the hand, and said, Two weeks more and you shall be mistress again. I asked him, if he spake true? He answered, Yes, and quickly you shall come to your master again; who had been gone from us three weeks. After many weary steps we came to Wachusett, where he was: and glad I was to see him. He asked me, When I washed me? I told him not this month, then he fetched me some water himself, and bid me wash, and gave me the glass to see how I looked; and bid his squaw give me something to eat: so she gave me a mess of beans and meat, and a little ground nut cake. I was wonderfully revived with this favor showed me, Psalms 106.46, *He made them also to be pitied, of all those that carried them captives.*

My master had three squaws, living sometimes with one, and some-times with another one, this old squaw, at whose wigwam I was, and with whom my master had been those three weeks. Another was Weetamoo, with whom I had lived and served all this while: a severe and proud dame she was, bestowing every day in dressing herself neat as much time as any of the gentry of the land: powdering her hair, and painting her face, going with necklaces, with jewels in her ears, and bracelets upon her hands: when she had dressed herself, her work was to make girdles of wampum and beads. The third squaw was a younger one, by whom he had two papooses. By that time I was refreshed by the old squaw, with whom my master was, Weetamoo's maid came to call me home, at which I fell a-weeping. Then the old squaw told me, to encourage me, that if I wanted victuals, I should come to her, and that I should lie there in her wigwam. Then I went with the maid, and quickly came again and lodged there. The squaw laid a mat under me, and a good rug over me; the first time I had any such kindness showed me. I understood that Weetamoo thought, that if she should let me go and serve with the old squaw, she would be in dan-ger to lose, not only my service, but the redemption pay also. And I was not a little glad to hear this; being by it raised in my hopes, that in God's due time there would be an end of this sorrowful hour. Then in came an Indian, and asked me to knit him three pair of stockings, for which I had a hat, and a silk handkerchief. Then another asked me to make her a shift, for which she gave me an apron.

Then came Tom and Peter, with the second letter from the Council, about the captives. Though they were Indians, I got them by the hand, and burst out into tears; my heart was so full that I could not speak to them; but recovering myself, I asked them how my husband did, and all my friends and acquaintance: They said, They are all very well, but melan-choly. They brought me two biscuits, and a pound of tobacco. The tobacco I quickly gave away; when it was all gone, one asked me to give him a pipe of tobacco, I told him it was all gone; then began he to rant and threaten. I told him when my husband came I would give him some: Hang him rogue (says he) I will knock out his brains, if he comes here. And then again, in the same breath they would say, That if there should come an hundred without guns, they would do them no hurt. So unstable and like mad-men they were. So that fearing the worst, I durst not send to my husband, though there were some thoughts of his coming to redeem and fetch me, not knowing what might follow. For there was little more trust to them than to the master they served. When the letter was come, the sagamores met to consult about the captives, and called me to them to inquire how much my husband would give to redeem me. When I came I sat down among them, as I was wont to do, as their manner is: then they bade me stand up, and said they were the General Court. They bid me speak what I thought he would give. Now knowing that all we had was destroyed by the Indians, I was in a great strait: I thought if I should speak of but a little, it would be slighted, and hinder the matter; if of a great sum, I knew not where it would be procured: yet at a venture, I said twenty pounds, yet desired them to take less; but they would not hear of that, but sent that message to Boston, that for twenty pounds I should be redeemed. It was a Praying Indian that wrote their letter for them. There was another Praying Indian, who told me, that he had a brother, that would not eat horse; his conscience was so tender and scrupulous (though as large as hell, for the destruction of poor Christians). Then he said, he read that scripture to him, 2 Kings, 6.25, *There was a famine in Samaria, and behold they besieged it, until an ass's head was sold for fourscore pieces of silver, and the fourth part of a kab of dove's dung, for five pieces of silver.* He expounded this place to his brother, and showed him that it was lawful to eat that in a famine which is not at another time. And now, says he, he will eat horse with any Indian of them all. There was another Praying Indian, who when he had done all the mischief that he could, betrayed his own father into the English hands, thereby to purchase his own life. Another Praying Indian was at Sudbury fight, though, as he deserved, he was afterward hanged for it. There was another Praying Indian, so wicked and cruel, as to wear a string about his neck, strung with Christians' fingers. Another Praying Indian, when they went to Sudbury fight, went with them, and his squaw also with him, with her papoose at her back: before they went to that fight they got a company together to powwow; the manner was as followeth. There was one that kneeled upon a deerskin, with the company round him in a ring who kneeled, and striking upon the ground with their hands, and with sticks, and muttering or humming with their mouths; beside him who kneeled in the ring, there also stood one with a gun in his hand: then he on the deerskin made a speech, and all manifested assent to it: and so they did many times together. Then they bade him with the gun go out of the ring, which he did, but when he was out, they called him in again; but he seemed to make a stand, then they called the more earnestly, till he returned again: then they all sang. Then they gave him two guns, in either hand one: and so he on the deerskin began again; and at the end of every sentence in his speaking, they all assented, humming or muttering with their mouths, and striking upon the ground with their hands. Then they bade him with the two guns go out of the ring again; which he did, a little way. Then they called him in again, but he made a stand; so they called him with greater earnestness; but he stood reeling and wavering as if he knew not whither he should stand or fall, or which way to go. Then they called him with exceeding great vehemency, all of them, one and another: after a little while he turned in, staggering as he went, with his arms stretched out, in either hand a gun. As soon as he came in, they all sang and rejoiced exceedingly a while. And then he upon the deerskin, made another speech unto which they all assented in a rejoicing manner: and so they ended their business, and forthwith went to Sudbury fight. To my thinking they went without any scruple, but that they should prosper, and gain the victory. And they went out not so rejoicing, but they came home with as great a victory. For they said they had killed two captains, and almost an hundred men. One Englishman they brought along with them: and he said, it was too true, for they had made sad work at Sudbury, as indeed it proved. Yet they came home without that rejoicing and triumphing over their victory, which they were wont to show at other times, but rather like dogs (as they say) which have lost their ears. Yet I could not perceive that it was for their own loss of men: they said, they had not lost above five or six: and I missed none, except in one wigwam. When they went, they acted as if the devil had told them that they should gain the victory: and now they acted, as if the devil had told them they should have a fall. Whether it were so or no, I cannot tell, but so it proved, for quickly they began to fall, and so held on that summer, till they came to utter ruin. They came home on a Sabbath day, and the pow-wow that kneeled upon the deerskin came home (I may say, without abuse) as black as the devil. When my master came home, he came to me and bid me make a shirt for his papoose, of a holland-laced pillowbeer. About that time there came an Indian to me and bid me come to his wigwam, at night, and he would give me some pork and ground nuts. Which I did, and as I was eating, another Indian said to me, he seems to be your good friend, but he killed two Englishmen at Sudbury, and there lie their clothes behind you: I looked behind me, and there I saw bloody clothes, with bullet holes in them, yet the Lord suffered not this wretch to do me any hurt; yea, instead of that, he many times refreshed me: five or six times did he and his squaw refresh my feeble carcass. If I went to their wigwam at any time, they would always give me something, and yet they were strangers that I never saw before. Another squaw gave me a piece of fresh pork, and a little salt with it, and lent me her pan to fry it in; and I cannot but remember what a sweet, pleasant and delightful relish that bit had to me, to this day. So little do we prize common mercies when we have them to the full.

The Twentieth Remove

It was their usual manner to remove, when they had done any mischief, lest they should be found out: and so they did at this time. We went about three or four miles, and there they built a great wigwam, big enough to hold a hundred Indians, which they did in preparation to a great day of dancing. They would say now amongst themselves, that the governor would be so angry for his loss at Sudbury, that he would send no more about the captives, which made me grieve and tremble. My sister being not far from the place where we now were, and hearing that I was here, desired her master to let her come and see me, and he was willing to it, and would go with her: but she being ready before him, told him she would go before, and was come within a mile or two of the place; then he overtook her, and began to rant as if he had been mad; and made her go back again in the rain; so that I never saw her till I saw her in Charlestown. But the Lord requited many of their ill doings, for this Indian her master, was hanged after at Boston. The Indians now began to come from all quarters, against their merry dancing day. Among some of them came one Goodwife Kettle: I told her my heart was so heavy that it was ready to break: so is mine too, said she, but yet said, I hope we shall hear some good news shortly. I could hear how earnestly my sister desired to see me, and I as earnestly desired to see her: and yet neither of us could get an opportunity. My daughter was also now about a mile off, and I had not seen her in nine or ten weeks, as I had not seen my sister since our first taking. I earnestly desired them to let me go and see them: yea, I entreated, begged, and persuaded them, but to let me see my daughter; and yet so hard-hearted were they, that they would not suffer it. They made use of their tyrannical power whilst they had it: but through the Lord's wonderful mercy, their time was now but short.

On a Sabbath day, the sun being about an hour high in the afternoon, came Mr. John Hoar (the Council permitting him, and his own foreward spirit inclining him) together with the two forementioned Indians, Tom and Peter, with their third letter from the Council. When they came near, I was abroad: though I saw them not, they presently called me in, and bade me sit down and not stir. Then they caught up their guns, and away they ran, as if an enemy had been at hand; and the guns went off apace. I manifested some great trouble, and they asked me what was the matter? I told them, I thought they had killed the Englishman (for they had in the meantime informed me that an Englishman was come), they said, No; they shot over his horse, and under, and before his horse; and they pushed him this way and that way, at their pleasure, showing what they could do: then they let them come to their wigwams. I begged of them to let me see the Englishman, but they would not. But there was I fain to sit their pleasure. When they had talked their fill with him, they suffered me to go to him. We asked each other of our welfare, and how my husband did, and all my friends? He told me they were all well, and would be glad to see me. Amongst other things which my husband sent me, there came a pound of tobacco: which I sold for nine shillings in money: for many of the Indians for want of tobacco, smoked hemlock, and ground ivy. It was a great mistake in any, who thought I sent for tobacco: for through the favor of God, that desire was overcome. I now asked them, whether I should go home with Mr. Hoar? They answered No, one and another of them: and it being night, we lay down with that answer; in the morning, Mr. Hoar invited the sagamores to dinner; but when we went to get it ready, we found that they had stolen the greatest part of the provision Mr. Hoar had brought, out of his bags, in the night. And we may see the wonderful power of God, in that one passage, in that when there was such a great number of the Indians together, and so greedy of a little good food; and no English there, but Mr. Hoar and myself: that there they did not knock us in the head, and take what we had: there being not only some provision, but also trading cloth, a part of the twenty pounds agreed upon: but instead of doing us any mischief, they seemed to be ashamed of the fact, and said, it were some matchit Indian that did it. Oh that we could believe that there is nothing too hard for God! God showed his power over the heathen in this, as he did over the hungry lions when Daniel was cast into the den. Mr. Hoar called them betime to dinner, but they ate very little, they being so busy in dressing themselves, and getting ready for their dance: which was carried on by eight of them, four men and four squaws; my master and mistress being two. He was dressed in his holland shirt, with great laces sewed at the tail of it, he had his silver buttons, his white stockings, his garters were hung round with shillings, and he had girdles of wampum upon his head and shoulders. She had a kersey coat, and covered with girdles of wampum from the loins upward: her arms from her elbows to her hands were covered with bracelets; there were handfuls of necklaces about her neck, and several sorts of jewels in her ears. She had fine red stockings, and white shoes, her hair powdered and face painted red, that was always before black. And all the dancers were after the same manner. There were two other singing and knocking on a kettle for their music. They kept hopping up and down one after another, with a kettle of water in the midst, standing warm upon some embers, to drink of when they were dry. They held on till it was almost night, throwing out wampum to the standers-by. At night I asked them again, if I should go home? They all as one said No, except my husband would come for me. When we were lain down, my master went out of the wigwam, and by and by sent in an Indian called James the Printer, who told Mr. Hoar, that my master would let me go home tomorrow, if he would [let] him have one pint of liquors. Then Mr. Hoar called his own Indians, Tom and Peter, and bid them go and see whether he would promise before them three: and if he would, he should have it; which he did, and he had it. Then Philip smelling the business called me to him, and asked me what I would give him, to tell me some good news, and speak a good word for me. I told him, I could not tell what to give him, I would [give] anything I had, and asked him what he would have? He said, two coats and twenty shillings in money, and half a bushel of seed corn, and some tobacco. I thanked him for his love: but I knew the good news as well as the crafty fox. My master after he had had his drink, quickly came ranting into the wigwam again, and called for Mr. Hoar, drinking to him, and saying, He was a good man: and then again he would say, Hang him, rogue: being almost drunk, he would drink to him, and yet presently say he should be hanged. Then he called for me. I trembled to hear him, yet I was fain to go to him, and he drank to me, showing no incivility. He was the first Indian I saw drunk all the while that I was amongst them. At last his squaw ran out, and he after her, around the wigwam, with his money jingling at his knees: but she escaped him: but having an old squaw he ran to her: and so through the Lord's mercy, we were no more troubled that night.

Yet I had not a comfortable night's rest: for I think I can say, I did not sleep for three nights together. The night before the letter came from the Council, I could not rest, I was so full of fears and troubles, God many times leaving us most in the dark, when deliverance is nearest: yea, at this time I could not rest night nor day. The next night I was overjoyed, Mr. Hoar being come, and that with such good tidings. The third night I was even swallowed up with the thoughts of things, *viz.* that ever I should go home again; and that I must go, leaving my children behind me in the wilderness; so that sleep was now almost departed from my eyes.

On Tuesday morning they called their General Court (as they call it) to consult and determine, whether I should go home or no: and they all as one man did seemingly consent to it, that I should go home; except Philip, who would not come among them.

But before I go any further, I would take leave to mention a few remarkable passages of providence, which I took special notice of in my afflicted time.

1. Of the fair opportunity lost in the long march, a little after the fort fight, when our English army was so numerous, and in pursuit of the enemy, and so near as to take several and destroy them: and the enemy in such distress for food, that our men might track them by their rooting in the earth for ground nuts, whilst they were flying for their lives. I say, that then our army should want provision, and be forced to leave their pursuit and return homeward; and the very next week the enemy came upon our town, like bears bereft of their whelps, or so many ravenous wolves, rending us and our lambs to death. But what shall I say? God seemed to leave His people to themselves, and order all things for His own holy ends. *Shall there be evil in the city and the Lord hath not done it? They are not grieved for the affliction of Joseph, therefore shall they go captive, with the first that go captive.* It is the Lord's doing, and it should be marvelous in our eyes.

2. I cannot but remember how the Indians derided the slowness, and dullness of the English army, in its setting out. For after the desolations at Lancaster and Medfield, as I went along with them, they asked me when I thought the English army would come after them? I told them I could not tell: It may be they will come in May, said they. Thus did they scoff at us, as if the English would be a quarter of a year getting ready.

3. Which also I have hinted before, when the English army with new supplies were sent forth to pursue after the enemy, and they understanding

it, fled before them till they came to Baquag River, where they forthwith went over safely: that that river should be impassable to the English. I can but admire to see the wonderful providence of God in preserving the heathen for further affliction to our poor country. They could go in great numbers over, but the English must stop: God had an overruling hand in all those things.

4. It was thought, if their corn were cut down, they would starve and die with hunger: and all their corn that could be found, was destroyed, and they driven from that little they had in store, into the woods in the midst of winter; and yet how to admiration did the Lord preserve them for his Holy ends, and the destruction of many still amongst the English! Strangely did the Lord provide for them; that I did not see (all the time I was among them) one man, woman, or child, die with hunger.

Though many times they would eat that, that a hog or a dog would hardly touch; yet by that God strengthened them to be a scourge to His people.

The chief and commonest food was ground nuts: they eat also nuts and acorns, artichokes, lily roots, ground beans, and several other weeds and roots, that I know not.

They would pick up old bones, and cut them to pieces at the joints, and if they were full of worms and maggots, they would scald them over the fire to make the vermin come out, and then boil them, and drink up the liquor, and then beat the great ends of them in a mortar, and so eat them. They would eat horse's guts, and ears, and all sorts of wild birds which they could catch: also bear, venison, beaver, tortoise, frogs, squirrels, dogs, skunks, rattlesnakes; yea, the very bark of trees; besides all sorts of creatures, and provision which they plundered from the English. I can but stand in admiration to see the wonderful power of God, in providing for such a vast number of our enemies in the wilderness, where there was nothing to be seen, but from hand to mouth. Many times in a morning, the generality of them would eat up all they had, and yet have some further supply against what they wanted. It is said, Psalms 81.13–14, *Oh, that my people had hearkened to me, and Israel had walked in my ways, I should soon have subdued their enemies, and turned my hand against their adversaries.* But now our perverse and evil carriages in the sight of the Lord, have so offended Him, that instead of turning His hand against them, the Lord feeds and nourishes them up to be a scourge to the whole land.

5. Another thing that I would observe is, the strange providence of God, in turning things about when the Indians were at the highest, and the English at the lowest point. I was with the enemy eleven weeks and five days, and not one week passed without the fury of the enemy, and some desolation by fire and sword upon one place or other. They mourned (with their black faces) for their own losses, yet triumphed and rejoiced in their inhuman, and many times devilish cruelty to the English. They would boast much of their victories; saying, that in two hours time they had destroyed such a captain, and his company at such a place; and such a captain and his company, in such a place; and such a captain and his company in such a place: and boast how many towns they had destroyed, and then scoff, and say, They had done them a good turn, to send them to heaven so soon. Again, they would say, This summer that they would knock all the rogues in the head, or drive them into the sea, or make them fly the country: thinking surely, Agag-like, *The bitterness of death is past.* Now the heathen begin to think all is their own, and the poor Christians' hopes to fail (as to man) and now their eyes are more to God, and their hearts sigh heavenward: and to say in good earnest, *Help Lord, or we perish:* When the Lord had brought His people to this, that they saw no help in anything but Himself: then He takes the quarrel into His own hand: and though they had made a pit, in their own imaginations, as deep as hell for the Christians that summer, yet the Lord hurled themselves into it. And the Lord had not so many ways before to preserve them, but now He hath as many to destroy them.

But to return again to my going home, where we may see a remarkable change of providence: at first they were all against it, except my husband would come for me; but afterward they assented to it, and seemed much to rejoice in it; some asked me to send them some bread, others some tobacco, others shaking me by the hand, offering me a hood and scarf to ride in; not one moving hand or tongue against it. Thus hath the Lord answered my poor desire, and the many earnest requests of others put up unto God for me. In my travels an Indian came to me, and told me, if I were willing, he and his squaw would run away, and go home along with me: I told him No: I was not willing to run away, but desired to wait God's time, that I might go home quietly, and without fear. And now God hath granted me my desire. O the wonderful power of God that I have seen, and the experience that I have had: I have been in the midst of those roaring lions, and savage bears, that feared neither God, nor man, nor the devil, by night and day, alone and in company: sleeping all sorts together, and yet not one of them ever offered me the least abuse of unchastity to me, in word or action. Though some are ready to say, I speak it for my own credit; but I speak it in the presence of God, and to His Glory. God's power is as great now, and as sufficient to save, as when he preserved Daniel in the lion's den; or the three children in the fiery furnace. I may well say as his Psalms 136.1, *Oh give thanks unto the Lord for he is good, for His mercy endureth forever.* Let the redeemed of the Lord say so, whom He hath redeemed from the hand of the enemy, especially that I should come away in the midst of so many hundreds of enemies quietly and peaceably, calm and not a dog moving his tongue. So I took my leave of them, and in coming along my heart melted into tears, more than all the while I was with them, and I was almost swallowed up with the thoughts that ever I should go home again. About the sun going down, Mr. Hoar, and myself, and the two Indians came to Lancaster, and a solemn sight it was to me. There had I lived many comfortable years amongst my relations and neighbors, and now not one Christian to be seen, nor one house left standing. We went on to a farm house that was yet standing, where we lay all night: and a comfortable lodging we had, though nothing but straw to lie on. The Lord preserved us in safety that night, and raised us up again in the morning, and carried us along, that before noon, we came to Concord. Now was I full of joy, and yet not without sorrow: joy to see such a lovely sight, so many Christians together, and some of them my neighbors: there I met with my brother, and my brother-in-law, who asked me, if I knew where his wife was? Poor heart! He had helped to bury her, and knew it not; she being shot down by the house was partly burnt: so that those who were at Boston at the desolation of the town, and came back afterward, and buried the dead, did not know her. Yet I was not without sorrow, to think how many were looking and longing, and my own children amongst the rest, to enjoy that deliverance that I had now received, and I did not know whether ever I should see them again. Being recruited with food and raiment we went to Boston that day, where I met with my dear husband, but the thoughts of our dear children, one being dead, and the other we could not tell where, abated our comfort each to other. I was not before so much hemmed in with the merciless and cruel heathen, but now as much with pitiful, tender-hearted and compassionate Christians. In that poor, and distressed, and beggarly condition I was received in, I was kindly entertained in several houses: so much love I received from several (some of whom I knew, and others I knew not) that I am not capable to declare it. But the Lord knows them all by name: the Lord reward them sevenfold into their bosoms of His spirituals, for their temporals! The twenty pounds the price of my redemption was raised by some Boston gentlemen, and Mrs. Usher, whose bounty and religious charity, I would not forget to make mention of. Then Mr. Thomas Shepard of Charlestown received us into his house, where we continued eleven weeks; and a father and mother they were to us. And many more tender-hearted friends we met with in that place. We were now in the midst of love, yet not without much and frequent heaviness of heart for our poor children, and other relations, who were still in affliction. The week following, after my coming in, the governor and Council sent forth to the Indians again; and that not without success; for they brought in my sister, and goodwife Kettle: their not knowing where our children were, was a sore trial to us still, and yet we were not without secret hopes that we should see them again. That which was dead lay heavier upon my spirit, than those which were alive and amongst the heathen; thinking how it suffered with its wounds, and I was no way able to relieve it; and how it was buried by the heathen in the wilderness from among all Christians. We were hurried up and down in our thoughts, sometime we should hear a report that they were gone this way, and sometimes that; and that they were come in, in this place or that: we kept inquiring and listening to hear concerning them, but no certain news as yet. About this time the Council had ordered a day of public thanksgiving: though I thought I had still cause of mourning, and being unsettled in our minds, we thought we would ride toward the eastward, to see if we could hear anything concerning our children. And as we were riding along (God is the wise disposer of all things) between Ipswich and Rowley we met with Mr. William Hubbard, who told us that our son Joseph was come in to Major Waldron's, and another with him, which was my sister's son. I asked him how he knew it? He said, the Major himself told him so. So along we went till we came to Newbury; and their minister being absent, they desired my husband to preach the thanksgiving for them. But he was not willing to stay there that night, but would go over to Salisbury, to hear further, and come again in the morning, which he did, and preached there that day. At night, when he had done, one came and told him that his daughter was come in at Providence: here was mercy on both hands: now hath God fulfilled that precious scripture which was such a comfort to me in my distressed condition. When my heart was ready to sink into the earth (my children being gone I could not tell whither) and my knees trembled under me, and I was walking through the valley of the shadow of death: then the Lord brought, and now has fulfilled that reviving word unto me: *Thus saith the Lord, Refrain thy voice from weeping, and thine eyes from tears, for thy work shall be rewarded, saith the Lord, and they shall come again from the land of the enemy.* Now we were between them, the one on the east, and the other on the west: our son being nearest, we went to him first, to Portsmouth, where we met with him, and with the major also: who told us he had done what he could, but could not redeem him under seven pounds; which the good people thereabouts were pleased to pay. The Lord reward the major, and all the rest, though unknown to me, for their labor of love. My sister's son was redeemed for four pounds, which the Council gave order for the payment of. Having now received one of our children, we hastened toward the other; going back through Newbury, my husband preached there on the Sabbath day: for which they rewarded him many-fold.

On Monday we came to Charlestown, where we heard that the governor of Rhode Island had sent over for our daughter, to take care of her, being now within his jurisdiction: which should not pass without our acknowledgments. But she being nearer Rehoboth than Rhode Island, Mr. Newman went over, and took care of her, and brought her to his own house. And the goodness of God was admirable to us in our low estate, in that he raised up passionate friends on every side to us, when we had nothing to recompense any for their love. The Indians were now gone that way, that it was apprehended dangerous to go to her: but the carts which carried provision to the English army, being guarded, brought her with them to Dorchester, where we received her safe: blessed be the Lord for it, for great is His power, and He can do whatsoever seemeth Him good. Her coming in was after this manner: she was travelling one day with the Indians, with her basket at her back; the company of Indians were got before her, and gone out of sight, all except one squaw; she followed the squaw till night, and then both of them lay down, having nothing over them but the heavens, and under them but the earth. Thus she travelled three days together, not knowing whither she was going: having nothing to eat or drink but water, and green hurtleberries. At last they came into Providence, where she was kindly entertained by several of that town. The Indians often said, that I should never have her under twenty pounds: but now the Lord hath brought her in upon free-cost, and given her to me the second time. The Lord make us a blessing indeed, each to others. Now have I seen that scripture also fulfilled, Deuteronomy 30.4, 7, *If any of thine be driven out to the outmost parts of heaven, from thence will the Lord thy God gather thee, and from thence will he fetch thee. And the Lord thy God will put all these curses upon thine enemies, and on them which hate thee, which persecuted thee.* Thus hath the Lord brought me and mine out of that horrible pit, and hath set us in the midst of tender-hearted and compassionate Christians. It is the desire of my soul, that we may walk worthy of the mercies received, and which we are receiving.

Our family being now gathered together (those of us that were living) the South Church in Boston hired a house for us: then we removed from Mr. Shepard's, those cordial friends, and went to Boston, where we continued about three-quarters of a year: still the Lord went along with us, and provided graciously for us. I thought it somewhat strange to set up housekeeping with bare walls; but as Solomon says, *Money answers all things;* and that we had through the benevolence of Christian friends, some in this town, and some in that, and others: and some from England, that in a little time we might look, and see the house furnished with love. The Lord hath been exceeding good to us in our low estate, in that when we had neither house nor home, nor other necessaries, the Lord so moved the hearts of these and those toward us, that we wanted neither food, nor raiment for ourselves or ours, Proverbs 18.24, *There is a friend which sticketh closer than a brother.* And how many such friends have we found, and are now living amongst? And truly such a friend have we found him to be unto us, in whose house we lived, *viz.* Mr. James Whitecomb, a friend unto us near hand, and afar off.

I can remember the time, when I used to sleep quietly without workings in my thoughts, whole nights together, but now it is other ways with me. When all are fast about me, and no eye open, but His who ever waketh, my thoughts are upon things past, upon the awful dispensation of the Lord toward us; upon His wonderful power and might, in carrying of us through so many difficulties, in returning us in safety, and suffering none to hurt us. I remember in the night season, how the other day I was in the midst of thousands of enemies, and nothing but death before me: it is then hard work to persuade myself, that ever I should be satisfied with bread again. But now we are fed with the finest of the wheat, and, as I may say, with honey out of the rock: instead of the husk, we have the fatted calf: the thoughts of these things in the particulars of them, and of the love and goodness of God toward us, make it true of me, what David said of himself, Psalms 6.6, *I watered my couch with my tears.* Oh! the wonderful power of God that mine eyes have seen, affording matter enough for my thoughts to run in, that when others are sleeping mine are weeping.

I have seen the extreme vanity of this world: one hour I have been in health, and wealth, wanting nothing: but the next hour in sickness and wounds, and death, having nothing but sorrow and affliction.

Before I knew what affliction meant, I was ready sometimes to wish for it. When I lived in prosperity, having the comforts of the world about me, my relations by me, my heart cheerful, and taking little care for anything; and yet seeing many, whom I preferred before myself, under many trials and afflictions, in sickness, weakness, poverty, losses, crosses, and cares of the world, I should be sometimes jealous lest I should not have my portion in this life, and that scripture would come to my mind, Hebrews 12.6, *For whom the Lord loveth he chasteneth, and scourgeth every son whom he receiveth.* But now I see the Lord had his time to scourge and chasten me. The portion of some is to have their afflictions by drops, now one drop and then another; but the dregs of the cup, the wine of astonishment, like a sweeping rain that leaveth no food, did the Lord prepare to be my portion. Affliction I wanted, and affliction I had, full measure (I thought) pressed down and running over; yet I see, when God calls a person to anything, and through never so many difficulties, yet He is fully able to carry them through and make them see, and say they have been gainers thereby. And I hope I can say in some measure, as David did, *It is good for me that I have been afflicted.* The Lord hath showed me the vanity of these outward things. That they are the vanity of vanities, and vexation of spirit; that they are but a shadow, a blast, a bubble, and our whole dependance must be upon Him. If trouble from smaller matters begin to arise in me, I have something at hand to check myself with, and say, why am I troubled? It was but the other day that if I had had the world, I would have given it for my freedom, or to have been a servant to a Christian. I have learned to look beyond present and smaller troubles, and to be quieted under them, as Moses said, Exodus 14.13, *Stand still and see the salvation of the Lord.*

1741

Yet for decades such expression was an anomaly in America. Before the Revolutionary War, most of the literature produced by Americans was composed by preachers who had been taught by their Puritan forebears that their job was not to embellish or elaborate on the word of God, but rather to stay out of its way—an aesthetic belief that led to the development of the Puritan "plaine style," a kind of writing that rendered most early American prose into icy, indifferent, and mathematically precise texts. The typical sermon of this period features three distinct sections: the first quotes a passage from the Bible for consideration; the second offers a sensible interpretation of that passage; and the third suggests how the passage may be applied to real life. Like most young men in eighteenth-century America, however, Jonathan Edwards is studying as much science as he is theology, and he knows therefore that there is a difference between having a "notional" understanding of something and a true "sense" of it—a difference, Edwards once wrote, between understanding the concept of honey and actually tasting its sweetness. So when Edwards grows up to become the best-known minister in the American colonies, he tries to give his audience a new approach to spirituality, a new path, a new sound, and a more palpably resonant theological experience. His most famous essay demonstrates this dramatically. It's a text that doesn't dismiss the traditional structure of the plaine style, but instead makes a point of carefully obeying the rules of that convention so that he might later break them to spectacular effect. After quoting Deuteronomy, he starts with a thesis statement, one that slyly hints at a theological threat but which nevertheless remains only placidly rhetorical: "There is nothing that keeps wicked men at any one moment out of hell, but the mere pleasure of God." Eventually, however, Edwards concludes this section of his essay with a surprisingly breathless, exasperated, and gratuitously graphic sentence that relentlessly pounds away at a single, horrifying, and inescapable image:

> So that, thus it is that natural men are held in the hand of God, over the pit of hell; they have deserved the fiery pit, and are already sentenced to it; and God is dreadfully provoked, His anger is as great towards them as to those that are actually suffering the executions of the fierceness of His wrath in hell, and they have done nothing in the least to appease or abate that anger, neither is God in the least bound by any promise to hold them up one moment; the devil is waiting for them, hell is gaping for them, the flames gather and flash about them, and would fain lay hold on them, and swallow them up; the fire pent up in their own hearts is struggling to break out: and they have no interest in any Mediator, there are no means within reach that can be any security to them. In short, they have no refuge, nothing to take hold of; all that preserves them every moment is the mere arbitrary will, and uncovenanted, unobliged forbearance of an incensed God.

With each succeeding semicolon here, Edwards sinks us deeper into condemnation, spiraling so quickly into doom that we probably don't even notice that his sentence is grammatically flawed: one giant run-on that starts to lose its footing after the first couple of lines. Or maybe we do notice this flaw, and maybe that's the point. Maybe we can't quite put our finger on what is wrong with the sentence, but we feel that something's wrong—our anxiety increasing as the wobble in its syntax becomes more and more unstable, and as we slowly start to realize that the reassuring composure of the essay's formulaic structure has betrayed us, has tricked us, has lured us into territory that is more than just uncomfortable: it feels like it wants to kill us. Indeed, accounts from those who were present on that Wednesday summer morning when Edwards first delivered "Sinners in the Hands of an Angry God" suggest that nothing like this essay had ever been heard before. "There was great moaning and crying throughout ye whole House," one visiting reverend reflected afterward in his journal. "'What shall I do to be Saved?' 'Oh, I am going to Hell!' 'What shall I do for Christ?' Their shrieks & cries were Piercing & Amazing." And even long after its first delivery, Jonathan Edwards's essay could still affect an audience. Harriet Beecher Stowe is said to have bolted out of a church when her father began delivering his own version of "Sinners." James Joyce supposedly based his hellfire sermon in *A Portrait of the Artist as a Young Man* on Edwards's masterpiece. And even *Pollyanna,* the 1960 Disney film starring Hayley Mills, borrows heavily from the essay in order to give its preacher something menacing to say. As one scholar has noted, long before the Revolution riled up Americans, Jonathan Edwards was tapping into the emotional turbulence roiling beneath society by composing rhythms that burrow so deeply into our bodies that before we can comprehend the argument they are making, we have already understood the proposition of their sounds.

JONATHAN EDWARDS

Sinners in the Hands
of an Angry God

Their foot shall slide in due time.

DEUTERONOMY 32.35

In this verse is threatened the vengeance of God on the wicked unbeliev-
ing Israelites, who were God's visible people, and who lived under the
means of grace, but who, notwithstanding all God's wonderful works
towards them, remained (as in verse 28.) void of counsel, having no understanding in them. Under all the cultivations of heaven, they brought forth
bitter and poisonous fruit, as in the two verses next preceding the text. The
expression I have chosen for my text, "Their foot shall slide in due time,"
seems to imply the following things, relating to the punishment and destruction to which these wicked Israelites were exposed.

1. That they were always exposed to destruction; as one that stands or
walks in slippery places is always exposed to fall. This is implied in the
manner of their destruction coming upon them, being represented by their
foot sliding. The same is expressed, Psalm 73.18: "Surely thou didst set them
in slippery places; thou castedst them down into destruction."

2. It implies that they were always exposed to sudden unexpected destruction. As he that walks in slippery places is every moment liable to fall,
he cannot foresee one moment whether he shall stand or fall the next; and
when he does fall, he falls at once without warning. Which is also expressed
in Psalm 73.18–19: "Surely thou didst set them in slippery places; thou
castedst them down into destruction: How are they brought into desolation as in a moment!"

3. Another thing implied is, that they are liable to fall of themselves,

without being thrown down by the hand of another; as he that stands or walks on slippery ground needs nothing but his own weight to throw him down.

4. That the reason why they are not fallen already, and do not fall now, is only that God's appointed time is not come. For it is said, that when the due time, or appointed time comes, their foot shall slide. Then they shall be left to fall, as they are inclined by their own weight. God will not hold them up in these slippery places any longer, but will let them go; and then, at that very instant, they shall fall into destruction; as he that stands on such slippery declining ground, on the edge of a pit, he cannot stand alone, when he is let go he immediately falls and is lost.

The observation from the words that I would now insist upon is this. "There is nothing that keeps wicked men at any one moment out of hell, but the mere pleasure of God." By the mere pleasure of God, I mean His sovereign pleasure, His arbitrary will, restrained by no obligation, hindered by no manner of difficulty, any more than if nothing else but God's mere will had in the least degree, or in any respect whatsoever, any hand in the preservation of wicked men one moment. The truth of this observation may appear by the following considerations.

1. There is no want of power in God to cast wicked men into hell at any moment. Men's hands cannot be strong when God rises up. The strongest have no power to resist Him, nor can any deliver out of His hands. He is not only able to cast wicked men into hell, but He can most easily do it. Sometimes an earthly prince meets with a great deal of difficulty to subdue a rebel, who has found means to fortify himself, and has made himself strong by the numbers of his followers. But it is not so with God. There is no fortress that is any defense from the power of God. Though hand join in hand, and vast multitudes of God's enemies combine and associate themselves, they are easily broken in pieces. They are as great heaps of light chaff before the whirlwind; or large quantities of dry stubble before devouring flames. We find it easy to tread on and crush a worm that we see crawling on the earth; so it is easy for us to cut or singe a slender thread that any thing hangs by: thus easy is it for God, when he pleases, to cast His enemies down to hell. What are we, that we should think to stand before him, at whose rebuke the earth trembles, and before whom the rocks are thrown down?

2. They deserve to be cast into hell; so that divine justice never stands in the way, it makes no objection against God's using His power at any

moment to destroy them. Yea, on the contrary, justice calls aloud for an infinite punishment of their sins. Divine justice says of the tree that brings forth such grapes of Sodom, "Cut it down, why cumbereth it the ground?" Luke 13.7. The sword of divine justice is every moment brandished over their heads, and it is nothing but the hand of arbitrary mercy, and God's will, that holds it back.

3. They are already under a sentence of condemnation to hell. They do not only justly deserve to be cast down thither, but the sentence of the law of God, that eternal and immutable rule of righteousness that God has fixed between Him and mankind, is gone out against them, and stands against them; so that they are bound over already to hell. John 3.18: "He that believeth not is condemned already." So that every unconverted man properly belongs to hell; that is his place; from thence he is, John 8.23: "Ye are from beneath." And thither he is bound; it is the place that justice, and God's word, and the sentence of his unchangeable law assign to him.

4. They are now the objects of that very same anger and wrath of God that is expressed in the torments of hell. And the reason why they do not go down to hell at each moment is not because God, in whose power they are, is not then very angry with them as angry as He is with many miserable creatures now tormented in hell, who there feel and bear the fierceness of His wrath. Yea, God is a great deal more angry with great numbers that are now on earth: yea, doubtless, with many that are now in this congregation, who it may be are at ease, than He is with many of those that are now in the flames of hell.

So that it is not because God is unmindful of their wickedness, and does not resent it, that He does not let loose His hand and cut them off. God is not altogether such an one as themselves, though they may imagine Him to be so. The wrath of God burns against them, their damnation does not slumber; the pit is prepared, the fire is made ready, the furnace is now hot, ready to receive them; the flames do now rage and glow. The glittering sword is whet, and held over them, and the pit hath opened its mouth under them.

5. The devil stands ready to fall upon them, and seize them as his own, at what moment God shall permit him. They belong to him; he has their souls in his possession, and under his dominion. The scripture represents them as his goods, Luke 11.12. The devils watch them; they are ever by them at their right hand; they stand waiting for them, like greedy hungry lions

that see their prey, and expect to have it, but are for the present kept back. If God should withdraw His hand, by which they are restrained, they would in one moment fly upon their poor souls. The old serpent is gaping for them; hell opens it mouth wide to receive them; and if God should permit it, they would be hastily swallowed up and lost.

6. There are in the souls of wicked men those hellish principles reigning that would presently kindle and flame out into hell fire, if it were not for God's restraints. There is laid in the very nature of carnal men a foundation for the torments of hell. There are those corrupt principles, in reigning power in them, and in full possession of them, that are seeds of hell fire. These principles are active and powerful, exceeding violent in their nature, and if it were not for the restraining hand of God upon them, they would soon break out, they would flame out after the same manner as the same corruptions, the same enmity does in the hearts of damned souls, and would beget the same torments as they do in them. The souls of the wicked are in scripture compared to the troubled sea, Isaiah 57.20. For the present, God restrains their wickedness by His mighty power, as He does the raging waves of the troubled sea, saying, "Hitherto shalt thou come, and but further;" but if God should withdraw that restraining power, it would soon carry all before it. Sin is the ruin and misery of the soul; it is destructive in its nature; and if God should leave it without restraint, there would need nothing else to make the soul perfectly miserable. The corruption of the heart of man is immoderate and boundless in its fury; and while wicked men live here, it is like fire pent up by God's restraints, whereas if it were let loose, it would set on fire the course of nature; and as the heart is now a sink of sin, so if sin was not restrained, it would immediately turn the soul into a fiery oven, or a furnace of fire and brimstone.

7. It is no security to wicked men for one moment that there are no visible means of death at hand. It is no security to a natural man that he is now in health and that he does not see which way he should now immediately go out of the world by any accident, and that there is no visible danger in any respect in his circumstances. The manifold and continual experience of the world in all ages, shows this is no evidence that a man is not on the very brink of eternity, and that the next step will not be into another world. The unseen, unthought-of ways and means of persons going suddenly out of the world are innumerable and inconceivable. Unconverted men walk over the pit of hell on a rotten covering, and there are innumerable places

in this covering so weak that they will not bear their weight, and these places are not seen. The arrows of death fly unseen at noonday; the sharpest sight cannot discern them. God has so many different unsearchable ways of taking wicked men out of the world and sending them to hell, that there is nothing to make it appear that God had need to be at the expense of a miracle, or go out of the ordinary course of His providence, to destroy any wicked man at any moment. All the means that there are of sinners going out of the world are so in God's hands, and so universally and absolutely subject to His power and determination, that it does not depend at all the less on the mere will of God whether sinners shall at any moment go to hell than if means were never made use of or at all concerned in the case.

8. Natural men's prudence and care to preserve their own lives, or the care of others to preserve them, do not secure them a moment. To this, divine providence and universal experience do also bear testimony. There is this clear evidence that men's own wisdom is no security to them from death, that if it were otherwise we should see some difference between the wise and politic men of the world, and others, with regard to their liableness to early and unexpected death: but how is it in fact? Ecclesiastes 2.16: "How dieth the wise man? even as the fool."

9. All wicked men's pains and contrivance which they use to escape hell, while they continue to reject Christ, and so remain wicked men, do not secure them from hell one moment. Almost every natural man that hears of hell, flatters himself that he shall escape it; he depends upon himself for his own security; he flatters himself in what he has done, in what he is now doing, or what he intends to do. Every one lays out matters in his own mind how he shall avoid damnation, and flatters himself that he contrives well for himself, and that his schemes will not fail. They hear indeed that there are but few saved, and that the greater part of men that have died heretofore are gone to hell; but each one imagines that he lays out matters better for his own escape than others have done. He does not intend to come to that place of torment; he says within himself that he intends to take effectual care, and to order matters so for himself as not to fail.

But the foolish children of men miserably delude themselves in their own schemes, and in confidence in their own strength and wisdom; they trust to nothing but a shadow. The greater part of those who heretofore have lived under the same means of grace, and are now dead, are undoubtedly gone to hell; and it was not because they were not as wise as those who are now alive: it was not because they did not lay out matters as well for themselves to secure their own escape. If we could speak with them, and inquire of them, one by one, whether they expected, when alive, and when they used to hear about hell, ever to be the subjects of that misery, we doubtless, should hear one and another reply, "No, I never intended to come here: I had laid out matters otherwise in my mind; I thought I should contrive well for myself: I thought my scheme good. I intended to take effectual care; but it came upon me unexpected; I did not look for it at that time, and in that manner; it came as a thief: Death outwitted me: God's wrath was too quick for me. Oh, my cursed foolishness! I was flattering myself, and pleasing myself with vain dreams of what I would do hereafter; and when I was saying, peace and safety, then suddenly destruction came upon me."

10. God has laid Himself under no obligation by any promise to keep any natural man out of hell one moment. God certainly has made no promises either of eternal life or of any deliverance or preservation from eternal death but what are contained in the covenant of grace, the promises that are given in Christ, in whom all the promises are yea and amen. But surely they have no interest in the promises of the covenant of grace who are not the children of the covenant, who do not believe in any of the promises, and have no interest in the Mediator of the covenant.

So that, whatever some have imagined and pretended about promises made to natural men's earnest seeking and knocking, it is plain and manifest that whatever pains a natural man takes in religion, whatever prayers he makes, till he believes in Christ, God is under no manner of obligation to keep him a moment from eternal destruction.

So that, thus it is that natural men are held in the hand of God, over the pit of hell; they have deserved the fiery pit, and are already sentenced to it; and God is dreadfully provoked, His anger is as great towards them as to those that are actually suffering the executions of the fierceness of His wrath in hell, and they have done nothing in the least to appease or abate that anger, neither is God in the least bound by any promise to hold them up one moment; the devil is waiting for them, hell is gaping for them, the flames gather and flash about them, and would fain lay hold on them, and swallow them up; the fire pent up in their own hearts is struggling to break out: and they have no interest in any Mediator, there are no means within reach that can be any security to them. In short, they have no refuge, nothing to take hold of; all that preserves them every moment is the mere arbitrary will, and uncovenanted, unobliged forbearance of an incensed God.

Application

The use of this awful subject may be for awakening unconverted persons in this congregation. This that you have heard is the case of every one of you that are out of Christ. That world of misery, that lake of burning brimstone is extended abroad under you. There is the dreadful pit of the glowing flames of the wrath of God; there is hell's wide-gaping mouth open; and you have nothing to stand upon, nor any thing to take hold of; there is nothing between you and hell but the air; it is only the power and mere pleasure of God that holds you up.

You probably are not sensible of this; you find you are kept out of hell, but do not see the hand of God in it; but look at other things, as the good state of your bodily constitution, your care of your own life, and the means you use for your own preservation. But indeed these things are nothing; if God should withdraw His hand, they would avail no more to keep you from falling, than the thin air to hold up a person that is suspended in it.

Your wickedness makes you as it were heavy as lead, and to tend downwards with great weight and pressure towards hell; and if God should let you go, you would immediately sink and swiftly descend and plunge into the bottomless gulf, and your healthy constitution, and your own care and prudence, and best contrivance, and all your righteousness, would have no more influence to uphold you and keep you out of hell, than a spider's web would have to stop a fallen rock. Were it not for the sovereign pleasure of God, the earth would not bear you one moment; for you are a burden to it; the creation groans with you; the creature is made subject to the bondage of your corruption, not willingly; the sun does not willingly shine upon you to give you light to serve sin and Satan; the earth does not willingly yield her increase to satisfy your lusts; nor is it willingly a stage for your wickedness to be acted upon; the air does not willingly serve you for breath to maintain the flame of life in your vitals, while you spend your life in the service of God's enemies. God's creatures are good, and were made for men to serve God with, and do not willingly subserve to any other purpose, and groan when they are abused to purposes so directly contrary to their nature and end. And the world would spew you out, were it not for the sovereign hand of Him who hath subjected it in hope. There are black clouds of God's wrath now hanging directly over your heads, full of the dreadful storm, and big with thunder; and were it not for the restraining hand of God, it would immediately burst forth upon you. The sovereign pleasure of God, for the present, stays His rough wind; otherwise it would come with fury, and your destruction would come like a whirlwind, and you would be like the chaff of the summer threshing floor.

The wrath of God is like great waters that are dammed for the present; they increase more and more, and rise higher and higher, till an outlet is given; and the longer the stream is stopped, the more rapid and mighty is its course when once it is let loose. It is true that judgment against your evil works has not been executed hitherto; the floods of God's vengeance have been withheld; but your guilt in the meantime is constantly increasing, and you are every day treasuring up more wrath; the waters are constantly rising, and waxing more and more mighty; and there is nothing but the mere pleasure of God that holds the waters back, that are unwilling to be stopped, and press hard to go forward. If God should only withdraw His hand from the floodgate, it would immediately fly open, and the fiery floods of the fierceness and wrath of God, would rush forth with inconceivable fury and would come upon you with omnipotent power; and if your strength were ten thousand times greater than it is, yea, ten thousand times greater than the strength of the stoutest, sturdiest devil in hell, it would be nothing to withstand or endure it.

The bow of God's wrath is bent, and the arrow made ready on the string, and justice bends the arrow at your heart, and strains the bow, and it is nothing but the mere pleasure of God, and that of an angry God, without any promise or obligation at all, that keeps the arrow one moment from being made drunk with your blood. Thus all you that never passed under a great change of heart, by the mighty power of the Spirit of God upon your souls, all you that were never born again, and made new creatures, and raised from being dead in sin, to a state of new, and before altogether unexperienced light and life, are in the hands of an angry God. However you may have reformed your life in many things, and may have had religious affections, and may keep up a form of religion in your families and closets, and in the house of God, it is nothing but His mere pleasure that keeps you from being this moment swallowed up in everlasting destruction. However unconvinced you may now be of the truth of what you hear, by and by you will be fully convinced of it. Those that are gone from being in the like circumstances with you see that it was so with them; for destruction came suddenly upon most of them; when they expected nothing of it and while they were saying, peace and safety: now they see that those things on which they depended for peace and safety, were nothing but thin air and empty shadows.

The God that holds you over the pit of hell, much as one holds a spider or some loathsome insect over the fire, abhors you, and is dreadfully provoked: His wrath towards you burns like fire; He looks upon you as worthy of nothing else but to be cast into the fire; He is of purer eyes than to bear to have you in His sight; you are ten thousand times more abominable in His eyes than the most hateful venomous serpent is in ours. You have offended Him infinitely more than ever a stubborn rebel did his prince; and yet it is nothing but His hand that holds you from falling into the fire every moment. It is to be ascribed to nothing else, that you did not go to hell the last night; that you was suffered to awake again in this world, after you closed your eyes to sleep. And there is no other reason to be given, why you have not dropped into hell since you arose in the morning, but that God's hand has held you up. There is no other reason to be given why you have not gone to hell since you have sat here in the house of God, provoking His pure eyes by your sinful wicked manner of attending His solemn worship. Yea, there is nothing else that is to be given as a reason why you do not this very moment drop down into hell.

O sinner! Consider the fearful danger you are in: it is a great furnace of wrath, a wide and bottomless pit, full of the fire of wrath, that you are held over in the hand of that God, whose wrath is provoked and incensed as much against you, as against many of the damned in hell. You hang by a slender thread, with the flames of divine wrath flashing about it, and ready every moment to singe it, and burn it asunder; and you have no interest in any Mediator, and nothing to lay hold of to save yourself, nothing to keep off the flames of wrath, nothing of your own, nothing that you ever have done, nothing that you can do, to induce God to spare you one moment. And consider here more particularly, several things concerning that wrath that you are in such danger of.

1. Whose wrath it is? It is the wrath of the infinite God. If it were only the wrath of man, though it were of the most potent prince, it would be comparatively little to be regarded. The wrath of kings is very much dreaded, especially of absolute monarchs, who have the possessions and lives of

their subjects wholly in their power, to be disposed of at their mere will. Proverbs 20.2: "The fear of a king is as the roaring of a lion: Whoso provoketh him to anger, sinneth against his own soul." The subject that very much enrages an arbitrary prince, is liable to suffer the most extreme torments that human art can invent, or human power can inflict. But the greatest earthly potentates in their greatest majesty and strength, and when clothed in their greatest terrors, are but feeble, despicable worms of the dust, in comparison of the great and almighty Creator and King of heaven and earth. It is but little that they can do, when most enraged, and when they have exerted the utmost of their fury. All the kings of the earth, before God, are as grasshoppers; they are nothing and less than nothing: both their love and their hatred is to be despised. The wrath of the great King of kings, is as much more terrible than theirs, as His majesty is greater. Luke 12.4–5: "And I say unto you, my friends, Be not afraid of them that kill the body, and after that, have no more that they can do. But I will forewarn you whom you shall fear: fear him, which after he hath killed, hath power to cast into hell: yea, I say unto you, Fear him."

2. It is the fierceness of His wrath that you are exposed to. We often read of the fury of God; as in Isaiah 59.18: "According to their deeds, accordingly he will repay fury to his adversaries." So Isaiah 66.15: "For behold, the Lord will come with fire, and with his chariots like a whirlwind, to render his anger with fury, and his rebuke with flames of fire." And in many other places. So Revelation 19.15: we read of "the wine press of the fierceness and wrath of Almighty God." The words are exceeding terrible. If it had only been said, "the wrath of God," the words would have implied that which is infinitely dreadful: but it is "the fierceness and wrath of God." The fury of God! the fierceness of Jehovah! Oh, how dreadful must that be! Who can utter or conceive what such expressions carry in them! But it is also "the fierceness and wrath of Almighty God." As though there would be a very great manifestation of His almighty power in what the fierceness of His wrath should inflict, as though omnipotence should be as it were enraged, and exerted, as men are wont to exert their strength in the fierceness of their wrath. Oh! then, what will be the consequence! What will become of the poor worms that shall suffer it! Whose hands can be strong? And whose heart can endure? To what a dreadful, inexpressible, inconceivable depth of misery must the poor creature be sunk who shall be the subject of this!

Consider this, you that are here present that yet remain in an unregenerate state. That God will execute the fierceness of His anger implies that He will inflict wrath without any pity. When God beholds the ineffable extremity of your case, and sees your torment to be so vastly disproportioned to your strength, and sees how your poor soul is crushed, and sinks down, as it were, into an infinite gloom; He will have no compassion upon you, He will not forbear the executions of His wrath, or in the least lighten His hand; there shall be no moderation or mercy, nor will God then at all stay His rough wind; He will have no regard to your welfare, nor be at all careful lest you should suffer too much in any other sense, than only that you shall not suffer beyond what strict justice requires. Nothing shall be withheld because it is so hard for you to bear. Ezekiel 8.18: "Therefore will I also deal in fury: mine eye shall not spare, neither will I have pity; and though they cry in mine ears with a loud voice, yet I will not hear them." Now God stands ready to pity you; this is a day of mercy; you may cry now with some encouragement of obtaining mercy. But when once the day of mercy is past, your most lamentable and dolorous cries and shrieks will be in vain; you will be wholly lost and thrown away of God as to any regard to your welfare. God will have no other use to put you to, but only to suffer misery; you shall be continued in being to no other end; for you will be a vessel of wrath fitted to destruction; and there will be no other use of this vessel, but to be filled full of wrath. God will be so far from pitying you when you cry to Him, that it is said He will only "laugh and mock." Proverbs 1.25–26, etc.

How awful are those words, Isaiah 63.3, which are the words of the great God: "I will tread them in mine anger, and will trample them in my fury, and their blood shall be sprinkled upon my garments, and I will stain all my raiment." It is perhaps impossible to conceive of words that carry in them greater manifestations of these three things, viz., contempt, and hatred, and fierceness of indignation. If you cry to God to pity you, He will be so far from pitying you in your doleful case, or showing you the least regard or favor, that instead of that, He will only tread you under foot. And though He will know that you cannot bear the weight of omnipotence treading upon you, yet He will not regard that, but He will crush you under His feet without mercy; He will crush out your blood, and make it fly and it shall be sprinkled on His garments, so as to stain all His raiment. He will not only hate you, but He will have you in the utmost contempt: no place shall be thought fit for you, but under His feet to be trodden down as the mire of the streets.

3. The misery you are exposed to is that which God will inflict to that end, that He might show what that wrath of Jehovah is. God hath had it on His heart to show to angels and men both how excellent His love is, and also how terrible His wrath is. Sometimes earthly kings have a mind to show how terrible their wrath is, by the extreme punishments they would execute on those that provoke them. Nebuchadnezzar, that mighty and haughty monarch of the Chaldean empire, was willing to show his wrath when enraged with Shadrach, Meshech, and Abednego; and accordingly gave orders that the burning fiery furnace should be heated seven times hotter than it was before; doubtless, it was raised to the utmost degree of fierceness that human art could raise it. But the great God is also willing to show His wrath and magnify His awful majesty and mighty power in the extreme sufferings of His enemies. Romans 9.22: "What if God, willing to show his wrath, and to make his power known, endure with much long-suffering the vessels of wrath fitted to destruction?" And seeing this in His design, and what He has determined, even to show how terrible the restrained wrath, the fury and fierceness of Jehovah is, He will do it to effect. There will be something accomplished and brought to pass that will be dreadful with a witness. When the great and angry God hath risen up and executed His awful vengeance on the poor sinner, and the wretch is actually suffering the infinite weight and power of His indignation, then will God call upon the whole universe to behold that awful majesty and mighty power that is to be seen in it. Isaiah 33.12–14: "And the people shall be as the burnings of lime, as thorns cut up shall they be burnt in the fire. Hear ye that are far off, what I have done; yet that are near, acknowledge my might. The sinners in Zion are afraid; fearfulness hath surprised the hypocrites," etc.

Thus it will be with you that are in an unconverted state, if you continue in it; the infinite might, and majesty, and terribleness of the omnipotent God shall be magnified upon you, in the ineffable strength of your torments. You shall be tormented in the presence of the holy angels, and in the presence of the Lamb; and when you shall be in this state of suffering, the glorious inhabitants of heaven shall go forth and look on the awful spectacle, that they may see what the wrath and fierceness of the Almighty is; and when they have seen it, they will fall down and adore that great power and majesty. Isaiah 66.23–24: "And it shall come to pass, that from one new moon to another, and from one sabbath to another, shall flesh come to worship before me, saith the Lord. And they shall go forth and look upon the carcasses of the men that have transgressed against me; for their worm shall not die, neither shall their fire be quenched, and they shall be an abhorring unto all flesh."

4. It is everlasting wrath. It would be dreadful to suffer this fierceness and wrath of Almighty God one moment; but you must suffer it to all eternity. There will be no end to this exquisite horrible misery. When you look forward, you shall see a long forever, a boundless duration before you, which will swallow up your thoughts, and amaze your soul; and you will absolutely despair of ever having any deliverance, any end, any mitigation, any rest at all. You will know certainly that you must wear out long ages, millions of millions of ages, in wrestling and conflicting with this almighty merciless vengeance; and then when you have done so, when so many ages have actually been spent by you in this manner, you will know that all is but a point to what remains. So that your punishment will indeed be infinite. Oh, who can express what the state of a soul in such circumstances is! All that we can possibly say about it gives but a very feeble, faint representation of it; it is inexpressible and inconceivable: For "who knows the power of God's anger?"

How dreadful is the state of those that are daily and hourly in danger of this great wrath and infinite misery! But this is the dismal case of every soul in this congregation that has not been born again, however moral and strict, sober and religious, they may otherwise be. Oh that you would consider it, whether you be young or old! There is reason to think that there are many in this congregation now hearing this discourse that will actually be the subjects of this very misery to all eternity. We know not who they are, or in what seats they sit, or what thoughts they now have. It may be they are now at ease, and hear all these things without much disturbance, and are now flattering themselves that they are not the persons, promising themselves that they shall escape. If they knew that there was one person, and but one, in the whole congregation, that was to be the subject of this misery, what an awful thing would it be to think of! If we knew who it was, what an awful sight would it be to see such a person! How might all the rest of the congregation lift up a lamentable and bitter cry over him! But, alas! instead of one, how many is it likely will remember this discourse in hell? And it would be a wonder, if some that are now present should not be in hell in a very short time, even before this year is out. And it would be no wonder, if some persons, that now sit here, in some seats of this meetinghouse, in health, quiet and secure, should be there before tomorrow morning. Those of you that finally continue in a natural condition, that shall keep out of hell longest will be there in a little time! your damnation does not slumber; it will come swiftly, and, in all probability, very suddenly upon many of you. You have reason to wonder that you are not already in hell. It is doubtless the case of some whom you have seen and known, that never deserved hell more than you, and that heretofore appeared likely to have been now alive as you. Their case is past all hope; they are crying in extreme misery and perfect despair; but here you are in the land of the living and in the house of God, and have an opportunity to obtain salvation. What would not those poor damned hopeless souls give for one day's opportunity as you now enjoy!

And now you have an extraordinary opportunity, a day wherein Christ has thrown the door of mercy wide open, and stands in calling and crying with a loud voice to poor sinners; a day wherein many are flocking to Him, and pressing into the kingdom of God. Many are daily coming from the east, west, north and south; many that were very lately in the same miserable condition that you are in are now in a happy state, with their hearts filled with love to Him who has loved them, and washed them from their sins in His own blood, and rejoicing in hope of the glory of God. How awful is it to be left behind at such a day! To see so many others feasting, while you are pining and perishing! To see so many rejoicing and singing for joy of heart, while you have cause to mourn for sorrow of heart and howl for vexation of spirit! How can you rest one moment in such a condition? Are not your souls as precious as the souls of the people at Suffield, where they are flocking from day to day to Christ?

Are there not many here who have lived long in the world, and are not to this day born again? and so are aliens from the commonwealth of Israel, and have done nothing ever since they have lived, but treasure up wrath against the day of wrath? Oh, sirs, your case, in an especial manner, is extremely dangerous. Your guilt and hardness of heart is extremely great. Do you not see how generally persons of your years are passed over and left, in the present remarkable and wonderful dispensation of God's mercy? You had need to consider yourselves, and wake thoroughly out of sleep. You cannot bear the fierceness and wrath of the infinite God. And you, young men, and young women, will you neglect this precious season which you now enjoy, when so many others of your age are renouncing all youthful vanities, and flocking to Christ? You especially have now an extraordinary opportunity; but if you neglect it, it will soon be with you as with those persons who spent all the precious days in youth in sin, and are now come to such a dreadful pass in blindness and hardness. And you, children, who are unconverted, do not you know that you are going down to hell, to bear the dreadful wrath of that God, who is now angry with you every day and every night? Will you be content to be the children of the devil, when so many other children in the land are converted, and are become the holy and happy children of the King of kings?

And let everyone that is yet of Christ, and hanging over the pit of hell, whether they be old men and women, or middle-aged, or young people, or little children, now hearken to the loud calls of God's word and providence. This acceptable year of the Lord, a day of such great favors to some, will doubtless be a day of as remarkable vengeance to others. Men's hearts harden, and their guilt increases apace at such a day as this, if they neglect their souls; and never was there so great danger of such persons being given up to hardness of heart and blindness of mind. God seems now to be hastily gathering in His elect in all parts of the land; and probably the greater part of adult persons that ever shall be saved, will be brought in now in a little time, and that it will be as it was on that great outpouring of the Spirit upon the Jews in the apostles' days; the election will obtain, and the rest will be blinded. If this should be the case with you, you will eternally curse this day, and will curse the day that ever you was born, to see such a season of the pouring out of God's Spirit, and will wish that you had died and gone to hell before you had seen it. Now undoubtedly it is, as it was in the days of John the Baptist, the axe is in an extraordinary manner laid at the root of the trees, that every tree which brings not forth good fruit, may be hewn down and cast into the fire.

Therefore, let everyone that is out of Christ, now awake and fly from the wrath to come. The wrath of Almighty God is now undoubtedly hanging over a great part of this congregation: Let everyone fly out of Sodom: "Haste and escape for your lives, look not behind you, escape to the mountain, lest you be consumed."

1782

"Where do passions find room in so diminutive a body?" asks J. Hector St. John in *Letters from an American Farmer*. He is speaking here about a hummingbird that he sees on his family farm, but he might as well be describing himself in the book. In *American Farmer*, St. John warns us that we should not expect "the style of the learned, the reflections of the patriot, the discussions of the politician, the curious observations of the naturalist, or the pleasing garb of the man of taste," but rather the undistorted, unguarded, and sincere observations of "a cultivator of the earth." If he is a hummingbird, it's accidental. If there be metaphors in his book, they've snuck in without his knowing:

> Sometimes, from what motives I know not, it will tear and lacerate flowers into a hundred pieces, for, strange to tell, they are the most irascible of the feathered tribe. Where do passions find room in so diminutive a body? They often fight with the fury of lions until one of the combatants falls a sacrifice and dies.

It's an observation in which many readers have nevertheless found metaphors for a young America populated by the old blood of Europe, yet one that has suddenly become untethered from the traditions and institutions of European thinking. And indeed, on closer inspection *Letters from an American Farmer* by J. Hector St. John is a narrative that is rife with symbol, so much so that scholars have now started to classify the book as an epistolary novel rather than as a memoir, an essay, or even a loose history. His name, scholars note, is not really "J. Hector St. John," but Michel Guillaume Jean de Crèvecoeur, and he was born not in eastern Pennsylvania, but in Normandy, France. He lived in America for only fifteen years, farmed for fewer than six, and took up writing not by accident but because that's what he was trained to do at the Collège Royal de Bourbon in France. Indeed, the structure of his book is consciously modeled on Montesquieu's *Persian Letters,* a popular epistolary novel that was published while Crèvecoeur was a student. So as far as authenticity goes, there might not be a single nonfiction entry in the American literary canon that is more manufactured than "*Letters from an American Farmer,* by J. Hector St. John." And yet, does that mean we ought to reassign the book's genre? When does a letter become "epistolary"? When does a person turn into a "persona"? And when does the use of form, structure, character, or voice turn an imaginative exploration of a personal experience into something that is "inauthentic"? As with any work of literature, the true value of Crèvecoeur's book lies not in the supposed naïveté of its speaker, but rather in the talents of its maker. We see this most powerfully at the end of the book, by which time the construction of "St. John"'s world and the realities of Crèvecoeur's life begin to intersect at jagged angles. A war has broken out between the colonists and the British, and Crèvecoeur tells us that he has tried to remain neutral. But as the Americans creep closer to revolution they begin to view his unwillingness to choose sides as suspicious. He is jailed. His farm is burned. His wife is killed. The children he never mentions by name are swept up into the chaos of war and lost. *Where do passions find room in so diminutive a body?* It is not really a question about hummingbirds, after all, nor about American pluck, the tenacity of "St. John," or even the hubris of Crèvecoeur. It's a question instead about being human. It's about our capacity to shape the raw and bloody materiality of our world into quietly profound and resonant meditations. It's about those tiny green portions of our individual lives that we somehow manage to transform into things that are even greater than themselves: into metaphor.

J. Hector St. John

On Snakes; and
On the Humming-Bird

Why would you prescribe this task; you know that what we take up our-selves seems always lighter than what is imposed on us by others. You insist on my saying something about our snakes; and in relating what I know concerning them, were it not for two singularities, the one of which I saw and the other I received from an eyewitness, I should have but very little to observe. The southern provinces are the countries where Nature has formed the greatest variety of alligators, snakes, serpents, and scorpions from the smallest size up to the pine barren, the largest species known here. We have but two, whose stings are mortal, which deserve to be mentioned; as for the black one, it is remarkable for nothing but its industry, agility, beauty, and the art of enticing birds by the power of its eyes. I admire it much and never kill it, though its formidable length and appearance often get the better of the philosophy of some people, particularly Europeans. The most dangerous one is the pilot, or copperhead, for the poison of which no remedy has yet been discovered. It bears the first name because it always precedes the rattlesnake, that is, quits its state of torpidity in the spring a week before the other. It bears the second name on account of its head being adorned with many copper-coloured spots. It lurks in rocks near the water and is extremely active and dangerous. Let man beware of it! I have heard only of one person who was stung by a copperhead in this country. The poor wretch instantly swelled in a most dreadful manner; a multitude of spots of different hues alternately appeared and vanished on different parts of his body; his eyes were filled with madness and rage; he cast them on all present with the most vindictive looks; he thrust out his tongue as the snakes do; he hissed through his teeth with inconceivable strength and became an object of terror to all bystanders. To the lividness of a corpse he united the desperate force of a maniac; they hardly were able to fasten him so as to guard themselves from his attacks, when in the space of two hours death relieved the poor wretch from his struggles and the spectators from their apprehensions. The poison of the rattlesnake is not mortal in so short a space, and hence there is more time to procure relief; we are acquainted with several antidotes with which almost every family is provided. They are extremely inactive, and if not touched, are perfectly inoffensive. I once saw, as I was travelling, a great cliff which was full of them; I handled several, and they appeared to be dead; they were all entwined together, and thus they remain until the return of the sun. I found them out by following the track of some wild hogs which had fed on them; and even the Indians often regale on them. When they find them asleep, they put a small forked stick over their necks, which they keep immovably fixed on the ground, giving the snake a piece of leather to bite; and this they pull back several times with great force until they observe their two poisonous fangs torn out. Then they cut off the head, skin the body, and cook it as we do eels; and their flesh is extremely sweet and white. I once saw a *tamed one,* as gentle as you can possibly conceive a reptile to be; it took to the water and swam whenever it pleased; and when the boys to whom it belonged called it back, their summons was readily obeyed. It had been deprived of its fangs by the preceding method; they often stroked it with a soft brush, and this friction seemed to cause the most pleasing sensations, for it would turn on its back to enjoy it, as a cat does before the fire. One of this species was the cause, some years ago, of a most deplorable accident, which I shall relate to you as I had it from the widow and mother of the victims. A Dutch farmer of the Minisink went to mowing, with his Negroes, in his boots, a precaution used to prevent being stung. Inadvertently he trod on a snake, which immediately flew at his legs; and as it drew back in order to renew its blow, one of his Negroes cut it in two with his scythe. They prosecuted their work and returned home; at night the farmer pulled off his boots and went to bed, and was soon after attacked with a strange sickness at his stomach; he swelled, and before a physician could be sent for, died. The sudden death of this man did not cause much inquiry; the neighbourhood wondered, as is usual in such cases, and without any further examination, the corpse was buried. A few days after, the son put on his father's boots and went to the meadow; at night he pulled them off, went to bed, and was attacked with the same symptoms about the same time, and died in the morning. A little before he expired, the doctor came, but was not able to assign what could be the cause of so singular a disorder; however, rather than appear wholly at a loss before the country people, he pronounced both father and son to have been bewitched. Some weeks after, the widow sold all the movables for the benefit of the younger children, and the farm was leased. One of the neighbours, who bought the boots, presently put them on, and was attacked in the same manner as the other two had been; but this man's wife, being alarmed by what had happened in the former family, despatched one of her Negroes for an eminent physician, who, fortunately having heard something of the dreadful affair, guessed at the cause, applied oil, etc., and recovered the man. The boots which had been so fatal were then carefully examined and he found that the two fangs of the snake had been left in the leather after being wrenched out of their sockets by the strength with which the snake had drawn back its head. The bladders which contained the poison and several of the small nerves were still fresh and adhered to the boot. The unfortunate father and son had been poisoned by pulling off these boots, in which action they imperceptibly scratched their legs with the points of the fangs, through the hollow of which some of this astonishing poison was conveyed. You have no doubt heard of their rattles if you have not seen them; the only observation I wish to make is that the rattling is loud and distinct when they are angry and, on the contrary, when pleased, it sounds like a distant trepidation, in which nothing distinct is heard. In the thick settlements, they are now become very scarce, for wherever they are met with, open war is declared against them, so that in a few years there will be none left but on our mountains. The black snake, on the contrary, always diverts me because it excites no idea of danger. Their swiftness is astonishing; they will sometimes equal that of a horse; at other times they will climb up trees in quest of our tree toads or glide on the ground at full length. On some occasions they present themselves half in the reptile state, half erect; their eyes and their heads in the erect posture appear to great advantage; the former display a fire which I have often admired, and it is by these they are enabled to fascinate birds and squirrels. When they have fixed their eyes on an animal, they become immovable, only turning their head sometimes to the right and sometimes to the left, but still with their sight invariably directed to the object. The distracted victim, instead of flying its enemy, seems to be arrested by some invincible power;

it screams; now approaches and then recedes; and after skipping about with unaccountable agitation, finally rushes into the jaws of the snake and is swallowed, as soon as it is covered with a slime or glue to make it slide easily down the throat of the devourer.

One anecdote I must relate, the circumstances of which are as true as they are singular. One of my constant walks when I am at leisure is in my lowlands, where I have the pleasure of seeing my cattle, horses, and colts. Exuberant grass replenishes all my fields, the best representative of our wealth; in the middle of that track I have cut a ditch eight feet wide, the banks of which Nature adorns every spring with the wild salendine and other flowering weeds, which on these luxuriant grounds shoot up to a great height. Over this ditch I have erected a bridge, capable of bearing a loaded waggon; on each side I carefully sow every year some grains of hemp, which rise to the height of fifteen feet, so strong and so full of limbs as to resemble young trees; I once ascended one of them four feet above the ground. These produce natural arbours, rendered often still more compact by the assistance of an annual creeping plant, which we call a vine, that never fails to entwine itself among their branches and always produces a very desirable shade. From this simple grove I have amused myself a hundred times in observing the great number of humming-birds with which our country abounds: the wild blossoms everywhere attract the attention of these birds, which like bees subsist by suction. From this retreat I distinctly watch them in all their various attitudes, but their flight is so rapid that you cannot distinguish the motion of their wings. On this little bird Nature has profusely lavished her most splendid colours; the most perfect azure, the most beautiful gold, the most dazzling red, are forever in contrast and help to embellish the plumes of his majestic head. The richest palette of the most luxuriant painter could never invent anything to be compared to the variegated tints with which this insect bird is arrayed. Its bill is as long and as sharp as a coarse sewing needle; like the bee, Nature has taught it to find out in the calyx of flowers and blossoms those mellifluous particles that serve it for sufficient food; and yet it seems to leave them untouched, undeprived of anything that our eyes can possibly distinguish. When it feeds, it appears as if immovable, though continually on the wing; and sometimes, from what motives I know not, it will tear and lacerate flowers into a hundred pieces, for, strange to tell, they are the most irascible of the feathered tribe. Where do passions find room in so diminutive a body? They often fight with the fury of lions until one of the combatants falls a sacrifice and dies. When fatigued, it has often perched within a few feet of me, and on such favourable opportunities I have surveyed it with the most minute attention. Its little eyes appear like diamonds, reflecting light on every side; most elegantly finished in all parts, it is a miniature work of our Great Parent, who seems to have formed it the smallest, and at the same time the most beautiful of the winged species.

As I was one day sitting solitary and pensive in my primitive arbour, my attention was engaged by a strange sort of rustling noise at some paces distant. I looked all around without distinguishing anything, until I climbed one of my great hemp stalks, when to my astonishment I beheld two snakes of considerable length, the one pursuing the other with great celerity through a hemp-stubble field. The aggressor was the black kind, six feet long; the fugitive was a water snake, nearly of equal dimensions. They soon met, and in the fury of their first encounter, they appeared in an instant firmly twisted together; and whilst their united tails beat the ground, they mutually tried with open jaws to lacerate each other. What a fell aspect did they present! Their heads were compressed to a very small size, their eyes flashed fire; and after this conflict had lasted about five minutes, the second found means to disengage itself from the first and hurried toward the ditch. Its antagonist instantly assumed a new posture, and half creeping and half erect, with a majestic mien, overtook and attacked the other again, which placed itself in the same attitude and prepared to resist. The scene was uncommon and beautiful; for thus opposed, they fought with their jaws, biting each other with the utmost rage; but notwithstanding this appearance of mutual courage and fury, the water snake still seemed desirous of retreating toward the ditch, its natural element. This was no sooner perceived by the keen-eyed black one, than twisting its tail twice round a stalk of hemp and seizing its adversary by the throat, not by means of its jaws but by twisting its own neck twice round that of the water snake, pulled it back from the ditch. To prevent a defeat, the latter took hold likewise of a stalk on the bank, and by the acquisition of that point of resistance, became a match for its fierce antagonist. Strange was this to behold; two great snakes strongly adhering to the ground, mutually fastened together by means of the writhings which lashed them to each other, and stretched at their full length, they pulled but pulled in vain; and in the moments of greatest exertions, that part of their bodies which was entwined seemed extremely small, while the rest appeared inflated and now and then convulsed with strong undulations, rapidly following each other. Their eyes seemed on fire and ready to start out of their heads; at one time the conflict seemed decided; the water snake bent itself into two great folds and by that operation rendered the other more than commonly outstretched; the next minute the new struggles of the black one gained an unexpected superiority; it acquired two great folds likewise, which necessarily extended the body of its adversary in proportion as what it had contracted its own. These efforts were alternate; victory seemed doubtful, inclining sometimes to the one side and sometimes to the other, until at last the stalk to which the black snake fastened suddenly gave way, and in consequence of this accident they both plunged into the ditch. The water did not extinguish their vindictive rage; for by their agitations I could trace, though not distinguish, their mutual attacks. They soon reappeared on the surface twisted together, as in their first onset; but the black snake seemed to retain its wonted superiority, for its head was exactly fixed above that of the other, which it incessantly pressed down under the water, until it was stifled and sunk. The victor no sooner perceived its enemy incapable of farther resistance than, abandoning it to the current, it returned on shore and disappeared.

1783

This year, Washington Irving is born just a few days before the end of the Revolutionary War, and so he and America are both new to the world at a time when London is fifteen hundred years old, Beijing is over two thousand years old, and Jerusalem is nearing four thousand. It's from the weight of this kind of history that Irving will free Americans in his satirical and best-selling *A History of New York,* a book that lampoons history itself by preposterously insisting that in order to tell the story of Manhattan—an island with a population of twelve thousand people—he must first "proceed to notice the cosmogony or formation of this our globe":

> And now I give my readers fair warning, that I am about to plunge for a chapter or two, into as complete a labyrinth as ever historian was perplexed withal; therefore I advise them to take fast hold of my skirts, and keep close at my heels, venturing neither to the right hand nor to the left, least they get bemired in a slough of unintelligible learning, or have their brains knocked out, by some of those hard Greek names which will be flying about in all directions.

And so he continues, for two volumes, seven books, and fifty-seven individual chapters, to pile so much significance onto the city of New York that by the end of his *History* the city is crushed by the burden of history, and thus ultimately freed from it. This is just what America needs. After all, the United

States won't even elect its first president until five years from now. There's no currency, no court system, and no functioning federal government. When the temporary Confederation Congress tries to convene this year, it manages to rustle up only a quorum of representatives for five days out of its five months of scheduled meetings. It's a period that one historian subsequently called "the First Great American Identity Crisis"—the result of an apprehension, perhaps, about the realization that the democratic experiment that had been promised during the war would now have to be wrangled into existence. And no one is cheering them on. The most popular book in Europe at this time is a six-thousand-page work of natural history called *Histoire naturelle* by a Frenchman named Georges-Louis Leclerc, the comte de Buffon, who writes in volume six of his sweeping world treatise that

> in America, animated Nature is weaker, less active, and more circumscribed in the variety of her productions; for we perceive, from the enumeration of the American animals, that the numbers of species is not only fewer, but that, in general, all the animals are much smaller than those of the Old Continent. No American animal can be compared to the elephant, the rhinoceros, the hippopotamus, the giraffe, the lion, the tiger

—a claim Buffon formally names "the Theory of American Degeneracy," extending his indictment to include therefore not only America's puny animals but its inferior humans as well. It's a criticism that Americans take painfully to heart, chief among them Thomas Jefferson, who dedicates a chapter of his book *Notes on the State of Virginia* to debunking Buffon's theory, arguing that any differences between the Old World and the New shouldn't be interpreted as a degeneracy in the latter,

> as if both sides were not warmed by the same genial sun; as if a soil of the same chemical composition, was less capable of elaboration into animal nutriment; . . . The truth is, that a Pigmy and a Patagonian . . . derive their dimensions from the same nutritive juices.

Jefferson enlisted friends, soldiers, scouts, and hunters to help him find an animal that might prove Buffon's theory wrong—a quest he even took into the presidency with him, when he doubled the country's size with the Louisiana Purchase, urging Lewis and Clark to, among other things, bring him back the carcass of a beast. So one year during that presidency, when a Philadelphia painter is invited to New York to sketch some giant bones a farmer has dug up, it's clear there is more than just a portrait at stake. Charles Willson Peale will eventually become known as the curator of America's first great museum, but right now he is merely an enthusiastic patriot, and when he first sees the bones of an animal "jutting out of the Earth like a great mountain of promise," he knows what he has to do. Peale buys the bones for $2,500, combines them with the bones from a similar local find, and slowly reconstructs them into the shape of an animal that his young and struggling nation could be proud of having spawned.

"The Largest of Terrestrial Beings," Peale calls the beast, which quickly becomes known as the largest reconstructed fossilized skeleton in the world. It helps, of course, that Peale takes liberties in putting together the skeleton, padding each joint with a bit of extra "cartilage" and thus increasing the animal's size by more than a few feet. Nevertheless, the thing is big, and it ignites the imagination of an insecure America—a single, monstrous, in-your-face refutation of the claim that America is inferior to Europe. Nobody knows what kind of animal the bones belong to at this point, so scientists simply call it "the American incognitum"—"the American unknown"—a conveniently mysterious name that allows the young nation to fantasize about a beast that "stalks the western wilds," according to the American Philosophical Society, "laying waste to whole forests . . . as the groans of expiring animals are heard quivering in its wake." The idea of extinction doesn't exist yet, of course, since the idea that God's creations could be flawed is still a blasphemy. This is before Darwin, before paleontology. And so for many years the American incognitum roams around America bounded only by the imagination of the nation's inhabitants. And yet gradually, as America pushes farther west, and as explorers continue to return without sightings of the beast, Americans begin to realize that the source of their new pride may not actually exist. "We are forced to submit to concurring facts," Charles Willson Peale adds to the plaque beneath the skeleton, that "the bones exist, but the animal does not." A statement that is as remarkable as it is obvious, because what it does—by acknowledging not only that God was in error but that Americans had misdirected their aspirations in the past—is declare that the New World is categorically not the Old. "History fades into fable," Washington Irving once wrote, and then proceeded to imagine the country that he wanted his country to be.

WASHINGTON IRVING

A History of New York

Chapter I

*In which the Author ventures a Description of the World,
from the best Authorities.*

The world in which we dwell is a huge, opake, reflecting, inanimate mass, floating in the vast etherial ocean of infinite space. It has the form of an orange, being an oblate spheroid, curiously flattened at opposite parts, for the insertion of two imaginary poles, which are supposed to penetrate and unite at the centre; thus forming an axis on which the mighty orange turns with a regular diurnal revolution.

The transitions of light and darkness, whence proceed the alternations of day and night, are produced by this diurnal revolution, successively presenting the different parts of the earth to the rays of the sun. The latter is, according to the best, that is to say, the latest, accounts, a luminous or fiery body, of a prodigious magnitude, from which this world is driven by a centrifugal or repelling power, and to which it is drawn by a centripetal or attractive force; otherwise termed the attraction of gravitation; the combination, or rather the counteraction of these two opposing impulses producing a circular and annual revolution. Hence result the vicissitudes of the seasons, *viz.* spring, summer, autumn, and winter.

I am fully aware, that I expose myself to the cavillings of sundry dead philosophers, by adopting the above theory. Some will entrench themselves behind the ancient opinion, that the earth is an extended plain, supported by vast pillars; others, that it rests on the head of a snake, or the back of a huge tortoise; and others, that it is an immense flat pancake, and rests upon whatever it pleases God—formerly a pious Catholic opinion, and sanctioned by a formidable *bull,* dispatched from the vatican by a most holy and infallible pontiff. Others will attack my whole theory, by declaring with the Brahmins, that the heavens rest upon the earth, and that the sun and moon swim therein like fishes in the water, moving from east to west by day, and gliding back along the edge of the horizon to their original stations during the night time. While others will maintain, with the Pauranicas of India, that it is a vast plain, encircled by seven oceans of milk, nectar and other delicious liquids; that it is studded with seven mountains, and ornamented in the centre by a mountainous rock of burnished gold; and that a great dragon occasionally swallows up the moon, which accounts for the phenomena of lunar eclipses.

I am confident also, I shall meet with equal opposition to my account of the sun; certain ancient philosophers having affirmed that it is a vast wheel of brilliant fire, others that it is merely a mirror or sphere of transparent chrystal; and a third class, at the head of whom stands Anaxagoras, having maintained, that it is nothing but a huge ignited rock or stone, an opinion which the good people of Athens have kindly saved me the trouble of confuting, by turning the philosopher neck and heels out of their city. Another set of philosophers, who delight in variety, declare, that certain fiery particles exhale constantly from the earth, which concentrating in a single point of the firmament by day, constitute the sun, but being scattered, and rambling about in the dark at night, collect in various points and form stars. These are regularly burnt out and extinguished, like the lamps in our streets, and require a fresh supply of exhalations for the next occasion.

It is even recorded that at certain remote and obscure periods, in consequence of a great scarcity of fuel, (probably during a severe winter) the sun has been completely burnt out, and not rekindled for a whole month. A most melancholy occurrence, the very idea of which gave vast concern to Heraclitus, the celebrated weeping Philosopher, who was a great stickler for this doctrine. Beside these profound speculations, others may expect me to advocate the opinion of Herschel, that the sun is a most magnificent, habitable abode; the light it furnishes, arising from certain empyreal, luminous or phosphoric clouds, swimming in its transparent atmosphere. But to save dispute and altercation with my readers—who I already perceive, are a captious, discontented crew, and likely to give me a world of trouble—I now, once for all, wash my hands of all and every of these theories, declining entirely and unequivocally, any investigation of their merits. The subject of the present chapter is merely the Island, on which is built the goodly city of New York,—a very honest and substantial Island, which I do not expect to find in the sun, or moon; as I am no land speculator, but a plain matter of fact historian. I therefore renounce all lunatic, or solaric excursions, and confine myself to the limits of this terrene or earthly globe; somewhere on the surface of which I pledge my credit as a historian—(which heaven and my landlord know is all the credit I possess) to detect and demonstrate the existence of this illustrious island to the conviction of all reasonable people.

Proceeding on this discreet and considerate plan, I rest satisfied with having advanced the most approved and fashionable opinion on the form of this earth and its movements; and I freely submit it to the cavilling of any Philo, dead or alive, who may choose to dispute its correctness. I must here intreat my unlearned readers (in which class I humbly presume to include nine tenths of those who shall pore over these instructive pages) not to be discouraged when they encounter a passage above their comprehension; for as I shall admit nothing into my work that is not pertinent and absolutely essential to its well being, so likewise I shall advance no theory or hypothesis, that shall not be elucidated to the comprehension of the dullest intellect. I am not one of those churlish authors, who do so enwrap their works in the mystic fogs of scientific jargon, that a man must be as wise as themselves to understand their writings; on the contrary, my pages, though abounding with sound wisdom and profound erudition, shall be written with such pleasant and urbane perspicuity, that there shall not even be found a country justice, an outward alderman, or a member of congress, provided he can read with tolerable fluency, but shall both understand and profit by my labours. I shall therefore, proceed forthwith to illustrate by experiment, the complexity of motion just ascribed to this our rotatory planet.

Professor Von Poddingcoft (or Puddinghead as the name may be rendered into English) was long celebrated in the college of New York, for most profound gravity of deportment, and his talent at going to sleep in the midst of examinations; to the infinite relief of his hopeful students, who thereby worked their way through college with great ease and little study. In the course of one of his lectures, the learned professor, seizing a bucket of water swung it round his head at arms length; the impulse with which he threw the vessel from him, being a centrifugal force, the retention of his arm operating as a centripetal power, and the bucket, which was a substitute for the earth, describing a circular orbit round about the globular head and ruby visage of Professor Von Poddingcoft, which formed no bad representation of the sun. All of these particulars were duly explained to the class of gaping students around him. He apprised them moreover, that the same principle of gravitation, which retained the water in the bucket, restrains the ocean from flying from the earth in its rapid revolutions; and he further informed them that should the motion of the earth be suddenly checked, it would incontinently fall into the sun, through the centripetal force of gravitation; a most ruinous event to this planet, and one which would also obscure, though it most probably would not extinguish the solar luminary. An unlucky stripling, one of those vagrant geniuses, who seem sent into the world merely to annoy worthy men of the puddinghead order, desirous of ascertaining the correctness of the experiment, suddenly arrested the arm of the professor, just at the moment that the bucket was in its zenith, which immediately descended with astonishing precision, upon the philosophic head of the instructor of youth. A hollow sound, and a red-hot hiss attended the contact, but the theory was in the amplest manner illustrated, for the unfortunate bucket perished in the conflict, but the blazing countenance of Professor Von Poddingcoft, emerged from amidst the waters, glowing fiercer than ever with unutterable indignation— whereby the students were marvellously edified, and departed considerably wiser than before.

It is a mortifying circumstance, which greatly perplexes many a pains taking philosopher, that nature often refuses to second his most profound and elaborate efforts; so that often after having invented one of the most ingenious and natural theories imaginable, she will have the perverseness to act directly in the teeth of his system, and flatly contradict his most favorite positions. This is a manifest and unmerited grievance, since it throws the censure of the vulgar and unlearned entirely upon the philosopher; whereas the fault is not to be ascribed to his theory, which is unquestionably correct, but to the waywardness of dame nature, who with the proverbial fickleness of her sex, is continually indulging in coquetries and caprices, and seems really to take pleasure in violating all philosophic rules, and jilting the most learned and indefatigable of her adorers. Thus it happened with respect to the foregoing satisfactory explanation of the motion of our planet; it appears that the centrifugal force has long since ceased to operate, while its antagonist remains in undiminished potency: the world therefore, according to the theory as it originally stood, ought in strict propriety to tumble into the sun—Philosophers were convinced that it would do so, and awaited in anxious impatience, the fulfilment of their prognostications. But the untoward planet, pertinaciously continued her course, notwithstanding that she had reason, philosophy, and a whole university of learned professors opposed to her conduct. The philo's were all at a non plus, and it is apprehended they would never have fairly recovered from the slight and affront which they conceived offered to them by the world, had not a good natured professor kindly officiated as mediator between the parties, and effected a reconciliation.

Finding the world would not accommodate itself to the theory, he wisely determined to accomodate the theory to the world: he therefore informed his brother philosophers, that the circular motion of the earth round the sun was no sooner engendered by the conflicting impulses above described, than it became a regular revolution, independent of the causes which gave it origin—in short, that madam earth having once taken it into her head to whirl round, like a young lady of spirit in a high dutch waltz, the duivel himself could not stop her. The whole board of professors of the university of Leyden joined in the opinion, being heartily glad of any explanation that would decently extricate them from their embarrassment—and immediately decreed the penalty of expulsion against all who should presume to question its correctness: the philosophers of all other nations gave an unqualified assent, and ever since that memorable era the world has been left to take her own course, and to revolve around the sun in such orbit as she thinks proper.

Chapter II

Cosmogony or Creation of the World.
With a multitude of excellent Theories, by which the
Creation of a World is shewn to be no such difficult
Matter as common Folks would imagine.

Having thus briefly introduced my reader to the world, and given him some idea of its form and situation, he will naturally be curious to know from whence it came, and how it was created. And indeed these are points absolutely essential to be cleared up, in as much as if this world had not been formed, it is more than probable, nay I may venture to assume it as a maxim or postulate at least, that this renowned island on which is situated the city of New York, would never have had an existence. The regular course of my history therefore, requires that I should proceed to notice the cosmogony or formation of this our globe.

And now I give my readers fair warning, that I am about to plunge for a chapter or two, into as complete a labyrinth as ever historian was perplexed withal; therefore I advise them to take fast hold of my skirts, and keep close at my heels, venturing neither to the right hand nor to the left, least they get bemired in a slough of unintelligible learning, or have their brains knocked out, by some of those hard Greek names which will be flying about in all directions. But should any of them be too indolent or chicken-hearted to accompany me in this perilous undertaking, they had better take a short cut round, and wait for me at the beginning of some smoother chapter.

Of the creation of the world, we have a thousand contradictory accounts; and though a very satisfactory one is furnished us by divine revelation, yet every philosopher feels himself in honour bound, to furnish us with a better. As an impartial historian, I consider it my duty to notice their several theories, by which mankind have been so exceedingly edified and instructed.

Thus it was the opinion of certain ancient sages, that the earth and the whole system of the universe, was the deity himself; a doctrine most strenuously maintained by Zenophanes and the whole tribe of Eleatics, as also by Strato and the sect of peripatetic or vagabondizing philosophers. Pythagoras likewise inculcated the famous numerical system of the monad, dyad and triad, and by means of his sacred quaternary elucidated the formation of the world, the arcana of nature and the principles both of music and morals. Other sages adhered to the mathematical system of squares and triangles; the cube, the pyramid and the sphere; the tetrahedron, the octahedron, the icosahedron and the dodecahedron. While others advocated the great elementary theory, which refers the construction of our globe and all that it contains, to the combinations of four material elements, air, earth, fire and water; with the assistance of a fifth, an immaterial and vivifying principle; by which I presume the worthy theorist meant to allude to that vivifying spirit contained in gin, brandy, and other potent liquors, and which has such miraculous effects, not only on the ordinary operations of nature, but likewise on the creative brains of certain philosophers.

Nor must I omit to mention the great atomic system taught by old Moschus before the siege of Troy; revived by Democritus of laughing memory; improved by Epicurus that king of good fellows, and modernised by the fanciful Descartes. But I decline enquiring, whether the atoms, of which the earth is said to be composed, are eternal or recent; whether they are animate or inanimate; whether, agreeably to the opinion of the Atheists, they were fortuitously aggregated, or as the Theists maintain, were arranged by a supreme intelligence. Whether in fact the earth is an insensate clod, or whether it is animated by a soul; which opinion was strenuously maintained by a host of philosophers, at the head of whom stands the great Plato, that temperate sage, who threw the cold water of philosophy on the form of sexual intercourse, and inculcated the doctrine of Platonic affection, or the art of making love without making children.—An exquisitely refined intercourse, but much better adapted to the ideal inhabitants of his imaginary island of Atlantis, than to the sturdy race, composed of rebellious flesh and blood, who populate the little matter of fact island which we inhabit.

Besides these systems, we have moreover the poetical theogeny of old Hesiod, who generated the whole Universe in the regular mode of procreation, and the plausible opinion of others, that the earth was hatched from the great egg of night, which floated in chaos, and was cracked by the horns of the celestial bull. To illustrate this last doctrine, Bishop Burnet in his Theory of the Earth, has favored us with an accurate drawing and description, both of the form and texture of this mundane egg; which is found to bear a miraculous resemblance to that of a *goose!* Such of my readers as take a proper interest in the origin of this our planet, will be pleased to learn, that the most profound sages of antiquity, among the Egyptians, Chaldeans, Persians, Greeks and Latins, have alternately assisted at the hatching of this strange bird, and that their cacklings have been caught, and continued in different tones and inflections, from philosopher to philosopher, unto the present day.

But while briefly noticing long celebrated systems of ancient sages, let me not pass over with neglect, those of other philosophers; which though less universal and renowned, have equal claims to attention, and equal chance for correctness. Thus it is recorded by the Brahmins, in the pages of their inspired Shastah, that the angel Bistnoo transforming himself into a great boar, plunged into the watery abyss, and brought up the earth on his tusks. Then issued from him a mighty tortoise, and a mighty snake; and

Bistnoo placed the snake erect upon the back of the tortoise, and he placed the earth upon the head of the snake.

The negro philosophers of Congo affirm, that the world was made by the hands of angels, excepting their own country, which the Supreme Being constructed himself, that it might be supremely excellent. And he took great pains with the inhabitants, and made them very black, and beautiful; and when he had finished the first man, he was well pleased with him, and smoothed him over the face, and hence his nose and the nose of all his descendants became flat.

The Mohawk Philosophers tell us that a pregnant woman fell down from heaven, and that a tortoise took her upon its back, because every place was covered with water; and that the woman sitting upon the tortoise paddled with her hands in the water, and raked up the earth, whence it finally happened that the earth became higher than the water.

Beside these and many other equally sage opinions, we have likewise the profound conjectures of ABOUL-HASSAN-ALY, son of Al Khan, son of Aly, son of Abderrahman, son of Abdallah, son of Masoud-el-Hadheli, who is commonly called MASOUDI, and surnamed Cothbeddin, but who takes the humble title of Laheb-ar-rasoul, which means the companion of the ambassador of God. He has written an universal history entitled "Mouroudge-ed-dhahrab, or the golden meadows and the mines of precious stones." In this valuable work he has related the history of the world, from the creation down to the moment of writing; which was, under the Khaliphat of Mothi Billah, in the month Dgioumadi-el-aoual of the 336th year of the Hegira or flight of the Prophet. He informs us that the earth is a huge bird, Mecca and Medina constituting the head, Persia and India the right wing, the land of Gog the left wing, and Africa the tail. He informs us moreover, that an earth has existed before the present, (which he considers as a mere chicken of 7000 years) that it has undergone divers deluges, and that, according to the opinion of some well informed Brahmins of his acquaintance, it will be renovated every seventy thousandth hazarouam; each hazarouam consisting of 12,000 years.

But I forbear to quote a host more of these ancient and outlandish philosophers, whose deplorable ignorance, in despite of all their erudition, compelled them to write in languages which but few of my readers can understand; and I shall proceed briefly to notice a few more intelligible and fashionable theories of their modern successors.

And first I shall mention the great Buffon, who conjectures that this globe was originally a globe of liquid fire, scintillated from the body of the sun, by the percussion of a comet, as a spark is generated by the collision of flint and steel. That at first it was surrounded by gross vapours, which cooling and condensing in process of time, constituted, according to their densities, earth, water and air; which gradually arranged themselves, according to their respective gravities, round the burning or vitrified mass, that formed their centre, &c.

Hutton, on the contrary, supposes that the waters at first were universally paramount; and he terrifies himself with the idea that the earth must be eventually washed away, by the force of rain, rivers and mountain torrents, untill it is confounded with the ocean, or in other words, absolutely dissolves into itself.—Sublime idea! far surpassing that of the tender-hearted damsel of antiquity who wept herself into a fountain; or the good dame of Narbonne in France, who for a volubility of tongue unusual in her sex, was doomed to peel five hundred thousand and thirty-nine ropes of onions, and actually ran out at her eyes, before half the hideous task was accomplished.

Whiston, the same ingenious philosopher who rivalled Ditton in his researches after the longitude, (for which the mischief-loving Swift discharged on their heads a stanza as fragrant as an Edinburgh nosegay) has distinguished himself by a very admirable theory respecting the earth. He conjectures that it was originally a *chaotic comet,* which being selected for the abode of man, was removed from its excentric orbit, and whirled round the sun in its present regular motion; by which change of direction, order succeeded to confusion in the arrangement of its component parts. The philosopher adds, that the deluge was produced by an uncourteous salute from the watery tail of another comet; doubtless through sheer envy of its improved condition; thus furnishing a melancholy proof that jealousy may prevail, even among the heavenly bodies, and discord interrupt that celestial harmony of the spheres, so melodiously sung by the poets.

But I pass over a variety of excellent theories, among which are those of Burnet, and Woodward, and Whitehurst; regretting extremely that my time will not suffer me to give them the notice they deserve—And shall conclude with that of the renowned Dr. Darwin, which I have reserved to the last for the sake of going off *with a report.* This learned Theban, who is as much distinguished for rhyme as reason, and for good natured credulity as serious research, and who has recommended himself wonderfully to the good graces of the ladies, by letting them into all the gallantries, amours, debaucheries, and other topics of scandal of the court of Flora; has fallen upon a theory worthy of his combustible imagination. According to his opinion, the huge mass of chaos took a sudden occasion to explode, like a barrel of gunpowder, and in that act exploded the sun—which in its flight by a similar explosion expelled the earth—which in like guise exploded the moon—and thus by a concatenation of explosions, the whole solar system was produced, and set most systematically in motion!

By the great variety of theories here alluded to, every one of which, if thoroughly examined, will be found surprisingly consistent in all its parts; my unlearned readers will perhaps be led to conclude, that the creation of a world is not so difficult a task as they at first imagined. I have shewn at least a score of ingenious methods in which a world could be constructed; and I have no doubt, that had any of the Philo's above quoted, the use of a good manageable comet, and the philosophical ware-house *chaos* at his command, he would engage, by the aid of philosophy to manufacture a planet as good, or if you would take his word for it, better than this we inhabit.

And here I cannot help noticing the kindness of Providence, in creating comets for the great relief of bewildered philosophers. By their assistance more sudden evolutions and transitions are affected in the system of nature, than are wrought in a pantomimic exhibition, by the wonder-working sword of Harlequin. Should one of our modern sages, in his theoretical flights among the stars, ever find himself lost in the clouds, and in danger of tumbling into the abyss of nonsense and absurdity, he has but to seize a comet by the beard, mount astride of its tail, and away he gallops in triumph, like an enchanter on his hyppogriff, or a Connecticut witch on her broomstick, "to sweep the cobwebs out of the sky."

It is an old and vulgar saying, about a "beggar on horse back," which I would not for the world have applied to our most reverend philosophers; but I must confess, that some of them, when they are mounted on one of these fiery steeds, are as wild in their curvettings as was Phæton of yore, when he aspired to manage the chariot of Phœbus. One drives his comet at full speed against the sun, and knocks the world out of him with the mighty concussion; another more moderate, makes his comet a kind of beast of burden, carrying the sun a regular supply of food and faggots—a third, of more combustible disposition, threatens to throw his comet, like a bombshell into the world, and blow it up like a powder magazine; while a fourth, with no great delicacy to this respectable planet, and its inhabitants, insinuates that some day or other, his comet—my modest pen blushes while I write it—shall absolutely turn tail upon our world and deluge it with water!—Surely as I have already observed, comets were bountifully provided by Providence for the benefit of philosophers, to assist them in manufacturing theories.

When a man once doffs the straight waistcoat of common sense, and trusts merely to his imagination, it is astonishing how rapidly he gets forward. Plodding souls, like myself, who jog along on the two legs nature has given them, are sadly put to it to clamber over the rocks and hills, to toil through the mud and mire, and to remove the continual obstructions, that abound in the path of science. But your adventurous philosopher launches his theory like a balloon, and having inflated it with the smoke and vapours of his own heated imagination, mounts it in triumph, and soars away to his congenial regions in the moon. Every age has furnished its quota of these adventurers in the realms of fancy, who voyage among the clouds for a season and are stared at and admired, until some envious rival assails their air blown pageant, shatters its crazy texture, lets out the smoke, and tumbles the adventurer and his theory into the mud. Thus one race of philosophers demolish the works of their predecessors, and elevate more splendid fantasies in their stead, which in their turn are demolished and replaced by the air castles of a succeeding generation. Such are the grave eccentricities of genius, and the mighty soap bubbles, with which the grown up children of science amuse themselves— while the honest vulgar, stand gazing in stupid admiration, and dignify these fantastic vagaries with the name of wisdom!—surely old Socrates was right in his opinion that philosophers are but a soberer sort of madmen, busying themselves in things which are totally incomprehensible, or which, if they could be comprehended, would be found not worth the trouble of discovery.

And now, having adduced several of the most important theories that occur to my recollection, I leave my readers at full liberty to choose among them. They are all the serious speculations of learned men—all differ essentially from each other—and all have the same title to belief. For my part, (as I hate an embarrassment of choice) until the learned have come to an agreement among themselves, I shall content myself with the account handed us down by the good old Moses; in which I do but follow the example of our ingenious neighbours of Connecticut; who at their first settlement proclaimed, that the colony should be governed by the laws of God—until they had time to make better.

One thing however appears certain—from the unanimous authority of the before quoted philosophers, supported by the evidence of our own senses, (which, though very apt to deceive us, may be cautiously admitted as additional testimony) it appears I say, and I make the assertion deliberately, without fear of contradiction, that this globe really *was created,* and that it is composed of *land and water.* It further appears that it is curiously divided and parcelled out into continents and islands, among which I boldly declare the renowned ISLAND OF NEW YORK, will be found, by any one who seeks for it in its proper place.

Thus it will be perceived, that like an experienced historian I confine myself to such points as are absolutely essential to my subject—building up my work, after the manner of the able architect who erected our theatre; beginning with the foundation, then the body, then the roof, and at last perching our snug little island like the little cupola on the top. Having dropt upon this simile by chance I shall make a moment's further use of it, to illustrate the correctness of my plan. Had not the foundation, the body, and the roof of the theatre first been built, the cupola could not have had existence as a cupola—it might have been a centry-box—or a watchman's box—or it might have been placed in the rear of the Manager's house and have formed—a temple;—but it could never have been considered a cupola. As therefore the building of the theatre was necessary to the existence of the cupola, as a cupola—so the formation of the globe and its internal construction, were first necessary to the existence of this island, as an island— and thus the necessity and importance of this part of my history, which in a manner is no part of my history, is logically proved.

Chapter III

How that famous navigator, Admiral Noah,
was shamefully nick-named; and how he committed
an unpardonable oversight in not having four sons.
With the great trouble of philosophers caused
thereby, and the discovery of America.

Noah, who is the first sea-faring man we read of, begat three sons, Shem, Ham, and Japhet. Authors it is true, are not wanting, who affirm that the patriarch had a number of other children. Thus Berosus makes him father of the gigantic Titans, Methodius gives him a son called Jonithus, or Jonicus, (who was the first inventor of Johnny cakes,) and others have mentioned a son, named Thuiscon, from whom descended the Teutons or Teutonic, or in other words, the Dutch nation.

I regret exceedingly that the nature of my plan will not permit me to gratify the laudable curiosity of my readers, by investigating minutely the history of the great Noah. Indeed such an undertaking would be attended with more trouble than many people would imagine; for the good old patriarch seems to have been a great traveller in his day, and to have passed under a different name in every country that he visited. The Chaldeans for instance give us his story, merely altering his name into Xisuthrus—a trivial alteration, which to an historian skilled in etymologies, will appear wholly unimportant. It appears likewise, that he had exchanged his tarpawlin and quadrant among the Chaldeans, for the gorgeous insignia of royalty, and appears as a monarch in their annals. The Egyptians celebrate him under the name of Osiris; the Indians as Menu; the Greek and Roman writers confound him with Ogyges, and the Theban with Deucalion and Saturn. But the Chinese, who deservedly rank among the most extensive and authentic historians, inasmuch as they have known the world ever since some millions of years before it was created, declare that Noah was no other than Fohi, a worthy gentleman, descended from an ancient and respectable family of Hong merchants, that flourished in the middle ages of the empire. What gives this assertion some air of credibility is, that it is a fact, admitted by the most enlightened literati, that Noah travelled into China, at the time of the building of the Tower of Babel (probably to improve himself in the study of languages) and the learned Dr. Shackford gives us the additional information, that the ark rested upon a mountain on the frontiers of China.

From this mass of rational conjectures and sage hypotheses, many satisfactory deductions might be drawn; but I shall content myself with the unquestionable fact stated in the Bible, that Noah begat three sons—Shem, Ham, and Japhet.

It may be asked by some inquisitive readers, not much conversant with the art of history writing, what have Noah and his sons to do with the subject of this work? Now though, in strict justice, I am not bound to satisfy such querulous spirits, yet as I have determined to accommodate my book to every capacity, so that it shall not only delight the learned, but likewise instruct the simple, and edify the vulgar; I shall never hesitate for a moment to explain any matter that may appear obscure.

Noah we are told by sundry very credible historians, becoming sole surviving heir and proprietor of the earth, in fee simple, after the deluge, like a good father portioned out his estate among his children. To Shem he gave Asia, to Ham, Africa, and to Japhet, Europe. Now it is a thousand times to be lamented that he had but three sons, for had there been a fourth, he would doubtless have inherited America; which of course would have been dragged forth from its obscurity on the occasion; and thus many a hard working historian and philosopher, would have been spared a prodigious mass of weary conjecture, respecting the first discovery and population of this country. Noah, however, having provided for his three sons, looked in all probability, upon our country as mere wild unsettled land, and said nothing about it, and to this unpardonable taciturnity of the patriarch may we ascribe the misfortune, that America did not come into the world, as early as the other quarters of the globe.

It is true some writers have vindicated him from this misconduct towards posterity, and asserted that he really did discover America. Thus it was the opinion of Mark Lescarbot, a French writer possessed of that ponderosity of thought, and profoundness of reflection, so peculiar to his nation, that the immediate descendants of Noah peopled this quarter of the globe, and that the old patriarch himself, who still retained a passion for the sea-faring life, superintended the transmigration. The pious and enlightened father Charlevoix, a French Jesuit, remarkable for his veracity and an aversion to the marvellous, common to all great travelers, is conclusively of the same opinion; nay, he goes still further, and decides upon the manner in which the discovery was effected, which was by sea, and under the immediate direction of the great Noah. "I have already observed," exclaims the good father in a tone of becoming indignation, "that it is an arbitrary supposition that the grand children of Noah were not able to penetrate into the new world, or that they never thought of it. In effect, I can see no reason that can justify such a notion. Who can seriously believe, that Noah and his immediate descendants knew less than we do, and that the builder and pilot of the greatest ship that ever was, a ship which was formed to traverse an unbounded ocean, and had so many shoals and quicksands to guard against, should be ignorant of, or should not have communicated to his descendants the art of sailing on the ocean?" Therefore they did sail on the ocean—therefore they sailed to America—therefore America was discovered by Noah!

Now all this exquisite chain of reasoning, which is so strikingly characteristic of the good father, being addressed to the faith, rather than the understanding, is flatly opposed by Hans De Laet, who declares it a real and most ridiculous paradox, to suppose that Noah ever entertained the thought of discovering America; and as Hans is a Dutch writer, I am inclined to believe he must have been much better acquainted with the worthy crew of the ark than his competitors, and of course possessed of more accurate sources of information. It is astonishing how intimate historians daily become with the patriarchs and other great men of antiquity. As intimacy improves with time, and as the learned are particularly inquisitive and familiar in their acquaintance with the ancients, I should not be surprised, if some future writers should gravely give us a picture of men and manners as they existed before the flood, far more copious and accurate than the Bible; and that, in the course of another century, the log book of old Noah should be as current among historians, as the voyages of Captain Cook, or the renowned history of Robinson Crusoe.

I shall not occupy my time by discussing the huge mass of additional suppositions, conjectures and probabilities respecting the first discovery of this country, with which unhappy historians overload themselves, in their endeavours to satisfy the doubts of an incredulous world. It is painful to see these laborious wights panting and toiling, and sweating under an enormous burthen, at the very outset of their works, which on being opened, turns out to be nothing but a mighty bundle of straw. As, however, by unwearied assiduity, they seem to have established the fact, to the satisfaction of all the world, that this country *has been discovered,* I shall avail myself of their useful labours to be extremely brief upon this point.

I shall not therefore stop to enquire, whether America was first discovered by a wandering vessel of that celebrated Phœnecian fleet, which, according to Herodotus, circumnavigated Africa; or by that Carthagenian expedition, which Pliny, the naturalist, informs us, discovered the Canary Islands; or whether it was settled by a temporary colony from Tyre, as hinted by Aristotle and Seneca. I shall neither enquire whether it was first discovered by the Chinese, as Vossius with great shrewdness advances, nor by the Norwegians in 1002, under Biorn; nor by Behem, the German navigator, as Mr. Otto has endeavoured to prove to the Sçavans of the learned city of Philadelphia.

Nor shall I investigate the more modern claims of the Welsh, founded on the voyage of Prince Madoc in the eleventh century, who having never returned, it has since been wisely concluded that he must have gone to America, and that for a plain reason—if he did not go there, where else could he have gone?—a question which most Socratically shuts out all further dispute.

Laying aside, therefore, all the conjectures above mentioned, with a multitude of others, equally satisfactory, I shall take for granted, the vulgar opinion that America was discovered on the 12th of October, 1492, by Christovallo Colon, a Genoese, who has been clumsily nick-named Columbus, but for what reason I cannot discern. Of the voyages and adventures of this Colon, I shall say nothing, seeing that they are already sufficiently known. Nor shall I undertake to prove that this country should have been called Colonia, after his name, that being notoriously self evident.

Having thus happily got my readers on this side of the Atlantic, I picture them to myself, all impatience to enter upon the enjoyment of the land of promise, and in full expectation that I will immediately deliver it into their possession. But if I do, may I ever forfeit the reputation of a regular bred historian. No—no—most curious and thrice learned readers, (for thrice learned ye are if ye have read all that goes before, and nine times learned shall ye be, if ye read all that comes after) we have yet a world of work before us. Think you the first discoverers of this fair quarter of the globe, had nothing to do but go on shore and find a country ready laid out and cultivated like a garden, wherein they might revel at their ease? No such thing—they had forests to cut down, underwood to grub up, marshes to drain, and savages to exterminate.

In like manner, I have sundry doubts to clear away, questions to resolve, and paradoxes to explain, before I permit you to range at random; but these difficulties, once overcome, we shall be enabled to jog on right merrily through the rest of our history. Thus my work shall, in a manner, echo the nature of the subject, in the same manner as the sound of poetry has been found by certain shrewd critics, to echo the sense—this being an improvement in history, which I claim the merit of having invented.

Chapter IV

Shewing the great toil and contention
which Philosophers have had in peopling America.—
And how the Aborigines came to be begotten by accident—
to the great satisfaction and relief of the author.

Bless us!—what a hard life we historians have of it, who undertake to satisfy the doubts of the world!—Here have I been toiling and moiling through three pestiferous chapters, and my readers toiling and moiling at my heels; up early and to bed late, poring over worm-eaten, obsolete, good-for-nothing books, and cultivating the acquaintance of a thousand learned authors, both ancient and modern, who, to tell the honest truth, are the stupidest companions in the world—and after all, what have we got by it?—Truly the mighty valuable conclusion, that this country does actually exist, and has been discovered; a self-evident fact not worth a hap'worth of gingerbread. And what is worse, we seem just as far off from the city of New York now, as we were at first. Now for myself, I would not care the value of a brass button, being used to this dull and learned company; but I feel for my unhappy readers, who seem most woefully jaded and fatigued.

Still, however, we have formidable difficulties to encounter, since it yet remains, if possible, to show how this country was originally peopled—a point fruitful of incredible embarrassment, to us scrupulous historians, but absolutely indispensable to our works. For unless we prove that the Aborigines did absolutely come from some where, it will be immediately asserted in this age of scepticism, that they did not come at all; and if they did not come at all, then was this country never populated—a conclusion perfectly agreeable to the rules of logic, but wholly irreconcilable to every feeling of humanity, inasmuch as it must syllogistically prove fatal to the innumerable Aborigines of this populous region.

To avert so dire a sophism, and to rescue from logical annihilation so many millions of fellow creatures, how many wings of geese have been plundered! what oceans of ink have been benevolently drained! and how many capacious heads of learned historians have been addled and forever confounded! I pause with reverential awe, when I contemplate the ponderous tomes in different languages, with which they have endeavoured to solve this question, so important to the happiness of society, but so involved in clouds of impenetrable obscurity. Historian after historian has engaged in the endless circle of hypothetical argument, and after leading us a weary chace through octavos, quartos, and folios, has let us out at the end of his work, just as wise as we were at the beginning. It was doubtless some philosophical wild goose chace of the kind, that made the old poet Macrobius rail in such a passion at curiosity, which he anathematizes most heartily, as "an irksome agonizing care, a superstitious industry about unprofitable things, an itching humour to see what is not to be seen, and to be doing what signifies nothing when it is done."

But come my lusty readers, let us address ourselves to our task and fall vigorously to work upon the remaining rubbish that lies in our way; but I warrant, had master Hercules, in addition to his seven labors, been given as an eighth to write a genuine American history, he would have been fain to abandon the undertaking, before he got over the threshold of his work.

Of the claims of the children of Noah to the original population of this country I shall say nothing, as they have already been touched upon in my last chapter. The claimants next in celebrity, are the descendants of Abraham. Thus Christoval Colon (vulgarly called Columbus) when he first discovered the gold mines of Hispaniola immediately concluded, with a shrewdness that would have done honour to a philosopher, that he had found the ancient Ophir, from whence Solomon procured the gold for embellishing the temple at Jerusalem; nay Colon even imagined that he saw the remains of furnaces of veritable Hebraic construction, employed in refining the precious ore.

So golden a conjecture, tinctured with such fascinating extravagance, was too tempting not to be immediately snapped at by the gudgeons of learning, and accordingly, there were a host of profound writers, ready to swear to its correctness, and to bring in their usual load of authorities, and wise surmises, wherewithal to prop it up. Vetablus and Robertus Stephens declared nothing could be more clear—Arius Montanus without the least hesitation asserts that Mexico was the true Ophir, and the Jews the early settlers of the country. While Possevin, Becan, and a host of other sagacious writers, lug in a *supposed* prophecy of the fourth book of Esdras, which being inserted in the mighty hypothesis, like the key stone of an arch, gives it, in their opinion, perpetual durability.

Scarce however, have they completed their goodly superstructure, than in trudges a phalanx of opposite authors, with Hans De Laet the great

Dutchman at their head, and at one blow, tumbles the whole fabric about their ears. Hans in fact, contradicts outright all the Israelitish claims to the first settlement of this country, attributing all those equivocal symptoms, and traces of Christianity and Judaism, which have been said to be found in divers provinces of the new world, to the *Devil,* who has always affected to counterfeit the worship of the true Deity. "A remark," says the knowing old Padre d'Acosta, "made by all good authors who have spoken of the religion of nations newly discovered, and founded besides on the authority of the *fathers of the church.*"

Some writers again, among whom it is with great regret I am compelled to mention Lopez de Gomara, and Juan de Leri, insinuate that the Canaanites, being driven from the land of promise by the Jews, were seized with such a panic, that they fled without looking behind them, until stopping to take breath they found themselves safe in America. As they brought neither their national language, manners nor features, with them, it is supposed they left them behind in the hurry of their flight—I cannot give my faith to this opinion.

I pass over the supposition of the learned Grotius, who being both an ambassador and a Dutchman to boot, is entitled to great respect; that North America, was peopled by a strolling company of Norwegians, and that Peru was founded by a colony from China—Manco or Mungo Capac, the first Incas, being himself a Chinese. Nor shall I more than barely mention that father Kircher, ascribes the settlement of America to the Egyptians, Rudbeck to the Scandinavians, Charron to the Gauls, Juffredus Petri to a skaiting party from Friesland, Milius to the Celtæ, Marinocus the Sicilian to the Romans, Le Compte to the Phœnicians, Postel to the Moors, Martyn d'Angleria to the Abyssinians, together with the sage surmise of De Laet, that England, Ireland and the Orcades may contend for that honour.

Nor will I bestow any more attention or credit to the idea that America is the fairy region of Zipangri, described by that dreaming traveller Marco Polo the Venetian; or that it comprises the visionary island of Atlantis, described by Plato. Neither will I stop to investigate the heathenish assertion of Paracelsus, that each hemisphere of the globe was originally furnished with an Adam and Eve. Or the more flattering opinion of Dr. Romayne supported by many nameless authorities, that Adam was of the Indian race—or the startling conjecture of Buffon, Helvetius, and Darwin, so highly honourable to mankind, and peculiarly complimentary to the

French nation, that the whole human species are accidentally descended from a remarkable family of monkies!

This last conjecture, I must own, came upon me very suddenly and very ungraciously. I have often beheld the clown in a pantomime, while gazing in stupid wonder at the extravagant gambols of a harlequin, all at once electrified by a sudden stroke of the wooden sword across his shoulders. Little did I think at such times, that it would ever fall to my lot to be treated with equal discourtesy, and that while I was quietly beholding these grave philosophers, emulating the excentric transformations of the parti-coloured hero of pantomime, they would on a sudden turn upon me and my readers, and with one flourish of their conjectural wand, metamorphose us into beasts! I determined from that moment not to burn my fingers with any more of their theories, but content myself with detailing the different methods by which they transported the descendants of these ancient and respectable monkeys, to this great field of theoretical warfare.

This was done either by migrations by land or transmigrations by water. Thus Padre Joseph D'Acosta enumerates three passages by land, first by the north of Europe, secondly by the north of Asia and thirdly by regions southward of the straits of Magellan. The learned Grotius marches his Norwegians by a pleasant route across frozen rivers and arms of the sea, through Iceland, Greenland, Estotiland and Naremberga. And various writers, among whom are Angleria, De Hornn and Buffon, anxious for the accommodation of these travellers, have fastened the two continents together by a strong chain of deductions—by which means they could pass over dry shod. But should even this fail, Pinkerton, that industrious old gentleman, who compiles books and manufactures Geographies, and who erst flung away his wig and cane, frolicked like a naughty boy, and committed a thousand etourderies, among the *petites filles* of Paris—he I say, has constructed a natural bridge of ice, from continent to continent, at the distance of four or five miles from Behring's straits—for which he is entitled to the grateful thanks of all the wandering aborigines who ever did, or ever will pass over it.

It is an evil much to be lamented, that none of the worthy writers above quoted, could ever commence his work, without immediately declaring hostilities against every writer who had treated of the same subject. In this particular, authors may be compared to a certain sagacious bird, which in building its nest, is sure to pull to pieces the nests of all the birds in its neighbourhood. This unhappy propensity tends grievously to impede the progress of sound knowledge. Theories are at best but brittle productions, and when once committed to the stream, they should take care that like the notable pots which were fellow voyagers, they do not crack each other. But this literary animosity is almost unconquerable. Even I, who am of all men the most candid and liberal, when I sat down to write this authentic history, did all at once conceive an absolute, bitter and unutterable contempt, a strange and unimaginable disbelief, a wondrous and most ineffable scoffing of the spirit, for the theories of the numerous literati, who have treated before me, of this country. I called them jolter heads, numsculls, dunderpates, dom cops, bottericks, domme jordans, and a thousand other equally indignant appellations. But when I came to consider the matter coolly and dispassionately, my opinion was altogether changed. When I beheld these sages gravely accounting for unaccountable things, and discoursing thus wisely about matters forever hidden from their eyes, like a blind man describing the glories of light, and the beauty and harmony of colours, I fell back in astonishment at the amazing extent of human ingenuity.

If—cried I to myself, these learned men can weave whole systems out of nothing, what would be their productions were they furnished with substantial materials—if they can argue and dispute thus ingeniously about subjects beyond their knowledge, what would be the profundity of their observations, did they but know what they were talking about! Should old Radamanthus, when he comes to decide upon their conduct while on earth, have the least idea of the usefulness of their labours, he will undoubtedly class them with those notorious wise men of Gotham, who milked a bull, twisted a rope of sand, and wove a velvet purse from a sow's ear.

My chief surprise is, that among the many writers I have noticed, no one has attempted to prove that this country was peopled from the moon—or that the first inhabitants floated hither on islands of ice, as white bears cruize about the northern oceans—or that they were conveyed here by balloons, as modern æreonauts pass from Dover to Calais—or by witchcraft, as Simon Magus posted among the stars—or after the manner of the renowned Scythian Abaris, who like the New England witches on full-blooded broomsticks, made most unheard of journeys on the back of a golden arrow, given him by the Hyperborean Apollo.

But there is still one mode left by which this country could have been peopled, which I have reserved for the last, because I consider it worth all the rest, it is—*by accident!* Speaking of the islands of Solomon, New Guinea, and New Holland, the profound father Charlevoix observes, "in fine, all these countries are peopled, and *it is possible,* some have been so *by accident.* Now if it could have happened in that manner, why might it not have been at the *same time,* and by the *same means,* with *the other* parts of the globe?" This ingenious mode of deducing certain conclusions from possible premises, is an improvement in syllogistic skill, and proves the good father superior even to Archimedes, for he can turn the world without any thing to rest his lever upon. It is only surpassed by the dexterity with which the sturdy old Jesuit, in another place, demolishes the gordian knot—"Nothing" says he, "is more easy. The inhabitants of both hemispheres are certainly the descendants of the same father. The common father of mankind, received an express order from Heaven, to people the world, and *accordingly it has been peopled.* To bring this about, it was necessary to overcome all difficulties in the way, and *they have also been overcome!*" Pious Logician! How does he put all the herd of laborious theorists to the blush, by explaining in fair words, what it has cost them volumes to prove they knew nothing about!

They have long been picking at the lock, and fretting at the latch, but the honest father at once unlocks the door by bursting it open, and when he has it once a-jar, he is at full liberty to pour in as many nations as he pleases. This proves to a demonstration that a little piety is better than a cart-load of philosophy, and is a practical illustration of that scriptural promise—"By faith ye shall move mountains."

From all the authorities here quoted, and a variety of others which I have consulted, but which are omitted through fear of fatiguing the unlearned reader—I can only draw the following conclusions, which luckily however, are sufficient for my purpose—First, That this part of the world has actually *been peopled* (Q. E. D.) to support which, we have living proofs in the numerous tribes of Indians that inhabit it. Secondly, That it has been peopled in five hundred different ways, as proved by a cloud of authors, who from the positiveness of their assertions seem to have been eye witnesses to the fact—Thirdly, That the people of this country had a *variety of fathers,* which as it may not be thought much to their credit by the common run of readers, the less we say on the subject the better. The question therefore, I trust, is forever at rest.

Chapter V

In which the Author puts a mighty Question to the rout,
by the assistance of the Man in the Moon—which not only
delivers thousands of people from great embarrassment,
but likewise concludes this introductory book.

The writer of a history may, in some respects, be likened unto an adventurous knight, who having undertaken a perilous enterprize, by way of establishing his fame, feels bound in honour and chivalry, to turn back for no difficulty nor hardship, and never to shrink or quail whatever enemy he may encounter. Under this impression, I resolutely draw my pen and fall to, with might and main, at those doughty questions and subtle paradoxes, which, like fiery dragons and bloody giants, beset the entrance to my history, and would fain repulse me from the very threshold. And at this moment a gigantic question has started up, which I must take by the beard and utterly subdue, before I can advance another step in my historick undertaking—but I trust this will be the last adversary I shall have to contend with, and that in the next book, I shall be enabled to conduct my readers in triumph into the body of my work.

The question which has thus suddenly arisen is, what right had the first discoverers of America to land, and take possession of a country, without asking the consent of its inhabitants, or yielding them an adequate compensation for their territory?

My readers shall now see with astonishment, how easily I will vanquish this gigantic doubt, which has so long been the terror of adventurous writers; which has withstood so many fierce assaults, and has given such great distress of mind to multitudes of kind-hearted folks. For, until this mighty question is totally put to rest, the worthy people of America can by no means enjoy the soil they inhabit, with clear right and title, and quiet, unsullied consciences.

The first source of right, by which property is acquired in a country, is DISCOVERY. For as all mankind have an equal right to any thing, which has never before been appropriated, so any nation, that discovers an uninhabited country, and takes possession thereof, is considered as enjoying full property, and absolute, unquestionable empire therein.

This proposition being admitted, it follows clearly, that the Europeans who first visited America, were the real discoverers of the same; nothing being necessary to the establishment of this fact, but simply to prove that it was totally uninhabited by man. This would at first appear to be a point of some difficulty, for it is well known, that this quarter of the world abounded with certain animals, that walked erect on two feet, had something of the human countenance, uttered certain unintelligible sounds, very much like language, in short, had a marvellous resemblance to human beings. But the host of zealous and enlightened fathers, who accompanied the discoverers, for the purpose of promoting the kingdom of heaven, by establishing fat monasteries and bishopricks on earth, soon cleared up this point, greatly to the satisfaction of his holiness the pope, and of all Christian voyagers and discoverers.

They plainly proved, and as there were no Indian writers arose on the other side, the fact was considered as fully admitted and established, that the two legged race of animals before mentioned, were mere cannibals, detestable monsters, and many of them giants—a description of vagrants, that since the times of Gog, Magog and Goliath, have been considered as outlaws, and have received no quarter in either history, chivalry or song; indeed, even the philosopher Bacon, declared the Americans to be people proscribed by the laws of nature, inasmuch as they had a barbarous custom of sacrificing men, and feeding upon man's flesh.

Nor are these all the proofs of their utter barbarism: among many other writers of discernment, the celebrated Ulloa tells us "their imbecility is so visible, that one can hardly form an idea of them different from what one has of the brutes. Nothing disturbs the tranquillity of their souls, equally insensible to disasters, and to prosperity. Though half naked, they are as contented as a monarch in his most splendid array. Fear makes no impression on them, and respect as little."—All this is furthermore supported by the authority of M. Bouguer. "It is not easy," says he, "to describe the degree of their indifference for wealth and all its advantages. One does not well know what motives to propose to them when one would persuade them to any service. It is vain to offer them money, they answer that they are not hungry." And Vanegas confirms the whole, assuring us that "ambition, they have none, and are more desirous of being thought strong, than valiant. The objects of ambition with us, honour, fame, reputation, riches, posts and distinctions are unknown among them. So that this powerful spring of action, the cause of so much *seeming* good and *real* evil in the world has no power over them. In a word, these unhappy mortals may be compared to children, in whom the development of reason is not completed."

Now all these peculiarities, though in the unenlightened states of Greece, they would have entitled their possessors to immortal honour, as having reduced to practice those rigid and abstemious maxims, the mere talking about which, acquired certain old Greeks the reputation of sages and philosophers;—yet were they clearly proved in the present instance, to betoken a most abject and brutified nature, totally beneath the human character. But the benevolent fathers, who had undertaken to turn these unhappy savages into dumb beasts, by dint of argument, advanced still stronger proofs; for as certain divines of the sixteenth century, and among the rest Lullus affirm—the Americans go naked, and have no beards!—"They have nothing," says Lullus, "of the reasonable animal, except the mask."—And even that mask was allowed to avail them but little, for it was soon found that they were of a hideous copper complexion—and being of a copper complexion, it was all the same as if they were negroes—and negroes are black, "and black" said the pious fathers, devoutly crossing themselves, "is the colour of the Devil!" Therefore so far from being able to own property, they had no right even to personal freedom, for liberty is too radiant a deity, to inhabit such gloomy temples. All which circumstances plainly convinced the righteous followers of Cortes and Pizarro, that these miscreants had no title to the soil that they infested—that they were a perverse, illiterate, dumb, heardless, bare-bottomed *black-seed*—mere wild beasts of the forests, and like them should either be subdued or exterminated.

From the foregoing arguments therefore, and a host of others equally conclusive, which I forbear to enumerate, it was clearly evident, that this fair quarter of the globe when first visited by Europeans, was a howling wilderness, inhabited by nothing but wild beasts; and that the transatlantic visitors acquired an incontrovertible property therein, by the *right of Discovery.*

This right being fully established, we now come to the next, which is the right acquired by *cultivation.* "The cultivation of the soil" we are told "is an obligation imposed by nature on mankind. The whole world is appointed for the nourishment of its inhabitants; but it would be incapable of doing it, was it uncultivated. Every nation is then obliged by the law of nature to cultivate the ground that has fallen to its share. Those people like the ancient Germans and modern Tartars, who having fertile countries, disdain to cultivate the earth, and choose to live by rapine, are wanting to themselves, and *deserve to be exterminated as savage and pernicious beasts."*

Now it is notorious, that the savages knew nothing of agriculture, when first discovered by the Europeans, but lived a most vagabond, disorderly, unrighteous life,—rambling from place to place, and prodigally rioting upon the spontaneous luxuries of nature, without tasking her generosity to yield them any thing more; whereas it has been most unquestionably shewn, that heaven intended the earth should be ploughed and sown, and manured, and laid out into cities and towns and farms, and country seats, and pleasure grounds, and public gardens, all which the Indians knew nothing about—therefore they did not improve the talents providence had bestowed on them—therefore they were careless stewards—therefore they had no right to the soil—therefore they deserved to be exterminated.

It is true the savages might plead that they drew all the benefits from the land which their simple wants required—they found plenty of game to hunt, which together with the roots and uncultivated fruits of the earth, furnished a sufficient variety for their frugal table;—and that as heaven merely designed the earth to form the abode, and satisfy the wants of man; so long as those purposes were answered, the will of heaven was accomplished.— But this only proves how undeserving they were of the blessings around them—they were so much the more savages, for not having more wants; for knowledge is in some degree an increase of desires, and it is this superiority both in the number and magnitude of his desires, that distinguishes the man from the beast. Therefore the Indians, in not having more wants, were very unreasonable animals; and it was but just that they should make way for the Europeans, who had a thousand wants to their one, and therefore would turn the earth to more account, and by cultivating it, more truly fulfil the will of heaven. Besides—Grotius and Lauterbach, and Puffendorff and Titius and a host of wise men besides, who have considered the matter properly, have determined, that the property of a country cannot be acquired by hunting, cutting wood, or drawing water in it—nothing but precise demarcation of limits, and the intention of cultivation, can establish the possession. Now as the savages (probably from never having read the authors above quoted) had never complied with any of these necessary forms, it plainly follows that they had no right to the soil, but that it was completely at the disposal of the first comers, who had more knowledge and more wants than themselves—who would portion out the soil, with churlish boundaries; who would torture nature to pamper a thousand fantastic humours and capricious appetites; and who of course were far more rational animals than themselves. In entering upon a newly discovered, uncultivated country therefore, the new comers were but taking possession of what, according to the aforesaid doctrine, was their own property—therefore in opposing them, the savages were invading their just rights, infringing the immutable laws of nature and counteracting the will of heaven—therefore they were guilty of impiety, burglary and trespass on the case,—therefore they were hardened offenders against God and man— therefore they ought to be exterminated.

But a more irresistible right than either that I have mentioned, and one which will be the most readily admitted by my reader, provided he is blessed with bowels of charity and philanthropy, is the right acquired by civilization. All the world knows the lamentable state in which these poor savages were found. Not only deficient in the comforts of life, but what is still worse, most piteously and unfortunately blind to the miseries of their situation. But no sooner did the benevolent inhabitants of Europe behold their sad condition than they immediately went to work to ameliorate and improve it. They introduced among them the comforts of life, consisting of rum, gin and brandy—and it is astonishing to read how soon the poor savages learnt to estimate these blessings—they likewise made known to them a thousand remedies, by which the most inveterate diseases are alleviated and healed, and that they might comprehend the benefits and enjoy the comforts of these medicines, they previously introduced among them the diseases, which they were calculated to cure. By these and a variety of other methods was the condition of these poor savages, wonderfully improved; they acquired a thousand wants, of which they had before been ignorant, and as he has most sources of happiness, who has most wants to be gratified, they were doubtlessly rendered a much happier race of beings.

But the most important branch of civilization, and which has most strenuously been extolled, by the zealous and pious fathers of the Roman Church, is the introduction of the Christian faith. It was truly a sight that might well inspire horror, to behold these savages, stumbling among the dark mountains of paganism, and guilty of the most horrible ignorance of religion. It is true, they neither stole nor defrauded, they were sober, frugal, continent, and faithful to their word; but though they acted right habitually, it was all in vain, unless they acted so from precept. The new comers therefore used every method, to induce them to embrace and practice the true religion—except that of setting them the example.

But notwithstanding all these complicated labours for their good, such was the unparalleled obstinacy of these stubborn wretches, that they ungratefully refused, to acknowledge the strangers as their benefactors, and persisted in disbelieving the doctrines they endeavoured to inculcate; most insolently alledging, that from their conduct, the advocates of Christianity did not seem to believe in it themselves. Was not this too much for human patience?—would not one suppose, that the foreign emigrants from Europe, provoked at their incredulity and discouraged by their stiff-necked obstinacy, would forever have abandoned their shores, and consigned them to their original ignorance and misery?—But no—so zealous were they to effect the temporal comfort and eternal salvation of these pagan infidels, that they even proceeded from the milder means of persuasion, to the more painful and troublesome one of persecution—Let loose among them, whole troops of fiery monks and furious blood-hounds—purified them by fire and sword, by stake and faggot; in consequence of which indefatigable measures, the cause of Christian love and charity were so rapidly advanced, that in a very few years, not one fifth of the number of unbelievers existed in South America, that were found there at the time of its discovery.

Nor did the other methods of civilization remain unenforced. The Indians improved daily and wonderfully by their intercourse with the whites. They took to drinking rum, and making bargains. They learned to cheat, to lie, to swear, to gamble, to quarrel, to cut each others throats, in short, to excel in all the accomplishments that had originally marked the superiority of their Christian visitors. And such a surprising aptitude have they shewn for these acquirements, that there is very little doubt that in a century more, provided they survive so long, the irresistible effects of civilization; they will equal in knowledge, refinement, knavery, and debauchery, the most enlightened, civilized and orthodox nations of Europe.

What stronger right need the European settlers advance to the country than this. Have not whole nations of uninformed savages been made acquainted with a thousand imperious wants and indispensible comforts of which they were before wholly ignorant—Have they not been literally hunted and smoked out of the dens and lurking places of ignorance and infidelity, and absolutely scourged into the right path. Have not the temporal things, the vain baubles and filthy lucre of this world, which were too apt to engage their worldly and selfish thoughts, been benevolently taken from them; and have they not in lieu thereof, been taught to set their affections on things above—And finally, to use the words of a reverend Spanish father, in a letter to his superior in Spain—"Can any one have the presumption to say, that these savage Pagans, have yielded any thing more than an inconsiderable recompense to their benefactors; in surrendering to them a little pitiful tract of this dirty sublunary planet, in exchange for a glorious inheritance in the kingdom of Heaven!"

Here then are three complete and undeniable sources of right established, any one of which was more than ample to establish a property in the newly discovered regions of America. Now, so it has happened in certain parts of this delightful quarter of the globe, that the right of discovery has been so strenuously asserted—the influence of cultivation so industriously extended, and the progress of salvation and civilization so zealously prosecuted, that, what with their attendant wars, persecutions, oppressions, diseases, and other partial evils that often hang on the skirts of great benefits—the savage aborigines have, some how or another, been utterly annihilated—and this all at once brings me to a fourth right, which is worth all the others put together—For the original claimants to the soil bring all dead and buried, and no one remaining to inherit or dispute the soil, the Spaniards as the next immediate occupants entered upon the possession, as clearly as the hang-man succeeds to the clothes of the malefactor—and as they have Blackstone, and all the learned expounders of the law on their side, they may set all actions of ejectment at defiance—and this last right may be entitled, the RIGHT BY EXTERMINATION, or in other words, the RIGHT BY GUNPOWDER.

But lest any scruples of conscience should remain on this head, and to settle the question of right forever, his holiness Pope Alexander VI, issued one of those mighty bulls, which bear down reason, argument and every thing before them; by which he generously granted the newly discovered quarter of the globe, to the Spaniards and Portuguese; who, thus having law and gospel on their side, and being inflamed with great spiritual zeal, shewed the Pagan savages neither favour nor affection, but prosecuted the work of discovery, colonization, civilization, and extermination, with ten times more fury than ever.

Thus were the European worthies who first discovered America, clearly entitled to the soil; and not only entitled to the soil, but likewise to the

eternal thanks of these infidel savages, for having come so far, endured
so many perils by sea and land, and taken such unwearied pains, for no
other purpose under heaven but to improve their forlorn, uncivilized and
heathenish condition—for having made them acquainted with the comforts of life, such as gin, rum, brandy, and the small-pox; for having introduced among them the light of religion, and finally—for having hurried
them out of the world, to enjoy its reward!

But as argument is never so well understood by us selfish mortals, as
when it comes home to ourselves, and as I am particularly anxious that this
question should be put to rest forever, I will suppose a parallel case, by way
of arousing the candid attention of my readers.

Let us suppose then, that the inhabitants of the moon, by astonishing advancement in science, and by a profound insight into that ineffable
lunar philosophy, the mere flickerings of which, have of late years, dazzled
the feeble optics, and addled the shallow brains of the good people of our
globe—let us suppose, I say, that the inhabitants of the moon, by these
means, had arrived at such a command of their *energies,* such an enviable
state of *perfectability,* as to controul the elements, and navigate the boundless regions of space. Let us suppose a roving crew of these soaring philosophers, in the course of an ærial voyage of discovery among the stars, should
chance to alight upon this outlandish planet.

And here I beg my readers will not have the impertinence to smile, as is
too frequently the fault of volatile readers, when perusing the grave speculations of philosophers. I am far from indulging in any sportive vein at
present, nor is the supposition I have been making so wild as many may
deem it. It has long been a very serious and anxious question with me, and
many a time, and oft, in the course of my overwhelming cares and contriv-
ances for the welfare and protection of this my native planet, have I lain
awake whole nights, debating in my mind whether it was most probable
we should first discover and civilize the moon, or the moon discover and
civilize our globe. Neither would the prodigy of sailing in the air and cruis-
ing among the stars be a whit more astonishing and incomprehensible to
us, than was the European mystery of navigating floating castles, through
the world of waters, to the simple savages. We have already discovered the
art of coasting along the ærial shores of our planet, by means of balloons,
as the savages had, of venturing along their sea coasts in canoes; and the
disparity between the former, and the ærial vehicles of the philosophers

from the moon, might not be greater, than that, between the bark canoes of the savages, and the mighty ships of their discoverers. I might here pursue an endless chain of very curious, profound and unprofitable speculations; but as they would be unimportant to my subject, I abandon them to my reader, particularly if he is a philosopher, as matters well worthy of his attentive consideration.

To return then to my supposition—let us suppose that the ærial visitants I have mentioned, possessed of vastly superior knowledge to ourselves; that is to say, possessed of superior knowledge in the art of extermination—riding on Hypogriffs, defended with impenetrable armour—armed with concentrated sun beams, and provided with vast engines, to hurl enormous moon stones: in short, let us suppose them, if our vanity will permit the supposition, as superior to us in knowledge, and consequently in power, as the Europeans were to the Indians, when they first discovered them. All this is very possible, it is only our self-sufficiency, that makes us think otherwise; and I warrant the poor savages, before they had any knowledge of the white men, armed in all the terrors of glittering steel and tremendous gun-powder, were as perfectly convinced that they themselves, were the wisest, the most virtuous, powerful and perfect of created beings, as are, at this present moment, the lordly inhabitants of old England, the volatile populace of France, or even the self-satisfied citizens of this most enlightened republick.

Let us suppose, moreover, that the ærial voyagers, finding this planet to be nothing but a howling wilderness, inhabited by us, poor savages and wild beasts, shall take formal possession of it, in the name of his most gracious and philosophic excellency, the man in the moon. Finding however, that their numbers are incompetent to hold it in complete subjection, on account of the ferocious barbarity of its inhabitants; they shall take our worthy President, the King of England, the Emperor of Hayti, the mighty little Bonaparte, and the great King of Bantam, and returning to their native planet, shall carry them to court, as were the Indian chiefs led about as spectacles in the courts of Europe.

Then making such obeisance as the etiquette of the court requires, they shall address the puissant man in the moon, in, as near as I can conjecture, the following terms:

"Most serene and mighty Potentate, whose dominions extend as far as eye can reach, who rideth on the Great Bear, useth the sun as a looking glass and maintaineth unrivalled controul over tides, madmen and sea-crabs. We thy liege subjects have just returned from a voyage of discovery, in the course of which we have landed and taken possession of that obscure little scurvy planet, which thou beholdest rolling at a distance. The five uncouth monsters, which we have brought into this august presence, were once very important chiefs among their fellow savages; for the inhabitants of the newly discovered globe are totally destitute of the common attributes of humanity, inasmuch as they carry their heads upon their shoulders, instead of under their arms—have two eyes instead of one—are utterly destitute of tails, and of a variety of unseemly complexions, particularly of a horrible whiteness—whereas all the inhabitants of the moon are pea green!

We have moreover found these miserable savages sunk into a state of the utmost ignorance and depravity, every man shamelessly living with his own wife, and rearing his own children, instead of indulging in that community of wives, enjoined by the law of nature, as expounded by the philosophers of the moon. In a word they have scarcely a gleam of true philosophy among them, but are in fact, utter heretics, ignoramuses and barbarians. Taking compassion therefore on the sad condition of these sublunary wretches, we have endeavoured, while we remained on their planet, to introduce among them the light of reason—and the comforts of the moon.—We have treated them to mouthfuls of moonshine and draughts of nitrous oxide, which they swallowed with incredible voracity, particularly the females; and we have likewise endeavoured to instil into them the precepts of lunar Philosophy. We have insisted upon their renouncing the contemptible shackles of religion and common sense, and adoring the profound, omnipotent, and all perfect energy, and the extatic, immutable, immoveable perfection. But such was the unparalleled obstinacy of these wretched savages, that they persisted in cleaving to their wives and adhering to their religion, and absolutely set at naught the sublime doctrines of the moon—nay, among other abominable heresies they even went so far as blasphemously to declare, that this ineffable planet was made of nothing more nor less than green cheese!"

At these words, the great man in the moon (being a very profound philosopher) shall fall into a terrible passion, and possessing equal authority over things that do not belong to him, as did whilome his holiness the Pope, shall forthwith issue a formidable bull,—specifying, "That—whereas a certain crew of Lunatics have lately discovered and taken possession of that little dirty planet, called *the earth*—and that whereas it is inhabited by none but a race of two legged animals, that carry their heads on their shoulders instead of under their arms; cannot talk the lunatic language; have two eyes instead of one; are destitute of tails, and of a horrible whiteness, instead of pea green—therefore and for a variety of other excellent reasons—they are considered incapable of possessing any property in the planet they infest, and the right and title to it are confirmed to its original discoverers.—And furthermore, the colonists who are now about to depart to the aforesaid planet, are authorized and commanded to use every means to convert these infidel savages from the darkness of Christianity, and make them thorough and absolute lunatics."

In consequence of this benevolent bull, our philosophic benefactors go to work with hearty zeal. They seize upon our fertile territories, scourge us from our rightful possessions, relieve us from our wives, and when we are unreasonable enough to complain, they will turn upon us and say—miserable barbarians! ungrateful wretches!—have we not come thousands of miles to improve your worthless planet—have we not fed you with moon shine—have we not intoxicated you with nitrous oxyde—does not our moon give you light every night and have you the baseness to murmur, when we claim a pitiful return for all these benefits? But finding that we not only persist in absolute contempt to their reasoning and disbelief in their philosophy, but even go so far as daringly to defend our property, their patience shall be exhausted, and they shall resort to their superior powers of argument—hunt us with Hypogriffs, transfix us with concentrated sunbeams, demolish our cities with moonstones; until having by main force, converted us to the true faith, they shall graciously permit us to exist in the torrid deserts of Arabia, or the frozen regions of Lapland, there to enjoy the blessings of civilization and the charms of lunar philosophy—in much the same manner as the reformed and enlightened savages of this country, are kindly suffered to inhabit the inhospitable forests of the north, or the impenetrable wildernesses of South America.

Thus have I clearly proved, and I hope strikingly illustrated, the right of the early colonists to the possession of this country—and thus is this gigantic question, completely knocked in the head—so having manfully surmounted all obstacles, and subdued all opposition, what remains but that I should forthwith conduct my impatient and way-worn readers, into the renowned city, which we have so long been in a manner besieging.—But hold, before I proceed another step, I must pause to take breath and recover from the excessive fatigue I have undergone, in preparing to begin this most accurate of histories. And in this I do but imitate the example of the celebrated Hans Von Dunderbottom, who took a start of three miles for the purpose of jumping over a hill, but having been himself out of breath by the time he reached the foot, sat himself quietly down for a few moments to blow, and then walked over it at his leisure.

1836

If Washington Irving gave Americans permission to not be British, then Ralph Waldo Emerson gave them the means to be American. "To be yourself in a world that is constantly trying to make you something else," he wrote, "is the greatest accomplishment."

RALPH WALDO EMERSON

Nature

A subtle chain of countless rings
The next unto the farthest brings;
The eye reads omens where it goes,
And speaks all languages the rose;
And, striving to be man, the worm
Mounts through all the spires of form.

Introduction

Our age is retrospective. It builds the sepulchres of the fathers. It writes biographies, histories, and criticism. The foregoing generations beheld God and nature face to face; we, through their eyes. Why should not we also enjoy an original relation to the universe? Why should not we have a poetry and philosophy of insight and not of tradition, and a religion by revelation to us, and not the history of theirs? Embosomed for a season in nature, whose floods of life stream around and through us, and invite us, by the powers they supply, to action proportioned to nature, why should we grope among the dry bones of the past, or put the living generation into masquerade out of its faded wardrobe? The sun shines to-day also. There is more wool and flax in the fields. There are new lands, new men, new thoughts. Let us demand our own works and laws and worship.

Undoubtedly we have no questions to ask which are unanswerable. We must trust the perfection of the creation so far as to believe that whatever curiosity the order of things has awakened in our minds, the order of things can satisfy. Every man's condition is a solution in hieroglyphic to those inquiries he would put. He acts it as life, before he apprehends it as truth. In like manner, nature is already, in its forms and tendencies, describing its own design. Let us interrogate the great apparition that shines so peacefully around us. Let us inquire, to what end is nature?

All science has one aim, namely, to find a theory of nature. We have theories of races and of functions, but scarcely yet a remote approach to an idea of creation. We are now so far from the road to truth, that religious teachers dispute and hate each other, and speculative men are esteemed unsound and frivolous. But to a sound judgment, the most abstract truth is the most practical. Whenever a true theory appears, it will be its own evidence. Its test is, that it will explain all phenomena. Now many are thought not only unexplained but inexplicable; as language, sleep, madness, dreams, beasts, sex.

Philosophically considered, the universe is composed of Nature and the Soul. Strictly speaking, therefore, all that is separate from us, all which Philosophy distinguishes as the NOT ME, that is, both nature and art, all other men and my own body, must be ranked under this name, NATURE. In enumerating the values of nature and casting up their sum, I shall use the word in both senses;—in its common and in its philosophical import. In inquiries so general as our present one, the inaccuracy is not material; no confusion of thought will occur. *Nature,* in the common sense, refers to essences unchanged by man; space, the air, the river, the leaf. *Art* is applied to the mixture of his will with the same things, as in a house, a canal, a statue, a picture. But his operations taken together are so insignificant, a little chipping, baking, patching, and washing, that in an impression so grand as that of the world on the human mind, they do not vary the result.

I

To go into solitude, a man needs to retire as much from his chamber as from society. I am not solitary whilst I read and write, though nobody is with me. But if a man would be alone, let him look at the stars. The rays that come from those heavenly worlds will separate between him and what he touches. One might think the atmosphere was made transparent with this design, to give man, in the heavenly bodies, the perpetual presence of the sublime. Seen in the streets of cities, how great they are! If the stars should appear one night in a thousand years, how would men believe and adore; and preserve for many generations the remembrance of the city of

God which had been shown! But every night come out these envoys of beauty, and light the universe with their admonishing smile.

The stars awaken a certain reverence, because though always present, they are inaccessible; but all natural objects make a kindred impression, when the mind is open to their influence. Nature never wears a mean appearance. Neither does the wisest man extort her secret, and lose his curiosity by finding out all her perfection. Nature never became a toy to a wise spirit. The flowers, the animals, the mountains, reflected the wisdom of his best hour, as much as they had delighted the simplicity of his childhood.

When we speak of nature in this manner, we have a distinct but most poetical sense in the mind. We mean the integrity of impression made by manifold natural objects. It is this which distinguishes the stick of timber of the wood-cutter from the tree of the poet. The charming landscape which I saw this morning is indubitably made up of some twenty or thirty farms. Miller owns this field, Locke that, and Manning the woodland beyond. But none of them owns the landscape. There is a property in the horizon which no man has but he whose eye can integrate all the parts, that is, the poet. This is the best part of these men's farms, yet to this their warranty-deeds give no title.

To speak truly, few adult persons can see nature. Most persons do not see the sun. At least they have a very superficial seeing. The sun illuminates only the eye of the man, but shines into the eye and the heart of the child. The lover of nature is he whose inward and outward senses are still truly adjusted to each other; who has retained the spirit of infancy even into the era of manhood. His intercourse with heaven and earth becomes part of his daily food. In the presence of nature a wild delight runs through the man, in spite of real sorrows. Nature says,—he is my creature, and maugre all his impertinent griefs, he shall be glad with me. Not the sun or the summer alone, but every hour and season yields its tribute of delight; for every hour and change corresponds to and authorizes a different state of the mind, from breathless noon to grimmest midnight. Nature is a setting that fits equally well a comic or a mourning piece. In good health, the air is a cordial of incredible virtue. Crossing a bare common, in snow puddles, at twilight, under a clouded sky, without having in my thoughts any occurrence of special good fortune, I have enjoyed a perfect exhilaration. I am glad to the brink of fear. In the woods, too, a man casts off his years, as the snake his slough, and at what period soever of life is always a child. In the woods is perpetual youth. Within these plantations of God, a decorum and sanctity reign, a perennial festival is dressed, and the guest sees not how he should tire of them in a thousand years. In the woods, we return to reason and faith. There I feel that nothing can befall me in life,—no disgrace, no calamity (leaving me my eyes), which nature cannot repair. Standing on the bare ground,—my head bathed by the blithe air and uplifted into infinite space,—all mean egotism vanishes. I become a transparent eyeball; I am nothing; I see all; the currents of the Universal Being circulate through me; I am part or parcel of God. The name of the nearest friend sounds then foreign and accidental: to be brothers, to be acquaintances, master or servant, is then a trifle and a disturbance. I am the lover of uncontained and immortal beauty. In the wilderness, I find something more dear and connate than in streets or villages. In the tranquil landscape, and especially in the distant line of the horizon, man beholds somewhat as beautiful as his own nature.

The greatest delight which the fields and woods minister is the suggestion of an occult relation between man and the vegetable. I am not alone and unacknowledged. They nod to me, and I to them. The waving of the boughs in the storm is new to me and old. It takes me by surprise, and yet is not unknown. Its effect is like that of a higher thought or a better emotion coming over me, when I deemed I was thinking justly or doing right.

Yet it is certain that the power to produce this delight does not reside in nature, but in man, or in a harmony of both. It is necessary to use these pleasures with great temperance. For nature is not always tricked in holiday attire, but the same scene which yesterday breathed perfume and glittered as for the frolic of the nymphs is overspread with melancholy to-day. Nature always wears the colors of the spirit. To a man laboring under calamity, the heat of his own fire hath sadness in it. Then there is a kind of contempt of the landscape felt by him who has just lost by death a dear friend. The sky is less grand as it shuts down over less worth in the population.

II

Commodity

Whoever considers the final cause of the world will discern a multitude of uses that enter as parts into that result. They all admit of being thrown into one of the following classes: Commodity; Beauty; Language; and Discipline.

Under the general name of commodity, I rank all those advantages which our senses owe to nature. This, of course, is a benefit which is temporary and mediate, not ultimate, like its service to the soul. Yet although low, it is perfect in its kind, and is the only use of nature which all men apprehend. The misery of man appears like childish petulance, when we explore the steady and prodigal provision that has been made for his support and delight on this green ball which floats him through the heavens. What angels invented these splendid ornaments, these rich conveniences, this ocean of air above, this ocean of water beneath, this firmament of earth between? this zodiac of lights, this tent of dropping clouds, this striped coat of climates, this fourfold year? Beasts, fire, water, stones, and corn serve him. The field is at once his floor, his work-yard, his play-ground, his garden, and his bed.

> *"More servants wait on man*
> *Than he'll take notice of."*

Nature, in its ministry to man, is not only the material, but is also the process and the result. All the parts incessantly work into each other's hands for the profit of man. The wind sows the seed; the sun evaporates the sea; the wind blows the vapor to the field; the ice, on the other side of the planet, condenses rain on this; the rain feeds the plant; the plant feeds the animal; and thus the endless circulations of the divine charity nourish man.

The useful arts are reproductions or new combinations by the wit of man, of the same natural benefactors. He no longer waits for favoring gales, but by means of steam, he realizes the fable of Æolus's bag, and carries the two and thirty winds in the boiler of his boat. To diminish friction, he paves the road with iron bars, and, mounting a coach with a ship-load of men, animals, and merchandise behind him, he darts through the country, from town to town, like an eagle or a swallow through the air. By the aggregate of these aids, how is the face of the world changed, from the era of Noah to that of Napoleon! The private poor man hath cities, ships, canals, bridges, built for him. He goes to the post-office, and the human race run on his errands; to the book-shop, and the human race read and write of all that happens, for him; to the court-house, and nations repair his wrongs. He sets his house upon the road, and the human race go forth every morning, and shovel out the snow, and cut a path for him.

But there is no need of specifying particulars in this class of uses. The catalogue is endless, and the examples so obvious, that I shall leave them to the reader's reflection, with the general remark, that this mercenary benefit is one which has respect to a farther good. A man is fed, not that he may be fed, but that he may work.

III

Beauty

A nobler want of man is served by nature, namely, the love of Beauty.

The ancient Greeks called the world *κόσμος,* beauty. Such is the constitution of all things, or such the plastic power of the human eye, that the primary forms, as the sky, the mountain, the tree, the animal, give us a delight *in and for themselves;* a pleasure arising from outline, color, motion, and grouping. This seems partly owing to the eye itself. The eye is the best of artists. By the mutual action of its structure and of the laws of light, perspective is produced, which integrates every mass of objects, of what character soever, into a well colored and shaded globe, so that where the particular objects are mean and unaffecting, the landscape which they compose is round and symmetrical. And as the eye is the best composer, so light is the first of painters. There is no object so foul that intense light will not make beautiful. And the stimulus it affords to the sense, and a sort of infinitude which it hath, like space and time, make all matter gay. Even the corpse has its own beauty. But besides this general grace diffused over nature, almost all the individual forms are agreeable to the eye, as is proved by our endless imitations of some of them, as the acorn, the grape, the pine-cone, the wheat-ear, the egg, the wings and forms of most birds, the lion's claw, the serpent, the butterfly, sea-shells, flames, clouds, buds, leaves, and the forms of many trees, as the palm.

For better consideration, we may distribute the aspects of Beauty in a threefold manner.

1. First, the simple perception of natural forms is a delight. The influence of the forms and actions in nature is so needful to man, that, in its lowest functions, it seems to lie on the confines of commodity and beauty. To the body and mind which have been cramped by noxious work or company, nature is medicinal and restores their tone. The tradesman, the at-

torney comes out of the din and craft of the street and sees the sky and the woods, and is a man again. In their eternal calm, he finds himself. The health of the eye seems to demand a horizon. We are never tired, so long as we can see far enough.

But in other hours, Nature satisfies by its loveliness, and without any mixture of corporeal benefit. I see the spectacle of morning from the hill-top over against my house, from daybreak to sunrise, with emotions which an angel might share. The long slender bars of cloud float like fishes in the sea of crimson light. From the earth, as a shore, I look out into that silent sea. I seem to partake its rapid transformations; the active enchantment reaches my dust, and I dilate and conspire with the morning wind. How does Nature deify us with a few and cheap elements! Give me health and a day, and I will make the pomp of emperors ridiculous. The dawn is my Assyria; the sunset and moonrise my Paphos, and unimaginable realms of faerie; broad noon shall be my England of the senses and the understand-ing; the night shall be my Germany of mystic philosophy and dreams.

Not less excellent, except for our less susceptibility in the afternoon, was the charm, last evening, of a January sunset. The western clouds di-vided and subdivided themselves into pink flakes modulated with tints of unspeakable softness, and the air had so much life and sweetness that it was a pain to come within doors. What was it that nature would say? Was there no meaning in the live repose of the valley behind the mill, and which Homer or Shakespeare could not re-form for me in words? The leafless trees become spires of flame in the sunset, with the blue east for their back-ground, and the stars of the dead calices of flowers, and every withered stem and stubble rimed with frost, contribute something to the mute music.

The inhabitants of cities suppose that the country landscape is pleasant only half the year. I please myself with the graces of the winter scenery, and believe that we are as much touched by it as by the genial influences of summer. To the attentive eye, each moment of the year has its own beauty, and in the same field, it beholds, every hour, a picture which was never seen before, and which shall never be seen again. The heavens change every mo-ment, and reflect their glory or gloom on the plains beneath. The state of the crop in the surrounding farms alters the expression of the earth from week to week. The succession of native plants in the pastures and roadsides, which makes the silent clock by which time tells the summer hours, will make even the divisions of the day sensible to a keen observer. The tribes of birds and insects, like the plants punctual to their time, follow each other, and the year has room for all. By watercourses, the variety is greater. In July, the blue pontederia or pickerel-weed blooms in large beds in the shallow parts of our pleasant river, and swarms with yellow butterflies in continual motion. Art cannot rival this pomp of purple and gold. Indeed the river is a perpetual gala, and boasts each month a new ornament.

But this beauty of Nature which is seen and felt as beauty, is the least part. The shows of day, the dewy morning, the rainbow, mountains, or-chards in blossom, stars, moonlight, shadows in still water, and the like, if too eagerly hunted, become shows merely, and mock us with their unreal-ity. Go out of the house to see the moon, and 't is mere tinsel; it will not please as when its light shines upon your necessary journey. The beauty that shimmers in the yellow afternoons of October, who ever could clutch it? Go forth to find it, and it is gone; 't is only a mirage as you look from the windows of diligence.

2. The presence of a higher, namely, of the spiritual element is essential to its perfection. The high and divine beauty which can be loved without effeminacy, is that which is found in combination with the human will. Beauty is the mark God sets upon virtue. Every natural action is graceful. Every heroic act is also decent, and causes the place and the bystanders to shine. We are taught by great actions that the universe is the property of every individual in it. Every rational creature has all nature for his dowry and estate. It is his, if he will. He may divest himself of it; he may creep into a corner, and abdicate his kingdom, as most men do, but he is entitled to the world by his constitution. In proportion to the energy of his thought and will, he takes up the world into himself. "All those things for which men plough, build, or sail, obey virtue," said Sallust. "The winds and waves," said Gibbon, "are always on the side of the ablest navigators." So are the sun and moon and all the stars of heaven. When a noble act is done,—perchance in a scene of great natural beauty; when Leonidas and his three hundred martyrs consume one day in dying, and the sun and moon come each and look at them once in the steep defile of Thermopylæ; when Arnold Winkelried, in the high Alps, under the shadow of the avalanche, gathers in his side a sheaf of Austrian spears to break the line for his comrades; are not these heroes entitled to add the beauty of the scene to the beauty of the deed? When the bark of Columbus nears the shore of America;—before it the beach lined with savages, fleeing out of all their huts of cane; the sea behind; and the

purple mountains of the Indian Archipelago around, can we separate the man from the living picture? Does not the New World clothe his form with her palm-groves and savannahs as fit drapery? Ever does natural beauty steal in like air, and envelope great actions. When Sir Harry Vane was dragged up the Tower-hill, sitting on a sled, to suffer death as the champion of the English laws, one of the multitude cried out to him, "You never sate on so glorious a seat!" Charles II., to intimidate the citizens of London, caused the patriot Lord Russell to be drawn in an open coach through the principal streets of the city on his way to the scaffold. "But," his biographer says, "the multitude imagined they saw liberty and virtue sitting by his side." In private places, among sordid objects, an act of truth or heroism seems at once to draw to itself the sky as its temple, the sun as its candle. Nature stretches out her arms to embrace man, only let his thoughts be of equal greatness. Willingly does she follow his steps with the rose and the violet, and bend her lines of grandeur and grace to the decoration of her darling child. Only let his thoughts be of equal scope, and the frame will suit the picture. A virtuous man is in unison with her works, and makes the central figure of the visible sphere. Homer, Pindar, Socrates, Phocion, associate themselves fitly in our memory with the geography and climate of Greece. The visible heavens and earth sympathize with Jesus. And in common life whosoever has seen a person of powerful character and happy genius, will have remarked how easily he took all things along with him,—the persons, the opinions, and the day, and nature became ancillary to a man.

3. There is still another aspect under which the beauty of the world may be viewed, namely, as it becomes an object of the intellect. Beside the relation of things to virtue, they have a relation to thought. The intellect searches out the absolute order of things as they stand in the mind of God, and without the colors of affection. The intellectual and the active powers seem to succeed each other, and the exclusive activity of the one generates the exclusive activity of the other. There is something unfriendly in each to the other, but they are like the alternate periods of feeding and working in animals; each prepares and will be followed by the other. Therefore does beauty, which, in relation to actions, as we have seen, comes unsought, and comes because it is unsought, remain for the apprehension and pursuit of the intellect; and then again, in its turn, of the active power. Nothing divine dies. All good is eternally reproductive. The beauty of nature re-forms itself in the mind, and not for barren contemplation, but for new creation.

All men are in some degree impressed by the face of the world; some men even to delight. This love of beauty is Taste. Others have the same love in such excess, that, not content with admiring, they seem to embody it in new forms. The creation of beauty is Art.

The production of a work of art throws a light upon the mystery of humanity. A work of art is an abstract or epitome of the world. It is the result or expression of nature, in miniature. For although the works of nature are innumerable and all different, the result or the expression of them all is similar and single. Nature is a sea of forms radically alike and even unique. A leaf, a sunbeam, a landscape, the ocean, make an analogous impression on the mind. What is common to them all,—that perfectness and harmony, is beauty. The standard of beauty is the entire circuit of natural forms,—the totality of nature; which the Italians expressed by defining beauty "il più nell' uno." Nothing is quite beautiful alone; nothing but is beautiful in the whole. A single object is only so far beautiful as it suggests this universal grace. The poet, the painter, the sculptor, the musician, the architect, seek each to concentrate this radiance of the world on one point, and each in his several work to satisfy the love of beauty which stimulates him to produce. Thus is Art a nature passed through the alembic of man. Thus in art does Nature work through the will of a man filled with the beauty of her first works.

The world thus exists to the soul to satisfy the desire of beauty. This element I call an ultimate end. No reason can be asked or given why the soul seeks beauty. Beauty, in its largest and profoundest sense, is one expression for the universe. God is the all-fair. Truth, and goodness, and beauty, are but different faces of the same All. But beauty in nature is not ultimate. It is the herald of inward and eternal beauty, and is not alone a solid and satisfactory good. It must stand as a part, and not as yet the last or highest expression of the final cause of Nature.

IV

Language

Language is a third use which Nature subserves to man. Nature is the vehicle of thought, and in a simple, double, and three-fold degree.

1. Words are signs of natural facts.
2. Particular natural facts are symbols of particular spiritual facts.

3. Nature is the symbol of spirit.

1. Words are signs of natural facts. The use of natural history is to give us aid in supernatural history; the use of the outer creation, to give us language for the beings and changes of the inward creation. Every word which is used to express a moral or intellectual fact, if traced to its root, is found to be borrowed from some material appearance. *Right* means *straight; wrong* means *twisted. Spirit* primarily means *wind; transgression,* the crossing of a *line; supercilious,* the *raising of the eyebrow.* We say the *heart* to express emotion, the *head* to denote thought; and *thought* and *emotion* are words borrowed from sensible things, and now appropriated to spiritual nature. Most of the process by which this transformation is made, is hidden from us in the remote time when language was framed; but the same tendency may be daily observed in children. Children and savages use only nouns or names of things, which they convert into verbs, and apply to analogous mental acts.

2. But this origin of all words that convey a spiritual import,—so conspicuous a fact in the history of language,—is our least debt to nature. It is not words only that are emblematic; it is things which are emblematic. Every natural fact is a symbol of some spiritual fact. Every appearance in nature corresponds to some state of the mind, and that state of the mind can only be described by presenting that natural appearance as its picture. An enraged man is a lion, a cunning man is a fox, a firm man is a rock, a learned man is a torch. A lamb is innocence; a snake is subtle spite; flowers express to us the delicate affections. Light and darkness are our familiar expression for knowledge and ignorance; and heat for love. Visible distance behind and before us, is respectively our image of memory and hope.

Who looks upon a river in a meditative hour and is not reminded of the flux of all things? Throw a stone into the stream, and the circles that propagate themselves are the beautiful type of all influence. Man is conscious of a universal soul within or behind his individual life, wherein, as in a firmament, the natures of Justice, Truth, Love, Freedom, arise and shine. This universal soul he calls Reason: it is not mine, or thine, or his, but we are its; we are its property and men. And the blue sky in which the private earth is buried, the sky with its eternal calm, and full of everlasting orbs, is the type of Reason. That which intellectually considered we call Reason, considered in relation to nature, we call Spirit. Spirit is the Creator. Spirit hath life in itself. And man in all ages and countries embodies it in his language as the FATHER.

It is easily seen that there is nothing lucky or capricious in these analogies, but that they are constant, and pervade nature. These are not the dreams of a few poets, here and there, but man is an analogist, and studies relations in all objects. He is placed in the centre of beings, and a ray of relation passes from every other being to him. And neither can man be understood without these objects, nor these objects without man. All the facts in natural history taken by themselves, have no value, but are barren, like a single sex. But marry it to human history, and it is full of life. Whole floras, all Linnæus' and Buffon's volumes, are dry catalogues of facts; but the most trivial of these facts, the habit of a plant, the organs, or work, or noise of an insect, applied to the illustration of a fact in intellectual philosophy, or in any way associated to human nature, affects us in the most lively and agreeable manner. The seed of a plant,—to what affecting analogies in the nature of man is that little fruit made use of, in all discourse, up to the voice of Paul, who calls the human corpse a seed,—"It is sown a natural body; it is raised a spiritual body." The motion of the earth round its axis and round the sun, makes the day and the year. These are certain amounts of brute light and heat. But is there no intent of an analogy between man's life and the seasons? And do the seasons gain no grandeur or pathos from that analogy? The instincts of the ant are very unimportant considered as the ant's; but the moment a ray of relation is seen to extend from it to man, and the little drudge is seen to be a monitor, a little body with a mighty heart, then all its habits, even that said to be recently observed, that it never sleeps, become sublime.

Because of this radical correspondence between visible things and human thoughts, savages, who have only what is necessary, converse in figures. As we go back in history, language becomes more picturesque, until its infancy, when it is all poetry; or all spiritual facts are represented by natural symbols. The same symbols are found to make the original elements of all languages. It has moreover been observed, that the idioms of all languages approach each other in passages of the greatest eloquence and power. And as this is the first language, so is it the last. This immediate dependence of language upon nature, this conversion of an outward phenomenon into a type of somewhat in human life, never loses its power to affect us. It is this which gives that piquancy to the conversation of a strong-natured farmer or backwoodsman, which all men relish.

A man's power to connect his thought with its proper symbol, and so to utter it, depends on the simplicity of his character, that is, upon his love of truth and his desire to communicate it without loss. The corruption of man is followed by the corruption of language. When simplicity of character and the sovereignty of ideas is broken up by the prevalence of secondary desires,—the desire of riches, of pleasure, of power, and of praise,—and duplicity and falsehood take the place of simplicity and truth, the power over nature as an interpreter of the will is in a degree lost; new imagery ceases to be created, and old words are perverted to stand for things which are not; a paper currency is employed, when there is no bullion in the vaults. In due time the fraud is manifest, and words lose all power to stimulate the understanding or the affections. Hundreds of writers may be found in every long-civilized nation who for a short time believe and make others believe that they see and utter truths, who do not of themselves clothe one thought in its natural garment, but who feed unconsciously on the language created by the primary writers of the country, those, namely, who hold primarily on nature.

But wise men pierce this rotten diction and fasten words again to visible things; so that picturesque language is at once a commanding certificate that he who employs it is a man in alliance with truth and God. The moment our discourse rises above the ground line of familiar facts and is inflamed with passion or exalted by thought, it clothes itself in images. A man conversing in earnest, if he watch his intellectual processes, will find that a material image more or less luminous arises in his mind, contemporaneous with every thought, which furnishes the vestment of the thought. Hence, good writing and brilliant discourse are perpetual allegories. This imagery is spontaneous. It is the blending of experience with the present action of the mind. It is proper creation. It is the working of the Original Cause through the instruments he has already made.

These facts may suggest the advantage which the country-life possesses, for a powerful mind, over the artificial and curtailed life of cities. We know more from nature than we can at will communicate. Its light flows into the mind evermore, and we forget its presence. The poet, the orator, bred in the woods, whose senses have been nourished by their fair and appeasing changes, year after year, without design and without heed,—shall not lose their lesson altogether, in the roar of cities or the broil of politics. Long hereafter, amidst agitation and terror in national councils,—in the hour of revolution,—these solemn images shall reappear in their morning lustre, as fit symbols and words of the thoughts which the passing events shall awaken. At the call of a noble sentiment, again the woods wave, the pines murmur, the river rolls and shines, and the cattle low upon the mountains, as he saw and heard them in his infancy. And with these forms, the spells of persuasion, the keys of power are put into his hands.

3. We are thus assisted by natural objects in the expression of particular meanings. But how great a language to convey such pepper-corn informations! Did it need such noble races of creatures, this profusion of forms, this host of orbs in heaven, to furnish man with the dictionary and grammar of his municipal speech? Whilst we use this grand cipher to expedite the affairs of our pot and kettle, we feel that we have not yet put it to its use, neither are able. We are like travellers using the cinders of a volcano to roast their eggs. Whilst we see that it always stands ready to clothe what we would say, we cannot avoid the question whether the characters are not significant of themselves. Have mountains, and waves, and skies, no significance but what we consciously give them when we employ them as emblems of our thoughts? The world is emblematic. Parts of speech are metaphors, because the whole of nature is a metaphor of the human mind. The laws of moral nature answer to those of matter as face to face in a glass. "The visible world and the relation of its parts, is the dial plate of the invisible." The axioms of physics translate the laws of ethics. Thus, "the whole is greater than its part;" "reaction is equal to action;" "the smallest weight may be made to lift the greatest, the difference of weight being compensated by time;" and many the like propositions, which have an ethical as well as physical sense. These propositions have a much more extensive and universal sense when applied to human life, than when confined to technical use.

In like manner, the memorable words of history and the proverbs of nations consist usually of a natural fact, selected as a picture or parable of a moral truth. Thus; A rolling stone gathers no moss; A bird in the hand is worth two in the bush; A cripple in the right way will beat a racer in the wrong; Make hay while the sun shines; 'T is hard to carry a full cup even; Vinegar is the son of wine; The last ounce broke the camel's back; Long-lived trees make roots first;—and the like. In their primary sense these are trivial facts, but we repeat them for the value of their analogical import. What is true of proverbs, is true of all fables, parables, and allegories.

This relation between the mind and matter is not fancied by some poet, but stands in the will of God, and so is free to be known by all men.

It appears to men, or it does not appear. When in fortunate hours we ponder this miracle, the wise man doubts if at all other times he is not blind and deaf;

> *"Can such things be,*
> *And overcome us like a summer's cloud,*
> *Without our special wonder?"*

for the universe becomes transparent, and the light of higher laws than its own shines through it. It is the standing problem which has exercised the wonder and the study of every fine genius since the world began; from the era of the Egyptians and the Brahmins, to that of Pythagoras, of Plato, of Bacon, of Leibnitz, of Swedenborg. There sits the Sphinx at the road-side, and from age to age, as each prophet comes by, he tries his fortune at reading her riddle. There seems to be a necessity in spirit to manifest itself in material forms; and day and night, river and storm, beast and bird, acid and alkali, preëxist in necessary Ideas in the mind of God, and are what they are by virtue of preceding affections in the world of spirit. A Fact is the end or last issue of spirit. The visible creation is the terminus or the circumference of the invisible world. "Material objects," said a French philosopher, "are necessarily kinds of *scoriæ* of the substantial thoughts of the Creator, which must always preserve an exact relation to their first origin; in other words, visible nature must have a spiritual and moral side."

This doctrine is abstruse, and though the images of "garment," "scoriae," "mirror," etc., may stimulate the fancy, we must summon the aid of subtler and more vital expositors to make it plain. "Every scripture is to be interpreted by the same spirit which gave it forth,"—is the fundamental law of criticism. A life in harmony with Nature, the love of truth and of virtue, will purge the eyes to understand her text. By degrees we may come to know the primitive sense of the permanent objects of nature, so that the world shall be to us an open book, and every form significant of its hidden life and final cause.

A new interest surprises us, whilst, under the view now suggested, we contemplate the fearful extent and multitude of objects; since "every object rightly seen, unlocks a new faculty of the soul." That which was unconscious truth, becomes, when interpreted and defined in an object, a part of the domain of knowledge,—a new weapon in the magazine of power.

V
Discipline

In view of the significance of nature, we arrive at once at a new fact, that nature is a discipline. This use of the world includes the preceding uses, as parts of itself.

Space, time, society, labor, climate, food, locomotion, the animals, the mechanical forces, give us sincerest lessons, day by day, whose meaning is unlimited. They educate both the Understanding and the Reason. Every property of matter is a school for the understanding,—its solidity or resistance, its inertia, its extension, its figure, its divisibility. The understanding adds, divides, combines, measures, and finds nutriment and room for its activity in this worthy scene. Meantime, Reason transfers all these lessons into its own world of thought, by perceiving the analogy that marries Matter and Mind.

1. Nature is a discipline of the understanding in intellectual truths. Our dealing with sensible objects is a constant exercise in the necessary lessons of difference, of likeness, of order, of being and seeming, of progressive arrangement; of ascent from particular to general; of combination to one end of manifold forces. Proportioned to the importance of the organ to be formed, is the extreme care with which its tuition is provided,—a care pretermitted in no single case. What tedious training, day after day, year after year, never ending, to form the common sense; what continual reproduction of annoyances, inconveniences, dilemmas; what rejoicing over us of little men; what disputing of prices, what reckonings of interest,—and all to form the Hand of the mind;—to instruct us that "good thoughts are no better than good dreams, unless they be executed!"

The same good office is performed by Property and its filial systems of debt and credit. Debt, grinding debt, whose iron face the widow, the orphan, and the sons of genius fear and hate;—debt, which consumes so much time, which so cripples and disheartens a great spirit with cares that seem so base, is a preceptor whose lessons cannot be foregone, and is needed most by those who suffer from it most. Moreover, property, which has been well compared to snow,—"if it fall level to-day, it will be blown into drifts to-morrow,"—is the surface action of internal machinery, like the index on the face of a clock. Whilst now it is the gymnastics of the understanding, it is hiving, in the foresight of the spirit, experience in profounder laws.

The whole character and fortune of the individual are affected by the least inequalities in the culture of the understanding; for example, in the perception of differences. Therefore is Space, and therefore Time, that man may know that things are not huddled and lumped, but sundered and individual. A bell and a plough have each their use, and neither can do the office of the other. Water is good to drink, coal to burn, wool to wear; but wool cannot be drunk, nor water spun, nor coal eaten. The wise man shows his wisdom in separation, in gradation, and his scale of creatures and of merits is as wide as nature. The foolish have no range in their scale, but suppose every man is as every other man. What is not good they call the worst, and what is not hateful, they call the best.

In like manner, what good heed Nature forms in us! She pardons no mistakes. Her yea is yea, and her nay, nay.

The first steps in Agriculture, Astronomy, Zoölogy (those first steps which the farmer, the hunter, and the sailor take), teach that Nature's dice are always loaded; that in her heaps and rubbish are concealed sure and useful results.

How calmly and genially the mind apprehends one after another the laws of physics! What noble emotions dilate the mortal as he enters into the counsels of the creation, and feels by knowledge the privilege to Be! His insight refines him. The beauty of nature shines in his own breast. Man is greater that he can see this, and the universe less, because Time and Space relations vanish as laws are known.

Here again we are impressed and even daunted by the immense Universe to be explored. "What we know is a point to what we do not know." Open any recent journal of science, and weigh the problems suggested concerning Light, Heat, Electricity, Magnetism, Physiology, Geology, and judge whether the interest of natural science is likely to be soon exhausted.

Passing by many particulars of the discipline of nature, we must not omit to specify two.

The exercise of the Will, or the lesson of power, is taught in every event. From the child's successive possession of his several senses up to the hour when he saith, "Thy will be done!" he is learning the secret that he can reduce under his will not only particular events but great classes, nay, the whole series of events, and so conform all facts to his character. Nature is thoroughly mediate. It is made to serve. It receives the dominion of man as meekly as the ass on which the Saviour rode. It offers all its kingdoms to man as the raw material which he may mould into what is useful. Man is never weary of working it up. He forges the subtile and delicate air into wise and melodious words, and gives them wing as angels of persuasion and command. One after another his victorious thought comes up with and reduces all things, until the world becomes at last only a realized will,—the double of the man.

2. Sensible objects conform to the premonitions of Reason and reflect the conscience. All things are moral; and in their boundless changes have an unceasing reference to spiritual nature. Therefore is nature glorious with form, color, and motion; that every globe in the remotest heaven, every chemical change from the rudest crystal up to the laws of life, every change of vegetation from the first principle of growth in the eye of a leaf, to the tropical forest and antediluvian coal-mine, every animal function from the sponge up to Hercules, shall hint or thunder to man the laws of right and wrong, and echo the Ten Commandments. Therefore is Nature ever the ally of Religion: lends all her pomp and riches to the religious sentiment. Prophet and priest, David, Isaiah, Jesus, have drawn deeply from this source. This ethical character so penetrates the bone and marrow of nature, as to seem the end for which it was made. Whatever private purpose is answered by any member or part, this is its public and universal function, and is never omitted. Nothing in nature is exhausted in its first use. When a thing has served an end to the uttermost, it is wholly new for an ulterior service. In God, every end is converted into a new means. Thus the use of commodity, regarded by itself, is mean and squalid. But it is to the mind an education in the doctrine of Use, namely, that a thing is good only so far as it serves; that a conspiring of parts and efforts to the production of an end is essential to any being. The first and gross manifestation of this truth is our inevitable and hated training in values and wants, in corn and meat.

It has already been illustrated, that every natural process is a version of a moral sentence. The moral law lies at the centre of nature and radiates to the circumference. It is the pith and marrow of every substance, every relation, and every process. All things with which we deal, preach to us. What is a farm but a mute gospel? The chaff and the wheat, weeds and plants, blight, rain, insects, sun,—it is a sacred emblem from the first furrow of spring to the last stack which the snow of winter overtakes in the fields. But the sailor, the shepherd, the miner, the merchant, in their several resorts, have each an experience precisely parallel, and leading to the same conclusion: because all organizations are radically alike. Nor can it be doubted that this moral sentiment which thus scents the air, grows in the grain, and impregnates the waters of the world, is caught by man and sinks into his soul. The moral influence of nature upon every individual is that amount of truth which it illustrates to him. Who can estimate this? Who can guess how much firmness the sea-beaten rock has taught the fisherman? how much tranquillity has been reflected to man from the azure sky, over whose unspotted deeps the winds forevermore drive flocks of stormy clouds, and leave no wrinkle or stain? how much industry and providence and affection we have caught from the pantomime of brutes? What a searching preacher of self-command is the varying phenomenon of Health!

Herein is especially apprehended the unity of Nature,—the unity in variety,—which meets us everywhere. All the endless variety of things make an identical impression. Xenophanes complained in his old age, that, look where he would, all things hastened back to Unity. He was weary of seeing the same entity in the tedious variety of forms. The fable of Proteus has a cordial truth. A leaf, a drop, a crystal, a moment of time, is related to the whole, and partakes of the perfection of the whole. Each particle is a microcosm, and faithfully renders the likeness of the world.

Not only resemblances exist in things whose analogy is obvious, as when we detect the type of the human hand in the flipper of the fossil saurus, but also in objects wherein there is great superficial unlikeness. Thus architecture is called "frozen music," by De Staël and Goethe. Vitruvius thought an architect should be a musician. "A Gothic church," said Coleridge, "is a petrified religion." Michael Angelo maintained, that, to an architect, a knowledge of anatomy is essential. In Haydn's oratorios, the notes present to the imagination not only motions, as of the snake, the stag, and the elephant, but colors also; as the green grass. The law of harmonic sounds reappears in the harmonic colors. The granite is differenced in its laws only by the more or less of heat from the river that wears it away. The river, as it flows, resembles the air that flows over it; the air resembles the light which traverses it with more subtle currents; the light resembles the heat which rides with it through Space. Each creature is only a modification of the other; the likeness in them is more than the difference, and their radical law is one and the same. A rule of one art, or a law of one organization, holds true throughout nature. So intimate is this Unity, that, it is easily seen, it lies under the undermost garment of Nature, and betrays its source in Universal Spirit. For it pervades Thought also. Every universal truth which we express in words, implies or supposes every other truth. *Omne verum vero consonat.* It is like a great circle on a sphere, comprising all possible circles; which, however, may be drawn and comprise it in like manner. Every such truth is the absolute Ens seen from one side. But it has innumerable sides.

The central Unity is still more conspicuous in actions. Words are finite organs of the infinite mind. They cannot cover the dimensions of what is in truth. They break, chop, and impoverish it. An action is the perfection and publication of thought. A right action seems to fill the eye, and to be related to all nature. "The wise man, in doing one thing, does all; or, in the one thing he does rightly, he sees the likeness of all which is done rightly."

Words and actions are not the attributes of brute nature. They introduce us to the human form, of which all other organizations appear to be degradations. When this appears among so many that surround it, the spirit prefers it to all others. It says, "From such as this have I drawn joy and knowledge; in such as this have I found and beheld myself; I will speak to it; it can speak again; it can yield me thought already formed and alive." In fact, the eye,—the mind,—is always accompanied by these forms, male and female; and these are incomparably the richest informations of the power and order that lie at the heart of things. Unfortunately every one of them bears the marks as of some injury; is marred and superficially defective. Nevertheless, far different from the deaf and dumb nature around them, these all rest like fountain-pipes on the unfathomed sea of thought and virtue whereto they alone, of all organizations, are the entrances.

It were a pleasant inquiry to follow into detail their ministry to our education, but where would it stop? We are associated in adolescent and adult life with some friends, who, like skies and waters, are coextensive with our idea; who, answering each to a certain affection of the soul, satisfy our desire on that side; whom we lack power to put at such focal distance from us, that we can mend or even analyze them. We cannot choose but love them. When much intercourse with a friend has supplied us with a standard of excellence, and has increased our respect for the resources of God who thus sends a real person to outgo our ideal; when he has, moreover, become an object of thought, and, whilst his character retains all its unconscious effect, is converted in the mind into solid and sweet wisdom,—it is a sign to us that his office is closing, and he is commonly withdrawn from our sight in a short time.

VI

Idealism

Thus is the unspeakable but intelligible and practicable meaning of the world conveyed to man, the immortal pupil, in every object of sense. To this one end of Discipline, all parts of nature conspire.

A noble doubt perpetually suggests itself,—whether this end be not the Final Cause of the Universe; and whether nature outwardly exists. It is a sufficient account of that Appearance we call the World, that God will teach a human mind, and so makes it the receiver of a certain number of congruent sensations, which we call sun and moon, man and woman, house and trade. In my utter impotence to test the authenticity of the report of my senses, to know whether the impressions they make on me correspond with outlying objects, what difference does it make, whether Orion is up there in heaven, or some god paints the image in the firmament of the soul? The relations of parts and the end of the whole remaining the same, what is the difference, whether land and sea interact, and worlds revolve and intermingle without number or end,—deep yawning under deep, and galaxy balancing galaxy, throughout absolute space,—or whether, without relations of time and space, the same appearances are inscribed in the constant faith of man? Whether nature enjoy a substantial existence without, or is only in the apocalypse of the mind, it is alike useful and alike venerable to me. Be it what it may, it is ideal to me so long as I cannot try the accuracy of my senses.

The frivolous make themselves merry with the Ideal theory, as if its consequences were burlesque; as if it affected the stability of nature. It surely does not. God never jests with us, and will not compromise the end of nature by permitting any inconsequence in its procession. Any distrust of the permanence of laws would paralyze the faculties of man. Their permanence is sacredly respected, and his faith therein is perfect. The wheels and springs of man are all set to the hypothesis of the permanence of nature. We are not built like a ship to be tossed, but like a house to stand. It is a natural consequence of this structure, that so long as the active powers predominate over the reflective, we resist with indignation any hint that nature is more short-lived or mutable than spirit. The broker, the wheelwright, the carpenter, the tollman, are much displeased at the intimation.

But whilst we acquiesce entirely in the permanence of natural laws, the question of the absolute existence of nature still remains open. It is the uniform effect of culture on the human mind, not to shake our faith in the stability of particular phenomena, as of heat, water, azote; but to lead us to regard nature as phenomenon, not a substance; to attribute necessary existence to spirit; to esteem nature as an accident and an effect.

To the senses and the unrenewed understanding, belongs a sort of instinctive belief in the absolute existence of nature. In their view man and nature are indissolubly joined. Things are ultimates, and they never look beyond their sphere. The presence of Reason mars this faith. The first effort of thought tends to relax this despotism of the senses which binds us to nature as if we were a part of it, and shows us nature aloof, and, as it were, afloat. Until this higher agency intervened, the animal eye sees, with wonderful accuracy, sharp outlines and colored surfaces. When the eye of Reason opens, to outline and surface are at once added grace and expression. These proceed from imagination and affection, and abate somewhat of the angular distinctness of objects. If the Reason be stimulated to more earnest vision, outlines and surfaces become transparent, and are no longer seen; causes and spirits are seen through them. The best moments of life are these delicious awakenings of the higher powers, and the reverential withdrawing of nature before its God.

Let us proceed to indicate the effects of culture.

1. Our first institution in the Ideal philosophy is a hint from Nature herself.

Nature is made to conspire with spirit to emancipate us. Certain mechanical changes, a small alteration in our local position, apprizes us of a dualism. We are strangely affected by seeing the shore from a moving ship, from a balloon, or through the tints of an unusual sky. The least change in our point of view gives the whole world a pictorial air. A man who seldom rides, needs only to get into a coach and traverse his own town, to turn the street into a puppet-show. The men, the women,—talking, running, bartering, fighting,—the earnest mechanic, the lounger, the beggar, the boys, the dogs, are unrealized at once, or, at least, wholly detached from all relation to the observer, and seen as apparent, not substantial beings. What new thoughts are suggested by seeing a face of country quite familiar, in the rapid movement of the railroad car! Nay, the most wonted objects, (make a very slight change in the point of vision,) please us most. In a camera obscura, the butcher's cart, and the figure of one of our own family amuse us. So a portrait of a well-known face gratifies us. Turn the eyes upside down, by looking at the landscape through your legs, and how agreeable is the picture, though you have seen it any time these twenty years!

In these cases, by mechanical means, is suggested the difference between the observer and the spectacle—between man and nature. Hence arises a pleasure mixed with awe; I may say, a low degree of the sublime is felt, from the fact, probably, that man is hereby apprized that whilst the world is a spectacle, something in himself is stable.

2. In a higher manner, the poet communicates the same pleasure. By a few strokes he delineates, as on air, the sun, the mountain, the camp, the city, the hero, the maiden, not different from what we know them, but only lifted from the ground and afloat before the eye. He unfixes the land and the sea, makes them revolve around the axis of his primary thought, and disposes them anew. Possessed himself by a heroic passion, he uses matter as symbols of it. The sensual man conforms thoughts to things; the poet conforms things to his thoughts. The one esteems nature as rooted and fast; the other, as fluid, and impresses his being thereon. To him, the refractory world is ductile and flexible; he invests dust and stones with humanity, and makes them the words of the Reason. The Imagination may be defined to be the use which the Reason makes of the material world. Shakespeare possesses the power of subordinating nature for the purposes of expression, beyond all poets. His imperial muse tosses the creation like a bauble from hand to hand, and uses it to embody any caprice of thought that is uppermost in his mind. The remotest spaces of nature are visited, and the farthest sundered things are brought together, by a subtile spiritual connection. We are made aware that magnitude of material things is relative, and all objects shrink and expand to serve the passion of the poet. Thus in his sonnets, the lays of birds, the scents and dyes of flowers he finds to be the *shadow* of his beloved; time, which keeps her from him, is his *chest;* the suspicion she has awakened, is her *ornament;*

> *The ornament of beauty is Suspect,*
> *A crow which flies in heaven's sweetest air.*

His passion is not the fruit of chance; it swells, as he speaks, to a city, or a state.

> *No, it was builded far from accident;*
> *It suffers not in smiling pomp, nor falls*
> *Under the brow of thralling discontent;*
> *It fears not policy, that heretic,*
> *That works on leases of short numbered hours,*
> *But all alone stands hugely politic.*

In the strength of his constancy, the Pyramids seem to him recent and transitory. The freshness of youth and love dazzles him with its resemblance to morning;

> *Take those lips away*
> *Which so sweetly were forsworn;*
> *And those eyes,—the break of day,*
> *Lights that do mislead the morn.*

The wild beauty of this hyperbole, I may say in passing, it would not be easy to match in literature.

This transfiguration which all material objects undergo through the passion of the poet,—this power which he exerts to dwarf the great, to magnify the small,—might be illustrated by a thousand examples from his Plays. I have before me the Tempest, and will cite only these few lines.

> *ARIEL. The strong based promontory*
> *Have I made shake, and by the spurs plucked up*
> *The pine and cedar.*

Prospero calls for music to soothe the frantic Alonzo, and his companions;

> *A solemn air, and the best comforter*
> *To an unsettled fancy, cure thy brains*
> *Now useless, boiled within thy skull.*

Again;

> *The charm dissolves apace,*
> *And, as the morning steals upon the night,*
> *Melting the darkness, so their rising senses*
> *Begin to chase the ignorant fumes that mantle*
> *Their clearer reason.*
>
> *Their understanding*
> *Begins to swell: and the approaching tide*
> *Will shortly fill the reasonable shores*
> *That now lie foul and muddy.*

The perception of real affinities between events (that is to say, of *ideal* affinities, for those only are real), enables the poet thus to make free with the most imposing forms and phenomena of the world, and to assert the predominance of the soul.

3. Whilst thus the poet animates nature with his own thoughts, he differs from the philosopher only herein, that the one proposes Beauty as his main end; the other Truth. But the philosopher, not less than the poet, postpones the apparent order and relations of things to the empire of thought. "The problem of philosophy," according to Plato, "is, for all that exists conditionally, to find a ground unconditioned and absolute." It proceeds on the faith that a law determines all phenomena, which being known, the phenomena can be predicted. That law, when in the mind, is an idea. Its beauty is infinite. The true philosopher and the true poet are one, and a beauty, which is truth, and a truth, which is beauty, is the aim of both. Is not the charm of one of Plato's or Aristotle's definitions strictly like that of the Antigone of Sophocles? It is, in both cases, that a spiritual life has been imparted to nature; that the solid seeming block of matter has been pervaded and dissolved by a thought; that this feeble human being has penetrated the vast masses of nature with an informing soul, and recognized itself in their harmony, that is, seized their law. In physics, when this is attained, the memory disburthens itself of its cumbrous catalogues of particulars, and carries centuries of observation in a single formula.

Thus even in physics, the material is degraded before the spiritual. The astronomer, the geometer, rely on their irrefragable analysis, and disdain the results of observation. The sublime remark of Euler on his law of arches,

"This will be found contrary to all experience, yet is true;" had already transferred nature into the mind, and left matter like an outcast corpse.

4. Intellectual science has been observed to beget invariably a doubt of the existence of matter. Turgot said, "He that has never doubted the existence of matter, may be assured he has no aptitude for metaphysical inquiries." It fastens the attention upon immortal necessary uncreated natures, that is, upon Ideas; and in their presence we feel that the outward circumstance is a dream and a shade. Whilst we wait in this Olympus of gods, we think of nature as an appendix to the soul. We ascend into their region, and know that these are the thoughts of the Supreme Being. "These are they who were set up from everlasting, from the beginning, or ever the earth was. When he prepared the heavens, they were there; when he established the clouds above, when he strengthened the fountains of the deep. Then they were by him, as one brought up with him. Of them took he counsel."

Their influence is proportionate. As objects of science they are accessible to few men. Yet all men are capable of being raised by piety or by passion, into their region. And no man touches these divine natures, without becoming, in some degree, himself divine. Like a new soul, they renew the body. We become physically nimble and lightsome; we tread on air; life is no longer irksome, and we think it will never be so. No man fears age or misfortune or death in their serene company, for he is transported out of the district of change. Whilst we behold unveiled the nature of Justice and Truth, we learn the difference between the absolute and the conditional or relative. We apprehend the absolute. As it were, for the first time, *we exist.* We become immortal, for we learn that time and space are relations of matter; that with a perception of truth or a virtuous will they have no affinity.

5. Finally, religion and ethics, which may be fitly called the practice of ideas, or the introduction of ideas into life, have an analogous effect with all lower culture, in degrading nature and suggesting its dependence on spirit. Ethics and religion differ herein; that the one is the system of human duties commencing from man; the other, from God. Religion includes the personality of God; Ethics does not. They are one to our present design. They both put nature under foot. The first and last lesson of religion is, "The things that are seen, are temporal; the things that are unseen, are eternal." It puts an affront upon nature. It does that for the unschooled, which philosophy does for Berkeley and Viasa. The uniform language that may be heard in the churches of the most ignorant sects, is,—"Contemn the

unsubstantial shows of the world; they are vanities, dreams, shadows, unrealities; seek the realities of religion." The devotee flouts nature. Some theosophists have arrived at a certain hostility and indignation towards matter, as the Manichean and Plotinus. They distrusted in themselves any looking back to these flesh-pots of Egypt. Plotinus was ashamed of his body. In short, they might all say of matter, what Michael Angelo said of external beauty, "It is the frail and weary weed, in which God dresses the soul which he has called into time."

It appears that motion, poetry, physical and intellectual science, and religion, all tend to affect our convictions of the reality of the external world. But I own there is something ungrateful in expanding too curiously the particulars of the general proposition, that all culture tends to imbue us with idealism. I have no hostility to nature, but a child's love to it. I expand and live in the warm day like corn and melons. Let us speak her fair. I do not wish to fling stones at my beautiful mother, nor soil my gentle nest. I only wish to indicate the true position of nature in regard to man, wherein to establish man all right education tends; as the ground which to attain is the object of human life, that is, of man's connection with nature. Culture inverts the vulgar views of nature, and brings the mind to call that apparent which it uses to call real, and that real which it uses to call visionary. Children, it is true, believe in the external world. The belief that it appears only, is an afterthought, but with culture this faith will as surely arise on the mind as did the first.

The advantage of the ideal theory over the popular faith is this, that it presents the world in precisely that view which is most desirable to the mind. It is, in fact, the view which Reason, both speculative and practical, that is, philosophy and virtue, take. For seen in the light of thought, the world always is phenomenal; and virtue subordinates it to the mind. Idealism sees the world in God. It beholds the whole circle of persons and things, of actions and events, of country and religion, not as painfully accumulated, atom after atom, act after act, in an aged creeping Past, but as one vast picture which God paints on the instant eternity for the contemplation of the soul. Therefore the soul holds itself off from a too trivial and microscopic study of the universal tablet. It respects the end too much to immerse itself in the means. It sees something more important in Christianity than the scandals of ecclesiastical history or the niceties of criticism; and, very incurious concerning persons or miracles, and not at all disturbed by chasms of historical evidence, it accepts from God the phenomenon, as it finds it, as the pure and awful form of religion in the world. It is not hot and passionate at the appearance of what it calls its own good or bad fortune, at the union or opposition of other persons. No man is its enemy. It accepts whatsoever befalls, as part of its lesson. It is a watcher more than a doer, and it is a doer, only that it may the better watch.

VII

Spirit

It is essential to a true theory of nature and of man, that it should contain somewhat progressive. Uses that are exhausted or that may be, and facts that end in the statement, cannot be all that is true of this brave lodging wherein man is harbored, and wherein all his faculties find appropriate and endless exercise. And all the uses of nature admit of being summed in one, which yields the activity of man an infinite scope. Through all its kingdoms, to the suburbs and outskirts of things, it is faithful to the cause whence it had its origin. It always speaks of Spirit. It suggests the absolute. It is a perpetual effect. It is a great shadow pointing always to the sun behind us.

The aspect of Nature is devout. Like the figure of Jesus, she stands with bended head, and hands folded upon the breast. The happiest man is he who learns from nature the lesson of worship.

Of that ineffable essence which we call Spirit, he that thinks most, will say least. We can foresee God in the coarse, and, as it were, distant phenomena of matter; but when we try to define and describe himself, both language and thought desert us, and we are as helpless as fools and savages. That essence refuses to be recorded in propositions, but when man has worshipped him intellectually, the noblest ministry of nature is to stand as the apparition of God. It is the organ through which the universal spirit speaks to the individual, and strives to lead back the individual to it.

When we consider Spirit, we see that the views already presented do not include the whole circumference of man. We must add some related thoughts.

Three problems are put by nature to the mind: What is matter? Whence is it? and Whereto? The first of these questions only, the ideal theory answers. Idealism saith: matter is a phenomenon, not a substance. Idealism acquaints us with the total disparity between the evidence of our own being and the evidence of the world's being. The one is perfect; the other, incapable of any assurance; the mind is a part of the nature of things; the world is a divine dream, from which we may presently awake to the glories and certainties of day. Idealism is a hypothesis to account for nature by other principles than those of carpentry and chemistry. Yet, if it only deny the existence of matter, it does not satisfy the demands of the spirit. It leaves God out of me. It leaves me in the splendid labyrinth of my perceptions, to wander without end. Then the heart resists it, because it balks the affections in denying substantive being to men and women. Nature is so pervaded with human life that there is something of humanity in all and in every particular. But this theory makes nature foreign to me, and does not account for that consanguinity which we acknowledge to it.

Let it stand then, in the present state of our knowledge, merely as a useful introductory hypothesis, serving to apprize us of the eternal distinction between the soul and the world.

But when, following the invisible steps of thought, we come to inquire, Whence is matter? and Whereto? many truths arise to us out of the recesses of consciousness. We learn that the highest is present to the soul of man; that the dread universal essence, which is not wisdom, or love, or beauty, or power, but all in one, and each entirely, is that for which all things exist, and that by which they are; that spirit creates; that behind nature, throughout nature, spirit is present; one and not compound it does not act upon us from without, that is, in space and time, but spiritually, or through ourselves: therefore, that spirit, that is, the Supreme Being, does not build up nature around us, but puts it forth through us, as the life of the tree puts forth new branches and leaves through the pores of the old. As a plant upon the earth, so a man rests upon the bosom of God; he is nourished by unfailing fountains, and draws at his need inexhaustible power. Who can set bounds to the possibilities of man? Once inhale the upper air, being admitted to behold the absolute natures of justice and truth, and we learn that man has access to the entire mind of the Creator, is himself the creator in the finite. This view, which admonishes me where the sources of wisdom and power lie, and points to virtue as to

> "*The golden key*
> *Which opes the palace of eternity,*"

carries upon its face the highest certificate of truth, because it animates me to create my own world through the purification of my soul.

The world proceeds from the same spirit as the body of man. It is a remoter and inferior incarnation of God, a projection of God in the unconscious. But it differs from the body in one important respect. It is not, like that, now subjected to the human will. Its serene order is inviolable by us. It is, therefore, to us, the present expositor of the divine mind. It is a fixed point whereby we may measure our departure. As we degenerate, the contrast between us and our house is more evident. We are as much strangers in nature as we are aliens from God. We do not understand the notes of birds. The fox and the deer run away from us; the bear and tiger rend us. We do not know the uses of more than a few plants, as corn and the apple, the potato and the vine. Is not the landscape, every glimpse of which hath a grandeur, a face of him? Yet this may show us what discord is between man and nature, for you cannot freely admire a noble landscape if laborers are digging in the field hard by. The poet finds something ridiculous in his delight until he is out of the sight of men.

VIII

Prospects

In inquiries respecting the laws of the world and the frame of things, the highest reason is always the truest. That which seems faintly possible, it is so refined, is often faint and dim because it is deepest seated in the mind among the eternal verities. Empirical science is apt to cloud the sight, and by the very knowledge of functions and processes to bereave the student of the manly contemplation of the whole. The savant becomes unpoetic. But the best read naturalist who lends an entire and devout attention to truth, will see that there remains much to learn of his relation to the world, and that it is not to be learned by any addition or subtraction or other comparison of known quantities, but is arrived at by untaught sallies of the spirit, by a continual self-recovery, and by entire humility. He will perceive that there are far more excellent qualities in the student than preciseness and infallibility; that a guess is often more fruitful than an indisputable affirmation, and that a dream may let us deeper into the secret of nature than a hundred concerted experiments.

For the problems to be solved are precisely those which the physiologist and the naturalist omit to state. It is not so pertinent to man to know all the individuals of the animal kingdom, as it is to know whence and whereto is this tyrannizing unity in his constitution, which evermore separates and classifies things, endeavoring to reduce the most diverse to one form. When I behold a rich landscape, it is less to my purpose to recite correctly the order and superposition of the strata, than to know why all thought of multitude is lost in a tranquil sense of unity. I cannot greatly honor minuteness in details, so long as there is no hint to explain the relation between things and thoughts; no ray upon the *metaphysics* of conchology, of botany, of the arts, to show the relation of the forms of flowers, shells, animals, architecture, to the mind, and build science upon ideas. In a cabinet of natural history, we become sensible of a certain occult recognition and sympathy in regard to the most unwieldly and eccentric forms of beast, fish, and insect. The American who has been confined, in his own country, to the sight of buildings designed after foreign models, is surprised on entering York Minster or St. Peter's at Rome, by the feeling that these structures are imitations also,—faint copies of an invisible archetype. Nor has science sufficient humanity, so long as the naturalist overlooks that wonderful congruity which subsists between man and the world; of which he is lord, not because he is the most subtile inhabitant, but because he is its head and heart, and finds something of himself in every great and small thing, in every mountain stratum, in every new law of color, fact of astronomy, or atmospheric influence which observation or analysis lays open. A perception of this mystery inspires the muse of George Herbert, the beautiful psalmist of the seventeenth century. The following lines are part of his little poem on Man.

> *Man is all symmetry,*
> *Full of proportions, one limb to another,*
> *And all to all the world besides.*
> *Each part may call the farthest, brother;*
> *For head with foot hath private amity,*
> *And both with moons and tides.*
>
> *Nothing hath got so far*
> *But man hath caught and kept it as his prey;*
> *His eyes dismount the highest star:*

He is in little all the sphere.
Herbs gladly cure our flesh, because that they
Find their acquaintance there.

For us, the winds do blow,
The earth doth rest, heaven move, and fountains flow;
Nothing we see, but means our good,
As our delight, or as our treasure;
The whole is either our cupboard of food,
Or cabinet of pleasure.

The stars have us to bed:
Night draws the curtain; which the sun withdraws.
Music and light attend our head.
All things unto our flesh are kind,
In their descent and being; to our mind,
In their ascent and cause.

More servants wait on man
Than he'll take notice of. In every path,
He treads down that which doth befriend him
When sickness makes him pale and wan.
Oh mighty love! Man is one world, and hath
Another to attend him.

The perception of this class of truths makes the attraction which draws men to science, but the end is lost sight of in attention to the means. In view of this half-sight of science, we accept the sentence of Plato, that "poetry comes nearer to vital truth than history." Every surmise and vaticination of the mind is entitled to a certain respect, and we learn to prefer imperfect theories, and sentences which contain glimpses of truth, to digested systems which have no one valuable suggestion. A wise writer will feel that the ends of study and composition are best answered by announcing undiscovered regions of thought, and so communicating, through hope, new activity to the torpid spirit.

I shall therefore conclude this essay with some traditions of man and nature, which a certain poet sang to me; and which, as they have always been in the world, and perhaps reappear to every bard, may be both history and prophecy.

'The foundations of man are not in matter, but in spirit. But the element of spirit is eternity. To it, therefore, the longest series of events, the oldest chronologies are young and recent. In the cycle of the universal man, from whom the known individuals proceed, centuries are points, and all history is but the epoch of one degradation.

'We distrust and deny inwardly our sympathy with nature. We own and disown our relation to it, by turns. We are like Nebuchadnezzar, dethroned, bereft of reason, and eating grass like an ox. But who can set limits to the remedial force of spirit?

'A man is a god in ruins. When men are innocent, life shall be longer, and shall pass into the immortal as gently as we awake from dreams. Now, the world would be insane and rabid, if these disorganizations should last for hundreds of years. It is kept in check by death and infancy. Infancy is the perpetual Messiah, which comes into the arms of fallen men, and pleads with them to return to paradise.

'Man is the dwarf of himself. Once he was permeated and dissolved by spirit. He filled nature with his overflowing currents. Out from him sprang the sun and moon; from man the sun; from woman the moon. The laws of his mind, the periods of his actions externized themselves into day and night, into the year and the seasons. But, having made for himself this huge shell, his waters retired; he no longer fills the veins and veinlets; he is shrunk to a drop. He sees that the structure still fits him, but fits him colossally. Say, rather, once it fitted him, now it corresponds to him from far and on high. He adores timidly his own work. Now is man the follower of the sun, and woman the follower of the moon. Yet sometimes he starts in his slumber, and wonders at himself and his house, and muses strangely at the resemblance betwixt him and it. He perceives that if his law is still paramount, if still he have elemental power, if his word is sterling yet in nature, it is not conscious power, it is not inferior but superior to his will. It is instinct." Thus my Orphic poet sang.

At present, man applies to nature but half his force. He works on the world with his understanding alone. He lives in it and masters it by a penny-wisdom; and he that works most in it is but a half-man, and whilst his arms are strong and his digestion good, his mind is imbruted, and he is a selfish savage. His relation to nature, his power over it, is through the

understanding, as by manure; the economic use of fire, wind, water, and
the mariner's needle; steam, coal, chemical agriculture; the repairs of the
human body by the dentist and the surgeon. This is such a resumption
of power as if a banished king should buy his territories inch by inch, instead of vaulting at once into his throne. Meantime, in the thick darkness,
there are not wanting gleams of a better light,—occasional examples of the
action of man upon nature with his entire force,—with reason as well as
understanding. Such examples are, the traditions of miracles in the earliest antiquity of all nations; the history of Jesus Christ; the achievements
of a principle, as in religious and political revolutions, and in the aboli-
tion of the slave-trade; the miracles of enthusiasm, as those reported of
Swedenborg, Hohenlohe, and the Shakers; many obscure and yet con-
tested facts, now arranged under the name of Animal Magnetism; prayer;
eloquence; self-healing; and the wisdom of children. These are examples of
Reason's momentary grasp of the sceptre; the exertions of a power which
exists not in time or space, but an instantaneous in-streaming causing
power. The difference between the actual and the ideal force of man is happily figured by the schoolmen, in saying, that the knowledge of man is
an evening knowledge, *vespertina cognitio,* but that of God is a morning
knowledge, *matutina cognitio.*

The problem of restoring to the world original and eternal beauty is
solved by the redemption of the soul. The ruin or the blank that we see
when we look at nature, is in our own eye. The axis of vision is not coinci-
dent with the axis of things, and so they appear not transparent but opaque.
The reason why the world lacks unity, and lies broken and in heaps, is
because man is disunited with himself. He cannot be a naturalist until he
satisfies all the demands of the spirit. Love is as much its demand as perception. Indeed, neither can be perfect without the other. In the uttermost
meaning of the words, thought is devout, and devotion is thought. Deep
calls unto deep. But in actual life, the marriage is not celebrated. There are
innocent men who worship God after the tradition of their fathers, but
their sense of duty has not yet extended to the use of all their faculties. And
there are patient naturalists, but they freeze their subject under the wintry
light of the understanding. Is not prayer also a study of truth,—a sally of
the soul into the unfound infinite? No man ever prayed heartily without
learning something. But when a faithful thinker, resolute to detach every
object from personal relations, and see it in the light of thought, shall, at

the same time, kindle science with the fire of the holiest affections, then will God go forth anew into the creation.

It will not need, when the mind is prepared for study, to search for objects. The invariable mark of wisdom is to see the miraculous in the common. What is a day? What is a year? What is summer? What is woman? What is a child? What is sleep? To our blindness, these things seem unaffecting. We make fables to hide the baldness of the fact and conform it, as we say, to the higher law of the mind. But when the fact is seen under the light of an idea, the gaudy fable fades and shrivels. We behold the real higher law. To the wise, therefore, a fact is true poetry, and the most beautiful of fables. These wonders are brought to our own door. You also are a man. Man and woman and their social life, poverty, labor, sleep, fear, fortune, are known to you. Learn that none of these things is superficial, but that each phenomenon has its roots in the faculties and affections of the mind. Whilst the abstract question occupies your intellect, nature brings it in the concrete to be solved by your hands. It were a wise inquiry for the closet, to compare, point by point, especially at remarkable crises in life, our daily history with the rise and progress of ideas in the mind.

So shall we come to look at the world with new eyes. It shall answer the endless inquiry of the intellect,—What is truth? and of the affections,—What is good? by yielding itself passive to the educated Will. Then shall come to pass what my poet said: "Nature is not fixed but fluid. Spirit alters, moulds, makes it. The immobility or bruteness of nature is the absence of spirit; to pure spirit it is fluid, it is volatile, it is obedient. Every spirit builds itself a house, and beyond its house a world, and beyond its world a heaven. Know then that the world exists for you. For you is the phenomenon perfect. What we are, that only can we see. All that Adam had, all that Caesar could, you have and can do. Adam called his house, heaven and earth; Caesar called his house, Rome; you perhaps call yours, a cobbler's trade; a hundred acres of ploughed land; or a scholar's garret. Yet line for line and point for point your dominion is as great as theirs, though without fine names. Build therefore your own world. As fast as you conform your life to the pure idea in your mind, that will unfold its great proportions. A correspondent revolution in things will attend the influx of the spirit. So fast will disagreeable appearances, swine, spiders, snakes, pests, mad-houses, prisons, enemies, vanish; they are temporary and shall be no more seen. The sordor and filths of nature, the sun shall dry up and the wind exhale.

As when the summer comes from the south the snow-banks melt and the face of the earth becomes green before it, so shall the advancing spirit create its ornaments along its path, and carry with it the beauty it visits and the song which enchants it; it shall draw beautiful faces, warm hearts, wise discourse, and heroic acts, around its way, until evil is no more seen. The kingdom of man over nature, which cometh not with observation,—a dominion such as now is beyond his dream of God,—he shall enter without more wonder than the blind man feels who is gradually restored to perfect sight.'

1841

And likewise, if Emerson's role was that of the enthusiastic lecturer—mapping out a different path for Americans in the world—then Thoreau was the first writer to start tromping down that path. This is the year when scientists first use the word *dinosaur*. It's also the first year they start using the word *scientist*. It's when James Braid develops a technique for inducing hypnosis, when Thomas Cook opens the world's first travel agency, and when a group of transcendentalists start a commune in Boston and invite the young Thoreau to manage the project's farm. He turns them down, however, opting instead to move in with Emerson's family as a tutor. "What are you doing now?" reads the first entry in Thoreau's journal. Most scholars insist that what we hear in that first line is actually Emerson's prodding of his young protégé. Yet whoever poses the question, it's Thoreau who spends the rest of his life trying to answer it. In nineteen subsequent volumes of his journal, Thoreau tells us that he spent at least four hours every day on some sort of walk. Indeed, many of his best essays are occasioned by a journey—a hike, a canoe trip, sometimes even a horseback ride—"sauntering," as he put it, through the world and through his mind. A walk for Thoreau was akin to writing an essay, he often said, a departure from the familiar in the service of discovery. In a bit of fanciful etymology, Thoreau claims that *sauntering* is derived from the French *Sainte Terre,* which is what crusaders called the Holy Land in the Middle Ages. A walk is a crusade, in other words, demanding that the walker leave his life behind in the "spirit of undying adventure, never to return." To walk—or to essay—is to change one's life forever. "If, about the last of October," Thoreau writes, "you ascend any hill in the outskirts of the town, and look over the forest, you will see, amid the brown of other oaks, which are now withered, and the green of the pines, the bright-red tops or crescent of the scarlet oaks, very equally and thickly distributed on all sides, even to the horizon." Leaf peeping, in other words. Yet New England's pretty foliage is not really the subject of Thoreau's meditation. For even though the essay advocates for wildness, and has inspired a rallying cry for today's environmentalists— "in Wildness is the preservation of the world"—Thoreau is foremost concerned with the world at risk within us. *If,* he says, *you look . . . then,* he says, *you'll see.* It's the contingency of this idea that Thoreau is crusading for—not the comfort of an observation after it's been made, but the force that propels an inquiry before we know where it will lead.

Walking

I wish to speak a word for Nature, for absolute freedom and wildness, as contrasted with a freedom and culture merely civil,—to regard man as an inhabitant, or a part and parcel of Nature, rather than a member of society. I wish to make an extreme statement, if so I may make an emphatic one, for there are enough champions of civilization: the minister and the school-committee and every one of you will take care of that.

I have met with but one or two persons in the course of my life who under-stood the art of Walking, that is, of taking walks,—who had a genius, so to speak, for *sauntering:* which word is beautifully derived "from idle people who roved about the country, in the Middle Ages, and asked charity, under pretense of going *à la Sainte Terre,*" to the Holy Land, till the children ex-claimed, "There goes a *Sainte-Terrer,*" a Saunterer, a Holy-Lander. They who never go to the Holy Land in their walks, as they pretend, are indeed mere idlers and vagabonds; but they who do go there are saunterers in the good sense, such as I mean. Some, however, would derive the word from *sans terre,* without land or a home, which, therefore, in the good sense, will mean, having no particular home, but equally at home everywhere. For this is the secret of successful sauntering. He who sits still in a house all the time may be the greatest vagrant of all; but the saunterer, in the good sense, is no more vagrant than the meandering river, which is all the while sedu-lously seeking the shortest course to the sea. But I prefer the first, which, indeed, is the most probable derivation. For every walk is a sort of crusade, preached by some Peter the Hermit in us, to go forth and reconquer this Holy Land from the hands of the Infidels.

It is true, we are but faint-hearted crusaders, even the walkers, nowadays, who undertake no persevering, never-ending enterprises. Our expeditions are but tours, and come round again at evening to the old hearth-side from which we set out. Half the walk is but retracing our steps. We should go forth on the shortest walk, perchance, in the spirit of undying adventure, never to return,—prepared to send back our embalmed hearts only as relics to our desolate kingdoms. If you are ready to leave father and mother, and brother and sister, and wife and child and friends, and never see them again, if you have paid your debts, and made your will, and settled all your affairs, and are a free man, then you are ready for a walk.

To come down to my own experience, my companion and I, for I sometimes have a companion, take pleasure in fancying ourselves knights of a new, or rather an old, order,—not Equestrians or Chevaliers, not Ritters or riders, but Walkers, a still more ancient and honorable class, I trust. The chivalric and heroic spirit which once belonged to the Rider seems now to reside in, or perchance to have subsided into, the Walker,—not the Knight, but Walker Errant. He is a sort of fourth estate, outside of Church and State and People.

We have felt that we almost alone hereabouts practiced this noble art; though, to tell the truth, at least if their own assertions are to be received, most of my townsmen would fain walk sometimes, as I do, but they cannot. No wealth can buy the requisite leisure, freedom, and independence, which are the capital in this profession. It comes only by the grace of God. It requires a direct dispensation from Heaven to become a walker. You must be born into the family of the Walkers. *Ambulator nascitur, non fit.* Some of my townsmen, it is true, can remember and have described to me some walks which they took ten years ago, in which they were so blessed as to lose themselves for half an hour in the woods; but I know very well that they have confined themselves to the highway ever since, whatever pretensions they may make to belong to this select class. No doubt they were elevated for a moment as by the reminiscence of a previous state of existence, when even they were foresters and outlaws.

> *"When he came to grene wode,*
> *In a mery mornynge,*
> *There he herde the notes small*
> *Of byrdes mery syngynge.*

"It is ferre gone, sayd Robyn,
   That I was last here;
Me lyste a lytell for to shote
   At the donne dere."

I think that I cannot preserve my health and spirits, unless I spend four hours a day at least,—and it is commonly more than that,—sauntering through the woods and over the hills and fields, absolutely free from all worldly engagements. You may safely say, A penny for your thoughts, or a thousand pounds. When sometimes I am reminded that the mechanics and shopkeepers stay in their shops not only all the forenoon, but all the afternoon too, sitting with crossed legs, so many of them,—as if the legs were made to sit upon, and not to stand or walk upon,—I think that they deserve some credit for not having all committed suicide long ago.

I, who cannot stay in my chamber for a single day without acquiring some rust, and when sometimes I have stolen forth for a walk at the eleventh hour of four o'clock in the afternoon, too late to redeem the day, when the shades of night were already beginning to be mingled with the daylight, have felt as if I had committed some sin to be atoned for,—I confess that I am astonished at the power of endurance, to say nothing of the moral insensibility, of my neighbors who confine themselves to shops and offices the whole day for weeks and months, ay, and years almost together. I know not what manner of stuff they are of,—sitting there now at three o'clock in the afternoon, as if it were three o'clock in the morning. Bonaparte may talk of the three-o'clock-in-the-morning courage, but it is nothing to the courage which can sit down cheerfully at this hour in the afternoon over against one's self whom you have known all the morning, to starve out a garrison to whom you are bound by such strong ties of sympathy. I wonder that about this time, or say between four and five o'clock in the afternoon, too late for the morning papers and too early for the evening ones, there is not a general explosion heard up and down the street, scattering a legion of antiquated and house-bred notions and whims to the four winds for an airing,—and so the evil cure itself.

How womankind, who are confined to the house still more than men, stand it I do not know; but I have ground to suspect that most of them do not *stand* it at all. When, early in a summer afternoon, we have been shaking the dust of the village from the skirts of our garments, making haste past those houses with purely Doric or Gothic fronts, which have such an air of repose about them, my companion whispers that probably about these times their occupants are all gone to bed. Then it is that I appreciate the beauty and the glory of architecture, which itself never turns in, but forever stands out and erect, keeping watch over the slumberers.

No doubt temperament, and, above all, age, have a good deal to do with it. As a man grows older, his ability to sit still and follow indoor occupations increases. He grows vespertinal in his habits as the evening of life approaches, till at last he comes forth only just before sundown, and gets all the walk that he requires in half an hour.

But the walking of which I speak has nothing in it akin to taking exercise, as it is called, as the sick take medicine at stated hours,—as the swinging of dumb-bells or chairs; but is itself the enterprise and adventure of the day. If you would get exercise, go in search of the springs of life. Think of a man's swinging dumb-bells for his health, when those springs are bubbling up in far-off pastures unsought by him!

Moreover, you must walk like a camel, which is said to be the only beast which ruminates when walking. When a traveller asked Wordsworth's servant to show him her master's study, she answered, "Here is his library, but his study is out of doors."

Living much out of doors, in the sun and wind, will no doubt produce a certain roughness of character,—will cause a thicker cuticle to grow over some of the finer qualities of our nature, as on the face and hands, or as severe manual labor robs the hands of some of their delicacy of touch. So staying in the house, on the other hand, may produce a softness and smoothness, not to say thinness of skin, accompanied by an increased sensibility to certain impressions. Perhaps we should be more susceptible to some influences important to our intellectual and moral growth, if the sun had shone and the wind blown on us a little less; and no doubt it is a nice matter to proportion rightly the thick and thin skin. But methinks that is a scurf that will fall off fast enough,—that the natural remedy is to be found in the proportion which the night bears to the day, the winter to the summer, thought to experience. There will be so much the more air and sunshine in our thoughts. The callous palms of the laborer are conversant with finer tissues of self-respect and heroism, whose touch thrills the heart, than the languid fingers of idleness. That is mere sentimentality that lies abed by day and thinks itself white, far from the tan and callus of experience.

When we walk, we naturally go to the fields and woods: what would become of us, if we walked only in a garden or a mall? Even some sects of philosophers have felt the necessity of importing the woods to themselves, since they did not go to the woods. "They planted groves and walks of Platanes," where they took *subdiales ambulationes* in porticos open to the air. Of course it is of no use to direct our steps to the woods, if they do not carry us thither. I am alarmed when it happens that I have walked a mile into the woods bodily, without getting there in spirit. In my afternoon walk I would fain forget all my morning occupations and my obligations to society. But it sometimes happens that I cannot easily shake off the village. The thought of some work will run in my head, and I am not where my body is,—I am out of my senses. In my walks I would fain return to my senses. What business have I in the woods, if I am thinking of something out of the woods? I suspect myself, and cannot help a shudder, when I find myself so implicated even in what are called good works,—for this may sometimes happen.

My vicinity affords many good walks; and though for so many years I have walked almost every day, and sometimes for several days together, I have not yet exhausted them. An absolutely new prospect is a great happiness, and I can still get this any afternoon. Two or three hours' walking will carry me to as strange a country as I expect ever to see. A single farmhouse which I had not seen before is sometimes as good as the dominions of the King of Dahomey. There is in fact a sort of harmony discoverable between the capabilities of the landscape within a circle of ten miles' radius, or the limits of an afternoon walk, and the threescore years and ten of human life. It will never become quite familiar to you.

Nowadays almost all man's improvements, so called, as the building of houses, and the cutting down of the forest and of all large trees, simply deform the landscape, and make it more and more tame and cheap. A people who would begin by burning the fences and let the forest stand! I saw the fences half consumed, their ends lost in the middle of the prairie, and some worldly miser with a surveyor looking after his bounds, while heaven had taken place around him, and he did not see the angels going to and fro, but was looking for an old post-hole in the midst of paradise. I looked again, and saw him standing in the middle of a boggy, stygian fen, surrounded by devils, and he had found his bounds without a doubt, three little stones, where a stake had been driven, and looking nearer, I saw that the Prince of Darkness was his surveyor.

I can easily walk ten, fifteen, twenty, any number of miles, commencing at my own door, without going by any house, without crossing a road except where the fox and the mink do: first along by the river, and then the brook, and then the meadow and the wood-side. There are square miles in my vicinity which have no inhabitants. From many a hill I can see civilization and the abodes of man afar. The farmers and their works are scarcely more obvious than woodchucks and their burrows. Man and his affairs, church and state and school, trade and commerce, and manufactures and agriculture, even politics, the most alarming of them all,—I am pleased to see how little space they occupy in the landscape. Politics is but a narrow field, and that still narrower highway yonder leads to it. I sometimes direct the traveller thither. If you would go to the political world, follow the great road,—follow that market-man, keep his dust in your eyes, and it will lead you straight to it; for it, too, has its place merely, and does not occupy all space. I pass from it as from a bean-field into the forest, and it is forgotten. In one half-hour I can walk off to some portion of the earth's surface where a man does not stand from one year's end to another, and there, consequently, politics are not, for they are but as the cigar-smoke of a man.

The village is the place to which the roads tend, a sort of expansion of the highway, as a lake of a river. It is the body of which roads are the arms and legs,—a trivial or quadrivial place, the thoroughfare and ordinary of travellers. The word is from the Latin *villa,* which together with *via,* a way, or more anciently *ved* and *vella,* Varro derives from *veho,* to carry, because the villa is the place to and from which things are carried. They who got their living by teaming were said *vellaturam facere.* Hence, too, apparently the Latin word *vilis* and our vile; also *villain.* This suggests what kind of degeneracy villagers are liable to. They are wayworn by the travel that goes by and over them, without travelling themselves.

Some do not walk at all; others walk in the highways; a few walk across lots. Roads are made for horses and men of business. I do not travel in them much, comparatively, because I am not in a hurry to get to any tavern or grocery or livery-stable or depot to which they lead. I am a good horse to travel, but not from choice a roadster. The landscape-painter uses the figures of men to mark a road. He would not make that use of my figure. I walk out into a Nature such as the old prophets and poets, Menu, Moses, Homer, Chaucer, walked in. You may name it America, but it is not America: neither Americus Vespucius, nor Columbus, nor the rest were the discoverers of it. There is a truer account of it in mythology than in any history of America, so called, that I have seen.

However, there are a few old roads that may be trodden with profit, as if they led somewhere now that they are nearly discontinued. There is the Old Marlborough Road, which does not go to Marlborough now, methinks, unless that is Marlborough where it carries me. I am the bolder to speak of it here, because I presume that there are one or two such roads in every town.

THE OLD MARLBOROUGH ROAD.

Where they once dug for money,
But never found any;
Where sometimes Martial Miles
　Singly files,
　And Elijah Wood,
　I fear for no good:
No other man,
Save Elisha Dugan,—
O man of wild habits,
Partridges and rabbits,
Who hast no cares
Only to set snares,
Who liv'st all alone,
Close to the bone,
And where life is sweetest
Constantly eatest.
When the spring stirs my blood
　With the instinct to travel,
　I can get enough gravel
On the Old Marlborough Road.
　Nobody repairs it,
　For nobody wears it;
　It is a living way,

As the Christians say.
Not many there be
    Who enter therein,
Only the guests of the
    Irishman Quin.
What is it, what is it,
    But a direction out there,
And the bare possibility
    Of going somewhere?
    Great guide-boards of stone,
    But travellers none;
    Cenotaphs of the towns
    Named on their crowns.
    It is worth going to see
    Where you might *be.*
    What king
    Did the thing,
    I am still wondering;
    Set up how or when,
    By what selectmen,
    Gourgas or Lee,
    Clark or Darby?
    They're a great endeavor
    To be something forever;
    Blank tablets of stone,
    Where a traveller might groan,
    And in one sentence
    Grave all that is known;
    Which another might read,
    In his extreme need.
    I know one or two
    Lines that would do,
    Literature that might stand
    All over the land,
    Which a man could remember
    Till next December,
    And read again in the spring,

> *After the thawing.*
> *If with fancy unfurled*
> *You leave your abode,*
> *You may go round the world*
> *By the Old Marlborough Road.*

At present, in this vicinity, the best part of the land is not private property; the landscape is not owned, and the walker enjoys comparative freedom. But possibly the day will come when it will be partitioned off into so-called pleasure-grounds, in which a few will take a narrow and exclusive pleasure only,—when fences shall be multiplied, and man-traps and other engines invented to confine men to the *public* road, and walking over the surface of God's earth shall be construed to mean trespassing on some gentleman's grounds. To enjoy a thing exclusively is commonly to exclude yourself from the true enjoyment of it. Let us improve our opportunities, then, before the evil days come.

What is it that makes it so hard sometimes to determine whither we will walk? I believe that there is a subtle magnetism in Nature, which, if we unconsciously yield to it, will direct us aright. It is not indifferent to us which way we walk. There is a right way; but we are very liable from heedlessness and stupidity to take the wrong one. We would fain take that walk, never yet taken by us through this actual world, which is perfectly symbolical of the path which we love to travel in the interior and ideal world; and sometimes, no doubt, we find it difficult to choose our direction, because it does not yet exist distinctly in our idea.

When I go out of the house for a walk, uncertain as yet whither I will bend my steps, and submit myself to my instinct to decide for me, I find, strange and whimsical as it may seem, that I finally and inevitably settle southwest, toward some particular wood or meadow or deserted pasture or hill in that direction. My needle is slow to settle,—varies a few degrees, and does not always point due southwest, it is true, and it has good authority for this variation, but it always settles between west and south-southwest. The future lies that way to me, and the earth seems more unexhausted and richer on that side. The outline which would bound my walks would be, not a circle, but a parabola, or rather like one of those cometary orbits which have been thought to be non-returning curves, in this case opening westward, in which my house occupies the place of the sun. I turn round and round irresolute sometimes for a quarter of an hour, until I decide, for a thousandth time, that I will walk into the southwest or west. Eastward I go only by force; but westward I go free. Thither no business leads me. It is hard for me to believe that I shall find fair landscapes or sufficient wildness and freedom behind the eastern horizon. I am not excited by the prospect of a walk thither; but I believe that the forest which I see in the western horizon stretches uninterruptedly toward the setting sun, and there are no towns nor cities in it of enough consequence to disturb me. Let me live where I will, on this side is the city, on that the wilderness, and ever I am leaving the city more and more, and withdrawing into the wilderness. I should not lay so much stress on this fact, if I did not believe that something like this is the prevailing tendency of my countrymen. I must walk toward Oregon, and not toward Europe. And that way the nation is moving, and I may say that mankind progress from east to west. Within a few years we have witnessed the phenomenon of a southeastward migration, in the settlement of Australia; but this affects us as a retrograde movement, and, judging from the moral and physical character of the first generation of Australians, has not yet proved a successful experiment. The eastern Tartars think that there is nothing west beyond Thibet. "The world ends there," say they, "beyond there is nothing but a shoreless sea." It is unmitigated East where they live.

We go eastward to realize history and study the works of art and literature, retracing the steps of the race; we go westward as into the future, with a spirit of enterprise and adventure. The Atlantic is a Lethean stream, in our passage over which we have had an opportunity to forget the Old World and its institutions. If we do not succeed this time, there is perhaps one more chance for the race left before it arrives on the banks of the Styx; and that is in the Lethe of the Pacific, which is three times as wide.

I know not how significant it is, or how far it is an evidence of singularity, that an individual should thus consent in his pettiest walk with the general movement of the race; but I know that something akin to the migratory instinct in birds and quadrupeds,—which, in some instances, is known to have affected the squirrel tribe, impelling them to a general and mysterious movement, in which they were seen, say some, crossing the broadest rivers, each on its particular chip, with its tail raised for a sail, and bridging narrower streams with their dead,—that something like the *furor*

which affects the domestic cattle in the spring, and which is referred to a
worm in their tails,—affects both nations and individuals, either perenni-
ally or from time to time. Not a flock of wild geese cackles over our town,
but it to some extent unsettles the value of real estate here, and, if I were a
broker, I should probably take that disturbance into account.

> *"Than longen folk to gon on pilgrimages,*
> *And palmeres for to seken strange strondes."*

Every sunset which I witness inspires me with the desire to go to a West
as distant and as fair as that into which the sun goes down. He appears
to migrate westward daily, and tempt us to follow him. He is the Great
Western Pioneer whom the nations follow. We dream all night of those
mountain-ridges in the horizon, though they may be of vapor only, which
were last gilded by his rays. The island of Atlantis, and the islands and gardens of the Hesperides, a sort of terrestrial paradise, appear to have been
the Great West of the ancients, enveloped in mystery and poetry. Who has
not seen in imagination, when looking into the sunset sky, the gardens of
the Hesperides, and the foundation of all those fables?

Columbus felt the westward tendency more strongly than any before.
He obeyed it, and found a New World for Castile and Leon. The herd of
men in those days scented fresh pastures from afar.

> *"And now the sun had stretched out all the hills,*
> *And now was dropped into the western bay;*
> *At last he rose, and twitched his mantle blue;*
> *To-morrow to fresh woods and pastures new."*

Where on the globe can there be found an area of equal extent with that
occupied by the bulk of our States, so fertile and so rich and varied in its
productions, and at the same time so habitable by the European, as this is?
Michaux, who knew but part of them, says that "the species of large trees
are much more numerous in North America than in Europe; in the United
States there are more than one hundred and forty species that exceed thirty
feet in height; in France there are but thirty that attain this size." Later
botanists more than confirm his observations. Humboldt came to America
to realize his youthful dreams of a tropical vegetation, and he beheld it in

its greatest perfection in the primitive forests of the Amazon, the most gigantic wilderness on the earth, which he has so eloquently described. The geographer Guyot, himself a European, goes farther,—farther than I am ready to follow him; yet not when he says,—"As the plant is made for the animal, as the vegetable world is made for the animal world, America is made for the man of the Old World . . . The man of the Old World sets out upon his way. Leaving the highlands of Asia, he descends from station to station towards Europe. Each of his steps is marked by a new civilization superior to the preceding, by a greater power of development. Arrived at the Atlantic, he pauses on the shore of this unknown ocean, the bounds of which he knows not, and turns upon his footprints for an instant." When he has exhausted the rich soil of Europe, and reinvigorated himself, "then recommences his adventurous career westward as in the earliest ages." So far Guyot.

From this western impulse coming in contact with the barrier of the Atlantic sprang the commerce and enterprise of modern times. The younger Michaux, in his "Travels West of the Alleghanies in 1802," says that the common inquiry in the newly settled West was, "'From what part of the world have you come?' As if these vast and fertile regions would naturally be the place of meeting and common country of all the inhabitants of the globe."

To use an obsolete Latin word, I might say, *Ex Oriente lux; ex Occidente FRUX.* From the East light; from the West fruit.

Sir Francis Head, an English traveller and a Governor-General of Canada, tells us that "in both the northern and southern hemispheres of the New World, Nature has not only outlined her works on a larger scale, but has painted the whole picture with brighter and more costly colors than she used in delineating and in beautifying the Old World . . . The heavens of America appear infinitely higher, the sky is bluer, the air is fresher, the cold is intenser, the moon looks larger, the stars are brighter, the thunder is louder, the lightning is vivider, the wind is stronger, the rain is heavier, the mountains are higher, the rivers longer, the forests bigger, the plains broader." This statement will do at least to set against Buffon's account of this part of the world and its productions.

Linnaeus said long ago, "Nescio quae facies *laeta, glabra* plantis Americanis: I know not what there is of joyous and smooth in the aspect of American plants;" and I think that in this country there are no, or at most very few, *Africanae bestiae,* African beasts, as the Romans called them, and that in this respect also it is peculiarly fitted for the habitation of man. We are told that within three miles of the centre of the East-Indian city of Singapore, some of the inhabitants are annually carried off by tigers; but the traveller can lie down in the woods at night almost anywhere in North America without fear of wild beasts.

These are encouraging testimonies. If the moon looks larger here than in Europe, probably the sun looks larger also. If the heavens of America appear infinitely higher, and the stars brighter, I trust that these facts are symbolical of the height to which the philosophy and poetry and religion of her inhabitants may one day soar. At length, perchance, the immaterial heaven will appear as much higher to the American mind, and the intimations that star it as much brighter. For I believe that climate does thus react on man,—as there is something in the mountain-air that feeds the spirit and inspires. Will not man grow to greater perfection intellectually as well as physically under these influences? Or is it unimportant how many foggy days there are in his life? I trust that we shall be more imaginative, that our thoughts will be clearer, fresher, and more ethereal, as our sky,—our understanding more comprehensive and broader, like our plains,—our intellect generally on a grander scale, like our thunder and lightning, our rivers and mountains and forests,—and our hearts shall even correspond in breadth and depth and grandeur to our inland seas. Perchance there will appear to the traveller something, he knows not what, of *laeta* and *glabra*, of joyous and serene, in our very faces. Else to what end does the world go on, and why was America discovered?

To Americans I hardly need to say,—

> *"Westward the star of empire takes its way."*

As a true patriot, I should be ashamed to think that Adam in paradise was more favorably situated on the whole than the backwoodsman in this country.

Our sympathies in Massachusetts are not confined to New England; though we may be estranged from the South, we sympathize with the West. There is the home of the younger sons, as among the Scandinavians they took to the sea for their inheritance. It is too late to be studying Hebrew; it is more important to understand even the slang of to-day.

Some months ago I went to see a panorama of the Rhine. It was like a dream of the Middle Ages. I floated down its historic stream in something more than imagination, under bridges built by the Romans, and repaired by later heroes, past cities and castles whose very names were music to my ears, and each of which was the subject of a legend. There were Ehrenbreitstein and Rolandseck and Coblentz, which I knew only in history. They were ruins that interested me chiefly. There seemed to come up from its waters and its vine-clad hills and valleys a hushed music as of Crusaders departing for the Holy Land. I floated along under the spell of enchantment, as if I had been transported to an heroic age, and breathed an atmosphere of chivalry.

Soon after, I went to see a panorama of the Mississippi, and as I worked my way up the river in the light of to-day, and saw the steamboats wooding up, counted the rising cities, gazed on the fresh ruins of Nauvoo, beheld the Indians moving west across the stream, and, as before I had looked up the Moselle now looked up the Ohio and the Missouri, and heard the legends of Dubuque and of Wenona's Cliff,—still thinking more of the future than of the past or present,—I saw that this was a Rhine stream of a different kind; that the foundations of castles were yet to be laid, and the famous bridges were yet to be thrown over the river; and I felt that *this was the heroic age itself,* though we know it not, for the hero is commonly the simplest and obscurest of men.

The West of which I speak is but another name for the Wild; and what I have been preparing to say is, that in Wildness is the preservation of the World. Every tree sends its fibres forth in search of the Wild. The cities import it at any price. Men plough and sail for it. From the forest and wilderness come the tonics and barks which brace mankind. Our ancestors were savages. The story of Romulus and Remus being suckled by a wolf is not a meaningless fable. The founders of every State which has risen to eminence have drawn their nourishment and vigor from a similar wild source. It was because the children of the Empire were not suckled by the wolf that they were conquered and displaced by the children of the Northern forests who were.

I believe in the forest, and in the meadow, and in the night in which the corn grows. We require an infusion of hemlock-spruce or arborvitae in our tea. There is a difference between eating and drinking for strength and from mere gluttony. The Hottentots eagerly devour the marrow of the koodoo and other antelopes raw, as a matter of course. Some of our Northern Indians eat raw the marrow of the Arctic reindeer, as well as various other parts, including the summits of the antlers, as long as they are soft. And herein, perchance, they have stolen a march on the cooks of Paris. They get what usually goes to feed the fire. This is probably better than stall-fed beef and slaughter-house pork to make a man of. Give me a wildness whose glance no civilization can endure,—as if we lived on the marrow of koodoos devoured raw.

There are some intervals which border the strain of the wood-thrush, to which I would migrate,—wild lands where no settler has squatted; to which, methinks, I am already acclimated.

The African hunter Cummings tells us that the skin of the eland, as well as that of most other antelopes just killed, emits the most delicious perfume of trees and grass. I would have every man so much like a wild antelope, so much a part and parcel of Nature, that his very person should thus sweetly advertise our senses of his presence, and remind us of those parts of Nature which he most haunts. I feel no disposition to be satirical, when the trapper's coat emits the odor of musquash even; it is a sweeter scent to me than that which commonly exhales from the merchant's or the scholar's garments. When I go into their wardrobes and handle their vestments, I am reminded of no grassy plains and flowery meadows which they have frequented, but of dusty merchants' exchanges and libraries rather.

A tanned skin is something more than respectable, and perhaps olive is a fitter color than white for a man,—a denizen of the woods. "The pale white man!" I do not wonder that the African pitied him. Darwin the naturalist says, "A white man bathing by the side of a Tahitian was like a plant bleached by the gardener's art, compared with a fine, dark green one, growing vigorously in the open fields."

Ben Jonson exclaims,—

"How near to good is what is fair!"

So I would say,—

"How near to good is what is wild!*"*

Life consists with wildness. The most alive is the wildest. Not yet subdued to man, its presence refreshes him. One who pressed forward incessantly and never rested from his labors, who grew fast and made infinite demands on life, would always find himself in a new country or wilderness, and surrounded by the raw material of life. He would be climbing over the prostrate stems of primitive forest-trees.

Hope and the future for me are not in lawns and cultivated fields, not in towns and cities, but in the impervious and quaking swamps. When, formerly, I have analyzed my partiality for some farm which I had contemplated purchasing, I have frequently found that I was attracted solely by a few square rods of impermeable and unfathomable bog,—a natural sink in one corner of it. That was the jewel which dazzled me. I derive more of my subsistence from the swamps which surround my native town than from the cultivated gardens in the village. There are no richer parterres to my eyes than the dense beds of dwarf andromeda *(Cassandra calyculata)* which cover these tender places on the earth's surface. Botany cannot go farther than tell me the names of the shrubs which grow there,—the high blueberry, panicled andromeda, lamb-kill, azalea, and rhodora,—all standing in the quaking sphagnum. I often think that I should like to have my house front on this mass of dull red bushes, omitting other flower plots and borders, transplanted spruce and trim box, even gravelled walks,—to have this fertile spot under my windows, not a few imported barrow-fulls of soil only to cover the sand which was thrown out in digging the cellar. Why not put my house, my parlor, behind this plot, instead of behind that meagre assemblage of curiosities, that poor apology for a Nature and Art, which I call my front-yard? It is an effort to clear up and make a decent appearance when the carpenter and mason have departed, though done as much for the passer-by as the dweller within. The most tasteful front-yard fence was never an agreeable object of study to me; the most elaborate ornaments, acorn-tops, or what not, soon wearied and disgusted me. Bring your sills up to the very edge of the swamp, then (though it may not be the best place for a dry cellar,) so that there be no access on that side to citizens. Front-yards are not made to walk in, but, at most, through, and you could go in the back way.

Yes, though you may think me perverse, if it were proposed to me to dwell in the neighborhood of the most beautiful garden that ever human art contrived, or else of a Dismal swamp, I should certainly decide for the swamp. How vain, then, have been all your labors, citizens, for me!

My spirits infallibly rise in proportion to the outward dreariness. Give me the ocean, the desert or the wilderness! In the desert, pure air and solitude compensate for want of moisture and fertility. The traveller Burton says of it,—"Your *morale* improves; you become frank and cordial, hospitable and single-minded . . . In the desert, spirituous liquors excite only disgust. There is a keen enjoyment in a mere animal existence." They who have been travelling long on the steppes of Tartary say, "On reëntering cultivated lands, the agitation, perplexity, and turmoil of civilization oppressed and suffocated us; the air seemed to fail us, and we felt every moment as if about to die of asphyxia." When I would recreate myself, I seek the darkest wood, the thickest and most interminable, and, to the citizen, most dismal swamp. I enter a swamp as a sacred place,—a *sanctum sanctorum*. There is the strength, the marrow, of Nature. The wild-wood covers the virgin mould,—and the same soil is good for men and for trees. A man's health requires as many acres of meadow to his prospect as his farm does loads of muck. There are the strong meats on which he feeds. A town is saved, not more by the righteous men in it than by the woods and swamps that surround it. A township where one primitive forest waves above, while another primitive forest rots below,—such a town is fitted to raise not only corn and potatoes, but poets and philosophers for the coming ages. In such a soil grew Homer and Confucius and the rest, and out of such a wilderness comes the Reformer eating locusts and wild honey.

To preserve wild animals implies generally the creation of a forest for them to dwell in or resort to. So it is with man. A hundred years ago they sold bark in our streets peeled from our own woods. In the very aspect of those primitive and rugged trees there was, methinks, a tanning principle which hardened and consolidated the fibres of men's thoughts. Ah! already I shudder for these comparatively degenerate days of my native village, when you cannot collect a load of bark of good thickness,—and we no longer produce tar and turpentine.

The civilized nations—Greece, Rome, England—have been sustained by the primitive forests which anciently rotted where they stand. They survive as long as the soil is not exhausted. Alas for human culture! little is to be expected of a nation, when the vegetable mould is exhausted, and it is compelled to make manure of the bones of its fathers. There the poet sustains himself merely by his own superfluous fat, and the philosopher comes down on his marrow-bones.

It is said to be the task of the American "to work the virgin soil," and that "agriculture here already assumes proportions unknown everywhere else."

I think that the farmer displaces the Indian even because he redeems the meadow, and so makes himself stronger and in some respects more natural. I was surveying for a man the other day a single straight line one hundred and thirty-two rods long, through a swamp, at whose entrance might have been written the words which Dante read over the entrance to the infernal regions,—"Leave all hope, ye that enter,"—that is, of ever getting out again; where at one time I saw my employer actually up to his neck and swimming for his life in his property, though it was still winter. He had another similar swamp which I could not survey at all, because it was completely under water, and nevertheless, with regard to a third swamp, which I did *survey* from a distance, he remarked to me, true to his instincts, that he would not part with it for any consideration, on account of the mud which it contained. And that man intends to put a girdling ditch round the whole in the course of forty months, and so redeem it by the magic of his spade. I refer to him only as the type of a class.

The weapons with which we have gained our most important victories, which should be handed down as heirlooms from father to son, are not the sword and the lance, but the bush-whack, the turf-cutter, the spade, and the bog hoe, rusted with the blood of many a meadow, and begrimed with the dust of many a hard-fought field. The very winds blew the Indian's cornfield into the meadow, and pointed out the way which he had not the skill to follow. He had no better implement with which to intrench himself in the land than a clam-shell. But the farmer is armed with plough and spade.

In Literature it is only the wild that attracts us. Dulness is but another name for tameness. It is the uncivilized free and wild thinking in "Hamlet" and the "Iliad," in all the Scriptures and Mythologies, not learned in the schools, that delights us. As the wild duck is more swift and beautiful than the tame, so is the wild—the mallard—thought, which 'mid falling dews wings its way above the fens. A truly good book is something as natural, and as unexpectedly and unaccountably fair and perfect, as a wild flower discovered on the prairies of the West or in the jungles of the East. Genius is a light which makes the darkness visible, like the lightning's flash, which perchance shatters the temple of knowledge itself,—and not a taper lighted at the hearth-stone of the race, which pales before the light of common day.

English literature, from the days of the minstrels to the Lake Poets,— Chaucer and Spenser and Milton, and even Shakespeare, included,—breathes no quite fresh and in this sense wild strain. It is an essentially tame and civilized literature, reflecting Greece and Rome. Her wilderness is a green wood,—her wild man a Robin Hood. There is plenty of genial love of Nature, but not so much of Nature herself. Her chronicles inform us when her wild animals, but not when the wild man in her, became extinct.

The science of Humboldt is one thing, poetry is another thing. The poet to-day, notwithstanding all the discoveries of science, and the accumulated learning of mankind, enjoys no advantage over Homer.

Where is the literature which gives expression to Nature? He would be a poet who could impress the winds and streams into his service, to speak for him; who nailed words to their primitive senses, as farmers drive down stakes in the spring, which the frost has heaved; who derived his words as often as he used them,—transplanted them to his page with earth adhering to their roots; whose words were so true and fresh and natural that they would appear to expand like the buds at the approach of spring, though they lay half-smothered between two musty leaves in a library,— ay, to bloom and bear fruit there, after their kind, annually, for the faithful reader, in sympathy with surrounding Nature.

I do not know of any poetry to quote which adequately expresses this yearning for the Wild. Approached from this side, the best poetry is tame. I do not know where to find in any literature, ancient or modern, any account which contents me of that Nature with which even I am acquainted. You will perceive that I demand something which no Augustan nor Elizabethan age, which no *culture,* in short, can give. Mythology comes nearer to it than anything. How much more fertile a Nature, at least, has Grecian mythology its root in than English literature! Mythology is the crop which the Old World bore before its soil was exhausted, before the fancy and imagination were affected with blight; and which it still bears, wherever its pristine vigor is unabated. All other literatures endure only as the elms which overshadow our houses; but this is like the great dragon-tree of the Western Isles, as old as mankind, and, whether that does or not, will endure as long; for the decay of other literatures makes the soil in which it thrives.

The West is preparing to add its fables to those of the East. The valleys of the Ganges, the Nile, and the Rhine having yielded their crop, it remains to be seen what the valleys of the Amazon, the Plate, the Orinoco, the St. Lawrence, and the Mississippi will produce. Perchance, when, in the course of ages, American liberty has become a fiction of the past,—as it is to some extent a fiction of the present,—the poets of the world will be inspired by American mythology.

The wildest dreams of wild men, even, are not the less true, though they may not recommend themselves to the sense which is most common among Englishmen and Americans to-day. It is not every truth that recommends itself to the common sense. Nature has a place for the wild clematis as well as for the cabbage. Some expressions of truth are reminiscent—others merely *sensible,* as the phrase is,—others prophetic. Some forms of disease, even, may prophesy forms of health. The geologist has discovered that the figures of serpents, griffins, flying dragons, and other fanciful embellishments of heraldry, have their prototypes in the forms of fossil species which were extinct before man was created, and hence "indicate a faint and shadowy knowledge of a previous state of organic existence." The Hindoos dreamed that the earth rested on an elephant, and the elephant on a tortoise, and the tortoise on a serpent; and though it may be an unimportant coincidence, it will not be out of place here to state, that a fossil tortoise has lately been discovered in Asia large enough to support an elephant. I confess that I am partial to these wild fancies, which transcend the order of time and development. They are the sublimest recreation of the intellect. The partridge loves peas, but not those that go with her into the pot.

In short, all good things are wild and free. There is something in a strain of music, whether produced by an instrument or by the human voice,—take the sound of a bugle in a summer night, for instance,—which by its wildness, to speak without satire, reminds me of the cries emitted by wild beasts in their native forests. It is so much of their wildness as I can understand. Give me for my friends and neighbors wild men, not tame ones. The wildness of the savage is but a faint symbol of the awful ferity with which good men and lovers meet.

I love even to see the domestic animals reassert their native rights,—any evidence that they have not wholly lost their original wild habits and vigor; as when my neighbor's cow breaks out of her pasture early in the spring and boldly swims the river, a cold, gray tide, twenty-five or thirty rods wide, swollen by the melted snow. It is the buffalo crossing the Mississippi. This exploit confers some dignity on the herd in my eyes,—already dignified. The seeds of instinct are preserved under the thick hides of cattle and horses, like seeds in the bowels of the earth, an indefinite period.

Any sportiveness in cattle is unexpected. I saw one day a herd of a dozen bullocks and cows running about and frisking in unwieldy sport, like huge rats, even like kittens. They shook their heads, raised their tails, and rushed up and down a hill, and I perceived by their horns, as well as by their activity, their relation to the deer tribe. But, alas! a sudden loud *Whoa!* would have damped their ardor at once, reduced them from venison to beef, and stiffened their sides and sinews like the locomotive. Who but the Evil One has cried, "Whoa!" to mankind? Indeed, the life of cattle, like that of many men, is but a sort of locomotiveness; they move a side at a time, and man, by his machinery, is meeting the horse and the ox half-way. Whatever part the whip has touched is thenceforth palsied. Who would ever think of a *side* of any of the supple cat tribe, as we speak of a *side* of beef?

I rejoice that horses and steers have to be broken before they can be made the slaves of men, and that men themselves have some wild oats still left to sow before they become submissive members of society. Undoubtedly, all men are not equally fit subjects for civilization; and because the majority, like dogs and sheep, are tame by inherited disposition, this is no reason why the others should have their natures broken that they may be reduced to the same level. Men are in the main alike, but they were made several in order that they might be various. If a low use is to be served, one man will do nearly or quite as well as another; if a high one, individual excellence is to be regarded. Any man can stop a hole to keep the wind away, but no other man could serve so rare a use as the author of this illustration did. Confucius says,—"The skins of the tiger and the leopard, when they are tanned, are as the skins of the dog and the sheep tanned." But it is not the part of a true culture to tame tigers, any more than it is to make sheep ferocious; and tanning their skins for shoes is not the best use to which they can be put.

When looking over a list of men's names in a foreign language, as of military officers, or of authors who have written on a particular subject, I am reminded once more that there is nothing in a name. The name Menschikoff, for instance, has nothing in it to my ears more human than a whisker, and it may belong to a rat. As the names of the Poles and Russians are to us, so are ours to them. It is as if they had been named by the child's rigmarole,— *Iery wiery ichery van, tittle-tol-tan.* I see in my mind a herd of wild creatures swarming over the earth, and to each the herdsman has affixed some barbarous sound in his own dialect. The names of men are of course as cheap and meaningless as *Bose* and *Tray,* the names of dogs.

Methinks it would be some advantage to philosophy, if men were named merely in the gross, as they are known. It would be necessary only to know the genus and perhaps the race or variety, to know the individual. We are not prepared to believe that every private soldier in a Roman army had a name of his own,—because we have not supposed that he had a character of his own. At present our only true names are nicknames. I knew a boy who, from his peculiar energy, was called "Buster" by his playmates, and this rightly supplanted his Christian name. Some travellers tell us that an Indian had no name given him at first, but earned it, and his name was his fame; and among some tribes he acquired a new name with every new exploit. It is pitiful when a man bears a name for convenience merely, who has earned neither name nor fame.

I will not allow mere names to make distinctions for me, but still see men in herds for all them. A familiar name cannot make a man less strange to me. It may be given to a savage who retains in secret his own wild title earned in the woods. We have a wild savage in us, and a savage name is perchance somewhere recorded as ours. I see that my neighbor, who bears the familiar epithet William, or Edwin, takes it off with his jacket. It does not adhere to him when asleep or in anger, or aroused by any passion or inspiration. I seem to hear pronounced by some of his kin at such a time his original wild name in some jaw-breaking or else melodious tongue.

Here is this vast, savage, hovering mother of ours, Nature, lying all around, with such beauty, and such affection for her children, as the leopard; and yet we are so early weaned from her breast to society, to that culture which is exclusively an interaction of man on man,—a sort of breeding in and in, which produces at most a merely English nobility, a civilization destined to have a speedy limit.

In society, in the best institutions of men, it is easy to detect a certain precocity. When we should still be growing children, we are already little men. Give me a culture which imports much muck from the meadows, and deepens the soil,—not that which trusts to heating manures, and improved implements and modes of culture only!

Many a poor sore-eyed student that I have heard of would grow faster, both intellectually and physically, if, instead of sitting up so very late, he honestly slumbered a fool's allowance.

There may be an excess even of informing light. Niépce, a Frenchman, discovered "actinism," that power in the sun's rays which produces a chemical effect,—that granite rocks, and stone structures, and statues of metal "are all alike destructively acted upon during the hours of sunshine, and, but for provisions of Nature no less wonderful, would soon perish under the delicate touch of the most subtile of the agencies of the universe." But he observed that "those bodies which underwent this change during the daylight possessed the power of restoring themselves to their original conditions during the hours of night, when this excitement was no longer influencing them." Hence it has been inferred that "the hours of darkness are as necessary to the inorganic creation as we know night and sleep are to the organic kingdom." Not even does the moon shine every night, but gives place to darkness.

I would not have every man nor every part of a man cultivated, any more than I would have every acre of earth cultivated: part will be tillage, but the greater part will be meadow and forest, not only serving an immediate use, but preparing a mould against a distant future, by the annual decay of the vegetation which it supports.

There are other letters for the child to learn than those which Cadmus invented. The Spaniards have a good term to express this wild and dusky knowledge, —*Gramática parda*, tawny grammar,— a kind of mother-wit derived from that same leopard to which I have referred.

We have heard of a Society for the Diffusion of Useful Knowledge. It is said that knowledge is power; and the like. Methinks there is equal need of a Society for the Diffusion of Useful Ignorance, what we will call Beautiful Knowledge, a knowledge useful in a higher sense: for what is most of our boasted so-called knowledge but a conceit that we know something, which robs us of the advantage of our actual ignorance? What we call knowledge is often our positive ignorance; ignorance our negative knowledge. By long years of patient industry and reading of the newspapers,—for what are the libraries of science but files of newspapers?—a man accumulates a myriad facts, lays them up in his memory, and then when in some spring of his life he saunters abroad into the Great Fields of thought, he, as it were, goes to grass like a horse, and leaves all his harness behind in the stable. I would say to the Society for the Diffusion of Useful Knowledge, sometimes,—Go to grass. You have eaten hay long enough. The spring has come with its green crop. The very cows are driven to their country pastures before the end of May; though I have heard of one unnatural farmer who kept his cow in the barn and fed her on hay all the year round. So, frequently, the Society for the Diffusion of Useful Knowledge treats its cattle.

A man's ignorance sometimes is not only useful, but beautiful,—while his knowledge, so called, is oftentimes worse than useless, besides being ugly. Which is the best man to deal with,—he who knows nothing about a subject, and, what is extremely rare, knows that he knows nothing, or he who really knows something about it, but thinks that he knows all?

My desire for knowledge is intermittent; but my desire to bathe my head in atmospheres unknown to my feet is perennial and constant. The highest that we can attain to is not Knowledge, but Sympathy with Intelligence. I do not know that this higher knowledge amounts to anything more definite than a novel and grand surprise on a sudden revelation of the insufficiency of all that we called Knowledge before,—a discovery that there are more things in heaven and earth than are dreamed of in our philosophy. It is the lighting up of the mist by the sun. Man cannot *know* in any higher sense than this, any more than he can look serenely and with impunity in the face of sun: "You will not perceive that, as perceiving a particular thing," say the Chaldean Oracles.

There is something servile in the habit of seeking after a law which we may obey. We may study the laws of matter at and for our convenience, but a successful life knows no law. It is an unfortunate discovery certainly, that of a law which binds us where we did not know before that we were bound. Live free, child of the mist,—and with respect to knowledge we are all children of the mist. The man who takes the liberty to live is superior to all the laws, by virtue of his relation to the law-maker. "That is active duty," says the Vishnu Purana, "which is not for our bondage; that is knowledge which is for our liberation: all other duty is good only unto weariness; all other knowledge is only the cleverness of an artist."

It is remarkable how few events or crises there are in our histories; how little exercised we have been in our minds; how few experiences we have had. I would fain be assured that I am growing apace and rankly, though my very growth disturb this dull equanimity,—though it be with struggle through long, dark, muggy nights or seasons of gloom. It would be well, if all our lives were a divine tragedy even, instead of this trivial comedy or farce. Dante, Bunyan, and others, appear to have been exercised in their minds more than we: they were subjected to a kind of culture such as our district schools and colleges do not contemplate. Even Mahomet, though many may scream at his name, had a good deal more to live for, ay, and to die for, than they have commonly.

When, at rare intervals, some thought visits one, as perchance he is walking on a railroad, then, indeed, the cars go by without his hearing them. But soon, by some inexorable law, our life goes by and the cars return.

> *"Gentle breeze, that wanderest unseen,*
> *And bendest the thistles round Loira of storms,*
> *Traveller of the windy glens,*
> *Why hast thou left my ear so soon?"*

While almost all men feel an attraction drawing them to society, few are attracted strongly to Nature. In their relation to Nature men appear to me for the most part, notwithstanding their arts, lower than the animals. It is not often a beautiful relation, as in the case of the animals. How little appreciation of the beauty of the landscape there is among us! We have to be told that the Greeks called the world Beauty, or Order, but we do not see clearly why they did so, and we esteem it at best only a curious philological fact.

For my part, I feel that with regard to Nature I live a sort of border life, on the confines of a world into which I make occasional and transitional and transient forays only, and my patriotism and allegiance to the State into whose territories I seem to retreat are those of a moss-trooper. Unto a life which I call natural I would gladly follow even a will-o'-the-wisp through bogs and sloughs unimaginable, but no moon nor fire-fly has shown me the causeway to it. Nature is a personality so vast and universal that we have never seen one of her features. The walker in the familiar fields which stretch around my native town sometimes finds himself in another land than is described in their owners' deeds, as it were in some far-away field on the confines of the actual Concord, where her jurisdiction ceases, and the idea which the word Concord suggests ceases to be suggested. These farms which I have myself surveyed, these bounds which I have set up, appear dimly still as through a mist; but they have no chemistry to fix them; they fade from the surface of the glass; and the picture which the painter painted stands out dimly from beneath. The world with which we are commonly acquainted leaves no trace, and it will have no anniversary.

I took a walk on Spaulding's Farm the other afternoon. I saw the setting sun lighting up the opposite side of a stately pine wood. Its golden rays straggled into the aisles of the wood as into some noble hall. I was impressed as if some ancient and altogether admirable and shining family had settled there in that part of the land called Concord, unknown to me,—to whom the sun was servant,—who had not gone into society in the village,—who had not been called on. I saw their park, their pleasure-ground, beyond through the wood, in Spaulding's cranberry-meadow. The pines furnished them with gables as they grew. Their house was not obvious to vision; the trees grew through it. I do not know whether I heard the sounds of a suppressed hilarity or not. They seemed to recline on the sunbeams. They have sons and daughters. They are quite well. The farmer's cart-path, which leads directly through their hall, does not in the least put them out,—as the muddy bottom of a pool is sometimes seen through the reflected skies. They never heard of Spaulding, and do not know that he is their neighbor,—notwithstanding I heard him whistle as he drove his team through the house. Nothing can equal the serenity of their lives. Their coat of arms is simply a lichen. I saw it painted on the pines and oaks. Their attics were in the tops of the trees. They are of no politics. There was no noise of labor. I did not perceive that they were weaving or spinning. Yet I did detect, when the wind lulled and hearing was done away, the finest imaginable sweet musical hum,—as of a distant hive in May, which perchance was the sound of their thinking. They had no idle thoughts, and no one without could see their work, for their industry was not as in knots and excrescences embayed.

But I find it difficult to remember them. They fade irrevocably out of my mind even now while I speak and endeavor to recall them, and recollect myself. It is only after a long and serious effort to recollect my best thoughts that I become again aware of their cohabitancy. If it were not for such families as this, I think I should move out of Concord.

We are accustomed to say in New England that few and fewer pigeons visit us every year. Our forests furnish no mast for them. So, it would seem, few and fewer thoughts visit each growing man from year to year, for the grove in our minds is laid waste,—sold to feed unnecessary fires of ambition, or sent to mill,—and there is scarcely a twig left for them to perch on. They no longer build nor breed with us. In some more genial season, perchance, a faint shadow flits across the landscape of the mind, cast by the *wings* of some thought in its vernal or autumnal migration, but, looking up, we are unable to detect the substance of the thought itself. Our winged thoughts are turned to poultry. They no longer soar, and they attain only to a Shanghai and Cochin-China grandeur. Those *gra-a-ate thoughts,* those *gra-a-ate* men you hear of!

We hug the earth,—how rarely we mount! Methinks we might elevate ourselves a little more. We might climb a tree, at least. I found my account in climbing a tree once. It was a tall white pine, on the top of a hill; and though I got well pitched, I was well paid for it, for I discovered new mountains in the horizon which I had never seen before,—so much more of the earth and the heavens. I might have walked about the foot of the tree for three-score years and ten, and yet I certainly should never have seen them. But, above all, I discovered around me,—it was near the end of June,—on the ends of the topmost branches only, a few minute and delicate red cone-like blossoms, the fertile flower of the white pine looking heavenward. I carried straightway to the village the topmost spire, and showed it to stranger jurymen who walked the streets,—for it was court-week,—and to farmers and lumber-dealers and wood-choppers and hunters, and not one had ever seen the like before, but they wondered as at a star dropped down. Tell of ancient architects finishing their works on the tops of columns as perfectly as on the lower and more visible parts! Nature has from the first expanded the minute blossoms of the forest only toward the heavens, above men's heads and unobserved by them. We see only the flowers that are under our feet in the meadows. The pines have developed their delicate blossoms on the highest twigs of the wood every summer for ages, as well over the heads of Nature's red children as of her white ones; yet scarcely a farmer or hunter in the land has ever seen them.

Above all, we cannot afford not to live in the present. He is blessed over all mortals who loses no moment of the passing life in remembering the past. Unless our philosophy hears the cock crow in every barn-yard within our horizon, it is belated. That sound commonly reminds us that we are growing rusty and antique in our employments and habits of thought. His philosophy comes down to a more recent time than ours. There is something suggested by it that is a newer testament,—the gospel according to this moment. He has not fallen astern; he has got up early and kept up early, and to be where he is to be in season, in the foremost rank of time. It is an expression of the health and soundness of Nature, a brag for all the world,—healthiness as of a spring burst forth, a new fountain of the Muses, to celebrate this last instant of time. Where he lives no fugitive slave laws are passed. Who has not betrayed his master many times since last he heard that note?

The merit of this bird's strain is in its freedom from all plaintiveness. The singer can easily move us to tears or to laughter, but where is he who can excite in us a pure morning joy? When, in doleful dumps, breaking the awful stillness of our wooden sidewalk on a Sunday, or, perchance, a watcher in the house of mourning, I hear a cockerel crow far or near, I think to myself, "There is one of us well, at any rate,"—and with a sudden gush return to my senses.

We had a remarkable sunset one day last November. I was walking in a meadow, the source of a small brook, when the sun at last, just before setting, after a cold gray day, reached a clear stratum in the horizon, and the softest, brightest morning sunlight fell on the dry grass and on the stems of the trees in the opposite horizon, and on the leaves of the shrub-oaks on the hill-side, while our shadows stretched long over the meadow eastward, as if we were the only motes in its beams. It was such a light as we could not have imagined a moment before, and the air also was so warm and serene that nothing was wanting to make a paradise of that meadow. When we reflected that this was not a solitary phenomenon, never to happen again, but that it would happen forever and ever an infinite number of evenings, and cheer and reassure the latest child that walked there, it was more glorious still.

The sun sets on some retired meadow, where no house is visible, with all the glory and splendor that it lavishes on cities, and perchance, as it has never set before,—where there is but a solitary marsh-hawk to have his wings gilded by it, or only a musquash looks out from his cabin, and there is some little black-veined brook in the midst of the marsh, just beginning to meander, winding slowly round a decaying stump. We walked in so pure and bright a light, gilding the withered grass and leaves, so softly and serenely bright, I thought I had never bathed in such a golden flood, without a ripple or a murmur to it. The west side of every wood and rising ground gleamed like the boundary of Elysium, and the sun on our backs seemed like a gentle herdsman driving us home at evening.

So we saunter toward the Holy Land, till one day the sun shall shine more brightly than ever he has done, shall perchance shine into our minds and hearts, and light up our whole lives with a great awakening light, as warm and serene and golden as on a bank-side in autumn.

1851

During its twenty-five-year run in the mid-1800s, P. T. Barnum's American Museum in New York City sold forty-five million tickets—roughly forty-four million more tickets than there were people in New York. He sold to both the lower class and the upper class, to "native-borns" and recent immigrants, and at a time when different races seldom mixed in American society Barnum also sold tickets to both blacks and whites. In many ways, the American Museum transcended difference while simultaneously exploiting the exoticness of "others" through a hodgepodge of exhibits of tattooed children, acrobatic fleas, minstrel shows, ventriloquists, contortionists, magicians, a mermaid, a white whale, a lady with a beard, and a tree under which—it was claimed on a plaque—Jesus's disciples once sat. Nothing else like it had ever existed in America. This was a time when there were few parks in the country, or beaches, sports teams, concert halls, etc. Most Americans worked at least six days a week, and so even the idea of a "weekend" was not widely known. Barnum's museum was unique, therefore, in the way it promoted an individual's right to indulge his curiosity about the grotesque and sublime: at two o'clock a performance of Shakespeare's *Othello;* at four o'clock an exhibition of Cheng and Eng, the Siamese twins. When P. T. Barnum's American Museum was destroyed by a fire in 1865, an editorial in the *Nation* magazine bid farewell to the institution. "We desire to give the American Museum all the credit it deserves, for it needs it all," the editorial began, and then passive-aggressively went on to propose a new kind of museum for the city of New York, an institution that was more fitting for "a first-class city," committed to the "seriousness" and "sobriety" of natural history—botany, zoology, geology, mineralogy—the myriad specializations that were beginning to emerge as the nineteenth century sought to carve up the world into easily knowable substrata of meanings:

> It is one thing to love shells and minerals, and to enjoy collections of them, but quite another to enjoy *every* collection of them. The more truly one loves a collection well arranged, the more he will be offended by a chaotic, dusty, dishonored collection. The more one loves the order and system of scientific enquiry, the more he will feel personally injured by disorder and lack of system among the materials of scientific enquiry. . . . Without scientific arrangement, without a catalogue, without attendants, without even labels, in very many instances, the heterogeneous heap of "curiosities," valuable and worthless well mixed up together, could not attract our students very often or detain them long.

What P. T. Barnum understood, however, is that the "valuable" and the "worthless," when mixed together, can inspire one to find brand-new meanings of one's own. From the Greek word *mouseion*—"the home of the Muses"—museums have always been places for amusement, music, and musing, spaces in which one can get lost in one's thoughts, wandering between ideas both grotesque and sublime. This might be the era when the word *scientist* is coined, but it's also when the term *haute couture* is introduced, when Lewis Carroll publishes *Alice's Adventures in Wonderland,* when a bike-riding frenzy overtakes the United States, and when we first read that intimately fateful opening sentence "Call me Ishmael," and feel ourselves compelled into service to help unravel the two strands in Herman Melville's epic story: the voyage of the *Pequod* to kill Moby Dick, and Ishmael's own voyage to make sense of that adventure. "Some years ago—never mind how long precisely," Ishmael continues in the second sentence of the book, signaling to us with his very next breath which of those two voyages will really matter in this book: *Never mind how long precisely.* This is a book that wanders, that muses, that uses facts and information to help expand its curiosity rather than to dictate the limits of ours. "Still we can hypothesize," Ishmael tells us at one point in the book, "even if we cannot prove and establish." And so while Captain Ahab drives toward a triumphant end to his quest, Ishmael revels in the endless minutiae of cetology, the hieroglyphic significance of the scars on Moby Dick's body, an analysis of a painting in the Spouter-Inn, and a meditation on the meaning of the color white. As many scholars have explained, Ishmael's proclivity for interpreting everything comes close to exhausting the virtues of interpretation. But what we eventually begin to realize, thanks to Ishmael's doggedness, is that with so many possible interpretations out there, perhaps there is no single "right" way to see anything, that more than one answer might exist to a question, that while the color white looks empty and vacuous and devoid of any meaning, it is actually a conflagration of all the other colors—that place on the spectrum where all light merges.

The Whiteness of the Whale

What the White Whale was to Ahab, has been hinted; what, at times, he was to me, as yet remains unsaid.

Aside from those more obvious considerations touching Moby Dick, which could not but occasionally awaken in any man's soul some alarm, there was another thought, or rather vague, nameless horror concerning him, which at times by its intensity completely overpowered all the rest; and yet so mystical and well nigh ineffable was it, that I almost despair of putting it in a comprehensible form. It was the whiteness of the whale that above all things appalled me. But how can I hope to explain myself here; and yet, in some dim, random way, explain myself I must, else all these chapters might be naught.

Though in many natural objects, whiteness refiningly enhances beauty, as if imparting some special virtue of its own, as in marbles, japonicas, and pearls; and though various nations have in some way recognised a certain royal pre-eminence in this hue; even the barbaric, grand old kings of Pegu placing the title "Lord of the White Elephants" above all their other magniloquent ascriptions of dominion; and the modern kings of Siam unfurling the same snow-white quadruped in the royal standard; and the Hanoverian flag bearing the one figure of a snow-white charger; and the great Austrian Empire, Cæsarian, heir to overlording Rome, having for the imperial color the same imperial hue; and though this pre-eminence in it applies to the human race itself, giving the white man ideal mastership over every dusky tribe; and though, besides all this, whiteness has been even made significant of gladness, for among the Romans a white stone marked a joyful day; and though in other mortal sympathies and symbolizings, this same hue is made the emblem of many touching, noble things—the innocence of brides, the benignity of age; though among the Red Men of America the giving of the white belt of wampum was the deepest pledge of honor; though in many climes, whiteness typifies the majesty of Justice in the ermine of the Judge, and contributes to the daily state of kings and queens drawn by milk-white steeds; though even in the higher mysteries of the most august religions it has been made the symbol of the divine spotlessness and power; by the Persian fire worshippers, the white forked flame being held the holiest on the altar; and in the Greek mythologies, Great Jove himself being made incarnate in a snow-white bull; and though to the noble Iroquois, the midwinter sacrifice of the sacred White Dog was by far the holiest festival of their theology, that spotless, faithful creature being held the purest envoy they could send to the Great Spirit with the annual tidings of their own fidelity; and though directly from the Latin word for white, all Christian priests derive the name of one part of their sacred vesture, the alb or tunic, worn beneath the cassock; and though among the holy pomps of the Romish faith, white is specially employed in the celebration of the Passion of our Lord; though in the Vision of St. John, white robes are given to the redeemed, and the four-and-twenty elders stand clothed in white before the great white throne, and the Holy One that sitteth there white like wool; yet for all these accumulated associations, with whatever is sweet, and honorable, and sublime, there yet lurks an elusive something in the innermost idea of this hue, which strikes more of panic to the soul than that redness which affrights in blood.

This elusive quality it is, which causes the thought of whiteness, when divorced from more kindly associations, and coupled with any object terrible in itself, to heighten that terror to the furthest bounds. Witness the white bear of the poles, and the white shark of the tropics; what but their smooth, flaky whiteness makes them the transcendent horrors they are? That ghastly whiteness it is which imparts such an abhorrent mildness, even more loathsome than terrific, to the dumb gloating of their aspect. So that not the fierce-fanged tiger in his heraldic coat can so stagger courage as the white-shrouded bear or shark.[1]

---

1. With reference to the Polar bear, it may possibly be urged by him who would fain go still deeper into this matter, that it is not the whiteness, separately regarded, which heightens the intolerable hideousness of that brute; for, analysed, that heightened hideousness, it might be said, only arises from the circumstance, that the irresponsible ferociousness of the creature stands invested in the fleece of celestial innocence and love; and hence, by bringing together two such opposite emotions in our minds, the Polar bear frightens us with so un-

Bethink thee of the albatross, whence come those clouds of spiritual wonderment and pale dread, in which that white phantom sails in all imaginations? Not Coleridge first threw that spell; but God's great, unflattering laureate, Nature.[2]

---

natural a contrast. But even assuming all this to be true; yet, were it not for the whiteness, you would not have that intensified terror.

As for the white shark, the white gliding ghostliness of repose in that creature, when beheld in his ordinary moods, strangely tallies with the same quality in the Polar quadruped. This peculiarity is most vividly hit by the French in the name they bestow upon that fish. The Romish mass for the dead begins with "Requiem eternam" (eternal rest), whence *Requiem* denominating the mass itself, and any other funeral music. Now, in allusion to the white, silent stillness of death in this shark, and the mild deadliness of his habits, the French call him *Requin*.

2. I remember the first albatross I ever saw. It was during a prolonged gale, in waters hard upon the Antarctic seas. From my forenoon watch below, I ascended to the overclouded deck; and there, dashed upon the main hatches, I saw a regal, feathery thing of unspotted whiteness, and with a hooked, Roman bill sublime. At intervals, it arched forth its vast archangel wings, as if to embrace some holy ark. Wondrous flutterings and throbbings shook it. Though bodily unharmed, it uttered cries, as some king's ghost in supernatural distress. Through its inexpressible, strange eyes, methought I peeped to secrets which took hold of God. As Abraham before the angels, I bowed myself; the white thing was so white, its wings so wide, and in those for ever exiled waters, I had lost the miserable warping memories of traditions and of towns. Long I gazed at that prodigy of plumage. I cannot tell, can only hint, the things that darted through me then. But at last I awoke; and turning, asked a sailor what bird was this. A goney, he replied. Goney! I never had heard that name before; is it conceivable that this glorious thing is utterly unknown to men ashore! never! But some time after, I learned that goney was some seaman's name for albatross. So that by no possibility could Coleridge's wild Rhyme have had aught to do with those mystical impressions which were mine, when I saw that bird upon our deck. For neither had I then read the Rhyme, nor knew the bird to be an albatross. Yet, in saying this, I do but indirectly burnish a little brighter the noble merit of the poem and the poet.

I assert, then, that in the wondrous bodily whiteness of the bird chiefly lurks the secret of the spell; a truth the more evinced in this, that by a solecism of terms there are birds called grey albatrosses; and these I have frequently seen, but never with such emotions as when I beheld the Antarctic fowl.

But how had the mystic thing been caught? Whisper it not, and I will tell; with a treacherous hook and line, as the fowl floated on the sea. At last the Captain made a postman of it; tying a lettered, leathern tally round its neck, with the ship's time and place; and then letting it escape. But I doubt not, that leathern tally, meant for man, was taken off in Heaven, when the white fowl flew to join the wing-folding, the invoking, and adoring cherubim!

Most famous in our Western annals and Indian traditions is that of the White Steed of the Prairies; a magnificent milk-white charger, large-eyed, small-headed, bluff-chested, and with the dignity of a thousand monarchs in his lofty, overscorning carriage. He was the elected Xerxes of vast herds of wild horses, whose pastures in those days were only fenced by the Rocky Mountains and the Alleghanies. At their flaming head he westward trooped it like that chosen star which every evening leads on the hosts of light. The flashing cascade of his mane, the curving comet of his tail, invested him with housings more resplendent than gold and silver-beaters could have furnished him. A most imperial and archangelical apparition of that unfallen, western world, which to the eyes of the old trappers and hunters revived the glories of those primeval times when Adam walked majestic as a god, bluff-bowed and fearless as this mighty steed. Whether marching amid his aides and marshals in the van of countless cohorts that endlessly streamed it over the plains, like an Ohio; or whether with his circumambient subjects browsing all around at the horizon, the White Steed gallopingly reviewed them with warm nostrils reddening through his cool milkiness; in whatever aspect he presented himself, always to the bravest Indians he was the object of trembling reverence and awe. Nor can it be questioned from what stands on legendary record of this noble horse, that it was his spiritual whiteness chiefly, which so clothed him with divineness; and that this divineness had that in it which, though commanding worship, at the same time enforced a certain nameless terror.

But there are other instances where this whiteness loses all that accessory and strange glory which invests it in the White Steed and Albatross.

What is it that in the Albino man so peculiarly repels and often shocks the eye, as that sometimes he is loathed by his own kith and kin! It is that whiteness which invests him, a thing expressed by the name he bears. The Albino is as well made as other men—has no substantive deformity—and yet this mere aspect of all-pervading whiteness makes him more strangely hideous than the ugliest abortion. Why should this be so?

Nor, in quite other aspects, does Nature in her least palpable but not the less malicious agencies, fail to enlist among her forces this crowning attribute of the terrible. From its snowy aspect, the gauntleted ghost of the Southern Seas has been denominated the White Squall. Nor, in some historic instances, has the art of human malice omitted so potent an auxiliary. How wildly it heightens the effect of that passage in Froissart, when, masked in the snowy symbol of their faction, the desperate White Hoods of Ghent murder their bailiff in the marketplace!

Nor, in some things, does the common, hereditary experience of all mankind fail to bear witness to the supernaturalism of this hue. It cannot well be doubted, that the one visible quality in the aspect of the dead which most appals the gazer, is the marble pallor lingering there; as if indeed that pallor were as much like the badge of consternation in the other world, as of mortal trepidation here. And from that pallor of the dead, we borrow the expressive hue of the shroud in which we wrap them. Nor even in our superstitions do we fail to throw the same snowy mantle round our phantoms; all ghosts rising in a milk-white fog—Yea, while these terrors seize us, let us add, that even the king of terrors, when personified by the evangelist, rides on his pallid horse.

Therefore, in his other moods, symbolize whatever grand or gracious thing he will by whiteness, no man can deny that in its profoundest idealized significance it calls up a peculiar apparition to the soul.

But though without dissent this point be fixed, how is mortal man to account for it? To analyse it, would seem impossible. Can we, then, by the citation of some of those instances wherein this thing of whiteness—though for the time either wholly or in great part stripped of all direct associations calculated to import to it aught fearful, but nevertheless, is found to exert over us the same sorcery, however modified;—can we thus hope to light upon some chance clue to conduct us to the hidden cause we seek?

Let us try. But in a matter like this, subtlety appeals to subtlety, and without imagination no man can follow another into these halls. And though, doubtless, some at least of the imaginative impressions about to be presented may have been shared by most men, yet few perhaps were entirely conscious of them at the time, and therefore may not be able to recall them now.

Why to the man of untutored ideality, who happens to be but loosely acquainted with the peculiar character of the day, does the bare mention of Whitsuntide marshal in the fancy such long, dreary, speechless processions of slow-pacing pilgrims, downcast and hooded with new-fallen snow? Or, to the unread, unsophisticated Protestant of the Middle American States, why does the passing mention of a White Friar or a White Nun, evoke such an eyeless statue in the soul?

Or what is there apart from the traditions of dungeoned warriors and kings (which will not wholly account for it) that makes the White Tower

of London tell so much more strongly on the imagination of an un-
travelled American, than those other storied structures, its neighbors—the
Byward Tower, or even the Bloody? And those sublimer towers, the White
Mountains of New Hampshire, whence, in peculiar moods, comes that
gigantic ghostliness over the soul at the bare mention of that name, while
the thought of Virginia's Blue Ridge is full of a soft, dewy, distant dreami-
ness? Or why, irrespective of all latitudes and longitudes, does the name
of the White Sea exert such a spectralness over the fancy, while that of the
Yellow Sea lulls us with mortal thoughts of long lacquered mild afternoons
on the waves, followed by the gaudiest and yet sleepiest of sunsets? Or, to
choose a wholly unsubstantial instance, purely addressed to the fancy, why,
in reading the old fairy tales of Central Europe, does "the tall pale man"
of the Hartz forests, whose changeless pallor unrustlingly glides through
the green of the groves—why is this phantom more terrible than all the
whooping imps of the Blocksburg?

Nor is it, altogether, the remembrance of her cathedral-toppling earth-
quakes; nor the stampedoes of her frantic seas; nor the tearlessness of
arid skies that never rain; nor the sight of her wide field of leaning spires,
wrenched cope-stones, and crosses all adroop (like canted yards of an-
chored fleets); and her suburban avenues of house-walls lying over upon
each other, as a tossed pack of cards;—it is not these things alone which
make tearless Lima, the strangest, saddest city thou can'st see. For Lima has
taken the white veil; and there is a higher horror in this whiteness of her
woe. Old as Pizarro, this whiteness keeps her ruins for ever new; admits not
the cheerful greenness of complete decay; spreads over her broken ramparts
the rigid pallor of an apoplexy that fixes its own distortions.

I know that, to the common apprehension, this phenomenon of whiteness is not confessed to be the prime agent in exaggerating the terror of
objects otherwise terrible; nor to the unimaginative mind is there aught
of terror in those appearances whose awfulness to another mind almost
solely consists in this one phenomenon, especially when exhibited under
any form at all approaching to muteness or universality. What I mean by
these two statements may perhaps be respectively elucidated by the following examples.

First: The mariner, when drawing nigh the coasts of foreign lands, if by
night he hear the roar of breakers, starts to vigilance, and feels just enough
of trepidation to sharpen all his faculties; but under precisely similar cir-

cumstances, let him be called from his hammock to view his ship sailing through a midnight sea of milky whiteness—as if from encircling head-lands shoals of combed white bears were swimming round him, then he feels a silent, superstitious dread; the shrouded phantom of the whitened waters is horrible to him as a real ghost; in vain the lead assures him he is still off soundings; heart and helm they both go down; he never rests till blue water is under him again. Yet where is the mariner who will tell thee, "Sir, it was not so much the fear of striking hidden rocks, as the fear of that hideous whiteness that so stirred me?"

Second: To the native Indian of Peru, the continual sight of the snow-howdahed Andes conveys naught of dread, except, perhaps, in the mere fancying of the eternal frosted desolateness reigning at such vast altitudes, and the natural conceit of what a fearfulness it would be to lose oneself in such inhuman solitude. Much the same is it with the backwoodsman of the West, who with comparative indifference views an unbounded prairie sheeted with driven snow, no shadow of tree or twig to break the fixed trance of whiteness. Not so the sailor, beholding the scenery of the Antarctic seas; where at times, by some infernal trick of legerdemain in the powers of frost and air, he, shivering and half shipwrecked, instead of rainbows speaking hope and solace to his misery, views what seems a boundless church-yard grinning upon him with its lean ice monuments and splintered crosses.

But thou sayest, methinks that white-lead chapter about whiteness is but a white flag hung out from a craven soul; thou surrenderest to a hypo, Ishmael.

Tell me, why this strong young colt, foaled in some peaceful valley of Vermont, far removed from all beasts of prey—why is it that upon the sun-niest day, if you but shake a fresh buffalo robe behind him, so that he can-not even see it, but only smells its wild animal muskiness—why will he start, snort, and with bursting eyes paw the ground in phrensies of affright? There is no remembrance in him of any gorings of wild creatures in his green northern home, so that the strange muskiness he smells cannot recall to him anything associated with the experience of former perils; for what knows he, this New England colt, of the black bisons of distant Oregon?

No: but here thou beholdest even in a dumb brute, the instinct of the knowledge of the demonism in the world. Though thousands of miles from Oregon, still when he smells that savage musk, the rending, goring bison herds are as present as to the deserted wild foal of the prairies, which this instant they may be trampling into dust.

Thus, then, the muffled rollings of a milky sea; the bleak rustlings of the festooned frosts of mountains; the desolate shiftings of the windrowed snows of prairies; all these, to Ishmael are as the shaking of that buffalo robe to the frightened colt!

Though neither knows where lie the nameless things of which the mystic sign gives forth such hints; yet with me, as with the colt, somewhere those things must exist. Though in many of its aspects this visible world seems formed in love, the invisible spheres were formed in fright.

But not yet have we solved the incantation of this whiteness, and learned why it appeals with such power to the soul; and more strange and far more portentous—why, as we have seen, it is at once the most meaning symbol of spiritual things, nay, the very veil of the Christian's Deity; and yet should be as it is, the intensifying agent in things the most appalling to mankind.

Is it that by its indefiniteness it shadows forth the heartless voids and immensities of the universe, and thus stabs us from behind with the thought of annihilation, when beholding the white depths of the milky way? Or is it, that as in essence whiteness is not so much a color as the visible absence of color, and at the same time the concrete of all colors; is it for these reasons that there is such a dumb blankness, full of meaning, in a wide landscape of snows—a colorless, all-color of atheism from which we shrink? And when we consider that other theory of the natural philosophers, that all other earthly hues—every stately or lovely emblazoning—the sweet tinges of sunset skies and woods; yea, and the gilded velvets of butterflies, and the butterfly cheeks of young girls; all these are but subtile deceits, not actually inherent in substances, but only laid on from without; so that all deified Nature absolutely paints like the harlot, whose allurements cover nothing but the charnel-house within; and when we proceed further, and consider that the mystical cosmetic which produces every one of her hues, the great principle of light, for ever remains white or colorless in itself, and if operating without medium upon matter, would touch all objects, even tulips and roses, with its own blank tinge—pondering all this, the palsied universe lies before us a leper; and like wilful travellers in Lapland, who refuse to wear colored and coloring glasses upon their eyes, so the wretched infidel gazes himself blind at the monumental white shroud that wraps all the prospect around him. And of all these things the Albino Whale was the symbol. Wonder ye then at the fiery hunt?

1854

In 1770 a frustrated inventor named Wolfgang von Kempelen built a contraption that would become the world's most famous robot. It was an automaton designed to resemble a sorcerer—full-sized, bearded, and wearing a silk turban— and when cranked up by von Kempelen it was able to play a remarkably skilled game of chess. The Turk, as it was called, permanently sat beside a large wooden cabinet, inside of which were housed the elaborate brass gears that made his mind tick. For almost a hundred years, and under four different owners, the Turk played countless exquisite games of chess, supposedly losing only to a young Russian soldier after a five-hour match. The Turk played against Voltaire, and won. Against Catherine the Great, and won. Against Benjamin Franklin, King George III, and even Napoleon Bonaparte—who supposedly tried to cheat three times— beating them all in a pinch. It's said that during a tour of Great Britain the Turk even beat Charles Babbage, the British mathematician who would go on to invent the earliest known principles for computer programming. This was an age of wonder, after all, a period that inspired the hot air balloon, the sewing machine, the elevator, the rifle. Observers weren't sure whether the Turk was alive, possessed, or a machine merely mimicking the movements of a man, but there it was, before their eyes, a marvel of modernity that seemed to be harkening, as one witness put it, "the arrival of inanimate reason." I often wonder, when I'm reading about the

Turk, whether his audiences would have been as convinced of his intelligence if his chess playing hadn't been as good as it apparently was. In other words, was his attempting to play chess what impressed the Turk's audience, or would attempting to play chess—but losing all his matches—not be proof enough of the Turk's intelligence? What are the signs of a mind at work? And what is it that we really want from intelligence: the problem solved, or the problem solving? At the height of the Turk's popularity, he traveled across the Atlantic for a series of matches in America, stopping in Boston, Philadelphia, New York, and then Baltimore, where a twenty-six-year-old writer paid a dollar to watch the Turk, and then walked back to his apartment to write "The Turkish Chess Player," an essay that exposed for the first time in print that the chess-playing Turk was actually a hoax: just a puppet being manipulated by a man in a box. In this investigatory essay, Edgar Allan Poe developed a style of inquiry that he later made famous in his popular "tales of ratiocination"—"The Purloined Letter," "The Murders in the Rue Morgue," and "The Mystery of Marie Roget"—a series of stories that are propelled through their mysteries by a consciousness that evolves before our eyes on the page. It wonders, it riffs, it asks questions and then asks more. It follows the whims of a theory, backs off, tries again, stumbles into something that feels solid, and holds on. "The theme of these stories," Poe once wrote, "is the exercise of ingenuity in trying to solve a problem." When he claimed in his essay that the Turk was a hoax, he was right—it was—but the details of his theory were wrong.

It isn't until this year, when the Turk is finally lost in a fire, that the last man who owned him reveals in *Chess Monthly* how the Turk appeared so real. But by the time of this explanation, the Turk is already ash, and there is no way to prove what he actually was.

A Chapter on Autography

The MS. of Mr. Irving has little about it indicative of his genius. Certainly, no one could suspect from it any nice finish in the writer's composition; nor is this nice finish to be found. The letters now before us vary remarkably in appearance; and those of late date are not nearly so well written as the more antique. Mr. Irving has traveled much, has seen many vicissitudes, and has been so thoroughly satiated with fame as to grow slovenly in the performance of his literary tasks. This slovenliness has affected his handwriting. But even from his earlier MSS. there is little to be gleaned, except the ideas of simplicity and precision. It must be admitted, however, that this fact, in itself, is characteristic of the literary manner, which, however excellent, has no prominent or very remarkable feature.

Mr. Bryant's MS. puts us entirely at fault. It is one of the most commonplace clerk's hands which we ever encountered, and has no character about it beyond that of the day book and ledger. He writes, in short, what mercantile men and professional penmen call a fair hand, but what artists term an abominable one. Among its regular up and down strokes, waving lines and hair lines, systematic taperings and flourishes, we look in vain for the force, polish, and decision of the poet. The picturesque, to be sure, is equally deficient in his chirography and in his poetical productions.

H. W. Longfellow, Professor of Moral Philosophy at Harvard, is entitled to the first place among the poets of America—certainly to the first place among those who have put themselves prominently forth as poets. His good qualities are all of the highest order, while his sins are chiefly those of affectation and imitation—an imitation sometimes verging on downright theft. His MS. is remarkably good, and is fairly exemplified in the signature. We see here plain indications of the force, vigor, and glowing richness of his literary style; the delicate and steady finish of his compositions. The man who writes thus may not accomplish much, but what he does, will always be thoroughly done. The main beauty, or at least one great beauty of his poetry, is that of proportion; another, is a freedom from extraneous embellishment. He oftener runs into affectation through his endeavors at simplicity, than through any other cause. Now this rigid simplicity and proportion are easily perceptible in the MS., which, altogether, is a very excellent one.

Mr. Everett's MS. is a noble one. It has about it an air of deliberate precision emblematic of the statesman, and a mingled grace and solidity betokening the scholar. Nothing can be more legible, and nothing need be more uniform. The man who writes thus will never grossly err in judgment, otherwise; but we may also venture to say that he will never attain the loftiest pinnacle of renown. The letters before us have a seal of red wax, with an oval device bearing the initials E. E., and surrounded with a scroll, inscribed with some Latin words which are illegible.

Mr. Cooper's MS. is very bad—unformed, with little of distinction character about it, and varying greatly in different epistles. In most of those before us a steel pen has been employed, the lines are crooked, and the whole chirography has a constrained and schoolboyish air. The paper is fine, and of a bluish tint. A wafer is always used. Without appearing ill-natured, we could scarcely draw any inferences from such a MS. Cooper has seen many vicissitudes, and it is probable that he has not always written thus. Whatever are his faults, his genius cannot be doubted.

Professor Palfrey is known to the public principally through his editorship of the *North American Review*. He has a reputation for scholarship; and many of the articles which are attributed to his pen evince that this reputation is well based, so far as the common notion of scholarship extends. For the best, he seems to dwell altogether within the narrow world of his own conceptions; imprisoning them by the very barrier which he has erected against the conceptions of others. His MS. shows a total deficiency in the sense of the beautiful. It has great pretension—great straining after effect; but is altogether one of the most miserable MSS. in the world—forceless, graceless, tawdry, vacillating, and unpicturesque. The signature conveys but a faint idea of its extravagance. However much we may admire the mere knowledge of the man who writes thus, it will not do to place any dependence upon his wisdom or upon his tatste.

Professor Henry, of Bristol College, is chiefly known by his contributions to our Quarterlies, and as one of the originators of the *New York Review*, in conjunction with Dr. Hawks and Prof. Anthon. His chirography is now neat and picturesque (much resembling that of Judge Tucker), and now excessively scratchy, clerky and slovenly, so that it is nearly impossible to say anything about it, except that it indicates a vacillating disposition, with unsettled ideas of the beautiful. None of his epistles, in regard to their chirography, end as well as they begin. This trait denotes fatigability. His signature, which is bold and decided, conveys not the faintest idea of the general MS.

Mr. Ralph Waldo Emerson belongs to a class of gentlemen with whom we have no patience whatever—the mystics for mysticism's sake. Quintilian mentions a pedant who taught obscurity, and who once said to a pupil, "This is excellent, for I do not understand it myself." How the good man would have chuckled over Mr. E! His present rôle seems to be the out-Carlyling Carlyle. Lycophron Tenebrosus is a fool to him. The best answer to his twaddle is *cui bono?*—a very little Latin phrase very generally mistranslated and misunderstood—*cui bono?*—to whom is it a benefit! If not to Mr. Emerson individually, then surely to no man living. His love of the obscure does not prevent him, nevertheless, from the composition of occasional poems in which beauty is apparent by flashes. Several of his effusions appeared in the *Western Messenger*—more in the *Dial,* of which he is the soul—or the sun—or the shadow. We remember the "Sphynx," the "Problem," the "Snow Storm," and some fine old verses entitled, "Oh, fair and stately maid whose eye." His MS. is bad, sprawling, illegible, and irregular, although sufficiently bold. This latter may be, and no doubt is, only a portion of his general affectation.

Mr. Horace Greeley, present editor of the *Tribune,* and formerly of the *New Yorker,* has for many years been remarked as one of the most able and honest of American editors. He has written much and invariably well. His political knowledge is equal to that of any of his contemporaries—his general information extensive. As a *belles lettres* critic he is entitled to high respect. His MS. is a remarkable one—having about it a peculiarity that we know not how better to designate than to converse of the picturesque. His characters are scratchy and irregular, ending with an abrupt taper—if we may be allowed this contradiction in terms, where we have the facsimile to prove that there is no contradiction in fact. All abrupt MSS., save this, have square or concise terminations of the letters. The whole chirography puts us in mind of a jig. We can fancy the writer jerking up his hand from the paper, at the end of each word, and indeed, of each letter. What mental idiosyncrasy lies *perdu* beneath all this, is more than we can say, but we will venture to assert that Mr. Greeley (whom we do not know personally) is, personally, a very remarkable man.

John Greenleaf Whittier is placed by his particular admirers in the very front rank of American poets. We are not disposed, however, to agree with their decision in every respect. Mr. Whittier is a fine versifier, so far as strength is regarded, independently of modulation. His subjects, too, are usually chosen with the view of affording scope to a certain *vivida vis* of expression, which seems to be his *forte;* but in taste, and especially in imagination, which Coleridge has just styled the soul of all poetry, he is even remarkably deficient. His themes are never to our liking. His chirography is an ordinary clerk's hand, affording little indication of character.

The chirography of Ex-President Adams (whose poem, "The Wants of Man," has, of late, attracted much attention), is remarkable for a certain steadiness of purpose pervading the whole, and overcoming even the constitutional tremulousness of the writer's hand. Wavering in every letter, the MS. has yet a firm, regular, and decisive appearance. It is also very legible.

1 8 5 8

This year, at three o'clock one morning, two ships are an-
chored in the middle of the Atlantic, idling stern-to-stern: an
American navy frigate and a British marines steamer, each carrying beneath their decks miles of spun copper wire, wrapped
in black iron, coated in black rubber. Without any speeches
or drumrolls, a soldier takes the ends of the two ships' wires
and solders between them a single penny before lifting up the
wire and then throwing it overboard. For the next nine days,
while sailing back to their respective ports, the two ships send
messages to each other across the black slack and the space
that is widening along it. This is the first time in human history that people have been able to remain in direct communication beyond the edges of each other's horizons. Messages
that had once taken weeks to cross the ocean are now traveling electrically at nearly the speed of light. It is the year that
Gray's Anatomy is first published in London, the year Charles
Darwin presents a paper on natural selection, and the year a
single nerve cell is first glimpsed beneath a microscope, allowing all those thoughts in all those minds throughout the
world—thrumming and sparking and jolting inside us all—to
be recognized for the first time as electrical themselves. Eventually this discovery will teach us about neurons, and how
they tingle with messages throughout their own bodies, electrical signals that speed across the surface of each neuron—
starting at the tip of their axon, zipping to the edge of their
dendrite—until, having felt their way across that body, the

signals pause for a moment before they leap out into a void and onto the next neuron, breaching the tiny space that separates it from others. Every new thought, we learn this year, requires a leap of faith. "Wonder—" writes Emily Dickinson, "is not precisely Knowing and not precisely Knowing not—"

EMILY DICKINSON

To Recipient Unknown

1

Dear Master

I am ill—but grieving more that you are ill, I make my stronger hand work long eno' to tell you—I thought perhaps you were in Heaven, and when you spoke again, it seemed quite sweet, and wonderful, and surprised me so—I wish that you were well. I would that all I love, should be weak no more. The Violets are by my side—the Robin very near—and "Spring"—they say, Who is she—going by the door—Indeed it is God's house—and these are gates of Heaven, and to and fro, the angels go, with their sweet postillions—I wish that I were great, like Mr. Michael Angelo, and could paint for you. You ask me what my Flowers said—then they were disobedient—I gave them messages—They said what the lips in the West, say, when the sun goes down, and so says the Dawn—Listen again, Master—I did not tell you that today had been the Sabbath Day. Each Sabbath on the sea, makes me count the Sabbaths, till we meet on the shore—and whether the hills will look as blue as the sailors say—I cannot stay any longer tonight, for this pain denies me—How strong when weak to recollect, and easy quite, to love. Will you tell me, please to tell me, soon as you are well—

2

oh—did I offend it—Daisy—Daisy—offend it—who bends her smaller life to his meeker every day—who only asks—a task—something to do for love of it—some little way she cannot guess to make that master glad—A love so big it scares her, rushing among her small heart—pushing aside the

blood—and leaving her (all) faint and white in the gust' arm—Daisy—
who never flinched thro' that awful parting—but held her life so tight he
should not see the wound—who would have sheltered him in her childish
bosom—only it was'nt big eno' for a Guest so large—*This* Daisy—grieve
her Lord—and yet it (she) often blundered—perhaps she grieved (grazed)
his taste—perhaps her odd—Backwoodsman (ways) (teased) his finer sense
(nature)—Daisy knows all that—but must she go unpardoned—teach her
grace—(preceptor) teach her majesty—Slow (Dull) at patrician things—
Even the wren open her nest learns (knows) more than Daisy dares—
Low at the knee that bore her once unto (wordless) rest, Daisy kneels, a
culprit—tell her her fault—Master—if it is small eno to cancel with *her
life,* she is satisfied—but punish—dont banish her—Shut her in prison—
Sir—only pledge that you will forgive—sometime—before the grave, and
Daisy will not mind—she will awake in your likeness—Wonder stings me
more than the Bee—who did never sting me—but made gay music with
his might wherever I did go—Wonder wastes my pound, you said I had
no size to spare—You send the water over the Dam in my brown eyes—
I've got a cough as big as a thimble—but I dont care for that—I've got a
Tomahawk in my side but that dont hurt me much, Her Master stabs her
more—Wont he come to her—or will he let her seek him, never minding
so long wandering (, if) to him at last—Oh how the sailor strains, when his
boat is filling—Oh how the dying tug, till the angel comes. Master—open
your life wide, and take me in forever, I will never be tired—I will never be
noisy when you want to be still—I will be your best little girl—nobody else
will see me, but you—but that is enough—I shall not want any more—and
all that Heaven will (only) disappoint me—(because) will be it's not so dear

3

Master,
If you saw a bullet hit a bird—and he told you he was'nt shot—you might
weep at his courtesy, but you would certainly doubt his word—One drop
more from the gash that stains your Daisy's bosom—then would you
believe? Thomas' faith in anatomy—was stronger than his faith in faith.
God made me—(Master—) I did'nt be—myself—*I* dont know how it
was done—He built the heart in me—Bye and bye it outgrow me—and
like the little mother—with the big child—I got tired holding him—I

heard of a thing called "Redemption"—which rested men and women—
You remember I asked you for it—you gave me something else—I forgot the
Redemption (and) was tired—no more—I am older—tonight, Master—
but the love is the same so are the moon and the crescent—if it had been
God's will that I might breathe where you breathed—and find the place—
myself—at night—if I (can) never forget that I am not with you and
that sorrow and frost are nearer than I—if I wish with a might I cannot
repress—that mine were the Queen's place—the love of the—Plantagenet
is my only apology—To come nearer than Presbyteries—and nearer than
the new coat—that the Tailor made—the prank of the Heart at play on the
Heart—in holy Holiday—is forbidden me—You make me say it over—I
fear you laugh—when I do not see—"Chillon" is not funny. Have you the
Heart in your breast—Sir—is it set like mine—a little to the left—has it
the misgiving—if it wake in the night—perchance—itself to it—a timbrel
is it—itself to it a tune? These things are (holy), Sir, I tough them (hallowed), but persons who pray—dare remark "Father!" You say I do not
tell you all—Daisy "confessed—and denied not." Vesuvius dont talk—
Etna—dont—said a syllable—one of them—a thousand years ago, and
Pompeii heard it, and hid forever—She could'nt look the world in the
face, afterward—I suppose—Bashful Pompeii! "Tell you of the want"—
you know what a leech is, dont you—and Daisy's arm is small—and you
have felt the Horizon—hav'nt you—and did the sea—(n)ever come so
close as to make you dance? I dont know what you can do for It—thank
you—Master—but if I had the Beard on my cheek—(like you—)and
you— had Daisy's petals—and you cared so for me—what would become
of you? Could you forget me in fight, or flight—or the foreign land? Could
Carlo, and you and I walk in the meadows an hour—and nobody care
but the Bobolink—and *his*—a *silver* scruple? I used to think when I died
I could see you—so I died as fast as I could—but the "Corporation" are
going (too)—so Heaven wont be sequestered—at all (now)—Say I may
wait for you—Say I need to go with no stranger to the to me—untried
(fold) I waited a long time—Master—but I can wait more—wait till my
hazel hair is dappled—and you carry the cane—then I can look at my
watch—and if the Day is too far declined—we can take the chances (for)
Heaven—What would you do with me if I came "in white"? Have you the
little chest to put the alive—in? I want to see you more—Sir—than all I
wish for in this world—and the wish—altered a little—will be my only

one—for the skies—Could you come to New England—(Would) you come to Amherst—Would you like to come—Master? Would Daisy disappoint you—no she would'nt—Sir—it were comfort forever—just to look in your face, while you looked in mine—then I could play in the woods— till Dark—till you take me where sundown cannot find us—and the true keep coming—till the town is full. I did'nt think to tell you, you did'nt come to me "in white"—nor ever told me why—No rose, yet felt myself a' bloom, No Bird—yet rode in Ether.

1865

This is the last year of the Civil War and there is still little knowledge of antiseptics. Soldiers are dying from gangrene more frequently than from bullets, their bodies slowly putrefying out from under them into mush. Before the start of the war, the new Washington Monument had just begun to emerge, but construction on it has stalled now at fewer than a hundred feet. Walt Whitman can almost see it as he stares out a window in a makeshift hospital: a white rectangular box sticking up out of the ground, its peak not yet completed, its direction unknown. By the end of the war, more than six hundred thousand soldiers will be dead, more American casualties in just four years than during the American Revolution, the War of 1812, the Mexican-American War, the Spanish-American War, World War I, World War II, and the Korean War combined. "It is everywhere," Whitman wrote, no longer willing to acknowledge death by name. It is not just present in the numbers one hears between battles; it's also cloaked around the hundreds of thousands of women who wear nothing but mourning black, in the photographs of battlefields that make corpses works of art, in the daily lists of casualties filling up the local papers—"slightly, in the shoulder," "severely, in the groin," "mortally, in the breast"—in one of which Whitman found his own brother's name. That's why he initially came to Washington, DC. But now it's three years later, and Walt Whitman is nearing his six hundredth visit to an army hospital, his one hundred thousandth patient. From here on out, he will never again write confidently about the future of his country. He will never write brashly about the destiny of its people, or of freedom, or of hope. He will write a lot more prose. In *Memoranda During the War,* a small collection of essays he self-published and gave away, he focuses intentionally on very small subjects—a soldier from Kansas, a soldier from Brooklyn, bugle calls, pencils, lamplight, weather—as if chastening his earlier proclivity for a gesture that might make sense of the whole war at once. "Its interior history," Whitman says of the war, "will not only never be written . . . but can never even be suggested." Instead, he tries sharing his own private experience of the war, focusing on the things that left him baffled, anxious, outraged, changed. On the weather that he notices in the capital, for example, Whitman writes,

> The sky, dark blue, the transparent night, the planets, the moderate west wind, the elastic temperature, the unsurpassable miracle of that great star, and the young and swelling moon swimming in the west, suffused the soul.

It is a simple sentence, and one that may seem characteristic of those catalogues Whitman unfurled in his youth as he made his way processionally toward some big idea. But there's also a lot of tension here. Lurking behind the prettiness of the catalogue and its parts is a pressure that builds with each successive clause, postponing that predicate just a little bit longer—and then a little bit more—straining against our capacity to keep track of those parts, to measure their meaning, to hold things together—our breath, our faith, a country, etc.—until, finally, or maybe too late, Whitman gives us a verb, "suffused," a word to help release all the pressure in the sentence, syntactically, barometrically, maybe even in our souls. What I love about this sentence is that I'm never quite sure, every time when I reach it, whether or not it has worked, whether or not I believe it.

WALT WHITMAN

The Weather—Does it Sympathize with These Times?

Whether the rains, the heat and cold, and what underlies them all, are affected with what affects man in masses, and follow his play of passionate action, strain'd stronger than usual, and on a larger scale than usual—whether this, or no, it is certain that there is now, and has been for twenty months or more on this American Continent North, many a remarkable, many an unprecedented expression of the subtile world of air above us and around us. There, since this War, and the wide and deep National agitation, strange analogies, different combinations, a different sunlight, or absence of it; different products even out of the ground. After every great battle, a great storm. Even civic events, the same. On Saturday last, a forenoon like whirling demons, dark, with slanting rain, full of rage; and then the afternoon, so calm, so bathed with flooding splendor from heaven's most excellent sun, with atmosphere of sweetness; so clear, it show'd the stars, long, long before they were due. As the President came out on the Capitol portico, a curious little white cloud, the only one in that part of the sky, appear'd like a hovering bird, right over him.

Indeed, the heavens, the elements, all the meteorological influences, have run riot for weeks past. Such caprices, abruptest alternation of frowns and beauty, I never knew. It is a common remark that (as last Summer was different in its spells of intense heat from any proceeding it,) the Winter just completed has been without parallel. It has remain'd so down to the hour I am writing. Much of the day-time of the past month was sulky, with leaden heaviness, fog, interstices of bitter cold, and some insane storms. But there have been samples of another description. Nor earth, nor sky ever knew spectacles of superber beauty than some of the nights have lately been here.

The western star, Venus, in the earlier hours of evening, has never been so large, so clear; it seems as if it told something, as if it held rapport indulgent with humanity, with us Americans. Five or six nights since, it hung close by the moon, then a little past its first quarter. The star was wonderful, the moon like a young mother. The sky, dark blue, the transparent night, the planets, the moderate west wind, the elastic temperature, the unsurpassable miracle of that great star, and the young and swelling moon swimming in the west, suffused the soul. Then I heard, slow and clear, the deliberate notes of a bugle come up out of the silence, sounding so good through the night's mystery, no hurry, but firm and faithful, floating along, rising, falling leisurely, with here and there a long-drawn note; the bugle, well play'd, sounding tattoo, in one of the army Hospitals near here, where the wounded (some of them personally so dear to me,) are lying in their cots, and many a sick boy come down to the war from Illinois, Michigan, Wisconsin, Iowa, and the rest.

1874

Fifty years from now, in 1920, the poet William Carlos Williams will publish *Kora in Hell,* a book that is composed almost entirely of prose. Written in short imaginative bursts during which Williams allowed his mind to move freely "from one thing to another," the book is an attempt to illustrate how the imagination really works, allowing us as readers to bear witness to the messiness of a mind as it bumps into new discoveries, new feelings, new freedoms. Today, *Kora in Hell* is considered one of the most successful realizations of Williams's belief that "a new rhythm is a new mind," but at the time of its publication the book was widely criticized by contemporary writers who had considered themselves champions of the "new." Wallace Stevens called it "rubbish." H.D. said it was "flippant." And Ezra Pound, who two years later would help T. S. Eliot edit and publish *The Waste Land,* called the book "incoherent." So let me propose a field trip to help us gain some perspective. This year, in Paris, there's been such tremendous political upheaval since the beheading of King Louis XVI that over the past few decades the country has seen a constitutional monarchy, a republic, a restoration of the monarchy, a socialist regime, and an erstwhile Napoleon. In response, some artists have tried to counter these disruptions by continuing to produce the same monumental, genteel, and smooth-surfaced paintings that Europe has perfected over the past three centuries: realistic depictions of historical events, Christian mythology, and very rich people.

In fact, these are paintings that look so real we feel as if we could step through their frames and march into battle with Charlemagne. And they are meant to. They want us to forget that what we are looking at are representations of things, so that we can believe without distraction in what those things represent: patriotism, morality, the divine presence of Christ in France. The paintings are propaganda, in other words. And after that, maybe they're decorative. So this year, when half a dozen artists stage an exhibition of their paintings that have been composed improvisationally, outside of their studios, in natural light, without models or props or the crutch of trans- parent cultural archetypes, the leading art critic of the day calls the show "an exhibition of moral depravity." The most popular painter in France warns the public that the artists behind these paintings are trying to "pollute the nation's treasures with unhealthy decadence." And a member of the Senate likens the exhibit to "the end of France as we know it." After all, these paintings are bucking the status quo in France by trying to not be realistic. They are trying, instead, to be representations. Their themes are indefinite—sunsets, flow- ers, rivers, air—their colors are unnatural—pastel shimmers, purple shadows, lime-and-mauve suns—and their brush- strokes are broken and visibly rough—dabs, dots, smears, and blobs—so that their canvases end up looking as if they were vibrating before us, thrumming, glistening, dripping, shifting, and therefore drawing our attention to the fact that they are art, they are made, this is painting, that is canvas, these are not replications of nonfictional realities, but expressions, renditions, interpretations, impressions. In the fin de siècle world of the French Impressionists, the reality that's depicted on these blurry but bold canvases is variable, porous, and purposely unstable, emphasizing therefore not what is being depicted but how each of us individually processes perception, how experience is layered, and knowledge uncertain.

A Matisse

On the french grass, in that room on Fifth Ave., lay that woman who had never seen my own poor land. The dust and noise of Paris had fallen from her with the dress and underwear and shoes and stockings which she had just put aside to lie bathing in the sun. So too she lay in the sunlight of the man's easy attention. His eye and the sun had made day over her. She gave herself to them both for there was nothing to be told. Nothing is to be told to the sun at noonday. A violet clump before her belly mentioned that it was spring. A locomotive could be heard whistling beyond the hill. There was nothing to be told. Her body was neither classic nor whatever it might be supposed. There she lay and her curving torso and thighs were close upon the grass and violets.

So he painted her. The sun had entered his head in the color of sprays of flaming palm leaves. They had been walking for an hour or so after leaving the train. They were hot. She had chosen the place to rest and he had painted her resting, with interest in the place she had chosen.

It had been a lovely day in the air.—What pleasant women are these girls of ours! When they have worn clothes and take them off it is with an effect of having performed a small duty. They return to the sun with a gesture of accomplishment.—Here she lay in this spot today not like Diana or Aphrodite but with better proof than they of regard for the place she was in. She rested and he painted her.

It was the first of summer. Bare as was his mind of interest in anything save the fullness of his knowledge, into which her simple body entered as into the eye of the sun himself, so he painted her. So she came to America.

No man in my country has seen a woman naked and painted her as if he knew anything except that she was naked. No woman in my country is naked except at night.

In the french sun, on the french grass, in a room on Fifth Ave., a french girl lies and smiles at the sun without seeing us.

1882

Some day in the future, a descendant of those Impressionists will mix his paints with hydrochloric acid, splatter them onto a canvas, and wait to see what happens. Within seconds of hitting the canvas, the acid-mixed paints will start to corrode and disappear, eventually leaving nothing but a very fancy frame around a very empty hole—a work of art that hangs today in a gallery of the Tate Modern. There will also be a piece of music called *Drip,* composed of running water, an empty vessel, and a page of sheet music containing just a five-word sentence: "Fill the vessel with water." In the future, some poems will be composed of just one word, or they'll be typographically shaped to look like a bird, or presented as lists of the chemical compounds found in the paper on which they are printed. There will be a performer who sits silently in the atrium of a building for 736 hours, inviting people to come and sit across from her as she stares into their eyes. A fourteen-foot-long shark suspended in formaldehyde will be called *The Physical Impossibility of Death in the Mind of Someone Living,* and we will take it seriously. As we will a three hundred page novel that never uses the letter *e;* a novel containing four hundred thousand words, seven hundred pages, and only one sentence; and another that will be tattooed, one word at a time, on 2,095 people. These works of art will come from mediums that will undergo revolutions at some point in their futures, and they are mediums that will continue to evolve, far beyond the horizons that any artists imagine today. The history of art is a history of expansion, after all. If art is to grow, to survive, to remain culturally relevant, it has to question the rules that it's inherited from earlier generations. It has to break those rules when necessary, find new rules with which to challenge itself, new reasons and new strategies for breaking those new rules, and then brand-new sets of rules to grapple with again. Before the Impressionists were ever acknowledged as genuine artists, they were derided as frauds because they "ignored the elementary rules of painting." As one critic succinctly put it,

> Without the integrity of the line, it is impossible to reproduce any form, and without realistic colors one cannot give form the appearance of reality. . . . The challenge for the true painter is to fulfill his vision within the constraints of line and color, otherwise he is not painting.

This is the kind of criticism that will be lodged against every new movement in art. In fact, replace the word *painter* with the word *poet* in the criticism above, and the words *line and color* with *meter and form,* and we are reading the same sort of criticism that will be written about free-verse poets at the end of the nineteenth century. Replace those same words with *novelist* and *plot and character,* and we're back at the start of the twentieth century, when Joyce was struggling against the claims that all he wrote was doggerel. Replace them with *musician* and *serialism and tone,* or *choreographer* and *rhythm and beauty,* or *filmmaker* and *sequencing and point of view,* and it's clear that we've got anxiety when it comes to breaking rules. And yet this is the year when Virginia Woolf is born, when Igor Stravinsky is born, when Robert Goddard is born, and when God is declared dead. What better time, therefore, to begin to get over our anxieties about art, to start realizing as a culture that those artists who test boundaries and the conventions of their art forms are doing so as visionaries on behalf of the human spirit, exploring what else is possible in these forms we've all inherited.

1888

Which is why we should return to America now: here, in the middle of the country, on a bank of the Mississippi, at the exact spot where Lewis and Clark departed from St. Louis in pursuit of the western wilds of the Louisiana Purchase. Their mission in 1804 was to find a water route to the Pacific Ocean, to evaluate the five hundred million acres that the United States had acquired, and to determine what to do with all that new space. Almost immediately upon the expedition's return, St. Louis became known as America's symbolic gateway to that frontier, the last major city that pioneers would encounter before entering the terra incognita of their maps—that wide western margin in the nation's imagination. Eighty years later, however, that margin now contains Topeka, Denver, Salt Lake City, and San Francisco. By now there is a railroad running across the country, and sixty million Americans filling two billion acres. When T. S. Eliot is born in St. Louis this year, the city is in its heyday, but it will never be great again. "The American frontier is closed," the U.S. Census Bureau will declare. According to that office, "At present all unsettled areas have been broken into by isolated bodies . . . such that there can hardly be said any longer to be a frontier line." Thanks to American exceptionalism, and thanks to Manifest Destiny, and thanks to the Monroe Doctrine, the country is now filled up. Frederick Jackson Turner will famously write about this moment, explaining that "the American frontier created the American identity . . . by breaking the bonds of

European customs, by offering new and unique experiences, and by calling on the formation of new institutions to accommodate these activities." And so, as Turner wonders, if the source of this creativity has already been exhausted, where will Americans find their creativity now? Those white American settlers who have started to make their homes west of the Mississippi will find upon arriving there mounds of buffalo bodies. For centuries, buffalo were the most important source of food for Native American tribes, but over the past few decades, both the buffalo and the Natives have started to disappear. In Kansas one year, the winner of a shooting contest killed two hundred ten buffalo in just forty-one minutes. Hunting parties convened on trains to ride through massive herds and decimate thousands at a time. And Buffalo Bill Cody once bragged to reporters that he killed four thousand single-handedly in one year alone. When Yellowstone National Park took a tally of its buffalo in 1890, it found that there were only twenty-three animals left. It is not a coincidence, say historians, that Native populations have also dropped by more than 50 percent. "The buffalo hunter," says one army general, "has done more to defeat the Indian nations in a few years' time than our soldiers have done in fifty." The buffalo were eradicated to thin out the Indians, and the Indians were eradicated to make way for the whites, and now those whites are gathering up those giant buffalo bodies—the carcasses of animals that had once run so densely across the country that "they darkened the whole earth," as Horace Greeley once put it—and are processing them for hides, soap, fuel, and glue in factories that are suddenly springing up across the country. One of those factories covers a hundred acres, processes five thousand tons of buffalo every month, and this year records a profit in excess of $17 million. One of its largest exports is something called bone black, a very expensive kind of paint that's made by charring the bones of buffalo, pulverizing them into dust, and then mixing in a binder such as urine, fat, or blood. It is a very dark color. According to artists, it is the purest, deepest, most mysterious black there is, something we can find in Picasso, Rembrandt, Caravaggio, Lascaux. It's been prized by artists for as long as art has existed, because it is a black that reflects nothing else. As Kandinsky once put it, it contains the possibility of every kind of silence, and never betrays any of them to us. Which is why, in a few years' time, when all those carcasses disappear, the pioneers who reached the Midwest and decided to settle down, supplementing their farming by gathering up and selling those buffalo by the ton, will begin to raid the burial grounds of the Indians who had lived there, selling the human bones for a few cents apiece. How many shadows and cloaks and dark nights in paintings have inside them hiding the bones of something else? "I said to my soul, be still, and wait . . ." T. S. Eliot once wrote, "So the darkness shall be the light." Silence is never silent, no matter what Kandinsky said. As the generation of modernists who are born this year will learn, when one frontier ends you must open up another.

T. S. ELIOT

The Dry Salvages

I

I do not know much about gods; but I think that the river
Is a strong brown god—sullen, untamed and intractable,
Patient to some degree, at first recognised as a frontier;
Useful, untrustworthy, as a conveyor of commerce;
Then only a problem confronting the builder of bridges.
The problem once solved, the brown god is almost forgotten
By the dwellers in cities—ever, however, implacable,
Keeping his seasons and rages, destroyer, reminder
Of what men choose to forget. Unhonoured, unpropitiated
By worshippers of the machine, but waiting, watching and waiting.
His rhythm was present in the nursery bedroom,
In the rank ailanthus of the April dooryard,
In the smell of grapes on the autumn table,
And the evening circle in the winter gaslight.

The river is within us, the sea is all about us;
The sea is the land's edge also, the granite
Into which it reaches, the beaches where it tosses
Its hints of earlier and other creation:
The starfish, the hermit crab, the whale's backbone;
The pools where it offers to our curiosity
The more delicate algae and the sea anemone.
It tosses up our losses, the torn seine,
The shattered lobsterpot, the broken oar
And the gear of foreign dead men. The sea has many voices,

Many gods and many voices.
                              The salt is on the briar rose,
The fog is in the fir trees.
                              The sea howl
And the sea yelp, are different voices
Often together heard; the whine in the rigging,
The menace and caress of wave that breaks on water,
The distant rote in the granite teeth,
And the wailing warning from the approaching headland
Are all sea voices, and the heaving groaner
Rounded homewards, and the seagull:
And under the oppression of the silent fog
The tolling bell
Measures time not our time, rung by the unhurried
Ground swell, a time
Older than the time of chronometers, older
Than time counted by anxious worried women
Lying awake, calculating the future,
Trying to unweave, unwind, unravel
And piece together the past and the future,
Between midnight and dawn, when the past is all deception,
The future futureless, before the morning watch
When time stops and time is never ending;
And the ground swell, that is and was from the beginning,
Clangs
The bell.

II

Where is there an end of it, the soundless wailing,
The silent withering of autumn flowers
Dropping their petals and remaining motionless;
Where is there an end to the drifting wreckage,
The prayer of the bone on the beach, the unprayable
Prayer at the calamitous annunciation?

There is no end, but addition: the trailing
Consequence of further days and hours,
While emotion takes to itself the emotionless
Years of living among the breakage
Of what was believed in as the most reliable—
And therefore the fittest for renunciation.

There is the final addition, the failing
Pride or resentment at failing powers,
The unattached devotion which might pass for devotionless,
In a drifting boat with a slow leakage,
The silent listening to the undeniable
Clamor of the bell of the last annunciation.

Where is the end of them, the fishermen sailing
Into the wind's tail, where the fog cowers?
We cannot think of a time that is oceanless
Or of an ocean not littered with wastage
Or of a future that is not liable
Like the past, to have no destination.

We have to think of them as forever bailing,
Setting and hauling, while the North East lowers
Over shallow banks unchanging and erosionless
Or drawing their money, drying sails at dockage;
Not as making a trip that will be unpayable
For a haul that will not bear examination.

There is no end of it, the voiceless wailing,
No end to the withering of withered flowers,
To the movement of pain that is painless and motionless,
To the drift of the sea and the drifting wreckage,
The bone's prayer to Death its God. Only the hardly, barely prayable
Prayer of the one Annunciation.

It seems, as one becomes older,
That the past has another pattern, and ceases to be a mere sequence—
Or even development: the latter a partial fallacy,
Encouraged by superficial notions of evolution,
Which becomes, in the popular mind, a means of disowning the past.
The moments of happiness—not the sense of well-being,
Fruition, fulfilment, security or affection,
Or even a very good dinner, but the sudden illumination—
We had the experience but missed the meaning,
And approach to the meaning restores the experience
In a different form, beyond any meaning
We can assign to happiness. I have said before
That the past experience revived in the meaning
Is not the experience of one life only
But of many generations—not forgetting
Something that is probably quite ineffable:
The backward look behind the assurance
Of recorded history, the backward half-look
Over the shoulder, towards the primitive terror.
Now, we come to discover that the moments of agony
(Whether, or not, due to misunderstanding,
Having hoped for the wrong things or dreaded the wrong things,
Is not in question) are likewise permanent
With such permanence as time has. We appreciate this better
In the agony of others, nearly experienced,
Involving ourselves, than in our own.
For our own past is covered by the currents of action,
But the torment of others remains an experience
Unqualified, unworn by subsequent attrition.
People change, and smile: but the agony abides.
Time the destroyer is time the preserver,
Like the river with its cargo of dead Negroes, cows and chicken coops,
The bitter apple and the bite in the apple.
And the ragged rock in the restless waters,
Waves wash over it, fogs conceal it;
On a halcyon day it is merely a monument,

In navigable weather it is always a seamark
To lay a course by: but in the sombre season
Or the sudden fury, is what it always was.

III

I sometimes wonder if that is what Krishna meant—
Among other things—or one way of putting the same thing:
That the future is a faded song, a Royal Rose or a lavender spray
Of wistful regret for those who are not yet here to regret,
Pressed between yellow leaves of a book that has never been opened.
And the way up is the way down, the way forward is the way back.
You cannot face it steadily, but this thing is sure,
That time is no healer: the patient is no longer here.
When the train starts, and the passengers are settled
To fruit, periodicals and business letters
(And those who saw them off have left the platform)
Their faces relax from grief into relief,
To the sleepy rhythm of a hundred hours.
Fare forward, travellers! not escaping from the past
Into different lives, or into any future;
You are not the same people who left that station
Or who will arrive at any terminus,
While the narrowing rails slide together behind you;
And on the deck of the drumming liner
Watching the furrow that widens behind you,
You shall not think "the past is finished"
Or "the future is before us."
At nightfall, in the rigging and the aerial,
Is a voice descanting (though not to the ear,
The murmuring shell of time, and not in any language)
"Fare forward, you who think that you are voyaging;
You are not those who saw the harbour
Receding, or those who will disembark.
Here between the hither and the farther shore
While time is withdrawn, consider the future

And the past with an equal mind.
At the moment which is not of action or inaction
You can receive this: 'on whatever sphere of being
The mind of a man may be intent
At the time of death'—that is the one action
(And the time of death is every moment)
Which shall fructify in the lives of others:
And do not think of the fruit of action.
Fare forward.
                    O voyagers, O seamen,
You who came to port, and you whose bodies
Will suffer the trial and judgement of the sea,
Or whatever event, this is your real destination."
So Krishna, as when he admonished Arjuna
On the field of battle.
                              Not fare well,
But fare forward, voyagers.

IV

Lady, whose shrine stands on the promontory,
Pray for all those who are in ships, those
Whose business has to do with fish, and
Those concerned with every lawful traffic
And those who conduct them.

   Repeat a prayer also on behalf of
Women who have seen their sons or husbands
Setting forth, and not returning:
Figlia del tuo figlio,
Queen of Heaven.

   Also pray for those who were in ships, and
Ended their voyage on the sand, in the sea's lips
Or in the dark throat which will not reject them
Or wherever cannot reach them the sound of the sea bell's
Perpetual angelus.

V

To communicate with Mars, converse with spirits,
To report the behaviour of the sea monster,
Describe the horoscope, haruspicate or scry,
Observe disease in signatures, evoke
Biography from the wrinkles of the palm
And tragedy from fingers; release omens
By sortilege, or tea leaves, riddle the inevitable
With playing cards, fiddle with pentagrams
Or barbituric acids, or dissect
The recurrent image into pre-conscious terrors—
To explore the womb, or tomb, or dreams; all these are usual
Pastimes and drugs, and features of the press:
And always will be, some of them especially
When there is distress of nations and perplexity
Whether on the shores of Asia, or in the Edgware Road.
Men's curiosity searches past and future
And clings to that dimension. But to apprehend
The point of intersection of the timeless
With time, is an occupation for the saint—
No occupation either, but something given
And taken, in a lifetime's death in love,
Ardour and selflessness and self-surrender.
For most of us, there is only the unattended
Moment, the moment in and out of time,
The distraction fit, lost in a shaft of sunlight,
The wild thyme unseen, or the winter lightning
Or the waterfall, or music heard so deeply
That it is not heard at all, but you are the music
While the music lasts. These are only hints and guesses,
Hints followed by guesses; and the rest
Is prayer, observance, discipline, thought and action.
The hint half guessed, the gift half understood, is Incarnation.
Here the impossible union.
Of spheres of existence is actual,
Here the past and future

Are conquered, and reconciled,
Where action were otherwise movement
Of that which is only moved
And has in it no source of movement—
Driven by daemonic, chthonic
Powers. And right action is freedom
From past and future also.
For most of us, this is the aim
Never here to be realised;
Who are only undefeated
Because we have gone on trying;
We, content at the last
If our temporal reversion nourish
(Not too far from the yew-tree)
The life of significant soil.

1903

So let's lay it out. I believe the goal of art is to break us all open, to make us all raw, to destabilize our understanding of ourselves and of our world so that we might experience both anew, with fresh eyes, and with the possibility of recognizing something that we had not recognized before. In over forty books, W. E. B. Du Bois will explore the issues of race, class, peace, and justice by harnessing a remarkable variety of literary forms, including newspaper invectives, stories, poems, memoirs, hymns, a children's book, a play, and even an encyclopedia that he left unfinished but in which he had hoped to embrace, as he put it, "absolutely everything I can." He was a polymath but also a perfectionist. An iconoclast who fiercely embraced tradition. A politician who refused to compromise. He's the man who not only helped found the NAACP, but who was fired as its president twice. He fought his whole life to pass the 1964 Civil Rights Act, yet died in Africa in self-imposed exile. He was an uncompromisingly independent thinker, in other words, which is a quality we can still powerfully experience in his essays because they make us feel as if we are privy to ideas and possibilities that may not exist anywhere else. So this year, when Du Bois publishes his masterful collection *The Souls of Black Folk,* it's not surprising to find in its midst an essay that is distinguished not only by the subtle potency of its argument but also by the fact that it isn't actually an essay. "Of the Coming of John" is a story, and yet Du Bois never referred to it as anything but an essay, as if he wanted to speak not only to the unity of races but perhaps of the genres too. "Between the sterner flights of logic," Du Bois once wrote about genre mingling, "I have sought to set some little alightings. . . . They are tributes to Beauty, and perhaps unworthy to stand alone; yet perversely, in my mind . . . I know not whether I mean the Thought for the Fancy, or the Fancy for the Thought, or why the book trails off to playing, rather than standing strong on unanswering fact."

W. E. B. Du Bois

Of the Coming of John

What bring they 'neath the midnight,
Beside the River–sea?
They bring the human heart wherein
No nightly calm can be;
That droppeth never with the wind,
Nor drieth with the dew;
O calm it, God; thy calm is broad
  To cover spirits too.
    The river floweth on.

Mrs. Browning.

Carlisle Street runs westward from the centre of Johnstown, across a great black bridge, down a hill and up again, by little shops and meat-markets, past single-storied homes, until suddenly it stops against a wide green lawn. It is a broad, restful place, with two large buildings outlined against the west. When at evening the winds come swelling from the east, and the great pall of the city's smoke hangs wearily above the valley, then the red west glows like a dreamland down Carlisle Street, and, at the tolling of the supper-bell, throws the passing forms of students in dark silhouette against the sky. Tall and black, they move slowly by, and seem in the sinister light to flit before the city like dim warning ghosts. Perhaps they are; for this is Wells Institute, and these black students have few dealings with the white city below.

And if you will notice, night after night, there is one dark form that ever hurries last and late toward the twinkling lights of Swain Hall,—for Jones is never on time. A long, straggling fellow he is, brown and hard-haired, who seems to be growing straight out of his clothes, and walks with a half-apologetic roll. He used perpetually to set the quiet dining-room into waves of merriment, as he stole to his place after the bell had tapped for prayers; he seemed so perfectly awkward. And yet one glance at his face made one forgive him much,—that broad, good-natured smile in which lay no bit of art or artifice, but seemed just bubbling good-nature and genuine satisfaction with the world.

He came to us from Altamaha, away down there beneath the gnarled oaks of Southeastern Georgia, where the sea croons to the sands and the sands listen till they sink half drowned beneath the waters, rising only here and there in long, low islands. The white folk of Altamaha voted John a good boy,—fine plough-hand, good in the rice-fields, handy everywhere, and always good-natured and respectful. But they shook their heads when his mother wanted to send him off to school. "It'll spoil him,—ruin him," they said; and they talked as though they knew. But full half the black folk followed him proudly to the station, and carried his queer little trunk and many bundles. And there they shook and shook hands, and the girls kissed him shyly and the boys clapped him on the back. So the train came, and he pinched his little sister lovingly, and put his great arms about his mother's neck, and then was away with a puff and a roar into the great yellow world that flamed and flared about the doubtful pilgrim. Up the coast they hurried, past the squares and palmettos of Savannah, through the cotton-fields and through the weary night, to Millville, and came with the morning to the noise and bustle of Johnstown.

And they that stood behind, that morning in Altamaha, and watched the train as it noisily bore playmate and brother and son away to the world, had thereafter one ever-recurring word,—"When John comes." Then what parties were to be, and what speakings in the churches; what new furniture in the front room,—perhaps even a new front room; and there would be a new schoolhouse, with John as teacher; and then perhaps a big wedding; all this and more—when John comes. But the white people shook their heads.

At first he was coming at Christmas-time,—but the vacation proved too short; and then, the next summer,—but times were hard and schooling costly, and so, instead, he worked in Johnstown. And so it drifted to the next summer, and the next,—till playmates scattered, and mother grew gray, and sister went up to the Judge's kitchen to work. And still the legend lingered,—"When John comes."

Up at the Judge's they rather liked this refrain; for they too had a John—a fair-haired, smooth-faced boy, who had played many a long summer's day to its close with his darker namesake. "Yes, sir! John is at Princeton, sir," said the broad-shouldered gray-haired Judge every morning as he marched down to the post-office. "Showing the Yankees what a Southern gentleman can do," he added; and strode home again with his letters and papers. Up at the great pillared house they lingered long over the Princeton letter,—the Judge and his frail wife, his sister and growing daughters. "It'll make a man of him," said the Judge, "college is the place." And then he asked the shy little waitress, "Well, Jennie, how's your John?" and added reflectively, "Too bad, too bad your mother sent him off—it will spoil him." And the waitress wondered.

Thus in the far-away Southern village the world lay waiting, half consciously, the coming of two young men, and dreamed in an inarticulate way of new things that would be done and new thoughts that all would think. And yet it was singular that few thought of two Johns,—for the black folk thought of one John, and he was black; and the white folk thought of another John, and he was white. And neither world thought the other world's thought, save with a vague unrest.

Up in Johnstown, at the Institute, we were long puzzled at the case of John Jones. For a long time the clay seemed unfit for any sort of moulding. He was loud and boisterous, always laughing and singing, and never able to work consecutively at anything. He did not know how to study; he had no idea of thoroughness; and with his tardiness, carelessness, and appalling good-humor, we were sore perplexed. One night we sat in faculty meeting, worried and serious; for Jones was in trouble again. This last escapade was too much, and so we solemnly voted "that Jones, on account of repeated disorder and inattention to work, be suspended for the rest of the term."

It seemed to us that the first time life ever struck Jones as a really serious thing was when the Dean told him he must leave school. He stared at the gray-haired man blankly, with great eyes. "Why,—why," he faltered, "but—I haven't graduated!" Then the Dean slowly and clearly explained, reminding him of the tardiness and the carelessness, of the poor lessons and neglected work, of the noise and disorder, until the fellow hung his head in confusion. Then he said quickly, "But you won't tell mammy and sister,—you won't write mammy, now will you? For if you won't I'll go out into the city and work, and come back next term and show you something." So the

Dean promised faithfully, and John shouldered his little trunk, giving neither word nor look to the giggling boys, and walked down Carlisle Street to the great city, with sober eyes and a set and serious face.

Perhaps we imagined it, but someway it seemed to us that the serious look that crept over his boyish face that afternoon never left it again. When he came back to us he went to work with all his rugged strength. It was a hard struggle, for things did not come easily to him,—few crowding memories of early life and teaching came to help him on his new way; but all the world toward which he strove was of his own building, and he builded slow and hard. As the light dawned lingeringly on his new creations, he sat rapt and silent before the vision, or wandered alone over the green campus peering through and beyond the world of men into a world of thought. And the thoughts at times puzzled him sorely; he could not see just why the circle was not square, and carried it out fifty-six decimal places one midnight,—would have gone further, indeed, had not the matron rapped for lights out. He caught terrible colds lying on his back in the meadows of nights, trying to think out the solar system; he had grave doubts as to the ethics of the Fall of Rome, and strongly suspected the Germans of being thieves and rascals, despite his text-books; he pondered long over every new Greek word, and wondered why this meant that and why it couldn't mean something else, and how it must have felt to think all things in Greek. So he thought and puzzled along for himself,—pausing perplexed where others skipped merrily, and walking steadily through the difficulties where the rest stopped and surrendered.

Thus he grew in body and soul, and with him his clothes seemed to grow and arrange themselves; coat sleeves got longer, cuffs appeared, and collars got less soiled. Now and then his boots shone, and a new dignity crept into his walk. And we who saw daily a new thoughtfulness growing in his eyes began to expect something of this plodding boy. Thus he passed out of the preparatory school into college, and we who watched him felt four more years of change, which almost transformed the tall, grave man who bowed to us commencement morning. He had left his queer thought-world and come back to a world of motion and of men. He looked now for the first time sharply about him, and wondered he had seen so little before. He grew slowly to feel almost for the first time the Veil that lay between him and the white world; he first noticed now the oppression that had not seemed oppression before, differences that erstwhile seemed natural, restraints and slights that in his boyhood days had gone unnoticed or been greeted with a laugh. He felt angry now when men did not call him "Mister," he clenched his hands at the "Jim Crow" cars, and chafed at the color-line that hemmed in him and his. A tinge of sarcasm crept into his speech, and a vague bitterness into his life; and he sat long hours wondering and planning a way around these crooked things. Daily he found himself shrinking from the choked and narrow life of his native town. And yet he always planned to go back to Altamaha,—always planned to work there. Still, more and more as the day approached he hesitated with a nameless dread; and even the day after graduation he seized with eagerness the offer of the Dean to send him North with the quartette during the summer vacation, to sing for the Institute. A breath of air before the plunge, he said to himself in half apology.

It was a bright September afternoon, and the streets of New York were brilliant with moving men. They reminded John of the sea, as he sat in the square and watched them, so changelessly changing, so bright and dark, so grave and gay. He scanned their rich and faultless clothes, the way they carried their hands, the shape of their hats; he peered into the hurrying carriages. Then, leaning back with a sigh, he said, "This is the World." The notion suddenly seized him to see where the world was going; since many of the richer and brighter seemed hurrying all one way. So when a tall, light-haired young man and a little talkative lady came by, he rose half hesitatingly and followed them. Up the street they went, past stores and gay shops, across a broad square, until with a hundred others they entered the high portal of a great building.

He was pushed toward the ticket-office with the others, and felt in his pocket for the new five-dollar bill he had hoarded. There seemed really no time for hesitation, so he drew it bravely out, passed it to the busy clerk, and received simply a ticket but no change. When at last he realized that he had paid five dollars to enter he knew not what, he stood stock-still amazed. "Be careful," said a low voice behind him; "you must not lynch the colored gentleman simply because he's in your way," and a girl looked up roguishly into the eyes of her fair-haired escort. A shade of annoyance passed over the escort's face. "You *will* not understand us at the South," he said half impatiently, as if continuing an argument. "With all your professions, one never sees in the North so cordial and intimate relations between white and black as are everyday occurrences with us. Why, I remember my closest playfellow in boyhood was a little Negro named after me, and surely no two,—*well!*" The man stopped short and flushed to the roots of his hair, for there directly beside his reserved orchestra chairs sat the Negro he had stumbled over in the hallway. He hesitated and grew pale with anger, called the usher and gave him his card, with a few peremptory words, and slowly sat down. The lady deftly changed the subject.

All this John did not see, for he sat in a half-daze minding the scene about him; the delicate beauty of the hall, the faint perfume, the moving myriad of men, the rich clothing and low hum of talking seemed all a part of a world so different from his, so strangely more beautiful than anything he had known, that he sat in dreamland, and started when, after a hush, rose high and clear the music of Lohengrin's swan. The infinite beauty of the wail lingered and swept through every muscle of his frame, and put it all a-tune. He closed his eyes and grasped the elbows of the chair, touching unwittingly the lady's arm. And the lady drew away. A deep longing swelled in all his heart to rise with that clear music out of the dirt and dust of that low life that held him prisoned and befouled. If he could only live up in the free air where birds sang and setting suns had no touch of blood! Who had called him to be the slave and butt of all? And if he had called, what right had he to call when a world like this lay open before men?

Then the movement changed, and fuller, mightier harmony swelled away. He looked thoughtfully across the hall, and wondered why the beautiful gray-haired woman looked so listless, and what the little man could be whispering about. He would not like to be listless and idle, he thought, for he felt with the music the movement of power within him. If he but had some master-work, some life-service, hard,—aye, bitter hard, but without the cringing and sickening servility, without the cruel hurt that hardened his heart and soul. When at last a soft sorrow crept across the violins, there came to him the vision of a far-off home,—the great eyes of his sister, and the dark drawn face of his mother. And his heart sank below the waters, even as the sea-sand sinks by the shores of Altamaha, only to be lifted aloft again with that last ethereal wail of the swan that quivered and faded away into the sky.

It left John sitting so silent and rapt that he did not for some time notice the usher tapping him lightly on the shoulder and saying politely, "Will you step this way, please, sir?" A little surprised, he arose quickly at the last tap, and, turning to leave his seat, looked full into the face of the fair-haired young man. For the first time the young man recognized his dark boyhood playmate, and John knew that it was the Judge's son. The white John started, lifted his hand, and then froze into his chair; the black John smiled lightly, then grimly, and followed the usher down the aisle. The manager was sorry, very, very sorry,—but he explained that some mistake had been made in selling the gentleman a seat already disposed of; he would refund the money, of course,—and indeed felt the matter keenly, and so forth, and—before he had finished John was gone, walking hurriedly across the square and down the broad streets, and as he passed the park he buttoned his coat and said, "John Jones, you're a natural-born fool." Then he went to his lodgings and wrote a letter, and tore it up; he wrote another, and threw it in the fire. Then he seized a scrap of paper and wrote: "Dear Mother and Sister—I am coming—John."

"Perhaps," said John, as he settled himself on the train, "perhaps I am to blame myself in struggling against my manifest destiny simply because it looks hard and unpleasant. Here is my duty to Altamaha plain before me; perhaps they'll let me help settle the Negro problems there,—perhaps they won't. 'I will go in to the King, which is not according to the law; and if I perish, I perish.'" And then he mused and dreamed, and planned a life-work; and the train flew south.

Down in Altamaha, after seven long years, all the world knew John was coming. The homes were scrubbed and scoured,—above all, one; the gardens and yards had an unwonted trimness, and Jennie bought a new gingham. With some finesse and negotiation, all the dark Methodists and Presbyterians were induced to join in a monster welcome at the Baptist Church; and as the day drew near, warm discussions arose on every corner as to the exact extent and nature of John's accomplishments. It was noon-tide on a gray and cloudy day when he came. The black town flocked to the depot, with a little of the white at the edges,—a happy throng, with "Good-mawnings" and "Howdys" and laughing and joking and jostling. Mother sat yonder in the window watching; but sister Jennie stood on the platform, nervously fingering her dress,—tall and lithe, with soft brown skin and loving eyes peering from out a tangled wilderness of hair. John rose gloomily as the train stopped, for he was thinking of the "Jim Crow" car; he stepped to the platform, and paused: a little dingy station, a black crowd gaudy and dirty, a half-mile of dilapidated shanties along a straggling ditch of mud. An overwhelming sense of the sordidness and narrowness of it all seized him; he looked in vain for his mother, kissed coldly the tall, strange girl who called him brother, spoke a short, dry word here and there; then, lingering neither for hand-shaking nor gossip, started silently up the street, raising his hat merely to the last eager old aunty, to her open-mouthed astonishment. The people were distinctly bewildered. This silent, cold man,—was this John? Where was his smile and hearty hand-grasp? "'Peared kind o' down in the mouf," said the Methodist preacher thoughtfully. "Seemed monstus stuck up," complained a Baptist sister. But the white postmaster from the edge of the crowd expressed the opinion of his folks plainly. "That damn Nigger," said he, as he shouldered the mail and arranged his tobacco, "has gone North and got plum full o' fool notions; but they won't work in Altamaha." And the crowd melted away.

The meeting of welcome at the Baptist Church was a failure. Rain spoiled the barbecue, and thunder turned the milk in the ice-cream. When the speaking came at night, the house was crowded to overflowing. The three preachers had especially prepared themselves, but somehow John's manner seemed to throw a blanket over everything,—he seemed so cold and preoccupied, and had so strange an air of restraint that the Methodist brother could not warm up to his theme and elicited not a single "Amen"; the Presbyterian prayer was but feebly responded to, and even the Baptist preacher, though he wakened faint enthusiasm, got so mixed up in his favorite sentence that he had to close it by stopping fully fifteen minutes sooner than he meant. The people moved uneasily in their seats as John rose to reply. He spoke slowly and methodically. The age, he said, demanded new ideas; we were far different from those men of the seventeenth and eighteenth centuries,—with broader ideas of human brotherhood and destiny. Then he spoke of the rise of charity and popular education, and particularly of the spread of wealth and work. The question was, then, he added reflectively, looking at the low discolored ceiling, what part the Negroes of this land would take in the striving of the new century. He sketched in vague outline the new Industrial School that might rise among these pines, he spoke in detail of the charitable and philanthropic work that might be organized, of money that might be saved for banks and business. Finally he urged unity, and deprecated especially religious and denominational bickering. "To-day," he said, with a smile, "the world cares little whether a man be Baptist or Methodist, or indeed a churchman at all, so long as he is good and true. What difference does it make whether a man be baptized in river or washbowl, or not at all? Let's leave all that little-ness, and look higher." Then, thinking of nothing else, he slowly sat down. A painful hush seized that crowded mass. Little had they understood of what he said, for he spoke an unknown tongue, save the last word about baptism; that they knew, and they sat very still while the clock ticked. Then at last a low suppressed snarl came from the Amen corner, and an old bent man arose, walked over the seats, and climbed straight up into the pulpit. He was wrinkled and black, with scant gray and tufted hair; his voice and hands shook as with palsy; but on his face lay the intense rapt look of the religious fanatic. He seized the Bible with his rough, huge hands; twice he raised it inarticulate, and then fairly burst into words, with rude and awful eloquence. He quivered, swayed, and bent; then rose aloft in perfect majesty, till the people moaned and wept, wailed and shouted, and a wild shrieking arose from the corners where all the pent-up feeling of the hour gathered itself and rushed into the air. John never knew clearly what the old man said; he only felt himself held up to scorn and scathing denunciation for trampling on the true Religion, and he realized with amazement that all unknowingly he had put rough, rude hands on something this little world held sacred. He arose silently, and passed out into the night. Down toward the sea he went, in the fitful starlight, half conscious of the girl who fol-lowed timidly after him. When at last he stood upon the bluff, he turned to his little sister and looked upon her sorrowfully, remembering with sudden pain how little thought he had given her. He put his arm about her and let her passion of tears spend itself on his shoulder.

Long they stood together, peering over the gray unresting water.

"John," she said, "does it make every one—unhappy when they study and learn lots of things?"

He paused and smiled. "I am afraid it does," he said.

"And, John, are you glad you studied?"

"Yes," came the answer, slowly but positively.

She watched the flickering lights upon the sea, and said thoughtfully, "I wish I was unhappy,—and—and," putting both arms about his neck, "I think I am, a little, John."

It was several days later that John walked up to the Judge's house to ask for the privilege of teaching the Negro school. The Judge himself met him at the front door, stared a little hard at him, and said brusquely, "Go 'round to the kitchen door, John, and wait." Sitting on the kitchen steps,

John stared at the corn, thoroughly perplexed. What on earth had come over him? Every step he made offended some one. He had come to save his people, and before he left the depot he had hurt them. He sought to teach them at the church, and had outraged their deepest feelings. He had schooled himself to be respectful to the Judge, and then blundered into his front door. And all the time he had meant right,—and yet, and yet, somehow he found it so hard and strange to fit his old surroundings again, to find his place in the world about him. He could not remember that he used to have any difficulty in the past, when life was glad and gay. The world seemed smooth and easy then. Perhaps,—but his sister came to the kitchen door just then and said the Judge awaited him.

The Judge sat in the dining-room amid his morning's mail, and he did not ask John to sit down. He plunged squarely into the business. "You've come for the school, I suppose. Well, John, I want to speak to you plainly. You know I'm a friend to your people. I've helped you and your family, and would have done more if you hadn't got the notion of going off. Now I like the colored people, and sympathize with all their reasonable aspirations; but you and I both know, John, that in this country the Negro must remain subordinate, and can never expect to be the equal of white men. In their place, your people can be honest and respectful; and God knows, I'll do what I can to help them. But when they want to reverse nature, and rule white men, and marry white women, and sit in my parlor, then, by God! we'll hold them under if we have to lynch every Nigger in the land. Now, John, the question is, are you, with your education and Northern notions, going to accept the situation and teach the darkies to be faithful servants and laborers as your fathers were,—I knew your father, John, he belonged to my brother, and he was a good Nigger. Well—well, are you going to be like him, or are you going to try to put fool ideas of rising and equality into these folks' heads, and make them discontented and unhappy?"

"I am going to accept the situation, Judge Henderson," answered John, with a brevity that did not escape the keen old man. He hesitated a moment, and then said shortly, "Very well,—we'll try you awhile. Good-morning."

It was a full month after the opening of the Negro school that the other John came home, tall, gay, and headstrong. The mother wept, the sisters sang. The whole white town was glad. A proud man was the Judge, and it was a goodly sight to see the two swinging down Main Street together. And yet all did not go smoothly between them, for the younger man could not and did not veil his contempt for the little town, and plainly had his heart set on New York. Now the one cherished ambition of the Judge was to see his son mayor of Altamaha, representative to the legislature, and— who could say?—governor of Georgia. So the argument often waxed hot between them. "Good heavens, father," the younger man would say after dinner, as he lighted a cigar and stood by the fireplace, "you surely don't expect a young fellow like me to settle down permanently in this—this God-forgotten town with nothing but mud and Negroes?" "*I* did," the Judge would answer laconically; and on this particular day it seemed from the gathering scowl that he was about to add something more emphatic, but neighbors had already begun to drop in to admire his son, and the conversation drifted.

"Heah that John is livenin' things up at the darky school," volunteered the postmaster, after a pause.

"What now?" asked the Judge, sharply.

"Oh, nothin' in particulah,—just his almighty air and uppish ways. B'lieve I did heah somethin' about his givin' talks on the French Revolution, equality, and such like. He's what I call a dangerous Nigger."

"Have you heard him say anything out of the way?"

"Why, no,—but Sally, our girl, told my wife a lot of rot. Then, too, I don't need to heah: a Nigger what won't say 'sir' to a white man, or—"

"Who is this John?" interrupted the son.

"Why, it's little black John, Peggy's son, your old playfellow."

The young man's face flushed angrily, and then he laughed.

"Oh," said he, "it's the darky that tried to force himself into a seat beside the lady I was escorting—"

But Judge Henderson waited to hear no more. He had been nettled all day, and now at this he rose with a half-smothered oath, took his hat and cane, and walked straight to the schoolhouse.

For John, it had been a long, hard pull to get things started in the rickety old shanty that sheltered his school. The Negroes were rent into factions for and against him, the parents were careless, the children irregular and dirty, and books, pencils, and slates largely missing. Nevertheless, he struggled hopefully on, and seemed to see at last some glimmering of dawn. The attendance was larger and the children were a shade cleaner this week. Even the booby class in reading showed a little comforting progress. So John settled himself with renewed patience this afternoon.

"Now, Mandy," he said cheerfully, "that's better; but you mustn't chop your words up so: 'If—the—man—goes.' Why, your little brother even wouldn't tell a story that way, now would he?"

"Naw, suh, he cain't talk."

"All right; now let's try again: 'If the man—'"

"John!"

The whole school started in surprise, and the teacher half arose, as the red, angry face of the Judge appeared in the open doorway.

"John, this school is closed. You children can go home and get to work. The white people of Altamaha are not spending their money on black folks to have their heads crammed with impudence and lies. Clear out! I'll lock the door myself."

Up at the great pillared house the tall young son wandered aimlessly about after his father's abrupt departure. In the house there was little to interest him; the books were old and stale, the local newspaper flat, and the women had retired with headaches and sewing. He tried a nap, but it was too warm. So he sauntered out into the fields, complaining disconsolately, "Good Lord! how long will this imprisonment last!" He was not a bad fellow,—just a little spoiled and self-indulgent, and as headstrong as his proud father. He seemed a young man pleasant to look upon, as he sat on the great black stump at the edge of the pines idly swinging his legs and smoking. "Why, there isn't even a girl worth getting up a respectable flirtation with," he growled. Just then his eye caught a tall, willowy figure hurrying toward him on the narrow path. He looked with interest at first, and then burst into a laugh as he said, "Well, I declare, if it isn't Jennie, the little brown kitchen-maid! Why, I never noticed before what a trim little body she is. Hello, Jennie! Why, you haven't kissed me since I came home," he said gaily. The young girl stared at him in surprise and confusion,—faltered something inarticulate, and attempted to pass. But a wilful mood had seized the young idler, and he caught at her arm. Frightened, she slipped by; and half mischievously he turned and ran after her through the tall pines.

Yonder, toward the sea, at the end of the path, came John slowly, with his head down. He had turned wearily homeward from the schoolhouse; then, thinking to shield his mother from the blow, started to meet his sister as she came from work and break the news of his dismissal to her. "I'll go away," he said slowly; "I'll go away and find work, and send for them. I cannot live here longer." And then the fierce, buried anger surged up into his throat. He waved his arms and hurried wildly up the path.

The great brown sea lay silent. The air scarce breathed. The dying day bathed the twisted oaks and mighty pines in black and gold. There came from the wind no warning, not a whisper from the cloudless sky. There was only a black man hurrying on with an ache in his heart, seeing neither sun nor sea, but starting as from a dream at the frightened cry that woke the pines, to see his dark sister struggling in the arms of a tall and fair-haired man.

He said not a word, but, seizing a fallen limb, struck him with all the pent-up hatred of his great black arm; and the body lay white and still beneath the pines, all bathed in sunshine and in blood. John looked at it dreamily, then walked back to the house briskly, and said in a soft voice, "Mammy, I'm going away—I'm going to be free."

She gazed at him dimly and faltered, "No'th, honey, is yo' gwine No'th agin?"

He looked out where the North Star glistened pale above the waters, and said, "Yes, mammy, I'm going—North."

Then, without another word, he went out into the narrow lane, up by the straight pines, to the same winding path, and seated himself on the great black stump, looking at the blood where the body had lain. Yonder in the gray past he had played with that dead boy, romping together under the solemn trees. The night deepened; he thought of the boys at Johnstown. He wondered how Brown had turned out, and Carey? And Jones,—Jones? Why, *he* was Jones, and he wondered what they would all say when they knew, when they knew, in that great long dining-room with its hundreds of merry eyes. Then as the sheen of the starlight stole over him, he thought of the gilded ceiling of that vast concert hall, heard stealing toward him the faint sweet music of the swan. Hark! was it music, or the hurry and shouting of men? Yes, surely! Clear and high the faint sweet melody rose and fluttered like a living thing, so that the very earth trembled as with the tramp of horses and murmur of angry men.

He leaned back and smiled toward the sea, whence rose the strange melody, away from the dark shadows where lay the noise of horses galloping, galloping on. With an effort he roused himself, bent forward, and looked steadily down the pathway, softly humming the "Song of the Bride,"—

"Freudig geführt, ziehet dahin."

Amid the trees in the dim morning twilight he watched their shadows dancing and heard their horses thundering toward him, until at last they came sweeping like a storm, and he saw in front that haggard white-haired man, whose eyes flashed red with fury. Oh, how he pitied him,—pitied him,—and wondered if he had the coiling twisted rope. Then, as the storm burst round him, he rose slowly to his feet and turned his closed eyes toward the Sea.

And the world whistled in his ears.

1909

The maritime measurement "mark twain," which is a depth of twelve feet, is the point at which dangerously shallow water becomes safe for riverboats. But it is also the point at which safe water can suddenly turn dangerous.

MARK TWAIN

Letters from the Earth

Letter I

1

The Creator sat upon the throne, thinking. Behind Him stretched the illimitable continent of heaven, steeped in a glory of light and color; before Him rose the black night of Space, like a wall. His mighty bulk towered rugged and mountain-like into the zenith, and His divine head blazed there like a distant sun. At His feet stood three colossal figures, diminished to extinction, almost, by contrast—archangels—their heads level with His ancle-bone.

When the Creator had finished thinking, He said,

"I have thought. Behold!"

He lifted His hand, and from it burst a fountain-spray of fire, a million stupendous suns, which clove the blackness and soared, away and away and away, diminishing in magnitude and intensity as they pierced the far frontiers of Space, until at last they were but as diamond nail-heads sparkling under the domed vast roof of the universe.

At the end of an hour the Grand Council was dismissed.

2

They left the Presence impressed and thoughtful, and retired to a private place, where they might talk with freedom. None of the three seemed to want to begin, though all wanted somebody to do it. Each was burning to discuss the great event, but would prefer not to commit himself till he should know how the others regarded it. So there was some aimless and halting conversation about matters of no consequence, and this dragged tediously along, arriving nowhere, until at last the archangel Satan gathered his courage together—of which he had a very good supply—and broke ground. He said—

"We know what we are here to talk about, my lords, and we may as well put pretence aside, and begin. If this is the opinion of the Council—"

"It is, it is!" said Gabriel and Michael, gratefully interrupting.

"Very well, then, let us proceed. We have witnessed a wonderful thing; as to that, we are necessarily agreed. As to the value of it—if it has any— that is a matter which does not personally concern us. We can have as many opinions about it as we like, but that is our limit. We have no vote. I think Space was well enough, just as it was, and useful, too. Cold and dark—a restful place, now and then, after a season of the over-delicate climate and trying splendors of heaven. But these are details of no considerable moment; the new feature, the immense feature, is—what, gentlemen?"

"The invention and introduction of automatic, unsupervised, self-regulating *law* for the government of those myriads of whirling and racing suns and worlds!"

"That is it!" said Satan. "You perceive that it is a stupendous idea. Nothing approaching it has been evolved from the Master Intellect before. Law—*automatic* Law—exact and unvarying Law—requiring no watching, no correcting, no readjusting while the eternities endure! He said those countless vast bodies would plunge through the wastes of Space ages and ages, at unimaginable speed, around stupendous orbits, yet never collide, and never lengthen nor shorten their orbital periods by so much as the hundredth part of a second in two thousand years! That is the new miracle, and the greatest of all—*Automatic Law!* And He gave it a name—the LAW OF NATURE—and said Natural Law is the LAW OF GOD—interchangeable names for one and the same thing."

"Yes," said Michael, "and He said He would establish Natural Law— the Law of God—throughout His dominions, and its authority should be supreme and inviolable."

"Also," said Gabriel, "He said He would by and by create animals, and place them, likewise, under the authority of that Law."

"Yes," said Satan, "I heard Him, but did not understand. What *is* animals, Gabriel?"

"Ah, how should I know? How should any of us know? It is a new word."

[Interval of three centuries, celestial time—the equivalent of a hundred million years, earthly time. Enter a messenger-Angel.]

"My lords, He is making animals. Will it please you to come and see?"

They went, they saw, and were perplexed. Deeply perplexed—and the Creator noticed it, and said—

"Ask. I will answer."

"Divine One," said Satan, making obeisance, "what are they for?"

"They are an experiment in Morals and Conduct. Observe them, and be instructed."

There were thousands of them. They were full of activities. Busy, all busy—mainly in persecuting each other. Satan remarked—after examining one of them through a powerful microscope—

"This large beast is killing weaker animals, Divine One."

"The tiger—yes. The law of his nature is ferocity. The law of his nature is the law of God. He cannot disobey it."

"Then in obeying it he commits no offence, Divine One?"

"No, he is blameless."

"This other creature here, is timid, Divine One, and suffers death without resisting."

"The rabbit—yes. He is without courage. It is the law of his nature—the law of God. He must obey it."

"Then he cannot honorably be required to go counter to his nature and resist, Divine One?"

"No. No creature can be honorably required to go counter to the law of his nature—the law of God."

After a long time and many questions, Satan said—

"The spider kills the fly, and eats it; the bird kills the spider and eats it; the wildcat kills the goose; the—well, they all kill each other. It is murder all along the line. Here are countless multitudes of creatures, and they all kill, kill, kill, they are all murderers. And they are not to blame, Divine One?"

"They are not to blame. It is the law of their nature. And always the law of nature is the law of God. Now—observe—behold! A new creature—and the masterpiece—*Man!*"

Men, women, children, they came swarming in flocks, in droves, in millions.

"What shall you do with them, Divine One?"

"Put into each individual, in differing shades and degrees, all the various Moral Qualities, in mass, that have been distributed, a single distinguishing characteristic at a time, among the nonspeaking animal world—courage, cowardice, ferocity, gentleness, fairness, justice, cunning, treachery, magnanimity, cruelty, malice, malignity, lust, mercy, pity, purity, selfishness, sweetness, honor, love, hate, baseness, nobility, loyalty, falsity, veracity, untruthfulness—each human being shall have *all* of these in him, and they will constitute his nature. In some, there will be high and fine characteristics which will submerge the evil ones, and those will be called good men; in others the evil characteristics will have dominion, and those will be called bad men. Observe—behold—they vanish!"

"Whither are they gone, Divine One?"

"To the earth—they and all their fellow-animals."

"What is the earth?"

"A small globe I made, a time, two times and half a time ago. You saw it, but did not notice it in the explosion of worlds and suns that sprayed from my hand. Man is an experiment, the other animals are another experiment. Time will show whether they were worth the trouble. The exhibition is over; you may take your leave, my lords."

3

Several days passed by.

This stands for a long stretch of (our) time, since in heaven a day is as a thousand years.

Satan had been making admiring remarks about certain of the Creator's sparkling industries—remarks which, being read between the lines, were sarcasms. He had made them confidentially to his safe friends the other archangels, but they had been overheard by some ordinary angels and reported at Headquarters.

He was ordered into banishment for a day—the celestial day. It was a punishment he was used to, on account of his too flexible tongue. Formerly he had been deported into Space, there being nowhither else to send him, and had flapped tediously around, there, in the eternal night and the arctic chill; but now it occurred to him to push on and hunt up the Earth and see how the Human-Race experiment was coming along.

By and by he wrote home—very privately—to St. Michael and St. Gabriel about it.

Satan's Letter.

This is a strange place, an extraordinary place, and interesting. There is nothing resembling it at home. The people are all insane, the other animals are all insane, the Earth is insane, Nature itself is insane. Man is a marvelous curiosity. When he is at his very very best he is a sort of low grade nickel-plated angel; at his worst he is unspeakable, unimaginable; and first and last and all the time he is a sarcasm. Yet he blandly and in all sincerity calls himself the "noblest work of God." This is the truth I am telling you. And this is not a new idea with him, he has talked it through all the ages, and believed it. Believed it, and found nobody among all his race to laugh at it.

Moreover—if I may put another strain upon you—he thinks he is the Creator's pet. He believes the Creator is proud of him; he even believes the Creator loves him; has a passion for him; sits up nights to admire him; yes, and watch over him and keep him out of trouble. He prays to Him, and thinks He listens. Isn't it a quaint idea? Fills his prayers with crude and bald and florid flatteries of Him, and thinks He sits and purrs over these extravagancies and enjoys them. He prays for help, and favor, and protection, every day; and does it with hopefulness and confidence, too, although no prayer of his has ever been answered. The daily affront, the daily defeat, do not discourage him, he goes on praying just the same. There is something almost fine about this perseverance. I must put one more strain upon you: he thinks he is going to heaven!

He has salaried teachers who tell him that. They also tell him there is a hell, of everlasting fire, and that he will go to it if he doesn't keep the Commandments. What are the Commandments? They are a curiosity. I will tell you about them by and by.

Letter II

1

I have told you nothing about man that is not true. You must pardon me if I repeat that remark now and then in these letters; I want you to take seriously the things I am telling you, and I feel that if I were in your place and you in mine, I should need that reminder from time to time, to keep my credulity from flagging.

For there is nothing about Man that is not strange to an Immortal. He looks at nothing as we look at it, his sense of proportion is quite different from ours, and his sense of values is so widely divergent from ours, that with all our large intellectual powers it is not likely that even the most gifted among us would ever be quite able to understand it.

For instance, take this sample: he has imagined a heaven, and has left entirely out of it the supremest of all his delights, the one ecstasy that stands first and foremost in the heart of every individual of his race—and of ours—sexual intercourse!

It is as if a lost and perishing person in a roasting desert should be told by a rescuer he might choose and have all longed-for things but one, and he should elect to leave out water!

His heaven is like himself: strange, interesting, astonishing, grotesque. I give you my word, it has not a single feature in it that he *actually values.* It consists—utterly and entirely—of diversions which he cares next to nothing about, here in the earth, yet is quite sure he will like in heaven. Isn't it curious? Isn't it interesting? You must not think I am exaggerating, for it is not so. I will give you details.

Most men do not sing, most men cannot sing, most men will not stay when others are singing if it be continued more than two hours. Note that.

Only about two men in a hundred can play upon a musical instrument, and not four in a hundred have any wish to learn how. Set that down.

Many men pray, not many of them like to do it. A few pray long, the others make a short cut.

More men go to church than want to.

To forty-nine men in fifty the Sabbath Day is a dreary, dreary bore.

Of all the men in a church on a Sunday, two-thirds are tired when the service is half over, and the rest before it is finished.

The gladdest moment for all of them is when the preacher uplifts his hands for the benediction. You can hear the soft rustle of relief that sweeps the house, and you recognize that it is eloquent with gratitude.

All nations look down upon all other nations.

All nations dislike all other nations.

All white nations despise all colored nations, of whatever hue, and oppress them when they can.

White men will not associate with "niggers," nor marry them.

They will not allow them in their schools and churches.

All the world hates the Jew, and will not endure him except when he is rich.

I ask you to note all those particulars.

Further. All sane people detest noise.

All people, sane or insane, like to have variety in their life. Monotony quickly wearies them.

Every man, according to the mental equipment that has fallen to his share, exercises his intellect constantly, ceaselessly, and this exercise makes up a vast and valued and essential part of his life. The lowest intellect, like the highest, possesses a skill of some kind and takes a keen pleasure in testing it, proving it, perfecting it. The urchin who is his comrade's superior in games is as diligent and as enthusiastic in his practice as are the sculptor, the painter, the pianist, the mathematician and the rest. Not one of them could be happy if his talent were put under an interdict.

Now then, you have the facts. You know what the human race enjoys, and what it doesn't enjoy. It has invented a heaven, out of its own head, all by itself. guess what it is like! In fifteen hundred eternities you couldn't do it. The ablest mind known to you or me in fifty million aeons couldn't do it. Very well, I will tell you about it.

2

1. First of all, I recall to your attention the extraordinary fact with which I began. To-wit, that the human being, like the immortals, naturally places sexual intercourse far and away above all other joys—yet he has left it out of his heaven! The very thought of it excites him; opportunity sets him wild; in this state he will risk life, reputation, everything—even his queer heaven itself—to make good that opportunity and ride it to the overwhelming climax. From youth to middle age all men and all women prize copulation above all other pleasures combined, yet it is actually as I have said: it is not in their heaven, prayer takes its place.

They prize it thus highly; yet, like all their so-called "boons," it is a poor thing. At its very best and longest the act is brief beyond imagination—the imagination of an immortal, I mean. In the matter of repetition the man is limited—oh, quite beyond immortal conception. We who continue the act *and* its supremest ecstasies unbroken and without withdrawal for centuries, will never be able to understand or adequately pity the awful poverty of these people in that rich gift which, possessed as we possess it, makes all other possessions trivial and not worth the trouble of invoicing.

2. In man's heaven *everybody sings!* There are no exceptions. The man who did not sing on earth, sings there; the man who could not sing on earth is able to do it there. The universal singing is not casual, not occasional, not relieved by intervals of quiet; it goes on, all day long, and every day, during a stretch of twelve hours. And *everybody stays;* whereas in the earth the place would be empty in two hours. The singing is of hymns alone. Nay, it is of *one* hymn alone. The words are always the same, in number they are only about a dozen, there is no rhyme, there is no poetry: "Hosannah, hosannah, hosannah, Lord God of Sabaoth, 'rah! 'rah! 'rah! ssht!—boom! . . . a-a-ah!"

3. Meantime, *every person* is playing on a harp—those millions and millions! whereas not more than twenty in the thousand of them could play an instrument in the earth, or ever *wanted* to.

Consider the deafening hurricane of sound—millions and millions of voices screaming at once, and millions and millions of harps gritting their teeth at the same time! I ask you—is it hideous, is it odious, is it horrible?

Consider further: it is a *praise* service; a service of compliment, of flattery, of adulation! Do you ask who it is that is willing to endure this strange compliment, this insane compliment; and who not only endures it but likes it, enjoys it, requires it, *commands* it? Hold your breath!

It is God! This race's God, I mean. He sits on his throne, attended by his four and twenty elders and some other dignitaries pertaining to his court, and looks out over his miles and miles of tempestuous worshippers, and smiles, and purrs, and nods his satisfaction northward, eastward, southward; as quaint and naif a spectacle as has yet been imagined in this universe, I take it.

It is easy to see that the inventor of the heaven did not originate the idea, but copied it from the show-ceremonies of some sorry little sovereign State up in the back settlements of the Orient somewhere.

All sane white people *hate noise;* yet they have tranquilly accepted this kind of heaven—without thinking, without reflection, without examination—and they actually want to go to it! Profoundly devout old gray-headed men put in a large part of their time dreaming of the happy day when they will lay down the cares of this life and enter into the joys of that place. Yet you can see how unreal it is to them, and how little it takes a grip upon them as being *fact,* for they make no practical preparation for the great change: you never see one of them with a harp, you never hear one of them sing.

As you have seen, that singular show is a service of divine worship—a service of praise: praise by hymn, praise by instrumental ecstasies, praise by prostration. It takes the place of "church." Now then, in the earth these people cannot stand much church—an hour and a quarter is the limit, and they draw the line at once a week. That is to say, Sunday. One day in seven; and even then they do not look forward to it with longing. And so—consider what their heaven provides for them: "church" that lasts forever, and a *Sabbath that has no end!* They quickly weary of this brief hebdomadal Sabbath here, yet they long for that eternal one; they dream of it, they talk about it, they *think* they think they are going to enjoy it—with all their simple hearts they think they think they are going to be happy in it!

It is because they do not think *at all;* they only think they think. Whereas they can't think; not two human beings in ten thousand have anything to think with. And as to imagination—oh, well, look at their heaven! They accept it, they approve it, they admire it. That gives you their intellectual measure.

4. The inventor of their heaven empties into it all the nations of the earth, in one common jumble. All are on an equality absolute, no one of them ranking another; they have to be "brothers," they have to mix together, pray together, harp together, hosannah together—whites, niggers, Jews, everybody—there's no distinction. Here in the earth all nations hate each other, and every one of them hates the Jew. Yet every pious person adores that heaven and wants to get into it. He really does. And when he is in a holy rapture he thinks he thinks that if he were only there he would take all the populace to his heart, and hug, and hug, and hug!

He is a marvel—man is! I would I knew who invented him.

5. Every man in the earth possesses some share of intellect, large or small; and be it large or be it small he takes pride in it. Also his heart swells at mention of the names of the majestic intellectual chiefs of his race, and he loves the tale of their splendid achievements. For he is of their blood, and in honoring themselves they have honored him. Lo, what the mind of man can do! he cries; and calls the roll of the illustrious of all the ages; and points to the imperishable literatures they have given to the world, and the mechanical wonders they have invented, and the glories wherewith they

have clothed science and the arts; and to them he uncovers, as to kings, and gives to them the profoundest homage, and the sincerest, his exultant heart can furnish—thus exalting intellect above all things else in his world, and enthroning it there under the arching skies in a supremacy unapproachable. And then he contrives a heaven that hasn't a rag of intellectuality in it anywhere!

Is it odd, is it curious, is it puzzling? It is exactly as I have said, incredible as it may sound. This sincere adorer of intellect and prodigal rewarder of its mighty services here in the earth has invented a religion and a heaven which pay no compliments to intellect, offer it no distinctions, fling to it no largess: in fact, never even mention it.

By this time you will have noticed that the human being's heaven has been thought out and constructed upon an absolute definite plan; and that this plan is, that it shall contain, in labored detail, each and every imaginable thing that is repulsive to a man, and not a single thing he likes!

Very well, the further we proceed the more will this curious fact be apparent.

Make a note of it: in man's heaven there are no exercises for the intellect, nothing for it to live upon. It would rot there in a year—rot and stink. Rot and stink—and at that stage become holy. A blessed thing: for only the holy can stand the joys of that bedlam.

Letter III

You have noticed that the human being is a curiosity. In times past he has had (and worn out and flung away) hundreds and hundreds of religions; to-day he has hundreds and hundreds of religions, and launches not fewer than three new ones every year. I could enlarge that number and still be within the facts.

One of his principle religions is called the Christian. A sketch of it will interest you. It is set forth in detail in a book containing 2,000,000 words, called the Old and New Testaments. Also it has another name—The Word of God. For the Christian thinks every word of it was dictated by God—the one I have been speaking of.

It is full of interest. It has noble poetry in it; and some clever fables; and some blood-drenched history; and some good morals; and some execrable morals; and a wealth of obscenity; and upwards of a thousand lies.

This Bible is built mainly out of the fragments of older Bibles that had their day and crumbled to ruin. So it noticeably lacks in originality, necessarily. Its three or four most imposing and impressive events all happened in earlier Bibles; all its best precepts and rules of conduct come also from those Bibles; there are only two new things in it: hell, for one, and that singular heaven I have told you about.

What shall we do? If we believe, with these people, that their God invented these cruel things, we slander him; if we believe that these people invented them themselves, we slander *them*. It is an unpleasant dilemma in either case, for neither of these parties has done *us* any harm.

For the sake of tranquillity, let us take a side. Let us join forces with the people and put the whole ungracious burden upon *him*—heaven, hell, Bible and all. It does not seem right, it does not seem fair; and yet when you consider that heaven, and how crushingly charged it is with everything that is repulsive to a human being, how *can* we believe a human being invented it? And when I come to tell you about hell, the stain will be greater still, and you will be likely to say *No*, a man would not provide *that* place, for either himself or anybody else; he simply *couldn't*.

That innocent Bible tells about the Creation. Of what—the universe? Yes, the universe. In *six days!*

God did it. He did not call it the universe—that name is modern. His whole attention was upon *this world*. He constructed it in five days—and then? It took him only *one* day to make *twenty million suns and eighty million planets!*

What were they for—according to his idea? To furnish light for this little toy-world. That was his whole purpose; he had no other. *One* of the 20,000,000 suns (the smallest one), was to light it in the day-time, the rest were to help *one* of the universe's countless moons modify the darkness of its nights.

It is quite manifest that he believed his fresh-made skies were diamond-sown with those myriads of twinkling stars the moment his first-day's sun sank below the horizon; whereas, in fact not a single star winked in that black vault until three years and a half after that memorable week's formidable industries had been completed. Then one star appeared, all solitary and alone, and began to blink. Three years later another one appeared. The two blinked together for more than four years before a third joined them.

At the end of the first hundred years there were not yet twenty-five stars twinkling in the wide wastes of those gloomy skies. At the end of a thousand years not enough stars were yet visible to make a show. At the end of a million years only half of the present array had sent their light over the telescopic frontiers, and it took another million for the rest to follow suit, as the vulgar phrase goes. There being at that time no telescope, their advent was not observed.

For three hundred years, now, the Christian astronomer has known that his Deity *didn't* make the stars in those tremendous six days; but the Christian astronomer does not enlarge upon that detail. Neither does the priest.

In his Book, God is eloquent in his praises of his mighty works, and calls them by the largest names he can find—thus indicating that he has a strong and just admiration of magnitudes; yet he made those millions of prodigious suns to light this wee little orb, instead of appointing this orb's little sun to dance attendance upon *them*. He mentions Arcturus in his Book—you remember Arcturus; we went there once. *It* is one of this earth's night-lamps!—that giant globe which is 50,000 times as large as the earth's sun, and compares with it as a melon compares with a cathedral.

However, the Sunday school still teaches the child that Arcturus was created to help light this earth, and the child grows up and continues to believe it long after he has found out that the probabilities are against it being so.

According to the Book and its servants the universe is only six thousand years old. It is only within the last hundred years that studious, inquiring minds have found out that it is nearer a hundred million.

During the Six Days, God created man and the other animals.

He made a man and a woman and placed them in a pleasant garden, along with the other creatures. They all lived together there in harmony and contentment and blooming youth for some time; then trouble came. God had warned the man and the woman that they must not eat of the fruit of a certain tree. And he added a most strange remark: he said that if they ate of it they should surely *die*. Strange, for the reason that inasmuch as they had never seen a sample of death they could not possibly know what he meant. Neither would he nor any other god have been able to make those ignorant children understand what was meant, without furnishing a sample. The mere *word* could have no meaning for them, any more than it would have for an infant of days.

Presently a serpent sought them out privately, and came to them walking upright, which was the way of serpents in those days. The serpent said the forbidden fruit would store their vacant minds with knowledge. So they ate it, which was quite natural, for man is so made that he eagerly *wants to know;* whereas the priest, like God, whose imitator and representative he is, has made it his business from the beginning to keep him *from* knowing any useful thing.

Adam and Eve ate the forbidden fruit, and at once a great light streamed into their dim heads. They had acquired knowledge. What knowledge—useful knowledge? No—merely knowledge that there was such a thing as good, and such a thing as evil, and how to *do* evil. They *couldn't* do it before, therefore all their acts up to this time had been without stain, without blame, without offence.

But *now* they could do evil—and suffer for it; *now* they had acquired what the Church calls an invaluable possession, the Moral Sense; that sense which differentiates man from the beast and sets him *above* the beast. Instead of *below* the beast—where one would suppose his proper place would be, since he is always foul-minded and guilty and the beast always clean-minded and innocent. It is like valuing a watch that *must* go wrong, above a watch that *can't.*

The Church still prizes the Moral Sense as man's noblest asset to-day, although the Church knows God had a distinctly poor opinion of it and did what he could in his clumsy way to keep his happy Children of the Garden from acquiring it.

Very well, Adam and Eve now knew what evil was, and how to do it. They knew how to do various kinds of wrong things, and among them one principal one—the one God had his mind on principally. That one was the art and mystery of sexual intercourse. To them it was a magnificent discovery, and they stopped idling around and turned their entire attention to it, poor exultant young things!

In the midst of one of these celebrations they heard God walking among the bushes, which was an afternoon custom of his, and they were smitten with fright. Why? Because they were naked. They had not known it before. They had not minded it before; neither had God.

In that memorable moment *immodesty* was born; and some people have valued it ever since, though it would certainly puzzle them to explain why.

Adam and Eve entered the world naked and unashamed—naked and pure-minded; and no descendant of theirs has ever entered it otherwise. All have entered it naked, unashamed, and clean in mind. They have entered it *modest*. They had to *acquire* immodesty and the soiled mind, there was no other way to get it. A Christian mother's first duty is to soil her child's mind, and she does not neglect it. Her lad grows up to be a missionary, and goes to the innocent savage and to the civilized Japanese, and soils their minds. Whereupon they adopt immodesty, they conceal their bodies, they stop bathing naked together.

The convention miscalled Modesty has no standard, and cannot have one, because it is opposed to nature and reason, and is therefore an artificiality and subject to anybody's whim, anybody's diseased caprice. And so, in India the refined lady covers her face and breasts and leaves her legs naked from the hips down, while the refined European lady covers her legs and exposes her face and her breasts. In lands inhabited by the innocent savage the refined European lady soon gets used to full-grown native stark-nakedness, and ceases to be offended by it. A highly cultivated French count and countess—unrelated to each other—who were marooned in their night clothes, by shipwreck, upon an uninhabited island in the eighteenth century, were soon naked. Also ashamed—for a week. After that their nakedness did not trouble them, and they soon ceased to think about it.

You have never seen a person with clothes on. Oh, well, you haven't lost anything.

To proceed with the Biblical curiosities. Naturally you will think the threat to punish Adam and Eve for disobeying was of course not carried out, since they did not create themselves, nor their natures nor their impulses nor their weaknesses, and hence were not properly subject to any one's commands, and not responsible to anybody for their acts. It will surprise you to know that the threat *was* carried out. Adam and Eve were punished, and that crime finds apologists unto this day. *The sentence of death was executed.*

As you perceive, the only person responsible for the couple's offence escaped; and not only escaped but became the executioner of the innocent.

In your country and mine we should have the privilege of making fun of this kind of morality, but it would be unkind to do it here. Many of these people have the reasoning faculty, but no one uses it in religious matters.

The best minds will tell you that when a man has begotten a child he is morally bound to tenderly care for it, protect it from hurt, shield it from disease, clothe it, feed it, bear with its waywardness, lay no hand upon it save in kindness and for its own good, and never in any case inflict upon it a wanton cruelty. God's treatment of his earthly children, every day and every night, is the exact opposite of all that, yet those best minds warmly justify these crimes, condone them, excuse them, and indignantly refuse to regard them as crimes at all, when *he* commits them. Your country and mine is an interesting one, but there is nothing there that is half so interesting as the human mind.

Very well, God banished Adam and Eve from the Garden, and eventually assassinated them. All for disobeying a command which he had no right to utter. But he did not stop there, as you will see. He has one code of morals for himself, and quite another for his children. He requires his children to deal justly—and gently—with offenders, and forgive them seventy-and-seven times; whereas he deals neither justly nor gently with any one, and he did not forgive the ignorant and thoughtless first pair of juveniles even their first small offence and say, "You may go free this time, I will give you another chance."

On the contrary! He elected to punish *their* children, all through the ages to the end of time, for a trifling offence committed by others before they were born. He is punishing them yet. In mild ways? No, in atrocious ones.

You would not suppose that this kind of a Being gets many compliments. Undeceive yourself: the world calls him the All-Just, the All-Righteous, the All-Good, the All-Merciful, the All-Forgiving, the All-Truthful, the All Loving, the Source of All Morality. These sarcasms are uttered daily, all over the world. But not as conscious sarcasms. No, they are meant seriously; they are uttered without a smile.

Letter IV

So the First Pair went forth from the Garden under a curse—a permanent one. They had lost every pleasure they had possessed before "The Fall;" and yet they were rich, for they had gained one worth all the rest: they knew the Supreme Art.

They practised it diligently, and were filled with contentment. The Deity *ordered* them to practise it. They obeyed, this time. But it was just as well it was not forbidden, for they would have practised it anyhow, if a thousand Deities had forbidden it.

Results followed. By the name of Cain and Abel. And these had some sisters; and knew what to do with them. And so there were some more results: Cain and Abel begot some nephews and nieces. These, in their turn, begot some second-cousins. At this point classification of relationships began to get difficult, and the attempt to keep it up was abandoned.

The pleasant labor of populating the world went on from age to age, and with prime efficiency; for in those happy days the sexes were still competent for the Supreme Art when by rights they ought to have been dead eight hundred years. The sweeter sex, the dearer sex, the lovelier sex was manifestly at its very best, then, for it was even able to attract gods. Real gods. They came down out of heaven and had wonderful times with those hot young blossoms. The Bible tells about it.

By help of those visiting foreigners the population grew and grew until it numbered several millions. But it was a disappointment to the Deity. He was dissatisfied with its morals; which in some respects were not any better than his own. Indeed they were an unflatteringly close imitation of his own. They were a very bad people, and as he knew of no way to reform them, he wisely concluded to abolish them. This is the only really enlightened and superior idea his Bible has credited him with, and it would have made his reputation for all time if he could only have kept to it and carried it out. But he was always unstable—except in his advertisements—and his good resolution broke down. He took a pride in man; man was his finest invention; man was his pet, after the housefly, and he could not bear to lose him wholly; so he finally decided to save a sample of him and drown the rest.

Nothing could be more characteristic of him. He created all those infamous people, and he alone was responsible for their conduct. Not one of them deserved death, yet it was certainly good policy to extinguish them; especially since in creating them the master crime had already been committed, and to allow them to go on procreating would be a distinct *addition* to the crime. But at the same time there could be no justice, no fairness, in any favoritism—*all* should be drowned or none.

No, he would not have it so; he would save half a dozen and try the race over again. He was not able to foresee that it would go rotten again, for he is only the Far-Sighted One in his advertisements.

He saved out Noah and his family, and arranged to exterminate the rest. He planned an Ark, and Noah built it. Neither of them had ever built an Ark before, nor knew anything about Arks; and so something out of the common was to be expected. It happened. Noah was a farmer, and although he knew what was required of the Ark he was quite incompetent to say whether this one would be large enough to meet the requirements or not (which it wasn't), so he ventured no advice. The Deity did not know it wasn't large enough, but took the chances and made no adequate measurements. In the end the ship fell far short of the necessities, and to this day the world still suffers for it.

Noah built the Ark. He built it the best he could, but left out most of the essentials. It had no rudder, it had no sails, it had no compass, it had no pumps, it had no charts, no lead-lines, no anchors, no log, no light, no ventilation, and as for cargo-room—which was the main thing—the less said about that the better. It was to be at sea eleven months, and would need fresh water enough to fill two Arks of its size—yet the additional Ark was not provided. Water from outside could not be utilized: half of it would be salt water, and men and land-animals could not drink it.

For not only was a sample of man to be saved, but business-samples of the other animals, too. You must understand that when Adam ate the apple in the Garden and learned how to multiply and replenish, the other animals learned the Art, too, by watching Adam. It was cunning of them, it was neat; for they got all that was worth having out of the apple without tasting it and afflicting themselves with the disastrous Moral Sense, the parent of all immoralities.

Letter V

Noah began to collect animals. There was to be one couple of each and every sort of creature that walked or crawled, or swam or flew, in the world of animated nature. We have to guess at how long it took to collect the creatures and how much it cost, for there is no record of these details. When Symmachus made preparation to introduce his young son to grown-up life in imperial Rome, he sent men to Asia, Africa and everywhere to collect wild animals for the arena-fights. It took the men three years to accumulate the animals and fetch them to Rome. Merely quadrupeds and alligators, you understand—no birds, no snakes, no frogs, no worms, no lice, no rats, no fleas, no ticks, no caterpillars, no spiders, no houseflies, no mosquitoes—nothing but just plain simple quadrupeds and alligators; and no quadrupeds except fighting ones. Yet it was as I have said: it took three years to collect them, and the cost of animals and transportation and the men's wages footed up $4,500,000.

How many animals? We do not know. But it was under 5,000, for that was the largest number *ever* gathered for those Roman shows, and it was Titus, not Symmachus, who made that collection. Those were mere baby-museums, compared to Noah's contract. Of birds and beasts and fresh-water creatures he had to collect 146,000 kinds; and of insects upwards of 2,000,000 species.

Thousands and thousands of those things are very difficult to catch, and if Noah had not given up and resigned, he would be on the job yet, as Leviticus used to say. However, I do not mean that he withdrew. No, he did not do that. He gathered as many creatures as he had room for, and then stopped.

If he had known all the requirements in the beginning, he would have been aware that what was needed was a fleet of Arks. But he did not know how many kinds of creatures there were, neither did his Chief. So he had no kangaroo, and no 'possum, and no Gila Monster, and no ornithorhynchus, and lacked a multitude of other indispensable blessings which a loving Creator had provided for man and forgotten about, they having long ago wandered to a side of this world which he had never seen and with whose affairs he was not acquainted. And so everyone of them came within a hair of getting drowned.

They only escaped by an accident: there was not water enough to go around. Only enough was provided to flood one small corner of the globe—the rest of the globe was not then known, and was supposed to be non-existent.

However, the thing that really and finally and definitely determined Noah to stop with enough species for purely business purposes and let the rest become extinct, was an incident of the last days: an excited stranger arrived with some most alarming news. He said he had been camping among some mountains and valleys about six hundred miles away, and he had seen a wonderful thing there: he stood upon a precipice overlooking a wide valley, and up the valley he saw a billowy black sea of strange animal life coming. Presently the creatures passed by, struggling, fighting, scrambling, screeching, snorting—horrible vast masses of tumultuous flesh! Sloths as big as an elephant; frogs as big as a cow; a megatherium and his harem, huge beyond belief; saurians and saurians and saurians, group after group, family after family, species after species—a hundred feet long, thirty feet high, and twice as quarrelsome; one of them hit a perfectly blameless Durham bull a thump with its tail and sent it whizzing three hundred feet into the air and it fell at the man's feet with a sigh and was no more. The man said that these prodigious animals had heard about the Ark and were coming. Coming to get saved from the flood. And not coming in pairs, they were *all* coming: they did not know the passengers were restricted to pairs, the man said, and wouldn't care a rap for the regulations, anyway—they would sail in that Ark or know the reason why. The man said the Ark would not hold the half of them; and moreover they were coming hungry, and would eat up everything there was, including the menagerie and the family.

All these facts were suppressed, in the Biblical account. You find not a hint of them there. The whole thing is hushed up. Not even the names of those vast creatures are mentioned. It shows you that when people have left a reproachful vacancy in a contract they can be as shady about it in Bibles as elsewhere. Those powerful animals would be of inestimable value to man now, when transportation is so hard pressed and expensive, but they are all lost to him. All lost, and by Noah's fault. They all got drowned. Some of them as much as eight million years ago.

Very well, the stranger told his tale, and Noah saw that he must get away before the monsters arrived. He would have sailed at once, but the upholsterers and decorators of the housefly's drawing room still had some finishing touches to put on, and that lost him a day. Another day was lost in getting the flies aboard, there being sixty-eight billions of them and the Deity still afraid there might not be enough. Another day was lost in stowing 40 tons of selected filth for the flies' sustenance.

Then at last, Noah sailed; and none too soon, for the Ark was only just sinking out of sight on the horizon when the monsters arrived, and added their lamentations to those of the multitude of weeping fathers and mothers and frightened little children who were clinging to the wave-washed rocks in the pouring rain and lifting imploring prayers to an All-Just and All-Forgiving and All-Pitying Being who had never answered a prayer since those crags were builded, grain by grain, out of the sands, and would still not have answered one when the ages should have crumbled them to sand again.

Letter VI

On the third day, about noon, it was found that a fly and been left behind. The return-voyage turned out to be long and difficult, on account of the lack of chart and compass, and because of the changed aspects of all coasts, the steadily rising water having submerged some of the lower landmarks and given to higher ones an unfamiliar look; but after sixteen days of earnest and faithful seeking, the fly was found at last, and received on board with hymns of praise and gratitude, the Family standing meanwhile uncovered, out of reverence for its divine origin. It was weary and worn, and had suffered somewhat from the weather, but was otherwise in good estate. Men and their families had died of hunger on barren mountain tops, but it had not lacked for food, the multitudinous corpses furnishing it in rank and rotten richness. Thus was the sacred bird providentially preserved.

Providentially. That is the word. For the fly had not been left behind by accident. No, the hand of Providence was in it. There are no accidents. All things that happen, happen for a purpose. They are foreseen from the beginning of time, they are ordained from the beginning of time. From the dawn of Creation the Lord had foreseen that Noah, being alarmed and confused by the invasion of the prodigious brevet Fossils, would prematurely fly to sea unprovided with a certain invaluable disease. He would have all the other diseases, and could distribute them among the new races of men as they appeared in the world, but he would lack one of the very best—typhoid fever; a malady which, when the circumstances are especially favorable, is able to utterly wreck a patient without killing him; for it can restore him to his feet with a long life in him, and yet deaf, dumb, blind, crippled and idiotic. The housefly is its main disseminator, and is more competent and more calamitously effective than all the other distributors of the dreaded scourge put together. And so, by foreordination from the beginning of time, this fly was left behind to seek out a typhoid corpse and feed upon its corruptions and gaum its legs with germs and transmit them to the repeopled world for permanent business. From that one housefly, in the ages that have since elapsed, billions of sickbeds have been stocked, billions of wrecked bodies sent tottering about the earth, and billions of cemeteries recruited with the dead.

It is most difficult to understand the disposition of the Bible God, it is such a confusion of contradictions; of watery instabilities and iron firmnesses; of goody-goody abstract morals made out of words, and concreted hell-born ones made out of *acts;* of fleeting kindness repented of in permanent malignities.

However, when after much puzzling you get at the key to his disposition, you do at last arrive at a sort of understanding of it. With a most quaint and juvenile and astonishing frankness he has furnished that key himself. It is *jealousy!*

I expect that to take your breath away. You are aware—for I have already told you in an earlier letter—that among human beings jealousy ranks distinctly as a *weakness;* a trade-mark of small minds; a property of *all* small minds, yet a property which even the smallest is ashamed of; and when accused of its possession will lyingly deny it and resent the accusation as an insult.

Jealousy. Do not forget it, keep it in mind. It is the key. With it you will come to partly understand God as we go along; without it nobody can understand him. As I have said, he has openly held up this treasonous key himself, for all to see. He says, naïvely, outspokenly, and without suggestion of embarrassment,

"I the Lord thy God am a jealous God."

You see, it is only another way of saying,

"I the Lord thy God am a small God; a small God, and fretful about small things."

He was giving a warning: he could not bear the thought of any other God getting some of the Sunday compliments of this comical little human race—he wanted all of them for himself. He valued them. To him they were riches; just as tin money is to a Zulu.

But wait—I am not fair; I am misrepresenting him; prejudice is beguiling me into saying what is not true. He did not say he wanted all of the adulations; he said nothing about not being willing to share them with his fellow-gods; what he said was,

"Thou shalt have no other gods *before* me."

It is a quite different thing, and puts him in a much better light—I confess it. There was an abundance of gods, the woods were full of them, as the saying is, and all he demanded was, that he should be ranked as high as the others—not above any of them, but not below any of them. He was willing that they should fertilize earthly virgins, but not on any better terms than he could have for himself in his turn. He wanted to be held their equal. This he insisted upon, in the clearest language: he would have no other gods *before* him. They could march abreast with him, but none of them could head the procession, and he did not claim the right to head it himself.

Do you think he was able to stick to that upright and creditable position? No. He could keep to a bad resolution forever, but he couldn't keep to a good one a month. By and by he threw this one aside and calmly claimed to be the only God in the entire universe.

As I was saying, jealousy is the key; all through his history it is present and prominent. It is the blood and bone of his disposition, it is the basis of his character. How small a thing can wreck his composure and disorder his judgment if it touches the raw of his jealousy! And nothing warms up this trait so quickly and so surely and so exaggeratedly as a suspicion that some competition with the god-Trust is impending. The fear that if Adam and Eve ate of the fruit of the Tree of Knowledge they would "be as gods," so fired his jealousy that his reason was affected, and he could not treat those poor creatures either fairly or charitably, or even refrain from dealing cruelly and criminally with their blameless posterity.

To this day his reason has never recovered from that shock; a wild nightmare of vengefulness has possessed him ever since, and he has almost bankrupted his native ingenuities in inventing pains and miseries and humiliations and heartbreaks wherewith to embitter the brief lives of Adam's descendants. Think of the diseases he has contrived for them! They are multitudinous; no book can name them all. And each one is a trap, set for an innocent victim.

The human being is a machine. An automatic machine. It is composed of thousands of complex and delicate mechanisms, which perform their functions harmoniously and perfectly, in accordance with laws devised for their governance, and over which the man himself has no authority, no mastership, no control. For each one of these thousands of mechanisms the Creator has planned an enemy, whose office is to harass it, pester it, persecute it, damage it, afflict it with pains, and miseries, and ultimate destruction. Not one has been overlooked.

From cradle to grave these enemies are always at work, they know no rest, night nor day. They are an army: an organized army; a besieging army; an assaulting army; an army that is alert, watchful, eager, merciless; an army that never relents, never grants a truce.

It moves by squad, by company, by battalion, by regiment, by brigade, by division, by army corps; upon occasion it masses its parts and moves upon mankind with its whole strength. It is the Creator's Grand Army, and he is the Commander in Chief. Along its battlefront its grisly banners wave their legends in the face of the sun: Disaster, Disease, and the rest.

Disease! that is the main force, the diligent force, the devastating force! It attacks the infant the moment it is born; it furnishes it one malady after another: croup, measles, mumps, bowel-troubles, teething-pains, scarlet fever, and other childhood specialties. It chases the child into youth and furnishes it some specialties for that time of life. It chases the youth into maturity, maturity into age, age into the grave.

With these facts before you will you now try to guess man's chiefest pet name for this ferocious Commander in Chief? I will save you the trouble— but you must not laugh. It is Our Father in Heaven!

It is curious—the way the human mind works. The Christian begins with this straight proposition, this definite proposition, this inflexible and uncompromising proposition: *God is all-knowing, and all-powerful.*

This being the case, nothing can happen without his knowing beforehand that it is going to happen; nothing happens without his permission; nothing can happen that he chooses to prevent.

That is definite enough, isn't it? It makes the Creator distinctly responsible for everything that happens, doesn't it?

The Christian concedes it in that italicised sentence. Concedes it with feeling, with enthusiasm.

Then, having thus made the Creator responsible for all those pains and diseases and miseries above enumerated, and which he could have prevented, the gifted Christian blandly calls him Our Father!

It is as I tell you. He equips the Creator with every trait that goes to the making of a fiend, and then arrives at the conclusion that a fiend and a father are the same thing! Yet he would deny that a malevolent lunatic and a Sunday school superintendent are essentially the same. What do you think of the human mind? I mean, in case you think there is a human mind.

Letter VII

Noah and his family were saved—if that could be called an advantage. I throw in the *if* for the reason that there has never been an intelligent person of the age of sixty who would consent to live his life over again. His or any one else's. The family were saved, yes, but they were not comfortable, for they were full of microbes. Full to the eyebrows; fat with them, obese with them; distended like balloons. It was a disagreeable condition, but it could not be helped, because enough microbes had to be saved to supply the future races of men with desolating diseases, and there were but eight persons on board to serve as hotels for them. The microbes were by far the most important part of the Ark's cargo, and the part the Creator was most anxious about and most infatuated with. They had to have good nourishment and pleasant accommodations. There were typhoid germs, and cholera germs, and hydrophobia germs, and lockjaw germs, and consumption germs, and black-plague germs, and some hundreds of other aristocrats, specially precious creations, golden bearers of God's love to man, blessed gifts of the infatuated Father to his children—all of which had to be sumptuously housed and richly entertained; these were located in the choicest places the interiors of the family could furnish: in the lungs, in the heart, in the brain, in the kidneys, in the blood, in the guts. In the guts particularly. The great intestine was the favorite resort. There they gathered, by countless billions, and worked, and fed, and squirmed, and sang hymns of praise and thanksgiving; and at night when it was quiet you could hear the soft murmur of it. The large intestine was in effect their heaven. They stuffed it solid; they made it as rigid as a coil of gaspipe. They took pride in this. Their principal hymn made gratified reference to it:

> "Constipation, O constipation,
> The joyful sound proclaim
> Till man's remotest entrail
> Shall praise its Makers' name"

The discomforts furnished by the Ark were many, and various. The family had to live right in the presence of the multitudinous animals, and breathe the distressing stench they made and be deafened day and night with the thunder-crash of noise their roarings and screechings produced; and in addition to these intolerable discomforts it was a peculiarly trying place for the ladies, for they could look in no direction without seeing some thousands of the creatures engaged in multiplying and replenishing. And then, there were the flies. They swarmed everywhere, and persecuted the family all day long. They were the first animals up, in the morning, and the last ones down, at night. But they must not be killed, they must not be injured, they were sacred, their origin was divine, they were the special pets of the Creator, his darlings.

By and by the other creatures would be distributed here and there about the earth—*scattered:* the tigers to India, the lion and the elephant to the vacant desert and the secret places of the jungle, the birds to the boundless regions of empty space, the insects to one or another climate, according to nature and requirement; but the fly? He is of no nationality; all the climates are his home, all the globe is his province, all creatures that breathe are his prey, and unto them all he is a scourge and a hell.

To man he is a divine ambassador, a minister plenipotentiary, the Creator's special representative. He infests him in his cradle; clings in bunches to his gummy eyelids; buzzes and bites and harries him, robbing him of his sleep and his weary mother of her strength in those long vigils which she devotes to protecting her child from this pest's persecutions. The fly harries the sick man in his home, in the hospital, even on his death-bed at his last gasp. Pesters him at his meals; previously hunts up patients suffering from loathsome and deadly diseases; wades in their sores, gaums its legs with a million death-dealing germs; then comes to that healthy man's table and wipes these things off on the butter and discharges a bowel-load of typhoid germs and excrement on his batter-cakes. The housefly wrecks more human constitutions and destroys more human lives than all God's multitude of misery messengers and death-agents put together.

Shem was full of hookworms. It is wonderful, the thorough and comprehensive study which the Creator devoted to the great work of making man miserable. I have said he devised a special affliction-agent for each and every detail of man's structure, overlooking not a single one, and I said the truth. Many poor people have to go barefoot, because they cannot afford shoes. The Creator saw his opportunity. I will remark, in passing, that he always has his eye on the poor. Nine-tenths of his disease-inventions were intended for the poor, and they *get* them. The well-to-do get only what is left over. Do not suspect me of speaking unheedfully, for it is not so: the vast bulk of the Creator's affliction-inventions are specially designed for the persecution of the poor. You could guess this by the fact that one of the pulpit's finest and commonest names for the Creator is "The Friend of the Poor." Under no circumstances does the pulpit ever pay the Creator a compliment that has a vestige of truth in it. The poor's most implacable and unwearying enemy is their Father in Heaven. The poor's only real friend is their fellow man. He is sorry for them, he pities them, and he shows it by his deeds. He does much to relieve their distresses; and in every case their Father in Heaven gets the credit of it.

Just so with diseases. If science exterminates a disease which has been working for God, it is God that gets the credit, and all the pulpits break into grateful advertising-raptures and call attention to how good he is! Yes, *he* has done it. Perhaps he has waited a thousand years before doing it. That is nothing; the pulpit says he was thinking about it all the time. When exasperated men rise up and sweep away an age-long tyranny and set a nation free, the first thing the delighted pulpit does is to advertise it as God's work, and invite the people to get down on their knees and pour out their thanks to him for it. And the pulpit says with admiring emotion, "Let tyrants understand that the Eye that never sleeps is upon them; and let them remember that the Lord our God will not always be patient, but will loose the whirlwinds of his wrath upon them in his appointed day."

They forget to mention that he is the slowest mover in the universe; that his Eye that never sleeps, might as well, since it takes it a century to see what any other eye would see in a week; that in all history there is not an instance where he thought of a noble deed *first,* but always thought of it just a little after somebody else had thought of it and *done* it. He arrives then, and annexes the dividend.

Very well, six thousand years ago Shem was full of hookworms. Microscopic in size, invisible to the unaided eye. All of the Creator's specially-deadly disease-producers are invisible. It is an ingenious idea. For thousands of years it kept man from getting at the roots of his maladies, and defeated his attempts to master them. It is only very recently that science has succeeded in exposing some of these treacheries.

The very latest of these blessed triumphs of science is the discovery and identification of the ambuscaded assassin which goes by the name of the hookworm. Its special prey is the barefooted poor. It lies in wait in warm regions and sandy places and digs its way into their unprotected feet.

The hookworm was discovered two or three years ago by a physician, who had been patiently studying its victims for a long time. The disease induced by the hookworm had been doing its evil work here and there in the earth ever since Shem landed on Ararat, but it was never suspected to *be* a disease at all. The people who had it were merely supposed to be *lazy,* and were therefore despised and made fun of, when they should have been pitied. The hookworm is a peculiarly sneaking and underhand invention, and has done its surreptitious work unmolested for ages; but that physician and his helpers will exterminate it now.

God is back of this. He has been thinking about it for six thousand years, and making up his mind. The idea of exterminating the hookworm was his. He came very near doing it before Dr. Charles Wardell Stiles did. But he is in time to get the credit of it. He always is.

It is going to cost a million dollars. He was probably just in the act of contributing that sum when a man pushed in ahead of him—as usual. Mr. Rockefeller. He furnishes the million, but the credit will go elsewhere—as usual. This morning's journal tells us something about the hookworm's operations:

> The hookworm parasites often so lower the vitality of those who are affected as to retard their physical and mental development, render them more susceptible to other diseases, make labor less efficient, and in the sections where the malady is most prevalent greatly increase the death rate from consumption, pneumonia, typhoid fever and malaria. It has been shown that the lowered vitality of multitudes, long attributed to malaria and climate and seriously affecting economic development, is in fact due in some districts to this parasite. The disease is by no means confined to any one class; it takes its toll of suffering and death from the highly intelligent and well to do as well as from the less fortunate. It is a conservative estimate that two millions of our people are affected by this parasite. The disease is more common and more serious in children of school age than in other persons.
>
> Widespread and serious as the infection is, there is still a most encouraging outlook. The disease can be easily recognized, readily and effectively treated and by simple and proper sanitary precautions successfully prevented, with God's help.

The poor children are under the Eye that never sleeps, you see. They have had that ill luck in all the ages. They and "the Lord's poor"—as the sarcastic phrase goes—have never been able to get away from that Eye's attentions.

Yes, the poor, the humble, the ignorant—they are the ones that catch it. Take the "sleeping sickness," of Africa. This atrocious cruelty has for its victims a race of ignorant and unoffending blacks whom God placed in a remote wilderness, and bent his parental Eye upon them—the one that never sleeps when there is a chance to breed sorrow for somebody. He arranged for these people before the Flood. The chosen agent was a fly, related to the tzetse; the tzetse is a fly which has command of the Zambezi country and stings cattle and horses to death, thus rendering that region uninhabitable by man. The tsetse's awful relative deposits a microbe which produces the Sleeping Sickness. Ham was full of these microbes, and when the voyage was over he discharged them in Africa and the havoc began, never to find amelioration until six thousand years should go by and science should pry into the mystery and hunt out the cause of the disease. The pious nations are now thanking God, and praising him for coming to the rescue of his poor blacks. The pulpit says the praise is due to him. He is surely a curious Being. He commits a fearful crime, continues that crime unbroken for six thousand years, and is then entitled to praise because he suggests to somebody else to modify its severities. He is called patient, and he certainly must be patient, or he would have sunk the pulpit in perdition ages ago for the ghastly compliments it pays him.

Science has this to say about the Sleeping Sickness, otherwise called the Negro Lethargy.

> It is characterised by periods of sleep recurring at intervals. The disease lasts from four months to four years, and is always fatal. The victim appears at first languid, weak, pallid, and stupid. His eyelids become puffy, an eruption appears on his skin. He falls asleep while talking, eating, or working. As the disease progresses he is fed with difficulty and becomes much emaciated. The failure of nutrition and the appearance of bedsores are followed by convulsions and death. Some patients become insane.

It is he whom Church and people call Our Father in Heaven who has invented the fly and sent him to inflict this dreary long misery and melancholy and wretchedness, and decay of body and mind, upon a poor savage who has done that Great Criminal no harm. There isn't a man in the world who doesn't pity that poor black sufferer, and there isn't a man that wouldn't make him whole if he could. To find the one person who has no pity for him you must go to heaven; to find the one person who is able to heal him and couldn't be persuaded to do it, you must go to the same place. There is only one father cruel enough to afflict his child with that horrible disease—only one. Not all the eternities can produce another one. Do you like reproachful poetical indignations warmly expressed? Here is one, hot from the heart of a slave:

> "Man's *inhumanity to man*
> *Makes countless thousands mourn!"*

I will tell you a pleasant tale which has in it a touch of pathos. A man got religion, and asked the priest what he must do to be worthy of his new estate. The priest said, "Imitate our Father in Heaven, learn to be like him." The man studied his Bible diligently and thoroughly and understandingly, and then with prayers for heavenly guidance instituted his imitations. He tricked his wife into falling down stairs, and she broke her back and became a paralytic for life; he betrayed his brother into the hands of a sharper, who robbed him of his all and landed him in the almshouse; he inoculated one son with hookworms, another with the sleeping sickness, another with the gonorrhea, he furnished one daughter with scarlet fever and ushered her into her teens deaf, dumb and blind for life; and after helping a rascal seduce the remaining one, he closed his doors against her and she died in a brothel cursing him. Then he reported to the priest, who said that *that* was no way to imitate his Father in Heaven. The convert asked wherein he had failed, but the priest changed the subject and inquired what kind of weather he was having, up his way.

Letter VIII

Man is without any doubt the most interesting fool there is. Also the most eccentric. He hasn't a single written law, in his Bible or out of it, which has any but just one purpose and intention—to *limit or defeat a law of God.*

He can seldom take a plain fact and get any but a wrong meaning out of it. He cannot help this; it is the way the confusion he calls his mind is constructed. Consider the things he concedes, and the curious conclusions he draws from them.

For instance, he concedes that God made man. Made him without man's desire or privity.

This seems to plainly and indisputably make God, and God alone, responsible for man's acts. But man denies this.

He concedes that God has made the angels perfect, without blemish, and immune from pain and death, and that he could have been similarly kind to man if he had wanted to, but denies that he was under any moral obligation to do it.

He concedes that man has no moral right to visit the child of his begetting with wanton cruelties, painful diseases and death, but refuses to limit God's privileges in this sort with the children of his begetting.

The Bible and man's statutes forbid murder, adultery, fornication, lying, treachery, robbery, oppression and other crimes, but contend that God is free of these laws and has a right to break them when he will.

He concedes that God gives to each man his temperament, his disposition, at birth; he concedes that man cannot by any process change this temperament, but must remain always under its dominion. Yet if it be full of dreadful passions, in one man's case, and barren of them in another man's, it is right and rational to punish the one for his crimes, and reward the other for abstaining from crime.

There—let us consider these curiosities.

Temperament (disposition.) Take two extremes of temperament—the goat and the tortoise.

Neither of these creatures makes its own temperament, but is born with it, like man, and can no more change it than can man.

Temperament is the *law of God,* written in the heart of every creature by God's own hand, and *must* be obeyed, and *will* be obeyed in spite of all restricting or forbidding statutes, let them emanate whence they may.

Very well, lust is the dominant feature of the goat's temperament, the law of God is in its heart, and it must obey it and *will* obey it the whole day long in the rutting season; without stopping to eat or drink. If the Bible said to the goat "Thou shalt not fornicate, thou shalt not commit adultery," even man—sapheaded man—would recognize the foolishness of the prohibition, and would grant that the goat ought not to be punished for obeying the law of his make. Yet he thinks it right and just that man should be put under the prohibition. *All* men. All alike.

On its face this is stupid, for, by temperament, which is the *real* law of God, many men are *goats* and can't *help* committing adultery when they get a chance; whereas there are numbers of men who, by temperament, can keep their purity and let an opportunity go by if the woman lacks in attractiveness. But the Bible doesn't allow adultery *at all,* whether a person can help it or not. It allows no distinction between goat and tortoise—the excitable goat, the emotional goat, that *has* to have some adultery every day or fade and die; and the tortoise, that cold calm puritan, that takes a treat only once in two years and then goes to sleep in the midst of it and doesn't wake up for sixty days. No lady goat is safe from criminal assault, even on the Sabbath Day, when there is a gentleman goat within three miles to leeward of her and nothing in the way but a fence fourteen feet high, whereas neither the gentleman tortoise nor the lady tortoise is ever hungry enough for solemn joys of fornication to be willing to break the Sabbath to get them. Now according to man's curious reasoning, the goat has earned punishment, and the tortoise praise.

"Thou shalt not commit adultery" is a command which makes no distinction between the following persons. They are all required to obey it:

Children at birth.

Children in the cradle.

School children.

Youths and maidens.

Fresh adults.

Older ones.

Men and women of 40.

Of 50.

Of 60.

Of 70.

Of 80.

Of 90.

Of 100.

The command does not distribute its burden equally, and cannot.

It is not hard upon the three sets of children.

It is hard—harder—still harder upon the next three sets—cruelly hard.

It is blessedly softened to the next three sets.

It has now done all the damage it can, and might as well be put out of commission.

Yet with comical imbecility it is continued, and the four remaining es-
tates are put under its crushing ban. Poor old wrecks, they couldn't disobey
if they tried. And think—because they holily refrain from adulterating
each other, they get praise for it! Which is nonsense; for even the Bible
knows enough to know that if the oldest veteran there could get his lost
hey-day back again for an hour he would cast that commandment to the
winds and ruin the first woman he came across, even though she were an
entire stranger.

It is as I have said: every statute in the Bible and in the law books is an
attempt to defeat a law of God—in other words an unalterable and indestructible law of nature. These people's God has shown them by a million
acts that he respects none of the Bible's statutes. He breaks every one of
them himself, adultery and all.

The law of God, as quite plainly expressed in woman's *construction* is this:

> There shall be *no limit* put upon your intercourse with the
> other sex sexually, at any time of life.

The law of God, as quite plainly expressed in *man's* construction is this:

> During your entire life you shall be under inflexible *limits
> and restrictions,* sexually.

During 27 days in every month (in the absence of pregnancy) from the
time a woman is seven years old till she dies of old age, she is ready for action, and *competent.* As competent as the candlestick is to receive the candle.
Competent every day, competent every night. Also she *wants* that candle—
yearns for it, longs for it, hankers after it, as commanded by the law of God
in her heart.

But man is only briefly competent; and only then in the moderate measure applicable to the word in *his* sex's case. He is competent from the age
of sixteen or seventeen thenceforward for thirty-five years. After 50 his
performance is of poor quality, the intervals between are wide, and its satis-
factions of no great value to either party; whereas his great-grandmother is
as good as new. There is nothing the matter with her plant. Her candlestick
is as firm as ever, whereas his candle is increasingly softened and weakened

by the weather of age, as the years go by, until at last it can no longer stand, and is mournfully laid to rest in the hope of a blessed resurrection which is never to come.

By the woman's make, her plant has to be out of service three days in the month, and during a part of her pregnancy. These are times of discomfort, often of suffering. For fair and just compensation she has the high privilege of unlimited adultery all the other days of her life.

That is the law of God, as revealed in her make. What becomes of this high privilege? Does she live in free enjoyment of it? No. Nowhere in the whole world. She is robbed of it everywhere. Who does this? Man. Man's statutes—ordained against her without allowing her a vote. Also God's statutes—if the Bible *is* the Word of God.

Now there you have a sample of man's "reasoning powers," as he calls them. He observes certain facts. For instance, that in all his life he never sees the day that he can satisfy *one* woman; also, that no woman ever sees the day that she can't overwork, and defeat, and put out of commission any *ten* masculine plants that can be put to bed to her.[1] He puts those strikingly-suggestive and luminous facts together, and from them draws this astonishing conclusion:

The Creator intended the woman to be restricted to one man.

So he concretes that singular conclusion into *law,* for good and all.

And he does it without consulting the woman, although she has a thousand times more at stake in the matter than he has. His procreative competency is limited to an average of 100 exercises per year for 50 years, hers is good for 3,000 a year for that whole time—and as many years longer as she may live. Thus his life-interest in the matter is 5,000 refreshments, while hers is 150,000; yet instead of fairly and honorably leaving the making of the law to the person who has an overwhelming interest at stake in it, this immeasurable hog, who has nothing at stake in it worth considering, makes it himself!

---

1. In the Sandwich Islands in 1866 a buxom royal princess died. Occupying a place of distinguished honor at her funeral were 36 splendidly built young native men. In a laudatory song which celebrated the various merits, achievements and accomplishments of the late princess those 36 stallions were called her *harem,* and the song said it had been her pride and her boast that she kept the whole of them busy, and that several times it had happened that more than one of them had been able to charge overtime.

You have heretofore found out, by my teachings, that man is a fool; you are now aware that woman is a *damned* fool.

Now if you or any other really intelligent person were arranging the fairnesses and justices between man and woman, you would give the man a one-fiftieth interest in one woman, and the woman a *harem*. Now wouldn't you? Necessarily. I give you my word, this creature with the decrepit candle has arranged it exactly the other way. Solomon, who was one of the Deity's favorites, had a copulation-cabinet composed of 700 wives and 300 concubines. To save his life he could not have kept two of these young creatures satisfactorily refreshed, even if he had had fifteen experts to help him. Necessarily almost the entire thousand had to go hungry years and years on a stretch. Conceive of a man hard-hearted enough to look daily upon all that suffering and not be moved to mitigate it. He even wantonly *added* a sharp pang to that pathetic misery; for he kept within those women's sight, always, stalwart watchmen whose splendid masculine forms made the poor lassies' mouths water but who hadn't anything to solace a candlestick with, these gentry being eunuchs. A eunuch is a person whose candle has been put out. By art.[2]

From time to time, as I go along, I will take up a Biblical statute and show you that it always violates a law of God, and then is imported into the law books of the nations, where it continues its violations. But those things will keep; there is no hurry.

Letter IX

The Ark continued its voyage, drifting around here and there and yonder, compassless and uncontrolled, the sport of the random winds and the swirling currents. And the rain, the rain, the rain! it kept on falling, pouring, drenching, flooding. No such rain had ever been seen before. Sixteen inches a day had been heard of, but that was nothing to this. This was a hundred and twenty inches a day—ten feet! At this incredible rate it rained forty days and forty nights, and submerged every hill that was 400 feet high. Then the heavens and even the angels went dry; no more water was to be had.

---

2. I am purpose publishing these Letters here in the world before I return to you. Two editions. One, unedited, for Bible readers and their children; the other, expurgated, for persons of refinement.

As a Universal Flood it was a disappointment, but there had been heaps of Universal Floods before, as is witnessed by all the Bibles of all the nations, and this was as good as the best one.

At last the Ark soared aloft and came to rest on top of Mount Ararat, 17,000 feet above the valley, and its living freight got out and went down the mountain.

Noah planted a vineyard, and drank of the wine and was overcome.

This person had been selected from all the populations because he was the best sample there was. He was to start the human race on a new basis. This was the new basis. The promise was bad. To go further with the experiment was to run a great and most unwise risk. Now was the time to do with these people what had been so judiciously done with the others—drown them. Anybody but the Creator would have seen this. But he didn't see it. That is, maybe he didn't.

It is claimed that from the beginning of time he foresaw everything that would happen in the world. If that is true, he foresaw that Adam and Eve would eat the apple; that their posterity would be unendurable and have to be drowned; that Noah's posterity would in their turn be unendurable, and that by and by he would have to leave his throne in heaven and come down and be crucified to save that same tiresome human race again. The whole of it? No! A part of it? Yes. How much of it? In each generation, for hundreds and hundreds of generations, a billion would die and all go to perdition except perhaps ten thousand out of the billion. The ten thousand would have to come from the little body of Christians, and only one in the hundred of that little body would stand any chance. None of them at all except such Roman Catholics as should have the luck to have a priest handy to sandpaper their souls at the last gasp, and here and there a Presbyterian. No others saveable. All the others damned. By the million.

Shall you grant that he foresaw all this? The pulpit grants it. It is the same as granting that in the matter of intellect the Deity is the Head Pauper of the Universe, and that in the matter of morals and character he is away down on the level of David.

Letter X

The two Testaments are interesting, each in its own way. The Old one gives us a picture of these people's Deity as he was before he got religion, the other one gives us a picture of him as he appeared afterward. The Old Testament is interested mainly in blood and sensuality. The New one in Salvation. Salvation by fire.

The first time the Deity came down to earth he brought life and death; when he came the second time, he brought hell.

Life was not a valuable gift, but death was. Life was a fever-dream made up of joys embittered by sorrows, pleasure poisoned by pain; a dream that was a nightmare-confusion of spasmodic and fleeting delights, ecstasies, exultations, happinesses, interspersed with long-drawn miseries, griefs, perils, horrors, disappointments, defeats, humiliations, and despairs—the heaviest curse devisable by divine ingenuity; but death was sweet, death was gentle, death was kind, death healed the bruised spirit and the broken heart, and gave them rest and forgetfulness; death was man's best friend; when man could endure life no longer, death came, and set him free.

In time, the Deity perceived that death was a mistake; a mistake, in that it was insufficient; insufficient, for the reason that while it was an admirable agent for the inflicting of misery upon the survivor, it allowed the dead person himself to escape from all further persecution in the blessed refuge of the grave. This was not satisfactory. A way must be contrived to pursue the dead beyond the tomb.

The Deity pondered this matter during four thousand years unsuccessfully, but as soon as he came down to earth and became a Christian his mind cleared and he knew what to do. *He invented hell,* and proclaimed it.

Now here is a curious thing. It is believed by everybody that while he was in heaven he was stern, hard, resentful, jealous, and cruel; but that when he came down to earth and assumed the name Jesus Christ, he became the opposite of what he was before: that is to say, he became sweet, and gentle, merciful, forgiving, and all harshness disappeared from his nature and a deep and yearning love for his poor human children took its place. Whereas it was as Jesus Christ that he devised hell and proclaimed it!

Which is to say, that as the meek and gentle Savior he was a thousand billion times crueler than ever he was in the Old Testament—oh, incomparably more atrocious than ever he was when he was at his very worst in those old days!

Meek and gentle? By and by we will examine this popular sarcasm by the light of the hell which he invented.

Letter XI

While it is true that the palm for malignity must be granted to Jesus, the inventor of hell, he was hard and ungentle enough for all godlike purposes even before he became a Christian. It does not appear that he ever stopped to reflect that *he* was to blame when a man went wrong, inasmuch as the man was merely acting in accordance with the disposition he had afflicted him with. No, he punished the man, instead of punishing himself. Moreover, the punishment usually oversized the offence. Often, too, it fell, not upon the doer of a misdeed, but upon somebody else—a chief man, the head of a community, for instance.

> And Israel abode in Shittim, and the people began to commit whoredom with the daughters of Moab.
>
> And the Lord said unto Moses, Take *all the heads of the people,* and hang them up before the Lord against the sun, that the fierce anger of the Lord may be turned away from Israel.

Does that look fair to you? It does not appear that the "heads of the people" got any of the adultery, yet it is they that are hanged, instead of "the people."

If it was fair and right in that day it would be fair and right to-day, for the pulpit maintains that God's justice is eternal and unchangeable; also that he is the Fountain of Morals; and that his morals are eternal and unchangeable. Very well, then, we must believe that if the people of New York should begin to commit whoredom with the daughters of New Jersey, it would be fair and right to set up a gallows in front of the city hall and hang the mayor and the sheriff and the judges and the archbishop on it, although they did not get any of it. It does not look right to me.

Moreover, you may be quite sure of one thing: *it couldn't happen.* These people would not allow it. They are better than their Bible. *Nothing* would happen here, except some lawsuits, for damages, if the incident couldn't be hushed up; and even down South they would not proceed against persons who did not get any of it; they would get a rope and hunt for the correspondents; and if they couldn't find them they would lynch a nigger.

Things have greatly improved since the Almighty's time, let the pulpit say what it may.

Will you examine the Deity's morals and disposition and conduct a little further? And will you remember that in the Sunday school the little children are urged to love the Almighty, and honor him, and praise him, and make him their model and try to be as like him as they can? Read:

1 And the LORD spake unto Moses, saying,

2 Avenge the children of Israel of the Midianites: afterward shalt thou be gathered unto thy people.

7 And they warred against the Midianites, as the LORD commanded Moses; and they slew all the males.

8 And they slew the kings of Midian, beside the rest of them that were slain; *namely,* Evi, and Rekem, and Zur, and Hur, and Reba, five kings of Midian: Balaam also the son of Beor they slew with the sword.

9 And the children of Israel took *all* the women of Midian captives, and their little ones, and took the spoil of all their cattle, and all their flocks, and all their goods.

10 And they burnt all their cities wherein they dwelt, and all their goodly castles, with fire.

11 And they took all the spoil, and all the prey, *both* of men and of beasts.

12 And they brought the captives, and the prey, and the spoil unto Moses, and Eleazar the priest, and unto the congregation of the children of Israel, unto the camp at the plains of Moab, which *are* by Jordan *near* Jericho.

13 And Moses, and Eleazar the priest, and all the princes of the congregation, went forth to meet them without the camp.

14 And Moses was wroth with the officers of the host, *with* the captains over thousands, and captains over hundreds, which came from the battle.

15 And Moses said unto them, Have ye saved all the women alive?

16 Behold, these caused the children of Israel, through the counsel of Balaam, to commit trespass against the LORD in the matter of Peor, and there was a plague among the congregation of the LORD.

17 Now therefore kill every male among the little ones, and kill every woman that hath known man by lying with him.

18 But all the women-children, that have not known a man by lying with him, keep alive for yourselves.

19 And do ye abide without the camp seven days: whosoever hath killed any person, and whosoever hath touched any slain, purify *both* yourselves and your captives on the third day, and on the seventh day.

20 And purify all *your* raiment, and all that is made of skins, and all work of goats' *hair*, and all things made of wood.

21 And Eleazar the priest said unto the men of war which went to the battle, This *is* the ordinance of the law which the LORD commanded Moses.

25 And the LORD spake unto Moses, saying,

26 Take the sum of the prey that was taken, *both* of man and of beast, thou, and Eleazar the priest, and the chief fathers of the congregation:

27 And divide the prey into two parts; between them that took the war upon them, who went out to battle, and between all the congregation:

28 And levy a tribute unto the LORD of the men of war which went out to battle.

31 And Moses and Eleazar the priest did as the LORD commanded Moses.

32 And the booty, *being* the rest of the prey which the men of war had caught, was six hundred thousand, and seventy thousand and five thousand sheep,

33 And threescore and twelve thousand beeves,

34 And threescore and one thousand asses,

35 And thirty and two thousand persons in all, of women that had not known man by lying with him.

40 And the persons *were* sixteen thousand; of which the LORD's tribute *was* thirty and two persons.

41 And Moses gave the tribute, *which was* the LORD's heave-offering, unto *Eleazar* the priest; as the Lord commanded Moses.

47 Even of the children of Israel's half, Moses took one portion of fifty, *both* of man and of beast, and gave them unto
the Levites, which kept the charge of the tabernacle of the
LORD; as the LORD commanded Moses.

10 When thou comest nigh unto a city to fight against it,
then proclaim peace unto it.

13 And when the LORD thy God hath delivered it into thine
hands, thou shalt smite every male thereof with the edge
of the sword:

14 But the women, and the little ones, and the cattle, and all
that is in the city, *even* all the spoil thereof, shalt thou take
unto thyself: and thou shalt eat the spoil of thine enemies,
which the LORD thy God hath given thee.

15 Thus shalt thou do unto all the cities *which* are very far off
from thee, which are not of the cities of these nations.

16 But of the cities of these people, which the LORD thy God
doth give thee for an inheritance, *thou shalt save alive*
NOTHING THAT BREATHETH.

The Biblical law says:
"Thou shalt not kill."
The law of God, planted in the heart of man at his birth, says:
"Thou *shalt* kill."
The chapter I have quoted, shows you that the book-statute is once
more a failure. It cannot set aside the more powerful law of nature.
According to the belief of these people, it was God himself who said:
"Thou shalt not kill."
Then it is plain that he cannot keep his own commandments.
He killed all those people—*every male.*
They had offended the Deity in some way. We know what the offence
was, without looking; that is to say, we know it was a trifle; some small
thing that no one but a god would attach any importance to. It is more
than likely that a Midianite had been duplicating the conduct of one
Onan, who was commanded to "go in unto his brother's wife"—which
he did; but instead of finishing, "he spilled it on the ground." The Lord slew
Onan for that, for the Lord could never abide indelicacy. The Lord slew

Onan, and to this day the Christian world cannot understand why he stopped with Onan, instead of slaying all the inhabitants for three hundred miles around—they being innocent of offence, and therefore the very ones he would usually slay. For that had always been his idea of fair dealing. If he had had a motto, it would have read, "Let no innocent person escape." You remember what he did in the time of the flood. There were multitudes and multitudes of tiny little children, and he knew they had never done him any harm; but their *relations* had, and that was enough for him: he saw the waters rise toward their screaming lips, he saw the wild terror in their eyes, he saw that agony of appeal in the mothers' faces which would have touched any heart but his, but he was after the guiltless particularly, and he drowned those poor little chaps.

And you will remember that in the case of Adam's posterity *all* the billions are innocent—*none* of them had a share in his offence, but the Deity holds them guilty to this day. None gets off, except by acknowledging that guilt—no cheaper lie will answer.

Some Midianite must have repeated Onan's act, and brought that dire disaster upon his nation. If that was not the indelicacy that outraged the feelings of the Deity, then I know what it was: some Midianite had been *pissing against the wall.* I am sure of it, for that was an impropriety which the Source of all Etiquette *never* could stand. A person could piss against a tree, he could piss on his mother, he could piss his own breeches, and get off, but he must not piss against the wall—that would be going quite too far. The origin of the divine prejudice against this humble crime is not stated; but we know that the prejudice was very strong—so strong that nothing but a wholesale massacre of the people inhabiting the region where the wall was defiled could satisfy the Deity.

Take the case of Jeroboam. "I will cut off from Jeroboam him that pisseth against the wall." It was done. And not only was the man that did it cut off, but everybody else.

The same with the house of Baasha: everybody was exterminated, kinsfolks, friends, and all, leaving "not one that pisseth against a wall."

In the case of Jeroboam you have a striking instance of the Deity's custom of not limiting his punishments to the guilty; the innocent are included. Even the "remnant" of that unhappy house was removed, even "as a man taketh away dung, till it be all gone." That includes the women, the young maids, and the little girls. All innocent, for *they* couldn't piss against a wall. Nobody of that sex can. None but members of the other sex can achieve that feat.

A curious prejudice. And it still exists. Protestant parents still keep the Bible handy in the house, so that the children can study it, and one of the first things the little boys and girls learn is to be righteous and holy and not piss against the wall. They study those passages more than they study any others, except those which incite to masturbation. *Those* they hunt out and study in private. No Protestant child exists who does not masturbate. That art is the earliest accomplishment his religion confers upon him. Also the earliest *her* religion confers upon *her*.

The Bible has this advantage over all other books that teach refinement and good manners: that it goes to the child: it goes to the mind at its most impressible and receptive age—the others have to wait.

> "Thou shalt have a paddle upon thy weapon; and it shall be,
> when thou wilt ease thyself abroad, thou shalt dig therewith,
> and shalt turn back and cover that which cometh from thee."

That rule was made in the old days because

> "The Lord thy God walketh in the midst of thy camp."

It is probably not worth while to try to find out, for certain, why the Midianites were exterminated. We can only be sure that it was for no large offence; for the cases of Adam, and the Flood, and the defilers of the wall, teach us that much. A Midianite may have left his paddle at home and thus brought on the trouble. However, it is no matter. The main thing is the trouble itself, and the morals of one kind and another that it offers for the instruction and elevation of the Christian of to-day.

God wrote upon the tables of stone—

"Thou shalt not kill."

Also—

"Thou shalt not commit adultery."

Paul, speaking by the divine voice, advised against sexual intercourse *altogether*. A great change from the divine view as it existed at the time of the Midianite incident.

Letter XII

Human history in all ages, is red with blood, and bitter with hate, and stained with cruelties; but not since Biblical times have these features been without a limit of some kind. Even the Church, which is credited with having spilt more innocent blood, since the beginning of its supremacy, than all the political wars put together have spilt, has observed a limit. A sort of limit. But you notice that when the Lord God of Heaven and Earth, adored Father of Man, goes to war, there is no limit. He is totally without mercy—he, who is called the Fountain of Mercy. He slays, slays, slays! all the men, all the beasts, all the boys, all the babies; also all the women and all the girls, except those that have not been deflowered.

He makes no distinction between innocent and guilty. The babies were innocent, the beasts were innocent, many of the men, many of the women, many of the boys, many of the girls, were innocent, yet they had to suffer with the guilty. What the insane Father required was blood and misery; he was indifferent as to who furnished it.

The heaviest punishment of all was meted out to persons who could not by any possibility have deserved so horrible a fate—the 32,000 virgins. Their naked privacies were probed, to make sure that they still possessed the hymen unruptured; after this humiliation they were sent away from the land that had been their home, to be sold into slavery; the worst of slaveries and the shamefulest, the slavery of prostitution; bed-slavery, to excite lust, and satisfy it with their bodies; slavery to any buyer, be he gentleman or be he a coarse and filthy ruffian.

It was the Father that inflicted this ferocious and undeserved punishment upon those bereaved and friendless virgins, whose parents and kindred he had slaughtered before their eyes. And were they praying to him for pity and rescue, meantime? Without a doubt of it.

These virgins were "spoil," plunder, booty. He claimed his share and got it. What use had *he* for virgins? Examine his later history and you will know.

His priests got a share of the virgins, too. What use could priests make of virgins? The private history of the Roman Catholic confessional can answer that question for you. The confessional's chief amusement has been seduction—in all the ages of the Church. Père Hyacinth testifies that of 100 priests confessed by him, 99 had used the confessional effectively for the seduction of married women and young girls. One priest confessed that of 900 girls and women whom he had served as father and confessor in his time, none had escaped his lecherous embrace but the elderly and the homely. The official list of questions which the priest is *required* to ask will overmasteringly excite any woman who is not a paralytic.

There is nothing in either savage or civilized history that is more utterly complete, more remorselessly sweeping than the Father of Mercy's campaign among the Midianites. The official report does not furnish the incidents, episodes, and minor details, it deals only in information in masses: *all* the virgins, *all* the men, *all* the babies, *all* "creatures *that breathe,*" all houses, *all* cities; it gives you just one vast picture, spread abroad here and there and yonder, as far as eye can reach, of charred ruin and storm-swept desolation; your imagination adds a brooding stillness, an aweful hush— the hush of death. But of course there *were* incidents. Where shall we get them?

Out of history of yesterday's date. Out of history made by the red Indian of America. He has duplicated God's work, and done it in the very spirit of God. In 1862 the Indians in Minnesota, having been deeply wronged and treacherously treated by the government of the United States, rose against the white settlers and massacred them; massacred all they could lay their hands upon, sparing neither age nor sex. Consider this incident:

Twelve Indians broke into a farm house at daybreak and captured the family. It consisted of the farmer and his wife and four daughters, the youngest aged fourteen and the eldest eighteen. They crucified the parents; that is to say, they stood them stark naked against the wall of the living room and nailed their hands to the wall. Then they stripped the daughters bare, stretched them upon the floor in front of their parents, and repeatedly ravished them. Finally they crucified the girls against the wall opposite the parents, and cut off their noses and their breasts. They also—but I will not go into that. There is a limit. There are indignities so atrocious that the pen cannot write them. One member of that poor crucified family—the father—was still alive when help came two days later.

Now you have *one* incident of the Minnesota massacre. I could give you fifty. They would cover all the different kinds of cruelty the brutal human talent has ever invented.

And now you know, by these sure indications, what happened under the personal direction of the Father of Mercies in his Midianite campaign. The Minnesota campaign was merely a duplicate of the Midianite raid. Nothing happened in the one that did not happen in the other.

No, that is not strictly true. The Indian was more merciful than was the Father of Mercies. He sold no virgins into slavery to minister to the lusts of the murderers of their kindred while their sad lives might last; he raped them, then charitably made their subsequent sufferings brief, ending them with the precious gift of death. He burned some of the houses, but not all of them. He carried off innocent dumb brutes, but he took the lives of none.

Would you expect this same conscienceless God, this moral bankrupt, to become a *teacher* of morals; of gentleness; of meekness; of righteousness; of purity? It looks impossible, extravagant; but listen to him. These are his own words:

> Blessed are the poor in spirit, for theirs is the kingdom of heaven.
> Blessed are they that mourn, for they shall be comforted.
> Blessed are the meek, for they shall inherit the earth.
> Blessed are they which do hunger and thirst after righteousness, for they shall be filled.
> *Blessed are the merciful,* for they shall obtain mercy.
> Blessed are the pure in heart, for they shall see God.
> *Blessed are the peace-makers,* for they shall be called *the children of God.*
> Blessed are they which are persecuted for righteousness' sake, for theirs is the kingdom of heaven.
> Blessed are ye, when men shall revile you, and persecute you, and say all manner of evil against you falsely for my sake.

The mouth that uttered these immense sarcasms, these giant hypocrisies, is the very same that ordered the wholesale massacre of the Midianitish men and babies and cattle; the wholesale destruction of house and city; the wholesale banishment of the virgins into a filthy and unspeakable slavery. This is the same person who brought upon the Midianites the fiendish cruelties which were repeated by the red Indians, detail by detail, in Minnesota eighteen centuries later. The Midianite episode filled him with joy. So did the Minnesota one, or he would have prevented it.

The Beatitudes and the quoted chapters from Numbers and Deuteronomy ought always to be read from the pulpit *together;* then the congregation would get an all-round view of Our Father in Heaven. Yet not in a single instance have I ever known a clergyman to do this.

1917

Some say that language calls the world into being, that until we have a word for it, a thing cannot exist. But others say that language has estranged us from the world, that the moment we start speaking—sucking in oxygen, wailing loudly upon birth—we are stuck in language, we are bound to the world by only symbol, by a representative relationship in which our words are only elegies for the things they cannot be. This year, when the United States enters the First World War, there is an exhibition of new artists in New York. What is the role of art in a world that is so cruel? In a culture that is wounded psychologically by war, how does one make art, beauty, expression, new life? How do you make a new world without colluding with the one around you? A hundred years from now, conceptual writer Kenneth Goldsmith will respond to that dilemma by transforming himself into what he'll call an "information manager," an artist obsessed with replicating, organizing, mirroring, archiving, reprinting, bootlegging, and plundering what exists. "The world is full of texts, more or less interesting," he'll write. "I do not wish to add any more." Here, says one of his ancestors this year. Please put this sculpture in your art exhibition. I call my work *Fountain*. It is a white porcelain urinal that I bought at a plumbing store. Here is where I signed it. No, I did not make it. I chose it, however. And now because I have chosen to call this work a sculpture, you will have to think of it as a sculpture as well. Even when you reject it, even when you attack it, even when you say that it is not really art because I did not really make it, you have already made it into something newer than what it originally was. Thank you for considering my work.

KENNETH GOLDSMITH

All the Numbers from Numbers

On the first,
Of the second,
In the second,
Head by head,
From twenty,
On the first,
Of the second,
From twenty,
Every male,
From twenty,
Were 46,500,
Every male,
From twenty,
Were 59,300,
From twenty,
Were 45,650,
From twenty,
Were 74,600,
From twenty,
Were 54,400,
From twenty,
Were 57,400,
From twenty,
Were 40,500,
From twenty,
Were 32,200,
From twenty,

Were 35,400,
From twenty,
Were 62,700,
From twenty,
Were 41,500,
From twenty,
Were 53,400,
Twelve men,
From twenty,
Were 603,550.
74,600
54,400
57,400
186,400
First,
46,500
59,300
45,650
151,450
Second,
40,500
32,200
35,400
108,100,
Third,
62,700
41,500
53,400
157,600
603,550
One.

The first,
Every first,
The first,
All the first,
A month,

A month old,
7,500.

A month old,
There were
8,600
A month old
Were 6,200
A month old
Were 22,000.

Every first,
From a month,
The first,
All the first,
From a month,
22,273,
All the first,
273,
Of the first,
Take five,
Twenty gerahs,
The first,
1,365.

From thirty,
To fifty.

From thirty,
To fifty.

From thirty,
To fifty,
From thirty,
To fifty,
Were 2,750,
From thirty,

To fifty,
Were 2,630,
From thirty,
To fifty,
Were 3,200,
From thirty,
To fifty,
Were 8,580.

One-fifth.

One-tenth
Of an ephah
Of barley,
A grain,
Place the
Grain,
The grain,
Take the
Grain,
Of the
Grain.

Bring two
turtledoves,
Two young
Pigeons,
A year old,
One,
A year old,
One,
A year old,
One,
One.

Ones,
Six,

Twelve,
Two,
Each one,
Two carts,
Four oxen,
Four carts,
Eight oxen,
One,
The one,
One
Silver dish,
One hundred thirty,
One
Silver bowl,
Seventy,
One
Gold Pan,
Ten,
One bull,
One ram,
One male lamb,
One year,
One male goat,
Two oxen,
Five rams,
Five male goats,
Five male lambs,
One year,
Second,
One silver dish,
One hundred
And thirty,
One silver bowl,
Seventy,
One gold Pan,
Ten,
One bull,

One ram,
One male lamb,
One year,
One male goat,
Two oxen,
Five rams,
Five male goats,
Five male lambs,
One,
Third,
One silver dish,
One hundred
And Thirty,
One silver bowl,
Seventy,
One gold Pan,
Ten,
One young bull,
One ram,
One male lamb,
One year,
One male goat,
Two oxen,
Five rams,
Five male goats,
Five male lambs,
One year,
Fourth,
One silver dish,
One hundred
And Thirty,
One silver bowl,
Seventy,
One gold Pan,
Ten,
One bull,

One male lamb,
One year,
One male goat,
Two oxen,
Five rams,
Five male goats,
Five male lambs,
One year,
Fifth,
One silver dish,
One hundred
And Thirty,
One silver bowl,
Seventy,
One gold Pan,
Ten,
One bull,
One ram,
One male lamb,
One year,
Sixth,
One silver dish,
One hundred
And Thirty,
One silver bowl,
Seventy,
One gold Pan,
Ten,
One bull,
One ram,
One male lamb,
One year,
One male goat,
Two oxen,
Five rams,
Five male goats,

Five male lambs,
One year,
Seventh,
One silver dish,
One hundred,
And Thirty,
One silver bowl,
Seventy,
One gold Pan,
Ten,
One bull,
One ram,
One male lamb,
One year,
One male goat,
Two oxen,
Five rams,
Five male goats,
Five male lambs,
One year,
Eighth,
One silver dish,
One hundred
And Thirty,
One silver bowl,
Seventy,
One gold Pan,
Ten,
One bull,
One ram,
One male lamb,
One year,
One male goat,
Two oxen,
Five rams,
Five male goats,

Five male lambs,
One year,
Ninth,
One silver dish,
One hundred
And Thirty,
One silver bowl,
Seventy,
One gold Pan,
Ten,
One bull,
One ram,
One male lamb,
One year,
One male goat,
Two oxen,
Five rams,
Five male goats,
Five male lambs,
One year,
Tenth,
One silver dish,
One hundred
And Thirty,
One silver bowl,
Seventy,
One gold Pan,
Ten,
One bull,
One ram,
One male lamb,
One year,
One male goat,
Two oxen,
Five rams,
Five male goats,

Five male lambs,
One year,
Eleventh,
One silver dish,
One hundred
And Thirty,
One silver bowl,
Seventy,
One gold Pan,
Ten,
One bull,
One ram,
One male lamb,
One year,
One male goat,
Two oxen,
Five rams,
Five male goats,
Five male lambs,
One year,
Twelfth,
One silver dish,
One hundred
And Thirty,
One silver bowl,
Seventy,
One gold Pan,
Ten,
One bull,
One ram,
One male lamb,
One year,
One male goat,
Two oxen,
Five rams,
Five male goats,

Five male lambs,
One year,
Twelve silver dishes,
Twelve silver bowls,
Twelve gold Pans,
One hundred
And Thirty,
Seventy,
2,400,
Twelve gold Pans,
Ten,
Twelve bulls,
Twelve,
One year,
Twelve,
Twelve,
24 bulls,
60,
60,
One year,
60,
Seven lamps.

A second,
The one,
The first,
Every first,
All the first,
First-born.

Twenty-five,
Fifty.

The first,
The second,
The fourteenth,

The first,
The second,
The fourteenth.

It was two,
A year.

Two trumpets,
The second,
First days.

The second year,
The second month,
On the twentieth,
The first time,
Set out first,
Three days' journey,
Three days.

Two millstones.

Me seventy,
Not one,
Nor two,
Nor five,
Nor ten,
Nor twenty,
But a
Whole month,
600,000,
Seventy,
Two men,
One was.

Two cubits,
Ten homers.

Then three,
Seven days?
Seven days,
For seven days.

Every one,
First ripe,
Built seven,
Two men.

At the end of
Forty days.

So they said to
One another.

One
The third,
And the
Fourth.

Twenty,
Forty,
Forty days,
Even
Forty years.

One-tenth,
One-fourth,
One-fourth,
Two-tenths,
One-third,
Three-tenths,
One-half.

One statute,
One law,

One ordinance,
One bull,
One male goat,
One year old,
One law.

Two hundred
And fifty,
Two hundred
And fifty,
Firepans,
Consumed
Two hundred
And fifty.

Those who
Died by the
Plague were
14,7000.
Twelve rods,
Twelve rods.

First-born
Of man,
First-born
Of unclean
Animals,
Five shekels,
Twenty gerahs,
First-born
Of an ox,
First-born
Of a goat.

The one
Who gathers,
The one

Who touches,
That one
Shall purify,
On the
Third day,
On the
Seventh day,
Seven days,
One slain,
On the
Third day,
On the
Seventh day.

Zin in the
First month.
Struck the
Rock twice.

Israel wept
For Aaron
Thirty days.

What have I
Done to you
That you have
Struck me
These
Three times?
Why have
You struck
Your donkey
These
Three times?
But the
Donkey saw
Me and turned

Aside from me
These
Three times.

Seven altars,
Seven bulls,
Seven rams,
Seven altars,
Seven altars,
Seven altars,
Seven bulls,
Seven rams.

Three times.

One,
And those
Who died by
The Plague
Were
24,000.

Twenty years old,
Twenty years old,
First,
43,730
250
22,200
40,500
76,500
64,300
60,500
52,700
32,500
45,600
64,400
53,400

45,400
601,730
23,000.

Two,
One,
One,
Tenth,
Fourth,
Two,
Three-tenths,
Two-tenths,
One,
A tenth,
One,
A tenth,
Half,
Third,
Fourth,
Fourteenth,
Fifteenth,
Seven,
First,
Two,
One,
Seven,
One,
Three-tenths,
Two-tenths,
A tenth,
Seven,
One,
Seven,
Seven,
Seventh,
First,
Two,

One,
Three-tenths,
Two-tenths,
One,
A tenth,
Seven,
One.

7th
1st
1,
1,
7,
1,
3/10,
2/10,
1/10,
7,
1,
10th,
7th,
1,
1,
7,
1,
3/10,
2/10,
1,
1/10,
7,
1,
15th,
7th,
7,
13,
2,
14,

1,
3/10,
2/10,
2,
1/10,
14,
1,
2nd,
12,
2,
14,
1,
1,
3rd,
11,
2,
14,
1,
1,
4th,
10,
1,
1,
5th,
9,
2,
14,
6th,
8,
2,
14,
1,
1,
7th,
7,
2,
14,

1,
1,
8th,
1,
1,
7,
1,
1.

1,000,
1,000,
1,000,
12,000,
1,000,
Thousands,
Hundreds,
Little ones,
Third,
Seventh,
Seventh.

One in
Five hundred,
675,000
Sheep,
72,000
Cattle,
61,000
Donkeys,
Persons were,
32,000,
And the half,
Sheep was
337,500,
Sheep was
675,
Cattle were

36,000,
Levy was 72,
Donkeys were
30,500,
Human beings were
16,000,
Half was
337,500,
Human beings were
16,000,
One drawn,
Every fifty,
The thousands,
The captains,
Of hundreds,
16,750 shekels,
Of thousands
And
Of hundreds.

Little ones,
Our little ones.

1,000,
2,000,
2,000,
2,000.

The six cities,
Five forty-two cities,
Forty-eight cities,
Your six cities.

1921

According to some, *to consider* something means "to know the stars." It's a word that comes from the Old English *cunnan,* meaning "to know," and the Latin *sidera,* which means "constellations." It's thought that the term emerged in the fourteenth century in reference to navigation, since to know one's way among the stars was as powerful a tool as any. But it's also possible that instead of deriving from the Old English, the *con* in *consider* comes from the Latin *cum,* which means "together" or "with," and which morphs into *con* when used as a prefix and placed before a consonant, like the *s* in Latin's *sidera.* This therefore transforms *consider* into a much different kind of word: "to be with the stars," "to commune with the stars," "to be one with the stars," "to dream." Sometimes the essay needs to be a place for emphatic certainty. But far more frequently, and much more desperately, the essay has been a safety zone for longing, wonder, and doubt: a refuge we can inhabit when we do not know, but want to; when we cannot feel, but must. "Perhaps," wrote Jean Toomer, "our lot on the earth is to seek and to search. Now and again we find just enough to enable us to carry on, but I doubt that any of us will completely find and be found in this life."

JEAN TOOMER

Blood-Burning Moon

1

Up from the skeleton stone walls, up from the rotting floor boards and the solid hand-hewn beams of oak of the pre-war cotton factory, dusk came. Up from the dusk the full moon came. Glowing like a fired pine-knot, it illumined the great door and soft showered the Negro shanties aligned along the single street of factory town. The full moon in the great door was an omen. Negro women improvised songs against its spell.

Louisa sang as she came over the crest of the hill from the white folks' kitchen. Her skin was the color of oak leaves on young trees in fall. Her breasts, firm and up-pointed like ripe acorns. And her singing had the low murmur of winds in fig trees. Bob Stone, younger son of the people she worked for, loved her. By the way the world reckons things, he had won her. By measure of that warm glow which came into her mind at thought of him, he had won her. Tom Burwell, whom the whole town called Big Boy, also loved her. But working in the fields all day, and far away from her, gave him no chance to show it. Though often enough of evenings he had tried to. Somehow, he never got along. Strong as he was with hands upon the ax or plow, he found it difficult to hold her. Or so he thought. But the fact was that he held her to factory town more firmly than he thought for. His black balanced, and pulled against, the white of Stone, when she thought of them. And her mind was vaguely upon them as she came over the crest of the hill, coming from the white folks' kitchen. As she sang softly at the evil face of the full moon.

A strange stir was in her. Indolently, she tried to fix upon Bob or Tom as the cause of it. To meet Bob in the canebrake, as she was going to do an hour or so later, was nothing new. And Tom's proposal which she felt on its

343

way to her could be indefinitely put off. Separately, there was no unusual significance to either one. But for some reason, they jumbled when her eyes gazed vacantly at the rising moon. And from the jumble came the stir that was strangely within her. Her lips trembled. The slow rhythm of her song grew agitant and restless. Rusty black and tan spotted hounds, lying in the dark corners of porches or prowling around back yards, put their noses in the air and caught its tremor. They began plaintively to yelp and howl. Chickens woke up and cackled. Intermittently, all over the countryside dogs barked and roosters crowed as if heralding a weird dawn or some ungodly awakening. The women sang lustily. Their songs were cotton-wads to stop their ears. Louisa came down into factory town and sank wearily upon the step before her home. The moon was rising towards a thick cloud-bank which soon would hide it.

> Red nigger moon. Sinner!
> Blood-burning moon. Sinner!
> Come out that fact'ry door.

2

Up from the deep dusk of a cleared spot on the edge of the forest a mellow glow arose and spread fan-wise into the low-hanging heavens. And all around the air was heavy with the scent of boiling cane. A large pile of cane-stalks lay like ribboned shadows upon the ground. A mule, harnessed to a pole, trudged lazily round and round the pivot of the grinder. Beneath a swaying oil lamp, a Negro alternately whipped out at the mule, and fed cane-stalks to the grinder. A fat boy waddled pails of fresh ground juice between the grinder and the boiling stove. Steam came from the copper boiling pan. The scent of cane came from the copper pan and drenched the forest and the hill that sloped to factory town, beneath its fragrance. It drenched the men in circle seated around the stove. Some of them chewed at the white pulp of stalks, but there was no need for them to, if all they wanted was to taste the cane. One tasted it in factory town. And from factory town one could see the soft haze thrown by the glowing stove upon the low-hanging heavens.

Old David Georgia stirred the thickening syrup with a long ladle, and ever so often drew it off. Old David Georgia tended his stove and told tales about the white folks, about moonshining and cotton picking, and about sweet nigger gals, to the men who sat there about his stove to listen to him. Tom Burwell chewed cane-stalk and laughed with the others till some one mentioned Louisa. Till some one said something about Louisa and Bob Stone, about the silk stockings she must have gotten from him. Blood ran up Tom's neck hotter than the glow that flooded from the stove. He sprang up. Glared at the men and said, "She's my gal." Will Manning laughed. Tom strode over to him. Yanked him up and knocked him to the ground. Several of Manning's friends got up to fight for him. Tom whipped out a long knife and would have cut them to shreds if they hadnt ducked into the woods. Tom had had enough. He nodded to Old David Georgia and swung down the path to factory town. Just then, the dogs started barking and the roosters began to crow. Tom felt funny. Away from the fight, away from the stove, chill got to him. He shivered. He shuddered when he saw the full moon rising towards the cloud-bank. He who didnt give a godam for the fears of old women. He forced his mind to fasten on Louisa. Bob Stone. Better not be. He turned into the street and saw Louisa sitting before her home. He went towards her, ambling, touched the brim of a marvelously shaped, spotted, felt hat, said he wanted to say something to her, and then found that he didnt know what he had to say, or if he did, that he couldnt say it. He shoved his big fists in his overalls, grinned, and started to move off.

"Youall want me, Tom?"

"Thats what us wants, sho, Louisa."

"Well, here I am—"

"An here I is, but that aint ahelpin none, all th same."

"You wanted to say something? . . ."

"I did that, sho. But words is like th spots on dice: no matter how y fumbles em, there's times when they jes wont come. I dunno why. Seems like th love I feels fo yo done stole m tongue. I got it now. Whee! Louisa, honey, I oughtnt tell y, I feel I oughtnt cause yo is young an goes t church an I has had other gals, but Louisa I sho do love y. Lil gal, Ise watched y from them first days when youall sat right here befo yo door befo th well an sang sometimes in a way that like t broke m heart. Ise carried y with me into th fields, day after day, an after that, an I sho can plow when yo is there, an I can pick cotton. Yassur! Come near beatin Barlo yesterday. I sho did. Yassur! An next year if ole Stone'll trust me, I'll have a farm. My own.

My bales will buy yo what y gets from white folks now. Silk stockings an purple dresses—course I dont believe what some folks been whisperin as t how y gets them things now. White folks always did do for niggers what they likes. An they jes cant help alikin yo, Louisa. Bob Stone likes y. Course he does. But not th way folks is awhisperin. Does he, hon?"

"I dont know what you mean, Tom."

"Course y dont. Ise already cut two niggers. Had t hon, t tell em so. Niggers always tryin t make somethin out a nothin. An then besides, white folks aint up t them tricks so much nowadays. Godam better not be. Leastawise not with yo. Cause I wouldnt stand f it. Nassur."

"What would you do, Tom?"

"Cut him jes like I cut a nigger."

"No, Tom—"

"I said I would an there aint no mo to it. But that aint th talk f now. Sing, honey Louisa, an while I'm listenin t y I'll be makin love."

Tom took her hand in his. Against the tough thickness of his own, hers felt soft and small. His huge body slipped down to the step beside her. The full moon sank upward into the deep purple of the cloud-bank. An old woman brought a lighted lamp and hung it on the common well whose bulky shadow squatted in the middle of the road, opposite Tom and Louisa. The old woman lifted the well-lid, took hold the chain, and began drawing up the heavy bucket. As she did so, she sang. Figures shifted, restlesslike, between lamp and window in the front rooms of the shanties. Shadows of the figures fought each other on the gray dust of the road. Figures raised the windows and joined the old woman in song. Louisa and Tom, the whole street, singing:

> *Red nigger moon. Sinner!*
> *Blood-burning moon. Sinner!*
> *Come out that fact'ry door.*

3

Bob Stone sauntered from his veranda out into the gloom of fir trees and magnolias. The clear white of his skin paled, and the flush of his cheeks turned purple. As if to balance this outer change, his mind became consciously a white man's. He passed the house with its huge open hearth which, in the days of slavery, was the plantation cookery. He saw Louisa bent over that hearth. He went in as a master should and took her. Direct, honest, bold. None of this sneaking that he had to go through now. The contrast was repulsive to him. His family had lost ground. Hell no, his family still owned the niggers, practically. Damned if they did, or he wouldnt have to duck around so. What would they think if they knew? His mother? His sister? He shouldnt mention them, shouldnt think of them in this connection. There in the dusk he blushed at doing so. Fellows about town were all right, but how about his friends up North? He could see them incredible, repulsed. They didnt know. The thought first made him laugh. Then, with their eyes still upon him, he began to feel embarrassed. He felt the need of explaining things to them. Explain hell. They wouldnt understand, and moreover, who ever heard of a Southerner getting on his knees to any Yankee, or anyone. No sir. He was going to see Louisa to-night, and love her. She was lovely—in her way. Nigger way. What way was that? Damned if he knew. Must know. He'd known her long enough to know. Was there something about niggers that you couldnt know? Listening to them at church didnt tell you anything. Looking at them didnt tell you anything. Talking to them didnt tell you anything— unless it was gossip, unless they wanted to talk. Of course, about farming, and licker, and craps—but those werent nigger. Nigger was something more. How much more? Something to be afraid of, more? Hell no. Who ever heard of being afraid of a nigger? Tom Burwell. Cartwell had told him that Tom went with Louisa after she reached home. No sir. No nigger had ever been with his girl. He'd like to see one try. Some position for him to be in. Him, Bob Stone, of the old Stone family, in a scrap with a nigger over a nigger girl. In the good old days . . . Ha! Those were the days. His family had lost ground. Not so much, though. Enough for him to have to cut through old Lemon's canefield by way of the woods, that he might meet her. She was worth it. Beautiful nigger gal. Why nigger? Why not, just gal? No, it was because she was nigger that he went to her. Sweet . . . The scent of boiling cane came to him. Then he saw the rich glow of the stove. He heard the voices of the men circled around it. He was about to skirt the clearing when he heard his own name mentioned. He stopped. Quivering. Leaning against a tree, he listened.

"Bad nigger. Yassur, he sho is one bad nigger when he gets started."

"Tom Burwell's been on th gang three times fo cuttin men."

"What y think he's agwine t do t Bob Stone?"

"Dunno yet. He aint found out. When he does— Baby!"

"Aint no tellin."

"Young Stone aint no quitter an I ken tell y that. Blood of th old uns in his veins."

"Thats right. He'll scrap, sho."

"Be gettin too hot f niggers round this away."

"Shut up, nigger. Y dont know what y talkin bout."

Bob Stone's ears burned as though he had been holding them over the stove. Sizzling heat welled up within him. His feet felt as if they rested on red-hot coals. They stung him to quick movement. He circled the fringe of the glowing. Not a twig cracked beneath his feet. He reached the path that led to factory town. Plunged furiously down it. Halfway along, a blindness within him veered him aside. He crashed into the bordering canebrake. Cane leaves cut his face and lips. He tasted blood. He threw himself down and dug his fingers in the ground. The earth was cool. Cane-roots took the fever from his hands. After a long while, or so it seemed to him, the thought came to him that it must be time to see Louisa. He got to his feet and walked calmly to their meeting place. No Louisa. Tom Burwell had her. Veins in his forehead bulged and distended. Saliva moistened the dried blood on his lips. He bit down on his lips. He tasted blood. Not his own blood; Tom Burwell's blood. Bob drove through the cane and out again upon the road. A hound swung down the path before him towards factory town. Bob couldnt see it. The dog loped aside to let him pass. Bob's blind rushing made him stumble over it. He fell with a thud that dazed him. The hound yelped. Answering yelps came from all over the countryside. Chickens cackled. Roosters crowed, heralding the bloodshot eyes of southern awakening. Singers in the town were silenced. They shut their windows down. Palpitant between the rooster crows, a chill hush settled upon the huddled forms of Tom and Louisa. A figure rushed from the shadow and stood before them. Tom popped to his feet.

"Whats y want?"

"I'm Bob Stone."

"Yassur—an I'm Tom Burwell. Whats y want?"

Bob lunged at him. Tom side-stepped, caught him by the shoulder, and flung him to the ground. Straddled him.

"Let me up."

"Yassur—but watch yo doins, Bob Stone."

A few dark figures, drawn by the sound of scuffle, stood about them. Bob sprang to his feet.

"Fight like a man, Tom Burwell, an I'll lick y."

Again he lunged. Tom side-stepped and flung him to the ground. Straddled him.

"Get off me, you godam nigger you."

"Yo sho has started somethin now. Get up."

Tom yanked him up and began hammering at him. Each blow sounded as if it smashed into a precious, irreplaceable soft something. Beneath them, Bob staggered back. He reached in his pocket and whipped out a knife.

"Thats my game, sho."

Blue flash, a steel blade slashed across Bob Stone's throat. He had a sweetish sick feeling. Blood began to flow. Then he felt a sharp twitch of pain. He let his knife drop. He slapped one hand against his neck. He pressed the other on top of his head as if to hold it down. He groaned. He turned, and staggered towards the crest of the hill in the direction of white town. Negroes who had seen the fight slunk into their homes and blew the lamps out. Louisa, dazed, hysterical, refused to go indoors. She slipped, crumbled, her body loosely propped against the woodwork of the well. Tom Burwell leaned against it. He seemed rooted there.

Bob reached Broad Street. White men rushed up to him. He collapsed in their arms.

"Tom Burwell . . ."

White men like ants upon a forage rushed about. Except for the taut hum of their moving, all was silent. Shotguns, revolvers, rope, kerosene, torches. Two high-powered cars with glaring search-lights. They came together. The taut hum rose to a low roar. Then nothing could be heard but the flop of their feet in the thick dust of the road. The moving body of their silence preceded them over the crest of the hill into factory town. It flattened the Negroes beneath it. It rolled to the wall of the factory, where it stopped. Tom knew that they were coming. He couldnt move. And then he saw the search-lights of the two cars glaring down on him. A quick shock went through him. He stiffened. He started to run. A yell went up from the mob. Tom wheeled about and faced them. They poured down on him. They swarmed. A large man with dead-white face and flabby cheeks came to him and almost jabbed a gun-barrel through his guts.

"Hands behind y, nigger."

Tom's wrists were bound. The big man shoved him to the well. Burn him over it, and when the woodwork caved in, his body would drop to the bottom. Two deaths for a godam nigger. Louisa was driven back. The mob pushed in. Its pressure, its momentum was too great. Drag him to the factory. Wood and stakes already there. Tom moved in the direction indicated. But they had to drag him. They reached the great door. Too many to get in there. The mob divided and flowed around the walls to either side. The big man shoved him through the door. The mob pressed in from the sides. Taut humming. No words. A stake was sunk into the ground. Rotting floor boards piled around it. Kerosene poured on the rotting floor boards. Tom bound to the stake. His breast was bare. Nails' scratches let little lines of blood trickle down and mat into the hair. His face, his eyes were set and stony. Except for irregular breathing, one would have thought him already dead. Torches were flung onto the pile. A great flare muffled in black smoke shot upward. The mob yelled. The mob was silent. Now Tom could be seen within the flames. Only his head, erect, lean, like a blackened stone. Stench of burning flesh soaked the air. Tom's eyes popped. His head settled downward. The mob yelled. Its yell echoed against the skeleton stone walls and sounded like a hundred yells. Like a hundred mobs yelling. Its yell thudded against the thick front wall and fell back. Ghost of a yell slipped through the flames and out the great door of the factory. It fluttered like a dying thing down the single street of factory town. Louisa, upon the step before her home, did not hear it, but her eyes opened slowly. They saw the full moon glowing in the great door. The full moon, an evil thing, an omen, soft showering the homes of folks she knew. Where were they, these people? She'd sing, and perhaps they'd come out and join her. Perhaps Tom Burwell would come. At any rate, the full moon in the great door was an omen which she must sing to:

> Red nigger moon. Sinner!
> Blood-burning moon. Sinner!
> Come out that fact'ry door.

1924

Until now, the photographs Ansel Adams has taken have not been very good: documentary records of an afternoon with friends, a tree that he admired, a sunset worth remembering. They are placeholders for meaning, but not particularly meaningful themselves. Of course, it isn't that Adams doesn't consider photography art. Rather, he hasn't figured out yet how to make photography work, how to render with light and luck the deep and powerful truths that he feels when in the mountains. As Adams will write toward the end of his life, "When I am ready to make a photograph, I think what I see in my mind's eye is something that is not literally there. What I am interested in expressing is something that is built up from within, rather than something extracted from without." *When I am ready to make a photograph.* Not just "take" one. Not just capture through hope and a lens whatever it is that the world might provide. As one critic will write about Adams's work, it is this acknowledgment of the difference between receiving information and actively making art that allows Adams eventually "to voice the moods of light, to use textures like different instruments, to make clouds float, waterfalls flash, snow reveal its hidden life, and grasses bend in infinite delicacy under dew." It is April. And once again Adams is in Yosemite National Park, halfway up the granite face of a cliff called Half Dome. He's on his way to a popular spot among hikers called the Diving Board, a long and narrow projection of rock from which you can look up and see the sharp sheer face of Half Dome rising high before you. Along the way, Adams stops to take some shots—his girl-friend, his buddies, a bird, his shoes—until he realizes upon reaching the Diving Board that he has only two pictures left. He positions the camera to face Half Dome, that great and monstrous cliff face that looks as if it had punctured the earth from the inside out. Wow, Adams thinks, then clicks. Immediately, however, he knows that the picture he has taken is not going to work, will not relay to viewers the true experience of Half Dome. So with only one picture left, Adams takes a risk. He allows himself to "revisualize" the scene. (His word.) He places over his lens a heavy red filter that immediately darkens the sky, darkens it even more than the cliff itself is, which immediately opens up an abyss beside the cliff, as if the brooding shelf of Half Dome had torn straight through it like a cleaver made of light, terrifying and bright. As Adams later puts it, this is the first time in his career that he has managed to make a mountain "look like how it feels." To do this, however, he has deeply manipulated the mountain he loves, he has wrangled the reality of the world around him into what he needed it to be. "Photography is really perception," he writes. "As with all art, the objective of photography is not the duplication of visual reality, but an investigation of the outer world and its influence on the inner world. . . . All of my photographs are photographs of myself."

GERTRUDE STEIN

If I Told Him:
A Completed Portrait of Picasso

If I told him would he like it. Would he like it if I told him.

Would he like it would Napoleon would Napoleon would would he like it.

If Napoleon if I told him if I told him if Napoleon. Would he like it if I told him if I told him if Napoleon. Would he like it if Napoleon if Napoleon if I told him. If I told him if Napoleon if Napoleon if I told him. If I told him would he like it would he like it if I told him.

Now.

Not now.

And now.

Now.

Exactly as as kings.

Feeling full for it.

Exactitude as kings.

So to beseech you as full as for it.

Exactly or as kings.

Shutters shut and open so do queens. Shutters shut and shutters and so shutters shut and shutters and so and so shutters and so shutters shut and so shutters shut and shutters and so. And so shutters shut and so and also. And also and so and so and also.

Exact resemblance to exact resemblance the exact resemblance as exact as a resemblance, exactly as resembling, exactly resembling, exactly in resemblance exactly a resemblance, exactly and resemblance. For this is so. Because.

Now actively repeat at all, now actively repeat at all, now actively repeat at all.

Have hold and hear, actively repeat at all.

I judge judge.

As a resemblance to him.

Who comes first. Napoleon the first.

Who comes too coming coming too, who goes there, as they go they share, who shares all, all is as all as as yet or as yet.

Now to date now to date. Now and now and date and the date.

Who came first Napoleon at first. Who came first Napoleon the first. Who came first, Napoleon first.

Presently.

Exactly do they do.

First exactly.

Exactly do they do too.

First exactly.

And first exactly.

Exactly do they do.

And first exactly and exactly.

And do they do.

At first exactly and first exactly and do they do.

The first exactly.

And do they do.

The first exactly.

At first exactly.

First as exactly.

At first as exactly.

Presently.

As presently.

As as presently.

He he he he and he and he and and he and he and he and and as and as he and as he and he. He is and as he is, and as he is and he is, he is and as he and he and as he is and he and he and and he and he.

Can curls rob can curls quote, quotable.

As presently.

As exactitude.

As trains.

Has trains.

Has trains.

As trains.

As trains.

Presently.

Proportions.

Presently.

As proportions as presently.

Father and farther.

Was the king or room.

Farther and whether.

Was there was there was there what was there was there what was there was there there was there.

Whether and in there.

As even say so.

One.

I land.

Two.

I land.

Three.

The land.

Three.

The land.

Three.

The land.

Two.

I land.

Two.

I land.

One.

I land.

Two.

I land.

As a so.

They cannot.

A note.

They cannot.

A float.

They cannot.

They dote.
They cannot.
They as denote.
Miracles play.
Play fairly.
Play fairly well.
A well.
As well.
As or as presently.
Let me recite what history teaches. History teaches.

1927

This year, physicist Werner Heisenberg writes a letter to a friend in which he describes a theory that becomes known as "the uncertainty principle," the idea that the act of observing something alters the reality of the thing being observed. In other words, it puts a limit on what we can know. At a moment in history when scientists are starting to figure out how to split the atom, erect hundred-story buildings, and launch rockets into space, this is an idea out of step with our ambitions. It suggests that some things will always be out of reach for humans, and that the world is a mystery after all. And so soon enough his theory is embraced by a new generation of writers who believe, as Laura Riding Jackson will write, that the world and the word are wholly incompatible:

> *This is not exactly what I mean*
> *Any more than the sun is the sun.*
> *But how to mean more closely*
> *If the sun shines but approximately?*
> *What a world of awkwardness!*
> *What hostile implements of sense!*
> *Perhaps this is as close a meaning*
> *As perhaps becomes such knowing.*
> *Else I think the world and I*
> *Must live together as strangers and die—*

The problem, however, is that the German word that Heisenberg actually uses in his letter is *Ungenauigkeit*—"imprecision"—

and I think that makes a difference. Heisenberg doesn't mean that knowledge isn't possible. He doesn't mean that the paper on which these words are printed cannot be proved to exist. He doesn't mean that just because a world war has ended, and Europe is in shambles, and communism is gaining in popularity around the world, nothing in our lives will be certain again. He means that when you probe the world closely enough, deeply enough, at so microscopic a level that even the light particles you're using are heavier than the things you are trying to see them with, it becomes even harder to really know what's going on. Light hits your target with such a brutal force that before you can glimpse what's beneath your microscope, it has already hurtled out of view, somewhere else. Knowledge isn't impossible, Heisenberg would insist. Knowing is.

LAURA RIDING JACKSON

In a Café

This is the second time I have seen that girl here. What makes me suspicious is that her manner has not changed. From her ears I should say she is Polish. If this is so, is it not dangerous to drink coffee here? Does anyone else think of this, I wonder? Yet why should I be suspicious? And why should her manner not remain unchanged? She has probably been cold, unhappy, unsuccessful or simply not alive ever since I saw her last. Quite honestly I wish her success. The man who is making sketches from pictures in the Art Magazine may find her little Polish ears not repulsive. For good luck I turn away and do not look at her again. I, who am neither sluttish nor genteel, like this place because it has brown curtains of a shade I do not like. Everything, even my position, which is not against the wall, is unsatisfactory and pleasing: the men coming too hurriedly, the women too comfortably from the lavatories, which are in an unnecessarily prominent position—all this is disgusting; it puts me in a sordid good-humour. This attitude I find to be the only way in which I can defy my own intelligence. Otherwise I should become barbaric and be a modern artist and intelligently mind everything, or I should become civilized and be a Christian Scientist and intelligently mind nothing. Plainly the only problem is to avoid that love of lost identity which drives so many clever people to hold difficult points of view—by *difficult* I mean big, hungry, religious points of view which absorb their personality. I for one am resolved to mind or not mind only to the degree where my point of view is no larger than myself. I can thus have a great number of points of view, like fingers, and which I can treat as I treat the fingers of my hand, to hold my cup, to tap the table for me and fold themselves away when I do not wish to think. If I fold them away now, then I am sitting here all this time (without ordering a second cup) because other people go on sitting here, not because I am thinking. It is all indeed, I admit, rather horrible. But if I remain a person instead of be-coming a point of view, I have no contact with horror. If I become a point of view, I become a force and am brought into direct contact with horror, another force. As well set one plague of cats loose upon another and expect peace of it. As a force I have power, as a person virtue. All forces eventually commit suicide with their power, while virtue in a person merely gives him a small though constant pain from being continuously touched, looked at, mentally handled; a pain by which he learns to recognize himself. Poems, being more like persons, probably only squirm every time they are read and wrap themselves round more tightly. Pictures and pieces of music, being more like forces, are soon worn out by the power that holds them together. To me pictures and music are always like stories told backwards: or like this I read in the newspaper: 'Up to the last she retained all her faculties and was able to sign cheques.'

It is surely time for me to go and yet I do not in the least feel like going. I have been through certain intimacies and small talk with everything here; when I go out I shall have to begin all over again in the street, in addition to wondering how many people are being run over behind me; when I get home I shall turn on the light and say to myself how glad I am it is winter, with no moths to kill. And I shall look behind the curtain where my clothes hang and think that I have done this ever since the homicidal red-haired boy confided his fear to me and I was sorry for him and went to his room and did it for him. And my first look round will be a Wuthering-Heights look; after that I shall settle down to work and forget about myself.

I am well aware that we form, all together, one monster. But I refuse to giggle and I refuse to be frightened and I refuse to be fierce. Nor will I feed or be fed on. I will simply think of other things. I will go now. Let them stare. I am well though eccentrically dressed.

1934

Maybe the only difference between an essayist and a journalist is the degree to which one becomes traumatized by facts. As a young man, Charles Reznikoff worked for a magazine called *Corpus Juris*—"a body of legal matters." For years it was Reznikoff's job to catalog the testimonies of thousands of court witnesses in hundreds of legal cases, methodically transcribing the statements of people who were allowed only to offer the raw facts of a case—what was said, what was seen, what was done, what was heard—and never their own thoughts about why those things had happened. They were statements being made in a temporary space—after an event had taken place, but before its meaning had been established—and so it was a space whose story was up for grabs. Reznikoff once said that what he admired about these texts was how they managed to affect him without doing anything but relaying observable fact. "Reading them is like witnessing something happen that did not actually happen to you," he explained, "and how that thing can still express something that you yourself feel." This year, while trying to evoke that same empathy in his own work, Reznikoff starts borrowing from the legal cases he had transcribed in his youth, stripping away the individualizing contexts of each case, breaking them into lines to accentuate common speech, and then merging them into an epic, dispassionate, impersonal narrative that attempts to record in clinically nonjudgmental detail the accidents, injustices, and disasters in American history. But when *Testimony* is finally published, the best that critics can say about it is that it's "uncluttered." At worst, it's "amoral," "crude," "astigmatic," "not art." "It is numbing," wrote one, "pointless in its cold recitation of savagery and murder . . . without the slightest saving grace of interpretation by the author." This is after the First World War, and just before the Second, and what critics seem to want from artists right now is an escape from the brutal repetition of history, a salve of indignation that might redeem humanity from what's inevitably to come. But as more recent critics have explained, Reznikoff knows that language can't revoke the events of the past any more than gas chambers can erase our memories of the dead. This is the year when a memoir called *Four Weeks in the Hands of Hitler's Hell-Hounds: The Nazi Murder Camp of Dachau* is written by a man who had escaped from the camp. It is published simultaneously in German, Russian, Spanish, and English more than two years before any nation is willing to acknowledge what the Nazis are actually doing. *How much do we know?* Charles Reznikoff asks. *How much can we know, choose to know, want to know, ignore?* By providing us with what feels like a blank slate of facts, Reznikoff neither eschews nor condones the atrocities he's collected, but instead creates a space of unmediated expression—"an intentionally neutral moral ground," as he once described it—that gradually starts to feel, as it grows and grows within us, a little too neutral, perhaps. Too blank, too objective, too unaffected by the facts of which it is composed, so that the blank slate begins to insist it be acknowledged, approached, examined, questioned, inhabited, experienced, and then finally judged. "I didn't invent the world," Charles Reznikoff once wrote, "but I felt it."

Testimony: The United States

I

Social Life

1

Before daybreak, Clay, a professional gambler,
went to a colored prostitute's tent
in the outskirts of town. About fifteen minutes after he got there,
sitting on the bed and taking off his shoes,
Ross, who "kept" her and whose mistress she was,
knocked on the screen door.
She called out that she had company
but Ross was drunk:
he jerked the screen door open
(it was only fastened by a hook over a nail),
kicked open the wooden door, closed but unlocked,
and came in.

The light in the tent was dim
but the two men knew each other:
Ross was also a gambler by profession
and had once gone to Clay's gaming-table
and punched a pistol in Clay's money
throwing it around.
Clay jumped up from the bed where he was sitting
and, pistol in hand,
asked Ross why he "broke in" on him.
Ross answered he didn't break in:

the door was "already open."
He had one hand at his mouth, holding a cigarette,
and asked Clay for a match.
Clay said he had no match,
but Cora got up from bed to get one
and Ross lit his cigarette.
Clay asked Ross if he had a "gun"
and Ross said no
and added that Clay was welcome to search him.
Clay did, Ross smiling during the search,
and Clay did not find a gun. He then caught Ross by the lapel of his
    coat
and told him, with a curse, that the best thing he could do was to go
    back to town,
and turned him loose.
The two men stood there facing each other for a few moments
and then Ross said that Clay had the best of him
but was acting like "a damn son of a bitch"—
and Clay shot him.

Cora ran out of the tent, screaming,
and heard three more shots.
When all was quiet in the tent again,
she came back.
The smoke blinded her for a minute or two
and then she saw Clay sitting astride Ross's body—
Ross was dead—
and striking the face a good "lick" with the handle of the pistol.
She begged Clay not to strike Ross again
and went down on the floor
and began talking to the dead man,
screaming, "Oh, my darling! Oh, my darling!"
And Clay put on his coat and left.

2
Late that night while they were upon the public highway,
he told her she could scream all she chose to

because there was nobody within three miles;
and then he stopped the buggy and got out
and took the lines and whip with him
and went around in front of the horse
and fastened the lines to the bridge railing.
Then he came back and asked her if she would get out without any
   trouble
and she said, "No!"

He said he would pull her out
and she told him he would not;
and he caught hold of her
and she caught hold of the buggy,
and he pulled her hands loose
and pulled her out of the buggy.

II

Domestic Scenes

1

She saw her father in the morning
as he came through the gate and up the steps.
She and her mother were in the kitchen
cooking breakfast;
and her father came in through the side door.
She had opened the door for him;
"Good morning, Pa," she said
and he had answered, pleasantly enough it seemed,
"Good morning."

Her mother was lifting the mush from the stove
and both were about to sit down at the small table in the kitchen
and have their breakfast.

Her father sat down. She took away his hat
and hung it on a nail in back of him,

and asked him to take off his overcoat
for it was warm in the room;
he did
and put it on a chair
and sat down again.

Then he asked his wife if she thought of coming back to him
and she answered that she had not been thinking anything of the
    kind just yet;
and his daughter spoke up and said,
as pleasantly as she could:
since they were both happier apart,
she thought they had best live apart and be friends—
it would be better for both of them.
At this her father jumped up
and she thought he was going to slap her
and ran out of the back door:
the door had a spring screen
and it slammed shut.

She turned to look at her father:
he was pulling a pistol from his pocket
and she heard her mother say, "Oh, George, don't shoot!"
But he did and shot her mother.
Then he went towards the back door and fired at his daughter—
she was out on the back porch looking in,
fixed to the spot.
He fired through the screen door
and the bullet struck his daughter through the left breast.

2

For several years Daffodil had been living with an Indian woman
and earning his living as a fisherman; living in a shack built upon a scow
moored to the shore of a river.
On the afternoon before Christmas,
they went in a rowboat to the home of her sister

who, with her husband, was also living in a shack
about five or six miles away.

They stayed until about eight o'clock Christmas night—
the company drinking much beer and some whiskey—
and while there Daffodil, jealous because of something the woman
     he was living with said,
struck her with his fists.
They left to go home:
he carried her
and threw her into the bottom of his boat.

Later that night, he was in a saloon near the waterfront,
only about a mile from the shack where they had been visiting,
and bought a dollar's worth of whiskey,
and went back to his boat.
They went on to their home
but, about midnight,
were still out on the bay
quite a distance from shore;
and he was seen striking the woman
who was seated near the stern
with something he held in his hand,
and those who watched
could hear the sound of the blows
and the woman screaming.

In a few days her body was found
in about eight feet of water
tied by a rope to the end of the scow
and held under water by a sack containing lead.

   3
Ned did not like his brother-in-law
because of a claim for money Ned said was due him
and among his threats were

he would "maul Jackson" and "stamp his guts out."
Stopping at Jackson's house one day
Ned told his sister that he had heard at a rodeo
someone charging Jackson with stealing hogs
and even stealing the salt to salt them with.
Ned went on
to spend the night with a friend camping a short distance away.
When Ned's friend broke camp next morning
and, as he had arranged with Jackson,
brought the camping utensils to Jackson for storage,
Ned went along.
Jackson and his wife had kept breakfast waiting for them
and now invited them to the meal.
The young men, however, had eaten their breakfast
before breaking camp
and so sat down on the threshold to the front room of the house
while Jackson and his wife went to their breakfast in the kitchen.
The door of the kitchen was open
and they could talk to each other.

Jackson asked Ned's friend if he had been at the rodeo, too,
and had heard him charged with the theft of hogs.
Ned's friend answered that he had been at the rodeo but had not
      heard the charge
and either Jackson—or his wife—then asked Ned who besides
      himself had heard it.
He gave them two or three names
and then wanted to know if his word was doubted
and not good enough for Jackson.
Jackson replied that of course his word was good enough
but he wanted to have someone else's word, too,
so that when he went for the man who had made the charge,
should the man deny making it,
the matter would not rest simply on the man's word against Ned's.
But Ned was angry
saying that Jackson was not big enough to question his word

and wanted him to come outside and settle their quarrel—
Ned younger and stronger.

Jackson said that he would not come out
and Ned said he would make him;
Jackson then said he wanted no trouble
and Ned replied he was going to have it.
Jackson rose from the breakfast table
and went into the front room; as he did so
Ned stepped out of the front door
and picked up an iron-bound singletree.
Jackson stopped at the open door
and told Ned to leave the ranch
and said again that he wanted no trouble.
Ned answered that he would not leave
and could not be put off,
and again challenged Jackson to come out.
Jackson asked him what he meant to do with the singletree
and Ned replied that he would show him.
Then Jackson picked up Ned's rifle
standing inside the door—
Ned had placed it near the threshold when he sat down—
and saying, "Damn you, I'll learn you to fight me!"
fired,
and Ned, standing eight or ten feet away,
fell to the ground.

Jackson left the house
and his wife went to find him,
leaving her little boy to take care of his uncle.
While she was gone,
Ned with his pocketknife
cut his own throat:
the bullet passing through his intestines
lodged in the hip bone
and he was in agonizing pain.

4

Mrs. Bell owned a quarter-section of land
and had used water from a ditch for irrigating;
but, some years before, a new ditch had been dug
and now the water of the old ditch was flowing through it.
Her brother had helped in the digging—
the new ditch passed through his land
next to that of his sister.

She claimed the right to use the water
but her brother said she could have none of it
until he was paid for his work;
and he built a dam on his own land
to stop the flow of water to hers.
And now the alfalfa upon the Bell place,
as well as the trees,
were suffering for lack of water.

Her husband said he would have the water
and her brother—
the stronger
and, overbearing and quarrelsome, he had beaten up Bell more than
    once—
said that if Bell interfered with the dam
he would put him in the ditch
and make a dam out of his body.

Bell went to the ditch and removed the dam
but later found that it had been replaced.
His brother-in-law had also fastened a rifle to a post
as a spring-gun,
running a cord from the trigger across the second dam
so that interference with it
would discharge the rifle and sound an alarm.
But the rifle was set not to cause any injury—
the muzzle pointed directly downward
about six inches from the ground.

After supper, on a night that was clear and still,
Bell and his wife drove to the dam in a buggy;
they carried a shovel
and under the seat Bell had placed his shotgun—
loaded.
Her brother and his wife had gone to bed,
but he heard the sound of the buggy,
dressed himself and went down to the dam.
His wife put out the light the better to see
and sat up in bed looking out of the window.

She saw a man in the buggy
and by his way of whistling
knew it was Bell.
She heard her husband and his sister talking
and Bell, too, but not what they were saying—
and suddenly there was a flash
and she heard the report of a gun.
She was sure it came from the buggy
and heard her husband crying out in pain,
"Oh, oh!"
Right afterwards, before she could get out of bed,
she heard a second shot;
and ran out of the house in her night clothes
towards her husband.
She could hear her sister-in-law saying,
"Go on, Papa; go on!"
and found her husband's body
near the post to which the spring-gun had been attached.

He had fallen across a barbed-wire fence
and was hanging over the wires;
still alive but gasping for breath.
And then he stopped breathing,
and she began to scream.
The string of the spring-gun
was under the body—

drawn and taut
and the rifle discharged.
So much for her story.

And this was Bell's story and that of his wife.
Neither knew about the spring-gun;
when they reached the dam,
she took the shovel and began to use it
because the land to be watered was hers.
When her brother came he took hold of her,
and pulled her towards the bank of the ditch;
there was a scuffle between them
and she fell on her knees.
Just then a shot was fired.
The horse hitched to the buggy lunged to the left,
and her husband shouted, "Whoa, whoa!" two or three times.
He believed that his wife was shot
and that he himself would be shot next;
holding the lines with his left hand,
he reached down with his right for the shotgun—
did not take the time to draw the gun to his shoulder—
and fired.
Her brother relaxed his hold on her arm
and fell limp in front of her:
just sank down.
She called to her sister-in-law
and when she came, her sister-in-law screamed
and then said: "You had better both go home!"

Did the first shot come from the spring-gun
set off by Mrs. Bell and her brother
scuffling on the bank of the ditch?
Or did Bell himself fire the first shot and was the second set off by his
    brother-in-law
as he fell dying?
Anyway, this is what the jury believed.

5

Watson was a mechanic, a hard-working man
earning from sixty to eighty dollars a month,
and, because of his work,
away from home much of the time.
His wife had died about ten years before
and there were three children—
twin girls of fifteen or sixteen and a boy of twelve.
Watson had to go to San Francisco
and stay there at work
several months. His daughters drew his wages—
and spent much of it for clothes
and theater tickets. When he came back
and found this out
he whipped his daughters with a leather strap he had;
and the next morning whipped them again
because breakfast was not ready.
They then decided to run away
and for three days hid in the basement of the house.

Later, he missed his silver watch
and asked his daughters about it;
at their answers
he charged them with lying
and beat them with a cane and a poker;
took one of them by the throat
and knocked her to the floor
and then kicked her in the side.
The next morning they ran away again
and lived for three weeks under the stairs
leading to an empty house.

6

The Mother-in-Law

His mother was much displeased by the marriage:
Jill was a country girl, the daughter of a farmer;

about twenty-six, and Jack a year younger.
Before the two left for the West,
Jack's mother got him to transfer his stocks and bonds to her.

Jack and his wife settled in Denver and, in two or three months,
Jack's mother came to Denver
to board and lodge in the same boarding-house.
For a while, she and Jill got along very well.
Jill hired a horse and buggy and drove her around;
and they went to church together.
Everything was pleasant enough
until, one evening, Jack wanted to go to a friend's house to play cards
and Jill objected: "Mrs. Tompkins is coming here tonight.
Can't you put your visit over until tomorrow?"
His mother heard them and said:
"If you want to go out, John, go out;
if you want to go to the theater
or to play cards with your friends,
do so.
She has no right to interfere with your pleasures!"

The next day, Jack's mother told Jill
that, from the letters she had been getting from Jack,
she didn't see how Jill and Jack could live together;
they would be better apart—
a good deal better for him and for her.
Her mother-in-law went on to tell her
there was no law in the land
that could compel a man to live with a woman
if he did not wish to—
as long as he paid her board.
She herself would pay Jill's way back to Brooklyn
or to her father's—
either way.
Jill said she would not go to her father's.
Then, her mother-in-law said, we will pay your way back to
    Brooklyn,

and offered Jill a hundred dollars
if she would give Jack a separation,
thinking that Jill might ask for two or three thousand
and she would pay it
and have done with Jill right away.

But Jill didn't say she would accept anything.
"Well, I am not going back," said her mother-in-law,
"and leave you two together;
I have all of Jack's money
and will leave him here without a cent—
without a red cent.
You should get a lawyer
and I will get my lawyer,
and they will draw up papers for a separation.
You have friends to advise you whom to go to."
Jill answered that she had no friends in Denver.
"You have friends in the boarding-house,"
and her mother-in-law added
that she had heard that Jill had been hanging around Jack
and that was why he had married her.

Jill began to cry—
as her mother-in-law explained afterwards,
"Of course, she did!
She could do that at any time"—
and got very angry.
"We are living happily together
and I don't see why we should separate!"
But her mother-in-law said coldly:
"I will give you three dollars a week to live on
for a separation,
and you must take that and live in Denver;
otherwise, I will leave you in Denver
without money or friends;
but you must not come back to New York.

You can go either to your sister's in Nevada or remain here,
but I don't want to lay eyes on you again!"

III

Children

1

The mining camp was near the top of a range of mountains;
no wagon road nearer than eight miles
and the rest of the way by trail
on foot or on the back of a horse or mule.
The community was under the rule of one man
whom they called their "Moses"—their teacher,
the teacher of all of them, parents and children.
The little boy was six years old
when he took a piece of a stove
and dropped it in the bushes,
and then said he had not taken it.
The "teacher" took the child
and ducked him in a pond
before six or more of the community
and the child's mother:
picked the boy up
and with one foot on the bank of the pond
and the other on a rock projecting above the water
dipped the boy into the pond
where it was shallow;
the child screamed in fright,
struggled
and held close to the man who was ducking him
and clutched at everything in sight;
when he was brought up
he had the mud and gravel at the bottom of the pond
clutched in his hands.

2

Nancy, all of twelve, living with her mother on the south side of the river,
was sent on an errand to her grandmother
who lived north of the railroad bridge;
and her brother, nine years of age, was sent with her.
When she reached the bridge, she stopped
to look and listen for a train,
for she knew trains were passing over the bridge
all hours of the day and night;
but she did not hear or see any
and with her brother started across.
When about halfway—
the bridge had no railing or planking
nothing except the ties to walk on—
she saw a train coming from the north
rounding the curve to the bridge.
The children were frightened
and began to run back,
but the little boy caught his foot in the ties
and fell.
His sister stopped, got him up,
and they ran a few steps farther.
Then she stopped again,
placed him on the end of a beam projecting from the bridge,
outside the rails for safety,
and kept on running
away from the train.

But when she was almost at the end of the bridge
she was struck by the engine
and, face up, pushed along the track about thirty feet
until the train stopped.

3

There were four machines for making horseshoes in the shop
and the boy—he was fifteen—

was put to work at one of them as "press boy."
The machines were worked by belts
running over a revolving shaft
and to reach the shaft—about twenty feet from the floor—
one had to go up a ladder.

The belt which ran the machine the boy was working at
was old. It broke twice
and the machinist went up and fixed it.
It broke again in the afternoon
and the machinist told the boy to go up and hold the belt
while he tried again to fix it.
The boy took the belt, weighing about forty or forty-five pounds,
on his shoulders
and started up the ladder;
when he got to the top he stepped off upon a plank
resting on a stringer of the building and on one of the uprights of
    the ladder
and walked along to the revolving shaft
where he was to hold the belt.

The shaft was running at full speed
as he put the ends of the belt over it
and dropped them down
and he was starting back when the machinist called up,
"Go back and hold that belt!"
He did and was holding the belt up from the shaft in a loop
for about ten minutes
when the machinist called up again,
"Wait! I am going to get some lacing."
The boy became tired and moving his feet a little
the plank turned—
and he fell on the shaft:
his right arm was caught between the belt and the shaft
and torn off at the elbow.

IV
Property

1

The Miles boy tore down Shelby's fence
so that the cattle got into the crop
and Shelby whipped him, "whipped him right":
fetched the boy up to the ranch,
said he wanted him to help put the fence up;
the boy stayed there that night
and the next morning was sitting in the kitchen,
peeling potatoes, when Shelby came in and put a gun at his head;
made him walk down to the barn, lie down on his belly,
tied a rope to him,
and tied him up to the "reach log" of the barn;
and when he was swinging there
took a blacksnake whip and whipped him a while;
then sat down on the sill of the barn,
rolled a cigarette and took a little rest,
and said, "As soon as I rest, I will whip you some more,"
and whipped him again;
and then let him down
and ordered him off the place.

The boy brought a damage suit against Shelby—
placed it in the hands of a lawyer—
and an information charging him with the crime of assault,
and Shelby had to give a bond for whipping him.

Hamilton was a young colored man, about twenty-two,
and had worked for Shelby. They met in a saloon in town
and had a drink together,
and Shelby said, "I want to see you in the wine-room a minute,"
and in the wine-room said to Hamilton:
"That Miles boy is in town
and he has had three or four indictments served on me.

Do you know anybody I could trust?"
"What for?," Hamilton asked.
"To get him out of the way—kill him."
"I don't," said Hamilton.
"My arm is hurt," said Shelby.
"I am just getting so I can ride
or I would have killed him long ago;
and rolled him up in a canvas
and thrown him into a burning coal bank."
Later, Hamilton heard Shelby say to a friend,
"If I could get that Miles boy in the hills
I would put his foot in a stirrup
and let the horse drag him to death."
And another time heard Shelby say, "I intended to get him to running
and rope him
and turn the other way and drag him to death."

Shelby was away in Chicago
and Mrs. Shelby had written Hamilton a letter to come up to the ranch.
The Miles boy and his brother were returning in a wagon with a
      four-horse team
along the main wagon road
to their home on a ranch, some fifty miles from town,
and on their way passed the Shelby ranch.
Mrs. Shelby was ironing in the kitchen
and saw them through her field-glasses.
"There comes the Miles boy!" she said to Hamilton,
and added that she did not want the boy to get back to town
and get on the witness stand
to swear against her husband.
"There's fifty dollars or more in it for you," she said to Hamilton,
"or anybody else that will do away with the Miles boy."
Hamilton said that he could not do it.
"Why not?" she said. "Aren't you going to do that for Mr. Shelby?
Go on and kill him!"
So she said, according to Hamilton.

He went to the dining-room and got the Winchester
from its case in a closet
and six cartridges right on the shelf above the gun,
and got on his horse;
put a black silk handkerchief over his face
into which he had cut holes with his pocketknife
and rode up behind the wagon
pointing his gun at the Miles boy,
and shot him through the body.
The Miles boy fell out of the wagon,
and Hamilton galloped around a big butte
and rode off to the hills.

When he got back to the ranch, he said, "Mrs. Shelby, I done it."
And she said: "I'm not a damn bit sorry.
He put us to a lot of trouble."
But Hamilton said, "I done something I am sorry for,"
and she said, "I am not,"
and took the black silk handkerchief, so he said,
and burnt it up in the kitchen stove.
But all this was not enough to find Shelby himself
guilty of the boy's death—so the judges held.

    2

Their bodies were found about a mile apart:
young Mrs. Thorsen's under the refuse of a hogpen
upon the farm of Jeremiah Saxon;
the body of her young husband in a trail made by cattle
close to some large logs,
in the hollow made by the cattle
jumping over the logs where the ground was swampy,
and covered by a little earth and some sods—
just enough to hide it.
Both had been shot through the head.

About a month before their death
they had made their home on government land,

next to Saxon's farm,
and were living in a boat-house floated up on some logs at high water.
The land had been occupied by several claimants
who had all abandoned it,
and Thorsen intended to clear the record of former filings
in the land-office; but the land was almost worthless
for any purpose.
The Saxon farm, however, over a hundred acres,
had a house on it, outbuildings, and an orchard;
it had been a farm for many years
and was used by Saxon as a place to keep cattle and poultry
and for raising supplies for his hotel in Bayview.
The country around the farm, however, was wild and uncultivated,
and the only means of travel by boat.
Jeremiah Saxon himself was now a man of seventy
and had lived in or near Bayview for many years;
about forty people were regular boarders at his hotel
and he was well-known to everybody in the neighborhood.

The school in Bayview closed at the end of January
and the school-mistress, before she left for her home in Oregon,
gave a dancing-party. She had been boarding at Saxon's hotel
and his son, Jim, now all of eighteen,
went about the stores in Bayview, Thursday afternoon, to get ham for
    the party
and, after supper that night, he and another young man and the
    school-mistress
were in the kitchen of the hotel until late
making cakes. Jim spent most of Friday
clearing out of a new building the debris left by the carpenters
to get the floor ready for dancing, and that afternoon
he went to the exhibition with which the school closed.
On Sunday, he took the school-mistress in his boat
to the village from which she left for home,
and after that, feeling blue, he stayed around the village,
in and out of the saloons, and was "pretty full of liquor."
About four or five in the afternoon,

he bought a pint of whiskey—which he could not pay for just then—
took the whiskey and his gun and left in his boat for his father's farm.
On the way to the farm he made up his mind to kill Thorsen.
He slept at the farm,
got up in the morning with his head feeling pretty bad,
finished the whiskey he had brought with him,
took his shotgun and went to Thorsen's house.
He told him that a calf had got its legs between two logs
and that he could not get the logs apart alone
and would Thorsen help him get the calf out?
Jim went ahead and Thorsen followed along the cattle trail.
When Jim got over the log where Thorsen's body was found,
he turned: Thorsen was just getting up on the log
and Jim said, "Look here, Thorsen!"
Jim had his gun ready and as Thorsen looked up
Jim fired. The charge struck Thorsen just below the eye
and he dropped dead.
Jim took whatever money Thorsen had in his pocket:
it was a little more than fifty-nine dollars.
Out of that money
he would buy several chances in the seal-skin lottery.
His father might ask him where he got that much money
and he would answer that the Land Company owed it
for work he had done in the fall and had just paid it.
As he started for the farm
Jim thought he had better do some more shooting
to make people think he was out hunting;
and so he shot away the rest of the cartridges he had with him.

He waited about the farm for an hour or so,
and then concluded he would have to kill Mrs. Thorsen, too,
because she had seen him going away with her husband,
and when Thorsen didn't come back there would be trouble.
He took the rifle kept in the house to kill cattle
and put a cartridge in it
and went down to the Thorsen house and told Mrs. Thorsen her husband
    had broken his leg

and he could not get him home
and that Mr. Thorsen wanted her to come right up to the house.
She put on her rubber boots and started along with Jim.
When they were near the hogpen, Jim held the rifle close to her temple
and fired.
He waited in the house until it was almost dark
and buried her under the manure pile at the hogpen;
next morning he went to Thorsen's body
and buried it just where it was lying.
In Thorsen's house, he found a pistol and more money on a shelf;
and then went back to Bayview and told those whom he happened to meet
that he had seen the Thorsens leave in a dinghy;
that, shortly after they left,
a squall came up and, after the squall was over,
he could see nothing more of the dinghy,
and thought it had been swamped and the Thorsens drowned.
Thorsen's pistol had a leather handle
and Jim cut the leather off
and also Thorsen's initials on the wood beneath the leather.
He kept the pistol under his bed and his mother found it.
When his father asked him where he got the pistol,
he answered that he had bought it from a man in Bayview.

The people of Bayview, now and then, went searching for the bodies of
    Thorsen and his wife—
they might have been washed ashore if not eaten by the seals—
and someone came upon Thorsen's body late in February.
Jim himself then pointed out where Mrs. Thorsen's body lay
and wanted to help the men digging it up.

The sheriff arrested Jim in the presence of his father
and the old man, naturally, was much agitated.
When the sheriff was taking his prisoner to the boat for the county-seat,
Saxon stepped up to his son and said:
"Now, Jim, don't you talk to anyone until you come up before the court,
and then tell the truth:
tell the court about seeing Thorsen and his wife go out in their boat,

and about the storm coming up and that you thought they were
    drowned."
And then Jim's father told those near them that Jim had wounded a wild
    goose near the farm
and had tied a string to its leg
so that it would draw other wild geese by its cries,
and Jim had managed to kill thirteen geese by the trick:
"I didn't know but what people would think it strange
that there was so much shooting going on up there,
and I thought I would tell you what it was
so that if anything was said about it you would know."
And he sent a young man along with his son to help protect him—
Gibbs had come to the neighborhood only three weeks before
where his work was slashing timber
and he boarded at Saxon's hotel—
for there was angry talk in the villages along the bay.
But when it was suggested that he go himself
he said he dared not: threats had been made against his own life, too,
for he would not help in the search for the Thorsens.

"My father," Jim told those who questioned him,
"wanted this land that Thorsen took.
He wanted Jones"—the young man his father had hired
to take care of the cattle at the farm—
"and Gibbs—one of the meanest men that ever came into this country—
to take the land
and pay out on it and then deed it over to him;
and Gibbs and Jones and my father
made it up how they would kill the Thorsens
My father came to me and said
he wanted me to go down with him to the farm next day
to look after some cattle. Gibbs stood near him
and said he would like to go down with us,
and so, next morning, we three went down to the farm,
and when we got there Father says to Jones,
'You better go up and get Thorsen to help bring the cattle down.'
As we walked along the bluff,

there was a hawk set up on a tree,
and Gibbs says to me,
'Give me your gun and I'll see if I can kill that hawk.'
I let him have the gun
and, after he shot the hawk, he kept the gun,
saying he might see some geese to shoot at.
We walked on until we got down by the cow trail,
and Gibbs walked ahead and Thorsen behind.
I heard Gibbs say to Thorsen, 'Look here, Thorsen!'
and just then he shot him, and I turned around and said,
'That's a pretty way to use a man
after calling him to drive the cattle up,'
and Gibbs says,
'That's the kind of cattle we came after.'

"After Gibbs shot Thorsen, Jones walked into the brush
and got a spade out,
and began to look around for a place to bury him—
it was in the cow trail—
and Father says, 'That's a good enough place right here.'
Jones went to work and dug the grave,
and I went off ten or fifteen feet
and never looked up at them until they had the grave ready,
and called me to help lay Thorsen in the grave.
They had his gum boots off and his gum coat,
and laid them down where he had dropped;
and I helped put him in the grave
and throwed over what loose dirt there was,
and then they pulled some grass sod up,
and put it on top of him,
and after that Father picked up Thorsen's gum coat and boots,
and throwed them down in the slough
where the tide flows in and out.

"As we walked along the beach to the house, Father said,
'Better hurry up and get Mrs. Thorsen down:
she may suspect something.'

And Jones said to me, 'Give me your shotgun.'
I told him I would not,
and Father commenced cursing and swearing at me
because I would not let Jones have it;
and Jones said: 'I will get the rifle.
Don't make any fuss about it.'
They was gone after Mrs. Thorsen about twenty minutes,
and I heard someone scream
and I went out and looked,
and saw her coming along the fence:
Father had hold of one arm
and Jones had hold of the other;
and just as they got inside the gate
Jones picked up the rifle. When they got inside,
Mrs. Thorsen asked what they had done with her husband.
Jones says, 'We shot him.'
And she says: 'Then kill me, too! I don't want to live any longer.'
Jones raised the rifle to her temple—
she never moved a muscle—
and shot her.

"They buried her right there behind the pigpen
and, after the grave was dug,
Father called me to help put her in the grave,
and we covered her up, and threw some sods on top of her,
so people would not see the loose dirt.
And Father and Jones went back to Thorsen's house
and when they came back Gibbs carried the pistol.
Father called me out to the front of the house,
and he had fifty dollars and gave it to me,
and said if he ever found out that I told this on him
I would be dead first;
and, what's more, if I went down to the farm next week,
and it came up stormy,
and anybody asked me what became of the Thorsens,
I was to say that I saw then go out on the day of the storm.
Before we left that evening,

Gibbs gave me the pistol.
I told him I did not want it
but he gave it to me and I kept it
Jones was to take Thorsen's boat out that night
and sink it—swamp it."

This is what Jim also told in court
when his father and Jones were tried for the murders—
and the jury believed him.

  3

Clark had a cabin a few miles from town:
a small building of boards,
battened with shingles. The lock on the door fitted loosely
and it could be pushed open
without unlocking it.
In December, Clark went into the mountains
for a hunting trip
to be gone most of the winter.
The morning he left he placed a loaded spring-gun
inside the cabin: the muzzle aimed at the door
so that someone standing in front of it
and putting his hand on the knob
would, upon pushing the door open a few inches,
get the charge in his body.
Clark then nailed up the door
and put a sign with the word "Danger"
over it. The best of what was in the cabin
had been taken to the house of a neighbor
and what was left was of little value.

Swenson and a companion had been several times to a construction camp,
looking for work. That morning they started for the camp again
and thought it best not to carry their blankets all the way
and left them in the stump of a tree near the cabin.
When they reached the camp, they found that they would have to go back
    to town

to find the man they had to see;
they found him and were to go to work the next day.

After that, Swenson and his companion bought a loaf of bread
and some sausage for supper
and began to walk back to camp.
By that time it was dark and raining and the road muddy.
When they came near the cabin,
Swenson said he did not think anybody had lived in it for a long time
and he would try to get in;
if they could, they had better get their blankets and sleep there,
instead of going on to the camp that night.
Pushing at the door—
the spring-gun was discharged
and the full charge
went through the door
and killed him.

4

Dr. Yard was a physician in Rhode Island,
and for some time had the management of Mrs. Lancaster's estate:
this amounted to more than a hundred thousand dollars,
most of it in stocks and bonds
all in the name of Dr. Yard;
for she had absolute confidence in his intregrity and business sagacity.
For years she had suffered from a partial paralysis
of one side of her body
and he had been her physician.
When at home, in Providence, she would visit his family—
his wife and aged mother—
and while traveling would write him often upon business and other
    matters:
her letters were always respectful and showed her esteem.
She had also left him a legacy of twenty-five thousand dollars
in the wills she had made,
and he was to be her sole executor—without bond.

His letters to her were of like character,
showing respect and esteem—
except two:
she was thinking of selling some of her stocks and bonds
and buying property in the Adirondacks,
near a place she used to go to—"The Ramble,"
under the management of friends.
He wrote her then that the executors of her late husband's estate
were much displeased with the plan
and would take steps to have a guardian appointed for her
if she persisted.

She had been traveling in California and, on the way home,
was stopping with the Craigs, her friends in Denver.
Shortly before her arrival, a package came for her by mail:
a bottle holding about half a pint of a dark liquid.
Some of those present when the package was opened
took it to be blackberry wine;
but, although it had been mailed at the end of March
and was not received until some time in April,
the bottle had the following inscription:
"Wish you a happy New Year!
Please accept this fine old whiskey
from your friends at The Ramble."

Before leaving Denver,
she spent a day in the country with Mrs. Craig
and came back to the house, very tired.
She took the bottle from her trunk to make "a couple of toddies,"
using no more than two spoonfuls of the contents for each;
and Mrs. Lancaster drank one and Mrs. Craig the other.
Soon after, both became sick
and their symptoms were those of arsenic poisoning;
in fact, when the fluid left in the bottle was examined
it showed a strong solution of arsenic.

The next morning, Mrs. Craig's daughter sat down by Mrs. Lancaster's
　　bedside:
Mrs. Lancaster seemed somewhat better and even inclined to talk:
yes, she knew that she had been poisoned.
The young woman asked if she supposed that her friends at The
　　Ramble could have sent it.
"No," she said. "Oh, no!"
"Have you any enemies that would do such a thing?"
"I don't know of an enemy in the world!"

She thought for a moment and then said,
"The last maid I had was angry at me:
she was not a lady and I did not care to keep her."
"How did you happen to employ her?"
"Dr. Yard employed her for me.
He was anxious that I should spend the winter in Cuba
with her as my companion, and I didn't want to go."
"Can you think of anyone who knows that they will benefit by your death?"
"I left Dr. Yard twenty-five thousand dollars in my will."
She went on to say that she didn't have as much confidence in Dr. Yard as
　　she used to have:
the medicine he had sent her lately
didn't seem to do her the good it used to;
and she didn't like the way she had been treated while in California:
she didn't get money when she wanted it,
and at one time she and her maid had only fifty cents between them.
"As soon as I am able to travel, I'll go East
and put this matter in the hands of a good detective."

But next day it was hard for her to breathe
and, after lingering several days in agony, she died.

5
She sold the twenty acres she had in Michigan
and this was the money she brought along to Portland—
seven hundred dollars in a draft of deposit on a bank
safe in her bosom.

She arrived in Portland with her three children
at seven in the morning, worn out by the long journey
and sick.
Her husband was at the depot to meet her
and brought her and the children to a lodging-house
run by a Mr. Flugel.
She had never seen the man before
but her husband told her he was a member of his family.

After breakfast, she went back to the room they had taken
to rest, and her husband told her Mr. Flugel had a place to sell—
a tract of ten acres near Portland—
and urged her to buy it. All his own own money was gone.
That evening, Flugel invited her into his room
and he, too, talked about the place he had for sale:
only eight miles from Portland along the road usually traveled,
and worth not less than fifteen hundred dollars in the market.
He would let her have it for fourteen hundred and fifty,
and take in part payment the draft of deposit she had with her,
and in the morning would take her out to see the place.
She said she didn't want to see it;
besides, she hadn't enough money,
and went back to her room.

But he came there that very night,
and she said she didn't want to see him—
she didn't want to buy the land.
At six in the morning, bright and early, he was back again
and said he was ready to take her out to see the place,
and had a team ready.
Before he left the room,
he said he would have a paper made out
by which he would let her have the place
for fourteen hundred and fifty dollars—
a good deal!
She became very nervous at that:
not sure that she understood him

or that he understood what she was saying—
a native of Germany, she was as yet uncertain about her English—
and sent the two eldest of her children after him
to tell him that she didn't want any paper drawn up.
The children caught up with him in the street
and told him: "Mother wants no paper, no writing today.
She is going crazy."
But he came back with the paper, anyway,
and brought along pen and ink.
She signed a contract to buy the land, finally—
she thought she was getting a deed—
and indorsed the draft in part payment.
But the tract of land was not worth even the part payment;
and, besides, it was mortgaged.

6

A Letter

Friend: has a young man in Ohio got a little nerve to come out to Montana?
There is a man here has got some scrub horses he thinks is fast—
range horses without any mark;
him and his friends will bet their money
as he is a man without any knowledge of horse racing.
Has been in the country a long time
and done business in the early days with the half-breed Indians;
now a saloonkeeper.

I want a man to come out and bring a good horse with him,
a pace or a trotter,
and we will match this man with a dead mortal cinch.
We can win several thousand dollars—
like finding it.
The way I would want to bring the horses in the country would be to
    sneak them in the town;
put a hair brand on them so they would appear range stock:
it is meat for someone.
The main object is to make it appear that the horses are undeveloped;
to give them a sure thing in the way of thinking.

It is a big snap for someone to match a horse race.
This is no josh: we have got the biggest sucker here in the state
and has got plenty of money.
Please don't send us your envelopes with your advertisements as a horseman,
or anything with your name on it.
Don't want these people to get on to anything that would throw us off.
Whatever business I have to do with you,
expect to be honorable and upright:
that is the only way for a person to transact business.

   7
Jacobs and a partner had a large store
but business was bad and the firm losing money.
One day, Jacobs left the store for lunch
and went to a restaurant in the neighborhood
with two companions—one a friend of many years.
They had just seated themselves at the table
when Jacobs got up and said he wanted to let his partner know where he was:
there was a telephone in the room
and he came back pale and excited
and wanted to leave at once.

On the way out, they stopped at the cigar-stand
and Jacobs bought cigars for himself and his companions
and managed to tell his friend
that he wanted to get rid of their companion
for the two of them to talk about a business matter;
and when their companion left them
the two went on towards Jacobs' place of business.

Jacobs became more excited than ever and said:
"They've got me!
The sheriff is in possession of the store right now
with an attachment!" And turning to his friend he said,
"I want you to promise me one thing:
be as good a friend to my wife as you have been to me."
His friend made up his mind to stay with Jacobs until he had calmed down

and, when they reached the store, Jacobs went inside
and his friend remained at the entrance.
It might be a good thing, his friend thought then, to see someone he had
    to see—who had an office nearby—
and be back in a few minutes.
When he was back, Jacobs had left the store.

There was a hotel nearby and Jacobs' friend, in his search for him,
went in and saw Jacobs' name on the register
and the number of the room he had been given.
His friend went up to the room at once
but found the door locked.

He finally got a boy who worked at the hotel
to go through the transom
and when the door was opened from the inside
they saw Jacobs lying on the bed,
flat on his back, dead:
he had taken off his shoes and coat, his vest was unbuttoned,
his necktie untied and the collar loosened;
and his head was thrown back,
mouth and eyes partly open.

There were brownish stains on his lips and chin.
On the dresser was a tumbler
with a little of a brownish liquid still in it—
about half a teaspoonful—
and it had a peculiar, unpleasant smell.

V

Railroads

1

The company was constructing a railroad
through mountainous country. It was the fall of the year
and it had been raining for days.

Several hundred laborers had been at work at the end of the track—
handling the ties and bedding them and laying track.
That morning it was raining again
and a number of the workmen
did not want to leave their boarding-camp.
But the head track-layer ordered them to leave:
they could go to work
or "get their time" and be discharged;
he wanted no "dudes" on the job
and he was "going to be in hell or in Aspen by Christmas!"

The construction train consisted of an engine and a tender,
a flatcar carrying two large water-tanks,
and another flatcar loaded with curved steel rails.
Forty or fifty men were on the engine, tender, and tank car
and two hundred or so crowded as close as they could stand
upon the car with steel rails.
The train was running about eight miles an hour down grade
when it reached a curve in the roadbed—now water-soaked and soft—
on an embankment that had been built along a gulch.
The tank car lurched to one side;
and when the flatcar with its heavy load of rails
came upon the embankment, the track slid
from the ties and the ends of the ties sank in the mud;
the front trucks of the car slipped into the gulch
and the steel rails began to slide from the car.

The men on the edges had a chance to jump
but those in the center were hemmed in and could not move;
Ryan was among those caught under the rails.
His body and hands were free
but his legs were caught fast and crushed:
blood was all over his overalls
and the raw flesh showed where they had been torn.
His legs had to be amputated
a few inches below the knee-joints;

and he was unable to straighten out the stumps
and use artificial legs.
Now his only way of getting about
was to drag himself along on his knees.

2

The boy was fourteen years of age and had been hired to carry water
to the men building and grading
the roadbed of the railroad.
The powder used for blasting often became frozen in the mountains,
even in May,
and it was the duty of the "gang boss" to thaw it.

The "gang boss" would thaw the powder
before an open fire. One day,
when he had to use a lot of it,
he laid about seventy-five sticks of the blasting-powder
against a log in front of the fire
and, as the powder became warm on one side,
turned the sticks to thaw them evenly;
and when they became sufficiently warm
laid them in a pile near the fire.

The water-boy came along with some tools from the blacksmith shop,
and stopped at the fire to warm himself;
and the "gang boss" picked up about forty sticks of the powder
and carried them in his arms to the boulder he was about to blast
leaving four or five sticks behind
for the boy to carry. When they reached the boulder,
the "boss" began putting the sticks of powder
in the hole drilled for it. He had put seven or eight sticks in the boulder
when someone called out, "The powder's on fire!"

A pile of logs and brush was between the fire and the "boss"
but he could see by the peculiar blaze
that some of the powder left at the fire was burning.

"Billy," he said to the boy, "run!"
"Throw the burning stick away!"
The boy jumped up and ran towards the fire.

When the smoke of the explosion cleared up
the boy's body was found
a few feet from where the fire had been.

3
The Favor

At midnight, when the freight train was about to start from Pueblo
a young man—a cripple with an artificial leg—
came up to the conductor in charge
and asked if he showed favors to crippled railroad men:
he wanted to go to his brother
who lived near the line between Pueblo and Denver
in order to make his living on a farm.
The conductor answered that he sometimes did a fellow railroad man
    a favor—
it depended—
and the young man showed him a letter:
he had been the brakeman on another road for ten or eleven months.
The conductor asked why he did not apply to the Brakemen's Brotherhood
    for aid,
and he answered that he had not been a brakeman long enough to get into
    the Brotherhood.
The conductor then said: no, he would not let him ride on the train;
besides, the letter was too old.

The conductor went up along the train
to take down the numbers of the cars
and did not come back to the caboose at the rear end
until the train had left Pueblo and was well under way.
He found the young man in the caboose
with two or three men traveling with live-stock on the train—
and left him there.

The train went on to Colorado Springs
where another railroad crossed the roadbed
and the train stopped at the crossing
to do some switching in the railroad yard.
The last six cars with the caboose were cut off
and left on the track.
Here the grade went downward
to a station they had passed;
two of the cars had air-brakes
and the conductor set these,
and ordered the rear brakeman to set the brakes on the other cars.
The brakeman noticed that the air-brakes were not holding
and set the hand-brakes on three, perhaps four, of the cars;
and the stockmen and the train crew left.
But the young man stayed in the caboose.

The brakes became loosened
and the cars started down the track:
they ran as far as the next station
and here crashed into the engine of another train.
The cars immediately in front of the caboose
were loaded with explosives—
these went off at the collision;
and the mangled body of the young man was found
by the side of the track.

4

At a stop, she left her seat in the "immigrant car" to stand near the stove
and get warm. When the train started with a jerk
she put out her hand to steady herself
and caught hold of a post beside the berths.
It might have been the newsboy going through the cars
or a friendly brakeman who had raised the upper berth
but had not pushed it up far enough
for the fastenings to catch,
and it came down—

and caught two of her fingers
and crushed them.

 5

As the train approached the station,
the family got up and stood at the door of the car
to be able to step off without delay.
As soon as the train stopped
they began to leave,
but the stop was so short
only some of the family were able to get off
and the train moved away
with the father still on it—
and his little girl and the baby on his arm.

The conductor of the train was on the platform of the car
and said: "Go to the next station.
It's only a short distance
and you can walk back."
At the next station
the man left the train;
he looked about and saw no way to get back
other than the roadbed of the railroad;
and, in fact, there was no other way:
on one side the water of the bay,
and on the other swamp.
There were two tracks, and he supposed that if a train would come along
it would be on the east track,
for the train he had just left was on the other;
and began to walk along the west track,
carrying the baby on one arm
and holding the little girl, a child of six, by the hand.

He had gone several hundred feet
when he heard the noise of a train behind him
and looked back
but, because of a curve in the road,

could not see on what track the train was running.
He looked again
and saw that the train was on the track on which he was walking
and crossed to the other track,
all the time holding the little girl by the hand.
But, frightened by the swift approach of the train,
she broke away
and ran back to the track they had been on—
right in front of the engine—
and was struck by it.

VI

That morning when the stevedores came to work
they were told by the foreman
to go down into the hold of the vessel
and help stow away a cargo of coal
from the vessel alongside. The stevedores had to go forward
down to the steerage deck
and then along this deck to a stairway
leading to the orlop deck, and along the orlop deck
to the hatchway
where there was a ladder leading into the hold

The foot of the stairway to the orlop deck
was about ten feet from the coaming of the hatchway
and the deck was pitch dark.
When the hatchway of the main deck was open
the light from above lit up the orlop deck, too,
so that the hatchway and the ladder to the hold
could be seen; it was also usual
when the men were stowing coal in the hold
to have a lighted lamp hung near the hatchway—
but this morning the hatchway on the main deck was closed
and the lamp had not been lit.

The men went down the narrow stairway to the orlop deck
in single file
and, as each man reached the foot of the stairs,
he had to go on
to make room for the others behind him.
They had just commenced to light the lamp
but, before it was lit,
O'Brien was going along the orlop deck in the darkness—
the other behind him coming down from the steerage deck
pressing him forward—
and down he went into the hatchway
falling twenty feet into the hold.

VII

Mining

1

The miner was working in a shaft sunk to a depth of about ninety feet
from a tunnel in a silver mine;
there were no ladders for going up or down the shaft
and he had to use the cracks between the timbering—
green bark, wet and slippery.

He had placed a cartridge in the hole
drilled by him at the bottom of the shaft
and had fired the fuse, and then climbed up the timbering
to wait for the explosion.
When there had been time and enough for it,
he made his way down the shaft
to see if water had reached the drill-hole,
and stopped about ten feet above the bottom—
high enough to be safe should the cartridge explode.
Turning to look down,
he held on to the timbering with one hand:
the fuse was alight.

But, as he turned to go up the shaft again,
his foot slipped—
the timbering was close at this point—
and he fell.
At the bottom of the shaft, he reached at once for the fuse
to pull it out before the cartridge exploded;
but, before he could get his fingers on it,
the explosion—
rock now feeling like sand—
struck his face and arms
blinding him forever.

    2

Vic had been mining coal since he was fourteen;
now, all of seventeen,
he was working with John in the same room;
and Vic, the elder and more experienced,
did the talking.
John was looking at the rock overhead
and testing it with a pick—
pounding it with the head of the pick
for the purpose of sounding it
to tell if the rock was loose;
and John called Vic's attention
to a crack—or slip—in the rock.
Vic didn't think there was any danger
but they started to put a prop under it.
They had a prop that had been cut the day before
but this was too short
and they threw it away.
Vic told John to get a prop where the props were kept
but there were no props around;
and Vic went out himself to get some props that had been left
at a prospect hole along the creek,
but these, too, were gone.
Then he decided to wait
until he had loaded the car with coal—
after all, the roof was all a little cracked.

They had nearly finished work for the day
when Vic heard a crack
and jumped back—
he supposed that the coal was about to fall
from the face of the room;
but it was a rock that fell from the roof
and his right arm was caught under it and crushed.

The rock that fell was about fifteen feet long
and four feet wide at the widest part
and was near the center of the room.
If there had been a prop or two under it
and the rock was going to fall,
Vic would have had some warning:
the prop would have bent or broken—
and the rock might not have fallen at all.

3

Graham was working in the "silver room,"
where the silver was separated from lead and gold.
Although usually only three sets of tanks were used at the same time,
on that day all four sets in the room were being used
and the waste acid from all four was to be poured into the "waste tank"
    at the same time.
But there were only three hoses in the silver room
through which to pump it,
and the foreman fixed up a fourth hose
by connecting two pieces of short hose that had been lying about—
old hose, worn and eaten by the acid in which they had been used—
slipping one end of each piece of hose over a piece of lead pipe
so that the two ends met near the middle;
he did not tie them to the pipe by wire or twine
and they were held only by what elastic force was left in them.

Graham began using this improvised hose
but in about ten or fifteen minutes
it parted:

one of the pieces slipped from the lead pipe
and the scalding hot acid was emptied upon his shoulder and back.

VIII

Labor Troubles

Oaks, his son, and another man working for Oaks
were lathers at work in a building;
in the morning, two men came to the building and told Oaks to quit
    working.
He would not. "Why not?" they asked and he answered:
"We are not members of the Union and are not going to stick it out.
We stuck it out a week,
and are not going to stick it out any longer."

One of the two asked him if he was willing to pay his help three dollars
    a day—
that was what the Union journeymen were striking for:
three dollars a day for eighteen bunches of laths,
eighteen hundred laths for a day's work;
and Oaks said he was willing.
Then, said the man, if he would come down and join the Union,
he would get all the Union men he wanted.
But Oaks said he would not.

They came back about three or four in the afternoon
with forty men—fully forty.
Oaks and his son were at work on a stage in a bedroom
and the party of forty came up the narrow stairway.
The lower part of the walls was not yet lathed
and was open between the studding;
one of the crowd stuck his head through the partition
where it was open at the bottom
and said, "Don't you think you fellows have done enough today?"
And another in the crowd said, "Yes, we don't want no scab work!"

The elder Oaks turned around and said he was not a scab
and was not doing scab work;
but the first of the crowd to speak now spoke up and said, "You said enough!"
The younger Oaks asked his father to say no more—not to provoke them,
and the strikers told father and son to come off the stage,
three or four shouting, "Come down!"
And they did.

As they were making their way through the crowd to the stairs,
one of the men said to the younger Oaks:
"Get your father out of here!
They nearly killed a man on Post Street."
The younger Oaks turned to his father
and saw one of the strikers punch his father on the back of the head
and another man striking at his father's face;
the younger Oaks tried to make the man who held him
break his hold
to get where his father was,
but a couple of men caught him around the neck
and he went down on the floor.

The crowd left, all of them,
in a rush down the stairway,
and the younger Oaks went to his father:
the elder Oaks was much excited
and showed his son a mark on his nose
where he had been hit.
His son told him to come home right away
and they would see what they could do,
and they went down the stairway together.
The younger man was in a pretty "banged up" condition himself
and his father was pale, very pale,
and had a lump on the back of his head.

That night the elder Oaks complained of a headache
and could not eat his dinner,
and about twelve that night

got to breathing hard
and was soon unconscious.
In a few days he died.
His death, the doctors said, was caused by a broken artery:
it might have been caused by a blow on the side of his head
or just the excitement—or both.

IX

Klein, a peddler of spectacles,
rode to the next station on the railroad:
the country was desert with houses few and far between.
There was a platform from the station to the section-house
and he went towards it to sell his spectacles
but before he reached it the section foreman,
calling him "a spotter" and spy for the railroad,
began to beat him with a shovel.

The foreman followed Klein
and gave him five minutes to get away
or he would "kill him";
and Klein started to walk along the track.
Two men who had been "hanging around" the station
followed him
and a quarter of a mile away
took his satchel of spectacles and his pocketbook
and whatever money he had.

Klein went back to the railroad station
and the two men followed
but stopped near the pump-house.
He wanted the ticket-agent to send a telegram to Green River
telling of the holdup
but the section foreman told the ticket-agent not to,
and went across the track to where the two men were standing
and the three came into the waiting-room
and began beating up Klein.

He called for help
but none of the spectators helped him
and all the ticket agent did
was to order the four of them out of the waiting room.

X

Mexicans

1

Brown and Jackson, cowboys on neighboring ranches near the Mexican
    border,
had their saddles stolen,
and started on the trail of four Mexicans
who had camped close to one of the ranches
the night before.
The Mexicans left behind two old saddles.

On the road Brown and Jackson passed the Mexicans:
they had stopped to cook dinner
and the cowboys saw their own saddles on horses two of the Mexicans
    were riding.
Jackson left Brown to watch them
and rode back to hurry along
those who had promised to help make the arrest;
but he could not find them
and he and Brown followed on after the Mexicans.

Later in the afternoon,
the Mexicans who had gone into ambush near the road
rushed upon them.
Jackson and Brown fled—
galloping off in different directions
as the Mexicans kept firing;
two of the Mexicans went after Jackson
and the other two after Brown.

Jackson got away
and rode on back in search of help.

Those who had gathered to help him and Brown
found Brown's horse without its bridle
and not far off his hat.
There was a pool of blood on the road
and from it the trail of a body that had been dragged away.
They followed the drag
and came upon Brown's body
with two knife wounds in his breast:
the Mexicans must have overtaken
and lassoed him,
jerking him from his horse,
and then plunged their knives into his breast;
and with their lassoes
dragged the body off the road into the brush and grass.

  2
Campbell was over six feet tall and unusually strong,
Zapota small and slender.
He and his wife were milking in the cowpen
when Campbell came up
and ordered him to get the horses and go to work.
Zapota said that it was too cold——and raining.

Standing outside the fence, within a few feet of Zapota,
Campbell asked him again if he was going to go to work.
The Mexican stood up where he was milking,
in his hand only a milk can,
and refused.
Campbell aimed his Winchester at him
and Zapota's wife caught the gun
but Campbell jerked it away and struck her on the head with it,
knocking her down;
then turned and shot Zapota through the breast.

Zapota's wife carried her husband to their home nearby
and laid him on some cotton
and covered him with a quilt and blanket;
they had no bed—no furniture at all.
There was no fireplace and it was freezing.
A neighbor, when Campbell asked him to, called at the Mexican's house,
and found him sitting on the floor,
wrapped in the blanket,
and his wife squatting by a little fire under the shed
her head gashed and bleeding from the blow.

The neighbor told Campbell the Mexican was doing badly.
Campbell's house was fifty yards or so away
but neither Campbell nor his wife
sent food, medicine, or clothing to the Zapotas.
The day after the shooting
Campbell did ask a doctor to visit the wounded man
but the doctor never went;
and Campbell insisted that Zapota leave the place
and was so insistent
a try was made to move the dying man.
However, in an hour or two he died.

XI

Indians

Early in the spring it was nice weather
and the trees just budding;
the other Indians on the reservation were plowing
and had been plowing for several days
when an Indian on horse jack with a carbine
came to the tepee
and asked the Indian who lived there
to come along with him—
out riding or roaming around.

The other Indian got a sorrel horse belonging to his wife—
also a gun;
and both had belts with cartridges,
the kind soldiers use.
They went to still another Indian's tepee
and he, too, saddled up a horse and got his gun and some cartridges,
and the three of them started.
By this time it was the middle of the forenoon.
They followed the road along the river
until they came to a road that ran off into the hills
and took it, but did not find anything to shoot at
until they saw a bunch of five cows,
and one of them shot and killed a cow.
Then they all got off their horses and started to skin it,
cutting down the legs and getting ready to take the hide off;
their guns laid on the ground
and their horses held by ropes.
But a white man who must have heard the shot
came up close;
did not say anything
and went away.

Then the Indians said to each other:
this man has seen us
and will know us.
He will go and tell on us.
So they took their guns and got on their horses
and followed him—
keeping off quite a way—
until he got back to the sheep he was herding.
Then all three charged and shot at him.
He fell
but started to get up
and one of the Indians shot him again.

A little dog was running around
and they said to each other:

this dog will go down to the ranch
and they will search for the man.
And one of the Indians shot it,
and put it beside the body.
In four or five days some of the sheep strayed back to the ranch,
two or so miles away,
and the owner and his hands went in search of the herder.

Nothing was left of his body but the bones
with some flesh on the hands
and the hair of his head.
The bone of his left arm was broken
and his woolen shirt was burned where the bullet had entered his breast.

1936

Our feelings have always been a problem in this genre. Conventional essays tend to privilege expositional clarity—that arrowy delineation of thought that promises the logical development of ideas toward uncluttered and easily digestible meanings. What we don't tend to value in essays, in other words, is what the essay actually is: an attempt, a trial, an experiment that does not guarantee a result. After all, to genuinely "attempt" something, doesn't there need to be the genuine risk that we might fail? "There are always those to whom all self-revelation is contemptible," F. Scott Fitzgerald once wrote, "unless it ends with a noble thanks to the gods for the Unconquerable Soul." This year, the last great thing Fitzgerald ever writes is an essay about attempting to save his own life—something that he will fail at within a few short years.

F. Scott Fitzgerald

The Crack-Up

Of course all life is a process of breaking down, but the blows that do the dramatic side of the work—the big sudden blows that come, or seem to come, from outside—the ones you remember and blame things on and, in moments of weakness, tell your friends about, don't show their effect all at once. There is another sort of blow that comes from within—that you don't feel until it's too late to do anything about it, until you realize with finality that in some regard you will never be as good a man again. The first sort of breakage seems to happen quick—the second kind happens almost without your knowing it but is realized suddenly indeed.

Before I go on with this short history, let me make a general observation— the test of a first-rate intelligence is the ability to hold two opposed ideas in the mind at the same time, and still retain the ability to function. One should, for example, be able to see that things are hopeless and yet be determined to make them otherwise. This philosophy fitted on to my early adult life, when I saw the improbable, the implausible, often the "impossible," come true. Life was something you dominated if you were any good. Life yielded easily to intelligence and effort, or to what proportion could be mustered of both. It seemed a romantic business to be a successful literary man—you were not ever going to be as famous as a movie star but what note you had was probably longer-lived; you were never going to have the power of a man of strong political or religious convictions but you were certainly more independent. Of course within the practice of your trade you were forever unsatisfied—but I, for one, would not have chosen any other.

As the Twenties passed, with my own twenties marching a little ahead of them, my two juvenile regrets—at not being big enough (or good enough) to play football in college, and at not getting overseas during the war— resolved themselves into childish waking dreams of imaginary heroism that were good enough to go to sleep on in restless nights. The big problems of life seemed to solve themselves, and if the business of fixing them was difficult, it made one too tired to think of more general problems.

Life, ten years ago, was largely a personal matter. I must hold in balance the sense of futility of effort and the sense of the necessity to struggle; the conviction of the inevitability of failure and still the determination to "succeed"—and, more than these, the contradiction between the dead hand of the past and the high intentions of the future. If I could do this through the common ills—domestic, professional, and personal—then the ego would continue as an arrow shot from nothingness to nothingness with such force that only gravity would bring it to earth at last.

For seventeen years, with a year of deliberate loafing and resting out in the center—things went on like that, with a new chore only a nice prospect for the next day. I was living hard, too, but: "Up to forty-nine it'll be all right," I said. "I can count on that. For a man who's lived as I have, that's all you could ask."

—And then, ten years this side of forty-nine, I suddenly realized I had prematurely cracked.

Now a man can crack in many ways—can crack in the head, in which case the power of decision is taken from you by others; or in the body, when one can but submit to the white hospital world; or in the nerves. William Seabrook in an unsympathetic book tells, with some pride and a movie ending, of how he became a public charge. What led to his alcoholism, or was bound up with it, was a collapse of his nervous system. Though the present writer was not so entangled—having at the time not tasted so much as a glass of beer for six months—it was his nervous reflexes that were giving way—too much anger and too many tears.

Moreover, to go back to my thesis that life has a varying offensive, the realization of having cracked was not simultaneous with a blow, but with a reprieve.

Not long before, I had sat in the office of a great doctor and listened to a grave sentence. With what, in retrospect, seems some equanimity, I had gone on about my affairs in the city where I was then living, not caring much, not thinking how much had been left undone, or what would become of this and that responsibility, like people do in books; I was well insured and anyhow I had been only a mediocre caretaker of most of the things left in my hands, even of my talent.

But I had a strong sudden instinct that I must be alone. I didn't want to see any people at all. I had seen so many people all my life—I was an average mixer, but more than average in a tendency to identify myself, my ideas, my destiny, with those of all classes that I came in contact with. I was always saving or being saved—in a single morning I would go through the emotions ascribable to Wellington at Waterloo. I lived in a world of inscrutable hostiles and inalienable friends and supporters.

But now I wanted to be absolutely alone and so arranged a certain insulation from ordinary cares.

It was not an unhappy time. I went away and there were fewer people. I found I was good-and-tired. I could lie around and was glad to, sleeping or dozing sometimes twenty hours a day and in the intervals trying resolutely not to think—instead I made lists—made lists and tore them up, hundreds of lists: of cavalry leaders and football players and cities, and popular tunes and pitchers, and happy times, and hobbies and houses lived in and how many suits since I left the army and how many pairs of shoes (I didn't count the suit I bought in Sorrento that shrank, nor the pumps and dress shirt and collar that I carried around for years and never wore, because the pumps got damp and grainy and the shirt and collar got yellow and starch-rotted). And lists of women I'd liked, and of the times I had let myself be snubbed by people who had not been my betters in character or ability.

—And then suddenly, surprisingly, I got better.

—And cracked like an old plate as soon as I heard the news.

That is the real end of this story. What was to be done about it will have to rest in what used to be called the "womb of time." Suffice to say that after about an hour of solitary pillow-hugging, I began to realize that for two years my life had been a drawing on resources that I did not possess, that I had been mortgaging myself physically and spiritually up to the hilt. What was the small gift of life given back in comparison to that?— when there had once been a pride of direction and a confidence in enduring independence.

I realized that in those two years, in order to preserve something—an inner hush maybe, maybe not—I had weaned myself from all the things I used to love—that every act of life from the morning toothbrush to the friend at dinner had become an effort. I saw that for a long time I had not liked people and things, but only followed the rickety old pretense of liking. I saw that even my love for those closest to me had become only an attempt to love, that my casual relations—with an editor, a tobacco seller, the child of a friend, were only what I remembered I *should* do, from other days. All in the same month I became bitter about such things as the sound of the radio, the advertisements in the magazines, the screech of tracks, the dead silence of the country—contemptuous at human softness, immediately (if secretively) quarrelsome toward hardness—hating the night when I couldn't sleep and hating the day because it went toward night. I slept on the heart side now because I knew that the sooner I could tire that out, even a little, the sooner would come that blessed hour of nightmare which, like a catharsis, would enable me to better meet the new day.

There were certain spots, certain faces I could look at. Like most midwesterners, I have never had any but the vaguest race prejudices—I always had a secret yen for the lovely Scandinavian blondes who sat on porches in St. Paul but hadn't emerged enough economically to be part of what was then society. They were too nice to be "chickens" and too quickly off the farmlands to seize a place in the sun, but I remember going round blocks to catch a single glimpse of shining hair—the bright shock of a girl I'd never know. This is urban, unpopular talk. It strays afield from the fact that in these latter days I couldn't stand the sight of Celts, English, Politicians, Strangers, Virginians, Negroes (light or dark), Hunting People, or retail clerks, and middlemen in general, all writers (I avoided writers carefully because they can perpetuate trouble as no one else can)—and all the classes as classes and most of them as members of their class . . .

Trying to cling to something, I liked doctors and girl children up to the age of about thirteen and well-brought-up boy children from about eight years old on. I could have peace and happiness with these few categories of people. I forgot to add that I liked old men—men over seventy, sometimes over sixty if their faces looked seasoned. I liked Katharine Hepburn's face on the screen, no matter what was said about her pretentiousness, and Miriam Hopkins's face, and old friends if I only saw them once a year and could remember their ghosts.

All rather inhuman and undernourished, isn't it? Well, that, children, is the true sign of cracking up.

It is not a pretty picture. Inevitably it was carted here and there within its frame and exposed to various critics. One of them can only be described as a person whose life makes other people's lives seem like death—even this time when she was cast in the unusually unappealing role of Job's comforter. In spite of the fact that this story is over, let me append our conversation as a sort of postscript:

> "Instead of being so sorry for yourself, listen—" she said. (She always says "Listen," because she thinks while she talks—*really* thinks.) So she said: "Listen. Suppose this wasn't a crack in you—suppose it was a crack in the Grand Canyon."
>
> "The crack's in me," I said heroically.
>
> "Listen! The world only exists in your eyes—your conception of it. You can make it as big or as small as you want to. And you're trying to be a little puny individual. By God, if I ever cracked, I'd try to make the world crack with me. Listen! The world only exists through your apprehension of it, and so it's much better to say that it's not you that's cracked—it's the Grand Canyon."
>
> "Baby, et up all her Spinoza?"
>
> "I don't know anything about Spinoza. I know—" She spoke, then, of old woes of her own, that seemed, in telling, to have been more dolorous than mine, and how she had met them, overridden them, beaten them.

I felt a certain reaction to what she said, but I am a slow-thinking man, and it occurred to me simultaneously that of all natural forces, vitality is the incommunicable one. In days when juice came into one as an article without duty, one tried to distribute it—but always without success; to further mix metaphors, vitality never "takes." You have it or you haven't it, like health or brown eyes or honor or a baritone voice. I might have asked some of it from her, neatly wrapped and ready for home cooking and digestion, but I could never have got it—not if I'd waited around for a thousand hours with the tin cup of self-pity. I could walk from her door, holding myself very carefully like cracked crockery, and go away into the world of bitterness, where I was making a home with such materials as are found there—and quote to myself after I left her door:

> *"Ye are the salt of the earth. But if the salt hath lost its savour, wherewith shall it be salted?"*
>
> MATTHEW 5:13

Pasting It Together

In a previous article this writer told about his realization that what he had before him was not the dish that he had ordered for his forties. In fact—since he and the dish were one, he described himself as a cracked plate, the kind that one wonders whether it is worth preserving. Your editor thought that the article suggested too many aspects without regarding them closely, and probably many readers felt the same way—and there are always those to whom all self-revelation is contemptible, unless it ends with a noble thanks to the gods for the Unconquerable Soul.

But I had been thanking the gods too long, and thanking them for nothing. I wanted to put a lament in my record, without even the background of the Euganean Hills to give it color. There weren't any Euganean Hills that I could see.

Sometimes, though, the cracked plate has to be retained in the pantry, has to be kept in service as a household necessity. It can never again be warmed on the stove nor shuffled with the other plates in the dishpan; it will not be brought out for company, but it will do to hold crackers late at night or to go into the icebox under leftovers . . .

Hence this sequel—a cracked plate's further history.

Now the standard cure for one who is sunk is to consider those in actual destitution or physical suffering—this is an all-weather beatitude for gloom in general and fairly salutary daytime advice for everyone. But at three o'clock in the morning, a forgotten package has the same tragic importance as a death sentence, and the cure doesn't work—and in a real dark night of the soul it is always three o'clock in the morning, day after day. At that hour the tendency is to refuse to face things as long as possible by retiring into an infantile dream—but one is continually startled out of this by various contacts with the world. One meets these occasions as quickly and carelessly as possible and retires once more back into the dream, hoping that things will adjust themselves by some great material or spiritual bonanza. But as the withdrawal persists there is less and less chance of the bonanza—one is not waiting for the fade-out of a single sorrow, but rather being an unwilling witness of an execution, the disintegration of one's own personality . . .

Unless madness or drugs or drink come into it, this phase comes to a dead end, eventually, and is succeeded by a vacuous quiet. In this you can try to estimate what has been sheared away and what is left. Only when this quiet came to me did I realize that I had gone through two parallel experiences.

The first time was twenty years ago, when I left Princeton in junior year with a complaint diagnosed as malaria. It transpired, through an X-ray taken a dozen years later, that it had been tuberculosis—a mild case, and after a few months of rest I went back to college. But I had lost certain offices, the chief one was the presidency of the Triangle Club, a musical comedy idea, and also I dropped back a class. To me college would never be the same. There were to be no badges of pride, no medals, after all. It seemed on one March afternoon that I had lost every single thing I wanted—and that night was the first time that I hunted down the specter of womanhood that, for a little while, makes everything else seem unimportant.

Years later I realized that my failure as a big shot in college was all right—instead of serving on committees, I took a beating on English poetry; when I got the idea of what it was all about, I set about learning how to write. On Shaw's principle that "if you don't get what you like, you better like what you get," it was a lucky break—at the moment it was a harsh and bitter business to know that my career as a leader of men was over.

Since that day I have not been able to fire a bad servant, and I am astonished and impressed by people who can. Some old desire for personal dominance was broken and gone. Life around me was a solemn dream, and I lived on the letters I wrote to a girl in another city. A man does not recover from such jolts—he becomes a different person, and, eventually, the new person finds new things to care about.

The other episode parallel to my current situation took place after the war, when I had again overextended my flank. It was one of those tragic loves doomed for lack of money, and one day the girl closed it out on the basis of common sense. During a long summer of despair I wrote a novel instead of letters, so it came out all right, but it came out all right for a different reason. The man with the jingle of money in his pocket who married the girl a year later would always cherish an abiding distrust, an animosity, toward the leisure class—not the conviction of a revolutionist but the smoldering hatred of a peasant. In the years since then I have never been able to stop wondering where my friends' money came from, nor to stop thinking that at one time a sort of *droit du seigneur* might have been exercised to give one of them my girl.

For sixteen years I lived pretty much as this latter person, distrusting the rich, yet working for money with which to share their mobility and the grace that some of them brought into their lives. During this time I had plenty of the usual horses shot from under me—I remember some of their names—*Punctured Pride, Thwarted Expectation, Faithless, Show-off, Hard Hit, Never Again.* And after a while I wasn't twenty-five, then not even thirty-five, and nothing was quite as good. But in all these years I don't remember a moment of discouragement. I saw honest men through moods of suicidal gloom—some of them gave up and died; others adjusted themselves and went on to a larger success than mine; but my morale never sank below the level of self-disgust when I had put on some unsightly personal show. Trouble has no necessary connection with discouragement—discouragement has a germ of its own, as different from trouble as arthritis is different from a stiff joint.

When a new sky cut off the sun last spring, I didn't at first relate it to what had happened fifteen or twenty years ago. Only gradually did a certain family resemblance come through—an overextension of the flank, a burning of the candle at both ends; a call upon physical resources that I did not command, like a man overdrawing at his bank. In its impact this blow was more violent than the other two but it was the same in kind—a feeling that I was standing at twilight on a deserted range, with an empty rifle in my hands and the targets down. No problem set—simply a silence with only the sound of my own breathing.

In this silence there was a vast irresponsibility toward every obligation, a deflation of all my values. A passionate belief in order, a disregard of motives or consequences in favor of guesswork and prophecy, a feeling that craft and industry would have a place in any world—one by one, these and other convictions were swept away. I saw that the novel, which at my maturity was the strongest and supplest medium for conveying thought and emotion from one human being to another, was becoming subordinated to a mechanical and communal art that, whether in the hands of Hollywood merchants or Russian idealists, was capable of reflecting only the tritest thought, the most obvious emotion. It was an art in which words were subordinate to images, where personality was worn down to the inevitable low gear of collaboration. As long past as 1930, I had a hunch that the talkies would make even the best selling novelist as archaic as silent pictures. People still read, if only Professor Canby's book of the month—curious children nosed at the slime of Mr. Tiffany Thayer in the drugstore libraries—but there was a rankling indignity, that to me had become almost an obsession, in seeing the power of the written word subordinated to another power, a more glittering, a grosser power . . .

I set that down as an example of what haunted me during the long night—this was something I could neither accept nor struggle against, something which tended to make my efforts obsolescent, as the chain stores have crippled the small merchant, an exterior force, unbeatable—

(I have the sense of lecturing now, looking at a watch on the desk before me and seeing how many more minutes—)

Well, when I had reached this period of silence, I was forced into a measure that no one ever adopts voluntarily: I was impelled to think. God, was it difficult! The moving about of great secret trunks. In the first exhausted halt, I wondered whether I had ever thought. After a long time I came to these conclusions, just as I write them here:

(1) That I had done very little thinking, save within the problems of my craft. For twenty years a certain man had been my intellectual conscience. That was Edmund Wilson.

(2) That another man represented my sense of the "good life," though I saw him once in a decade, and since then he might have been hung. He is in the fur business in the Northwest and wouldn't like his name set down here. But in difficult situations I have tried to think what *he* would have thought, how *he* would have acted.

(3) That a third contemporary had been an artistic conscience to me— I had not imitated his infectious style, because my own style, such as it is, was formed before he published anything, but there was an awful pull toward him when I was on a spot.

(4) That a fourth man had come to dictate my relations with other people when these relations were successful: how to do, what to say. How to make people at least momentarily happy (in opposition to Mrs. Post's theories of how to make everyone thoroughly uncomfortable with a sort of systemized vulgarity). This always confused me and made me want to go out and get drunk, but this man had seen the game, analyzed it, and beaten it, and his word was good enough for me.

(5) That my political conscience had scarcely existed for ten years save as an element of irony in my stuff. When I became again concerned with the

system I should function under, it was a man much younger than myself who brought it to me, with a mixture of passion and fresh air.

So there was not an "I" anymore—not a basis on which I could organize my self-respect—save my limitless capacity for toil that it seemed I possessed no more. It was strange to have no self—to be like a little boy left alone in a big house, who knew that now he could do anything he wanted to do, but found that there was nothing that he wanted to do—

(The watch is past the hour and I have barely reached my thesis. I have some doubts as to whether this is of general interest, but if anyone wants more, there is plenty left, and your editor will tell me. If you've had enough, say so—but not too loud, because I have the feeling that someone, I'm not sure who, is sound asleep—someone who could have helped me to keep my shop open. It wasn't Lenin, and it wasn't God.)

Handle with Care

I have spoken in these pages of how an exceptionally optimistic young man experienced a crack-up of all values, a crack-up that he scarcely knew of until long after it occurred. I told of the succeeding period of desolation and of the necessity of going on, but without the benefit of Henley's familiar heroics, "my head is bloody but unbowed." For a checkup of my spiritual liabilities indicated that I had no particular head to be bowed or unbowed. Once I had had a heart but that was about all I was sure of.

This was at least a starting place out of the morass in which I floundered: "I felt—therefore I was." At one time or another there had been many people who had leaned on me, come to me in difficulties or written me from afar, believed implicitly in my advice and my attitude toward life. The dullest platitude monger or the most unscrupulous Rasputin who can influence the destinies of many people must have some individuality, so the question became one of finding why and where I had changed, where was the leak through which, unknown to myself, my enthusiasm and my vitality had been steadily and prematurely trickling away.

One harassed and despairing night I packed a briefcase and went off a thousand miles to think it over. I took a dollar room in a drab little town where I knew no one and sunk all the money I had with me in a stock of potted meat, crackers, and apples. But don't let me suggest that the change from a rather overstuffed world to a comparative asceticism was any Research Magnificent—I only wanted absolute quiet to think out why I had developed a sad attitude toward sadness, a melancholy attitude toward melancholy, and a tragic attitude toward tragedy—*why I had become identified with the objects of my horror or compassion.*

Does this seem a fine distraction? It isn't: identification such as this spells the death of accomplishment. It is something like this that keeps sane people from working. Lenin did not willingly endure the sufferings of his proletariat, nor Washington of his troops, nor Dickens of his London poor. And when Tolstoy tried some such merging of himself with the objects of his attention, it was a fake and a failure. I mention these because they are the men best known to us all.

It was dangerous mist. When Wordsworth decided that "there hath passed away a glory from the earth," he felt no compulsion to pass away with it, and the Fiery Particle Keats never ceased his struggle against T.B. nor in his last moments relinquished his hope of being among the English poets.

My self-immolation was something sodden-dark. It was very distinctly not modern—yet I saw it in others, saw it in a dozen men of honor and industry since the war. (I heard you, but that's too easy—there were Marxians among these men.) I had stood by while one famous contemporary of mine played with the idea of the Big Out for half a year; I had watched when another, equally eminent, spent months in an asylum unable to endure any contact with his fellow men. And of those who had given up and passed on I could list a score.

This led me to the idea that the ones who had survived had made some sort of clean break. This is a big word and is no parallel to a jailbreak when one is probably headed for a new jail or will be forced back to the old one. The famous "Escape" or "Run away from it all" is an excursion in a trap even if the trap includes the South Seas, which are only for those who want to paint them or sail them. A clean break is something you cannot come back from; that is irretrievable because it makes the past cease to exist. So, since I could no longer fulfill the obligations that life had set for me or that I had set for myself, why not slay the empty shell who had been posturing at it for four years? I must continue to be a writer because that was my only way of life, but I would cease any attempts to be a person—to be kind, just, or generous. There were plenty of counterfeit coins around that would pass instead of these and I knew where I could get them at a nickel on the dollar. In thirty-nine years an observant eye has learned to detect where the milk is watered and the sugar is sanded, the rhinestone passed for diamond and the stucco for stone. There was to be no more giving of myself—all giving was to be outlawed henceforth under a new name, and that name was Waste.

The decision made me rather exuberant, like anything that is both real and new. As a sort of beginning there was a whole shaft of letters to be tipped into the wastebasket when I went home, letters that wanted something for nothing—to read this man's manuscript, market this man's poem, speak free on the radio, indite notes of introduction, give this interview, help with the plot of this play, with this domestic situation, perform this act of thoughtfulness or charity.

The conjurer's hat was empty. To draw things out of it had long been a sort of sleight of hand, and now, to change the metaphor, I was off the dispensing end of the relief roll forever.

The heady villainous feeling continued.

I felt like the beady-eyed men I used to see on the commuting train from Great Neck fifteen years back—men who didn't care whether the world tumbled into chaos tomorrow if it spared their houses. I was one with them now, one with the smooth articles who said:

> *"I'm sorry but business is business."*
> Or:
> *"You ought to have thought of that before you got into this trouble."*
> Or:
> *"I'm not the person to see about that."*

And a smile—ah, I would get me a smile. I'm still working on that smile. It is to combine the best qualities of a hotel manager, an experienced old social weasel, a headmaster on visitors' day, a colored elevator man, a pansy pulling a profile, a producer getting stuff at half its market value, a trained nurse coming on a new job, a body-vender in her first rotogravure, a hopeful extra swept near the camera, a ballet dancer with an infected toe, and of course the great beam of loving kindness common to all those from Washington to Beverly Hills who must exist by virtue of the contorted pan.

The voice too—I am working with a teacher on the voice. When I have perfected it the larynx will show no ring of conviction except the conviction of the person I am talking to. Since it will be largely called upon for the elicitation of the word "Yes," my teacher (a lawyer) and I are concentrating on that, but in extra hours. I am learning to bring into it that polite acerbity that makes people feel that far from being welcome they are not even tolerated and are under continual and scathing analysis at every moment. These times will of course not coincide with the smile. This will be reserved exclusively for those from whom I have nothing to gain, old worn-out people or young struggling people. They won't mind—what the hell, they get it most of the time anyhow.

But enough. It is not a matter of levity. If you are young and you should write asking to see me and learn how to be a somber literary man writing pieces upon the state of emotional exhaustion that often overtakes writers in their prime—if you should be so young and fatuous as to do this, I would not do so much as acknowledge your letter, unless you were related to someone very rich and important indeed. And if you were dying of starvation outside my window, I would go out quickly and give you the smile and the voice (if no longer the hand) and stick around till somebody raised a nickel to phone for the ambulance, that is if I thought there would be any copy in it for me.

I have now at last become a writer only. The man I had persistently tried to be became such a burden that I have "cut him loose" with as little compunction as a Negro lady cuts loose a rival on Saturday night. Let the good people function as such—let the overworked doctors die in harness, with one week's "vacation" a year that they can devote to straightening out their family affairs, and let the underworked doctors scramble for cases at one dollar a throw; let the soldiers be killed and enter immediately into the Valhalla of their profession. That is their contract with the gods. A writer need have no such ideals unless he makes them for himself, and this one has quit. The old dream of being an entire man in the Goethe-Byron-Shaw tradition, with an opulent American touch, a sort of combination of J. P. Morgan, Topham Beauclerk, and St. Francis of Assisi, has been relegated to the junk heap of the shoulder pads worn for one day on the Princeton freshman football field and the overseas cap never worn overseas.

So what? This is what I think now: that the natural state of the sentient adult is a qualified unhappiness. I think also that in an adult the desire to be finer in grain than you are, "a constant striving" (as those people say who gain their bread by saying it), only adds to this unhappiness in the end—that end that comes to our youth and hope. My own happiness in the past often approached such an ecstasy that I could not share it even with the person dearest to me but had to walk it away in quiet streets and lanes with only fragments of it to distill into little lines in books—and I think that my happiness, or talent for self-delusion or what you will, was an exception. It was not the natural thing but the unnatural—unnatural as the Boom; and my recent experience parallels the wave of despair that swept the nation when the Boom was over.

I shall manage to live with the new dispensation, though it has taken some months to be certain of the fact. And just as the laughing stoicism which has enabled the American Negro to endure the intolerable conditions of his existence has cost him his sense of the truth—so in my case there is a price to pay. I do not any longer like the postman, nor the grocer, nor the editor, nor the cousin's husband, and he in turn will come to dislike me, so that life will never be very pleasant again, and the sign Cave Canem is hung permanently just above my door. I will try to be a correct animal though, and if you throw me a bone with enough meat on it I may even lick your hand.

1939

This year, when *Fortune* magazine asks James Agee to write an essay about Brooklyn, it has already rejected his work five times. It called an essay he wrote about a cruise to Cuba "too involved with its own style." A profile of a singer was "overwhelmingly detailed." And the essay that he composed about three families in Alabama—which eventually became *Let Us Now Praise Famous Men*—was rejected on the grounds that it was "arrogant, mannered, precious, and gross." James Agee is not a journalist, you see, and yet neither is he willing to assume any other label. In a letter to a friend he admits to "a total suspicion of both 'creative' and 'reportorial' attitudes and methods, which therefore will require the development of more or less an entirely new form of writing." The essay that he hands in to *Fortune* this year will be the last that it asks him to write. He calls it "a travelogue beyond the boundaries of its subject"; *Fortune* calls it "undisciplined." It is ten thousand words long, opening with a series of claustrophobic assertions that give us very little by way of a context. But then, very slowly, those assertions give way to observations, and those observations to scenes, and soon we're in the midst of an urban dreamscape that feels like it's perpetually revving up to something big, a simultaneously indulgent and inspiring litany of starts—hints of revelations that he dangles before our hearts, then yanks away suddenly in order to keep them alive. James Agee struggled throughout his life with suicide—"not just fooling with the idea," as he once told a friend, "but feeling very seriously on the edge of doing it"—and I think we can feel this palpably in the rise and fall of his modulating prose, that soaring aspiration that feels infinite when we're in it, but that Agee always cuts prematurely short. When he dies, alone, in the back of a taxicab, he is forty-six years old and the victim of a heart attack. But some say he is a victim of his own hand as well, decades after a life spent aggressively drunk. Years from now, a magazine will finally publish his essay about Brooklyn. It comes out the same year that New York City demolishes its landmark monument to Beaux-Arts architecture, Pennsylvania Station—a temple, as one critic described it, "not only to transportation, but to the sensation of freedom itself." It was made of granite, greeting the traveler at street level with an imposing phalanx of solid Doric columns, interrupted only occasionally by ten-foot-high doors. Inside, the echoing stone foyer distributed its travelers into dozens of different passageways, long and winding tunnels whose ceilings began to lower as their floors ramped into the earth. Maybe they were dark, overcrowded, too tight to turn around in, to pause to check your ticket, to stop to change your mind. Maybe the building squeezed you down as it sucked you toward its gut, and maybe this was intentional, a stylistic trick to prepare you for that moment when the tunnels disappeared and the ceiling lifted up and the walls widened out as you flashed into a gleaming white atrium of light, its thin iron archways supporting a glass ceiling that was seven acres wide—a roof of pure sky—the largest indoor public space anywhere in the world, and one that felt so suddenly unburdensome to travelers that moving from that foyer to the Great Hall, as it was called, physically felt like having something lifted from your shoulders, the architectural equivalent of traveling, in other words, and the literary equivalent of being inside a sentence that is held aloft by language, by a vim of curiosity, and maybe by a little bit of fear of what comes next.

Brooklyn Is

"City of homes and churches."
WHITMAN, WRITING OF BROOKLYN

"One of the great waste places of the world."
DOUGHTY, WRITING OF ARABIA

"And blights with plagues the marriage hearse."
BLAKE, WRITING OF LONDON

"Life is fundamentally composed of vegetable matter."
OBSOLETE TEXTBOOK OF BIOLOGY

Watching them in the trolleys, or along the inexhaustible reduplications of the streets of their small tradings and their sleep, one comes to notice, even in the most urgently poor, a curious quality in the eyes and at the corners of the mouth, relative to what is seen on Manhattan Island: a kind of drugged softness or narcotic relaxation. The same look may be seen in monasteries and on the lawns of sanitariums, and there must have been some similar look among soldiers convalescent of shell shock in institutionalized British gardens where, in a late summer dusk, a young man could mistake heat lightnings and the crumpling of hidden thunder for what he has left in France, and must return to. If there were not Manhattan, there could not be this Brooklyn look; for truly to appreciate what one escapes, it must be not only distant but near at hand. Only: all escapes are relative, and bestow their own peculiar forms of bondage.

It is the same of the physique and whole tone and meters of the city

433

itself. You have only to cross a bridge to know it: how behind you the whole of living is drawn up straining into verticals, tightened and badgered in nearly every face of man and child and building; and how where you are entering, even among the riverside throes of mechanisms and of tenements in the iron streets, this whole of living is nevertheless relaxed upon horizontalities, a deep taproot of stasis in each action and each building. Partly, it suggests the qualities of any small American city, the absorption in home, the casualness of the measuredly undistinguished; only this usual provincialism is powerfully enhanced here by the existence of Manhattan, upon which an inestimable swarm of Brooklyn's population depends for a living itself. And again, this small-city quality is confused in the deep underground atomic drone of the intertextured procedures upon blind time of more hundreds on hundreds of thousands of compacted individual human existences than the human imagination can comprehend or bear to comprehend.

It differs from most cities in this: that though it has perhaps a "center," and hands, and eyes, and feet, it is chiefly no whole or recognizable animal but an exorbitant pulsing mass of scarcely discernible cellular jellies and tissues; a place where people merely "live." A few American cities, Manhattan chief among them, have some mad magnetic energy which sucks all others into "provincialism"; and Brooklyn of all great cities is nearest the magnet, and is indeed "provincial": it is provincial as a land of rich earth and of this earth is an enormous farm, whose crop is far less "industrial" or "financial" or "notable" or in any way "distinguished" or "definable" than it is of human flesh and being. And this fact alone, which of itself makes Brooklyn so featureless, so little known, to many so laughable, or so ripe for patronage, this fact, that two million human beings are alive and living there, invests it with an extraordinarily high, piteous and inviolable dignity, well beyond touch of laughter, defense, or need of notice.

Manhattan is large, yet all its distances seem quick and available. Brooklyn is larger, seventy-one square miles as against twenty-two; but here you enter the paradoxes of the relative. You know, here only a few miles from wherever I stand, Brooklyn ends; only a few miles away is Manhattan; Brooklyn is walled with world-traveled wetness on west and south, and on north and east is the young beaverboard frontier of Queens; Brooklyn comes to an end: but actually, that is, in the conviction of the body, there seems almost no conceivable end to Brooklyn; it seems, on land as flat and huge as

Kansas, horizon beyond horizon forever unfolded, an immeasurable pro-
liferation of house on house and street by street; or seems as China does,
infinite in time in patience and in population as in space.

The collaborated creature of the insanely fungoid growth of fifteen or
twenty villages, now sewn and quilted edge to edge and lacking any center
in remote proportion to its mass, it is perhaps the most amorphous of all
modern cities; and at the same time, by virtue of its arterial streets, it has
continuities so astronomically vast as Paris alone or the suburbs south of
Chicago could match: on Flatbush Avenue, DeKalb, Atlantic, New Lots,
Church, any number more, a vista of low buildings and side streets of
glanded living sufficient to paralyze all conjecture; simply, far as the eye can
strain, no end of Brooklyn, and looking back, far as the eye can urge itself,
no end, nor imaginable shore; only, thrust upon the pride of heaven, the
monolith of the Empire State, a different mode of life; and even this, seen
here, has the smoky frailty of a half-remembered dream.

(Observing in subway stations, in any part of Brooklyn, not in an hour
of rush but in the leisured evening, you see this; how, wherever there is a
choice of staircases, one toward Manhattan, one away, without thought
or exception they descend the staircase toward the Island. An imaginative
designer would have foreseen this and would have omitted the alternatives
entirely.

(In Upper Flatbush, already two miles deep inland from the bridges, a
young woman of Manhattan asked a druggist how she might get into certain territory well south of there. Without thought of irony he began, "*Oh.
You want to go to Brooklyn.*")

More homes are owned in Brooklyn than in any other Borough; there
are more children per adult head; it is a great savings-bank town; there are
fewer divorces; it is by and large as profoundly domesticated, docile and
"stable" a population as one could conceive of, outside England. The horror of "unsuccessful" marriages—unsuccessful, that is, as shown by an open
or legal break; the lethal effort of Carry On is thought well of—this horror is such that there is a special bank to which husbands come one day to
deposit, estranged wives the next to be fertilized by this genteel equivalent
of alimony. It seems significant of Brooklyn that it is probably the only city
that has such a bank.

At the north brow of Prospect Park, where a vast number of these marriages are, in the medical sense, contracted and where, indeed, the whole

sweep of infancy, childhood, and the descending discords of family life is on display, there stands a piece of statuary. From away down Flatbush Avenue it suggests that cloven flame which spoke with Dante in hell but by a nearer view, it is a man and a nude woman in bronze and their plump child, eager for the Park, and it represents the beauty and stability of Brooklyn, and of human family life. The man and wife stand back to back, in the classical posture of domestic sleep. It is a thoroughly vulgar and sincere piece of work, and once one gets beyond the aesthete's sometimes myopic scorn, is the infallibly appropriate creation of the whole heart of Brooklyn. Michelangelo would have done much less well.

All the neighborhoods that make up this area; those well known, and those which are indicated on no official map.

The Hill, for instance: the once supremely solid housing of Clinton Avenue, broken with a light titter of doctors' shingles; the two big homes which are become the L. I. Grotto Pouch and the Pouch Annex; or the boarded brownstone opposite the decrepit bricks of the Adelphi Academy; or those blocks which have formed "protective associations" against the infiltration of Negroes.

Or Park Slope: the big Manhattan-style apartment buildings which now hem the Park, and on the streets of the upward slope, and on Eighth Avenue, the bland powerful regiments of grey-stone bays and the big single homes, standing with a locked look among mature trees and the curious quietudes of bourgeois Paris: and these confused among apartment buildings and among parochial schools, and the yellow bricks of post-tenements, and the subway of "rough" children.

Or the Heights: the enormous homes and the fine rows, a steadily narrower area remains inviolable, the top drawer of Brooklyn, disintegrated toward the stooping of the street toward the Squibb Building: great houses broken apart for roomers; a gradual degeneration into artists and journalists, Communists, bohemians and barbers, chiefly of Manhattan.

Or, among brownstones, between the last two-mile convergence of Fulton and Broadway, a swifter and swifter breakdown of the former middle classes, a steady thickening of Jews into the ultimacies of Brownsville and East New York.

Or that great range of brick and brownstone north of Fulton which in each two blocks falls upon more and more bad fortune; one last place, east of Fort Greene Park, the utmost magnificence of the brownstone style; and beyond-death at length in the Navy Yard district, the hardest in Brooklyn, harder even than Red Hook (the hardest neighborhood in Brooklyn was a pinched labyrinth of brick and frame within a jump of Borough Hall, but the W.P.A. cleared that one up).

Or Eastern Parkway, the Central Park West of Brooklyn; in its first stretches near Prospect Park, the dwelling of the most potent Jews of the city; a slow then more swift ironing out, and the end again in Brownsville.

Or Bay Ridge, and its genteel gentile apartment buildings, and the staid homes of Scandinavian seafarers.

Or Greenpoint and Williamsburg and Bushwick, the wood tenements, bare lots and broken vistas, the balanced weights and images of production and poverty; the headquarters of a municipal government as corrupt as any in the nation; everywhere the spindling Democratic clubs, the massive Roman churches; everywhere, in the eyes of men, in dark bars and on corners, knowledgeable appraising furtive light of hard machine politics; everywhere, the curious gaslit odor of Irish-American democracy.

Or Flatbush: or Brighton: or Sheepshead Bay: or the negligible downtown; or the view, from the Fulton Street Elevated, of the low-swung and convolved sea of the living, as much green as roofs; or of Brooklyn's nineteenth century backyard life, thousands of solitaries, chips, each floated in his green eddy: or the comparable military attentions of the stoned dead, the stern hieroglyphs of Jews, the thousands of gold Christs in the sun, the many churches focusing upon the frank secret star-demolished city, their stooplings and proud bulbs and triple crosses and sharp stars and square-flung roods moored high, light-ballasted, among the harboring homes, ships pointing out the sun on a single wind; or the mother who walks on Division Avenue whose infant hexes her from his carriage in a gargoyle frown of most intense suspicion; or the soft whistling of the sea off Coney Island; or the facade of the Academy of Music, a faded print of Boston's Symphony Hall; or the young pair who face each other astride a bicycle in Canarsie; or the lavender glow of brownstones in cloudy weather, or the chemical brilliance of jonquils in tamped dirt; or the haloed Sunday hats of little girls, as exquisite as those of their elders are pathologic: or the scornful cornices of dishonored homes; or the shade cord at whose end is a white home-crocheted Jewish star; or the hot-pants little Manhattan sweat-shop girls who come to Tony's Square Bar to meet the sailors and spend a few bearable hours a week; or the streaming of first-flight gentiles from

Poly Prep into Williams and Princeton, the second flight into Colgate or Cornell; or of the Jews whose whole families are breaking their hearts for it from Boys High into Brooklyn College and Brooklyn Law, and the luckiest of them into Harvard; or the finance editor of the *Eagle* who believes all journalists are gentlemen who are out of what he calls the Chosen, and who scabbed in the *Eagle* strike; or in the middle afternoon in whatever part of Brooklyn, the starlike amplitude of baby buggies and of strolling and lounging silent or soft-speaking women, the whole as vacant of masculinity as most urgent war; or in his window above the banging of DeKalb Avenue late on a hot Saturday afternoon the grizzling skullcapped Jew who knocks softly above the texts of his holiness, his lips moving in his unviolated beard, and who has been thus drowned in his pieties since early morning; or the grievings and the gracilities of the personalities at the zoo; or the bright fabric stretched of the confabulations of birds and children; or bed by bed and ward by ward along the sacred odors of the corridors of the twelve-street mass of the Kings County Hospital, those who burst with unspeakable vitality or who are floated faint upon dubiety or who wait to die. These, the sick, the fainted or fecund, the healthful, the young, the living and the dead, the buildings, the streets, the windows, the linings of the ward nests, the lethal chambers of the schools, the fumed and whining factories, the pitiless birds, the animals, that Bridge which stands up like God and makes music to himself by night and by day: all in the lordly, idiot light, these are inhabitants of Brooklyn.

Or Greenpoint; or Williamsburg; where from many mileages of the jungle of voided land, small factories, smokestacks, tenements, homes of irregular height and spacing, the foci are returned upon the eye, the blown dome and trebled crossage Greek church, and those massive gas reservoirs which seem to have more size than any building can; the hard trade avenues, intense with merchandisings of which none is above the taking of the working class: the bridal suites in modernistic veneers and hot-colored plushes, the dark little drugstores which smell like medicine spilled in a phone-booth mouthpiece; the ineffable baroques of gossamer in which little-girl-graduates and Brides of Heaven are clothed. Here, and still strongly in Bushwick and persistent too in East New York and Brownsville, there is an enormous number of tall-windowed three- and four-floor wood houses of the full-blown nineteenth century, a style indigenous to Brooklyn, the facades as handsome as anything in the history of American architecture; of these, few have been painted within a decade or more, none are above the rooming-house level, most are tenements, all are deathtraps to fire; their face is of that half-divine nobility which is absorptive of every humiliation, and is increased in each: many more of the tenements are those pallid or yellow bricks which are so much used all over Brooklyn as a mark of poverty; mixed among these many small houses of weathered wood, stucco, roofing; the stucco fronts are often Italian and usually un-colored, and suggest nevertheless the rich Italianate washes; some are washed brick red, the joints drawn in white; or the golden-oak doors of these neater homes, or the manifold and beautiful frontages of asphaltic shingles, some shinglings merely, but applied in strong imaginations of color and pattern, others simulative of slate or brick and more handsome than either; the knowledge, forced or vue, willing or no, that all street and domestic art is talented and powerful in proportion to poverty and disadvantage of blood; the care in the selection of curtains and window ornaments; white shades and tasseled shade cords, or tan venetian blinds, or curtains of starched wrecked lace, or red or gold or magenta sateen, little statues of comedy or faith, flowers, leaves and lamps; the names and faces of Irish, Italians, Jews and Slavs; and in the street the proud cries of children, the tightened eyes of fathers, the dissolving beauties of young wives, the deep enthronements of the aged, and along five thousand first-floor windows in their gloom, am-bushed behind drawn breathing shades, the staring into the single zoned street of crouched aging women, the look of tired lionesses in an endless zoo in a hot afternoon; and in the bleeding of early neons, the return of the typists, and of the students in careful suits, hard ties, carrying their hokey books, and the small bare crowding, where men gentle with weariness drink beer in the solace of each other's voices and the nickelodeon; and in the evenings, here almost in the warm Hebraic volubilities of Brownsville, such a swarm, affection, patience, bitterness and vitality in existence as words will not record.

Or the drive one afternoon, with a Brooklyn journalist, a too-well-born young man not long enough out of Harvard, which began in the vibrated shelters of Brooklyn Bridge and threaded the waterfront and at length sketched in motion the whole people of Brooklyn; the shore drive along Bay Ridge, Coney Island, Sheepshead Bay, and in darkness drove the nar-row vision of its needle steep northward through the whole body of the city, straight through Flatbush; those who gathered firewood on a vacant lot on Front Street; the huge warehouses, their walls a yard thick, which were built in the time of the clipper ships; a harvester addressed to Guaraquito, a Chevrolet on its way to Peru, stacks of scrap iron ready for loading to kill whom, where, this time; the calm leaning above earth of the *Hulda Maersk,* Isbrandtsen-Moller, the effulgence of her pale aluminum, her beautifully made bow; pine refugee crates, all of the utmost size permitted for the bringing away of the inappraisable objects of outrage, grief and remembrance, veiled in tarpaulin as if they were deaths and marked with that wineglass which is this planet's symbol for this end up; it is memorable, too, how half the houses in this section are deserted, the windows shattered, standing jagged as war among vacant lots, the ghosts of floors against their walls: and the dark hard bars at street corners, and men who watched the bland progress of this skimming sedan in cold, strychnine, deeply gratifying hate; and along the sheltered Atlantic Basin the warehouses stored with newsprint from Nova Scotia, Norway, Latvia, Finland; and further down the front the ships from South America and Africa and Japan; in the middle of a vacant lot a Negro who sat on a lard can and ate out of a newspaper; the mahogany odors of roasting coffee; the prow of the *Tai Yin,* dark as a planned murder above a heap of scrap; the funereally rusted prows also of the *Dundrum Castle* and the *Ohio;* how little of Grover Whalen there is in the clothing of the custom officials of a freight waterfront; how relaxed work is here as against the Manhattan waterfront, almost the sun-saturated ease of New Orleans; an enormous repaired diesel gentled along on a Williamsburg hauler, suggesting, in the middle of the street, an extracted heart; the negroid breath of a molasses factory; a glimpse of the Red Hook housing project which may or may not, unlike all former American housing projects, serve those for whom it is intended; on the curve of a new cinder track nine strong boys aslant in distance running, their aura part ancient Greece, part present Leningrad; the pale parade of the great structures of the Bush Terminal, powerful as barges; the hulls resting where the olive shipments used to be heavy; the journalist's efforts to get to the yachting docks ("the *Corsair* sometimes docks here"), but "they keep them pretty well barricaded"; the long jetty created of the ballast of returning clippers, stacked now with Pacific Coast lumber; the cheap white-sweated brick of the Red Hook Play Center; or the skinned land which was formerly a Hooverville, available to the totally derelict, but which under squarer dispensation wears W.P.A.'s usual credit line for having Cleaned this Area; or how the comfortable young man remarked of certain outrageously poor homes left standing, that they were not of the squatter class; these people have some right to be here but (laughing) imagine you or I living in such a way; and the drawbridge over the Gowanus Canal, its sheathings and angularities in motion as elegant as those of a starved cat; or how he remarked that one may find a good deal of prose in Brooklyn but precious little poetry, or again, of the whole region just traversed, "Good solid work here; no swank; not a part of town one comes to see much, but quite necessary to the community."

Or further, along the shore road, passing a stretch of rather Ducky middle-income houses, the "Tudor" type, his patronizing approval: "Here at least you can see some *attempt* at decency"; and a half-made park with the odd pubescent nudity of all new public efforts; and on the bay the pinched island Fort Lafayette with the minelaying equipment, and Hoffman Island, the quarantine for parrots and monkeys; the obsolete cannons of Fort Hamilton; a shutdown deserted block of middle-class housing of the Twenties, the blasted mansions of Victorian pleasance, boarded or broken out with gasolines and soft drinks; the San Carlo Bocce-Drome, rubbed earth in oil-green-tree shade, soft-stepping middle-aged Italians at play; a dismantled country club; the high, mild-breezed lift of the shore drive.

And on Coney, the drive along a back street past dirtied frames which suggest the poorer parts of the Jersey Shore and which are said to be the worst "slum" in greater New York; and his speaking, with limitless scorn and hatred, of Sea Gate, a *restricted* neighborhood; the *aristocracy, Mrs. Linkowitz, Mrs. Finkelstein;* and Sea Gate itself, at the west end of the island, a few wooden Victorians, the rest undersized pretensions of gaudiest, most betraying bricks, perhaps the most dreadfully piteous excrescence crystallization of snobbery I have ever seen; and in a barren place at the far end of the island, in a bright spring sun of six o'clock, the engine quiet, and the whole of the harbor paved the color of dawn and deep up the north the slow laboring pencil-mark shadow of an outgoing liner, and at profound distance, spoken out of the ocean water itself, a whistling, and light tolling.

And how at Landy's in Sheepshead Bay he outlined his plans for solidifying himself in the community before joining the Nazi *Bund.*

And in darkness, the deep, droned drive up the whole facade of the scarcely distinguishable city; the ascent of a diving bell.

And the hesitations and slow drivings around Brooklyn College; along the walk next the ball-field entrance the slowly moving crowd and the lighted placards with the key words, UNITY? WAR; and the new-appearing buildings of this great day college, bloomed with light of study, bad Georgian, the look of a unit of Harvard house plans with elephantiasis; and again skirting the ball field, trying to hear; in the middle of the field was one dark group and a speaker raised among them with his flag, on the far side another such group (could they be opponents?), and the placards; and again along the side of the field, as near as we could get, the fat motor idling, and the driver speaking hatefully of Jews; five students came along the walks glancing over, and crossed away in front of us, one of them saying "the Communist sons of bitches"; there was a thin mist through which all light seemed meager and the sky enormous, and in the faint field they stood dark, earnestly attentive, their placards oscillating; and above them, with the help I believe of a weak microphone, came the passionate incompetent speaking of the student. From where we were, only his deep sincerity and fear and the inadequacies of his particular mind and intonations were at first audible, but at length the greyed, desperate, salient words came through, in his brave uncertain hypnotized tenor, "war" . . . "democracy" . . . "unalterably opposed"; and the placards moved as masts in a harbor; it was the night before Hitler was to tell Roosevelt there would be no ten-year's peace, and I suggested that that must be the cause of the mass meeting. The journalist agreed it must be, added, "Let them. Let them yap about peace and democracy all they like. They're not going to impress Hitler one little bit."

(All over the city, on streets and walks and walls the children and the other true primitives of the race have established ancient, essential and ephemeral form of art, have set forth in chalk and crayon the names and images of their pride, love, preying, scorn, desire; the Negroes, Jews, Italians, Poles, most powerfully, these same poorest most abundantly, and in these are the characters of neighborhood and of race; on an iron door in Williamsburg: *Dominick says he will Screw Fanny.* On another: *Boys gang up on Don* and *Down with Don* and *Don is a Bull Artist.* Against green shingles of a Bushwick side door: *The Lady in this House is Nuts.* In an immaculate neighborhood of lower-middle-class Jews in East New York, against a new blood wash of drugstore brick, the one word *strike.* In Brighton, among Jews recently withdrawn from the ghetto, a child begins an abstract drawing and his mother quickly, "*Don't* do that," and a ten-year-old boy immediately, to a younger, in the same notation, "*Don't* do that." On Park Slope on a Sunday afternoon, not printed, but in an unskillful Palmer script: *Lois I have gone up the street. Don't forget to bring your skates.* In Williamsburg: *Ruby loves Max but Max hates Ruby.*

(And drawings, all over, of phalli, fellatio, ships, homes, airplanes, Western heroes, women, and monsters dredged out of the memories of the unspeakable sea journeys of the womb, all spangling the walks and walls, which each strong rain effaces.)

Or deep in Flatbush; in a warm middle afternoon.

I leave the trolley avenue and walk up a residential street; I have not gone a block before I recognize a silence so powerful and so specialized it has almost a fragrance of its own; it is the silence of having left a street of the open world and of having entered an empty church, and is much that fragrance; and there is in the silence an almost Brahmin tranquillity, weakening to the senses, and a subtly terrifying quality of suffocation and of the sacrosanct; and in a moment more, standing between these rows of neat homes, I know what this special sanctitude is; that this world is totally dedicated to tame marriages in their first ten years of youth, and that during the sweep of each working day these streets are yielded over to housewives and to young children and to infants so entirely that those who stroll these walks and sit in the sun are cloistral nuns, vestals, made fecund though they are, and govern a world in which returning men are made womanly in an odor of cherished floors, clean cloths, nationally advertised cosmetics, and the sharp stench of babies. Two youths, it is true, toss a ball back and forth in the street; but they do so as if this were a Puritan Sunday, or an area of crisis in sickness in which for relief the healthful must relax, but gently; the rest is as I have said; I see five closed cars, moored empty before doors; each is lately washed, the treads of the tires are sharp, they are all black, not one but is a Chevrolet, Ford or Plymouth; and on doorsteps dolls and the bright aerodynamic toys of the children of this decade; and it seems before every house, shining hearselike in the glare, an identical perambulator, deep, black, sleek with lacquer, brimmed with white cloths; and women: two who stroll abreast along the shadowless adolescence of saplings, serving their carriages; two more who sit in an open door and talk in stopped-down voices; another who sits alone, addling the sprung carriage and staring emptily upon the street; another who, drawing aside a sun-porch curtain, peers out upon my watching with the soft sterile alarm of one whose knight is East crusading; a laundry truck sneaks cushioning past and halts at a far door; far up the street I hear the voice of a child; in his shaded pram by the step, swollen with royalty, a baby sleeps; a half mile up Flatbush Avenue, the metal whine of a northbound trolley.

Some of the houses are ten to fifteen years old, some are much younger; all, in their several ways, perfect images of these matings: little doubles and singles of brick and shingle or of brick and stucco or of solid brick in rows; of these latter, five in a row, rather new, are cautiously ornate and are fronted in near patterns of bright brick the six colors of children's modeling clays; they are so prim, so undersized, they suggest dolls' homes or the illustrations of a storybook of pretty dreams for sexually ripened children; or as if through some kind of white magic they had been made of candy, to the wonder and delight of two who, lost and loving in a wilderness, came suddenly upon a home; "exposed beams," wrought-iron knockers, white concrete steps, oak doors with barred peeping shutters, little touches of the Elizabethan, the Colonial, the Byzantine; or the others, those peaked twins faced with shingles, or those of which the porch is wood, glass and brick, the first floor stucco, above that weatherboard or shingle; and of these kinds each has a sun porch, and at the door two whitewashed urns or boxes for flowers, and each a little six-by-four lawn and a low hedge; and these lawns are brightly seeded, and shrubbed with dark junipers, and are affectionately tended; and in the curtained or venetian-blinded windows of these sun porches there are bullfrogs and pelicans and Scotch terriers and swans of china and roadside potteries of green or yellow sprouting streaked reptilian leaves at whose roots are dainty cowries; and between the homes, or between each double, a streakless concrete lane, an exact width between the windowless walls to pass the sedan, and beyond, a garage; and in these backyards, bright in the sun on patented lines, the bedspreads and the pasteled undergarments of women to whom the natural-color advertisements have told their love of nice things, and this washing has been done in supreme suds which are incapable of damaging the most delicate fabrics and which keep these women unenvious of one another's hands, in electric machines which would flatter any motion picture's conception of a laboratory in an essay on the holiness of medical students.

Or more ordinarily perhaps, few or none of the most fairy story of these love nests, but solid regiments of the other types, or mixtures of types; both the uniform and the varied strongly exist; plain cubed double-houses of dark red or brindled brick of the Twenties is one kind, very common;

another, the wood doubles whose twin-peaked gables make an M above the partitioned sun porch; and some are faced entirely with stucco; and more often than not there is scarcely room between the walls for a child to get through and the sidewalk trees are developed well beyond the sapling stage; and quite frequently, too, there is at the corner a four- or a six-floor brick apartment building, with a small cement court in which the women sit in damp or Windsor chairs; and from one or two windows of these, some pouting betrayal of humility, a cerise mattress; or again for no good reason these buildings will thicken to occupy most of several blocks and there will be fewer mattresses and women at the sills or none and a higher rental, and fewer hatless women in spring coats over housedresses; on some streets there is an inexplicable mixture of "classes," and of "grades" of homes, Central Europeans, a sudden family of Negroes in a scarred frame house, facing the most laxatived of Anglo-Saxons; or again scarce-explicably, a block of solid working class, a row of upper porches, where a rubber tree takes the air and a child's stained sheets are spread, and a woman combs and fondles in the sun her long wild-ivory ghastly hair whose face, peering from this ambush, is the four staring holes of a drowned corpse, and the boys play ball more loudly and of two little boys, passing on limber legs, one is saying, just above a whisper, ". . . you know: back stairs. You know: down the back stairs. Back stairs. You know . . ." and at the end of the street a small factory without even a name moans like many flies; Or, too, there are streets of spaced homes, side lawns and heavy trees whose structures are columned wood, wide plates of glass, big porches, the thick Sunday dinner proprieties which succeeded the jigsaw period: or rows again of yellow brick, flat-faced or roundly bayed, rented dwellings, such as may be seen in every part of Brooklyn and in much of the eastern United States—enough variety, mixture, monotony, sudden change, that it is impossible to generalize Flatbush; and in all this variety nevertheless and in the actions and faces of those who live here the drive of an all but annihilative essential uniformity: such that it seems that the middle-class suburbs and residential streets of all the small cities of the continent are here set against one another and ironed to one scarcely wrinkled flatness and similitude. The "avenues," the arteries, are no less like themselves, immeasurable stretches of three-floor yellow-brick with ground-floor merchants of hosiery and Ex-Lax—for Brooklyn's "downtown," too, is ironed thin to every door; and in this lowness of all building and in the almost stellar vistas of the avenues, an incredible dilation of the sky and the flat horizon, and thus, paradoxic with the odors of suffocation, the open grandeurs almost of a ranch, the quietudes not only of paralysis but of the stratosphere; and so it is not surprising in a Flatbush husband that he feels the air is a lot cleaner out here; a decent place to raise your kids.

(In the gallery of one of the big second-run theatres in the downtown section of Flatbush Avenue, about ten in the evening, they were nearly all high-school boys. They all knew each other, as they don't in New York, and kept calling across to each other, and the way they tried to pick at my wife [she was alone] was different from New York, too: "Hey, miss, what time is it?" and "Hey, miss, what's your first name?" They teased the picture more volubly, too. It was a very ordinary thoroughbred show, Kentucky, etcetera, with the customary crimes against the talents of Zasu Pitts; but there was one sequence, a spring night, when the heroine was called from a party and waited, glowing in the darkness in her evening dress, while a champion colt was foaled, of a dying dam. Small-lighted men labored intensely in the dark stable over a dark mass almost in silence, and in the gabby balcony an extraordinary quiet, tender, premonitory incertitude took full hold. Out of this gentle, intuitive, questioning silence at length, in a mild naked voice, a boy in the front row realized: "The horse is having a baby," and a boy five rows back, in a thickened voice, cried: "Aww, why don't you shut up.")

Social note.

Brooklyn Heights: the dusk of the gods.

It was really very kind of them, but one can't help that; or must one? The facade was Heights nineteenth-century, but the extent of the daughter's revolt consisted in a renegade taste for the smuggest and safest in modernism, so the interiors were a little beyond her parents. They both had tall, large, narrow faces, and an almost oriental cruelty in the eyes and the ends of the lower lips; like many married couples each suggested an unflattering reflection of the other, and they had the strange corpsy dryness common to all whose living is contractive, anti-human. There were weak side-cars served by the usual gentle, refined, ruined girl of foreign extraction, one drink each and a half glass over for me, and we went down to dinner. On a wide, dry plate lay four high-grade Cattleyas, all directed at me; but I made no comment. The bay was soft-lighted against fair, slender palms, and the curtains, with that ostentatious good taste which is the worst taste of all, were drawn against the most magnificent view in greater New York. We ate exquisitely cooked boned squab, pecan-sized potatoes fried in a fine oil, asparagus without sauce, and an exceptionally good dessert of strawberries, baked egg white and ice cream whose aggregate name I lack the worldly wisdom to know: Baked Alaska, probably; and as the food came and went I developed the feeling, perhaps unfairly, that this was not the ordinary Tuesday-evening menu, and that the specialization was the result less of hospitality than of the wish to astound the bourgeois. Unfortunately the thing I think of most is the rotted meat which is freshened with embalming fluid and sold at a feasible price to the Negroes along Fulton Street, who, lacking the benefits of a thorough course in biology, and any other sniff at it while they are yet conscious, are not in a position to identify this odor as the alter ego of death. While we ate she talked. There is no room here to tell of it all (I refer you to Swift's *Polite Conversation*), but of some little it is impossible to refrain. About the private park, for instance, which the survivor of the Misses Pierrepont still holds open to the play of the appropriate children, each of whose mother is given a key, on the strict condition, of course, that no little friends be brought in, or not without express permission. Gramercy Park; yes; but so much more dear and private. Of course you've heard of the Stuart Washington; the one Lafayette spoke of as the best likeness. (So dear and private.) And at Bellport, my youngest has struck up the sweetest relationship with (a hardware merchant); calls him (by an upper-class seaboard-style pet name). I asked, with malice aforethought in the ambiguity, whether it is "mixed" at Bellport. She stiffened a little but recovering: "Oh no, they're all Americans." (One up for me, fat lady.) Of course heaven knows nowadays *what* one's daughters meet at Packer. Yet of course (yes of course) they learn to form their own groups; it's really rather a good exposure, rather a good training; after all, they'll have to be doing just that all their lives. (I nod. I think of the poor rich daughters of jewelers and contractors whose parents are responsible; and what is responsible for that crime in the parents.) And of course the Institute. (I pretend never to have heard of it.) 'Why the Institute of Arts and Sciences: . . . splendid . . . wonderful . . . Academy of Music . . . Boston Symphony . . . lectures . . . the Academy is filled whenever William Lyon Phelps (discovers Browning) . . . But of late, I gather, this is cracking. The new director insists on everyone's *mixing*; it's for *all* Brooklyn; of course there must be really *lovely* people on the *Hill,* and *Park Slope,* and down in *Flatbush,* whom one might never hear of otherwise, but really . . . one meets one's hairdresser . . . in brief, it appears that those ladies whose pleasurable illusion has been that the bloody distillations of the fury, innocence and the genius of the planet are their particular property are beginning to lose interest in "culture," that masked anti-Christ which in fact is of itself more than they have ever possessed.

After dinner there is no coffee: tardily, and with slight begrudging, cordials are offered, a choice of green Chartreuse and Grand Marnier. I am shown a charming glass-painting of early New York superior to any in the City Museum, decline a cigar (courteously) and am led upstairs to the library, and the serious talk of the evening. At the stairhead she turns, her voice lowered and sparkling in a hint of roguishness, by indescribable subtleties of manner leads me, as such women lead: "Mr. _____; oh Mr. A. I do hope when you write of Brooklyn you (beckoning) *won't* say that *all* the bedrooms in Brooklyn are (beckoning) dreadful, sordid, stuffy little places (her voice still more lowered, opening a door); look here."

The room is perhaps twenty-five by fifteen; the broad panes command the harbor and the complete lower island; the bed is low to the floor and eight feet square. I wonder what possible use it can be to them, and think of the limitations which poverty sets round the clean sensual talents of Jews and Negroes.

As we leave she reiterates, with just a touch of blackmail in the voice, her eager anticipation of the article, which she will most certainty read. I hope, madam, that it was not mere courtesy; and I wish I might have served more of your friends, however unimportant they may be.

I think I remember more vividly, though, her remark: ". . . *dreadful* neighborhood; dreadful: Negroes on Myrtle Avenue: Syrians within two blocks of us, nudging our elbows: *I do wish they'd clear them away.*"

The first settlers of what was to become Brooklyn landed on the Heights in 1636. By 1642 the only Indians on Long Island were huddled on the damp prow of Montauk Point.

Thirty-four years ago, when Mr. George Hobson, a gentle resident of the Hill neighborhood, began teaching Latin in Boys High School, there was hardly a Jew to be seen in the corridors.

Today one-sixteenth of the world's Jews reside in Brooklyn and comprise half the population of that city. If "society" in the Heights (Society meaning-of-the-word), has any significance whatever, which is at least open to question, every simple realist must agree that the Jewish "society" of the Eastern Parkway and the St. George Hotel ball and banquet room is incomparably more important, more powerful and more dignified than that which crouches at the crumbling edge of the Heights.

It is a pleasure to know that neither is quite acceptable among equivalent New Yorkers; and that the latter are still less securely presentable before both God and Man.

(Or, opposite a loud concrete playground in East New York, sitting in the kind sun in his infinitesimal lawn in a kitchen rocker, his dirty brocaded bathrobe drawn tight, the wasted workman of forty whose face still wears the alien touch of death; his chin is drawn in as far as it will go and he is staring with eyes like diamonds upon the vitalities of the schoolboys, frowning with furious sorrow, his mouth caught up one cheek in a kicking smile.)

Or in Bay Ridge, a sweet quiet of distance from the city, a flagstaff in the water breeze, the many apartment buildings ornate but in the safe-playing Nordic taste; the young woman waiting in the maroon roadster; the mother and child who stand at the subway mouth; and each five minutes, in a walking noise of dry leaves, the rising from underground of the gently or complacently docile: the young woman loses patience and drives away; the mother and her husband do not kiss when they meet; two middle-aged men come up talking together, but most of those who rise thus from the dead give no appearance of knowing one another but walk alone toward their suppers; and the unimaginable solitude of most families begins to suggest itself.

Or Bensonhurst, those double and single homes and whole towns of apartments of not unprosperous Jews along the well-shaded streets, as affable among one another, almost, as in the ghettos; the well-pleased wives, the sexuality in the eyes and garments of the high-school girls, the exceedingly richly fed children, their thighs thick in their trousers, the father who sits in his small lawn, his eyes naphthaline with ruinous adoration of his boy; the plump blond boys who pitch ball quietly in the street, with excellently cushioned gloves of yellow leather; the college student, trying to cancel his dark opulent features in sharp tweeds; the five mothers and seven children in an apartment court who all eat ice-cream cones, all raspberry;

the adolescent girl on the front steps whose eyes, glanced upward, are at once hot and pure; the reappearance of the tweed student, licking an ice-cream cone, raspberry flavor.

Or Brighton Beach, the flat-faced apartments chilled in their own shade and the gay candy-colored brick homes, in every one a room for rent, and the almost shacklike bungalows, and the parents watching for their children in front of the school; the hot orange and blue trim of the houses, the diminutive synagogues.

Or Sheepshead Bay, the blunt little launches still trestled, the colors and shapes of children's paintings; the hopeless desolation of the worn-out edge of Brooklyn; the criminally made row houses in the middle of nowhere; the desperately pathetic matchwood shacks stilted above the stench of the mudflats; the manhole turrets rising to that level at which Robert Moses will establish another of his parks, with reflecting pools, and an end of the shacks.

Or Canarsie, that full end-of-the-world, that joke even to Brooklyn, its far end; the abomination of desolation, the houses thinned to nothing, the blank sand, the shattered cabaret with the sign, 'The Girl You Bring is the Girl You Take Home,' the new cabaret in the middle of waste silence, with ambitious men aligning the brilliant trims; the shades along the last street and at its head a small young brick apartment, its first floor occupied; the row of dark peaked shingles which across a little park faces the declining sun and the bare land with the look, "somehow we have not been very successful in life"; and this park itself, brand-new, a made-island of green in all this grave ocean, and in this silence, a little noise. The leaves are blown aslant and in their shade a few lie prostrate on young grass, mothers, young girls, two boys together; and meditate, or talk inaudibly; on benches, men without color sit apart from one another in silence. A girl bounces a fat ball on the cement over and over and over. The wind is freshening and the sloped light is turning gold. Birds speak with each other in the hushed leaves and in the wind there are the soft calls of children, but these noises are blown by the wind and are finally almost impossible to hear.

In Prospect Park on Sunday they are all there, on the lake, along the bending walks, sown on the seas of lawn; the old, the weary, the loving, and the young; who move in the flotations of seeds upon placid winds; a family, gathering its blankets and its baskets, quarreling a little. Four young men hatless in dark coats walk rapidly across the vast grass in an air of purpose and of enigma; a little boy running alone who suddenly leaps into the air; another little boy and an elderly man and a rolled umbrella, hand in hand; the rear end of a metal swan, a tractor saddle and bicycle pedals; a working-class father of fifty who, leant to a tree, holds four identical hats by their elastics and watches toward the water with an iron and tender look; two little girls stand on two stones by the ruffed water and hesitate toward one another like courting insects; an old woman built like a bear sits alone on a bench with her fecund knees spread and her hands folded on her belly; she is intensely watching everything in sight and in silence the tears run freely down her face; three boys and three hard-fleshed girls in working-class clothes range past with the resourceful and sensitive eyes of wild animals; four couples in file, unaware of one another, push baby carriages along a walk; three are somber, one is mutual; a young man suddenly genuflects before a smiling girl in a gold blouse, his hands at the eye at his heart like a tenor; six delicately dressed Negro boys of eight to fourteen softly follow a seventh who pushes a virgin bicycle of cream and ultramarine and gold with an unsullied squirrel's tail smoking at the heel of the rear mudguard; he does not ride but continually hovers his lovely machine with the passion of a stallion and the reverence of a bridegroom; his eyes are dazed, and he is unspeakably touched and solitary; the young man, his photograph made, gets up and dusts his knee; within this range of lawn, each at wide distance from the others, five children are running rapidly with the young child's weakness at the knee; not one, from here, is larger than a gnat; in a deep walk alone, a boy with a meek nape abruptly kisses his thick-legged girl and they laugh and kiss again; she digs her dark head deeply against his neck and with arms tightened they walk on with the unsteadiness of drunks; in a walk alone, in the beauty of the Botanic Gardens, an elderly woman stands very still facing a robin who stands still, dabs at the pavement, and points his eye at her; when he is seen the woman smiles slyly yet timorously, as a child might who feared reprimand; all over those long-drawn heavings of fair lawn, each mirroring the whole mystery of one another's past and being and future and each blind to the signals of warning, they move in hundreds and in thousands in such spaciousness they scarcely seem a crowd but a whole race dispread upon a fresh green world, and their motions upon this space are those of a culture upon a microscopic slide.

And one by one, slowly disclosed in the speed of walking of Washington Avenue and the slow withdrawal of an apartment cornice, in gradual parade upon the facade of the Institute of Arts and Science and upon the iron sky, letter by letter, figure by figure, the names and images of the noble: Confucius, Lao-tze, Moses, David, Jeremiah, Isaiah, St. Peter, St. Paul, Mohammed, and, between columns, Sophocles, Pericles, Herodotus, Thucydides, Socrates, Demosthenes.

The great grey building static, the sky is slowly crowded to the left.

Or late in the day, in the zoo, the black bears with the muzzles of vaudeville tramps, and those who affectionately watch them; the empty pit; the desperate bawlings of the single polar bear, his eyes half crazy with loneliness, his whole focus on the pit of blacks; the quieting and softening of all light and the wonder this performs upon some animals; the sexy teasings and huggings of the round, masked bright-eyed coons and the delight there must be in the wrestlings of fat furred bodies: the deep moat where Hilda the elephant was pushed by her playful husband, to die in bewilderment of sacroiliac pain, and where he too recently fell; that cage in which three black metal eagles, hunch-backed with heart-cracking melancholia, fall clumsy as grounded buzzards from limb to limb of their small skinned tree, "Presented to the Children of New York by the Brooklyn Daily *Eagle*": and through the dusk the agonies of the bear; *Baw: Baww: Bawww!;* and the bumpings and kiddings of the gay coons; and the kangaroos, some orange and some fawn, whose eyes are lovely as those of giraffes or of Victorian heroines and who move like wheelchairs: and the deer.

It is late dusk now, with the lamps on; the sky is one clean pearl. There are almost no people left. Those kingly anarchists who have become symbols of journalism sit quite without motion. The bear is still crying: he has the sound of a baby who has been forgotten in the attic of an abandoned house. In their run the young among the deer are altered. They are no longer being watched and it is not only that: they are caught also at the heart and throughout their bodies with that breath-depriving mystical ecstasy which dusk excites in them and in young goats. Their eyes are sainted, innocent, as those of goats daemonic. They move tenderly, with a look of minnows about the head and body: then a sudden break, a strong-sprung sharp-hooved bouncing run in the soft dirt, the precisions of chisels and of Mozart: and in the midst of this one of them will suddenly leap high into the air, wrists high, tail waggling, wriggling his whole body upon itself in a blind spasm of self-delight (while the kangaroos amble and squat): and now, even; it is rapidly darkening: in a child's angry joy in life and furious reluctance in the death even of one day, a fawn tears out again on the empty run and three times over climbs the air and congratulates himself: and out of the fallen brightness of the air, low a long while then steadily rising, hammered and beaten mad hell with ceremonial bells, drawn in a whole periphery of this green park and this world, such a wild inexhaustible wailing as to freeze the root of the heart.

1940

Goethe once said that experience is only half of experience, by which I think he meant that merely living a fascinating life cannot guarantee a fascinating book. Art requires rendering, shaping, the construction of an experience. If artists received credit merely for being alive, for having stuff happen to them, for experience alone, could we really call what they produce "art"? The earliest source we have for that word is the Indo-European root *ar-*, which means "to fit together," "to cobble," "to join." Art, first and foremost, is the province of technicians, which is why this year is not particularly important to Walter Abish, despite the fact that it marks the enthronement of the fourteenth Dalai Lama, the discovery of cave paintings in Lascaux, France, the opening of the first McDonald's, and the opening of Auschwitz. It's also the year when Walter Abish and his parents flee Austria and the Nazis. And yet this still doesn't matter. Neither should it matter a few years later when Abish and his parents have to flee Italy, or then move out of France when the Germans take the Ardennes, or then move out of China when the Maoists take control . . . I think what I mean is that Walter Abish has experienced a lot in his life, and yet when he finally settles in America as a writer, the experiences he chooses to mine are not necessarily his own. Cobbling together texts from the lives of other writers— other people's memoirs, other people's letters, other people's journals, other people's lives—he creates collaged essays of a collective first person. An everyone, or a no one: it doesn't really matter. "I lie," Abish once wrote, "and I am lied to, but the result of my lie is mental leaps, memory, knowledge." He never tells us in his essays from whom he has borrowed the texts he is using. Instead, Abish only indicates how many words he has borrowed, a number that in most cases corresponds exactly to the number of words in each text. So the information that he gives us is manically unhelpful. It's as if he wants to emphasize the fact that we know the words aren't his, yet simultaneously smirk as he asks us, "Why's it matter?" Why does it matter? These are essays of penetrating heartbreak; never mind that the heartbreak belongs to someone else. It's a heartbreak that's achieved through the reassuring surfaces of quotidian experiences, which are undermined by the fact that we don't know whose they are—nor when, nor how, nor why they are occurring. They are ours for the moment. That is why they matter.

WALTER ABISH

What Else

Part I

95

I was twenty. I will let no one say it is the best time of life. Everything threatens a young man with ruin: love, ideas, the loss of his family, his entrance into the world of adults. It is hard to learn one's part in the world.

What was our world like? It was the chaos the Greeks put at the beginning of the universe in the midst of creation. Except that we thought it was the beginning of the end, the real end, and not the one that is the beginning of a beginning.

100

Often memories are nothing. As though a window curtain were to remain intact during a fire, the silliest images come down from the attic of recollections, while momentous ones remain there. One of my great memories is of having filched out of my grandfather's bedroom, after he died, a package of dreadful cigarettes, Nazilles or Nazirs, I can't remember which, and some kind of cigarette holder. I pocketed them all, and can still see myself at Maisons-Lafitte, among the paths and tall grass of the Place Sully, smoking that cigarette with the sovereign awareness of disobeying. I was happy.

92

I was told I was good looking and believed it. For some time I had a white speck in my right eye which was to blind it and make me squint; but this was not yet apparent. Hundreds of photographs were taken of me and my mother touched them up with colored pencils. In one, which has survived, I am fair and pink, with curls, my cheeks are plump and I am wearing a look of kindly deference to the established order; my mouth is swollen with hypocrisy: I know my worth.

79

I keep beginning again. I keep taking a fresh notebook. And each time I hope it will lead to something, that it will be a constructive experiment, that I shall open some door. It never happens. I stop before I get to a door, any door. The same invisible obstacle that stops me. I ought at least to try and keep the same notebook, to get to the last page. That would mean that I have said almost everything.

157

Yet I exist. Not of course, as an individual, since in this respect I am merely the stake—a stake perpetually at risk—in the struggle between another society, made up of several thousand million nerve cells lodged in the ant hill of my skull, and my body, which serves as its robot. Neither psychology nor metaphysics nor art can provide me with a refuge. There are myths, now open to internal investigation by a new kind of sociology which will emerge one day and will deal more gently with them than traditional sociology does. The self is not only hateful: there is no place between *us* and *nothing*. And if, in the last resort, I opt for *us,* even though it is no more than a semblance, the reason is that, unless I destroy myself—an act which would obliterate the conditions of the option—I have only one possible choice between this semblance and nothing.

132

I had taken an apartment at the back of a house, all the windows overlooking the court. On purpose! For one thing, I can't stand light, can't stand being drenched in strong natural rays; but then, too, in order to hide from men and women. "Always polite" was my slogan, "but few appearances and never without preparation." I had no telephone either, to make appointments impossible. I went to the usual parties, clinked glasses with the men, ran through the standard gossip with the ladies, and never let the flower girl pass without buying the bunch in season for the lady on your right. I don't think anyone thought of considering me improper. Of course, there was a lot of calculation and superstructures in all this, yet that was my own business.

169

My chief activity, literature, a term disparaged today. I do not hesitate to use it, however, for it is a question of fact: one is a literary man as one is a botanist, a philosopher, an astronomer, a physicist, a doctor. There is no point in inventing other terms, other excuses to justify one's predilection for writing: anyone who likes to think with a pen is a writer. The few books I have published, however, won me no fame. I do not complain of this, anymore than I brag of it, for I feel the same distaste for the "popular author" genre as for that of the "neglected poet."

Without being a traveler in the strict sense of the word, I have seen a certain number of cities: as a young man, Switzerland, Belgium, Holland, England; later, the Rhineland, Egypt, Greece, Italy and Spain; quite recently equatorial Africa. Yet I speak no foreign language fluently and this fact, along with others, gives me a sense of inadequacy and isolation.

198

I have long, indeed for years, played with the idea of setting out the sphere of life—bios—graphically on a map. First I envisaged an ordinary map, but now I would incline to a general staff's map of a city center, if such a thing existed. Doubtless, it does not, because of the ignorance of the theatre of future wars. I have evolved a system of signs, and on the gray background of such maps they would make a colorful show if I clearly marked in the houses of my friends and girlfriends, the assembly halls of various collectives, from the "debating chambers" of the Youth Movement to the gathering places of the Communist youth, the hotel and brothel rooms that I knew for one night, the decisive beaches in the Tiergarten, the ways to the different schools and the graves I saw filled, the sites of the prestigious cafés whose long forgotten names daily crossed our lips, the tennis courts where empty apartment blocks stand today, and the halls emblazoned with gold and stucco that the terrors of dancing classes made almost the equal of gymnasiums.

69

3 January. Epigraphs for the whole of my diaries:

a) Pascal, 71 & 72, in the Chevalier's editing. Montaigne's ". . . *je suis moy-mesmes la matiere de mon livre* . . ."

b) the opening of Kenko's *Tsurezure-gusa:* What a strange demented feeling it gives me when I realize that I have spent whole days before this inkstone, with nothing better to do, jotting down at random whatever nonsensical thoughts have entered my head!

274

Sunrise is a necessary concomitant of long railway journeys, just as are hard boiled eggs, illustrated papers, packs of cards, rivers upon which boats strain but make no progress. At a certain moment when I was turning over the thoughts that had filled my mind, in the preceding minutes, so as to discover whether I had just been asleep or not (and when the very uncertainty which made me ask myself the question was to furnish me with an affirmative answer), in the pale square of the window, over a small black wood I saw some ragged clouds whose fleecy edges were a fixed dead-pink not liable to change, like the color that dyes the wing which has grown to wear it, or the sketch upon which the artist's fancy has washed it. But I felt that, unlike them, this color was due neither to inertia nor to caprice but to necessity and life. Presently there gathered behind it reserves of light. It brightened; the sky turned to crimson which I strove, gluing my eyes to the window, to see more clearly, for I felt that it was related somehow to the most intimate life of nature, but, the course of the line altering, the train turned, the morning scene gave place in the frame of the window to a nocturnal village, its roofs still blue with moonlight, its ponds encrusted with the opalescent nacre of night, beneath a firmament still powdered with all its stars, and I was lamenting the loss of my strip of pink sky when I caught sight of it afresh, but red this time in the opposite window.

97

From the past, it is my childhood which fascinates me most; these images alone, upon inspection, fail to make me regret the time which has vanished. For it is not the irreversible I discover in childhood, it is the irreducible: everything which is still in me, by fits and starts; in the child I read quite openly the dark underside of myself—boredom, vulnerability, disposition to despair (in the plural, fortunately), inward excitement, cut off (unfortunately) from all expression.

Contemporaries: I was beginning to walk, Proust was still alive, and finishing *A la Recherche du Temps Perdu.*

92

It is not for me to ponder what is happening to the "shape of a city," even if the true city distracted and abstracted from the one I live in by the force of an element which is to my mind what air is supposed to be to life. Without regret, at this moment I see it change and even disappear. It slides, it burns, it sinks into the shudder of weeds along its barricades, into the dreams of curtains in its bedroom, where a man and a woman indifferently continue making love.

36

March 11

How time flies; another ten days and I have achieved nothing. It doesn't come off. A page now and then is successful, but I can't keep it up, the next day I am powerless.

49

My principle objection wasn't the *vanity* involved in writing one's auto-biography. Such books are like others: quickly forgotten if boring. What I was frightened of was deflowering the happy moments I've experienced by describing and dissecting them. Now that's what I certainly will *not* do—I'll skip them instead.

132

It must have been fine outside. The windows with their heavy curtains greasy with dust, gave unto a cool, shaded courtyard, as echoing as a well. At the end of this courtyard a man was clearing his throat; he cleared it carefully, for a long time, spat, and then began to sing quietly. The afternoon had that particular resonance which a very blue sky seems to give to Paris when it is rather empty. I was lying there, stretched out in silence, with my body calm and relaxed and the pleasant smell of a cigarette in my mouth, and I saw that afternoon (just as I had for the first time *seen* a painting); saw it purposeless, not devoid of charm, but unrelated to anything, floating like a flower on the water.

122

As far back as I remember myself (with interest, with amusement, seldom with admiration or disgust), I have been subject to mild hallucinations.

Some are aural, others are optical and by none have I profited much. The fatidic accents that restrained Socrates or egged on Joaneta Darc have degenerated with me to the level of something one happens to hear between lifting and clapping down the receiver of a busy party-line telephone. Just before falling asleep, I often become aware of a kind of one-sided conversation going on in an adjacent section of my mind, quite independently from the actual trend of my thoughts. It is a neutral, detached, anonymous voice, which I catch saying words of no importance whatever.

73

My only desire, at one time, was to be in the police. It seemed to me a fitting occupation for my sleepless, intriguing mind. I imagined that among criminals there were people worth fighting with, clever, crafty, desperate people. Later I recognized that it was a good thing that I gave up the idea; for almost everything the police have to deal with is concerned with poverty and misery—not criminals or gangsters.

113

When I was ten I went to the opera for the first time. They were playing *Il Trovatore,* and I was struck by the fact that these people suffered so much and that they were never calm and seldom gay. But I quickly felt at home in the pathetic style. I began to like the ravings of Leonora, and when her hands fumbled wildly about her mouth, I felt I recognized in this gesture a desperate grab at her dentures; I even saw the glitter of a few outflung teeth. In the Bible people used to rent their garments; why shouldn't pulling out your teeth be a beautiful and moving expression of despair?

168

All the abandoned cities and towns and beach resorts that keep returning to my fiction were there in that huge landscape, the area just around our camp, which was about seven or eight miles from Shanghai, out in the paddy fields in a former university. There was a period when we didn't know the war had ended, when the Japanese had more or less abandoned the whole zone and the Americans had yet to come in, then all of the images I keep using—the abandoned apartment houses and so forth—must have touched something in my mind. It was a very interesting zone psychologically, and it obviously has a big influence—as did the semitropical nature of the place: lush vegetation, a totally water-logged world, huge rivers, canals, paddies, great sheets of water everywhere. It was a dramatized landscape thanks to the war and to the collapse of the irrigation system—a landscape dramatized in a way that is difficult to find in say, Western Europe.

168

Her apartment: for reasons that are no longer clear to me, a few weeks after that first evening in her apartment, we moved the convertible couch from the north wall of the living room to the west wall. After we parted, but before we were married, the furniture was moved once again, as if to erase my former presence. I can understand the movement of the furniture as well as and as passionately as I understand Schubert's sonatas. The aquarium with its dozen guppies was by now long gone. After we were married but living apart, she once again moved the couch. I often wonder if I avoided sleeping with her after we were married for the sake of the text-to-be? I believe she had not read *The Sun Also Rises* but her parting words seemed straight out of that all too familiar exchange in the novel. Am I reading into her parting gift, Malraux's *The Voices of Silence,* a meaning that wasn't there? Why write?

135

I have not kept a journal for more than a year. I have lost the habit. I did not exactly promise myself to resume it, but all the same, I should like to try; for in the state in which I am at present, I fear that any other attempted production will be destined to failure. I have just reread with disgust a few pages I had written at Neuchatel; they smack of effort, and the tone strikes me as stilted. Doubtless they were not written naturally and they betray an anxiety to escape certain reproaches, which it is absurd to take into account. My great strength, even in the past, was being very little concerned with opinion and not trying to construct myself consistently; writing as simply as possible and without trying to prove anything.

97

I went down to have a look at the lake, and to see if it was doing anything wild. It wasn't. I went out of a sense of duty towards it. I have lost all pleasure in the lake, and indeed in the woods, since the soldiers came and invaded them and robbed them of all the privacy I so loved. You didn't understand when I minded the tanks cutting up the wild flowers. It was a thing of beauty now tarnished for ever—one of the few things I had preserved against the horrible new world.

III

I have a shelf on top of one of my bookcases at home that has my books— the first hardbound copy of each of my books that I have received (I believe ten of them in all). Each of them is significant to me; they have become totemic. I wrote my name in them and put them away. I have these ten books all in one place. And every once in a while, I look at them, especially the first ten, with a real sense of pleasure. I want to touch them. Sometimes I smell them. I like the smell—they are no longer fresh, some of them being very old.

115

Cora was lost, my marriage had failed, nothing had come of an attempted reconciliation. A mountain of rustling crackling paper remained behind in the room. Nothing had been made to last by these papers. I stood in a square in the center of the city, in a sharply outlined space lit by the sun in the middle of a crater of shadows, the pages of a torn newspaper fluttering across the main street in the gusty wind.

Irresolutely I went to the travel agency, stood for a while in front of the window, then walked in and only when the assistant behind the counter turned to me, did Paris occur to me as a destination.

41
July 31
One can imagine a face for the void. Then it strikes us how much the void resembles us. Is it myself I am staring at?

The dark is checked by the dark, as a hand by a stranger's hand.

70
As night fell, we were standing in the garden; deep in thought, we were almost motionless, at the most shifting our weight from one foot to the other,

now and then. From time to time, one of us took a sip of wine from a glass that seemed forgotten the moment he picked it up. We were so drained of emotion that sometimes we were afraid of dropping our glasses.

88

Here is a whole nervous breakdown in miniature. We came on Tuesday. Sank into a chair, could scarcely rise; everything insipid; tasteless, colorless. Enormous desire for rest. Wednesday—only wish to be alone in the open air. Air delicious—avoided speech; could not be read. Thought of my own power of writing with veneration, as of something incredible, belonging to someone else never again to be annoyed by one. Mind a blank. Slept in my chair. Thursday. No pleasure in life whatsoever; but felt perhaps more attuned to existence.

49

Dec. 20. Nothing so stupid as a journal, when you go scribbling in it without any real want. There is no pleasure in keeping a diary when you cannot lock it in a drawer and when absolutely anyone can read it every morning without understanding a word of it.

74

Even when we got happily swished and threw dishes out of the kitchen window—only to find them unbroken when the snows cleared—I was shocked by the satisfied violence with which she proclaimed an end to our marriage. I was a "three-time loser," which was obviously true. I heard it with relief. There was no doubt about it. I was not good at this marriage business. I looked forward to lonely freedom.

74   *18 July*

My dear Walter

As you see, I am still writing from here, and nothing came of the Scandinavian journey! I couldn't help smiling because I seem to notice that you are turning my own weapon against me. Heaven knows what you hit, but certainly not the "enemy"! What is all this about the soul? Or a Scandinavian journey? The most that could have done for me is provide me with some distraction.

Part II

198

I was on an English boat going from Siracusa in Sicily to Tunis in North
Africa. I had taken the cheapest passage and it was a voyage of two nights
and one day. We were no sooner out of the harbor than I found that in
my class no food was served. I sent a note to the captain saying I'd like
to change to another class. He sent a note back saying that I could not
change and, further, asking whether I had been vaccinated. I wrote back
that I had not been vaccinated and that I didn't intend to be. He wrote
back that unless I was vaccinated I would not be permitted to disembark
at Tunis. We had meanwhile gotten in a terrific storm. The waves were
higher than the boat. It was impossible to walk on the deck. The correspondence between the captain and myself continued in a deadlock. In
my last note to him, I stated my firm intention to get off his boat at the
earliest opportunity and without being vaccinated. He then wrote back
that I had been vaccinated and to prove it he sent along a certificate with
his signature.

66

The writer of this book is no misanthrope; today one pays too dearly for
hatred of man. If one would hate man the way man was hated formerly,
Timonically, wholly, without exception, with a full heart, and with the
whole love of hatred, then one would have to renounce contempt. And
how much fine joy, how much graciousness ever do we owe precisely to our
contempt!

121

I play my role. Only in the plane or hotel into which promoters have
booked me am I for a while alone and under no obligation to maintain
anything. I take a bath or a shower, then stand at the window—a view of
another city. A twinge of stage fright, every time. While reading, I forget
each word the moment I have read it. Afterward a cold buffet. To the same
questions I do not always return the same answers, for I do not find any of
my answers all that convincing. I watch a lady's nice teeth from close up
as she speaks to me; I hold a glass in my hand, and I sweat. This is not my
metier, I think to myself, but here I stand.

85
Sometimes the weary traveler suffering from jetlag prefers to be shown directly to his hotel to be sewn in the sheets from which no dreams ever befalls. Weary and heartsick, emotionally battered by the voyage, the eyes overcome with fatigue, unable to read the newspaper thoughtfully provided for him he teeters on the hem of sleep, disrobing this way or that, clenching in his teeth all these distraught objects of the recent past—the way someone looked at him, seeming not seeing but just seeing.

83
Since I have been famous, neckties, caps, handkerchiefs, and whole sentences complete with instruction for use have been stolen from me. (Fame is someone it seems to be fun to piss on.) The more famous a man gets the fewer friends he has. It can't be helped: fame isolates. When fame helps you he never lets you forget it. When he hurts you, he says something about the price you have to pay. I certify that fame is boring and only rarely amusing.

195
Sousse, Sfax, the great Ranan circus at El Djem, Kairouan, Djerba—I reach them all without difficulty by train, by bus and by boat. At Djerba, Ulysses had forgotten Penelope and Ithaca: the island was worthy of its legend. It was a cool orchard with a carpet of dappled grass; the glossy crowns of palms sheltered by the delicate blossoming trees; the edges of this garden were lashed by the sea. I was the only guest at the hotel and the owner spoiled me. She told me that the summer before, one of her boarders, a little English girl, had gone every day to a deserted beach to lie in the sun; one day she came back to lunch, her face all crumpled, and did not touch her food. "What's the matter?" my hostess asked; the girl burst into tears. Three Arabs who had been watching her for several days, had raped her, one by one. "I tried to cheer her up," the woman said. "I said to her: Oh! Mademoiselle, when you are travelling . . . Come now, calm yourself; after all, when you are travelling!" But she insisted on packing her bags that same evening.

92
A disturbed night in spite of the pill. Dreamt angrily of someone of whom I have never waking thought angrily.

Conrad's *Heart of Darkness* still a fine story, but its faults show now. The language too inflated for the situation. Kurtz never really comes alive. It is as if Conrad had taken an episode in his own life and tried to lend it, for the sake of "literature," a greater significance than it will hold. And how often he compares something concrete with something abstract. Is this a trick I have caught.

45
June 22.
Now the itch to write is over, the vacuum in my brain begins again. My novel is finished, I feel a twinge of rheumatism or arthritis. Is it that you can feel only one thing at a time, or do you imagine them?

154
The day before yesterday we were in the house of a woman who had two others there for us to lay. The place was dilapidated and open to all the winds and lit by the night-light, we could see a palm tree through the un-glassed window, and two Turkish women wore silk robes embroidered with gold. This is a great place for contrasts: splendid things gleaming in the dust. I performed on a mat that a family of cats had to be shooed off—a strange coitus, looking at each other without being able to exchange a word, and the exchange of looks is all the deeper for the curiosity and surprise. My brain was too stimulated for me to enjoy it otherwise. These shaved cunts make a strange effect—the flesh is as hard as bronze, and my girl has a splendid arse.
    Goodbye—Write to me, write to my mother sometimes . . .

148
Oct. 14
I get up early and go to the dining room for coffee. Everybody bows and I bow and I can't remember any of their names or what they are doing here. I know some of them are journalists, some of them are working for the government, and most of them are foreigners, but they swim as one except for a tall, pale young Frenchman and a German couple who shake hands with affection as they part each morning in front of the hotel. I have done nothing since I am here and I recognize the signs. I have presented my credentials, as one must, gone once to the Press Office where I was pleasantly welcomed by Constancia de la Mora, had two telephone calls from her sug-

gesting I come back to the office and meet people who might like to meet me, and have not gone.

143

Jackdaws inhabit the village. Two horses are feeding on the bark of a tree. Apples lie rotting in the wet clay soil around the trees, nobody is harvesting them. On one of the trees, which seemed from afar like the only tree left with any leaves, apples hung in mysterious clusters close to one another. There isn't a single leaf on the wet tree, just wet apples refusing to fall. I picked one, it tasted pretty sour, but the juice in it quenched my thirst. I threw the apple core against the tree, and the apples fell like rain. When the apples had becalmed again, restful on the ground, I thought to myself that no one could imagine such human loneliness. It is the loneliest day, the most isolated of all. So I went and shook the tree until it was utterly bare.

111

Back from Morocco, I once sat down with eyes closed and legs crossed in a corner of my room and tried to say "Allah! Allah! Allah!" over and over again for half-an-hour at the right speed and volume. I tried to imagine myself going on saying it for a whole day and a large part of the night; taking a short sleep and then beginning again; doing the same thing for days and weeks, months and years; growing older and older and living like that, and clinging tenaciously to that life; flying into a fury if something disturbed me in that life; wanting nothing else, sticking to it utterly.

97

There is something else too. When Doughty went to Arabia in the 1800s, he claimed somewhat grandly that it was to revive the expressive possibilities of the English language. Well, in a sense, I also went to the desert to solve a problem with language, although not as Doughty meant it. Perhaps I can put it this way. It's possible to think of language as the most versatile, and maybe the original, form of deception, a sort of fortunate fall: I lie and am lied to, but the result of my lie is mental leaps, memory, knowledge.

196

We got up and wandered across the square, looking at some acrobats and musicians, but as soon as one of the performers spotted us as tourists, he would rush over to demand money before we had even seen anything. We tried to watch a snake charmer who was holding a snake by the neck a few inches from his mouth, almost licking it with his tongue, while an assistant was beating a drum. He spotted us and right away came over for money. We gave him a 50 francs piece which he looked at with disdain. He brought over a snake and asked us to touch it. It felt strangely cool and smooth in spite of the slight roughness of its tiny scales. It would bring us good luck, he said. We gave him a 100 franc piece, whereupon with an unpleasant grin he hung the snake around poor Edwin's neck, stroking its head, saying that it would make him rich and always keep him out of trouble with the police. I gave him another 100 francs so he would take the snake off Edwin's neck and before he could put it around mine, we fled.

78

Friday 12th

Eating cherries today in front of the mirror I saw my idiotic face. Those self-contained bullets disappearing down my mouth made it look looser, more lascivious and contradictory than ever. It contains many elements of brutality, calm, slackness, boldness and cowardice, but as elements only, and it is more changeable and characterless than a landscape beneath scurrying clouds. That's why so many people find it so impossible to retain (You've too many of them, says Hedda).

137

6 Oct

Since I arrived in Paris, there isn't a day that goes by that I don't window-shop in the bookstores. Sometimes I even go in to look through the shelves of books on display. And bit by bit I am feeling a profound distaste for literature. I don't really know what its origin is. Is it the enormous number of books that are appearing, the thousands of novels translated from every language, and somewhat at random (for Eca de Queiroz, Pio Baroja, Rebreanu, etc., are still unknown)? Complete anarchy, chaos. And the artificial production of the "new wave." This too: a novel no longer interests the modern critic unless it's difficult, almost unreadable; or unless it illustrates a new theory of the novel or literature.

100

The cliché that clichés are cliché only because their truth is self-evident would seem self-evident. Yet from birth we're taught that things are not simple as they seem. The wise man's work is to undo complications: things are simple, truth blazes ("brightness falls from the air"), and the obvious way to prevent wars is not to fight. Thus, when I proclaim that I am never less alone than when I am by myself, and am met with a glazed stare, the stare is from one who abhors a vacuum—the look of nature. But I am complicating matters.

106

Yesterday I tried to let myself go completely. The result was that I fell into a deep sleep and experienced nothing except a great sense of refreshment, and the curious sensation of having seen something important while I was asleep. But what it was I could not remember; it had gone forever.

But today this pencil will prevent my going to sleep. I dimly see certain strange images that seem to have no connection with my past; an engine puffing up a steep incline dragging endless coaches after it. Where can it all come from? Where is it going? How did it get there at all?

13

Jean Jacques Rousseau confesses himself. It is less a need than an idea.

46

What tense would you choose to live in?

I want to live in the imperative of the future passive participle—in the "what ought to be."

I like to breathe that way. That's what I like. It suggests a kind of mounted, bandit-like equestrian honor . . .

1941

What's essential in the modern poem, T. S. Eliot once wrote, is "the expression of *significant* emotion, emotion which has its life in the poem and not in the life of the poet." What's significant about that line is the word *significant* itself, which doesn't mean "important" or "crucial," but means instead "symbolic." Your life, when you write about it, is not your life, once you write about it. You are a metaphor, says Eliot; your *I* is a persona. This is something poetry has understood from the get-go, but in essays the idea of a "persona" is still controversial. After all, the characteristically informal, associative, and digressive essay gives us the impression that the ruminations of its *I* are direct, raw, and utterly unrehearsed—a familiarity that we can trust because it feels so uncontrived, especially in comparison to the loudly pronounced formal conceits of a poem's lyric intimacy. And yet, for centuries essayists have been acknowledging the construction of their personae. "I may presently change," Montaigne said in the sixteenth century, "not only by chance, but also by intention." In the eighteenth century, William Hazlitt admitted to "the assumption of a character . . . which gives force and life to his writing." Virginia Woolf anguished over the contradiction that's inherent in "Never to be yourself and yet always—that is the problem." And E. B. White frequently proclaimed that "writing is a form of imposture: I'm not at all sure I am anything like the person I seem to a reader." He spent forty years as a staff writer for the *New Yorker* and *Harper's,* turning out essays of such casual

473

elegance that it's hard to believe his most famous essay, "Once More to the Lake," took him twenty-five years to write, a quarter of a century of sculpting, dismantling, reshaping, and perfecting a text that in its final form might feel on its surface like a sophisticated response to an assignment from school: *What did you do on your summer vacation?*

One summer morning, along about 1904, my father rented a camp on a lake in Maine and took us all there for the month of August.

Indeed, White did write a version of this essay for a high school assignment, a version you can find in White's papers at Cornell, and a version you can still feel him struggling with today in his essay that has since become a classic. For if we read a little more closely into its benign opening sentence, we can hear White trying to cast his essay into a space of fabled logic, an atmosphere of innocence that almost has the ring of "once upon a time," a tone White underscores with intentional imprecision—"along about 1904"—thus hurling the essay immediately into the imagination, thick into nostalgia, and therefore into a space that allows for a variety of personae: three different minds inside that single letter *I*. There is the persona of his son, whom he observes and also becomes; the persona of his father, whom he remembers and also becomes; and the persona of the writer, which is the most tragic of the three, because it recognizes far too late in his essay that a psychic rift has opened up that cannot be undone.

E. B. White

Once More to the Lake

One summer, along about 1904, my father rented a camp on a lake in Maine and took us all there for the month of August. We all got ringworm from some kittens and had to rub Pond's Extract on our arms and legs night and morning, and my father rolled over in a canoe with all his clothes on; but outside of that the vacation was a success and from then on none of us ever thought there was any place in the world like that lake in Maine. We returned summer after summer—always on August 1st for one month. I have since become a salt-water man, but sometimes in summer there are days when the restlessness of the tides and the fearful cold of the sea water and the incessant wind which blows across the afternoon and into the evening make me wish for the placidity of a lake in the woods. A few weeks ago this feeling got so strong I bought myself a couple of bass hooks and a spinner and returned to the lake where we used to go, for a week's fishing and to revisit old haunts.

I took along my son, who had never had any fresh water up his nose and who had seen lily pads only from train windows. On the journey over to the lake I began to wonder what it would be like. I wondered how time would have marred this unique, this holy spot—the coves and streams, the hills that the sun set behind, the camps and the paths behind the camps. I was sure that the tarred road would have found it out, and I wondered in what other ways it would be desolated. It is strange how much you can remember about places like that once you allow your mind to return into the grooves that lead back. You remember one thing, and that suddenly reminds you of another thing. I guess I remembered clearest of all the early mornings, when the lake was cool and motionless, remembered how the bedroom smelled of the lumber it was made of and of the wet woods whose scent entered through the screen. The partitions in the camp were thin and did not extend clear to the top of the rooms, and as I was always the first up I would dress softly so as not to wake the others, and sneak out into the sweet outdoors and start out in the canoe, keeping close along the shore in the long shadows of the pines. I remembered being very careful never to rub my paddle against the gunwale for fear of disturbing the stillness of the cathedral.

The lake had never been what you would call a wild lake. There were cottages sprinkled around the shores, and it was in farming country although the shores of the lake were quite heavily wooded. Some of the cottages were owned by nearby farmers, and you would live at the shore and eat your meals at the farmhouse. That's what our family did. But although it wasn't wild, it was a fairly large and undisturbed lake and there were places in it that, to a child at least, seemed infinitely remote and primeval.

I was right about the tar: it led to within half a mile of the shore. But when I got back there, with my boy, and we settled into a camp near a farmhouse and into the kind of summertime I had known, I could tell that it was going to be pretty much the same as it had been before—I knew it, lying in bed the first morning, smelling the bedroom, and hearing the boy sneak quietly out and go off along the shore in a boat. I began to sustain the illusion that he was I, and therefore, by simple transposition, that I was my father. This sensation persisted, kept cropping up all the time we were there. It was not an entirely new feeling, but in this setting it grew much stronger. I seemed to be living a dual existence. I would be in the middle of some simple act, I would be picking up a bait box or laying down a table fork, or I would be saying something, and suddenly it would be not I but my father who was saying the words or making the gesture. It gave me a creepy sensation.

We went fishing the first morning. I felt the same damp moss covering the worms in the bait can, and saw the dragonfly alight on the tip of my rod as it hovered a few inches from the surface of the water. It was the arrival of this fly that convinced me beyond any doubt that everything was as it always had been, that the years were a mirage and there had been no years. The small waves were the same, chucking the rowboat under the chin as we fished at anchor, and the boat was the same boat, the same color green and the ribs broken in the same places, and under the floor-boards the same fresh-water leavings and débris—the dead hellgrammite, the wisps of moss, the rusty discarded fishhook, the dried blood from yesterday's catch. We stared silently at the tips of our rods, at the dragonflies that came and went.

I lowered the tip of mine into the water, tentatively, pensively dislodging the fly, which darted two feet away, poised, darted two feet back, and came to rest again a little farther up the rod. There had been no years between the ducking of this dragonfly and the other one—the one that was part of memory. I looked at the boy, who was silently watching his fly, and it was my hands that held his rod, my eyes watching. I felt dizzy and didn't know which rod I was at the end of.

We caught two bass, hauling them in briskly as though they were mackerel, pulling them over the side of the boat in a businesslike manner without any landing net, and stunning them with a blow on the back of the head. When we got back for a swim before lunch, the lake was exactly where we had left it, the same number of inches from the dock, and there was only the merest suggestion of a breeze. This seemed an utterly enchanted sea, this lake you could leave to its own devices for a few hours and come back to, and find that it had not stirred, this constant and trustworthy body of water. In the shallows, the dark, watersoaked sticks and twigs, smooth and old, were undulating in clusters on the bottom against the clean ribbed sand, and the track of the mussel was plain. A school of minnows swam by, each minnow with its small individual shadow, doubling the attendance, so clear and sharp in the sunlight. Some of the other campers were in swimming, along the shore, one of them with a cake of soap, and the water felt thin and clear and insubstantial. Over the years there had been this person with the cake of soap, this cultist, and here he was. There had been no years.

Up to the farmhouse to dinner through the teeming, dusty field, the road under our sneakers was only a two-track road. The middle track was missing, the one with the marks of the hooves and the splotches of dried, flaky manure. There had always been three tracks to choose from in choosing which track to walk in; now the choice was narrowed down to two. For a moment I missed terribly the middle alternative. But the way led past the tennis court, and something about the way it lay there in the sun reassured me; the tape had loosened along the backline, the alleys were green with plantains and other weeds, and the net (installed in June and removed in September) sagged in the dry noon, and the whole place steamed with midday heat and hunger and emptiness. There was a choice of pie for dessert, and one was blueberry and one was apple, and the waitresses were the same country girls, there having been no passage of time, only the illusion of it as in a dropped curtain—the waitresses were still fifteen; their hair had been washed, that was the only difference—they had been to the movies and seen the pretty girls with the clean hair.

Summertime, oh summertime, pattern of life indelible, the fade-proof lake, the woods unshatterable, the pasture with the sweetfern and the juniper forever and ever, summer without end; this was the background, and the life along the shore was the design, the cottages with their innocent and tranquil design, their tiny docks with the flagpole and the American flag floating against the white clouds in the blue sky, the little paths over the roots of the trees leading from camp to camp and the paths leading back to the outhouses and the can of lime for sprinkling, and at the souvenir counters at the store the miniature birch-bark canoes and the post cards that showed things looking a little better than they looked. This was the American family at play, escaping the city heat, wondering whether the newcomers in the camp at the head of the cove were "common" or "nice," wondering whether it was true that the people who drove up for Sunday dinner at the farmhouse were turned away because there wasn't enough chicken.

It seemed to me, as I kept remembering all this, that those times and those summers had been infinitely precious and worth saving. There had been jollity and peace and goodness. The arriving (at the beginning of August) had been so big a business in itself, at the railway station the farm wagon drawn up, the first smell of the pine-laden air, the first glimpse of the smiling farmer, and the great importance of the trunks and your father's enormous authority in such matters, and the feel of the wagon under you for the long ten-mile haul, and at the top of the last long hill catching the first view of the lake after eleven months of not seeing this cherished body of water. The shouts and cries of the other campers when they saw you, and the trunks to be unpacked, to give up their rich burden. (Arriving was less exciting nowadays, when you sneaked up in your car and parked it under a tree near the camp and took out the bags and in five minutes it was all over, no fuss, no loud wonderful fuss about trunks.)

Peace and goodness and jollity. The only thing that was wrong now, really, was the sound of the place, an unfamiliar nervous sound of the outboard motors. This was the note that jarred, the one thing that would sometimes break the illusion and set the years moving. In those other summertimes all motors were inboard; and when they were at a little distance, the noise they made was a sedative, an ingredient of summer sleep. They were one-cylinder and two-cylinder engines, and some were make-and-break and some were jump-spark, but they all made a sleepy sound across the lake. The one-lungers throbbed and fluttered, and the twin-cylinder ones purred and purred, and that was a quiet sound too. But now the campers all had outboards. In the daytime, in the hot mornings, these motors made a petulant, irritable sound; at night, in the still evening when the afterglow lit the water, they whined about one's ears like mosquitoes. My boy loved our rented outboard, and his great desire was to achieve singlehanded mastery over it, and authority, and he soon learned the trick of choking it a little (but not too much), and the adjustment of the needle valve. Watching him I would remember the things you could do with the old one-cylinder engine with the heavy flywheel, how you could have it eating out of your hand if you got really close to it spiritually. Motor boats in those days didn't have clutches, and you would make a landing by shutting off the motor at the proper time and coasting in with a dead rudder. But there was a way of reversing them, if you learned the trick, by cutting the switch and putting it on again exactly on the final dying revolution of the flywheel, so that it would kick back against compression and begin reversing. Approaching a dock in a strong following breeze, it was difficult to slow up sufficiently by the ordinary coasting method, and if a boy felt he had complete mastery over his motor, he was tempted to keep it running beyond its time and then reverse it a few feet from the dock. It took a cool nerve, because if you threw the switch a twentieth of a second too soon you would catch the flywheel when it still had speed enough to go up past center, and the boat would leap ahead, charging bull-fashion at the dock.

We had a good week at the camp. The bass were biting well and the sun shone endlessly, day after day. We would be tired at night and lie down in the accumulated heat of the little bedrooms after the long hot day and the breeze would stir almost imperceptibly outside and the smell of the swamp drift in through the rusty screens. Sleep would come easily and in the morning the red squirrel would be on the roof, tapping out his gay routine. I kept remembering everything, lying in bed in the mornings—the small steamboat that had a long rounded stern like the lip of a Ubangi, and how quietly she ran on the moonlight sails, when the older boys played their mandolins and the girls sang and we ate doughnuts dipped in sugar, and how sweet the music was on the water in the shining night, and what it had felt like to think about girls then. After breakfast we would go up to the store and the things were in the same place—the minnows in a bottle, the plugs and spinners disarranged and pawed over by the youngsters from the boys' camp, the fig newtons and the Beeman's gum. Outside, the road was tarred and cars stood in front of the store. Inside, all was just as it had always been, except there was more Coca-Cola and not so much Moxie and root beer and birch beer and sarsaparilla. We would walk out with a bottle of pop apiece and sometimes the pop would backfire up our noses and hurt. We explored the streams, quietly, where the turtles slid off the sunny logs and dug their way into the soft bottom; and we lay on the town wharf and fed worms to the tame bass. Everywhere we went I had trouble making out which was I, the one walking at my side, the one walking in my pants.

One afternoon while we were there at that lake a thunderstorm came up. It was like the revival of an old melodrama that I had seen long ago with childish awe. The second-act climax of the drama of the electrical disturbance over a lake in America had not changed in any important respect. This was the big scene, still the big scene. The whole thing was so familiar, the first feeling of oppression and heat and a general air around camp of not wanting to go very far away. In mid-afternoon (it was all the same) a curious darkening of the sky, and a lull in everything that had made life tick; and then the way the boats suddenly swung the other way at their moorings with the coming of a breeze out of the new quarter, and the premonitory rumble. Then the kettle drum, then the snare, then the bass drum and cymbals, then crackling light against the dark, and the gods grinning and licking their chops in the hills. Afterward the calm, the rain steadily rustling in the calm lake, the return of light and hope and spirits, and the campers running out in joy and relief to go swimming in the rain, their bright cries perpetuating the deathless joke about how they were getting simply drenched, and the children screaming with delight at the new sensation of bathing in the rain, and the joke about getting drenched linking the generations in a strong indestructible chain. And the comedian who waded in carrying an umbrella.

When the others went swimming my son said he was going in too. He pulled his dripping trunks from the line where they had hung all through the shower, and wrung them out. Languidly, and with no thought of going in, I watched him, his hard little body, skinny and bare, saw him wince slightly as he pulled up around his vitals the small, soggy, icy garment. As he buckled the swollen belt, suddenly my groin felt the chill of death.

1950

This year, Joseph McCarthy suggests in a speech in West Virginia that the U.S. State Department is awash with Communists. In South Africa, the Population Registration Act has legalized apartheid. The Soviet Union has developed an atomic bomb, the People's Republic of China has just been founded in Beijing, and Diners Club International introduces the credit card. It's around this time that the composer John Cage visits the Acoustic Laboratory at Harvard University, home of the world's first anechoic chamber, a room whose ceiling, floor, and walls are designed to absorb the sounds of the world outside it. According to the Guinness Book of World Records, it is the world's quietest space, and so what the composer expects when he walks into the chamber is to "experience silence for the first time in my life." Instead, when the lab tech seals the soundproof door, John Cage says that he quickly starts to hear his own heart beating down his feet into the floor, the high spinning hiss of his own nervous system, and the persistent *whoosh-whoosh* of something thrumming in his head, which the lab technician tells John Cage is air molecules pounding on his ear drums by the billions. Within a year, Cage writes a piece of music that he calls *4'33"*, a composition that instructs musicians to perform the piece while sitting silently for four minutes and thirty-three seconds—the thermostatic equivalent of absolute zero. At its premiere in New York, the pianist methodically follows the score's seven pages with a stopwatch. Wind can be heard crinkling leaves outside the theater. Rain starts pattering on the windows and the roof. As they get restless, audience members rustle through the pages of their programs, squeak in wooden chairs, cough into their hands, sneeze into the air. Unbeknownst to them, the politely clapping audience at the end of the recital had collectively composed Cage's *4'33"*, contributing accidental accompaniments to his experimental score, and proving not so much that silence is never possible, but that music—that art—is absolutely everywhere.

JOHN CAGE

Lecture on Nothing

I am here   ,   and there is nothing to say   .

                                                                    If among you are
those who wish to get   somewhere   ,   let them leave at
any moment   .   What we re–quire   is
silence   ;   but what silence requires
        is   that I go on talking   .

                                                                    Give any one thought
                a push   :   it falls down easily
;   but the pusher   and the pushed   pro–duce   that enter–
tainment   called   a dis–cussion   .
                Shall we have one later   ?

                                        ♍

Or   ,   we could simply de–cide   not to have a dis–
cussion   .   What ever you like .   But
now   there are silences   and the
words   make   help make   the
silences   .

                                                        I have nothing to say
        and I am saying it   and that is
                        as I need it   .

                This space of time .   is organized
.   We need not fear these   silences, —
                                        ♍
we may love them   .

                                                                    This is a composed
talk   ,   for I am making it

                                        483

just as I make   a piece of music.   It is like a glass
        of milk   .   We need the   glass
and we need the   milk   .   Or again   it is like an
empty glass   into which   at any
moment   anything   may be poured
.   As we go along   ,   (who knows?)
            an i–dea may occur in this   talk   .
                        I have no idea   whether one will
            or not.   If one does,   let it.   Re–

                                        ♍

gard it as something   seen   momentarily   ,   as
though   from a window   while traveling   .
If across Kansas   ,   then, of course,   Kansas
.   Arizona   is more interesting,
almost too interesting ,   especially   for a New–Yorker   who is
being interested   in spite of himself   in everything.   Now he knows he
needs   the Kansas in him   .   Kansas is like
nothing on earth   ,   and for a New Yorker very refreshing.
It is like an empty glass ,   nothing but wheat   ,   or
is it corn   ?   Does it matter which   ?
Kansas   has this about it: at any instant,   one may leave it,
and whenever one wishes one may return to it   .

                                        ♍

Or you may leave it   forever   and never return to it   ,
            for we pos–sess nothing   .   Our poetry now
            is the reali–zation   that we possess   nothing
.   Anything   therefore   is a delight
(since we do not   pos–sess it)   and thus   need not fear its loss
.   We need not destroy the   past: it is gone;
at any moment,   it might reappear and   seem to be   and be the present
.   Would it be a   repetition?   Only if we thought we
owned it,   but since we don't,   it is free   and so are we
.   Most anybody knows a–bout the future
            and how un–certain it is   .

                                        ♍

What I am speaking   is often called   content.
I myself   have called   it form   .   It is the conti–

nuity   of a piece of music.   Continuity   today,
when it is necessary   ,   is a demonstration   of dis–
interestedness.   That is,   it is a proof   that our delight
lies in not   pos–sessing anything   .   Each moment
presents what happens .   How different
this form sense is   from that   which is bound up with
memory: themes   and secondary themes;   their struggle;
their development;   the climax;   the recapitulation   (which is the belief
that one may   own one's own home) .   But actually,
unlike the snail   ,   we carry our homes   within us,

ℳ

which enables us   to fly   or to stay
, —   to enjoy   each.   But beware of
that which is   breathtakingly   beautiful,   for at any moment
            the telephone   may ring   or the airplane
come down in a   vacant lot   .   A piece of string
or a sunset   ,   possessing neither   ,
each acts   and the continuity   happens
.   Nothing more than   nothing   can be said.
Hearing   or making this   in music   is not different
—   only simpler —   than living this way   .
            Simpler, that is   ,   for me, — because it happens
            that I write music   .

ℳ   ℳ

That music is   simple to make   comes from   one's willingness to accept   the limitations   of structure.   Structure is
simple   be–cause   it can be thought out,   figured out,
measured   .   It is a discipline   which,
accepted,   in return   accepts whatever   ,   even those
rare moments   of ecstasy,   which,   as sugar loaves train horses,
train us   to make what we make   .   How could I
better tell   what structure   is   than simply to
tell   about this,   this talk   which is
contained   within   a space of time   approximately
forty minutes   long   ?

ℳ

That forty minutes   has been divided into five   large parts,   and
each unit   is divided   likewise.   Subdivision   in–
volving   a square root   is the only   possible subdivision which
permits   this micro–macrocosmic   rhythmic structure   ,
which I find so   acceptable   and accepting   .
As you see,   I can say anything   .
It makes very little   difference   what I say   or even how I say it.
At   this par–ticular moment,   we are passing through the fourth
part   of a unit which is the   second unit in the second large
part of this talk   .   It is a little bit   like passing through Kansas
.   This, now, is the   end   of that second unit
.   .

                                        ♍

Now begins the   third unit   of the second   .
                                                                Now the

second part of that   third unit   .
                        Now its third part   .

                                                                Now its fourth
part   (which, by the way,   is just the same
length   as the third part)   .

                        Now the fifth   and last part   .

                                        ♍

You have just   ex–perienced   the structure   of this talk   from a
microcosmic   point of view   .   From a macrocosmic
point of view   we are just passing the halfway point   in the second
large part.   The first part   was a rather rambling discussion of
nothing   ,   of form,   and continuity
when it is the way we   now   need it.   This second
part   is about structure: how simple it is
,   what it is   and why   we should be willing   to
accept   its limitations.   Most speeches   are full   of
ideas.   This one   doesn't have to have   any
.   But at any moment   an idea   may come along
.   Then   we may enjoy it   .

         ♍

Structure   without life   is dead.   But Life   without
structure   is un–seen   .   Pure life
expresses itself   within   and through structure
.   Each moment   is absolute,   alive and sig–
nificant.   Blackbirds   rise   from a field making   a
sound   de–licious   be–yond   com–pare
.   I heard them
because   I ac–ccpted   the limitations   of an arts
conference   in a Virginia   girls' finishing school,   which limitations
allowed me   quite by accident   to hear the blackbirds
as they flew up and   overhead   .   There was a social
calendar   and hours for breakfast   ,   but one day I saw a

         ♍

cardinal   ,   and the same day   heard a woodpecker.
I also met   America's youngest   college president   .
However,   she has resigned,   and people say she is   going into politics
.   Let her.   Why shouldn't she?   I also had the
pleasure   of hearing an eminent   music critic   ex–claim
that he hoped   he would live long e–nough   to see the end
of this craze for Bach.   A pupil once   said to me: I
understand   what you say about   Beethoven   and I think
I agree   but I have a   very serious   question   to
ask you: How do you   feel   about Bach
?   Now we have come   to the end   of the
part   about structure   .

         ♍ ♍

However,   it oc–curs   to me to say more   about structure
.   Specifically   this: We are
now at   the be–ginning   of the third part   and that part
is not the part   devoted   to structure.   It's the part
about material.   But I'm still talking   about structure.   It must be
clear from that   that structure   has   no point,   and,
as we have seen,   form   has no point either.   Clearly we are be–
ginning to get   nowhere   .

     Unless some   other i–dea crops up   a–bout it that is

all I have   to say about structure   .
                                        ♍
Now about   material: is it interesting   ?
It is and it   isn't   .   But one thing is
certain.   If one is making   something   which is to be nothing
,   the one making must   love   and be patient   with
the material   he chooses.   Otherwise   he calls attention to the
material,   which is precisely something   ,   whereas it was
nothing   that was being made;   or   he calls attention to
himself,   whereas   nothing is anonymous   .
               The technique   of handling materials   is, on the sense level
what structure as a   discipline is   on the rational level   :
                    a means   of experiencing   nothing
.

                                        ♍
I remember loving   sound   before I ever   took a music lesson
.   And so we make our   lives   by what we love
.   (Last year   when I talked here   I made a short talk.
That was because   I was talking   about something   ;   but
this year   I am talking   about nothing   and
of course will go on   talking   for a long time   .)
                                        The other day a
pupil said,   after trying to compose   a melody   using only
three tones,   "I   felt limited   ."

               Had she   con–cerned herself   with the three tones—
her materials   —   she would not   have felt limited
                                        ♍
,   and   since materials   are without feeling,
there would not have   been   any limitation.   It was all in her
mind   ,   whereas it be–longed   in the
materials   .   It became something
by not being   nothing;   it would have been   nothing by being
something   .

                                        Should one use the
materials   characteristic   of one's time   ?
Now there's a question   that ought to get us   somewhere

.   It is an intel–   lectual question
.   I shall answer it   slowly   .   and
autobiographically   .

℞

I remember   as a child   loving   all the sounds
,   even the unprepared   ones.   I liked them
especially   when there was one at   a time   .
                    A five–finger exercise   for one hand was
full of beauty   .   Later on I
gradually liked   all the intervals   .

                                    As I look back
I realize   that I be–gan liking the octave   ;   I accepted the
major and minor   thirds.   Perhaps,   of all the intervals,
I liked these thirds   least   .   Through the music of
Grieg,   I became passionately   fond   of the fifth

.

℞

Or perhaps you could   call it   puppy–dog love   ,
            for the fifth did not make me   want to write music: it made me want to de–
vote my life to   playing the works of Grieg   .
                When later I heard   modern music,
I took, like a duck   to water, to all the   modern intervals: the sevenths,   the
seconds,   the tritone,   and the fourth   .
                I liked Bach too   a–bout this time   ,   but I
didn't like the sound   of the thirds and sixths.   What I admired in
Bach   was the way   many things   went together
.   As I keep on   re–membering,   I see that I never
really liked the   thirds,   and this explains   why I never really
liked Brahms   .

℞

Modern music   fascinated me   with all its modern   intervals: the
sevenths,   the seconds,   the tritone,   and the fourth   and
always,   every now and then,   there was a fifth,   and that pleased me
.   Sometimes there were single tones,   not intervals at
all,   and that was a de–   light.   There were so many in–
tervals in modern music that it fascinated   me rather than that I   loved it, and being
fascinated by it I   de–cided   to write it.   Writing it at

first   is difficult: that is,   putting the mind on it
takes the ear off it   .   However,   doing it alone,
I was free to hear   that a high sound   is different   from a
low sound even when both are called by the   same letter.   After several years of
working alone   ,   I began to feel   lonely.
                                            ♍

Studying with a   teacher,   I learned that the   intervals   have
meaning;   they are not just   sounds   but they imply
in their progressions   a sound   not actually present to the ear
.   Tonality.   I never liked tonality   .
I worked at it   .   Studied it.   But I never had any
feeling for it   :   for instance: there are some   pro—
gressions called   de—ceptive cadences.   The idea is this: progress in such a way
as to imply   the presence   of a tone not actually   land somewhere else.   present;   then
fool everyone by not   landing on it—   land somewhere else.   What is being
fooled   ?   Not the ear   but the mind
.   The whole question is   very intellectual   .
However   modern music   still fascinated me
                                            ♍

with all its modern   intervals   .   But in order to
have them   ,   the mind had fixed it   so that one had to a—
void having   pro—gressions that would   make one think of   sounds that were
not actually present   to the ear   .   Avoiding
did   not   ap—peal to me   .   I began to see
that the separation of   mind and ear   had spoiled   the sounds
, —   that a clean slate   was necessary.   This made me
not only contemporary ,   but "avant—garde."   I used noises
.   They had not been   in—tellectualized;   the ear could hear them
directly   and didn't have to go through any   abstraction   a—bout them
.   I found that I   liked noises   even more than I
liked intervals.   I liked noises   just as much as I had   liked single sounds
                                            ♍

.

                                            Noises, too
,   had been dis—criminated against   ;   and being American,
having been trained   to be sentimental,   I fought   for noises. I liked being
on the side of the   underdog   .

I got police   per–mission   to play sirens.   The most amazing noise
I ever found   was that produced by   means of a coil of wire attached to the
pickup arm   of a phonograph and then amplified.   It was shocking,
really shocking,   and thunderous   .   Half intellectually   and
half sentimentally   , when the war came a–long,   I decided to use
only   quiet sounds   .   There seemed to me
to be no truth,   no good,   in anything big   in society.

          ♏

But quiet sounds   were like loneliness   ,   or
love   or friendship   .   Permanent, I thought
,   values,   independent   at least from
Life, Time and   Coca–Cola   .   I must say
I still feel this way   ,   but something else is   happening
:   I begin to hear   the old sounds
—   the ones I had thought worn out,   worn out by
intellectualization—   I begin to hear   the old sounds   as
though they are   not worn out   .   Obviously, they are
not worn out   .   They are just as   audible   as the
new sounds.   Thinking   had worn them out   .
   And if one stops thinking about   them,   suddenly they are

          ♏

fresh   and new.   "If you think   you are a ghost
you will become a   ghost   ."   Thinking the sounds
worn out   wore them out   .   So you see
:   this question   brings us back
where we were: nowhere   ,   or,
if you like   ,   where we are   .
        I have a story: "There was once a man
standing on a high elevation. A company of several men who happened to be walking on the road
noticed from the distance the man standing on the high place and talked among themselves about
this man. One of them said: He must have lost his favorite animal. Another man said
:   No, it must be his friend whom he is looking for. A third one said:
He is just enjoying the cool air up there. The three could not   a–gree   and the dis–

          ♏

cussion   (Shall we have one   later?) went on until   they reached the high
place where the man   was   .   One of the three
asked: O, friend   standing up there   ,   have you not

lost your pet animal   ?   No, sir,   I have not lost any
.   The second man asked :   Have you not lost your friend
?   No, sir   ,   I have not lost my friend
either   .   The third man asked: Are you not enjoying
the fresh breeze   up there?   No, sir   ,
I am not   .   What, then
,   are you standing up there   for   ,
           if you say no   to all our
questions   ?   The man on high said :
                                        ♍

I just stand   ."

                                                             If there are
no questions,   there are no answers   .   If there are questions
,   then, of course,   there are answers   ,   but the
final answer   makes the   questions   seem absurd
,   whereas the questions,   up until then,   seem more intelligent
than the answers   .   Somebody asked   De–
bussy   how he wrote   music.   He said:
I take all the tones there are,   leave out the ones I don't want,   and
use all the others   .   Satie said   :
When I was young,   people told me: You'll see when   you're fifty years old
.   Now I'm fifty .   I've seen nothing   .
                                        ♍ ♍

Here we are now   at the beginning
           of the fourth large part   of this talk.
More and more   I have the feeling   that we are getting
nowhere.   Slowly   ,   as the talk goes on
,   we are getting   nowhere   and that is a pleasure
.   It is not irritating   to be where one is   .   It is
only irritating   to think one would like to be somewhere else. Here we are now
,   a little bit after the   beginning   of the
fourth large part   of this talk   .
                    More and more   we have the feeling
                    that I am getting   nowhere   .
                    Slowly   ,   as the talk goes on
                                        ♍

,   slowly   ,   we have the feeling

                    we are getting   nowhere.   That is a pleasure
                which will continue   .   If we are irritated
,   it is not a pleasure   .   Nothing is not   a
pleasure   if one is irritated ,   but suddenly
,   it is a pleasure   ,   and then more and more
                    it is not irritating   (and then more and more
                and slowly   ).   Originally
                    we were nowhere   ;   and now, again
,   we arc having   the pleasure
of being   slowly   nowhere.   If anybody
is sleepy   ,   let him go to sleep   .

                                            ♍

Here we are now   at the beginning   of the
third unit   of the fourth large part   of this talk.
More and more   I have the feeling   that we are getting
nowhere.   Slowly   ,   as the talk goes on
,   we are getting   nowhere   and that is a pleasure
.   It is not irritating   to be where one is   .   It is
only irritating   to think one would like to be somewhere else. Here we are now
,   a little bit after the   beginning   of the third unit   of the
fourth large part   of this talk
                                                                    .
                    More and more   we have the feeling
                    that I am getting   nowhere
                    Slowly   ,   as the talk goes on

                                            ♍

,   slowly   ,   we have the feeling
                    we are getting   nowhere   That is a pleasure
                which will continue   .   If we are irritated
,   it is not a pleasure   .   Nothing is not   a
pleasure   if one is irritated ,   but suddenly
,   it is a pleasure   ,   and then more and more
                    it is not irritating   (and then more and more
                and slowly   ).   Originally
                    we were nowhere   ;   and now, again
                    we are having   the pleasure
of being   slowly   nowhere.   If anybody
is sleepy   ,   let him go to sleep   .

♍

Here we are now   at the beginning   of the
fifth unit   of the fourth large part   of this talk.
More and more   I have the feeling   that we are getting
nowhere.   Slowly   ,   as the talk goes on
,   we are getting   nowhere   and that is a pleasure
.   It is not irritating   to be where one is   .   It is
only irritating   to think one would like   to be somewhere else.   Here we are now
,   a little bit after the   beginning   of the fifth unit   of the
fourth large part   of this talk   .
          More and more   we have the feeling
          that I am getting   nowhere   .
          Slowly   ,   as the talk goes on

♍

,   slowly   ,   we have the feeling
          we are getting   nowhere.   That is a pleasure
          which will continue   .   If we are irritated
,   it is not a pleasure   .   Nothing is not   a
pleasure   if one is irritated   ,   but suddenly
,   it is a pleasure   ,   and then more and more
          it is not irritating   (and then more and more
          and slowly   ).   Originally
          we were nowhere   ;   and now, again
,   we are having   the pleasure
of being   slowly   nowhere.   If anybody
is sleepy   ,   let him go to sleep   .

♍

Here we are now   at the middle
          of the fourth large part   of this talk.
More and more   I have the feeling   that we are getting
nowhere.   Slowly   ,   as the talk goes on
,   we are getting   nowhere   and that is a pleasure
.   It is not irritating   to be where one is   .   It is
only irritating   to think one would like   to be somewhere else.   Here we are now
,   a little bit after the   middle   of the
fourth large part   of this talk   .
          More and more   we have the feeling

that I am getting nowhere .

Slowly , as the talk goes on

℞

, slowly , we have the feeling

we are getting nowhere. That is a pleasure

which will continue . If we are irritated

, it is not a pleasure . Nothing is not a

pleasure if one is irritated , but suddenly

, it is a pleasure , and then more and more

it is not irritating (and then more and more

and slowly). Originally

we were nowhere ; and now, again

, we are having the pleasure

of being slowly nowhere. If anybody

is sleepy , let him go to sleep .

℞

Here we are now at the beginning of the

ninth unit of the fourth large part of this talk.

More and more I have the feeling that we are getting

nowhere. Slowly , as the talk goes on

, we are getting nowhere and that is a pleasure

, It is not irritating to be where one is . It is

only irritating to think one would like to be somewhere else. Here we are now

, a little bit after the beginning of the ninth unit of the

fourth large part of this talk .

More and more we have the feeling

that I am getting nowhere .

Slowly , as the talk goes on

℞

, slowly , we have the feeling

we are getting nowhere. That is a pleasure

which will continue . If we are irritated

, it is not a pleasure . Nothing is not a

pleasure if one is irritated , but suddenly

, it is a pleasure , and then more and more

it is not irritating (and then more and more

and slowly). Originally

we were nowhere   ;   and now, again
,   we are having   the pleasure
of being   slowly   nowhere.   If anybody
is sleepy   ,   let him go to sleep   .
                                            ♍

Here we are now   at the beginning   of the
eleventh unit   of the fourth large part   of this talk.
More and more   I have the feeling   that we are getting
nowhere.   Slowly   ,   as the talk goes on
,   we are getting   nowhere   and that is a pleasure
.   It is not irritating   to be where one is   .   It is
only irritating   to think one would like   to be somewhere else.   Here we are now
,   a little bit after the   beginning   of the eleventh unit   of the
fourth large part   of this talk   .
                More and more   we have the feeling
                that I am getting   nowhere   .
                Slowly   ,   as the talk goes on
                                            ♍

,   slowly   ,   -   we have the feeling
                we are getting   nowhere.   That is a pleasure
        which will continue   .   If we are irritated
,   it is not a pleasure   .   Nothing is not   a
pleasure   if one is irritated   ,   but suddenly
,   it is a pleasure   ,   and then more and more
                it is not irritating   (and then more and more
                and slowly   ).   Originally
                we were nowhere   ;   and now, again
,   we are having   the pleasure
of being   slowly   nowhere.   If anybody
is sleepy   ,   let him go to sleep   .
                                            ♍

Here we are now   at the beginning of the thir–
teenth unit   of the fourth large part   of this talk.
More and more   .   I have the feeling   that we are getting
nowhere.   Slowly   ,   as the talk goes on
,   we are getting   nowhere   and that is a pleasure
.   It is not irritating   to be where one is   .   It is

only irritating   to think one would like   to be somewhere else.   Here we are now
,   a little bit after the   beginning of the   thir–teenth unit   of the
fourth large part   of this talk   .
                           More and more   we have the feeling
                           that I am getting   nowhere   .
                           Slowly   ,   as the talk goes on
                                        ♍

,   slowly   ,   we have the feeling
                           we are getting   nowhere.   That is a pleasure
              which will continue   .   If we are irritated
,   it is not a pleasure   .   Nothing is not   a
pleasure   if one is irritated   ,   but suddenly
,   it is a pleasure   ,   and then more and more
                           it is not irritating   (and then more and more
                        and slowly   ).   Originally
                           we were nowhere   ;   and now, again
,   we are having   the pleasure
of being   slowly   nowhere.   If anybody
is sleepy   ,   let him go to sleep   .
                                        ♍ ♍

                                        ♍

♍

That is finished   now.   It was a pleasure   .
                          And now   ,   this is a pleasure.
"Read me that part   a–gain   where I disin–herit everybody   ."
                          The twelve–tone   row   is a method;   a
method is a control   of each   single
note.   There is too much   there there   .
There is not enough   of nothing in it   .   A structure is
like   a bridge from nowhere   to   nowhere   and
anyone may   go on it   :   noises or tones
,   corn or wheat   .   Does it matter which
?   I thought there were eighty–eight tones   .
              You can quarter them too   .

♍

If it were feet   ,   would it be a two–tone row
?   Or can we fly from here   to where
?   I have nothing   against the   twelve–tone row;
but it is a   method,   not a structure   .
    We really do need a structure   ,   so we can see
we are nowhere   .   Much of the music I   love
uses the twelve–tone   row   ,   but that is not why I
love it.   I love it   for no reason   .
                          I love it   for suddenly   I am nowhere
.   (My own music does that   quickly for me   .)
                          And it seems to me   I could   listen forever
to Japanese   shakuhachi music   or the Navajo

♍

Yeibitchai   .   Or I could sit or
stand   near Richard Lippold's   *Full Moon*
                          any length of time   .
                          Chinese bronzes   , —   how I love them

.

                                                                             But those beauties
,   which others   have made,   tend to stir up
              the need to possess   and I know
I possess   nothing   .
                          Record collections   , —
                          that is not music   .

℀

The phonograph   is a thing, —   not a musical   instrument

.   A thing leads to other things,   whereas a   musical instrument

leads to nothing   .

          Would you like to join a society called   Capitalists Inc.

?   (Just so no one would think we were   Communists.)

Anyone joining   automatically   becomes president   .

To join   you must show   you've destroyed   at least one hundred

records   or, in the case of   tape,   one sound mirror

.   To imagine you   own

any piece of music   is to miss   the whole point

.   There is no point   or the point   is nothing;

and even   a long–playing   record   is a thing.

℀

A lady   from Texas   said: I live in Texas   .

          We have no music   in Texas.   The reason they've no

music in Texas   is because   they have recordings

in Texas.   Remove the records from Texas

          and someone   will learn to sing   .

          Everybody   has a song

          which is   no   song at all :

          it is a process   of singing   ,

          and when you sing   ,

          you are   where you are   .

          All I know about method is that when I am not working I sometimes
think I know something, but when I am working, it is quite clear that I know nothing.

℀ ℀

1955

Rhetoricians would probably call at least some of these introductions "hypotactic" in structure (from the Greek words *hypo*—"under"—and *tassein*—"to arrange"). It's a style that suggests that each clause in a sentence, or every point in a paragraph, is the logical corollary to what comes before it. The style connotes control, in other words, confidently explaining to readers that the meanings they're being led toward are genuinely there to find: this statement is followed by this statement, which then brings me to this statement, which therefore leads me to the inevitable conclusion that 1950s America was itself hypotactic. For example, for the past decade the U.S. government has been explaining to Americans not only that the atom bomb brought a peaceful conclusion to World War II, but that it will also improve our lives for decades to come. The U.S. State Department has banned newspapers and magazines from publishing photographs of the people who were disfigured by atom bombs in Japan, while simultaneously promoting initiatives like Project Plowshare, an experiment to clear with nuclear bombs whole parcels of land for farming; or Atomium, a playground sculpture in the shape of a giant atom that teaches children at this year's world's fair that nuclear energy is fun; and Nucleon, a new car funded by the Department of Energy that Ford plans to equip with its own nuclear reactor. But the most powerful display of rhetoric deployed in the service of controlling the uncontrollable will come this year on *This Is Your Life,* a television show that will invite two women from Hiroshima to meet the American copilot who dropped the bomb on their city. They are still young, in their twenties, but because the bomb has melted their hands into claws and their necks into their shoulders and rearranged their faces just a little too much, they are shown in silhouette behind a screen on the stage. The pilot, Robert Lewis, walks out, makes a statement, shakes the hand of the man who has escorted the girls from Japan, and then gives the man a donation of fifty dollars for the girls. He is nervous, a little drunk, maybe scripted, and very cold. But whatever his demeanor, the chutzpah of his presence on the television that night makes a bold and brutal statement about America's new dominance over everyone, everywhere. "Easily the most dramatic and affecting entertainment of the week," *Time* magazine declares. What we do not see that night on *This Is Your Life*, however, is the journal Lewis kept while copiloting the *Enola Gay*, the journal he auctioned off for forty thousand dollars, and in which he recorded observations from his flight on the morning of August 6, 1945. They are observations that appear to be unrelated on the page—his notes about the clouds, temperature, time, speed, his view of a city from thirty thousand feet, and then his view of smoke rings expanding out of rubble—notes that rhetoricians would call "paratactic," which comes from the Greek word *para,* or "beside," because it denotes a style of writing that levels everything in it equally, refuses to assign significance, and refuses responsibility.

LEONARD MICHAELS

In the Fifties

In the fifties I learned to drive a car. I was frequently in love. I had more friends than now.

When Khrushchev denounced Stalin my roommate shit blood, turned yellow, and lost most of his hair.

I attended the lectures of the excellent E. B. Burgum until Senator McCarthy ended his tenure. I imagined N.Y.U. would burn. Miserable students, drifting in the halls, looked at one another.

In less than a month, working day and night, I wrote a bad novel.

I went to school—N.Y.U., Michigan, Berkeley—much of the time.

I had witty, giddy conversations, four or five nights a week, in a homosexual bar in Ann Arbor.

I read literary reviews the way people suck candy.

Personal relationships were more important to me than anything else.

I had a fight with a powerful fat man who fell on my face and was immovable.

I had personal relationships with football players, jazz musicians, assbandits, nymphomaniacs, non-specialized degenerates, and numerous Jewish premedical students.

I had personal relationships with thirty-five rhesus monkeys in an experiment on monkey addiction to morphine. They knew me as one who shot reeking crap out of cages with a hose.

With four other students I lived in the home of a chiropractor named Leo.

I met a man in Detroit who owned a submachine gun; he claimed to have hit Dutch Schultz. I saw a gangster movie that disproved his claim.

I knew two girls who had brains, talent, health, good looks, plenty to eat, and hanged themselves.

I heard of parties in Ann Arbor where everyone made it with everyone else, including the cat.

I knew card sharks and con men. I liked marginal types because they seemed original and aristocratic, living for an ideal or obliged to live it. Ordinary types seem fundamentally unserious. These distinctions belong to a romantic fop. I didn't think that way too much.

I worked for an evil vanity publisher in Manhattan.

I worked in a fish-packing plant in Massachusetts, on the line with a sincere Jewish poet from Harvard and three lesbians; one was beautiful, one grim; both loved the other, who was intelligent. I loved her too. I dreamed of violating her purity. They talked among themselves, in creepy whispers, always about Jung. In a dark corner, away from our line, old Portuguese men slit fish into open flaps, flicking out the bones. I could see only their eyes and knives. I'd arrive early every morning to dash in and out until the stench became bearable. After work I'd go to bed and pluck fish scales out of my skin.

I was a teaching assistant in two English departments. I graded thousands of freshman themes. One began like this: "Karl Marx, for that was his name . . ." Another began like this: "In Jonathan Swift's famous letter to the Pope . . ." I wrote edifying comments in the margins. Later I began to scribble "Awkward" beside everything, even spelling errors.

I got A's and F's as a graduate student. A professor of English said my attitude wasn't professional. He said that he always read a "good book" after dinner.

A girl from Indiana said this of me on a teacher-evaluation form: "It is bad enough to go to English class at eight in the morning, but to be instructed by a shabby man is horrible."

I made enemies on the East Coast, the West Coast, and in the Middle West. All now dead, sick, or out of luck.

I was arrested, photographed, and fingerprinted. In a soundproof room two detectives lectured me on the American way of life, and I was charged with the crime of nothing. A New York cop told me that detectives were called "defectives."

I had an automobile accident. I did the mambo. I had urethritis and mononucleosis.

In Ann Arbor, a few years before the advent of Malcolm X, a lot of my friends were black. After Malcolm X, almost all my friends were white. They admired John F. Kennedy.

In the fifties, I smoked marijuana, hash, and opium. Once I drank absinthe. Once I swallowed twenty glycerine caps of peyote. The social effects of "drugs," unless sexual, always seemed tedious. But I liked people who inclined the drug way. Especially if they didn't proselytize. I listened to long conversations about the phenomenological weirdness of familiar reality and the great spiritual questions this entailed—for example, "Do you think Wallace Stevens is a head?"

I witnessed an abortion.

I was godless, but I thought the fashion of intellectual religiosity more despicable. I wished that I could live in a culture rather than study life among the cultured.

I drove a Chevy Bel Air eighty-five miles per hour on a two-lane blacktop. It was nighttime. Intermittent thick white fog made the headlights feeble and diffuse. Four others in the car sat with the strict silent rectitude of catatonics. If one of them didn't admit to being frightened, we were dead. A Cadillac, doing a hundred miles per hour, passed us and was obliterated in the fog. I slowed down.

I drank Old Fashioneds in the apartment of my friend Julian. We talked about Worringer and Spengler. We gossiped about friends. Then we left to meet our dates. There was more drinking. We all climbed trees, crawled in the street, and went to a church. Julian walked into an elm, smashed his glasses, vomited on a lawn, and returned home to memorize Anglo-Saxon grammatical forms. I ended on my knees, vomiting into a toilet bowl, repeatedly flushing the water to hide my noises. Later I phoned New York so that I could listen to the voices of my parents, their Yiddish, their English, their logics.

I knew a professor of English who wrote impassioned sonnets in honor of Henry Ford.

I played freshman varsity basketball at N.Y.U. and received a dollar an hour for practice sessions and double that for games. It was called "meal money." I played badly, too psychological, too worried about not studying, too short. If pushed or elbowed during a practice game, I was ready to kill. The coach liked my attitude. In his day, he said, practice ended when there was blood on the boards. I ran back and forth, in urgent sneakers, through my freshman year. Near the end I came down with pleurisy, quit basketball, started smoking more.

I took classes in comparative anatomy and chemistry. I took classes in Old English, Middle English, and modern literature. I took classes and classes.

I fired a twelve-gauge shotgun down the hallway of a railroad flat into a couch pillow.

My roommate bought the shotgun because of his gambling debts. He expected murderous thugs to come for him. I'd wake in the middle of the night listening for a knock, a cough, a footstep, wondering how to identify myself as not him when they broke through our door.

My roommate was an expensively dressed kid from a Chicago suburb. Though very intelligent, he suffered in school. He suffered with girls though he was handsome and witty. He suffered with boys though he was heterosexual. He slept on three mattresses and used a sun lamp all winter. He bathed, oiled, and perfumed his body daily. He wanted soft, sweet joys in every part, but when some whore asked if he'd like to be beaten with a garrison belt, he said yes. He suffered with food, eating from morning to night, loading his pockets with fried pumpkin seeds when he left for class, smearing caviar paste on his filet mignons, eating himself into a monumental face of eating because he was eating. Then he killed himself.

A lot of young, gifted people I knew in the fifties killed themselves. Only a few of them continue walking around.

I wrote literary essays in the turgid, tumescent manner of darkest Blackmur.

I used to think that someday I would write a fictional version of my stupid life in the fifties.

I was a waiter in a Catskill hotel. The captain of the waiters ordered us to dance with the female guests who appeared in the casino without escorts and, as much as possible, fuck them. A professional *tummler* walked the ground. Whenever he saw a group of people merely chatting, he thrust in quickly and created a tumult.

I heard the Budapest String quartet, Dylan Thomas, Lester Young and Billie Holiday together, and I saw Pearl Primus dance, in a Village nightclub, in a space two yards square, accompanied by an African drummer about seventy years old. His hands moved in spasms of mathematical complexity at invisible speed. People left their tables to press close to Primus and see the expression in her face, the sweat, the muscles, the way her naked feet seized and released the floor.

Eventually I had friends in New York, Ann Arbor, Chicago, Berkeley, and Los Angeles.

I did the cha-cha, wearing a tux, at a New Year's party in Hollywood, and sat at a table with Steve McQueen. He'd become famous in a TV series about a cowboy with a rifle. He said he didn't know which he liked best, acting or driving a racing car. I thought he was a silly person and then realized he thought I was. I met a few other famous people who said something. One night, in a yellow Porsche, I circled Manhattan with Jack Kerouac. He recited passages, perfectly remembered from his book reviews, to the sky. His manner was ironical, sweet, and depressing.

I had a friend named Chicky who drove his chopped, blocked, stripped, dual-exhaust Ford convertible, while vomiting out the fly window, into a telephone pole. He survived, lit a match to see if the engine was all right, and it blew up in his face. I saw him in the hospital. Through his bandages he said that ever since high school he'd been trying to kill himself. Because his girlfriend wasn't good-looking enough. He was crying and laughing while he pleaded with me to believe that he had really been trying to kill himself because his girlfriend wasn't good-looking enough. I told him that I was going out with a certain girl and he told me that he had fucked her once but it didn't matter because I could take her away and live somewhere else. He was a Sicilian kid with a face like Caravaggio's angels of debauch. He'd been educated by priests and nuns. When his hair grew back and his face healed, his mind healed. He broke up with his girlfriend. He wasn't nearly as narcissistic as other men I knew in the fifties.

I knew one who, before picking up his dates, ironed his dollar bills and powdered his testicles. And another who referred to women as "cockless wonders" and used only their family names—for example, "I'm going to meet Goldberg, the cockless wonder." Many women thought he was extremely attractive and became his sexual slaves. Men didn't like him.

I had a friend who was dragged down a courthouse stairway, in San Francisco, by her hair. She'd wanted to attend the House Un-American hearings. The next morning I crossed the Bay Bridge to join my first protest demonstration. I felt frightened and embarrassed. I was bitter about what had happened to her and the others she'd been with. I expected to see thirty or forty people like me, carrying hysterical placards around the courthouse until the cops bludgeoned us into the pavement. About two thousand people were there. I marched beside a little kid who had a bag of marbles to throw under the hoofs of the horse cops. His mother kept saying, "Not yet, not yet." We marched all day. That was the end of the fifties.

1959

This year, on the night of November 15, two men break in to a Kansas farmhouse, then gag, stab, bludgeon, and shoot the four family members who are sleeping upstairs. The next morning, over breakfast, Truman Capote notices an article of just 335 words about the murder, and decides in that moment to spend the next six years collecting eight thousand pages of notes that he'll eventually shape into what he describes as an "immaculately factual" "nonfiction novel." Today we know that neither of those descriptions about *In Cold Blood* is right, but how much does that really matter? This is the middle of the twentieth century, and reinvention is all the rage. It's when pantyhose make their American debut, Miles Davis records his legendary album *Kind of Blue,* Castro becomes prime minister of Cuba, and Tom Wolfe begins to promote the idea that all of a sudden there is a "new journalism" in the world, a form of literature that "consumes devices that happen to have originated with the novel and mixes them with every other device known to prose. And all the while, quite beyond matters of technique, it enjoys an advantage so obvious, so built-in, one almost forgets what power it has: the simple fact that the reader knows *all this really happened.*" The "New Journalists" of this era want so badly to be journalists. Why aren't they satisfied with being known as essayists?

LILLIAN ROSS

The Yellow Bus

A few Sundays ago, in the late, still afternoon, a bright-yellow school bus, bearing the white-on-blue license plate of the State of Indiana and with the words "BEAN BLOSSOM TWP MONROE COUNTY" painted in black letters under the windows on each side, emerged into New York City from the Holland Tunnel. Inside the bus were eighteen members of the senior class of the Bean Blossom Township High School, who were coming to the city for their first visit. The windows of the bus, as it rolled out into Canal Street, were open, and a few of the passengers leaned out, deadpan and silent, for a look at Manhattan. The rest sat, deadpan and silent, looking at each other. In all, there were twenty-two people in the bus: eleven girls and seven boys of the senior class; their English teacher and her husband; and the driver (one of the regular bus drivers employed by the township for the school) and his wife. When they arrived, hundreds of thousands of the city's eight million inhabitants were out of town. Those who were here were apparently minding their own business; certainly they were not handing out any big hellos to the visitors. The little Bean Blossom group, soon to be lost in the shuffle of New York's resident and transient summer population, had no idea of how to elicit any hellos—or, for that matter, any goodbyes or how-are-yous. Their plan for visiting New York City was divided into three parts: one, arriving; two, staying two days and three nights; three, departing.

Well, they had arrived. To get here, they had driven eight hundred and forty miles in thirty-nine and a half hours, bringing with them, in addition to spending money of about fifty dollars apiece, a fund of $957.41, which the class had saved up collectively over the past six years. The money represented the profits from such enterprises as candy and ice-cream concessions at school basketball games, amusement booths at the class (junior) carnival, and ticket sales for the class (senior) play, "Mumbo-Jumbo." For six years, the members of the class had talked about how they would spend the money to celebrate their graduation. Early this year, they voted on it. Some of the boys voted for a trip to New Orleans, but they were outvoted by the girls, all of whom wanted the class to visit New York. The class figured that the cost of motels and hotels—three rooms for the boys, three rooms for the girls, one room for each of the couples—would come to about four hundred dollars. The bus driver was to be paid three hundred and fifty dollars for driving and given thirty for road, bridge, and tunnel tolls. Six members of the class, who were unable to participate in the trip, stayed home. If there should be any money left over, it would be divided up among all the class members when the travellers returned to Bean Blossom Township. The names of the eighteen touring class members were: R. Jay Bowman, Shelda Bowman (cousin of R. Jay), Robert Britton, Mary Jane Carter, Lynn Dillon, Ina Hough, Thelma Keller, Wilma Keller (sister of Thelma), Becky Kiser, Jeanne Molnar, Nancy Prather, Mike Richardson, Dennis Smith, Donna Thacker, Albert Warthan, Connie Williams, Larry Williams (not related to Connie), and Lela Young.

It was also a first visit to New York for the English teacher, a lively young lady of twenty-eight named Polly Watts, and for her husband, Thomas, thirty-two, a graduate student in political science at Indiana University, in Bloomington, which is about twelve miles from the Bean Blossom Township school. The only people on the bus who had been to New York before were the driver, a husky, uncommunicative man of forty-nine named Ralph Walls, and his wife, Margaret, thirty-nine and the mother of his seven children, aged twenty-one to two, all of whom were left at home. Walls was the only adviser the others had on what to do in New York. His advice consisted of where to stay (the Hotel Woodstock, on West Forty-third Street, near Times Square) and where to eat (Hector's Cafeteria, around the corner from the hotel).

The Bean Blossom Township school is in the village of Stinesville, which has three hundred and fifty-five inhabitants and a town pump. A couple of the seniors who made the trip live in Stinesville; the others live within a radius of fifteen miles or so, on farms or in isolated houses with vegetable gardens and perhaps a cow or two. At the start of the trip, the travellers gathered in front of their school shortly after midnight, and by one in the morning, with every passenger occupying a double seat in the bus (fifty-four-passenger, 1959 model), and with luggage under the seats, and suits and dresses hung on a homemade clothes rack in the back of the bus, they were on their way.

The senior-class president, R. (for Reginald) Jay Bowman, was in charge of all the voting on the trip. A wiry, energetic eighteen-year-old with a crew haircut, he had been president of the class for the past five years, and is one of two members of the class who intend to go to college. He wants to work, eventually, for the United States Civil Service, because a job with the government is a steady job. Or, in a very vague way, he thinks he may go into politics. With the help of a hundred-and-two-dollar-a-year scholarship, he plans to pay all his own expenses at Indiana University. The other student who is going to college has also chosen Indiana University. She is Nancy Prather, an outdoorsy, freckle-faced girl whose father raises dairy and beef cattle on a two-hundred-and-fifty-acre farm and who is the class salutatorian. As for the valedictorian, a heavyset, firm-mouthed girl named Connie Williams, she was planning to get married a week after returning home from New York. The other class members expected, for the most part, to get to work at secretarial or clerical jobs, or in automobile or electronic-parts factories in Bloomington. The New York trip was in the nature of a first and last fling.

Ralph Walls dropped the passengers and their luggage at the Woodstock and then took the bus to a parking lot on Tenth Avenue, where he was going to leave it for the duration of the visit. His job, he had told his passengers, was *to* drive to New York, not *in* it. He had also told them that when he got back to the Woodstock he was going to sleep, but had explained how to get around the corner to Hector's Cafeteria. The boys and girls signed the register and went to their rooms to get cleaned up. They all felt let down. They had asked Walls whether the tall buildings they saw as they came uptown from the Holland Tunnel made up the skyline, and Walls had said he didn't know. Then they had asked him which was the Empire State Building, and he had said they would have to take a tour to find out. Thus put off, they more or less resigned themselves to saving any further questions for a tour. Jay Bowman said that he would see about tours before the following morning.

Mrs. Watts and her husband washed up quickly and then, notwithstanding the bus driver's advice, walked around the Times Square area to see if they could find a reasonably priced and attractive place to have supper. They checked Toffenetti's, almost across the street from the hotel, but decided it was too expensive (hamburger dinners at two dollars and ten cents, watermelon at forty cents) and too formidable. When they reconvened with the senior class in the lobby of the Woodstock, they recommended that everybody have this first meal at Hector's. The party set out—for some reason, in Indian file—for Hector's, and the first one inside was Mike Richardson, a husky, red-haired boy with large, swollen-looking hands and sunburned forearms. A stern-voiced manager near the door, shouting "Take your check! Take your check!" at all incomers, gave the Indiana group the same sightless once-over he gave everybody else. The Bean Blossom faces, which had been puzzled, fearful, and disheartened since Canal Street, now took on a look of resentment. Mike Richardson led the line to the counter. Under a sign reading "BAKED WHITEFISH," a white-aproned counterman looked at Mike and said, "Come on, fella!" Mike glumly took a plate of fish and then filled the rest of his tray with baked beans, a roll, iced tea, and strawberry shortcake (check—$1.58). The others quickly and shakily filled their trays with fish, baked beans, a roll, iced tea, and strawberry shortcake. Sweating, bumping their trays and their elbows against other trays and other elbows, they found seats in twos and threes with strangers, at tables that still had other people's dirty dishes on them. Then, in a nervous clatter of desperate and noisy eating, they stuffed their food down.

"My ma cooks better than this," said Albert Warthan, who was sitting with Mike Richardson and Larry Williams. Albert, the eldest of seven children of a limestone-quarry worker, plans to join the Army and become a radar technician.

"I took this filet de sole? When I wanted somethin' else, I don't know what?" Mike said.

"I like the kind of place you just set there and decide what you want," said Larry, who is going to work on his grandfather's farm.

"My ma and pa told me to come home when it was time to come home, and not to mess around," Albert said. "I'm ready to chuck it and go home right now."

"The whole idea of it is just to see it and get it over with," Mike said.

"You got your money divided up in two places?" Albert asked. "So's you'll have some in one place if it gets stolen in t'other?"

The others nodded.

"Man, you can keep this New York," said Larry. "This place is too hustly, with everybody pushin' and no privacy. Man, I'll take the Big Boy any old day."

Frisch's Big Boy is the name of an Indiana drive-in chain, where a hamburger costs thirty cents. The general effect of Hector's Cafeteria was to give the Bean Blossom Class of 1960 a feeling of unhappiness about eating in New York and to strengthen its faith in the superiority of the Big Boys back home.

Jay Bowman went from table to table, polling his classmates on what they wanted to do that evening. At first, nobody wanted to do anything special. Then they decided that the only special thing they wanted to do was to go to Coney Island, but they wanted to save Coney Island for the wind-up night, their last night in New York. However, nobody could think of anything to do that first night, so Jay took a re-vote, and it turned out that almost all of them wanted to go to Coney Island right away. Everybody but three girls voted to go to Coney Island straight from Hector's. Mrs. Watts was mildly apprehensive about this project, but Mike Richardson assured her it was easy; somebody at the hotel had told him that all they had to do was go to the subway and ask the cashier in the booth which train to take, and that would be that. Mrs. Watts said she was going to walk around a bit with her husband. The three girls who didn't want to go to Coney Island explained that they firmly believed the class should "have fun" on its last night in the city, and not before. The three were Ina Hough, whose father works in an R.C.A.-television manufacturing plant in Indianapolis (about fifty miles from Stinesville); Lela Young, whose foster father works in a Chevrolet-parts warehouse in Indianapolis; and Jeanne Molnar, whose father is a draftsman at the Indiana Limestone Company, in Bloomington. All three already knew that they disliked New York. People in New York, they said, were all for themselves.

At nine o'clock, while most of their classmates were on the Brighton B.M.T. express bound for Coney Island, the three girls walked to Sixth Avenue and Fiftieth Street with Mr. and Mrs. Watts, who left them at that point to take a walk along Fifth Avenue. The girls stood in a long line of people waiting to get into the Radio City Music Hall. After twenty minutes, they got out of the line and walked over to Rockefeller Plaza, where they admired the fountain, and to St. Patrick's Cathedral, which looked bigger to them than any church they had ever seen. The main church attended by the Bean Blossom group is the Nazarene Church. No one in the senior class had ever talked to a Jew or to more than one Catholic, or— with the exception of Mary Jane Carter, daughter of the Nazarene minister in Stinesville—had ever heard of an Episcopalian. At ten o'clock, the three girls returned to the Music Hall line, which had dwindled, but when they got to the box office they were told that they had missed the stage show, so they decided to skip the Music Hall and take a subway ride. They took an Independent subway train to the West Fourth Street station, which a subway guard had told them was where to go for Greenwich Village. They decided against getting out and looking, and in favor of going uptown on the same fare and returning to their hotel. Back at the Woodstock, where they shared a room, they locked themselves in and started putting up their hair, telling each other that everybody in New York was rude and all for himself.

At Coney Island, the Indiana travellers talked about how they could not get over the experience of riding for forty-five minutes, in a shaking, noisy train, to get there.

"The long ride was a shock to what I expected," said Albert Warthan.

Nancy Prather said she didn't like the looks of the subway or the people on it. "You see so many different people," she said. "Dark-complected ones one minute, light-complected ones the next."

"I hate New York, actually," Connie Williams said. "I'm satisfied with what we got back home."

"Back home, you can do anything you please in your own back yard any time you feel like it, like hootin' and hollerin' or anything," said Larry Williams. "You don't ever get to feel all cooped up."

"I sort of like it here in Coney Island," said Dennis Smith. "I don't feel cooped up."

Dennis's buddies looked at him without saying anything. His "sort of liking" Coney Island was the first sign of defection from Indiana, and the others did not seem to know what to make of it. Dennis is a broad-shouldered boy with large, beautiful, wistful blue eyes and a gold front tooth.

"I hate it," Connie said.

Jay Bowman organized as many of the group as he could to take a couple of rides on the Cyclone. Most of the boys followed these up with a ride on the parachute jump, and then complained that it wasn't what they had expected at all. Some of the boys and girls went into the Spookorama. They all rode the bobsled, and to top the evening off they rode the bumper cars. "The Spookorama was too imitation to be frightening," Albert said. Before leaving Coney Island, Jay got to work among his classmates, polling them on how much money they were prepared to spend on a tour of the city the next day. They stayed in Coney Island about an hour. Nobody went up to the boardwalk to take a look at the ocean, which none of the class had ever seen. They didn't feel they had to look at the ocean. "We knew the ocean was there, and anyway we aim to see the ocean on the tour tomorrow," Jay said later.

When Ina, Lela, and Jeanne got in line for the Music Hall, the Wattses took their stroll along Fifth Avenue and then joined a couple of friends, Mike and Ardis Cavin. Mike Cavin plays clarinet with the United States Navy Band, in Washington, D.C., and is studying clarinet—as a commuter—at the Juilliard School of Music. At Madison Avenue and Forty-second Street, the two couples boarded a bus heading downtown, and while talking about where to get off they were taken in hand by an elderly gentleman sitting near them, who got off the bus when they did and walked two blocks with them, escorting them to their destination—the Jazz Gallery, on St. Mark's Place. Mike Cavin wanted to hear the tenor-saxophone player John Coltrane. The Wattses stayed at the Jazz Gallery with the Cavins for three hours, listening, with patient interest, to modern jazz. They decided that they liked modern jazz, and especially Coltrane. Leaving the Jazz Gallery after one o'clock, the two couples took buses to Times Square, walked around for twenty minutes looking for a place where they could get a snack, and finally, because every other place seemed to be closed, went to Toffenetti's. Back at the hotel, the Wattses ran into one of the Coney Island adventurers, who told them that Ina, Lela, and Jeanne were missing, or at least were not answering their telephone or knocks on their door. Mr. Watts got the room clerk, unlocked the girls' door, and found them sitting on their beds, still putting up their hair. Everybody was, more or less unaccountably, angry—the three girls who hadn't gone to Coney Island, the girls who had, the boys who had, the Wattses, and the room clerk. The Wattses got to bed at 3:30 A.M.

At 6:30 A.M., Mrs. Watts was called on the telephone. Message: One of the anti-Coney Island trio was lying on the floor of the room weeping and

hysterical. Mrs. Watts called the room clerk, who called a doctor practicing in the Times Square area, who rushed over to the hotel, talked with
the weeping girl for twenty minutes, and left her with a tranquillizing pill,
which she refused to take.

By the time everybody had settled down enough to eat breakfast in drugstores and get ready to start out, it was after nine in the morning, half an
hour behind time for the scheduled (by unanimous vote) all-day tour of
the city by chartered sightseeing bus, at six dollars per person. The tour was
held up further while Mrs. Watts persuaded the weeper to take a shower, in
an effort to encourage her to join the tour. After the shower, the unhappy
girl stopped crying and declared that she would go along. By the time the
group reached the Bowery, she felt fine, and in Chinatown, like the other
boys and girls, she bought a pair of chopsticks, for thirty-five cents. The
Cathedral of St. John the Divine was the highlight of the tour for many of
the students, who were delighted to hear that some of the limestone used
in the cathedral interior had very likely come from quarries near Stinesville.
Mrs. Watts, on the other hand, who had studied art, had taught art for five
years at Huntington College, in Huntington, Indiana, and had taken an
accredited art tour of Europe before her marriage, indignantly considered
the cathedral "an imitation of European marvels."

Mrs. Watts took the Bean Blossom teaching job, at thirty-six hundred
dollars a year, last fall, when her husband decided to abandon a concrete-
building-block business in Huntington in order to study for a Ph.D. in political science, a subject he wants to teach. Since he had decided that Indiana
University was the place to do this, they moved from Huntington—where
Mr. Watts had won the distinction of being the youngest man ever to hold
the job of chairman of the Republican Party of Huntington County—to
Bloomington. Mrs. Watts drives the twelve miles from Bloomington to
Stinesville every day. She teaches English to the tenth, eleventh, and twelfth
grades, and, because the school had no Spanish teacher when she signed
up for the job, she teaches Spanish, too. She considers the Bean Blossom
Township school the most democratic school she has ever seen. "They vote
on everything," she says. "We have an average of two votes on something
or other every day." Having thus been conditioned to voting as a way of
life, Mrs. Watts left the voting on day-to-day plans for the group visit in
the capable hands of Jay Bowman. He solved the problem of the tour's
late start that morning by taking a vote on whether or not to leave out the

Empire State Building. It was promptly voted out of the tour, and voted in for some later time as a separate undertaking.

The tour included a boat trip to the Statue of Liberty, where the group fell in with crushing mobs of people walking to the top of the torch. Mrs. Watts found the experience nightmarish, and quit at the base of the torch. Most of the boys and girls made it to the top. "There are a hundred and sixty-eight steps up the torch, and there were forty thousand people ahead of me, but I was determined to climb up it," Jay Bowman reported to Mrs. Watts. "It took me twenty minutes, and it was worthwhile. The thing of it was I had to do it."

For the tour, Jay, like the other boys, had put on dress-up clothes bought specially, at a cost of about twenty-five dollars an outfit, for the trip to New York—white beachcomber pants reaching to below the knee, white cotton-knit shirt with red and blue stripes and a pocket in one sleeve, white socks with red and blue stripes, and white sneakers. The girls wore cotton skirts, various kinds of blouses, white cardigan sweaters, and low-heeled shoes. Mrs. Watts wore high-heeled pumps, even for sightseeing. Everyone else on the tour was astonished at the way New York City people dressed. "They look peculiar," Nancy Prather said. "Girls wearing high heels in the daytime, and the boys here always got a regular suit on, even to go to work in."

"I wouldn't trade the girls back home for any of the girls here," Jay Bowman says. "New York girls wear too much makeup. Not that my interests are centered on any of the girls in the senior class. My interests are centered on Nancy Glidden. She's in the *junior* class. I take her to shows in Bloomington. We eat pizzas, listen to Elvis Presley—things of that nature—and I always get her home by twelve. Even though my interests are centered on the junior class, I'm proud to say my classmates are the finest bunch of people in the world."

Jay lives with his parents and two brothers in an old nine-room house on thirty acres of land owned by Jay's father, who works in the maintenance department of the Bridgeport Brass Company, in Indianapolis. His mother works in Bloomington, on the R.C.A. color-television-set assembly line. Jay's grandfather, who has worked in limestone quarries all his life, lives across the road, on five acres of his own land, where he has a couple of cows and raises beans and corn for the use of the family. The Bowman family had no plumbing in their house while Jay was a child, and took baths in a tub in the kitchen with water from a well, but a few years ago, with their own hands, they installed a bathroom and a plumbing system, and did other work on the house, including putting in a furnace. Jay's parents get up at four in the morning to go to work. Jay, who hasn't been sick one day since he had the mumps at the age of twelve, never sleeps later than seven. He is not in the least distressed at having to work his way through college. He plans to get to school in his own car. This is a 1950 Chevrolet four-door sedan, which he hopes to trade in, by paying an additional four hundred dollars, for a slightly younger model before the end of the year.

"The thing of it is I feel proud of myself," Jay says. "Not to be braggin' or anything. But I saved up better than a thousand dollars to send myself to college. That's the way it is. I scrubbed floors, put up hay, carried groceries, and this last winter I worked Saturdays and Sundays in a country store on the state highway and got paid a dollar an hour for runnin' it."

The Bowman family has, in addition to a kind of basic economic ambition, two main interests—basketball and politics. Jay, like most of the other boys on the trip, played basketball on the school basketball team, which won the first round in its section of the Wabash Valley tournament last season. Jay talks about basketball to his classmates but never about politics. Talk about the latter he saves for his family. His grandfather is a Democrat. "If it was up to my grandpa, he'd never want a single Republican in the whole country," he says. "And my Dad agrees with him. I agree with my Dad. My Dad thinks if Franklin D. Roosevelt was still President, this country wouldn't be in the trouble it finds itself in."

At 5 P.M. of this second day in the City of New York, the members of the Bean Blossom senior class returned to their hotel and stood in the lobby for a while, looking from some distance at a souvenir-and-gift stand across from the registration desk. The stand was stocked with thermometers in the form of the Statue of Liberty, in two sizes, priced at seventy-nine cents and ninety-eight cents; with silver-plated charm bracelets; with pins and compacts carrying representations of the Empire State Building; with scarves showing the R.C.A. Building and the U.N. Building; and with ashtrays showing the New York City skyline. Mike Richardson edged over to the stand and picked up a wooden plaque, costing ninety-eight cents, with the Statue of Liberty shown at the top, American flags at the sides, and, in the middle, a poem, inscribed "Mother," which read:

> *To one who bears the sweetest name*
> *And adds a luster to the same*
> *Who shares my joys*
> *Who cheers when sad*
> *The greatest friend I ever had*
> *Long life to her, for there's no other*
> *Can take the place of my dear mother.*

After reading the poem, Mike smiled.

"Where ya from?" the man behind the stand asked him.

"Indiana," Mike said, looking as though he were warming up. "We've been on this tour? The whole day?"

"Ya see everything?" the man asked.

"Everything except the Empire State Building," said Mike.

"Yeah," said the man, and looked away.

Mike was still holding the plaque. Carefully, he replaced it on the stand. "I'll come back for this later," he said.

Without looking at Mike, the man nodded.

Mike joined Dennis Smith and Larry Williams, who were standing with a tall, big-boned, handsome girl named Becky Kiser. Becky used to be a cheerleader for the Bean Blossom Township basketball team.

"We was talkin' about the way this place has people layin' in the streets on that Bowery sleepin'," Larry said. "You don't see people layin' in the streets back home."

"I seen that in Chicago," Dennis said. "I seen *women* layin' in the streets in Chicago. That's worse."

The others nodded. No argument.

Mike took a cigarette from his sleeve pocket and lit it with a match from the same pocket. He blew out a stream of smoke with strength and confidence. "I'll be glad when we light out of here," he said. "Nothin' here feels like the farm."

Becky Kiser, with an expression of terrible guilt on her attractive, wide-mouthed face, said, "I bet you'd never get bored here in New York. Back home, it's the same thing all the time. You go to the skating rink. You go to the Big Boy. In the winter, there's basketball. And that's all."

"When I was in Chicago, I seen a man who shot a man in a bar," Dennis said. "I stood right across the street while the man who was shot the people drug him out." He looked at Becky Kiser. The other boys were also looking at her, but with condemnation and contempt. Dennis gave Becky support. "In Stinesville, they see you on the streets after eleven, they run you home," he said. "Seems like here the city never closes."

"Man, you're just not lookin' ahead," Mike said to Dennis, ignoring Becky.

"You like it here?" Larry asked, in amazement. "Taxes on candy and on everything?"

The Nazarene minister's daughter, Mary Jane Carter, came over with Ina Hough.

"Dennis, here, likes New York," Mike announced.

"*I* don't," said Ina. "I like the sights, but I think they're almost ruined by the people."

"The food here is expensive, but I guess that's life," said Mary Jane, in a mood of forbearance.

"Oh, man!" said Mike.

"Oh, man!" said Larry. "Cooped up in New York."

Ina said stiffly, "Like the guide said today, you could always tell a New Yorker from a tourist because a New Yorker never smiles, and I agree with him."

"After a while, you'd kinda fit in," Dennis said mildly.

Before dinner that night, Mr. Watts walked through the Times Square area checking prices and menus at likely restaurants. He made tentative arrangements at The Californian for a five-course steak or chicken dinner, to cost $1.95 per person, and asked Jay Bowman to go around taking a vote on the proposition. Half an hour later, Jay reported to Mr. Watts that some of the boys didn't want to go to The Californian, because they thought they'd have to do their own ordering. So Mr. Watts talked to the boys in their rooms and explained that the ordering was taken care of; all they had to say was whether they wanted steak or chicken. On the next ballot, everybody was in favor of The Californian. The class walked over. When the fifth course was finished, it was agreed that the dinner was all right, but several of the boys said they thought the restaurant was too high-class.

After dinner, it started to rain, and it rained hard. The Wattses and seven of the girls decided that they wanted to see "The Music Man." The four other girls wanted to see "My Fair Lady." None of the boys wanted to see a musical show. In the driving rain, the Wattses and the girls ran to the theatres of their choice, all arriving soaked to the skin. By good luck, each group was able to buy seats. At "The Music Man," the Wattses and the seven girls with them sat in the balcony, in the direct path of an air-conditioning unit that blew icy blasts on their backs. At "My Fair Lady," the four girls sat in the balcony, where an air-conditioning unit blew icy blasts at their legs. The girls liked their shows. The "My Fair Lady" group was transported by the costumes. Ina Hough, who went to "The Music Man," thought that it was just like a movie, except for the way the scenes changed.

The boys split up, some of them taking the subway down to Greenwich Village, the others heading for the Empire State Building, where they paid a dollar-thirty for tickets to the observatory and, once up there, found that the fog and rain blotted out the view completely. "We stood there about an hour and a half messin' around, me and my buddies," Jay later told Mrs. Watts. "Wasn't no sense in leavin' at that price." In Greenwich Village, Mike Richardson, Dennis Smith, and Larry Williams walked along the narrow streets in a drizzling rain. All were still wearing their beachcomber outfits. Nobody talked to them. They didn't see anybody they wanted to talk to. They almost went into a small coffeehouse; they changed their minds because the prices looked too high. They went into one shop, a bookstore, and looked at some abstract paintings, which appealed to them. "Sort of interestin', the way they don't look like nothin'," Mike said. Then they took the subway back to Times Square, where they walked around for a while in the rain. Toward midnight, Mike and Dennis told each other they were lonesome for the smell of grass and trees, and, the rain having stopped, they walked up to Central Park, where they stayed for about an hour and got lost.

The next morning, a meeting of the class was held in the hotel lobby to take a vote on when to leave New York. Jay Bowman reported that they had enough money to cover an extra day in the city, plus a side trip to Niagara Falls on the way home. Or, he said, they could leave New York when they had originally planned to and go to Washington, D.C., for a day before heading home. The bus driver had told Jay that it was all one to him which they chose. The class voted for the extra day in New York and Niagara Falls.

"I'm glad," Becky Kiser said, with a large, friendly smile, to Dennis Smith. Several of her classmates overheard her and regarded her with a uniformly deadpan look. "I like it here," she went on. "I'd like to live here. There's so much to see. There's so much to do."

Her classmates continued to study her impassively until Dennis took their eyes away from her by saying, "You get a feelin' here of goin' wherever you want to. Seems the city never closes. I'd like to live here, I believe. People from everyplace are here."

"Limousines all over the joint," Albert Warthan said.

"Seems like you can walk and walk and walk," Dennis went on dreamily. "I like the way the big buildin's crowd you in. You want to walk and walk and never go to sleep."

"I hate it," Connie Williams said, with passion.

"Oh, man, you're just not lookin' ahead," Mike Richardson said to Dennis. "You got a romantic notion. You're not realistic about it."

"This place couldn't hold me," Larry Williams said. "I like the privacy of the farm."

"I want to go to new places," said Becky, who had started it. "I want to go to Europe."

"Only place I want to go is Texas," Larry said. "I got folks in Texas."

"There's no place like home," Mike said. "Home's good enough for me."

"I believe the reason of this is we've lived all of our lives around Stinesville," Dennis said. "If you took Stinesville out of the country, you wouldn't be hurt. But if you took New York out of the country, you'd be hurt. The way the guide said, all our clothes and everything comes from New York."

Becky said, "In Coney Island, I saw the most handsome man I ever saw in my whole life. I think he was a Puerto Rican or something, too."

Albert said, "When we get back, my pa will say, 'Well, how was it?' I'll say, 'It was fine.'"

"I'd like to come back, maybe stay a month," Jay Bowman said diplomatically. "One thing I'd like to do is come here when I can see a major-league baseball game."

"I'd like to see a major-league baseball game, but I wouldn't come back just to see it," Mike said.

"I hate New York," Connie said.

"Back home, everybody says 'Excuse me,'" Nancy Prather said.

"I like it here," Dennis said stubbornly.

This day was an open one, leaving the boys and girls free to do anything they liked, without prearranged plan or vote. Mike passed close by the souvenir-and-gift stand in the hotel lobby, and the proprietor urged him to take home the Statue of Liberty.

"I'd like to, but it won't fit in my suitcase," Mike said, with a loud laugh.

A group formed to visit the zoo in Central Park, got on the subway, had a loud discussion about where to get off, and were taken in hand by a stranger, who told them the zoo was in the Bronx. Only the boy named Lynn Dillon listened to the stranger. The others went to the zoo in Central Park. Lynn stayed on the subway till it reached the Bronx, and spent the entire day in the Bronx Zoo by himself. The rest of the zoo visitors, walking north after lunch in the cafeteria, ran into the Metropolitan Museum of Art and went in. "It was there, and it was free, so we did it," Nancy Prather said. "There were these suits of armor and stuff. Nothin' I go for myself."

That morning, the Wattses had tried to get some of the boys and girls to accompany them to the Guggenheim Museum or the Museum of Modern Art, but nobody had wanted to pay the price of admission. "Why pay fifty cents to see a museum when they got them free?" the class president asked. Mrs. Watts reported afterward that the Guggenheim was the most exciting museum she had ever seen, including all the museums she had seen in Europe on her accredited art tour. "There aren't big crowds in there, for one thing," she said. "And I don't think the building overpowers the paintings at all, as I'd heard." From the Guggenheim, the Wattses went to Georg Jensen's to look at silver, but didn't buy anything. Then they went to the Museum of Modern Art and had lunch in the garden. "Lovely lunch, fabulous garden, fabulous sculpture, but I'm disappointed in the museum itself," Mrs. Watts said. "Everything jammed into that small space! Impossible to get a good view of Picasso's 'Girl Before a Mirror.'"

By dinnertime, more than half of the Bean Blossomers had, to their relief, discovered the Automat. Jay Bowman had a dinner consisting of a ham sandwich (forty cents), a glass of milk (ten cents), and a dish of fresh strawberries (twenty cents). Then, with a couple of buddies, he bought some peanuts in their shells and some Cokes, and took them up to his room for the three of them to consume while talking about what to do that night. They decided, because they had not yet had a good view of the city from the Empire State observatory, that they would go back there. They were accompanied by most of the girls and the other boys, and this time the group got a cut rate of sixty-five cents apiece. Dennis went off wandering by himself. He walked up Fifth Avenue to Eighty-fifth Street, over to Park Avenue, down Park to Seventy-second Street, across to the West Side, down Central Park West to Sixty-sixth Street, over behind the Tavern-on-the-Green (where he watched people eating outdoors), and down Seventh Avenue to Times Square, where he stood around on corners looking at the people who bought papers at newsstands.

The Wattses had arranged to meet anybody who was interested under the Washington Arch at around nine-thirty for an evening in Greenwich Village. The boys had decided to take a walk up Broadway after leaving the Empire State Building, but the girls all showed up in Washington Square, along with two soldiers and three sailors they had met in the U.S.O. across the street from the Woodstock. The Wattses led the way to a coffeehouse, where everybody had coffee or lemonade. Then the girls and the servicemen left the Wattses, saying they were going to take a ride on the ferry to Staten Island. The Wattses went to the Five Spot, which their jazz friend had told them had good music.

After breakfast the following morning, the bus driver, Ralph Walls, showed up in the hotel lobby for the first time since the group's arrival in New York and told Jay Bowman to have everyone assembled at five-forty-five the following morning for departure at six o'clock on the dot. The driver said that he was spending most of his time sleeping, and that before they left he was going to do some more sleeping. He had taken his wife on a boat trip around Manhattan, though, he said, and he had taken a few walks on the streets. After reminding Jay again about the exact time planned for the departure, he went back upstairs to his room.

Mrs. Watts took nine of the girls (two stayed in the hotel to sleep) for a walk through Saks Fifth Avenue, just looking. Mr. Watts took three of the boys to Abercrombie & Fitch, just looking. Everybody walked every aisle on every floor in each store, looking at everything on the counters and in the showcases. Nobody bought anything. The two groups met at noon under the clock in Grand Central; lunched at an Automat; walked over to the United Nations Buildings, where they decided not to take the regular tour; and took a crosstown bus to the Hudson River and went aboard the liner S.S. Independence, where they visited every deck and every lounge on the boat, and a good many of the staterooms. Then they took the bus back to Times Square and scattered to do some shopping.

Mike Richardson bought all his gifts—eleven dollars' worth—at the hotel stand, taking not only the plaque for his mother but a set of salt and pepper shakers, with the Statue of Liberty on the salt and the Empire State Building on the pepper, also for his mother; a Statue of Liberty ashtray for his father; a George Washington Bridge teapot for his sister-in-law; a mechanical dog for his niece; a City Hall teapot-cup-and-saucer set for his grandparents; and a cigarette lighter stamped with the Great White Way for himself. At Macy's, Becky Kiser bought a dress, a blouse, and an ankle chain for herself, and a necklace with matching bracelet and earrings for her mother, a cuff-link-and-tie-clasp set for her father, and a bracelet for her younger sister. Albert Warthan bought a miniature camera for himself and a telephone-pad-and-pencil set stamped with the George Washington Bridge and a Statue of Liberty thermometer, large-size, as general family gifts, at the hotel stand. Jay Bowman bought an unset cultured pearl at Macy's for his girl friend in the junior class, as well as silver-looking earrings for his married sister and for his mother, and at a store called King of Slims, around the corner from the hotel, he bought four ties—a red toreador tie (very narrow) for his older brother, a black toreador tie for his younger brother, a conservative silk foulard for his father, and a white toreador tie for himself. Dennis Smith bought a Statue of Liberty ashtray for his mother and a Statue of Liberty cigarette lighter for his father. Connie Williams bought two bracelets and a Statue of Liberty pen for herself. The bus driver and his wife spent sixty dollars on clothes for their children, six of whom are girls. Nancy Prather didn't buy anything. The Wattses spent about a hundred dollars in the course of the visit, most of it on meals and entertainment.

On their last evening in New York, all the boys and girls, accompanied by the Wattses, went to the Radio City Music Hall, making it in time to see the stage show. Then they packed and went to bed. The bus driver, after an early dinner with his wife at Hector's Cafeteria, brought the yellow school bus over from Tenth Avenue and parked it right in front of the hotel, so that it would be there for the early start.

Next morning at five-forty-five, the Bean Blossomers assembled in the lobby; for the first time since the trip had started, nobody was late. The bus pulled out at exactly 6 A.M., and twenty minutes after that, heading west over the George Washington Bridge, it disappeared from the city.

1963

Norman Mailer genuinely grappled with that question as much as he cleverly toyed with it. Long after he'd won a Pulitzer Prize in *fiction* for his book about the life of an *actual* murderer, and then a Pulitzer in *nonfiction* for his third-person account of his *own* participation in antiwar demonstrations, Mailer wrote a book about Marilyn Monroe that was sold as a novel, described as a memoir, and framed as a diary in the late actress's voice. Anticipating outrage at his fiddling with categories that separate the genres, Mailer preempted critics by putting himself on trial in *New York* magazine:

> THE COURT: Mr. Mailer, I will remind you of the charge. It is criminal literary negligence . . .
>
> MR. MAILER: I am aware of the charge, Your Honor.
>
> PROSECUTOR: Mr. Mailer, I am holding in my hand a work entitled *Of Women and Their Elegance,* which has your name on the cover as author. Would you describe it? . . .
>
> MAILER: Originally, I wished to title it *Of Women and Their Elegance, by Marilyn Monroe as Told to Norman Mailer,* but it was decided the title could prove misleading to the public . . .
>
> PROSECUTOR: It is made up.
>
> MAILER: More or less made up.
>
> PROSECUTOR: Could you be more specific?
>
> MAILER: . . . We reconstruct the past by our recollections of the mood fully as much as by our grasp of

fact. When facts are skimpy, one hopes to do well
at sensing the mood . . .

PROSECUTOR: You wrote [this], knowing there was no
factual basis for [it]?

MAILER: No factual basis.

PROSECUTOR: What makes you think there is a fictional basis?

MAILER: I'm not sure a fictional basis is possible . . .

PROSECUTOR: Are you telling us that you doubt your
ethics?

MAILER: I call them in question.

PROSECUTOR: You think yourself guilty of literary
malpractice?

What Mailer grappled with openly and gleefully throughout
his writing life was the same question that lurks in every kind
of essay: How do you ford the confluence of chance and contrivance? It's a question that is sometimes acknowledged,
sometimes ignored, and sometimes perversely turned on its
head or deliriously denied to be relevant at all. But it's always
there, always, whether we like it or not. And this is what
makes journalists and essayists kindred spirits at heart.

NORMAN MAILER

Ten Thousand Words a Minute

Remember that old joke about three kinds of intelligence: human, animal, and military? Well, if there are three kinds of writers: novelists, poets, and *reporters,* there is certainly a gulf between the poet and the novelist; quite apart from the kind of living they make, poets invariably seem to be aristocrats, usually spoiled beyond repair; and novelists—even if they make a million, or have large talent—look to have something of the working class about them. Maybe it is the drudgery, the long, obsessive inner life, the day-to-day monotony of applying themselves to the middle of the same continuing job, or perhaps it is the business of being unappreciated at home—has anyone met a novelist who is happy with the rugged care provided by his wife?

Now, of course, I am tempted to round the image out and say reporters belong to the middle class. Only I do not know if I can push the metaphor. Taken one by one, it is true that reporters tend to be hardheaded, objective, and unimaginative. Their intelligence is sound but unexceptional and they have the middle-class penchant for collecting tales, stories, legends, accounts of practical jokes, details of negotiation, bits of memoir—all those capsules of fiction which serve the middle class as a substitute for ethics and/or culture. Reporters, like shopkeepers, tend to be worshipful of the fact which wins and so covers over the other facts. In the middle class, the remark, "He made a lot of money," ends the conversation. If you persist, if you try to point out that the money was made by digging through his grandmother's grave to look for oil, you are met with a middle-class shrug. "It's a question of taste whether one should get into the past," is the winning reply.

In his own person there is nobody more practical than a reporter. He exhibits the same avidity for news which a businessman will show for money.

No bourgeois will hesitate to pick up a dollar, even if he is not fond of the man with whom he deals: so, a reporter will do a nice story about a type he dislikes, or a bad story about a figure he is fond of. It has nothing to do with his feelings. There is a logic to news—on a given day, with a certain meteorological drift to the winds in the mass media, a story can only ride along certain vectors. To expect a reporter to be true to the precise detail of an event is kin to the sentimentality which asks a fast revolving investor to be faithful to a particular stock in his portfolio when it is going down and his others are going up.

But here we come to the end of our image. When the middle class gather for a club meeting or a social function, the atmosphere is dependably dull, whereas ten reporters come together in a room for a story are slightly hysterical, and two hundred reporters and photographers congregated for a press conference are as void of dignity, even stuffed-up, stodgy, middle-class dignity, as a slew of monkeys tearing through the brush. There is reason for this, much reason; there is always urgency to get some quotation which is usable for their story, and afterward, find a telephone: the habitat of a reporter, at its worst, is identical to spending one's morning, afternoon and evening transferring from the rush hour of one subway train to the rush hour of another. In time even the best come to remind one of the rush hour. An old fight reporter is a sad sight, he looks like an old prize-fight manger, which is to say, he looks like an old cigar butt.

Nor is this true only of sports reporters. They are gifted with charm compared to political reporters who give off an effluvium which is unadulterated cancer gulch. I do not think I exaggerate. There is an odor to any Press Headquarters which is unmistakable. One may begin by saying it is like the odor in small left-wing meeting halls, except it is worse, far worse, for there is no poverty to put a guilt-free iron into the nose; on the contrary, everybody is getting free rinks, free sandwiches, free news releases. Yet there is the unavoidable smell of flesh burning quietly and slowly in the service of a machine. Have any of you never been through the smoking car of an old coach early in the morning when the smokers sleep and the stale air settles into congelations of gloom? Well, that is a little like the scent of Press Headquarters. Yet the difference is vast, because Press Headquarters for any big American event is invariably a large room in a large hotel, usually the largest room in the largest hotel in town. Thus it is a commercial room in a commercial hotel. The walls must be pale green or pale pink, dirty by now, subtly dirty like the toe of a silk stocking. (Which is incidentally the smell of the plaster.) One could be meeting bureaucrats from Tashkent in the Palace of the Soviets. One enormous barefaced meeting room, a twenty-foot banner up, a proscenium arch at one end, with high Gothic windows painted within the arch—almost never does a window look out on the open air. (Hotels build banquet rooms on the *inside* of their buildings—it is the best way to fill internal space with revenue.)

This room is in fever. Two hundred, three hundred, I suppose even five hundred reporters get into some of these rooms, there to talk, there to drink, there to bang away on any one of fifty standard typewriters, provided by the people on Public Relations who have set up this Press Headquarters. It is like being at a vast party in Limbo—there is tremendous excitement, much movement and no sex at all. Just talk. Talk fed by cigarettes. One thousand to two thousand cigarettes are smoked every hour. The mind must keep functioning fast enough to offer up stories. (Reporters meet as in a marketplace to trade their stories—they barter an anecdote they cannot use about one of the people in the event in order to pick up a different piece which is usable by their paper. It does not matter if the story is true or altogether not true, it must merely be suitable and not too mechanically libelous.) So they char the inside of their bodies in order to scrape up news which can go out to the machine, that enormous machine, that intellectual leviathan which is obliged to eat each day, tidbits, gristle, gravel, garbage cans, charlotte russe, old rubber tires, T-bone steaks, wet cardboard, dry leaves, apple pie, broken bottles, dog food, shells, roach powder, dry ball-point pens, grapefruit juice. All the trash, all the garbage, all the slop and a little of the wealth go out each day and night into the belly of that old American goat, our newspapers.

So the reporters smell also of this work, they smell of the dishwasher and the pots, they are flesh burning themselves very quietly and slowly in the service of a machine which feeds goats, which feeds The Goat. One smells this collective odor on the instant one enters their meeting room. It is not a corrupt smell, it does not have enough of the meats, the savory, and the vitality of flesh to smell corrupt and fearful when it is bad, no, it is more the smell of excessive respect for power, the odor of flesh gutted by avidities which are electric and empty. I suppose it is the bleak smell one could find on the inside of one's head during a bad cold, full of fever, badly used, burned out of mood. The physical sensation of a cold often is one of power trapped corrosively inside, coils of strength being liquidated in some center of the self. The reporter hangs in a powerless-power—his voice directly, or via the rewrite desk indirectly, reaches out to millions of readers; the more readers he owns, the less he can say. He is forbidden by a hundred censors, most of them inside himself, to communicate notions which are not conformistically simple, simple like plastic is simple, that is to say, monotonous. Therefore a reporter forms a habit equivalent to lacerating the flesh: he learns to write what he does not naturally believe. Since he did not start presumably with the desire to be a bad writer or a dishonest writer, he ends by bludgeoning his brain into believing that something which is half true is in fact—since he creates a fact each time he puts something into a newspaper—nine-tenths true. A psyche is debauched—his own; a false fact is created. For which fact, sooner or later, inevitably, inexorably, the public will pay. A nation which forms detailed opinions on the basis of detailed fact which is askew from the subtle reality becomes a nation of citizens whose psyches are skewed, item by detailed item, away from *any* reality.

So great guilt clings to reporters. They know they help to keep America slightly insane. As a result perhaps they are a shabby-looking crew. The best of them are the shabbiest, which is natural if one thinks about it—a sensitive man suffers from the prosperous life of his lies more than a dull man. In fact the few dudes one finds among reporters tend to be semi-illiterates, or hatchet men, or cynics on two or three payrolls who do restrained public relations in the form of news stories. But this is to make too much of the extremes. Reporters along the middle of the spectrum are shabby, worried, guilty, and suffer each day from the damnable anxiety that they know all sorts of powerful information a half hour to twenty-four hours before anyone else in America knows it, not to mention the time clock ticking away in the vault of all those stories which cannot be printed or will not be printed. It makes for a livid view of existence. It is like an injunction to become hysterical once a day. Then they must write at lightning speed. It may be heavy-fisted but true, it may be slick as a barnyard slide, it may be great, it may be fill—what does it matter?. The matter rides out like oats in a conveyor belt, and the unconscious takes a ferocious pounding. Writing is of use to the psyche only if the writer discovers something he did not know he knew in the act itself of writing. That is why a few men will go through hell in order to keep writing—Joyce and Proust, for example. Being a writer can save one from insanity or cancer; being a bad writer can drive one smack into the center of the plague. Think of the poor reporter who does not have the leisure of the novelist or the poet to discover what he thinks. The unconscious gives up, buries itself, leaves the writer to his cliché, and saves the truth, or that part of it the reporter is yet privileged to find, for his colleagues and his friends. A good reporter is a man who must still tell you the truth privately; he has bright harsh eyes and can relate ten good stories in a row standing at a bar.

Still, they do not quit. That charge of adrenalin once a day, that hysteria, that sense of powerless-power close to the engines of history—they can do without powerless-power no more than a gentleman junkie on the main line can do without his heroin, doctor. You see, a reporter is close to the action. He is not *of* the action, but he is close to it, as close as a crab louse to the begetting of a child. One may never be President, but the photographer working for his paper has the power to cock a flashbulb and make the eyes of JFK go blink!

However, it is not just this lead-encased seat near the radiations of power which keeps the reporter hooked on a drug of new news to start new adrenalin; it is also the ride. It is the free ride. When we were children, there were those movies about reporters; they were heroes. While chasing a lead, they used to leap across empty elevator shafts, they would wrestle automatics out of mobsters' hands, and if they were Cary Grant, they would pick up a chair and stick it in the lion's face, since the lion had had the peculiar sense to walk into the editor's office. Next to being a cowboy, or a private eye, the most heroic activity in America was to be a reporter. Now it is the welfare state. Every last cigar-smoking fraud of a middle-aged reporter, pale with prison pallor, deep lines in his cheeks, writing daily pietisms for the sheet back home about free enterprise, is himself the first captive of the welfare state. It is the best free ride anyone will find since he left his family's chest. Your room is paid for by the newspaper, your trips to the particular spots attached to the event—in this case, the training camp at Elgin, Illinois, for Patterson, and the empty racetrack at Aurora Downs for Liston—are by chartered limousine. Who but a Soviet bureaucrat, a British businessman, a movie star, or an American reporter would ride in a chartered limousine? (They smell like funeral parlors.) Your typing paper is free if you want it; your seat at the fight, or your ticket to the convention is right up there, under the ropes; your meals if you get around to eating them are free, free sandwiches only but then a reporter has a stomach like

a shaving mug and a throat like a hog's trough: he couldn't tell steak tar-
tare from *guacamole*. And the drinks—if you are at a big fight—are without charge. If you are at a political convention, there is no free liquor. But
you do have a choice between free Pepsi-Cola and free Coca-Cola. The
principle seems to be that the reporting of mildly psychotic actions—such
as those performed by politicians—should be made in sobriety; whereas a
sane estimate of an athlete's chances are neatest on booze. At a fight Press
Headquarters, the drinks are very free, and the mood can even be half con-
vivial. At the Patterson-Liston Press Headquarters there was a head bartender working for Championship Sports whose name was Archie. He was
nice. He was a nice man. It was a pleasure to get a drink from him. You remember these things afterward, it's part of the nostalgia. The joy of the free
ride is the lack of worry. It's like being in an Army outfit which everyone's
forgotten. You get your food, you get your beer, you get your pay, the work
is easy, and leave to town is routine. You never had it so good—you're an
infant again: you can grow up a second time and improve the job.

That's the half and half of being a reporter. One half is addiction,
adrenalin, anecdote-shopping, deadlines, dread, cigar smoke, lung cancer,
vomit, feeding The Goat; the other is Aloha, Tahiti, old friends and the
free ride to the eleventh floor of the Sheraton-Chicago, Patterson-Liston
Press Headquarters, everything free. Even your news is free. If you haven't
done your homework, if you drank too late last night and missed the last
limousine out to Elgin or Aurora this morning, if there's no poop of your
own on Floyd's speed or Sonny's bad mood, you can turn to the handouts
given you in the Press Kit, dig, a *Kit,* kiddies, worked up for you by Harold
Conrad who's the Public Relations Director. It's not bad stuff, it's interesting material. No need to do your own research. Look at some of this: there's
the tale of the tape for each fighter with as many physical measurements
as a tailor in Savile Row might take; there's the complete record of each
fighter, how he won, how many rounds, who, the date, so forth; there's the
record of how much money they made on each fight, how their KO records
compare with the All-Time Knockout Artists, Rocky Marciano with 43 out
of 49, batting .878, Joe Louis at .761, Floyd at .725 (29 in 40) and Sonny
Liston going with 23 for 34, is down at .676, back of Jim Jeffries who comes
in at .696. There's a column there, there's another if you want to dig into
the biographies of each fighter, six single-spaced pages on Patterson, four
on Liston. There's a list of each and every fighter who won and lost the

Heavyweight Championship, and the year—remember? Remember Jake Kilrain and Marvin Hart (stopped Jack Root at Reno, Nevada, 12 rounds, July 3, 1905). You can win money with Marvin Hart betting in bars. And Tommy Burns. Jack O'Brien. In what year did Ezzard Charles first take Jersey Joe Walcott; in what town? You can see the different columns shaping up. If you got five columns to do on the fight, three can be whipped right up out of Graff/Reiner/Smith Enterprises, Inc. Sports News Release. Marvelous stuff. How Sonny Liston does his roadwork on railroad tracks, what Sonny's best weight is (206–212), what kind of poundages Floyd likes to give away—averages 10 pounds a bout—Floyd's style in boxing, Liston's style in boxing. It's part of the free list, an offering of facts with a little love from the Welfare State.

It is so easy, so much is done for you, that you remember these days with nostalgia. When you do get around to paying for yourself, going into a room like the Camelot Room at the Sheraton-Chicago, with its black-blood three-story mahogany paneling and its high, stained Gothic windows looking out no doubt on an air shaft, it is a joy to buy your own food, an odd smacking sensation to pay for a drink. It is the Welfare State which makes the pleasure possible. When one buys all one's own drinks, the sensation of paying cash is without much joy, but to pay for a drink occasionally—that's near bliss.

And because it is a fight, cancer gulch has its few oases. The Press Headquarters livens up with luminaries, the unhealthiest people in America now meet some of the healthiest, complete self-contained healthy bodies which pass modestly through: Ingemar Johansson and Archie Moore, Rocky Marciano, Barney Ross, Cassius Clay, Harold Johnson, Ezzard Charles, Dick Tiger on his way to San Francisco where he is to fight Gene Fullmer and beat him, Jim Braddock——big, heavy, grey, and guarded, looking as tough as steel drilled into granite, as if he were the toughest night watchman in America, and Joe Louis looking like the largest Chinaman in the world, still sleepy, still sad. That's part of the pleasure of Press Headquarters—the salty crystallized memories which are released from the past, the night ten or eleven years ago when Joe Louis, looking just as sleepy and as sad as he does now, went in to fight Rocky Marciano at the Garden, and was knocked out in eight. It was part of a comeback, but Louis was never able to get his fight going at all, he was lethargic that night, and Marciano, fighting a pure Italian street-fighter's style, throwing his punches as if he held a brick in each hand, taking Louis' few good shots with an animal joy, strong enough to eat bricks with his teeth, drove right through Joe Louis and knocked him out hard. Louis went over in a long, very inert fall, as if an old tree or a momentous institution were coming down, perhaps the side of a church wall hovering straight and slow enough in its drop for the onlooker to take a breath in the gulf of the bomb. And it had been a bomb. Louis' leg was draped over the rope. People were crying as they left Madison Square Garden that night. It was a little like the death of Franklin Delano Roosevelt: something generous had just gone out of the world. And now here was Marciano as well, in the couloirs and coffee shop and lobby of the Sheraton-Chicago, a man looking as different from the young contender he had been on his way to the championship as Louis now looked the same. Louis had turned old in the ring. Marciano retired undefeated, and so aged after he stopped. Now he seemed no longer to be carrying bricks but pillows. He had gotten very plump, his face was round and no longer lumpy, he was half bald, a large gentle monk with a bemused, misty, slightly tricky expression.

And there were others, Bill Hartack, Jack Kearns who at eighty-plus still looked to be one of the most intelligent men in America, Sammy Taub, the old radio announcer who used to talk as fast as the cars on the Indianapolis Speedway, "and he hits him another left to the belly, and another, and another, and a right to the head, and a left to the head." Taub made bums sound like champions—it is doubtful if there was ever a fighter who could throw punches fast enough to keep up with Taub, and now he was an old man, a grandfather, a bright, short man with a birdlike face, a little like a tiny older version of Leonard Lyons.

There were many, there were so many, preliminary fighters who got their money together to get to Chicago, and managers, and promoters. There were novelists, Jimmy Baldwin, Budd Schulberg, Gerald Kersh, Ben Hecht. As the fight approached, so did the Mob. That arid atmosphere of reporters alone with reporters and writers with writers gave way to a whiff of the deep. The Mob was like birds and beasts coming in to feed. Heavy types, bouncers, plug-uglies, flatteners, one or two speedy, swishing, Negro ex-boxers, for example, now blown up to the size of fat middleweights, slinky in their walk, eyes fulfilling the operative definition of razor slits, murder coming off them like scent comes off a skunk. You could feel death as they passed. It came wafting off. And the rest of the beasts as well—the strong-arm men, the head-kickers, the limb-breakers, the groin-stompers. If a clam had a muscle as large as a man, and the muscle grew eyes, you would get the mood. Those were the beasts. They were all orderly, they were all trained, they were dead to humor. They never looked at anyone they did not know, and when they were introduced they stared at the floor while shaking hands as if their own hand did not belong to them, but was merely a stuffed mitten to which their arm was attached.

The orders came from the birds. There were hawks and falcons and crows, Italian dons looking like little old shrunken eagles, gulls, pelicans, condors. The younger birds stood around at modest strategic points in the lobby, came up almost not at all to Press Headquarters, posted themselves out on the street, stood at the head of escalators, near the door of the barbershop, along the elevator strip, by the registration desk. They were all dressed in black gabardine topcoats, black felt hats, and very large dark sunglasses with expensive frames. They wore white scarves or black scarves. A few would carry a black umbrella. They stood there watching everyone who passed. They gave the impression of knowing exactly why they were standing there, what they were waiting to hear, how they were supposed to see, who they were supposed to watch. One had the certainty after a time that they knew the name of every man and woman who walked through the downstairs lobby and went into the Championship Sports office on the ground floor. If a figure said hello to a celebrity he was not supposed to know—at least not in the bird's private handbook—one could sense the new information being filed. Some were tall, some were short, but almost all were thin, their noses were aquiline, their chins were modest, their cheeks were subtly concave. They bore a resemblance to George Scott in *The Hustler*. Their aura was succinct. It said, "If you spit on my shoes, you're dead." It was a shock to realize that the Mob, in the flesh, was even more impressive than in the motion pictures.

There were also some fine old *mafiosos* with faces one had seen on the busts of Venetian doges in the Ducal Palace, subtle faces, insidious with the ingrowth of a curious culture built on treachery, dogma, the evil eye, and blood loyalty to clan. They were *don capos,* and did not wear black any longer, black was for subalterns. They were the leaders of the birds, fine old gentlemen in quiet grey suits, quiet intricate dark ties. Some had eyes which contained the humor of a cardinal; others were not so nice. There was an unhealthy dropsical type with pallor, and pink-tinted bifocal glasses—the kind who looked as if they owned a rich mortuary in a poor Italian neighborhood, and ran the local Republican club.

All the birds and beasts of the Mob seemed to be for Liston, almost without exception they were for Sonny. It was not because his prison record stirred some romantic allegiance in them, nothing of service in India together, sir, or graduates from the same campus; no, nor was it part necessarily and absolutely of some large syndicated plot to capture and run the Heavyweight Championship of the World so that the filaments of prestige which trail from such a crown would wind back into all the pizza parlors and jukeboxes of the continent, the gambling casinos, the after-hours joints, the contracting businesses, and the demolition businesses, the paving businesses, the music of the big bands, the traffic in what is legit and what is illegit—like junk and policy—no, in such a kingdom, the Heavyweight Championship is not worth that much, it's more like the Polish Corridor was to the Nazis, or Cuba to us, it's a broken boil. In their mind Patterson was a freak, some sort of vegetarian. It was sickening to see a post of importance held by a freak, or by the manager of a freak.

II

Before the fight much was made of the battle between good and evil, and the descriptions of the training camps underlined these differences. Patterson trained in a boys' camp up at Elgin which gave the impression of a charitable institution maintained by a religious denomination. The bungalows were small, painted white on their outside, and were of a miserable, dull stained-pine-color within. The atmosphere was humorless and consecrated. Nor was Patterson about. It was two days before the fight, and he had disappeared. Perhaps he was training, conceivably he was sleeping, maybe he was taking a long walk. But the gym up the hill was closed to reporters. So we gathered in one of the cottages, and watched a film which had been made of Patterson's fights. Since it had been put together by a public-relations man who was devoted to Patterson, the film caught most of Floyd's best moments and few of his bad ones.

At his best he was certainly very good. He had been an extraordinary club fighter. As a middleweight and light-heavyweight he had put together the feat of knocking out a good many of the best club fighters in America. Yvon Durelle, Jimmy Slade, Esau Ferdinand, Willie Troy, Archie McBride had been stopped by Patterson, and they were tough men. One reason a club fighter is a club fighter, after all, is because of his ability to take punishment and give a high, durable level of performance. The movies brought back the excitement there used to be watching Patterson on television in 1953 and 1954 when he would fight the main event at Eastern Parkway. I knew nothing about fights then, but the first time I saw Patterson, he knocked out a rugged fighter named Dick Wagner in five rounds, and there had been something about the way he did it which cut into my ignorance. I knew he was good. It was like seeing one's first exciting bullfight: at last one knows what everybody has been talking about. So I had an affection for Patterson which started early. When Patterson was bad he was unbelievably bad, he was Chaplinesque, simple, sheepish, eloquent in his clumsiness, sad like a clown, his knees looked literally to droop. He would seem precisely the sort of shy, stunned, somewhat dreamy Negro kid who never knew the answer in class. But when he was good, he seemed as fast as a jungle cat. He was the fastest heavyweight I had ever seen. Watching these movies, it was evident he could knock a man out with a left hook thrown from the most improbable position, leaping in from eight feet out, or wheeling to the left, his feet in the air, while he threw his hook across his body. He was like a rangy, hungry cat who starts to jump from a tree at some prey, and turns in flight to take an accurate, improvised swipe at a gorilla swinging by on a vine.

But the movies were only half pleasing. Because Patterson's fascination as a fighter was in his complex personality, in his alternations from high style to what—in a champion—could only be called buffoonery. The movies showed none of his bad fights, except for the famous third round with Ingemar Johansson in their first fight—an omission which not even a public-relations man would want to make. In the perspective of boxing history, those seven knockdowns were no longer damaging; Patterson's courage in getting up was underlined in one's memory by the way he came back in the next fight to knock Johansson out in the fifth round. So one was left with the disagreeable impression that this movie was too righteous.

Naturally I got into a debate with Cus D'Amato and a young gentleman named Jacobs, Jim Jacobs as I remember, who was built like a track man and had an expression which was very single-minded. He was the Public Relations Assistant, the man who had cut the movie, and a serious handball player too, as I learned later. In the debate, he ran me all over the court. It was one of those maddening situations where you know you are right, but the other man has the facts, and the religious conviction as well.

What about all the times Patterson has been knocked down, I started.

What times?

What times? Why . . . I was ready to stammer.

Name them.

Johansson, Rademacher.

Go on.

Roy Harris.

A slip. I could show you the film clips.

Tom McNeeley.

Also a slip, but Floyd's too nice a guy to claim it was, said Jacobs. As a matter of fact, Rademacher hit him when Floyd was tripping over his own foot as he was going backwards. That's why Floyd went down, Floyd's too much of a gentleman to take any of the credit for a knockdown away from a talented amateur like Rademacher.

"As a matter of fact," went on Jacobs, "there's one knockdown you haven't mentioned. Jacques Royer-Crecy knocked Floyd down to one knee with a left hook in the first round back in 1954."

"You better not argue with this guy," said Cus D'Amato with a happy grin. "He's seen so many movies, he knows more about Floyd's fights than I do. He can beat *me* in an argument." With that warning I should have known enough to quit, but it was Sunday and I was full of myself. The night before, at Medinah Temple, before thirty-six-hundred people (we grossed over $8000) I had had a debate with William F. Buckley, Jr. The sportswriters had put up Buckley as a 2½-to-1 favorite before our meet, but I was told they named me the winner. Eight, one, one even; seven rounds to three; six, three, one even; those were the scorecards *I* received. So at the moment, I was annoyed that this kid Jacobs, whom I started to call Mr. Facts, was racking me up.

Therefore, I heeded Cus D'Amato not at all and circled back to the fight. Jacobs was calling Patterson a great champion, I was saying he had yet to prove he was great—it was a dull argument until I said, "Why didn't he fight the kind of man Louis and Dempsey went up against?" A big mistake. Jacobs went through the record of every single fighter Jack Dempsey and Joe Louis fought as champions, and before we were done, by the laws of collected evidence, he had bludgeoned the court into accepting, against its better judgment, that Pete Rademacher was the equal of Buddy Baer, Tom McNeeley of Luis Firpo, Hurricane Jackson of Tony Galento, and that Brian London riding his much underrated bicycle could have taken a decision from Bill Brennan.

Jacobs was much too much for me. I quit. "I'm telling you," said Cus D'Amato, having enjoyed this vastly, "he beats me all the time in arguments."

While this had been going on, two small Negroes looking like starchy divinity students had been glowering at me and my arguments. Every time I said something which was not altogether in praise of Patterson, they looked back as if I were a member of the White Citizens Council. I never did get a chance to find out who they were, or what they represented (Jacobs was keeping me much too busy), but one could lay odds they were working for one of the more dogmatic Negro organizations devoted to the uplift of the race. They had none of the humor of the few Freedom Riders I had met, or the personal attractiveness some of the young Negroes around Martin Luther King seemed to have. No, these were bigots. They could have believed in anything from the Single Tax to the Brotherhood of Sleeping Car Porters for all I knew, but they were dead-eyed to any voice which did not give assent to what they believed already. So it was depressing to find them in Patterson's camp, and thus devoted to him. It fit with the small-trade-   .
union bigotry that hung over this establishment.

Outside, in the air, the view while dull was not so dogmatic. Sammy Taub, the radio announcer of my childhood, had a voice full of an old Jew's love for Patterson. "Oh, Floyd's got the real class," said Mr. Taub, "he's a gentleman. I've seen a lot of fighters, but Floyd's the gentleman of them all. I could tell you things about him, about how nice he is. He's going to take that big loudmouth Liston apart, punch by punch. And I'm going to be there to watch it!" he said with a grin and an old announcer's windup.

Next morning I spent more time with D'Amato on the way to Liston's camp. We went together in the limousine. It was the day before the fight, and D'Amato was going out as Patterson's representative to check on the gloves. There had been trouble with this already: D'Amato had objected to Liston's plan to wear a pair of gloves made by a Chicago manufacturer named Frager. It seems the eight-ounce Everlast gloves with curled horsehair for padding had not been large enough to fit Liston's hand. So his manager, Jack Nilon, had come up with gloves which had foam-rubber padding. D'Amato objected. His argument was that Liston's knuckles could punch closer to the surface of the glove riding in foam rubber than in horse-hair. The unspoken aim must have been to irritate Liston.

But one couldn't encourage D'Amato to talk about the challenger. D'Amato talked only about his own fighters. How he talked! He had stopped drinking years ago and so had enormous pent-up vitality. As a talker, he was one of the world's great weight lifters, not brilliant, but powerful, non-stop, and very solid. Talk was muscle. If you wanted to interrupt, you had to bend his arm off.

Under the force, however, he had a funny simple quality, something of that passionate dogmatism which some men develop when they have been, by their own count, true to their principles. He had the enthusiastic man-ner of a saint who is all works and no contemplation. His body was short and strong, his head was round, and his silver-white hair was cut in a short brush. He seemed to bounce as he talked. He reminded me of a cer-tain sort of very tough Italian kid one used to find in Brooklyn. They were sweet kids, and rarely mean, and they were fearless, at least by the measure of their actions they were fearless. They would fight anybody. Size, age, repu-tation did not make them hesitate. Because they were very single-minded, however, they were often the butt of the gang, and proved natural victims for any practical jokes. Afterward everyone would hide. They were the kind of kids who would go berserk if you were their friend or their leader and be-trayed them. They would literally rip up a sewer grating or a manhole cover in order to beat their way a little closer to you.

I was certain he had been this kind of kid, and later I heard a story that when D'Amato was little, he started once to walk through a small park at night and saw a huge shape waiting for him in the distance. He said he had the feeling he could not turn back. If he did, he would never be able to go near that park again. So he continued down the path. The huge shape was discovered to be a tree. D'Amato's critics would claim that he spent his en-tire life being brave with trees.

The likelihood, however, is that for a period D'Amato was one of the bravest men in America. He was a fanatic about boxing, and cared little about money. He hated the Mob. He stood up to them. A prizefight man-ager running a small gym with broken mirrors on East Fourteenth Street does not usually stand up for the Mob, any more than a chambermaid would tell the Duchess of Windsor to wipe her shoes before she enters her suite at the Waldorf.

D'Amato was the exception, however. The Mob ended by using two words to describe him: "He's crazy." The term is given to men who must be killed. Nobody killed D'Amato. For years, like a monk, he slept in the back room of his gym with a police dog for a room-mate. The legend is that he kept a gun under his pillow. During Patterson's last few weeks of training before fighting Archie Moore for the championship in 1956, a fight he was to win in five rounds, D'Amato bunked on a cot in front of the door to Floyd's room. He was certain that with the championship so close to them the Mob would try to hurt his fighter. What a movie this would have made. It could have ended with a zoom-away shot of the Mob in a burning barn.

The trial of it is that the story goes on. D'Amato was one of the most stubborn men in America. And he was determined that no fighter connected to the Mob in any way would get to fight Floyd. The only trouble was that the good heavyweights in America had managers who were not ready to irritate the men who ran boxing. If they took a match with Patterson, and he defeated their fighter, how could their ex-contender ever get a fight on television again? D'Amato may have had the vision of a Lenin—as he said with a grin, "They're always calling me a Communist"—but he never could get enough good managers to begin his new party. Patterson, who was conceivably the best young heavyweight in history at the moment he won the championship, now began to be wasted. He was an artist, and an artist is no greater than his material. The fighters D'Amato got for him now were without luster. So were the fights. After a few years, D'Amato's enemies began to spread the canard best calculated to alienate Patterson. They said D'Amato got him nothing but cripples to fight because Patterson was not good enough to go into the ring with a real heavyweight. To a champion who even now would look for a training camp which might bear resemblance to Wiltwyck, that charity school for near-delinquent adolescents where he first had learned to fight; to someone like Patterson, who as a child would weep when he was unjustly accused; who would get down and walk along the subway tracks on the Eighth Avenue El at High Street in Brooklyn because he had found a cubbyhole for workmen three feet off the rails where he could conceal himself from the world by pulling an iron door close to over him, lying there in darkness while the trains blasted by with apocalyptic noise; to a man who had been so shy as an adolescent that he could not speak to the thirteen-year-old girl who was later to become his wife and so brought a fast-talking friend along to fill the silence; who as a teen-age fighter, just beginning to go to the gym, was so delicate that his older brother Frank once told the reporter Lester Bromberg, "I can't get used to my kid brother being a name fighter. I remember him as the boy who would cry if I hit him too hard when we boxed in the gym"; to a champion who as a young professional had refused to look while his next opponent, Chester Mieszala, was sparring at Chicago's Midtown Gym because he considered it to be taking unfair advantage; to a man who would later sit in shame in a dark room for months after losing his championship to Johansson, the canard that he was a weak heavyweight kept in possession of his kingdom by the determination of his manager never to make a good fight must have been a story to taste like quicklime in his throat. Patterson had put his faith in D'Amato. If D'Amato didn't believe in him . . . It's the sort of story which belongs on radio at eleven in the morning or three in the afternoon.

The aftermath of the first Johansson fight, however, blew out the set. It was discovered that D'Amato directly or indirectly had gotten money for the promotion through a man named "Fat Tony" Salerno. D'Amato claimed to have been innocent of the connection, and indeed it was a most aesthetic way for the Mob to get him. It's equally possible that after years of fighting every windmill in town, D'Amato had come down to the hard Bolshevistic decision that you don't make an omelet without breaking eggs. Whatever the fact, D'Amato had his license suspended in New York. He was not allowed to work in Floyd's corner the night of the second Johansson fight. And thereafter Patterson kept him away. He gave D'Amato his managerial third of the money, but he didn't let him get too close to training.

If this partnership of Patterson and D'Amato had been made in Heaven, then God or man had failed again. The last sad item was the Liston fight. Patterson had delegated D'Amato to make some of the arrangements. According to the newspapers, Patterson then discovered that D'Amato was trying to delay the negotiations. Now D'Amato was accepted in camp only as a kind of royal jester who could entertain reporters with printable stories. He seemed to be kept in the cabin where I met him at the foot of the hill, forbidden access to the gymnasium the way a drunk is eighty-sixed from his favorite bar. It must have been a particularly Italian humiliation for a man like D'Amato to sit in that cabin and talk to journalists. There were any number of fight reporters who could not go into court and swear they had never had a free meal from the Mob. Some of the food may have been filet mignon. At least so one might judge by the violence of their printed reactions to D'Amato. A reporter can never forgive anyone he has attacked unjustly. Now D'Amato had to receive these cigar butts like a baron demoted to a concierge. He could speak, but he could not act.

Speak he did. If you listened to D'Amato talk, and knew nothing other, you would not get the impression D'Amato was no longer the center of Patterson's camp. He seemed to give off no sense whatever of having lost his liaison to Floyd. When he talked of making the Liston fight, one would never have judged he had tried to prevent it.

"I didn't," he swore to me. "I wanted the fight. Floyd came up to me, and said, 'Cus, you got to make this fight. Liston's going around saying I'm too yellow to fight him. I don't care if a fighter says he can beat me, but no man can say I'm yellow.'" D'Amato bobbed his head. "Then Floyd said, 'Cus, if this fight isn't made, I'll be scared to go out. I'll be afraid to walk into a restaurant and see Liston eating. Because if I see him, I'll have a fight with him right there in the restaurant, and I'll kill him.' I wouldn't try to keep Floyd from having a fight after he says something like that!" said D'Amato.

We were now arriving at Aurora Downs. The limousine took a turn off the highway, went down a blacktop road and then went through a gate onto a dirt road. There was a quick view of a grandstand and part of a small abandoned racetrack. Under the grandstand, the challenger's gym had been installed: it was there Liston had jumped rope to the sound of *Night Train,* performing with such hypnotic, suspended rage that the reporters gave most of their space to describe this talent.

We were meeting now in the clubhouse restaurant, its pari-mutuel windows boarded up, its floor empty of tables. It was a cold, chilly room, perhaps a hundred feet long, roped off at the rear to give privacy to Liston's quarters, and the surfaces all seemed made of picture-window glass, chromium, linoleum, and pastel plastics like Formica. The most prominent decorations were two cold-drink vending machines, side by side, large as telephone booths. They were getting small play from the reporters because the day was dank, one of those grey September days which seem to seep up from Lake Michigan and move west. As many as a hundred of us must have come out in our various limousines to see the finale of Everlast vs. Frager, and we gathered in an irritable circle, scrimmaging four and five deep for a view of the scales, an ordinary pair of office scales for small packages, and of two pairs of gloves on a plain wooden table. Disappointed with how I came out in the scrimmage, I pulled back far enough to stand on a chair. The view was now good. A thin man in a green sweater, a man with a long, hungry nose and a pocked, angry skin still alive from an adolescence where one hot boil had doubtless burst upon another, was now screaming at everybody in sight, at D'Amato whom he seemed ready to attack, at Nick Florio, brother of Dan Florio, Patterson's trainer, and at a man named Joe Triner who belonged to the Illinois State Athletic Commission. It developed he was Jack Nilon, Liston's manager or adviser, a Philadelphia caterer, wealthy in his own right, who had been brought together with Liston by various beneficent forces in Philadelphia who decided Sonny needed rehabilitation in his front window as much as in his heart. So Nilon represented American business, acting once again as big brother to a former convict with talent. How Nilon could scream! It turned out, bang-bang, that the new gloves for Liston were a fraction over eight ounces. Nilon was having none of that. Triner, the Commission man, looked sick. "They weighed eight ounces at the Commission's office today," he said.

"Don't give me none of that," screamed Nilon. "They got to weigh in right here. How do I know what kind of scale you use?"

"What do we want to cheat you on a quarter of an ounce for?" asked Triner.

"Just to get Sonny upset, just to get Sonny upset, that's all," screamed Nilon as if he were pouring boiling oil.

Liston now emerged from the depths of the clubhouse and walked slowly toward us. He was wearing a dark-blue sweat suit, and he moved with the languid pleasure of somebody who is getting the taste out of every step. First his heel went down, then his toe. He could not have enjoyed it more if he had been walking barefoot through a field. One could watch him picking the mood up out of his fingertips and toes. His handlers separated before him. He was a Presence.

"What the hell's going on?" Liston asked. He had a deep growl of a voice, rich, complex, well-modulated. His expression had the sort of holy disdain one finds most often on a very grand old lady.

They started to explain to him, and he nodded petulantly, half listening to the arguments. His expression seemed to say, "Which one of these bullshit artists is most full of it right now?"

While he was listening he pulled on one of the gloves, worked his fist about in it, and then slapped the glove down on the table. "It still don't fit," he cried out in the angry voice of a child. Everybody moved back a little. He stood there in disgust, but wary, alert, as if some deep enemy were in the room, someone who could damage him with a psychic bullet. His eyes bounced lightly, gracefully, from face to face. Which gave the opportunity to see into them for a moment. From the advance publicity one had expected to look into two cracks of dead glass, halfway between reptile and sleepy leopard, but they had the dark, brimming, eloquent, reproachful look one sees sometimes in the eyes of beautiful colored children, three or four years old. And in fact that was the shock of the second degree which none of the photographs had prepared one for: Liston was near to beautiful. For obvious reasons it is an unhappy word to use. But there is no other to substitute. One cannot think of more than a few men who have beauty. Charles Chaplin has it across a room, Krishna Menon across a table. Stephen Spender used to have it, Burt Lancaster oddly enough used to have it—there was no comparison between the way he looked in a movie and the way he looked in life. They say Orson Welles had it years ago, and President Eisenhower in person, believe it or not. At any rate, Liston had it. You did not feel you were looking at someone attractive, you felt you were looking at a creation. And this creation looked like it was building into a temper which would tear up the clubhouse at Aurora Downs. One knew he was acting, no contender would get violent the day before a championship fight, and yet everyone in the room was afraid of Liston. Even D'Amato did not speak too much, Liston had the stage and was using it. "Let's see that glove, let's weigh it again." They leaped to put it on the scales for him. He squatted and made a huge dumb show of scowling at the numbers as if he were just another blighted cotton picker. "Sheeet, who can read the numbers," he pretended to be saying to himself.

"He's not going in the ring with gloves over regulation weight," shouted another dragon, Pollino, the cut man for Liston, a lean Italian with an angry, chopped-up face.

"Well, this scale isn't the official scale," said D'Amato mildly. "The gloves are eight ounces."

Pollino looked like he'd leap across the table to get his hands on D'Amato's neck. "Wha' do you call official scale?" shouted Pollino. "There is no official scale. I'll bet you thousand dollars they're more than eight ounces."

Nilon came in like a shrike from the other side of Liston. "Why do you bother my fighter with this?" he screamed at the officials. "Why don't you go over to Patterson's camp and bother him the day before the fight? What's he doing? Sleeping? He doesn't have a hundred reporters looking down his throat."

"I don't want to stand much more of this," snapped Liston in the child's voice he used for display of temper. "This is the sort of thing gives reporters a chance to ask stupid questions." Was his dislike of reporters a reminder of the days when four or five policemen would have given him a going-over in a police station while the police reporter listening to the muffled thuds, would be playing cards in the next room? Liston did not talk to white reporters individually. At Press Headquarters the bitter name for him was Malcolm X. "Just stupid questions, that's all," he repeated, and yet his manner was changing still again. His mood could shift as rapidly as the panoramic scenes in a family film. Suddenly he was mild, now he was mild. He tapped the gloves on the table, and said in a gentle voice, "Oh, they're all right. Let's use them." Then lightly, sadly, he chuckled, and added in his richest voice, "I'm going to hit him so hard that extra quarter of an ounce isn't gonna be any more than just an extra quarter of an ounce he's being hit with." The voice came home to me. I knew which voice it was at last. It was the voice Clark Gable used his last ten years, that genial rum squire's voice, the indulgent "I've been around" voice. Headmasters in prep schools sometimes have it. Liston had it. He must have studied Gable over the years. Perhaps in the movies one sees in prison.

A little more bickering went on between Pollino and Florio. They were like guerrilla troops who have not heard that the armistice has been declared. Then quiet. We were done. But just as the meet was ready to break, Liston held up a hand and said, "I don't want to wear these gloves. I've changed my mind. We've had a special pair made for me. Bring the new gloves over." And he glowered at the officials and dropped his upper lip.

It was a very bad moment for the officials.

Two assistants marched in carrying a white boxing glove. It was half the size of a shark. A toot of relief went up from the press. Liston grinned. As photographers rushed to take his picture once more, he held the great white glove in his hands and studied it with solemnity.

When we got back to the car, D'Amato smiled. "Very unusual fellow," he said. "He's more intelligent than I thought. Good sense of humor."

I made a small speech in which I declared that Liston made me think not so much of a great fighter as of a great actor who was playing the role of the greatest heavyweight fighter who ever lived.

D'Amato listened attentively. We were in a space age, and the opinions of moon men and Martians had also to be considered. "Sonny's a good fighter," he said finally.

Then we talked of other things. I mentioned my four daughters. D'Amato came from a family of seven brothers. "I guess that's why I never got married," he said. "I don't know, I never could figure it out. No dame could ever get me. I wonder why?"

"A lady once told me she'd never marry a man she couldn't change."

"It's just as well I didn't get married," said D'Amato.

On the night of the fight I shared a cab to Comiskey Park with Pete Hamill of the New York *Post*. We caught a cabdriver who was for Patterson, and this worked to spoil the ride. As the fight approached, Hamill and I had been growing nervous in a pleasant way, we were feeling that mixture of apprehension and anticipation which is one of the large pleasures of going to a big fight. Time slows down, the senses become keyed, one's nose for magic is acute.

Such a mood had been building in each of us over the afternoon. About five we had gone to the Playboy Club with Gene Courtney of the Philadelphia *Inquirer*, and it had looked about the way one thought it would look. It was full of corporation executives, and after cancer gulch, the colors were lush, plum colors, velvet reds with the blood removed, a dash of cream, the flesh-orange and strawberry wine of a peach melba, Dutch chocolate colors, champagne colors, the beige of an onion in white wine sauce. The bunnies went by in their costumes, electric-blue silk, Kelly-green, flame-pink, pinups from a magazine, faces painted into sweetmeats, flower tops, tame lynx, piggie, poodle, a queen or two from a beauty contest. They wore a Gay-Nineties rig which exaggerated their hips, bound their waist in a ceinture, and lifted them into a phallic brassiere— each breast looked like the big bullet on the front bumper of a Cadillac. Long black stockings, long long stockings, up almost to the waist on each side, and to the back, on the curve of the can, as if ejected tenderly from the body, was the puff of chastity, a little white ball of a bunny's tail which bobbled as they walked. We were in bossland.

We drank, standing at the bar, talking about fights and fighters, and after a while we came to the fight we were to see that evening. Courtney had picked Liston by a knockout in the fifth, Hamill and I independently had arrived at Patterson in the sixth. So we had a mock fight to pay for a round of drinks. Courtney had bought a cigarette lighter in the Club—it was a slim, inexpensive black lighter with a white rabbit's face painted on the surface. When we put the lighter flat on the table and gave it a twirl, the ears would usually come to rest pointing toward one of us. We agreed that each spin would be a single round, and each time one ear pointed at Courtney or at me, it would count as a knockdown against our fighter. If both ears pointed at one of us, that would be the knockout.

Well, Liston knocked Patterson down in the first round. In the second round the ears pointed at no one. In the third round Patterson knocked Liston down. For the fourth, Liston dropped Patterson. "The fifth is the round," said Courtney, spinning the lighter. It went around and around and ended with one ear pointing at me. Liston had knocked Patterson down again, but had not knocked him out. I took the lighter and gave it a spin. The ears pointed at Courtney. Both ears. Patterson had knocked Liston out in the sixth round.

"Too much," said Hamill.

I had given an interview the day before to Leonard Shecter of the *Post*. I had said: "I think Liston is going to have Patterson down two, three, four times. And Patterson will have Liston down in the first, second, or third and end it with one punch in the sixth." The cigarette lighter had given me a perfect fight.

Well, the Playboy Club was the place for magic, and this mood of expectation, of omen and portent, stayed with us. All of one's small actions became significant. At the hotel, signaling for the cab which was to take us to the ball park, the choice felt wrong. One had the psychology of a ghost choosing the hearse he would ride to a funeral, or of a general, brain livid after days of combat, so identifying himself with his army that he decides to attack first with the corps on his left because it is his left foot which has stepped first into the command car. It is not madness exactly. It is not madness if Montgomery or Rommel thinks that way. If the world is a war between God and the Devil, and Destiny is the line of their battle, then a general may be permitted to think that God or the Devil or the agent of both, which is Magic, has entered his brain before an irrevocable battle. For why should the gods retire when the issue is great? Such a subject is virtually taboo, one must pass by it quickly, or pass for mad, but I had noticed that whenever I was overtired, a sensitivity to the magical would come into me. I now had had little sleep for ten days, and I had been drinking for the last three: when I was very short of sleep, liquor did not make me drunk so much as it gave a thin exaltation, a sensitivity not unlike the touch of drugs in the old days; it was like gasoline burning an orderly flame in the empty chambers of one's reserve. I think one begins to die a little when one has had but three or four hours of sleep each night for a week; some of the cells must die from overexcitement, some from overwork, and their death must bring some of the consciousness of death, some little part of the deep secret of death into the living, weary brain. So I took the cab because it was the second in line at the hotel, and the first cab had not wished to go to the ball park. But a feeling of gloom came over me as if I had committed a serious error.

The driver, as I have said, was for Patterson. He was a big round Negro about thirty with a pleasant face, sly yet not quite dishonest, but he had a pompous manner which seemed to fill the cab with psychic gas as dead as the exhaust from a bus. He was for Patterson, Hamill was for Patterson, I was for Patterson. We were left with nothing but the search for an imaginary conversationalist to argue for Sonny.

How this driver hated Liston! He went on about him at length, most of it not near to printable. "This guy Liston is no good," said the cabdriver. "I tell you the good Lord is going to look down and stop that man because he isn't worth the flesh and blood and muscle that was put into him. Now I don't care," said the cabdriver, going on comfortably, "that Liston was in prison, some of the best men in this country have come out of the can, I nearly did time myself, but I tell you, I don't like Liston, he's a bully and a hustler, and he's no good, he's no good at all, why if you were walking along the street and you saw a beautiful young child, why what would you think. You'd think, 'What a beautiful child.' That's what Patterson would think. He'd go up to that child and have a pleasant conversation or something, and go away, but what would Liston do, he'd have the same pleasant conversation, and then he'd get to thinking this is an awful good-looking kid, and if it's a good-looking kid it must have a good-looking mother. That man's an opportunist," said the driver severely, "and I tell you how I know, it's because I've been a hustler, I've hustled everything you can hustle, and there isn't anything anybody can tell me about Liston. That hustler is going to get ruined tonight."

Now the trouble with this speech was that it turned out to be as oppressive as it was amusing, and one's fine mood of excessive, even extreme sensitivity began to expire under the dull force of the exposition. It was hopeless to try to explain that Liston, whatever his virtues, however discovered his faults, could not possibly be as simple as the driver described him.

It was a fact, however, that Liston did not seem to be loved by the Negroes one talked to. It was not only the grey-haired Negroes with the silver-rimmed glasses and the dignity of the grave, the teachers, the deacons, the welfare workers, the camp directors, the church organists who were for Patterson, but indeed just about every Negro one talked to in Chicago. One of the pleasures preceding the fight had been to conduct a private poll. Of the twenty Negroes polled by our amateur, all but two or three were unsympathetic to Liston. The word was out—"You got to stick with the champion." I must have heard that phrase a dozen times. Of course the Negroes spoken to were employed; they were taxicab drivers, house servants, bellboys, waiters, college students, young professionals. Some answered cynically. There were a few with that snaky elegance one finds in colored people like Sugar Ray Robinson, and had seen at the fringes of Liston's court out at Aurora, the sort of Negro always seen standing on a key street corner in Harlem, the best-dressed Negro of the intersection. I had assumed they would instinctively be for Liston, and perhaps they were, but I was a strange white man asking questions—there is no need to assume the questions were asked so skillfully or decently that the truth was obliged to appear. Patterson, was the safe reply. It demanded nothing, especially if they were not going to see me again and so would suffer no loss of respect for their judgment. Patterson was a churchgoer, a Catholic convert (and so of course was Liston, but the cynical could remark that a Christmas candle in the window looks nice in a department store), Patterson was up tight with the NAACP, he was the kind of man who would get his picture taken with Jackie Robinson and Ralph Bunche (in fact he looked a little like Ralph Bunche), he would be photographed with Eleanor Roosevelt, and was; with Jack Kennedy, and was; with Adlai Stevenson if he went to the UN; he would campaign with Shelley Winters if she ever ran for Mayor of New York; he was a liberal's liberal. The worst to be said about Patterson is that he spoke with the same cow's cud as other liberals. Think what happens to a man with Patterson's reflexes when his brain starts to depend on the sounds of "introspective," "obligation," "responsibility," "inspiration," "commendation," "frustrated," "seclusion"—one could name a dozen others from his book. They are a part of his pride; he is a boy from the slums of Bedford-Stuyvesant who has acquired these words like stocks and bonds and income-bearing properties. There is no one to tell him it would be better to keep the psychology of the streets than to cultivate the contradictory desire to be a great fighter and a great, healthy, mature, autonomous, related, integrated individual. What a shabby gentility there has been to Patterson's endeavor. The liberals of America had been working for thirty years to create a state of welfare where the deserving could develop themselves. Patterson, as one of the deserving, as one of those who deserve profoundly to be enriched, ends with "introspective." The void in our culture does not know enough to give him "the agen-bite of inwit."

The cynical Negro, talking to a white stranger, would pick Patterson. Yet there was more to it than that. "You got to stick with the champion." They were working, they had jobs, they had something to hold on to; so did Patterson. They would be fierce toward anyone who tried to take what was theirs: family, home, education, property. So too they assumed would Patterson be fierce. They could hardly be expected to consider that the power to keep one's security loses force when it is too secure. Patterson earned $1,825 his first year as a professional fighter, $37,901 his second year, not quite $40,000 his third year when he was fighting main events at Madison Square Garden. By his fourth year, just before he won the title, it was $50,000. Since then he has made more than $3,500,000 in six years. For the Liston fight he would pick up another $2,000,000 from attendance, theatre television, and other rights. The payments would be spread over seventeen years. It was a long way to have come, but the psychic trip was longer. Responsibility, security, and institutional guilt was not necessarily the best tone for the reflexes in his leaping left hook.

But the deepest reason that Negroes in Chicago had for preferring Patterson was that they did not want to enter again the logic of Liston's world. The Negro had lived in violence, had grown in violence, and yet had developed a view of life which gave him life. But its cost was exceptional for the ordinary man. The majority had to live in shame. The demand for courage may have been exorbitant. Now as the Negro was beginning to come into the white man's world, he wanted the logic of the white man's world: annuities, mental hygiene, sociological jargon, committee solutions for the ills of the breast. He was sick of a whore's logic and a pimp's logic, he wanted no more of *mother-wit*, of *smarts*, or *playing the dozens*, of battling for true love into the diamond-hard eyes of every classy prostitute and hustler on the street. The Negro wanted Patterson, because Floyd was the proof a man could be successful and yet be secure. If Liston won, the old torment was open again. A man could be successful *or* he could be secure. He could not have both. If Liston had a saga, the average Negro wanted more of it.

Besides there was always the Mob. Liston had been a strong-arm man for the Mob—they were not so ready to forgive that. He represented the shadow of every bully who had run them off the street when they were children, he was part of the black limousines with four well-dressed men inside, sliding down the dark streets. One did not try to look into the eyes of the men who rode in those limousines.

But there was one reason beyond any other for picking Patterson, and it went deeper than the pretentions of his new dialogue or the professional liberalism of his ideas, his pronouncements or his associates. Patterson was the champion of every lonely adolescent and every man who had been forced to live alone, every protagonist who tried to remain unique in a world whose waters washed apathy and compromise into the pores. He was the hero of all those unsung romantics who walk the street at night seeing the vision of Napoleon while their feet trip over the curb, he was part of the fortitude which could sustain those who lived for principle, those who had gone to war with themselves and ended with discipline. He was the artist. He was the man who could not forgive himself if he gave less than his best chance for perfection. And so he aroused a powerful passion in those lonely people who wanted him to win. He was champion, he was a millionaire, but he was still an archetype of the underdog, an impoverished prince.

And Liston was looking to be king. Liston came from that world where you had no dream but making it, where you trusted no one because your knowledge of evil was too quick to its presence in everyone; Liston came from that world where a man with a dream was a drunk in the gutter, and the best idealism was found in a rabbit's foot blessed by a one-eyed child. Liston was voodoo, Liston was magic, Liston was the pet of the witch doctor; Liston knew that when the gods gathered to watch an event, you kept your mind open to the devils who might work for you. They would come neatly into your eye and paralyze your enemy with their curse. You were their slave, but they were working for you. Yes, Liston was the secret hero of every man who had ever given mouth to a final curse against the dispositions of the Lord and made a pact with Black Magic. Liston was Faust. Liston was the light of every racetrack tout who dug a number on the way to work. He was the hero of every man who would war with destiny for so long as he had his gimmick: the cigarette smoker, the lush, the junkie, the tea-head, the fixer, the bitch, the faggot, the switchblade, the gun, the corporation executive. Anyone who was fixed on power. It was due to Liston's style of fighting as much as anything else. He had no extreme elegance as a boxer, he was a hint slow, indeed he may not have been a natural boxer as was Patterson, but Liston had learned much and attached it to his large physical strength, he had a long and abnormally powerful left jab, a pounding left hook, a heavy right. He had lead in his fists. The only man who had ever defeated him, a club fighter named Marty Marshall, had said, "Every time he hit me, it hurt all over." In his last twenty-five fights Liston had knocked out the other man twenty-one times. So his force appealed to those who had enlisted with an external force. At the Playboy Club, drinking with Courtney and Hamill, I made a bet with a former Harvard man (Business School, no doubt), who told me Liston had it made. He put up fifty against my twenty-eight and we left the money in the bartender's till. I was not to go back.

So it approached. The battle of good and evil, that curious battle where decision is rare and never clear. As we got out of the cab, several blocks from Comiskey Park, two little Negroes, nine or ten years old, danced up to us in the dark, the light of a Halloween candle in their eye. "Give me silver," one of them cried in a Caribbean voice, "give silver, sir," and left us with an orange piece of paper, a throwaway from a nightclub. "Come to Club Jerico after the Fight," said the misspelled legend. "Come to Club Jerico." Je-rico. I—rich.

III

On the afternoon of the night Emile Griffith and Benny Paret were to fight a third time for the welterweight championship, there was murder in both camps. "I hate that kind of guy," Paret had said earlier to Pete Hamill about Griffith. "A fighter's got to look and talk and act like a man." One of the Broadway gossip columnists had run an item about Griffith a few days before. His girl friend saw it and said to Griffith, "Emile, I didn't know about you being that way." So Griffith hit her. So he said. Now at the weigh-in that morning, Paret had insulted Griffith irrevocably, touching him on the buttocks, while making a few more remarks about his manhood. They almost had their fight on the scales.

The accusation of homosexuality arouses a major passion in many men; they spend their lives resisting it with a biological force. There is a kind of man who spends every night of his life getting drunk in a bar, he rants, he brawls, he ends in a small rumble on the street; women say, "For God's sakes, he's homosexual. Why doesn't he just turn queer and get his suffering over with." Yet men protect him. It is because he is choosing not to become homosexual. It was put best by Sartre who said that a homosexual is a man who practices homosexuality. A man who does not, is not homosexual—he is entitled to the dignity of his choice. He is entitled to the fact that he chose not to become homosexual, and is paying presumably his price.

The rage in Emile Griffith was extreme. I was at the fight that night, I had never seen a fight like it. It was scheduled for fifteen rounds, but they fought without stopping from the bell which began the round to the bell which ended it, and then they fought after the bell, sometimes for as much as fifteen seconds before the referee could force them apart.

Paret was a Cuban, a proud club fighter who had become welterweight champion because of his unusual ability to take a punch. His style of fighting was to take three punches to the head in order to give back two. At the end of ten rounds, he would still be bouncing, his opponent would have a headache. But in the last two years, over the fifteen-round fights, he had started to take some bad maulings.

This fight had its turns. Griffith won most of the early rounds, but Paret knocked Griffith down in the sixth. Griffith had trouble getting up, but made it, came alive and was dominating Paret again before the round was over. Then Paret began to wilt. In the middle of the eighth round, after a clubbing punch had turned his back to Griffith, Paret walked three disgusted steps away, showing his hindquarters. For a champion, he took much too long to turn back around. It was the first hint of weakness Paret had ever shown, and it must have inspired a particular shame, because he fought the rest of the fight as if he were seeking to demonstrate that he could take more punishment than any man alive. In the twelfth, Griffith caught him. Paret got trapped in a corner. Trying to duck away, his left arm and his head became tangled on the wrong side of the top rope. Griffith was in like a cat ready to rip the life out of a huge boxed rat. He hit him eighteen right hands in a row, an act which took perhaps three or four seconds, Griffith making a pent-up whimpering sound all the while he attacked, the right hand whipping like a piston rod which has broken through the crankcase, or like a baseball bat demolishing a pumpkin. I was sitting in the second row of that corner—they were not ten feet away from me, and like everybody else, I was hypnotized. I had never seen one man hit another so hard and so many times. Over the referee's face came a look of woe as if some spasm had passed its way through him, and then he leaped on Griffith to pull him away. It was the act of a brave man. Griffith was uncontrollable. His trainer leaped into the ring, his manager, his cut man, there were four people holding Griffith, but he was off on an orgy, he had left the Garden, he was back on a hoodlum's street. If he had been able to break loose from his handlers and the referee, he would have jumped Paret to the floor and whaled on him there.

And Paret? Paret died on his feet. As he took those eighteen punches something happened to everyone who was in psychic range of the event. Some part of his death reached out to us. One felt it hover in the air. He was still standing in the ropes, trapped as he had been before, he gave some little half-smile of regret, as if he were saying, "I didn't know I was going to die just yet," and then, his head leaning back but still erect, his death came to breathe about him. He began to pass away. As he passed, so his limbs descended beneath him, and he sank slowly to the floor. He went down more slowly than any fighter had ever gone down, he went down like a large ship which turns on end and slides second by second into its grave. As he went down, the sound of Griffith's punches echoed in the mind like a heavy ax in the distance chopping into a wet log.

Paret lay on the ground, quivering gently, a small froth on his mouth. The house doctor jumped into the ring. He knelt. He pried Paret's eyelid open. He looked at the eyeball staring out. He let the lid snap shut. He reached into his satchel, took out a needle, jabbed Paret with a stimulant. Paret's back rose in a high arch. He writhed in real agony. They were calling him back from death. One wanted to cry out, "Leave the man alone. Let him die." But they saved Paret long enough to take him to a hospital where he lingered for days. He was in coma. He never came out of it. If he lived, he would have been a vegetable. His brain was smashed. But they held him in life for a week, they fed him chemicals, and made exploratory operations into his skull, and fed details of his condition to The Goat. And The Goat kicked clods of mud all over the place, and spoke harshly of prohibiting boxing. There was shock in the land. Children had seen the fight on television. There were editorials, gloomy forecasts that the Game was dead. The managers and the prizefighters got together. Gently, in thick, depressed hypocrisies, they tried to defend their sport. They did not find it easy to explain that they shared an unstated view of life which was religious.

It was of course not that religion which is called Judeo-Christian. It was an older religion, a more primitive one—a religion of blood, a murderous and sensitive religion which mocks the effort of the understanding to approach it, and scores the lungs of men like D. H. Lawrence, and burns the brain of men like Ernest Hemingway when they explore out into the mystery, searching to discover some part of the secret. It is the view of life which looks upon death as a condition which is more alive than life or unspeakably more deadening. As such it is not a very attractive notion to the Establishment. But then the Establishment has nothing very much of even the Judeo-Christian tradition. It has a respect for legal and administrative aspects of justice, and it is devoted to the idea of compassion for the poor. But the Establishment has no idea of death, no tolerance for Heaven or Hell, no comprehension of bloodshed. It sees no logic in pain. To the Establishment these notions are a detritus from the past.

Like a patient submerged beneath the plastic cover of an oxygen tent, boxing lives on beneath the cool, bored eyes of the doctors in the Establishment. It would not take too much to finish boxing off. Shut down the oxygen, which is to say, turn that switch in the mass media which still gives sanction to organized pugilism, and the fight game would be dead.

But the patient is permitted to linger for fear the private detectives of the Establishment, the psychiatrists and psychoanalysts, might not be able to neutralize the problem of gang violence. Not so well as the Game. Of course, the moment some piece of diseased turnip capable of being synthesized cheaply might prove to have the property of tranquilizing a violent young man for a year, the Establishment would wipe out boxing. Every time a punk was arrested, the police would prescribe a pill, and violence would walk the street sheathed and numb. Of course the Mob would lose revenue, but then the Mob is also part of the Establishment, it, and the labor unions and the colleges and the newspapers and the corporations are all part of the Establishment. The Establishment is never simple. It needs the Mob to grease the chassis on its chariot. Therefore, the Mob would be placated. In a society with strong central government, it is not so difficult to turn up a new source of revenue. What is more difficult is to enter the plea that violence may be an indispensable element of life. This is not the place to have the argument: it is enough to say that if the liberal Establishment is right in its unstated credo that death is a void, and man leads out his life suspended momentarily above that void, why then there is no argument at all. Whatever shortens life is monstrous. We have not the right to shorten life, since life is the only possession of the psyche, and in death we have only nothingness. What then can there be said in defense of sports-car racing, war, or six-ounce gloves?

But if we go from life into a death which is larger than our life has been, or into a death which is small, if death comes to nothing for one man because he swallowed his death in his life, and if for another death is alive with dimension, then the certitudes of the Establishment lose power. A drug which offers peace to a pain may dull the nerve which could have taught the mind how to carry that pain into the death which comes on the next day or on the decades that follow. A tranquilizer gives coma to an anxiety which may later smell of the dungeon, beneath the ground. If we are born into life as some living line of intent from an eternity which may have tortured us or nurtured us in death, then we may be obliged to go back to death with more courage and art than we left it. Or face the dim end of going back with less.

That is the existential venture, the unstated religious view of boxers trying to beat each other into unconsciousness or, ultimately, into death. It is the culture of the killer who sickens the air about him if he does not find some half-human way to kill a little in order not to deaden all. It is a defense against the plague, against that plague which comes from violence converted into the nausea of all that nonviolence which is void of peace. Paret's death was with horror, but not all the horror was in the beating, much was in the way his death was cheated. Which is to say that his death was twice a nightmare. I knew that something in boxing was spoiled forever for me, that there would be a fear in watching a fight now which was like the fear one felt for any *novillero* when he was having an unhappy day, the bull was dangerous, and the crowd was ugly. You knew he would get hurt. There is fascination in seeing that the first time, but it is not as enjoyable as one expects. It is like watching a novelist who has written a decent book get run over by a car.

Something in boxing was spoiled. But not the principle, not the right for one man to try to knock another out in the ring. That was perhaps not a civilized activity, but it belonged to the tradition of the humanist, it was a human activity, it showed a part of what man was like, it belonged to his ability to create art and artful movement on the edge of death or pain or danger or attack, and it had much to say about the subtleties of human style. For there are boxers whose bodies move like a fine brain, and there are others who pound the opposition down with the force of a trade-union leader, there are fools and wits and patient craftsmen among boxers, wild men full of a sense of outrage, and steady oppressive peasants, clever spoilers, dogged infantrymen who walk forward all night, hypnotists (like Liston), dancers, liners, mothers giving a scolding, horsemen high on their legs. There is knowledge to be found about our nature, and the nature of animals, of big cats, lions, tigers, gorillas, bears, walruses (Archie Moore), birds, elephants, jackals, bulls. No, I was not down on boxing, but I loved it with freedom no longer. It was more like somebody in your family was fighting now. And the feeling one had for a big fight was no longer clear of terror in its excitement. There was awe in the suspense.

But then there is nothing else very much like being at a Heavyweight Championship fight. It is to some degree the way a Hollywood premiere once ought to have been; it's a big party with high action—there is the same rich flush of jewelry, bourbon, bare shoulders, cha-cha, silk, the promise that a life or two will be changed by tonight; it is even a bit like a political convention; it is much more like an event none of us will ever see—conceive of sitting in a classic arena waiting for a limited war with real bullets to begin between a platoon of Marines and two mounted squads of Russian Cossacks—you'd have the sensation of what a Heavyweight Championship can promise. A great heavyweight fight could take place in the center of a circus.

Ideally, it should take place in New York. Because Broadway turns out and Hollywood flies in with Las Vegas on the hip, and many of the wings and dovecotes and banlieues of what even a couple of years ago was called Café Society is there, and International Set (always seeing their first fight), and Big Business, and every good-looking call girl in New York, and some not so good-looking, and all the figures from the history pages of prize-fighting in America, as well as ghosts there are some to claim—the ghost of Benny Leonard, the ghost of Harry Greb. Plus all the models, loose celebrities, socialites of high and lower rank, hierarchies from the racetrack, politicians, judges, and—one might offer a prayer if one really cared—one sociologist of wit and distinction ought to be there to capture for America the true status of its conflicting aristocracies: does Igor Cassini rate with Mickey Rooney or does Roger Blough get a row in front of Elizabeth Taylor? Is Frank Sinatra honored before Mrs. Woodward? Does Zsa Zsa Gabor come in ahead of Mayor Wagner? The First Sociologists of America are those professionals who sell the hot seats for a big fight in New York.

In Chicago, there was little of this. If there are nine circles to Hell, there were nine clouds over this fight. D'Amato was not licensed to manage in New York. Small matter. Patterson once again would fight in New York without him. But Liston was not cleared to fight by the State Boxing Commission—the shadow of the Establishment lay against him. So the fight was transferred to Chicago which promptly took fire. If Patterson-Liston was not clean enough for New York, it was not cool enough for Chicago. The local newspapers gave the kind of publicity one tastes in cold canned food. The stories on training were buried. Interest was greater outside the city than within. Yet little of Broadway arrived and less of Hollywood. You cannot get producers and movie stars to travel a distance to watch two Negroes fight. A bitch lives to see a white man fight a black man. She's not prejudiced—depending on the merits, she'll root for either, but a Negro against a Negro wets no juice.

And then there was poor weather. The day before the fight was misty, chilly. It rained on and off, and cleared inconclusively on Tuesday, which was cold. Fight night was cold enough to wear a topcoat. Comiskey Park was far from filled. It could hold fifty thousand for a big fight; it ended with less than twenty in paid admissions. Twenty-six thousand people showed. Proportions were poor. Because of theatre television, Patterson would make more money on this fight than any fighter had ever made, and there was much local interest in cities all over America. Parties were got up to go to the theatre, see it on television. The press coverage was larger than average, larger let us say than any of the three Johansson fights or the Marciano-Walcott fights. It was the biggest fight in ten years, it was conceivably the

biggest fight since Louis fought Schmeling the second time, and yet nobody in the city where it was fought seemed to care. Radio, with its roaring inside hysteria, had lost to television that grey eminence which now
instructed Americans in the long calm of Ecclesiastes: vanity of vanities, all
events are vanity.

So for a celebrity hunter, ringside was nothing formidable at this fight.
The good people of Chicago turned out modestly. The very good people—
which is to say, the very rich—turned out for ringside, and had a chance
to cross the outfield grass, luminous green in the half-light of the baseball
towers, and walk to their seats under the great folded wings of the grandstand. Ever since the Romans built the Colosseum, arenas take on a pre-
historic breath at night—one could be a black ant walking inside the circle
a pterodactyl must have made with its wing as it slept. Or is it hills like dark
elephants of which we speak?

I had a seat in the working press five rows from the ring. An empty seat
away was Jimmy Baldwin. There had been a chill between us in the last
year. Not a feud, but bad feeling. We had been glad, however, to see each
other in Chicago. Tacitly, settling no differences, not talking about it, we
had thought to be friendly. But the unsettled differences were still there.
Two nights ago, at a party, we had had a small fight. We each insulted
the other's good intentions and turned away. Now we sat with a hundred-
pound cake of ice on the empty seat between us. After ten minutes, I got up
and went for a walk around the ring.

The Press section occupied the first six rows. Back of us was an aisle
which made a larger square around the square of the ring. On the other
side of this aisle was the first row of ringside seats. This was as close as you
could come to the fight if you had entered by buying a ticket. So I took a
sampling of the house as I walked around the square. If this had been New
York, you would expect to find twelve movie stars in the front row. But this
was Chicago. Behind us were a muster of local Irish politicians, big men
physically in the mold of Jimmy Braddock, not unhappy tonight with their
good seats.

The front row to my right and the front row across the ring from me
was given over in part to the Mob. They were the most intricate faces one
would find this side of Carpaccio or Bellini, chins with hooks and chisels,
nostrils which seemed to screw the air up into the head, thin-lipped mouths
like thin-nosed pliers, eyes which behind their dark glasses scrutinized your

interior until they could find the tool in you which would work for them, and then would flip away like the turning of a card. Yes, those two rows of seats made up a right angle of *don capos* and a few very special Catholic priests, thin, ascetic, medieval in appearance, as well as a number of field officers dressed in black like subalterns, but older, leaner, with more guilds at their command. They were well-seated. They filled close to every seat around the corner.

It proved to be Patterson's corner.

That was art. They did not have to do much more. Sitting there, they could devote their study to Patterson. He would see them when he came back to his corner, his seconds would be obliged to look at them each time a new round began and they climbed down the steps from the corner. The back of the cornermen's necks would be open to detailed inspection, the calves of Patterson's leg, as he sat resting on the stool, would be a ready target for mental arrows. Like Lilliputians they could shoot thousands of pins into Gulliver.

I completed the tour. The last row, Liston's corner, was routine: muscle-men, mobsters, business-sporting, a random sample. Turning the angle I came back to my seat, and sat watching a preliminary, shivering a little in the cold. It was much too cold for a fight. The sensitivity to magic I had felt earlier in the evening would not come back. There was just a dull sense of apprehension. Everything was wrong.

The preliminaries ended. Visiting fighters were called up from the crowd to take a bow. Archie Moore drew a large hand: he was wearing a black-silk cape with a white lining and he twirled the cape with éclat. It said: "Go away, all solemn sorcerers, the magic man is here."

Patterson and Liston arrived within a minute of each other. The visiting fighters who were gathered in the ring said hello to each man, shook their gloves, and went back to their seats.

The Star-Spangled Banner was played. Liston stood in his corner with his handlers, the referee stood in the middle of the ring, and Cus D'Amato stood alone, eight feet away from Patterson and his seconds. Since D'Amato was across from me, I could see his face clearly. It was as pale as his white sweater. His face was lifted to the sky, his eyes were closed. While the anthem played, D'Amato held his hand to his heart as if he were in anguish. I had the impression he was praying with fear.

The anthem ended, the fighters took their instructions from the referee, and stripped their robes. Their bodies made a contrast. Liston, only an inch taller than Patterson, weighed 214 pounds to Patterson's 189. But the difference was not just in weight. Liston had a sleek body, fully muscled, but round. It was the body of a strong man, but the muscles looked to have been shaped by pleasure as much as by work. He was obviously a man who had had some very good times.

Whereas Patterson still had poverty in his muscles. He was certainly not weak, there was whipcord in the way he was put together, but it was still the dry, dedicated body of an athlete, a track man, a disciplinarian: it spoke little of leisure and much of the gym. There was a lack eating at it, some misery.

The bell rang

Liston looked scared.

Patterson looked grim.

They came together with no vast impact, trying for small gains. Each was moving with large respect for the other. Liston had the unhappy sweaty look in his eye of the loudest-talking champion on a city block—he has finally gotten into a fight with one of the Juniors, and he knows this Junior can fight. If he loses he's got much to lose. So Liston was trying to make Junior keep distance.

Patterson was not doing much. He threw a fast left hook which missed, then he circled a bit, fighting from a crouch. He lunged in once very low, trying to get under Liston's long jab and work to the stomach, but his timing was not acute and he drew back quickly. There had been no inspiration, no life, and a hint of clumsiness. But it had been intellectually sound. It caused no harm. Then he tried again, feinting a left hook, and slipping Liston's left jab, but as he came in close, Liston grabbed him with both arms, and they bulled back and forth until the referee separated them. Now, they each had an unhappy look on their faces as if they were big men who had gotten into an altercation in a bar, and didn't like the physical activity of fighting. Each of them looked like it would take three or four rounds to warm up.

All this had used a minute. Liston seemed to have gained the confidence that he was stronger, and he began crowding Patterson to the rope, throwing a good many punches, not left hooks, not left jabs, not uppercuts or straight rights, just thick, slow, clubbing punches. None of them landed on Patterson's body or head, they all banged on his arms, and occasionally Patterson would bang Liston back on the arm. It is a way of fighting. A strong slow fighter will sometimes keep hitting the other man on the shoulder or the biceps until his arms go dead. If the opponent is in condition, it is a long procedure. I was surprised at how slow Liston's punches were. From ringside, they looked easy to block. He had a way of setting himself and going "ahem" before he threw the punch. It is, of course, one thing to block punches from your seat at ringside, and another to block them in a ring, but when a fighter is punching with real speed and snap, you can't block the punches from where you sit. Even from thirty feet away, you are fooled.

All that was fooling me now was Patterson. He seemed sluggish. He was not getting hit with Liston's punches, but he was not hitting back, he seemed to miss one small opportunity after another. He was fighting like a college heavyweight who has gone in to work with a professional and is getting disheartened at the physical load of such sparring. He had the expression on his face of somebody pushing a Cadillac which has run out of gas.

Then occurred what may have been the most extraordinary moment ever seen in a championship fight. It was very spooky. Patterson, abruptly, without having been hurt in any visible way, stood up suddenly out of his crouch, his back a foot from the ropes, and seemed to look half up into the sky as if he had seen something there or had been struck by something from there, by some transcendent bolt, and then he staggered like a man caught in machine-gun fire, and his legs went, and he fell back into the ropes. His left glove became tangled in the top rope, almost as Paret's arm had been tangled, and that murmur of death, that visitation which had passed into Madison Square Garden on the moment Paret began to die, seemed a breath from appearing now. Patterson looked at Liston with one lost look, as if somehow he had been expecting this to happen ever since the night it happened to Paret; it was the look of a man saying, "Don't kill me," and then Liston hit him two or three ill-timed punches, banging a sloppy stake into the ground, and Patterson went down. And he was out. He was not faking. He had started to pass out at the moment he stood straight on his feet and was struck by that psychic bolt which had come from wherever it had come.

Patterson rolled over, he started to make an attempt to get to his feet, and Baldwin and I were each shouting, "Get up, get up!" But one's voice had no force in it, one's will had no life.

Patterson got up somewhere between a quarter and a half second too late. You could see the critical instant pass in the referee's body, and Patterson was still getting his glove off the ground. The fight was over: 2:06 of the First. It must have been the worst fight either fighter had ever had.

Liston looked like he couldn't believe what had happened. He was blank for two or three long seconds, and then he gave a whoop. It was an artificial, tentative whoop, but it seemed to encourage him because he gave another which sounded somewhat better, and then he began to whoop and whoop and laugh and shout because his handlers had come into the ring and were hugging him and telling him he was the greatest fighter that ever lived. And Patterson, covered quickly with his bathrobe, still stunned, turned and buried his head in Cus D'Amato's shoulder.

From the stands behind us came one vast wave of silence. Here and there sounded cheers or applause, but you could hear each individual voice or pair of hands clapping into the silence.

"What happened?" said Baldwin.

IV

What did happen? Everybody was to ask that question later. But in private.

The descriptions of the fight fed next morning to The Goat showed no uncertainty. They spoke of critical uppercuts and powerful left hooks and pulverizing rights. Liston talked of dominating Patterson with left hands, Patterson's people said it was a big right which did the job, some reporters called the punches crunching, others said they were menacing, brutal, demolishing. One did not read a description of the fight which was not authoritative. The only contradiction, a most minor contradiction, is that with one exception, a wire-service photograph used everywhere of a right hand by Liston which has apparently just left Patterson's chin, there were no pictures—and a point was made of looking at a good many— which show Liston putting a winning glove into Patterson's stomach, solar plexus, temple, nose, or jaw. In fact there is not a single picture of Liston's glove striking Patterson at all. It is not highly probable the photographers missed every decent punch. Fight photographers are capable of splitting the strictest part of a second in order to get the instant of impact. The fine possibility is that there was no impact. There was instead an imprecise beating, that is a beating which was not convincing if the men were anywhere near to equal in strength. Something had happened to Patterson, however. He fought as if he were down with jaundice. It was not that he did not do his best; he always did his determined best; he did just that against Liston. It is just that his best this night was off the spectrum of his normal condition. Something had struck at him. From inside himself or from without, in that instant he straightened from his crouch and stared at the sky, he had the surprise of a man struck by treachery.

Now I am forced to give a most improper testimony, because I felt as if I were a small part of that treachery and one despairs of trying to explain how that could be so.

A man turns to boxing because he discovers it is the best experience of his life. If he is a good fighter, his life in the center of the ring is more intense than it can be anywhere else, his mind is more exceptional than at any other time, his body has become a live part of his brain. Some men are geniuses when they are drunk; a good fighter feels a bit of genius when he is having a good fight. This illumination comes not only from the discipline he has put on his body or the concentration of his mind to getting ready for his half hour in the open, but no, it comes as well from his choice to occupy the stage on an adventure whose end is unknown. For the length of his fight, he ceases to be a man and becomes a Being, which is to say he is no longer finite in the usual sense, he is no longer a creature of a given size and dress with a name and some habits which are predictable. Liston-in-the-ring was not just Sonny Liston; much more he was the nucleus of that force at Comiskey Park (and indeed from everywhere in the world from which such desire could reach) which wished him to win or hated him with an impotence that created force, to wit, hated him less than it feared him, and so betrayed its hate since the telepathic logic of the unconscious makes us give our strength to those we think to hate but favor despite ourselves. Just so, Patterson-in-the-ring was not Floyd Patterson sparring in his gym, but was instead a vehicle of all the will and all the particular love which truly wished him to win, as well as a target of all the hatred which was not impotent but determined to strike him down.

When these universes collided, the impact if not clear was total. The world quivered in some rarefied accounting of subtle psychic seismographs, and the stocks of certain ideal archetypes shifted their status in our country's brain. Sex had proved superior to Love still one more time, the Hustler had taken another pool game from the Infantryman, the Syndicate rolled out the Liberal, the Magician hyped the Artist, and, since there were more than a few who insisted on seeing them simply as God and the Devil (whichever much or little of either they might be), then the Devil had shown that the Lord was dramatically weak.

The Goat would demand that this fight be reported in a veritable factology of detail. America could not listen to questions. The professional witnesses to the collision, the pipers of cancer gulch, were obliged to testify to a barrage of detailed punches, and the fighters reexamining their own history in such a mirror of prose would be forced to remake the event in their mind. Yet so long as one kept one's memory, the event was unclear. The result had been turned by betrayal. And it was by one's own person that the guilt was felt. I had been there with half a body from half a night of sleep for too many nights, and half a brain from too many bouts of drinking drinks I did not want that much, and dim in concentration because I was brooding about the loss of a friendship which it was a cruel and stupid waste to lose. And Baldwin too had been brooding. We had sat there like beasts of burden, empty of psychic force to offer our fighter.

Now, too late, in the bout's sudden wake, like angels whose wings are wet, we buried our quarrel; this time it might stay buried for a while. "My Lord," said Jimmy, "I lost seven hundred and fifty dollars tonight."

Well, we laughed. I had lost no more than a paltry thirty-eight.

Later, I went back to the dressing room. But Patterson's door was locked. Over a hundred reporters were jammed into Liston's room, so many that one could not see the new champion, one could only hear his voice. He was resounding very much like Clark Gable now, late Gable with the pit of his mannerism—that somewhat complacent jam of much too much love for the self. Liston had the movie star's way of making the remark which cuts, then balming it with salve. "Did you take your ugly pills?" says the actor to the leading lady, and gives his smile at her flush. "Why honey, dear child, I'm only kidding." So Liston said, "The one time he hurt me was when he got up to a knee at nine. I was afraid he would come all the way up." Which was class. It whipped. A minute later, some banana oil was uncorked. "Yessir," said Liston at large, "Floyd is a heck of a man."

I left that dressing room and tried to get into Patterson's, but the door was still locked. Ingemar Johansson was standing nearby. They were interviewing him over a pay telephone for a radio program. Johansson had a bewildered combative look as if someone had struck him on the back of the head with a loaded jack. He had knocked Patterson down for seven times in one round, there had been wild lightning and "toonder," but he had not been able to keep Patterson down. Now Liston had taken Floyd out with a punch or two or three no witness would agree upon.

"Do you think you can beat Liston," was the interviewer's question.

"I don't know," said Johansson.

"Do you think you have a chance?"

Johansson looked sad and Swedish. "One always has a chance," he said. "I would make my fight and fight it, that's all."

One never did get into Patterson's dressing room. After a while I left and walked around the empty ringside seats. It was cold now. Some of the events of the last few days were coming back to me in, the cold air of Comiskey Park. They were not agreeable to contemplate. I had done a few unattractive things. I did not want to count them.

But then in fact I had been doing so much that was wrong the last two days. If one is to talk of betrayal and try to explain what was yet to happen, the account must slip back a bit into what had happened already. On Monday, the New York *Times* had shown a story on the first page of the second section about William F. Buckley and myself and our debate on Saturday night. It had culled some dismembered remarks from the exchange, added a touch of wit from each of us, and called the result a draw. I did not take it well. For I had prepared for the debate, I had honed myself like a club fighter getting ready for the champion. I had been ready, and Buckley, who had been working at other things, was not as ready. He had been speaking in Texas the day before and flew into Chicago only that morning. The afternoon of our debate he was still writing his speech. Saturday night, Medinah Temple had held almost four thousand people. It was built like an opera house with an enormous apron on the stage, and balconies which made a turn around the house through more than half a circle. One spoke with the audience sitting deep to one's left and deep to one's right, close in front and high overhead. Despite its size it was not unlike the theatre in *Les Enfants du Paradis,* and it had been dramatic for our separate styles. Buckley, tall and thin, spoke from high on his toes, his long arm and long finger outstretched in condemnation, a lone shaft of light pointing down on him from above while he excoriated the Left for Cuba, and myself for "swinishness." In my turn I led an intellectual foray into the center of his positions, arguing that if conservatism was a philosophy which saw each person in his appointed place so that men were equal only before God and in Eternity, that the radical in his turn conceived the form

of the world as a record of the war between God and the Devil where man
served as God's agent and sought to shift the wealth of our universe in such
a way that the talent which was dying now by dim dull deaths in every poor
man alive would take its first breath and show what a mighty renaissance
was locked in the unconscious of the dumb.

Afterward, the people I met on the street and in restaurants or at a party
would congratulate me and say I had won. And I had felt exactly like a club
fighter who has won a very big fight. But the test of a poor man is profit,
and I squandered mine. Something pent up for years, dictatorial and harsh,
began to slip through my good humor after I read the verdict in the *Times*.
There might be other debates with Buckley in the spring. He would be
ready next time. It was raw to lose a victory. I did not take it well. Actors
speak of a motor inside themselves. I could not stop mine, one did not
want to now, and I drank because the drink was fuel.

Yes, I had done everything wrong since then, I had even had the fool's
taste to be pleased with the magic of the cigarette lighter. If I had been a part
of the psychic cadre guarding Patterson, I had certainly done everything to
make myself useless to him. I could even wonder at that moment, my mind
quick with bitterness toward the *Times,* whether the entire liberal persuasion of America had rooted for Floyd in the same idle, detached fashion as
myself, wanting him to win but finding Liston secretly more interesting, in
fact, and, indeed, demanding of Patterson that he win only because he was
good for liberal ideology. I had a moment of vast hatred then for that bleak
gluttonous void of the Establishment, that liberal power at the center of our
lives which gave jargon with charity, substituted the intolerance of mental
health for the intolerance of passion, alienated emotion from its roots, and
man from his past, cut the giant of our half-wakened arts to fit a bed of
Procrustes, Leonard Bernstein on the podium, John Cage in silence, offered
a National Art Center which would be to art as canned butter is to butter,
and existed in a terror of eternity which built a new religion of the psyche on a
God who died, old doctor Freud, of cancer. Yes, it was this Establishment
which defeated Patterson precisely because it supported him, because it was
able to give reward but not love, because it was ruled by a Goat who radiated
depression like fallout searches for milk.

A long night was to follow, of curious pockets and creepy encounters.
Too much magic had been put into one place, and now it was as if a bomb
had exploded prematurely, imperfectly. The turbulence of the air had eyes

of calm, and gave telepathic intensity to the dark. One would think of an event with rising concentration and around the turn of one's thought would appear, quite real, smacking of the flesh, some man or woman who belonged to the event. Walking through the Park, a person shouted my name. Then another cry. It was the voice of each of the men who had promoted the debate with Buckley, John Golden and Aaron Berlin. We took off extempore together to have a drink and go on to my party, and on the way, walking through the streets of the South Side near Comiskey Park, two gloomy Negro adolescents fell in and walked along with us. They were eighteen or nineteen, shabby. They wore flat leather caps. One had turned the short peak around to the back of his head. They had been blasted tonight by Floyd's defeat. Everything would be more difficult now. They did not want to hate Patterson, but they could hardly speak.

Poor Patterson. He was alienated from his own, from his own streets, his own vocabulary, his own manager, he was even alienated from his own nightmare. What could the Establishment tell him of that odyssey which set him once walking on subway tracks to discover a hole not too many inches away from where the trains went by. "Oh," said the Establishment, "he wanted to go back to the womb. How interesting!" But they could not tell one why he had this wish, nor why it was interesting. The womb was part of their void, of the liberal void, they would not begin to guess that a champion who could find a way to go to sleep minutes before a big fight must have learned early to live on the edge of his death. The psychic roar of a prizefight crowd was like the sound of the subway. Yes, Patterson had gone out early to explore because he had known, living in terror down in Bedford-Stuyvesant part of town, down in a world of curse, evil eye, blasted intent, that the forces of the past which had forced their way into the seed which made him now wanted no less than that he be extraordinary, that he be great, that be a champion of his people. But he had succeeded too quickly. He had come too early upon the scene. The Establishment had made him a Negroid white. His skin was black, his psychology had turned white, poor blasted man, twice cursed. He could have the consolation that his championship had gone on to another black.

But it was unfair. He deserved more than this, more than this gutted performance. One would now never know if he lost before he reached the ring, whipped by the oatmeal of the liberal line, or if the Devil had struck him down with vastly greater ease than the Devil had intended. No matter how, the result had been awful. That this brave, decent, sensitive, haunted man should have been defeated with such humiliation. It was awful.

The party was very big, and it was a good party. The music went all the way down into the hour or two before breakfast, but no one saw the dawn come in because the party was at Hugh Hefner's house which is one of the most extraordinary houses in America and the living room where much of the party was going was sixty feet long and more than thirty wide, and almost twenty high, yet there were no windows, at least I never saw the sky from that room, and so there was a timeless spaceless sensation. Staying as a houseguest in his home, there had been servants ready all twenty-four hours these last few days, one had been able to get the equivalent of any drink made at any bar at any hour of the world, one could have chili at four a.m. or ice cream at ten, the servants had been perfect, the peace when empty of the house was profound, one never saw one's host except for once or twice in some odd hour of the night. He had a quality not unlike Jay Gatsby, he looked and talked like a lean, rather modest cowboy of middle size; there was something of a mustang about Hefner. He was not the kind of man one would have expected to see as the publisher of his magazine, nor the owner of the Playboy Club, nor certainly as the undemanding host of his exceptional establishment. Timeless, spaceless, it was outward bound. One was in an ocean liner which traveled at the bottom of the sea, or on a spaceship wandering down the galaxy along a night whose duration was a year. The party went on, and I drank and I drank some more. The swimming pool was beneath the dance floor, and there were bathing suits for those who wanted them, and some did, and people went to look through the trapdoor in the living room which pried open over a fall of fifteen feet into a grotto of the pool below. Above was the orchestra and the dancers in a Twist. The Twist was not dead in Chicago, not hardly. If there were such a thing as sexual totalitarianism, then the Twist was its Horst Wessel, and all the girls with boy's bodies were twisting out their allegiance. I hated the Twist. Not because I had become a moralist on the stroke of twelve, not because I felt sex without love was determined to be bad, but because I hated too much life for sex without any possibility of love. The Twist spoke of some onanism which had gone on forever, some effort which had lost its beginning and labored to find no end, of an art which burned itself for fuel.

Now, after the knockout, in some fatigue-ridden, feverish whole vision of one's guilt and of Patterson's defeat—for of course the fighters spoke as well from the countered halves of my nature; what more had I to tell myself of sex versus love, magic against art, or the hustler and the infantryman?—out of a desire to end some war in myself, as if victory by Patterson might have given me discipline, and the triumph of Liston could now distract me only further, out of a fury to excise defeat, I began in the plot-ridden, romantic dungeons of my mind, all subterranean rhythms stirred by the beat of this party, to see myself as some sort of center about which all that had been lost must now rally. It was not simple egomania nor simple drunkenness, it was not even simple insanity: it was a kind of metaphorical leap across a gap. To believe the impossible may be won creates a strength from which the impossible may indeed be attacked. Fidel Castro alone in the jungle, with a dozen men left, seven-eighths of his landing party dead, lost, or captured, turned to his followers in the sugarcane and said, "The days of the dictatorship are numbered." If he had been killed that moment they would have said he died as a madman. He was not mad, he was merely all but impossible. But in his mind he saw a set of psychic steps which led to victory. And In my mind, half-gorged from juice, the beginning of a resolution was forming. I did not know it, but I was getting ready to tell myself that I must have a press conference next morning in which I would explain why Floyd Patterson still had an excellent chance to defeat Sonny Liston in their next fight, and why in fact—this would be indigestible for The Goat—why the fight which had taken place had been a mysterious dumb show substituted by inexplicable intervention for the real event. Opportunity came. This was a party like a pinball machine; there were bonuses on the turn of the lights, and a little later I was having a drink with a man from Championship Sports, I had drinks with several of them that night, but on the conversational ride we took together with the liquor, I dunned this man into some half-muttered acceptance of an idea which did not seem at all impractical at two in the morning. I would do publicity for the second Patterson-Liston fight, I was the only man in America who could save the second fight because I believed that Patterson had a true chance to beat Liston the next time they met. And it made sense: at that hour, in the blasted remains of the promotion, with no thought of a return at all promising, the confidence I offered was enough to trap the promise of a conference for the press. Liston was seeing reporters at eleven-thirty; I could have mine at eleven, a semifinal on the eleventh floor.

"And what will you say?" asked the reporters, a little later.

"I'll say it tomorrow."

But the party did not end until seven in the morning. I had the choice of sleeping for a few hours or not sleeping at all, and decided it would be easier not to fall asleep. So I talked for an hour or two with the housekeeper while the drinks began to fade, and then shaved very slowly and dressed and went out to walk the twelve or fifteen blocks from Hefner's house to the hotel. I was tired now, I felt something of the exhilaration a fighter must know in the twelfth or thirteenth round of a fifteen-round fight when he has fought his way into some terrain of the body which is beyond fatigue and is riding now like a roller coaster on the beating of his heart, while the flashbulbs ricochet their red-and-green echoes of light into his skull. The awe of his venture has fined down now into the joy that whether he wins or loses, he has finally lifted into flight, something in himself has come up free of the muck.

At the hotel, I went first to fight headquarters downstairs. In the eyes of the man from Championship Sports who had agreed last night to let me meet the press, I could now see a critical lack of delight.

"It's been changed," he said. "Sonny Liston is having his conference at eleven. You had better have yours afterward."

That would not work. After Liston talked to the reporters they would want to file their stories.

"What floor will it be on?"

"The ninth."

I thought to go to the ninth floor. It was a large mistake. Later I learned reporters were waiting for me on the eleventh. But an amateur's nose for the trap is pointed to the wrong place. I was afraid to go to the eleventh floor for fear the conference would begin two floors below. Naturally, Liston was late. On the ninth floor, in the banquet room, there were but a few reporters. I went up to the dais, sat down on a chair at one end. For several minutes nobody paid attention. Then one or two men became curious. What are you doing up there, they wanted to know. Well, I was going to sit up there, I told them, while the champion was having his press conference. Afterward I wanted to say a few things. To what effect? To the effect that I still thought Patterson was the better fighter.

A few of the movie cameramen here for TV newsreel began to take their interest. They came up with light meters, set cameras, measured distance. A flashbulb went off, another. The room was filling.

Now officials began to ask me to leave. They asked pleasantly, they asked with bewilderment, they asked in simple menace. I kept saying that I had been invited to speak at this conference, and so would not leave. Who had invited me? Reporters wanted to know. I had the sense to say I would not give the name until it was my turn to speak. I had some sense it would be bad for the man who invited me—I did not want to offer his name for nothing.

"If you don't leave," said the last official, "we'll have to remove you by force."

"Remove me by force."

"Would you give a statement, Mr. Mailer," said a reporter for the *Times.*

"Yes." The answer was formal Chinese. "I came here prepared to make a case that I am the only man in this country who can build the second Patterson-Liston fight into a $2,000,000 gate instead of a $200,000 dog in Miami. I wish to handle the press relations for this second fight. For various and private reasons I need to make a great deal of money in the next two months." Two or three journalists were now taking careful notes.

Then I felt a hand on my shoulder. Its touch was final—the end of a sequence. "Would you come with us?" On one side was a house detective. On the other side was another house detective.

"No."

"We'll have to carry you out."

"Carry me out."

They lifted the chair in which I was sitting. I had not expected this to happen. It was too simple. And there was no way to resist. The publicity from a scuffle would feed a circus. Nonetheless, if you are not a pacifist, to be transported in a chair is no happy work. Once we were quits of the dais, there was nothing to do but slip off. I walked to the elevator. Fifteen minutes of cool, reasonable debate went on downstairs before one of the detectives agreed to telephone up for permission. I would be allowed at least to see Sonny's conference with the press.

When we got back, Liston was much in command. He sat in the center of the long table, on the dais, flanked by four or five men on either side. Questions were admiring, routine. "What did you think of Patterson's punch?" someone asked, a reporter.

"He hits harder than I thought he would," said Liston.

"He never landed a punch."

"That's true," said Liston, "but he banged me on the arm. I could feel it there."

Someone asked a new question. Liston answered in a reasonable voice. Then he said something grim. About reporters.

"Well, I'm not a reporter," I shouted from the back of the room, "but I'd like to say . . ."

"You're worse than a reporter," said Liston.

"Shut the bum up," shouted some reporters.

"No," said Liston. "Let the bum speak."

"I picked Floyd Patterson to win by a one-punch knockout in the sixth round, and I still think I was right," I shouted to Liston.

"You're still drunk."

"Shut the bum up," shouted several reporters.

A reporter asked another question. Nilon was quick to answer it. I had had my moment, lost it. The conference went on. There were questions and answers about the finances of the fight. I was weary. After a while, I sat down. The faces of the people who looked at me were not friendly. When the conference ended, I went up to a reporter who was a friend. "Next time ask your question," he said. "Don't stand there posing."

An ego made of molybdenum could not have concealed from itself that one had better not quit now. The losses would be too great.

So I went back to the dais and tried to approach Liston.

Two very large Negroes stood in the way. "I want to talk to the champion," I said.

"Well, go up front. Don't try to approach him from behind," snapped one of the Negroes.

"Fair enough," I said, and went down the length of the table, turned around, and came up again to Sonny Liston from the front. A man was talking, and I waited ten or fifteen seconds till he was done, and then took a step forward.

"What did you do," said Liston, "go out and get another drink?"

He was sitting down, and I was standing. Since he sat there with his forearms parallel, laid out flat on the table in front of him, it gave to his body the magisterial composure of a huge cat with a man's face.

"Liston," I said, "I still say Floyd Patterson can beat you."

A smile came from the Sphinx. "Aw, why don't you stop being a sore loser?"

"You called me a bum."

Each of us was by now aware that there were reporters gathering around us.

Something unexpected and gentle came into Liston's voice. "Well, you *are* a bum," he said. "Everybody is a bum. I'm a bum, too. It's just that I'm a bigger bum than you are." He stood up and stuck out his hand. "Shake, bum," he said.

Now it came over me that I had not begun to have the strength this morning to be so very good as I had wanted to be. Once more I had tried to become a hero, and had ended as an eccentric. There would be argument later whether I was a monster or a clown. Could it be, was I indeed a bum? I shook his hand.

A few flashbulbs went off, and Liston's face looked red to me and then green and then red and green again before the flare of the light left my retina. His hand was large and very relaxed. It told little about him. But a devil came into my head. I pulled his hand toward me, and his weight was so balanced on his toes that his head and body came forward with his hand and we were not a foot apart. "Listen," said I, leaning my head closer, speaking from the corner of my mouth, as if I were whispering in a clinch, "I'm pulling this caper for a reason. I know a way to build the next fight from a $200,000 dog in Miami to a $2,000,000 gate in New York."

Out of Liston's eyes stared back the profound intelligence of a profound animal. Now we understood each other, now we could work as a team. "Say," said Liston, "that last drink really set you up. Why don't you go and get *me* a drink, you bum."

"I'm not your flunky," I said.

It was the first jab I'd slipped, it was the first punch I'd sent home. He loved me for it. The hint of a chuckle of corny old darky laughter, cotton-field giggles, peeped out a moment from his throat. "Oh, sheeet, man!" said the wit in his eyes. And for the crowd who was watching, he turned and announced at large, "I like this guy."

So I left that conference a modest man. Because now I knew that when it came to debate I had met our Zen master. I took a cab and rode the mile to Hefner's place, feeling the glow of fatigue which is finally not too unclean, and back at the mansion lunch was chili so hot it scorched the throat. I had a glass of milk, and Baldwin dropped by and we spoke in tired voices of the fight and after a while he inquired about the health of my sister and I replied that she was fine, she was looking beautiful, why didn't he consider marrying her, quick as that, which put me one up on old Jim again, and we shook our writer's hands and said good-by, each of us to go back to New York by separate flight, he to write his account, I to mine. Next day, and the following day, and even on the days of the next week, some favorite pets of The Goat kept taking little bites at me. First it was a red jaybird named Mr. Smith and then it was A. J. Liebling, a loverly owl. (One couldn't mind what an owl didn't see, but it was supposed to hear.) Then a wily old hamster named Winchell gobbled some of the remaining rump, and Dorothy Kilgallen, looking never in the least like a chinless lemur, took the largest bite of all. She wrote that I had tried to pick up a fight with Archie Moore. Well, I had never tried to pick a fight with Archie Moore because Mr. Moore had indicated already that he could manage to handle a pugilist like Mr. George Plimpton of *The Paris Review,* and Mr. Plimpton and I were much in the same league. Indeed, Mr. Moore had said, "I almost broke my back not hitting Mr. Plimpton."

It could have been very nice. Nobody minds if they read in the papers that they were thrown in a swimming pool when in fact they did not go near a glass of water. The lies of The Goat were not onerous and his pets were sweet: it was just that later one was called in to see a high probation official and was told that probation, about to end, would now be extended further. One would have to pay this bit for the caper. I did not mind so much. I had learned a lot and educations were paid for best in cash. But what I lost was also nice, I was sorry to see it gone. Some ghost of Don Quixote was laid to rest in me and now I could never be as certain as that morning on the walk whether Patterson indeed could ever bring in his return. To shake the hand of the Devil must quiver the hole: who knew any longer where Right was Left or who was Good and how Evil had hid? For if Liston was the agent of the Devil, what a raid had been made on God, what a royal black man had arisen. Sonny, the King of Hip, was Ace of Spades, and Patterson, ah, Patterson was now an archetype of all which was underdog. He would be a giant if he won. If he could rally from his flight and shave the beard he glued on his mouth; if he could taste those ashes, and swallow to the end, and never choke; if he could sleep through the aisles and enormities of each long night, pondering if the Devil had struck him down (and so might strike again—what fear could be worse than that!) or, even worse, be forced to wonder if the Lord had passed him by for Sonny, if Sonny were now the choice, having carried the blood of his Negritude through prison walls; if Floyd could sleep through those long dreams, and be cool to the power of the dead in Liston's fists (and the rents in his own psyche); if Patterson could keep from pulling apart and could put himself together; if he could shed the philosophy which drained him and learn to create for himself till he was once again the heavyweight with the fastest, hardest hands of our modern time; if he could go out into the ring with the sullen apathy of his followers now staring him in the eye; if he could move in and take that next fight away from Liston and knock Sonny out, then a great man would be with us, and a genius our champion rather than a king. So one would hope for Patterson one more time. Genius was more rare than royalty and so its light must reach a little further into our darkness down the deep waters of sleep, down one's long inner space. The first fight had been won by the man who knew the most about Evil; would the second reveal who had studied more of the Good? would they meet in the clangor of battle or the fiasco of a doomed dead cause? would we witness a dog in Miami or the lion of New York?

1963

"Perhaps the whole root of our trouble, the human trouble," James Baldwin once wrote, "is that we will sacrifice all the beauty of our lives, will imprison ourselves in totems, taboos, crosses, blood sacrifices, steeples, mosques, races, armies, flags, nations, in order to deny the fact of death, which is the only fact we have. . . . Art is here to prove, and to help one bear, the fact that all safety is an illusion."

JAMES BALDWIN

The Fight: Patterson vs. Liston

We, the writers—a word I am using in its most primitive sense—arrived in Chicago about ten days before the baffling, bruising, an unbelievable two minutes and six seconds at Comiskey Park. We will get to all that later. I know nothing whatever about the Sweet Science or the Cruel Profession or the Poor Boy's Game. But I know a lot about pride, the poor boy's pride, since that's my story and will, in some way, probably, be my end.

There was something vastly unreal about the entire bit, as though we had all come to Chicago to make various movies and then spent all our time visiting the other fellow's set—on which no cameras were rolling. Dispatches went out every day, typewriters clattered, phones rang; each day, carloads of journalists invaded the Patterson or Liston camps, hung around until Patterson or Liston appeared; asked lame, inane questions, always the same questions; went away again, back to those telephones and typewriters; and informed a waiting, anxious world, or at least a waiting, anxious editor, what Patterson and Liston had said or done that day. It was insane and desperate, since neither of them ever really *did* anything. There wasn't anything for them *to* do, except train for the fight. But there aren't many ways to describe a fighter in training—it's muscle and sweat and grace, it's the same thing over and over—and since neither Patterson nor Liston were doing much boxing, there couldn't be any interesting thumbnail sketches of their sparring partners. The "feud" between Patterson and Liston was as limp and tasteless as British roast lamb. Patterson is really far too much of a gentleman to descend to feuding with anyone, and I simply never believed, especially after talking with Liston, that he had the remotest grudge against Patterson. So there we were, hanging around, twiddling our thumbs, drinking Scotch, and telling stories, and trying to make copy out of nothing. And waiting, of course, for the Big Event, which would

585

justify the monumental amounts of time, money, and energy which were being expended in Chicago.

Neither Patterson nor Liston has the *color,* or the instinct for drama, which is possessed to such a superlative degree by the marvelous Archie Moore and the perhaps less marvelous, but certainly vocal, and rather charming, Cassius Clay. In the matter of color, a word which I am not now using in its racial sense, the press room far outdid the training camps. There were not only the sportswriters, who had come, as I say, from all over the world: there were also the boxing greats, scrubbed and sharp and easygoing, Rocky Marciano, Barney Ross, Ezzard Charles, and the King, Joe Louis, and Ingemar Johansson, who arrived just a little before the fight and did not impress me as being easygoing at all. Archie Moore's word for him is "desperate," and he did not say this with any affection. There were the ruined boxers, stopped by an unlucky glove too early in their careers, who seemed to be treated with the tense and embarrassed affection reserved for faintly unsavory relatives, who were being used, some of them, as sparring partners. There were the managers and trainers, who, in public anyway, and with the exception of Cus D'Amato, seemed to have taken, many years ago, the vow of silence. There were people whose functions were mysterious indeed, certainly unnamed, possibly unnamable, and, one felt, probably, if undefinably, criminal. There were hangers-on and protégés, a singer somewhere around, whom I didn't meet, owned by Patterson, and another singer owned by someone else—who couldn't sing, everyone agreed, but who didn't have to, being so loaded with personality—and there were some improbable-looking women, turned out, it would seem, by a machine shop, who didn't seem, really, to walk or talk, but rather to gleam, click, and glide, with an almost soundless meshing of gears. There were some pretty incredible girls, too, at the parties, impeccably blank and beautiful and rather incredibly vulnerable. There were the parties and the postmortems and the gossip and speculations and recollections and the liquor and the anecdotes, and dawn coming up to find you leaving somebody else's house or somebody else's room or the Playboy Club; and Jimmy Cannon, Red Smith, Milton Gross, Sandy Grady, and A. J. Liebling; and Norman Mailer, Gerald Kersh, Budd Schulberg, and Ben Hecht—who arrived, however, only for the fight and must have been left with a great deal of time on his hands—and Gay Talese (of the *Times*), and myself. Hanging around in Chicago, hanging on the lightest word, or action, of Floyd Patterson and Sonny Liston.

I am not an aficionado of the ring, and haven't been since Joe Louis lost his crown—he was the last great fighter for me—and so I can't really make comparisons with previous events of this kind. But neither, it soon struck me, could anybody else. Patterson was, in effect, the *moral* favorite—people *wanted* him to win, either because they liked him, though many people didn't, or because they felt that his victory would be salutary for boxing and that Liston's victory would be a disaster. But no one could be said to be enthusiastic about either man's record in the ring. The general feeling seemed to be that Patterson had never been tested, that he was the champion, in effect, by default; though, on the other hand, everyone attempted to avoid the conclusion that boxing had fallen on evil days and that Patterson had fought no worthy fighters because there were none. The desire to avoid speculating too deeply on the present state and the probable future of boxing was responsible, I think, for some very odd and stammering talk about Patterson's personality. (This led Red Smith to declare that he didn't feel that sportswriters had any business trying to be psychiatrists, and that he was just going to write down who hit whom, how hard, and where, and the hell with why.) And there was very sharp disapproval of the way he has handled his career, since he has taken over most of D'Amato's functions as a manager, and is clearly under no one's orders but his own. "In the old days," someone complained, "the manager told the fighter what to do, and he did it. You didn't have to futz around with the guy's *temperament,* for Christ's sake." Never before had any of the sportswriters been compelled to deal directly with the fighter instead of with his manager, and all of them seemed baffled by this necessity and many were resentful. I don't know how they got along with D'Amato when he was running the entire show— D'Amato can certainly not be described as either simple or direct—but at least the figure of D'Amato was familiar and operated to protect them from the oddly compelling and touching figure of Floyd Patterson, who is quite probably the least likely fighter in the history of the sport. And I think that part of the resentment he arouses is due to the fact that he brings to what is thought of—quite erroneously—as a simple activity a terrible note of complexity. This is his personal style, a style which strongly suggests that most un-American of attributes, privacy, the will to privacy; and my own guess is that he is still relentlessly, painfully shy—he lives gallantly with his scars, but not all of them have healed—and while he has found a way to master this, he has found no way to hide it; as, for example, another miraculously tough and tender man, Miles Davis, has managed to do. Miles's disguise would certainly never fool anybody with sense, but it keeps a lot of people away, and that's the point. But Patterson, tough and proud and beautiful, is also terribly vulnerable, and looks it.

I met him, luckily for me, with Gay Talese, whom he admires and trusts. I say "luckily" because I'm not a very aggressive journalist, don't know enough about boxing to know which questions to ask, and am simply not able to ask a man questions about his private life. If Gay had not been there, I am not certain how I would ever have worked up my courage to say anything to Floyd Patterson—especially after having sat through, or suffered, the first, for me, of many press conferences. I only sat through two with Patterson, silently, and in the back—he, poor man, had to go through it every day, sometimes twice a day. And if I don't know enough about boxing to know which questions to ask, I must say that the boxing experts are not one whit more imaginative, though they were, I thought, sometimes rather more insolent. It was a curious insolence, though, veiled, tentative, uncertain—they couldn't be sure that Floyd wouldn't give them as good as he got. And this led, again, to that curious resentment I mentioned earlier, for they were forced, perpetually, to speculate about the man instead of the boxer. It doesn't appear to have occurred yet to many members of the press that one of the reasons their relations with Floyd are so frequently strained is that he has no reason, on any level, to trust them, and no reason to believe that they would be capable of hearing what he had to say, even if he could say it. Life's far from being as simple as most sportswriters would like to have it. The world of sports, in fact, is far from being as simple as the sports pages often make it sound.

Gay and I drove out, ahead of all the other journalists, in a Hertz car, and got to the camp at Elgin while Floyd was still lying down. The camp was very quiet—bucolic, really—when we arrived: set in the middle of small, rolling hills; four or five buildings; a tethered goat, the camp mascot; a small green tent containing a Spartan cot; lots of cars. "They're very car-conscious here," someone said of Floyd's small staff of trainers and helpers. "Most of them have two cars." We ran into some of them standing around and talking on the grounds, and Buster Watson, a close friend of Floyd's, stocky, dark, and able, led us into the press room. Floyd's camp was actually Marycrest Farm, the twin of a Chicago settlement house, which works, on a smaller scale but in somewhat the same way, with disturbed and deprived children, as does Floyd's New York alma mater, the Wiltwyck School for Boys. It is a Catholic institution—Patterson is a converted Catholic—and the interior walls of the building in which the press conferences took place were decorated with vivid mosaics, executed by the children in colored beans, of various biblical events. There was an extraordinarily effective crooked cross, executed in charred wood, hanging high on one of the walls. There were two doors to the building in which the two press agents worked, one saying "Caritas," the other saying "Veritas." It seemed an incongruous setting for the life being lived there, and the event being prepared, but Ted Carroll, the Negro press agent, a tall man with white hair and a knowledge-able, weary, gentle face, told me that the camp was like the man. "The man lives a secluded life. He's like this place—peaceful and faraway." It was not all that peaceful, of course, except naturally; it was otherwise menaced and inundated by hordes of human beings, from small boys who wanted to be boxers to old men who remembered Jack Dempsey as a kid. The signs on the road pointing the way to Floyd Patterson's training camp were perpetu-ally carried away by souvenir hunters. ("At first," Ted Carroll said, "we were worried that maybe they were carrying them away for another reason—you know, the usual hassle—but no, they just want to put them in the rum-pus room.") We walked about with Ted Carroll for a while and he pointed out to us the house—white, with green shutters, somewhat removed from the camp and on a hill—in which Floyd Patterson lived. He was resting now, and the press conference had been called for three o'clock, which was nearly three hours away. But he would be working out before the confer-ence. Gay and I left Ted and wandered close to the house. I looked at the ring, which had been set up on another hill near the house, and examined the tent. Gay knocked lightly on Floyd's door. There was no answer, but Gay said that the radio was on. We sat down in the sun, near the ring, and speculated on Floyd's training habits, which kept him away from his family for such long periods of time.

Presently, here he came across the grass, loping, rather, head down, with a small, tight smile on his lips. This smile seems always to be there when he is facing people and disappears only when he begins to be comfortable. Then he can laugh, as I never heard him laugh at a press conference, and the face which he watches so carefully in public is then, as it were, permitted to be its boyish and rather surprisingly zestful self. He greeted Gay, and took sharp, covert notice of me, seeming to decide that if I were with Gay,

I was probably all right. We followed him into the gym, in which a large sign faced us, saying, "So we being many are one body in Christ." He went through his workout, methodically, rigorously, pausing every now and again to disagree with his trainer, Dan Florio, about the time—he insisted that Dan's stopwatch was unreliable—or to tell Buster that there weren't enough towels, to ask that the windows be closed. "You threw a good right hand that time," Dan Florio said; and, later, "Keep the right hand *up. Up!*" "We got a floor scale that's no good," Floyd said, cheerfully. "Sometimes I weigh two hundred, sometimes I weigh 'eighty-eight." And we watched him jump rope, which he must do according to some music in his head, very beautiful and gleaming and faraway, like a boy saint helplessly dancing and seen through the steaming windows of a storefront church.

We followed him into the house when the workout was over, and sat in the kitchen and drank tea; he drank chocolate. Gay knew that I was somewhat tense as to how to make contact with Patterson—my own feeling was that he had a tough enough row to hoe, and that everybody should just leave him alone; how would *I* like it if I were forced to answer inane questions every day concerning the progress of my work?—and told Patterson about some of the things I'd written. But Patterson hadn't heard of me, or read anything of mine. Gay's explanation, though, caused him to look directly at me, and he said, "I've seen you someplace before. I don't know where, but I know I've seen you." I hadn't seen him before, except once, with Liston, in the commissioner's office, when there had been a spirited fight concerning the construction of Liston's boxing gloves, which were "just about as flat as the back of my hand," according to a sportswriter, "just like wearing no gloves at all." I felt certain, considering the number of people and the tension in that room, that he could not have seen me *then*—but we do know some of the same people, and have walked very often on the same streets. Gay suggested that he had seen me on TV. I had hoped that the contact would have turned out to be more personal, like a mutual friend or some activity connected with the Wiltwyck School, but Floyd now remembered the subject of the TV debate he had seen—the race problem, of course—and his face lit up. "I *knew* I'd seen you somewhere!" he said, triumphantly, and looked at me for a moment with the same brotherly pride I felt—and feel—in him.

By now he was, with good grace but a certain tense resignation, preparing himself for the press conference. I gather that there are many people who enjoy meeting the press—and most of them, in fact, were presently in Chicago—but Floyd Patterson is not one of them. I think he hates being put on exhibition, he doesn't believe it is real; while he is terribly conscious of the responsibility imposed on him by the title which he held, he is also afflicted with enough imagination to be baffled by his position. And he is far from having acquired the stony and ruthless perception which will allow him to stand at once within and without his fearful notoriety. Anyway, we trailed over to the building in which the press waited, and Floyd's small, tight, shy smile was back.

But he has learned, though it must have cost him a great deal, how to handle himself. He was asked about his weight, his food, his measurements, his morale. He had been in training for nearly six months ("Is that necessary?" "I just like to do it that way"), had boxed, at this point, about 162 rounds. This was compared to his condition at the time of the first fight with Ingemar Johansson. "Do you believe that you were overtrained for that fight?" "Anything I say now would sound like an excuse." But, later, "I was careless—not overconfident, but careless." He had allowed himself to be surprised by Ingemar's aggressiveness. "Did you and D'Amato fight over your decision to fight Liston?" The weary smile played at the corner of Floyd's mouth, and though he was looking directly at his interlocutors, his eyes were veiled. "No." Long pause. "Cus knows that I do what I want to do—ultimately, he accepted it." Was he surprised by Liston's hostility? No. Perhaps it had made him a bit more determined. Had he anything against Liston personally? "No. I'm the champion and I want to remain the champion." Had he and D'Amato ever disagreed before? "Not in relation to my opponents." Had he heard it said that, as a fighter, he lacked viciousness? "Whoever said that should see the fights I've won without being vicious." And why was he fighting Liston? "Well," said Patterson, "it was my decision to take the fight. You gentlemen disagreed, but you were the ones who placed him in the number-one position, so I felt that it was only right. Liston's criminal record is behind him, not before him." "Do you feel that you've been accepted as a champion?" Floyd smiled more tightly than ever and turned toward the questioner. "No," he said. Then, "Well, I have to be accepted as the champion—but maybe not a good one." "Why do you say," someone else asked, "that the opportunity to become a great champion will never arise?" "Because," said Floyd, patiently, "you gentlemen will never let it arise." Someone asked him about his experiences when boxing in Europe—what kind of reception had he enjoyed? Much greater and much warmer than here, he finally admitted, but added, with a weary and humorous caution, "I don't want to say anything derogatory about the United States. I am satisfied." The press seemed rather to flinch from the purport of this grim and vivid little joke, and switched to the subject of Liston again. Who was most in awe of whom? Floyd had no idea, he said, but, "Liston's confidence is on the surface. Mine is within."

And so it seemed to be indeed, as, later, Gay and I walked with him through the flat midwestern landscape. It was not exactly that he was less tense—I think that he is probably always tense, and it is that, and not his glass chin, or a lack of stamina, which is his real liability as a fighter—but he was tense in a more private, more bearable way. The fight was very much on his mind, of course, and we talked of the strange battle about the boxing gloves, and the commissioner's impenetrable and apparent bias toward Liston, though the difference in the construction of the gloves, and the possible meaning of this difference, was clear to everyone. The gloves had been made by two different firms, which was not the usual procedure, and, though they were the same standard eight-ounce weight, Floyd's gloves were the familiar, puffy shape, with most of the weight of the padding over the fist, and Liston's were extraordinarily slender, with most of the weight of the padding over the wrist. But we didn't talk only of the fight, and I can't now remember all the things we *did* talk about. I mainly remember Floyd's voice, going cheerfully on and on, and the way his face kept changing, and the way he laughed; I remember the glimpse I got of him then, a man more complex than he was yet equipped to know, a hero for many children who were still trapped where he had been, who might not have survived without the ring, and who yet, oddly, did not really seem to belong there. I dismissed my dim speculations, that afternoon, as sentimental inaccuracies, rooted in my lack of knowledge of the boxing world, and corrupted with a guilty chauvinism. But now I wonder. He told us that his wife was coming in for the fight, against his will, "in order," he said, indescribably, "to *console* me if—" and he made, at last, a gesture with his hand, downward.

Liston's camp was very different, an abandoned racetrack in, or called, Aurora Downs, with wire gates and a uniformed cop, who lets you in, or doesn't. I had simply given up the press conference bit, since they didn't teach me much, and I couldn't ask those questions. Gay Talese couldn't help me with Liston, and this left me floundering on my own until Sandy Grady called up Liston's manager, Jack Nilon, and arranged for me to see Liston for a few minutes alone the next day. Liston's camp was far more outspoken concerning Liston's attitude toward the press than Patterson's. Liston didn't like most of the press, and most of them didn't like him. But I didn't, myself, see any reason why he *should* like them, or pretend to—they had certainly never been very nice to him, and I was sure that he saw in them merely some more ignorant, uncaring white people, who, no matter how fine we cut it, had helped to cause him so much grief. And this impression was confirmed by reports from people who *did* get along with him—Wendell Phillips and Bob Teague, who are both Negroes, but rather rare and salty types, and Sandy Grady, who is not a Negro, but is certainly rare, and very probably salty. I got the impression from them that Liston was perfectly willing to take people as they were, if they would do the same for him. Again, I was not particularly appalled by his criminal background, believing, rightly or wrongly, that I probably knew more about the motives and even the necessity of this career than most of the white press could. The only relevance Liston's—presumably previous—associations should have been allowed to have, it seemed to me, concerned the possible effect of these on the future of boxing. Well, while the air was thick with rumor and gospel on this subject, I really cannot go into it without risking, at the very least, being sued for libel; and so, one of the most fascinating aspects of the Chicago story will have to be left in the dark. But the Sweet Science is not, in any case, really so low on shady types as to be forced to depend on Liston. The question is to what extent Liston is prepared to cooperate with whatever powers of darkness there are in boxing; and the extent of his cooperation, we must suppose, must depend, at least partly, on the extent of his awareness. So that there is nothing unique about the position in which he now finds himself and nothing unique about the speculation which now surrounds him.

I got to his camp at about two o'clock one afternoon. Time was running out, the fight was not more than three days away, and the atmosphere in the camp was, at once, listless and electric. Nilon looked as though he had not slept and would not sleep for days, and everyone else rather gave the impression that they wished they could—except for three handsome Negro ladies, related, I supposed, to Mrs. Liston, who sat, rather self-consciously, on the porch of the largest building on the grounds. They may have felt as I did, that training camps are like a theater before the curtain goes up, and if you don't have any function in it, you're probably in the way.

Liston, as we all know, is an enormous man, but surprisingly trim. I had already seen him work out, skipping rope to a record of "Night Train," and, while he wasn't nearly, for me, as moving as Patterson skipping rope in silence, it was still a wonderful sight to see. The press has really maligned Liston very cruelly, I think. He is far from stupid; is not, in fact, stupid at all. And, while there is a great deal of violence in him, I sensed no cruelty at all. On the contrary, he reminded me of big, black men I have known who acquired the reputation of being tough in order to conceal the fact that they weren't hard. Anyone who cared to could turn them into taffy.

Anyway, I liked him, liked him very much. He sat opposite me at the table, sideways, head down, waiting for the blow: for Liston knows, as only the inarticulately suffering can, just how inarticulate he is. But let me clarify that: I say "suffering" because it seems to me that he has suffered a great deal. It is in his face, in the silence of that face, and in the curiously distant light in the eyes—a light which rarely signals because there have been so few answering signals. And when I say "inarticulate," I really do not mean to suggest that he does not know how to talk. He is inarticulate in the way we all are when more has happened to us than we know how to express; and inarticulate in a particularly Negro way—he has a long tale to tell which no one wants to hear. I said, "I can't ask you any questions because everything's been asked. Perhaps I'm only here, really, to say that I wish you well." And this was true, even though I wanted Patterson to win. Anyway, I'm glad I said it, because he looked at me then, really for the first time, and he talked to me for a little while.

And what had hurt him most, somewhat to my surprise, was not the general press reaction to him, but the Negro reaction. "Colored people," he said, with great sorrow, "say they don't want their children to look up to me. Well, they ain't teaching their children to look up to Martin Luther King, either." There was a pause. "I wouldn't be no bad example if I was up there. I could tell a lot of those children what they need to know—because—I passed that way. I could make them *listen*." And he spoke a little of what he would like to do for young Negro boys and girls, trapped in those circumstances which so nearly defeated him and Floyd, and from which neither can yet be said to have recovered. "I tell you one thing, though," he said, "if I was up there, I wouldn't bite my tongue." I could certainly believe that. And we discussed the segregation issue, and the role in it of those prominent Negroes who find him so distasteful. "I would never," he said, "go against my brother—we got to learn to stop fighting among our own." He lapsed into silence again. "They said they didn't want me to have the title. They didn't say that about Johansson." "They" were the Negroes. "*They* ought to know why I got some of the bum raps I got." But he was not suggesting that they were *all* bum raps. His wife came over, a very pretty woman, seemed to gather in a glance how things were going, and sat down. We talked for a little while of matters entirely unrelated to the fight, and then it was time for his workout, and I left. I felt terribly ambivalent, as many Negroes do these days, since we are all trying to decide, in one way or another, which attitude, in our terrible American dilemma, is the most effective: the disciplined sweetness of Floyd or the outspoken intransigence of Liston. *If I was up there, I wouldn't bite my tongue.* And Liston is a man aching for respect and responsibility. Sometimes we grow into our responsibilities and sometimes, of course, we fail them.

I left for the fight full of a weird and violent depression, which I traced partly to fatigue—it had been a pretty grueling time—partly to the fact that I had bet more money than I should have—on Patterson—and partly to the fact that *I* had had a pretty definitive fight with someone with whom I had hoped to be friends. And I was depressed about Liston's bulk and force and his twenty-five-pound weight advantage. I was afraid that Patterson might lose, and I really didn't want to see that. And it wasn't that I didn't like Liston. I just felt closer to Floyd.

I was sitting between Norman Mailer and Ben Hecht. Hecht felt about the same way that I did, and we agreed that if Patterson didn't get "stopped," as Hecht put it, "by a baseball bat," in the very beginning—if he could carry Liston for five or six rounds—he might very well hold the title. We didn't pay an awful lot of attention to the preliminaries—or I didn't; Hecht did; I watched the ballpark fill with people and listened to the vendors and the jokes and the speculations; and watched the clock.

From my notes: Liston entered the ring to an almost complete silence. Someone called his name, he looked over, smiled, and winked. Floyd entered, and got a hand. But he looked terribly small next to Liston, and my depression deepened.

My notes again: Archie Moore entered the ring, wearing an opera cape. Cassius Clay, in black tie, and as insolent as ever. Mickey Allen sang "The Star-Spangled Banner." When Liston was introduced, some people booed—

they cheered for Floyd, and I think I know how this made Liston feel. It promised, really, to be one of the worst fights in history.

Well, I was wrong; it was scarcely a fight at all, and I can't but wonder who on earth will come to see the rematch, if there is one. Floyd seemed all right to me at first. He had planned for a long fight, and seemed to be feeling out his man. But Liston got him with a few bad body blows, and a few bad blows to the head. And no one agrees with me on this, but at one moment, when Floyd lunged for Liston's belly—looking, it must be said, like an amateur, wildly flailing—it seemed to me that some unbearable tension in him broke, that he lost his head. And, in fact, I nearly screamed, "Keep your head, baby!" but it was really too late. Liston got him with a left, and Floyd went down. I could not believe it. I couldn't hear the count, and though Hecht said, "It's over," and picked up his coat and left, I remained standing, staring at the ring, and only conceded that the fight was really over when two other boxers entered the ring. Then I wandered out of the ballpark, almost in tears. I met an old colored man at one of the exits, who said to me, cheerfully, "I've been robbed," and we talked about it for a while. We started walking through the crowds, and A. J. Liebling, behind us, tapped me on the shoulder and we went off to a bar, to mourn the very possible death of boxing, and to have a drink, with love, for Floyd.

1964

So: Say you are a writer, and you are writing about the world. How do you reach out from your own imagination to grasp the edges of a legitimate world?

Tom Wolfe

The Kandy-Kolored Tangerine-Flake Streamline Baby

The first good look I had at customized cars was at an event called a "Teen Fair," held in Burbank, a suburb of Los Angeles beyond Hollywood. This was a wild place to be taking a look at art objects—eventually, I should say, you have to reach the conclusion that these customized cars *are* art objects, at least if you use the standards applied in a civilized society. But I will get to that in a moment. Anyway, about noon you drive up to a place that looks like an outdoor amusement park, and there are three serious-looking kids, like the cafeteria committee in high school, taking tickets, but the scene inside is quite mad. Inside, two things hit you. The first is a huge platform a good seven feet off the ground with a hully-gully band—everything is electrified, the bass, the guitars, the saxophones—and then behind the band, on the platform, about two hundred kids are doing frantic dances called the hully-gully, the bird, and the shampoo. As I said, it's noontime. The dances the kids are doing are very jerky. The boys and girls don't touch, not even with their hands. They just ricochet around. Then you notice that all the girls are dressed exactly alike. They have bouffant hairdos—all of them—and slacks that are, well, skin-tight does not get the idea across; it's more the conformation than how tight the slacks are. It's as if some lecherous old tailor with a gluteus-maximus fixation designed them, striation by striation. About the time you've managed to focus on this, you notice that out in the middle of the park is a huge, perfectly round swimming pool; really rather enormous. And there is a Chris-Craft cabin cruiser in the pool, going around and around, sending up big waves, with more of these bouffant babies bunched in the back of it. In the water, suspended like plankton, are kids in scuba-diving outfits; others are tooling around underwater, breathing through a snorkel. And all over the place are booths, put up by shoe companies and guitar companies and God knows who else, and there are kids dancing in all of them—dancing the bird, the hully-gully, and the shampoo—with the music of the hully-gully band piped all over the park through loudspeakers.

All this time, Tex Smith, from *Hot Rod Magazine,* who brought me over to the place, is trying to lead me to the customized-car exhibit—"Tom, I want you to see this car that Bill Cushenberry built, The Silhouette"— which is to say, here are two hundred kids ricocheting over a platform at high noon, and a speedy little boat barreling around and around and around in a round swimming pool, and I seem to be the only person who is distracted. The customized-car exhibit turns out to be the Ford Custom Car Caravan, which Ford is sending all over the country. At first, with the noise and peripheral motion and the inchoate leching you are liable to be doing, what with bouffant nymphets rocketing all over the place, these customized cars do not strike you as anything very special. Obviously they *are* very special, but the first thing you think of is the usual—you know, that the kids who own these cars are probably skinny little hoods who wear T shirts and carry their cigarette packs by winding them around in the T shirt up near the shoulder.

But after a while, I was glad I had seen the cars in this natural setting, which was, after all, a kind of Plato's Republic for teenagers. Because if you watched anything at this fair very long, you kept noticing the same thing. These kids are absolutely maniacal about form. They are practically religious about it. For example, the dancers: none of them ever smiled. They stared at each other's legs and feet, concentrating. The dances had no grace about them at all, they were more in the nature of a hoedown, but everybody was concentrating to do them exactly *right*. And the bouffant kids all had form, wild form, but form with rigid standards, one gathers. Even the boys. Their dress was prosaic—Levi's, Slim Jims, sport shirts, T shirts, polo shirts—but the form was consistent: a stove-pipe silhouette. And they all had the same hairstyle: some wore it long, some short, but none of them had a part; all that hair was brushed back straight from the hairline. I went by one of the guitar booths, and there was a little kid in there, about thirteen, playing the hell out of an electric guitar. The kid was named Cranston something or other. He looked like he ought to be named Kermet or Herschel; all his genes were kind of horribly Okie. Cranston was playing away and a big crowd was watching. But Cranston was slouched back with his spine bent like a sapling up against a table, looking gloriously bored. At thirteen, this kid was being fanatically cool. They all were. They were all wonderful slaves to form. They have created their own style of life, and they are much more authoritarian about enforcing it than are adults. Not only that, but today these kids—especially in California—have *money,* which, needless to say, is why all these shoe merchants and guitar sellers and the Ford Motor Company were at a Teen Fair in the first place. I don't mind observing that it is this same combination—money plus slavish devotion to form—that accounts for Versailles or St. Mark's Square. Naturally, most of the artifacts that these kids' money-plus-form produce are of a pretty ghastly order. But so was most of the paraphernalia that developed in England during the Regency. I mean, most of it was on the order of starched cravats. A man could walk into Beau Brummel's house at 11 A.M., and here would come the butler with a tray of wilted linen. "These were some of our failures," he confides. But then Brummel comes downstairs wearing one perfect starched cravat. Like one perfect iris, the flower of Mayfair civilization. But the Regency period did see some tremendous formal architecture. And the kids' formal society has also brought at least one substantial thing to a formal development of a high order—the customized cars. I don't have to dwell on the point that cars mean more to these kids than architecture did in Europe's great formal century, say, 1750 to 1850. They are freedom, style, sex, power, motion, color—everything is right there.

Things have been going on in the development of the kids' formal attitude toward cars since 1945, things of great sophistication that adults have not been even remotely aware of, mainly because the kids are so inarticulate about it, especially the ones most hipped on the subject. They are not from the levels of society that produce children who write sensitive analytical prose at age seventeen, or if they do, they soon fall into the hands of English instructors who put them onto Hemingway or a lot of goddamn-and-hungry-breast writers. If they ever right about a highway again, it's a rain-slicked highway and the sound of the automobiles passing over it is like the sound of tearing silk, not that one household in ten thousand has heard the sound of tearing silk since 1945.

Anyway, we are back at the Teen Fair and I am talking to Tex Smith and to Don Beebe, a portly young guy with a white sport shirt and Cuban

sunglasses. As they tell me about the Ford Custom Car Caravan, I can see
that Ford has begun to comprehend this teen-age style of life and its poten-
tial. The way Ford appears to figure it is this: Thousands of kids are getting
hold of cars and either hopping them up for speed or customizing them to
some extent, usually a little of both. Before they get married they pour *all*
their money into this. If Ford can get them hooked on Fords now, after the
kids are married they'll buy new Fords. Even the kids who aren't full-time
car nuts themselves will be influenced by which car is considered "boss."
They use that word a lot, "boss." The kids used to consider Ford the hot car,
but then, from 1955 to 1962, Chevrolet became the favorite. They had big
engines and were easy to hop up, the styling was simple, and the kids could
customize them easily. In 1959, and more so in 1960, Plymouth became a
hot car, too. In 1961 and 1962, it was all Chevrolet and Plymouth. Now
Ford is making a big push. A lot of the professional hot-rod and custom-
car people, adults, will tell you that now Ford is the hot car, but you have
to discount some of it, because Ford is laying money on everybody right
and left, in one form or another. In the Custom Car Caravan, all the cars
have been fashioned out of Ford bodies except the ones that are completely
handmade, like the aforementioned Silhouette.

Anyway, Don Beebe is saying, over a loudspeaker, "I hate to break up that
dancing, but let's have a little drag racing." He has a phonograph hooked
up to the loudspeaker, and he puts on a record, produced by Riverside
Records, of drag-strip sounds, mainly dragsters blasting off and squealing
from the starting line. Well, he doesn't really break up the dancing, but a
hundred kids come over, when they hear the drag-strip sounds, to where
Beebe has a slot-racing stand. Slot racing is a model-train-type game in
which two model drag racers, each about five inches long, powered by electricity, run down a model drag strip. Beebe takes a microphone and announces that Dick Dale, the singer, is here, and anybody who will race
Dick at the slot-racing stand will get one of his records. Dick Dale is pretty
popular among the kids out here because he sings a lot of "surfing" songs.
The surfers—surfboard riders—are a cult much admired by all the kids.
They have their own argot, with adjectives like "hang ten," meaning the
best there is. They also go in for one particular brand of customizing: they
take old wood-bodied station wagons, which they call "woodies," and fix
them up for riding, sleeping and hauling surfing equipment for their week-
ends at the beach. The surfers also get a hell of a bang out of slot racing for

some reason, so with Dick Dale slot racing at the Teen Fair, you have about three areas of the arcane teen world all rolled into one.

Dick Dale, rigged out in Byronic shirt and blue cashmere V-neck sweater and wraparound sunglasses, singer's mufti U.S.A., has one cord with a starter button, while a bouffant nymphet from Newport named Sherma, Sherma of the Capri pants, has the other one. Don Beebe flashes a starting light and Sherma lets out a cry, not a thrilled cry, just nerves, and a model 1963 Ford and a model dragster go running down the slot board, which is about chest high. The slot board is said to be one-twenty-fifth the actual size of a drag strip, which somehow reminds you of those incredible stamp-size pictures in the dictionary with the notation that this is one-hundreth the size of a real elephant. A hundred kids were packed in around the slot racers and did not find it incredible. That is, they were interested in who would win, Dick Dale or Sherma. I'm sure they had no trouble magnifying the slot racers twenty-five times to the size of the full-blown, esoteric world of hot rods and custom cars.

I met George Barris, one of the celebrities of the custom-car world, at the Teen Fair. Barris is the biggest name in customizing. He is a good example of a kid who grew up completely absorbed in this teen-age world of cars, who pursued the pure flame and its forms with such devotion that he emerged an artist. It was like Tiepolo emerging from the studios of Venice, where the rounded Grecian haunches of the murals on the Palladian domes hung in the atmosphere like clouds. Except that Barris emerged from the auto-body shops of Los Angeles.

Barris invited me out to his studio—only he would never think of calling it that, he calls it Kustom City—at 10811 Riverside Drive in North Hollywood. If there is a river within a thousand miles of Riverside Drive, I saw no sign of it. It's like every place else out there: endless scorched boulevards lined with one-story stores, shops, bowling alleys, skating rinks, tacos drive-ins, all of them shaped not like rectangles but like trapezoids, from the way the roofs slant up from the back and the plate-glass fronts slant out as if they're going to pitch forward on the sidewalk and throw up. The signs are great, too. They all stand free on poles outside. They have horribly slick dog-legged shapes that I call boomerang modern. As for Kustom City—Barris grew up at the time when it was considered sharp to change all the C's to K's. He also sells Kandy Lac to paint cars Kandy Kolors with, and I know that sibilant C in City must have bothered the hell out of him at some point. It's interesting, I think, that he still calls the place Kustom City, and still sells Kandy Kolors, because he is an intelligent person. What it means is, he is absolutely untouched by the big amoeba god of Anglo-European sophistication that gets you in the East. You know how it is in the East. One day you notice that the boss's button-down shirt has this sweet percale roll to it, while your own was obviously slapped together by some mass-production graph keepers who are saving an eighth of inch of cloth per shirt, twelve inches per bolt or the like, and this starts eating at you.

Barris, whose family is Greek, is a solid little guy, five feet seven, thirty-seven years old, and he looks just like Picasso. When he's working, which is most of the time, he wears a heavy white T-style shirt, faded off-white pants cut full with pleats in the manner of Picasso walking along in the wind on a bluff at Rapallo, and crepe-sole slipper-style shoes, also off-white. Picasso, I should add, means nothing to Barris, although he knows who he is. It's just that to Barris and the customizers there is no one great universe of form and design called Art. Yet that's the universe he's in. He's not building cars, he's creating forms.

Barris starts taking me through Kustom City, and the place looks like any other body shop at first, but pretty soon you realize you're in a *gallery*. This place is full of cars such as you have never seen before. Half of them will never touch the road. They're put on trucks and trailers and carted all over the country to be exhibited at hot-rod and custom-car shows. They'll run, if it comes to that—they're full of big, powerful, hopped-up chrome-plated motors, because all that speed and power, and all that lovely apparatus, has tremendous emotional meaning to everybody in customizing. But it's like one of these Picasso or Miró rugs. You don't walk on the damn things. You hang them on the wall. It's the same thing with Barris' cars. In effect, they're sculpture.

For example, there is an incredible object he built called the XPAK-400 air car. The customizers love all that X jazz. It runs on a cushion of air, which is beside the point, because it's a pure piece of curvilinear abstract sculpture. If Branusci is any good, then this thing belongs on a pedestal, too. There is not a straight line in it, and only one true circle, and those countless planes, and tremendous baroque fins, and yet all in all it's a rigid little piece of solid geometrical harmony. As a matter of fact, Branusci and Barris both developed out of a design concept that we can call Streamlined Modern or Thirties Curvilinear—via utterly different roads, of course—and Barris and most other custom artists are carrying this idea of the abstract curve, which is very tough to handle, on and on and on at a time when your conventional designer—from architects to the guys who lay out magazines— are all Mondrian. Even the young Detroit car stylists are all Mondrian. Only the aircraft designers have done anything more with the Streamline, and they have only because they're forced to by physics, and so on. I want to return to that subject in a minute, but first I want to tell you about another car Barris was showing me.

This was stuck back in a storeroom. Barris wasn't interested in it any more since he did it nine years ago. But this car—this old car, as far as Barris was concerned—was like a dream prefiguration of a very hot sports car, the Quantum, that Saab has come out with this year after a couple of years of consultation with all sorts of aerodynamic experts and advance-guard designers. They're beautiful cars—Saab's and Barris'. They're the same body, practically—with this lovely topology rolling down over the tunneled headlights, with the whole hood curving down very low to the ground in front. I told Barris about the similarity, but he just shrugged; he is quite used to some manufacturer coming up with one of his cars five or six years later.

Anyway, Barris and I were walking around the side of Kustom City, through the parking lot, when I saw an Avanti, the new Studebaker sports model, very expensive. This one had paper mock-ups added to the front and the rear, and so I asked Barris about it. That wasn't much, he said, starting with the paper mock-ups, it brought the hood out a foot with a chic slope to it. He was doing the same sort of thing in the back to eliminate that kind of loaf-of-bread look. It really makes the car. Barris doesn't regard this as a very major project. It may end up in something like a kit you can buy, similar to the old Continental kits, to rig up front and back.

If Barris and the customizers hadn't been buried in the alien and suspect underworld of California youth, I don't think they would seem at all unusual by now. But they've had access to almost nothing but the hot-rod press. They're like Easter Islanders. Suddenly you come upon the astonishing objects, and then you have to figure out how they got there and why they're there.

If you study the work of Barris or Cushenberry, the aforementioned Silhouette, or Ed Roth or Darryl Starbird, can you beat that name?, I think you come up with a fragment of art history. Somewhere back in the thirties, designers, automobile designers among them, came up with the idea of the Streamline. It sounded "functional," and on an airplane it is functional, but on a car it's not, unless you're making a Bonneville speed run. Actually, it's baroque. The Streamline is baroque abstract or baroque modern or whatever you want to call it. Well, about the time the Streamline got going—in the thirties, you may recall, we had curved buildings, like the showpieces later, at the World's Fair—in came the Bauhaus movement, which was blown-up Mondrian, really. Before you knew it, everything was Mondrian—the Kleenex box: Mondrian; the format of the cover of *Life* Magazine: Mondrian; those bled-to-the-edge photograph layouts in *Paris-Match:* Mondrian. Even automobiles: Mondrian. They call Detroit automobiles streamlined, but they're not. If you don't believe it, look down from an airplane at all the cars parked on a shopping-center apron, and except that all the colors are pastel instead of primary, what have you got? A Mondrian painting. The Mondrian principle, those straight edges, is very tight, very Apollonian. The Streamline principle, which really has no function, which curves around and swoops and flows just for the thrill of it, is very free Dionysian. For reasons I don't have to labor over, the kids preferred the Dionysian. And since Detroit blew the thing, the Dionysian principle in cars was left to people in the teen-age netherworld, like George Barris.

Barris was living in Sacramento when he started customizing cars in 1940. As the plot develops, you have the old story of the creative child, the break from the mold of the parents, the garret struggle, the bohemian life, the first success, the accolade of the esoteric following, and finally the money starts pouring in. With this difference: We're out on old Easter Island, in the buried netherworld of teen-age Californians, and those objects, those cars, they have to do with the gods and the spirit and a lot of mystic stuff in the community.

Barris told me his folks were Greeks who owned a restaurant, and "they wanted me to be a restaurant man, like every other typical Greek, I guess," he said. But Barris, even at ten, was wild about cars, carving streamlined cars out of balsa wood. After a few years, he got a car of his own, a 1925 Buick, then a 1932 Ford. Barris established many of the formal conventions of customizing himself. Early in the game he had clients, other kids who paid him to customize their cars. In 1943 he moved to Los Angeles and landed in the middle of the tremendous teen-age culture that developed there during the war. Family life was dislocated, as the phrase goes, but the money was pouring in, and the kids began to work up their own style of life—as they've been doing ever since—and to establish those fanatic forms and conventions I was talking about earlier. Right at the heart of it, of course, was the automobile. Cars were hard to come by, what with the war, so the kids were raiding junkyards for parts, which led to custom-built cars, mostly roadsters by the very nature of it, and also to a lot of radical, hopped-up engines. All teen-age car nuts had elements of both in their work—customizing and hot-rodding, form and power—but tended to concentrate on one or the other. Barris—and Ed Roth later told me it was the same with him—naturally gravitated toward customizing. In high school, and later for a brief time at Sacramento College and the Los Angeles Art Center, he was taking what he described to me as mechanical drawing, shop, and free art.

I like this term "free art." In Barris' world at the time, and now for that matter, there was no such thing as great big old fructuous Art. There was mechanical drawing and then there was free art, which did not mean that it was liberating in any way, but rather that it was footloose and free and not going anywhere in particular. The kind of art that appealed to Barris, and meant something to the people he hung around with, was the automobile.

Barris gets a wonderful reflective grin on his face when he starts talking about the old days—1944 to 1948. He was a hot-rodder when hot-rodders were hot-rodders, that's the kind of look he gets. They all do. The professional hot-rodders—such as the Petersen magazine syndicate (*Hot Rod Magazine* and many others) and the National Hot Rod Association—have gone to great lengths to obliterate the memory of the gamey hot-rod days, and they try to give everybody in the field transfusions of Halazone so that the public will look at the hot-rodders as nice boys with short-sleeved sport shirts just back from the laundry and a chemistry set, such an interesting hobby.

In point of fact, Barris told me, it was a lurid time. Everybody would meet in drive-ins, the most famous of them being the Piccadilly out near Sepulveda Boulevard. It was a hell of a show, all the weird-looking roadsters and custom cars, with very loud varoom-varoom motors. By this time Barris had a '36 Ford roadster with many exotic features.

"I had just come from Sacramento, and I wasn't supposed to know anything. I was a tourist, but my car was wilder than anything around. I remember one night this kid comes up with a roadster with no door handles.

It looked real sharp, but he had to kick the door from the inside to open it. You should have seen the look on his face when he saw mine—I had the same thing, only with electric buttons."

The real action, though, was the drag racing, which was quite, but quite, illegal.

"We'd all be at the Piccadilly or some place, and guys would start challenging each other. You know, a guy goes up to another guy's car and looks it up and down like it has gangrene or something, and he says: 'You wanna *go?*' Or, if it was a real grudge match for some reason, he'd say, 'You wanna go for pink slips?' The registrations on the cars were pink; in other words, the winner got the other guy's car.

"Well, as soon as a few guys had challenged each other, everybody would ride out onto this stretch of Sepulveda Boulevard or the old divided highway, in Compton, and the guys would start dragging, one car on one side of the center line, the other car on the other. Go a quarter of a mile. It was wild. Some nights there'd be a thousand kids lining the road to watch, boys and girls, all sitting on the sides of their cars with the lights shining across the highway."

But George, what happened if some ordinary motorist happened to be coming down the highway at this point?

"Oh, we'd block off the highway at each end, and if some guy wanted to get through anyway, we'd tell him, 'Well, Mister, there are going to be two cars coming down both sides of the road pretty fast in a minute, and you can go through if you want to, but you'll just have to take your best shot.'

"They always turned around, of course, and after a while the cops would come. Then you *really* saw something. Everybody jumped in their cars and took off, in every direction. Some guys would head right across a field. Of course, all our cars were so hopped up, the cops could never catch anybody.

"Then one night we got raided at the Piccadilly. It was one Friday night. The cops came in and just started loading everybody in the wagons. I was sitting in a car with a cop who was off duty—he was a hot-rodder himself—or they would have picked me up, too. Saturday night everybody came back to the Piccadilly to talk about what happened the night before, and the cops came back again and picked up three hundred and fifty that night. That pretty well ended the Piccadilly."

From the very moment he was on his own in Los Angeles, when he was about eighteen, Barris never did anything but customize cars. He never took any other kind of job. At first he worked in a body shop that took him on because so many kids were coming by wanting this and that done to their cars, and the boss really didn't know how to do it, because it was all esoteric teen-age stuff. Barris was making next to nothing at first, but he never remembers feeling hard up, nor does any kid out there today I talked to. They have a magic economy or something. Anyway, in 1945 Barris opened his own shop on Compton Avenue, in Los Angeles, doing nothing but customizing. There was that much demand for it. It was no sweat, he said; pretty soon he was making better than $100 a week.

Most of the work he was doing then was modifying Detroit cars—chopping and channeling. Chopping is lowering the top of the car, bringing it nearer to the hood line. Channeling is lowering the body itself down between the wheels. Also, they'd usually strip off all the chrome and the door handles and cover up the wheel openings in the back. At that time, the look the kids liked was to have the body lowered in the back and slightly jacked up in the front, although today it's just the opposite. The front windshield in those days was divided by a post, and so chopping the top gave the car a very sinister appearance. The front windshield always looked like a couple of narrow, slitty little eyes. And I think this, more than anything else, diverted everybody from what Barris and the others were really doing. Hot-rodders had a terrible reputation at that time, and no line was ever drawn between hot-rodders and custom-car owners, because, in truth, they were speed maniacs, too.

This was Barris' chopped-and-channeled Mercury period. Mercurys were his favorite. All the kids knew the Barris styling and he was getting a lot of business. What he was really doing, in a formal sense, was trying to achieve the kind of streamlining that Detroit, for all intents and purposes, had abandoned. When modified, some of the old Mercurys were more streamlined than any standard model that Detroit has put out to this day. Many of the coupes he modified had a very sleek slope to the back window that has been picked up just this year in the "fastback" look of the Rivieras, Sting Rays, and a few other cars.

At this point Barris and the other customizers didn't really have enough capital to do many completely original cars, but they were getting more and more radical in modifying Detroit cars. They were doing things Detroit didn't do until years later—tailfins, bubbletops, twin headlights, concealed headlights, "Frenched" headlights, the low-slung body itself. They lifted some twenty designs from him alone. One, for example, is the way cars now have the exhaust pipes exit through the rear bumper or fender. Another is the bullet-shaped, or breast-shaped if you'd rather, front bumpers on the Cadillac.

Barris says "lifted," because some are exact down to the most minute details. Three years ago when he was in Detroit, Barris met a lot of car designers and, "I was amazed," he told me. "They could tell me about cars I built in 1945. They knew all about the four-door '48 Studebaker I restyled. I chopped the top and dropped the hood and it ended up a pretty good-looking car. And the bubbletop I built in 1954—they knew all about it. And all this time we thought they frowned on us."

Even today—dealing with movie stars and auto manufacturers and all sorts of people on the outside—I think Barris, and certainly the others, still feel psychologically a part of the alien teen-age netherworld in which they grew up. All that while they were carrying the torch for the Dionysian Streamline. They were America's modern baroque designers—and, oddly enough, "serious" designers, Anglo-European-steeped designers, are just coming around to it. Take Saarinen, especially in something like his T.W.A. terminal at Kennedy. The man in his last years came around to baroque modern.

It's interesting that the customizers, like sports-car fans, have always wanted cars minus most of the chrome—but for different ideals. The sports-car owner thinks chrome trim interferes with the "classic" look of his car. In other words, he wants to simplify the thing. The customizer thinks chrome interferes with something else—the luxurious baroque Streamline. The sports-car people snigger at tailfins. The customizers love them and, looked at from a baroque standard of beauty, they are really not so trashy at all. They are an inspiration, if you will, a wonderful fantasy extension of the curved line, and since the car in America is half fantasy anyway, a kind of baroque extension of the ego, you can build up a good argument for them.

Getting back to Easter Island, here were Barris and the others with their blowtorches and hard-rubber mallets, creating their baroque sculpture, cut off from the rest of the world and publicized almost solely via the teen-age grapevine. Barris was making a fairly good living, but others were starving at this thing. The pattern was always the same: a guy would open a body shop and take on enough hack collision work to pay the rent so that he could slam the door shut at 2 P.M. and get in there and do his custom jobs, and pretty soon the guy got so he couldn't even face *any* collision work. Dealing with all those crusty old arteriosclerotic bastards takes up all your *time,* man, and so they're trying to make a living doing nothing but custom work, and they are starving.

The situation is a lot like that today, except that customizing is beginning to be rationalized, in the sense Max Weber used that word. This rationalization, or efficient exploitation, began in the late forties when an $80-a-week movie writer named Robert Peterson noticed all the kids pouring their money into cars in a little world they had created for themselves, and he decided to exploit it by starting *Hot Rod Magazine,* which clicked right away and led to a whole chain of hot-rod and custom-car magazines. Petersen, by the way, now has a pot of money and drives Maseratis and other high-status-level sports cars of the Apollonian sort, not the Dionysian custom kind. Which is kind of a shame, because he has the money to commission something really incredible.

Up to that time the only custom-car show in the country was a wild event Barris used to put on bereft of any sort of midwifery by forty-two-year-old promoters with Windsor-knot ties who usually run low-cost productions. This car show was utterly within the teen-age netherworld, with no advertising or coverage of any sort. It took place each spring—during the high-school Easter vacations—when all the kids, as they still do, would converge on the beach at Balboa for their beer-drinking-*Fasching* rites, or whatever the Germans call it. Barris would rent the parking lot of a service station on a corner for a week, and kids from all over California would come with their customized cars. First there would be a parade; the cars, about a hundred fifty of them, would drive all through the streets of Balboa, and the kids would line the sidewalks to watch them; then they'd drive back to the lot and park and be on exhibit for the week.

Barris still goes off to Balboa and places like that. He likes that scene. Last year at Pacific Ocean Park he noticed all these bouffant babies and got the idea of spraying all those great puffed-up dandelion heads with fluorescent water colors, the same Kandy Kolors he uses on the cars. Barris took out an air gun, the girls all lined up and gave him fifty cents per, and he sprayed them with these weird, brilliant color combinations all afternoon

until he ran out of colors. Each girl would go skipping and screaming away
out onto the sidewalks and the beaches. Barris told me, "It was great that
night to take one of the rides, like the Bubble Ride, and look down and see
all those fluorescent colors. The kids were bopping [dancing] and running
around."

The Bubble is a ride that swings out over the ocean. It is supposed to be
like a satellite in orbit.

"But the fellows sky-diving got the best look as they came down by
parachute."

In 1948 Petersen put on the first custom-car show in the Los Angeles
armory, and this brought customizing out into the open a little. A wild-
looking Buick Barris had remodeled was one of the hits of the show, and
he was on his way, too.

At some point in the fifties a lot of Hollywood people discovered Barris
and the customizers. It was somewhat the way the literary set had discovered the puppeteer Tony Sarg during the thirties and deified him in a very
arty, in-groupy way, only I think in the case of Hollywood and Barris there
was something a lot more in-the-grain about it. The people who end up
in Hollywood are mostly Dionysian sorts and they feel alien and resentful when confronted with the Anglo-European ethos. They're a little slow
to note the difference between top-sides and sneakers, but they appreciate
Cuban sunglasses.

In his showroom at Kustom City, down past the XPAK-400 air car,
Barris has a corner practically papered with photographs of cars he has customized or handmade for Hollywood people: Harry Karl, Jayne Mansfield,
Elvis Presley, Liberace, and even celebrities from the outside like Barry
Goldwater (a Jaguar with a lot of airplane-style dials on the dashboard) and
quite a few others. In fact, he built most of the wild cars that show-business
people come up with for publicity purposes. He did the "diamond-dust"
paint job on the Bobby Darin Dream Car, which was designed and built by
Andy DiDia of Detroit. That car is an example par excellence of baroque
streamlining, by the way. It was badly panned when pictures of it were first
published, mainly because it looked like Darin was again forcing his ego
on the world. But as baroque modern sculpture—again, given the fantasy
quotient in cars to begin with—it is pretty good stuff.

As the hot-rod and custom-car show idea began catching on, and there
are really quite a few big ones now, including one at the Coliseum up at

Columbus Circle last year, it became like the culture boom in the other arts. The big names, particularly Barris and Roth but also Starbird, began to make a lot of money in the same thing Picasso has made a lot of money in: reproductions. Barris' creations are reproduced by AMT Models as model cars. Roth's are reproduced by Revel. The way people have taken to these models makes it clearer still that what we have here is no longer a car but a design object, an *objet,* as they say.

Of course, it's not an unencumbered art form like oil painting or most conventional modern sculpture. It carries a lot of mental baggage with it, plain old mechanical craftsmanship, the connotations of speed and power and the aforementioned mystique that the teen-age netherworld brings to cars. What you have is something more like sculpture in the era of Benvenuto Cellini, when sculpture was always more tied up with religion and architecture. In a lot of other ways it's like the Renaissance, too. Young customizers have come to Barris' shop, for example, like apprentices coming to the feet of the master. Barris said there were eleven young guys in Los Angeles right now who had worked for him and then gone out on their own, and he doesn't seem to begrudge them that.

"But they take on too much work," he told me. "They want a name, fast, and they take on a lot of work, which they do for practically nothing, just to get a name. They're usually undercapitalized to begin with, and they take on too much work, and then they can't deliver and they go bankrupt."

There's another side to this, too. You have the kid from the small town in the Midwest who's like the kid from Keokuk who wants to go to New York and live in the Village and be an artist and the like—he means, you know, things around home are but *hopelessly,* totally square; home and all that goes with it. Only the kid from the Midwest who wants to be a custom-car artist goes to Los Angeles to do it. He does pretty much the same thing. He lives a kind of suburban bohemian life and takes odd jobs and spends the rest of his time at the feet of somebody like Barris, working on cars.

I ran into a kid like that at Barris'. We were going through his place, back into his interiors—car interiors—department, and we came upon Ronny Camp. Ronny is twenty-two, but he looks about eighteen because he has teen-age posture. Ronny is, in fact, a bright and sensitive kid with an artistic eye, but at first glance he seems always to have his feet propped up on a table or something so you can't walk past, and you have to kind of bat them down, and he then screws up his mouth and withdraws his eyeballs to the optic chiasma and glares at you with his red sulk. That was the misleading first impression.

Ronny was crazy over automobiles and nobody in his hometown, Lafayette, Indiana, knew anything about customizing. So one day Ronny packs up and tells the folks, This is it, I'm striking out for hip territory, Los Angeles, where a customizing artist is an artist. He had no idea where he was going, you understand, all he knew was that he was going to Barris' shop and make it from there. So off he goes in his 1960 Chevrolet.

Ronny got a job at a service station and poured every spare cent into getting the car customized at Barris'. His car was right there while we were talking, a fact I was very aware of, because he never looked at me. He never took his eyes off that car. It's what is called semi-custom. Nothing has been done to it to give it a really sculptural quality, but a lot of streamlining details have been added. The main thing you notice is the color—tangerine flake. This paint—one of Barris' Kandy Kolor concoctions—makes the car look like it has been encrusted with chips of some kind of semi-precious ossified tangerine, all coated with a half-inch of clear lacquer. There used to be very scholarly and abstruse studies of color and color symbolism around the turn of the century, and theorists concluded that preferences for certain colors were closely associated with rebelliousness, and these are the very same colors many of the kids go for—purple, carnal yellow, various violets and lavenders and fuchsias and many other of these Kandy Kolors.

After he got his car fixed up, Ronny made a triumphal progress back home. He won the trophy in his class at the national hot-rod and custom-car show in Indianapolis, and he came tooling into Lafayette, Indiana, and down the main street in his tangerine-flake 1960 Chevrolet. It was like Ezra Pound going back to Hamilton, New York, with his Bollingen plaque and saying, Here I am, Hamilton, New York. The way Ronny and Barris tell it, the homecoming was a big success—all the kids thought Ronny was all right, after all, and he made a big hit at home. I can't believe the part about home. I mean, I can't really believe Ronny made a hit with a tangerine-flake Chevrolet. But I like to conjecture about his parents. I don't know anything about them, really. All I know is, *I* would have had a hell of a lump in my throat if I had seen Ronny coming up to the front door in his tangerine-flake car, bursting so flush and vertical with triumph that no one would ever think of him as a child of the red sulk—Ronny, all the way back from California with his grail.

Along about 1957, Barris started hearing from the Detroit auto manu-facturers.

"One day," he said, "I was working in the shop—we were over in Lynwood then—and Chuck Jordan from Cadillac walked in. He just walked in and said he was from Cadillac. I thought he meant the local agency. We had done this Cadillac for Liberace, the interior had his songs, all the notes, done in black and white Moroccan leather, and I thought he wanted to see something about that. But he said he was from the Cadillac styling center in Detroit and they were interested in our colors. Chuck—he's up there pretty good at Cadillac now, I think—said he had read some articles about our colors, so I mixed up some samples for him. I had developed a trans-lucent paint, using six different ingredients, and it had a lot of brilliance and depth. That was what interested them. In this paint you look through a clear surface into the color, which is very brilliant. Anyway, this was the first time we had any idea they even knew who we were."

Since then Barris has made a lot of trips to Detroit. The auto compa-nies, mainly GM and Ford, pump him for ideas about what the kids are going for. He tells them what's wrong with their cars, mainly that they aren't streamlined and sexy enough.

"But, as they told me, they have to design a car they can sell to the farmer in Kansas as well as the hot dog in Hollywood."

For that reason—the inevitable compromise—the customizers do not dream of working as stylists for the Detroit companies, although they deal with them more and more. It would be like René Magritte or somebody going on the payroll of Continental Can to do great ideas of Western man. This is an old story in art, of course, genius vs. the organization. But the customizers don't think of corporate bureaucracy quite the way your conventional artist does, whether he be William Gropper or Larry Rivers, namely, as a lot of small-minded Babbitts, venal enemies of culture, etc. They just think of the big companies as part of that vast mass of *adult* America, sclerotic from years of just being too old, whose rules and ideas weigh down upon Youth like a vast, bloated sac. Both Barris and Roth have met Detroit's Young Stylists, and seem to look upon them as monks from another country. The Young Stylists are designers Detroit recruits from the art schools and sets up in a room with clay and styluses and tells to go to it—start carving models, dream cars, new ideas. Roth especially cannot conceive of anyone having any valid concepts about cars who hasn't come out of the teen-age netherworld. And maybe he's right. While the Young Stylists sit in a north-lit studio smoothing out little Mondrian solids, Barris and Roth carry on in the Dionysian loop-the-loop of streamlined baroque modern.

I've mentioned Ed Roth several times in the course of this without really telling you about him. And I want to, because he, more than any other of the customizers, has kept alive the spirit of alienation and rebellion that is so important to the teen-age ethos that customizing grew up in. He's also the most colorful, and the most intellectual, and the most capricious. Also the most cynical. He's the Salvador Dalí of the movement—a surrealist in his designs, a showman by temperament, a prankster. Roth is really too bright to stay within the ethos, but he stays in it with a spirit of luxurious obstinacy. Any style of life is going to produce its celebrities if it sticks to its rigid standards, but in the East a talented guy would most likely be drawn into the Establishment in one way or another. That's not so inevitable in California.

I had been told that Roth was a surly guy who never bathed and was hard to get along with, but from the moment I first talked to him on the telephone he was an easy guy and very articulate. His studio—he calls it a studio, by the way—is out in Maywood, on the other side of the city from North Hollywood, in what looked to me like a much older and more run-down section. When I walked up, Roth was out on the apron of his place doing complicated drawings and lettering on somebody's ice-cream truck with an airbrush. I knew right away it was Roth from pictures I had seen of him; he has a beatnik-style beard. "Ed Roth?" I said. He said yeah and we started talking and so forth. A little while later we were sitting in a diner having a couple of sandwiches and Roth, who was wearing a short-sleeved T shirt, pointed to this huge tattoo on his left arm that says "Roth" in the lettering style with big serifs that he uses as his signature. "I had that done a couple of years ago because guys keep coming up to me saying, 'Are you Ed Roth?'"

Roth is a big, powerful guy, about six feet four, two hundred seventy pounds, thirty-one years old. He has a constant sort of court attendant named Dirty Doug, a skinny little guy who blew in from out of nowhere, sort of like Ronny Camp over at Barris'. Dirty Doug has a job of sweeping up in a steel mill, but what he obviously lives for is the work he does around Roth's. Roth seems to have a lot of sympathy for the Ronny Camp–Dirty Doug syndrome and keeps him around as a permanent fixture. At Roth's behest, apparently, Dirty Doug has dropped his last name, Kinney, altogether, and refers to himself as Dirty Doug—not Doug. The relationship between Roth and Dirty Doug—which is sort of Quixote and Sancho Panza, Holmes and Watson, Lone Ranger and Tonto, Raffles and Bunny—is part of the folklore of the hot-rod and custom-car kids. It even crops up in the hot-rod comic books, which are an interesting phenomenon in themselves. Dirty Doug, in this folklore, is every rejected outcast little kid in the alien netherworld, and Roth is the understanding, if rather overly pranksterish, protective giant or Robin Hood—you know, a good-bad giant, not part of the Establishment.

Dirty Doug drove up in one of his two Cadillacs one Saturday afternoon while I was at Roth's, and he had just gone through another experience of rejection. The police had hounded him out of Newport. He has two Cadillacs, he said, because one is always in the shop. Dirty Doug's cars, like most customizers', are always in the process of becoming. The streaks of "primer" paint on the Cadillac he was driving at the time had led to his rejection in Newport. He had driven to Newport for the weekend. "All the cops have to do is see paint like that and already you're 'one of those hot-rodders,'" he said. "They practically followed me down the street and gave me a ticket every twenty-five feet. I was going to stay the whole weekend, but I came on back."

At custom-car shows, kids are always asking Roth, "Where's Dirty Doug?" and if Dirty Doug couldn't make it for some reason, Roth will recruit any kid around who knows the pitch and install him as Dirty Doug, just to keep the fans happy.

Thus Roth protects the image of Dirty Doug even when the guy's not around, and I think it becomes a very important piece of mythology. The thing is, Roth is not buying the act of the National Hot Rod Association, which for its own reasons, not necessarily the kids' reasons, is trying to assimilate the hot-rod ethos into conventional America. It wants to make all the kids look like candidates for the Peace Corps or something.

The heart of the contretemps between the NHRA Establishment and Roth can be illustrated in their slightly different approach to drag racing on the streets. The Establishment tries to eliminate the practice altogether and restricts drag racing to certified drag strips and, furthermore, lets the people know about that. They encourage the hot-rod clubs to help out little old ladies whose cars are stuck in the snow and then hand them a card reading something like, "You have just been assisted by a member of the Blue Bolt Hot Rod Club, an organization of car enthusiasts dedicated to promoting safety on our highways."

Roth's motto is: "Hell, if a guy wants to go, let him *go*."

Roth's designs are utterly baroque. His air car—the Rotar—is not nearly as good a piece of design as Barris', but his beatnik Bandit is one of the great *objets* of customizing. It's a very Rabelaisian *tour de force*—a twenty-first-century version of a '32 Ford hot-rod roadster. And Roth's new car, the Mysterion, which he was working on when I was out there, is another *tour de force,* this time in the hottest new concept in customizing, asymmetrical design. Asymmetrical design, I gather, has grown out of the fact that the driver sits on one side of the car, not in the middle, thereby giving a car an eccentric motif to begin with. In Roth's Mysterion—a bubbletop coupe powered by two 406-horsepower Thunderbird motors—a thick metal arm sweeps up to the left from the front bumper level, as from the six to the three on a clock, and at the top of it is an elliptical shape housing a bank of three headlights. No headlights on the right side at all; just a small clearance light to orient the oncoming driver. This big arm, by the way, comes up in a spherical geometrical arc, not a flat plane. Balancing this, as far as the design goes, is an arm that comes up over the back of the bubbletop on the right side, like from the nine to the twelve on a clock, also in a spherical arc, if you can picture all this. Anyway, this car takes the Streamline and the abstract curve and baroque curvilinear one step further, and I wouldn't be surprised to see it inspiring Detroit designs in the years to come.

Roth is a brilliant designer, but as I was saying, his conduct and his attitude dilute the Halazone with which the Establishment is trying to transfuse the whole field. For one thing, Roth, a rather thorough-going bohemian, kept turning up at the car shows in a T shirt. That was what he wore at the big National Show at the New York Coliseum, for example. Roth also insists on sleeping in a car or station wagon while on the road, even though he is making a lot of money now and could travel first class. Things came to a head early this year when Roth was out in Terre Haute, Indiana, for a show. At night Roth would just drive his car out in a cornfield, lie back on the front seat, stick his feet out the window and go to sleep. One morning some kid came by and saw him and took a picture while Roth was still sleeping and sent it to the model company Roth has a contract with, Revel, with a note saying, "Dear Sirs: Here.is a picture of the man you say on your boxes is the King of Customizers." The way Roth tells it, it must have been an extraordinarily good camera, because he says, with considerable pride, "There were a bunch of flies flying around my feet, and this picture showed all of them."

Revel asked Roth if he wouldn't sort of spruce up a little bit for the image and all that, and so Roth entered into a kind of reverse rebellion. He bought a full set of tails, silk hat, boiled shirt, cuff links, studs, the whole apparatus, for $215, also a monocle, and now he comes to all the shows like that. "I bow and kiss all the girls' hands," he told me. "The guys get pretty teed off about that, but what can they do? I'm being a perfect gentleman."

To keep things going at the shows, where he gets $1000 to $2000 per appearance—he's that much of a drawing card—Roth creates and builds one new car a year. This is the Dalí pattern, too. Dalí usually turns out one huge and (if that's possible any more) shocking painting each year or so and ships it on over to New York, where they install it in Carstairs or hire a hall if the thing is too big, and Dalí books in at the St. Regis and appears on television wearing a rhinoceros horn on his forehead. The new car each year also keeps Roth's model-car deal going. But most of Roth's income right now is the heavy business he does in Weirdo and Monster shirts. Roth is very handy with the airbrush—has a very sure hand—and one day at a car show he got the idea of drawing a grotesque cartoon on some guy's sweat shirt with the airbrush, and that started the Weirdo shirts. The typical Weirdo shirt is in a vein of draftsmanship you might call Mad Magazine Bosch, very slickly done for something so grotesque, and will show a guy who looks like Frankenstein, the big square steam-shovel jaw and all, only he has a wacky leer on his face, at the wheel of a hot-rod roadster, and usually he has a round object up in the air in his right hand that looks like it is attached to the dashboard by a cord. This, it turns out, is the gearshift. It doesn't look like a gearshift to me, but every kid knows immediately what it is.

"Kids *love* dragging a car," Roth told me. "I mean they really love it. And what they love most is when they shift from low to second. They get so they can practically *feel* the r.p.m.'s. They can shift without hardly hitting the clutch at all."

These shirts always have a big caption, and usually something rebellious or at least alienated, something like "MOTHER IS WRONG" or "BORN TO LOSE."

"A teen-ager always has resentment to adult authority," Roth told me. "These shirts are like a tattoo, only it's a tattoo they can take off if they want to."

I gather Roth doesn't look back on his own childhood with any great relish. Apparently his father was pretty strict and never took any abiding interest in Roth's creative flights, which were mostly in the direction of cars, like Barris'.

"You've got to be real careful when you raise a kid," Roth told me several times. "You've got to spend time with him. If he's working on something, building something, you've got to work with him." Roth's early career was almost exactly like Barris', the hot rods, the drive-ins, the drag racing, the college (East Los Angeles Junior College and UCLA), taking mechanical drawing, the chopped and channeled '32 Ford (a big favorite with all the hot-rodders), purple paint, finally the first custom shop, one stall in a ten-stall body shop.

"They threw me out of there," Roth said, "because I painted a can of Lucky Lager beer on the wall with an airbrush. I mean, it was a perfect can of Lucky Lager beer, all the details, the highlights, the seals, the small print, the whole thing. Somehow this can of Lucky Lager beer really bugged the guy who owned the place. Here was this can of Lucky Lager beer on *his* wall."

The Establishment can't take this side of Roth, just as no Establishment could accommodate Dadaists for very long. Beatniks more easily than Dadaists. The trick has always been to absorb them somehow. So far Roth has resisted absorption.

"We were the real gangsters of the hot-rod field," Roth said. "They keep telling us we have a rotten attitude. We have a different attitude, but that doesn't make us rotten."

Several times, though, Roth would chuckle over something, usually some particularly good gesture he had made, like the Lucky Lager, and say, "I am a real rotten guy."

Roth pointed out, with some insight, I think, that the kids have a revealing vocabulary. They use the words "rotten," "bad" and "tough" in a very fey, ironic way. Often a particularly baroque and sleek custom car will be called a "big, bad Merc" (for Mercury) or something like that. In this case "bad" means "good," but it also retains some of the original meaning of "bad." The kids know that to adults, like their own parents, this car is going to look sinister and somehow like an assault on their style of life. Which it is. It's rebellion, which the parents don't go for—"bad," which the kids *do* go for, "bad" meaning "good."

Roth said that Detroit is beginning to understand that there are just a hell of a lot of these bad kids in the United States and that they are growing up. "And they want a better car. They don't want an old man's car."

Roth has had pretty much the same experience as Barris with the motor companies. He has been taken to Detroit and feted and offered a job as a designer and a consultant. But he never took it seriously.

"I met a lot of the young designers," said Roth. "They were nice guys and they know a lot about design, but none of them has actually done a car. They're just up there working away on those clay models."

I think this was more than the craftsman's scorn of the designer who never actually does the work, like some of the conventional sculptors today who have never chiseled a piece of stone or cast anything. I think it was more that the young Detroit stylists came to the automobile strictly from art school and the abstract world of design—rather than via the teen-age mystique of the automobile and the teen-age ethos of rebellion. This status-group feeling is very important to Roth, and to Barris, for that matter, because it was only because of the existence of this status group—and this style of life—that custom car sculpture developed at all.

With the Custom Car Caravan on the road—it has already reached Freedomland—the manufacturers may well be on the way to routinizing the charisma, as Max Weber used to say, which is to say, bringing the whole field into a nice, safe, vinyl-glamorous marketable ball of polyethylene. It's probably already happening. The customizers will end up like those poor bastards in Haiti, the artists, who got too much, too soon, from Selden Rodman and the other folk-doters on the subject of primitive genius, so they're all down there at this moment carving African masks out of mahogany—what I mean is, they never *had* an African mask in Haiti before Selden Rodman got there.

I think Roth has a premonition that something like that is liable to happen, although it will happen to him last, if at all. I couldn't help but get a kick out of what Roth told me about his new house. We had been talking about how much money he was making, and he told me how his taxable income was only about $6200 in 1959, but might hit $15,000 this year, maybe more, and he mentioned he was building a new house for his wife and five kids down at Newport, near the beach. I immediately asked him for details, hoping to hear about an utterly baroque piece of streamlined architecture.

"No, this is going to be my wife's house, the way she wants it, nothing way out; I mean, she has to do the home scene." He has also given her a huge white Cadillac, by the way, unadorned except for his signature— "Roth"—with those big serifs, on the side. I saw the thing, it's huge, and in the back seat were his children, very sweet-looking kids, all drawing away on drawing pads.

But I think Roth was a little embarrassed that he had disappointed me on the house, because he told me his idea of the perfect house—which turned out to be a kind of ironic parable:

"This house would have this big, round living room with a dome over it, you know? Right in the middle of the living room would be a huge television set on a swivel so you could turn it and see it from wherever you are in the room. And you have this huge easy chair for yourself, you know the kind that you can lean back to about ninety-three different positions and it vibrates and massages your back and all that, and this chair is on tracks, like a railroad yard.

"You can take one track into the kitchen, which just shoots off one side of the living room, and you can ride backward if you want to and watch the television all the time, and of course in the meantime you've pressed a lot of buttons so your TV dinner is cooking in the kitchen and all you have to do is go and take it out of the oven.

"Then you can roll right back into the living room, and if somebody rings the doorbell you don't move at all. You just press a button on this big automatic console you have by your chair and the front door opens, and you just yell for the guy to come in, and you can keep watching television.

"At night, if you want to go to bed, you take another track into the bedroom, which shoots off on another side, and you just kind of roll out of the chair into the sack. On the ceiling above your bed you have another TV set, so you can watch all night."

Roth is given, apparently, to spinning out long Jean Shepherd stories like this with a very straight face, and he told me all of this very seriously. I guess I didn't look like I was taking it very seriously, because he said, "I have a TV set over the bed in my house right now—you can ask my wife."

I met his wife, but I didn't ask her. The funny thing is, I did find my-self taking the story seriously. To me it was a sort of parable of the Bad Guys, and the Custom Sculpture. The Bad Guys built themselves a little world and got onto something good and then the Establishment, all sorts of Establishments, began closing in, with a lot of cajolery, thievery and hypnosis, and in the end, thrown into a vinyl Petri dish, the only way left to tell the whole bunch of them where to head in was to draw them a huge asinine picture of themselves, which they were sure to like. After all, Roth's dream house is nothing more than his set of boiled shirt and tails expanded into a whole universe. And he is not really very hopeful about that either.

1965

In some ways, twenty-five hundred years ago, Plato asked the same question. In *Symposium,* he tells us a relatively simple story about some friends at a dinner party who talk about love. Surrounding Plato's story about that party, however, is the philosopher's own story about how he heard the story. According to Plato, a man named Aristodemus, who had attended the dinner party, told his friends Apollodorus and Phonix about the conversation that evening. Phonix then told his friend about the party, and that friend told it to Glaucon, and then Glaucon told it to Plato. But Glaucon isn't sure that he remembers the story correctly, so he looks to Apollodorus to clarify some details, even though Apollodorus wasn't actually at the party, but instead had only heard about it from Aristodemus, who was. Why is this important? At first it's hard to say why any of it is important, and so we temporarily forget about these elaborate machinations once Plato starts telling us about the party itself. What we learn is that several people made speeches at the party, and all of them had opinions about the meaning of love. Socrates also happened to be at the dinner party, and when he finally speaks up he tells his dinner companions about a woman named Diotima, a priestess whom he knew while growing up in Athens and who had once shared with Socrates her own thoughts about love. When we're young, she said, we begin by loving a body, and then we learn eventually how to love different bodies, and then how to love souls, and then customs, and then finally knowledge. Love, it turns out, is multilayered, like most things. But by the time we learn this in Plato's *Symposium,* we're hearing it from a fifth-hand source, and so the story is a little fuzzy. On top of this, the story comes from a party that took place back when Socrates was still alive—fifteen years earlier than when Plato was writing *Symposium*—and the crux of Plato's essay isn't even that story about the party itself, but the story that's told at the party by Socrates about his youth—a story within a story within an essay, it turns out—remembered from a moment in Socrates's life that happened sixty years before he shares it with his friends. So seventy-five years and six retellings later, what we learn in the *Symposium* is that knowledge is layered, too. It's complicated, multi-dimensional, unpredictable, very messy, and we probably couldn't agree on what it even is or how it's even made or the best way to frame it for someone else to appreciate. And this is why the *Symposium* is itself so complicated. Knowledge—real knowledge—is problematized the moment we start trying to nail it down.

GAY TALESE

Frank Sinatra Has a Cold

Frank Sinatra, holding a glass of bourbon in one hand and a cigarette in the other, stood in a dark corner of the bar between two attractive but fading blondes who sat waiting for him to say something. But he said nothing; he had been silent during much of the evening, except now in this private club in Beverly Hills he seemed even more distant, staring out through the smoke and semidarkness into a large room beyond the bar where dozens of young couples sat huddled around small tables or twisted in the center of the floor to the clamorous clang of folk-rock music blaring from the stereo. The two blondes knew, as did Sinatra's four male friends who stood nearby, that it was a bad idea to force conversation upon him when he was in this mood of sullen silence, a mood that had hardly been uncommon during this first week of November, a month before his fiftieth birthday.

Sinatra had been working in a film that he now disliked, could not wait to finish; he was tired of all the publicity attached to his dating the twenty-year-old Mia Farrow, who was not in sight tonight; he was angry that a CBS television documentary of his life, to be shown in two weeks, was reportedly prying into his privacy, even speculating on his possible friendship with Mafia leaders; he was worried about his starring role in an hour-long NBC show entitled *Sinatra—A Man and His Music,* which would require that he sing eighteen songs with a voice that at this particular moment, just a few nights before the taping was to begin, was weak and sore and uncertain. Sinatra was ill. He was the victim of an ailment so common that most people would consider it trivial. But when it gets to Sinatra it can plunge him into a state of anguish, deep depression, panic, even rage. Frank Sinatra had a cold.

Sinatra with a cold is Picasso without paint, Ferrari without fuel—only worse. For the common cold robs Sinatra of that uninsurable jewel, his voice, cutting into the core of his confidence, and it affects not only his own psyche but also seems to cause a kind of psychosomatic nasal drip within dozens of people who work for him, drink with him, love him, depend on him for their own welfare and stability. A Sinatra with a cold can, in a small way, send vibrations through the entertainment industry and beyond as surely as a President of the United States, suddenly sick, can shake the national economy.

For Frank Sinatra was now involved with many things involving many people—his own film company, his record company, his private airline, his missile-parts firm, his real-estate holdings across the nation, his personal staff of seventy-five—which are only a portion of the power he is and has come to represent. He seemed now to be also the embodiment of the fully emancipated male, perhaps the only one in America, the man who can do anything he wants, anything, can do it because he has money, the energy, and no apparent guilt. In an age when the very young seem to be taking over, protesting and picketing and demanding change, Frank Sinatra survives as a national phenomenon, one of the few prewar products to withstand the test of time. He is the champ who made the big comeback, the man who had everything, lost it, then got it back, letting nothing stand in his way, doing what few men can do: he uprooted his life, left his family, broke with everything that was familiar, learning in the process that one way to hold a woman is not to hold her. Now he has the affection of Nancy and Ava and Mia, the fine female produce of three generations, and still has the adoration of his children, the freedom of a bachelor, he does not feel old, he makes old men feel young, makes them think that if Frank Sinatra can do it, it can be done; not that they could do it, but it is still nice for other men to know, at fifty, that it can be done.

But now, standing at this bar in Beverly Hills, Sinatra had a cold, and he continued to drink quietly and he seemed miles away in his private world, not even reacting when suddenly the stereo in the other room switched to a Sinatra song, "In the Wee Small Hours of the Morning."

It is a lovely ballad that he first recorded ten years ago, and it now inspired many young couples who had been sitting, tired of twisting, to get up and move slowly around the dance floor, holding one another very close. Sinatra's intonation, precisely clipped, yet full and flowing, gave a deeper meaning to the simple lyrics—"In the wee small hours of the morning / while the whole wide world is fast asleep / you lie awake, and think about the girl . . ."—it was like so many of his classics, a song that evoked loneliness and sensuality, and when blended with the dim light and the alcohol and nicotine and late-night needs, it became a kind of airy aphrodisiac. Undoubtedly the words from this song, and others like it, had put millions in the mood, it was music to make love by, and doubtless much love had been made by it all over America at night in cars, while the batteries burned down, in cottages by the lake, on beaches during balmy summer evenings, in secluded parks and exclusive penthouses and furnished rooms, in cabin cruisers and cabs and cabanas—in all places where Sinatra's songs could be heard were these words that warmed women, wooed and won them, snipped the final thread of inhibition and gratified the male egos of ungrateful lovers; two generations of men had been the beneficiaries of such ballads, for which they were eternally in his debt, for which they may eternally hate him. Nevertheless here he was, the man himself, in the early hours of the morning in Beverly Hills, out of range.

The two blondes, who seemed to be in their middle thirties, were preened and polished, their matured bodies softly molded within tight dark suits. They sat, legs crossed, perched on the high bar stools. They listened to the music. Then one of them pulled out a Kent and Sinatra quickly placed his gold lighter under it and she held his hand, looked at his fingers: they were nubby and raw, and the pinkies protruded, being so stiff from arthritis that he could barely bend them. He was, as usual, immaculately dressed. He wore an oxford-grey suit with a vest, a suit conservatively cut on the outside but trimmed with flamboyant silk within; his shoes, British, seemed to be shined even on the bottom of the soles. He also wore, as everybody seemed to know, a remarkably convincing black hairpiece, one of sixty that he owns, most of them under the care of an inconspicuous little grey-haired lady who, holding his hair in a tiny satchel, follows him around whenever he performs. She earns $400 a week. The most distinguishing thing about Sinatra's face are his eyes, clear blue and alert, eyes that within seconds can go cold with anger, or glow with affection, or, as now, reflect a vague detachment that keeps his friends silent and distant.

Leo Durocher, one of Sinatra's closest friends, was now shooting pool in the small room behind the bar. Standing near the door was Jim Mahoney, Sinatra's press agent, a somewhat chunky young man with a square jaw and narrow eyes who would resemble a tough Irish plainclothesman if it were not for the expensive continental suits he wears and his exquisite shoes often adorned with polished buckles. Also nearby was a big, broad-shouldered two-hundred-pound actor named Brad Dexter who seemed always to be thrusting out his chest so that his gut would not show.

Brad Dexter has appeared in several films and television shows, displaying fine talent as a character actor, but in Beverly Hills he is equally known for the role he played in Hawaii two years ago when he swam a few hundred yards and risked his life to save Sinatra from drowning in a riptide. Since then Dexter has been one of Sinatra's constant companions and has been made a producer in Sinatra's film company. He occupies a plush office near Sinatra's executive suite. He is endlessly searching for literary properties that might be converted into new starring roles for Sinatra. Whenever he is among strangers with Sinatra he worries because he knows that Sinatra brings out the best and worst in people—some men will become aggressive, some women will become seductive, others will stand around skeptically appraising him, the scene will be somehow intoxicated by his mere presence, and maybe Sinatra himself, if feeling as badly as he was tonight, might become intolerant or tense, and then: headlines. So Brad Dexter tries to anticipate danger and warn Sinatra in advance. He confesses to feeling very protective of Sinatra, admitting in a recent moment of self-revelation: "I'd kill for him."

While this statement may seem outlandishly dramatic, particularly when taken out of context, it nonetheless expresses a fierce fidelity that is quite common within Sinatra's special circle. It is a characteristic that Sinatra, without admission, seems to prefer: All the Way; All or Nothing at All. This is the Sicilian in Sinatra; he permits his friends, if they wish to remain that, none of the easy Anglo-Saxon outs. But if they remain loyal, then there is nothing Sinatra will not do in turn—fabulous gifts, personal kindnesses, encouragement when they're down, adulation when they're up. They are wise to remember, however, one thing. He is Sinatra. The boss. Il Padrone.

I had seen something of this Sicilian side of Sinatra last summer at Jilly's saloon in New York, which was the only other time I'd gotten a close view of him prior to this night in this California club. Jilly's, which is on West Fifty-second Street in Manhattan, is where Sinatra drinks whenever he is in New York, and there is a special chair reserved for him in the back room against the wall that nobody else may use. When he is occupying it, seated behind a long table flanked by his closest New York friends—who include the saloonkeeper, Jilly Rizzo, and Jilly's azure-haired wife, Honey, who is known as the "Blue Jew"—a rather strange ritualistic scene develops. That night dozens of people, some of them casual friends of Sinatra's, some mere acquaintances, some neither, appeared outside of Jilly's saloon. They approached it like a shrine. They had come to pay respect. They were from New York, Brooklyn, Atlantic City, Hoboken. They were old actors, young actors, former prizefighters, tired trumpet players, politicians, a boy with a cane. There was a fat lady who said she remembered Sinatra when he used to throw the *Jersey Observer* onto her front porch in 1933. There were middle-aged couples who said they had heard Sinatra sing at the Rustic Cabin in 1938 and "We knew then that he really had it!" Or they had heard him when he was with Harry James's band in 1939, or with Tommy Dorsey in 1941 ("Yeah, that's the song, 'I'll Never Smile Again'—he sang it one night in this dump near Newark and we danced . . ."); or they remembered that time at the Paramount with the swooners, and him with those bow ties, The Voice; and one woman remembered that awful boy she knew then—Alexander Dorogokupetz, an eighteen-year-old heckler who had thrown a tomato at Sinatra and the bobby-soxers in the balcony had tried to flail him to death. Whatever became of Alexander Dorogokupetz? The lady did not know.

And they remembered when Sinatra was a failure and sang trash like "Mairzy Doats," and they remembered his comeback and on this night they were all standing outside Jilly's saloon, dozens of them, but they could not get in. So some of them left. But most of them stayed, hoping that soon they might be able to push or wedge their way into Jilly's between the elbows and backsides of the men drinking three-deep at the bar, and they might be able to peek through and see him sitting back there. This is all they really wanted; they wanted to see him. And for a few moments they gazed in silence through the smoke and they stared. Then they turned, fought their way out of the bar, went home.

Some of Sinatra's close friends, all of whom are known to the men guarding Jilly's door, do manage to get an escort into the back room. But once they are there they, too, must fend for themselves. On the particular evening, Frank Gifford, the former football player, got only seven yards in three tries. Others who had somehow been close enough to shake Sinatra's hand did not shake it; instead they just touched him on the shoulder or sleeve, or they merely stood close enough for him to see them and, after he'd given them a wink of recognition or a wave or a nod or called out their names (he had a fantastic memory for first names), they would then turn and leave. They had checked in. They had paid their respects. And as I watched this ritualistic scene, I got the impression that Frank Sinatra was dwelling simultaneously in two worlds that were not contemporary.

On the one hand he is the swinger—as he is when talking and joking with Sammy Davis, Jr., Richard Conte, Liza Minelli, Bernie Massi, or any of the other show-business people who get to sit at the table; on the other, as when he is nodding or waving to his paisanos who are close to him (Al Silvani, a boxing manager who works with Sinatra's film company; Dominic Di Bona, his wardrobe man; Ed Pucci, a 300-pound former football lineman who is his aide-de-camp), Frank Sinatra is Il Padrone. Or better still, he is what in traditional Sicily have long been called uomini rispettati—men of respect: men who are both majestic and humble, men who are loved by all and are very generous by nature, men whose hands are kissed as they walk from village to village, men who would personally go out of their way to redress a wrong.

Frank Sinatra does things personally. At Christmas time, he will personally pick dozens of presents for his close friends and family, remembering the type of jewelry they like, their favorite colors, the sizes of their shirts and dresses. When a musician friend's house was destroyed and his wife was killed in a Los Angeles mud slide a little more than a year ago, Sinatra personally came to his aid, finding the musician a new home, paying whatever hospital bills were left unpaid by the insurance, then personally supervising the furnishing of the new home down to the replacing of the silverware, the linen, the purchase of new clothing.

The same Sinatra who did this can, within the same hour, explode in a towering rage of intolerance should a small thing be incorrectly done for him by one of his paisanos. For example, when one of his men brought him a frankfurter with catsup on it, which Sinatra apparently abhors, he angrily threw the bottle at the man, splattering catsup all over him. Most of the men who work around Sinatra are big. But this never seems to intimidate Sinatra nor curb his impetuous behavior with them when he is mad. They will never take a swing back at him. He is Il Padrone.

At other times, aiming to please, his men will overreact to his desires: when he casually observed that his big orange desert jeep in Palm Springs seemed in need of a new painting, the word was swiftly passed down through the channels, becoming ever more urgent as it went, until finally it was a command that the jeep be painted now, immediately, yesterday. To accomplish this would require the hiring of a special crew of painters to work all night, at overtime rates; which, in turn, meant that the order had to be bucked back up the line for further approval. When it finally got back to Sinatra's desk, he did not know what it was all about; after he had figured it out he confessed, with a tired look on his face, that he did not care when the hell they painted the jeep.

Yet it would have been unwise for anyone to anticipate his reaction, for he is a wholly unpredictable man of many moods and great dimension, a man who responds instantaneously to instinct—suddenly, dramatically, wildly he responds, and nobody can predict what will follow. A young lady named Jane Hoag, a reporter at *Life*'s Los Angeles bureau who had attended the same school as Sinatra's daughter, Nancy, had once been invited to a party at Mrs. Sinatra's California home at which Frank Sinatra, who maintains very cordial relations with his former wife, acted as host. Early in the party Miss Hoag, while leaning against a table, accidentally with her elbow knocked over one of a pair of alabaster birds to the floor, smashing it to pieces. Suddenly, Miss Hoag recalled, Sinatra's daughter cried, "Oh, that was one of my mother's favorite . . ."—but before she could complete the sentence, Sinatra glared at her, cutting her off, and while forty other guests in the room all stared in silence, Sinatra walked over, quickly with his finger flicked the other alabaster bird off the table, smashing it to pieces, and then put an arm gently around Jane Hoag and said, in a way that put her completely at ease, "That's okay, kid."

Now Sinatra said a few words to the blondes. Then he turned from the bar and began to walk toward the poolroom. One of Sinatra's other men friends moved in to keep the girls company. Brad Dexter, who had been standing in the corner talking to some other people, now followed Sinatra.

The room cracked with the clack of billiard balls. There were about a dozen spectators in the room, most of them young men who were watching Leo Durocher shoot against two other aspiring hustlers who were not very good. This private drinking club has among its membership many actors, directors, writers, models, nearly all of them a good deal younger than Sinatra or Durocher and much more casual in the way they dress for the evening. Many of the young women, their long hair flowing loosely below their shoulders, wore tight, fanny-fitting Jax pants and very expensive sweaters; and a few of the young men wore blue or green velour shirts with high collars and narrow tight pants, and Italian loafers.

It was obvious from the way Sinatra looked at these people in the pool-room that they were not his style, but he leaned back against a high stool that was against the wall, holding his drink in his right hand, and said nothing, just watched Durocher slam the billiard balls back and forth. The younger men in the room, accustomed to seeing Sinatra at this club, treated him without deference, although they said nothing offensive. They were a cool young group, very California-cool and casual, and one of the coolest seemed to be a little guy, very quick of movement, who had a sharp profile, pale blue eyes, blondish hair, and squared eyeglasses. He wore a pair of brown corduroy slacks, a green shaggy-dog Shetland sweater, a tan suede jacket, and Game Warden boots, for which he had recently paid $60.

Frank Sinatra, leaning against the stool, sniffling a bit from his cold, could not take his eyes off the Game Warden boots. Once, after gazing at them for a few moments, he turned away; but now he was focused on them again. The owner of the boots, who was just standing in them watching the pool game, was named Harlan Ellison, a writer who had just completed work on a screenplay, *The Oscar*.

Finally Sinatra could not contain himself.

"Hey," he yelled in his slightly harsh voice that still had a soft, sharp edge. "Those Italian boots?"

"No," Ellison said.

"Spanish?"

"No."

"Are they English boots?"

"Look, I donno, man," Ellison shot back, frowning at Sinatra, then turning away again.

Now the poolroom was suddenly silent. Leo Durocher who had been poised behind his cue stick and was bent low just froze in that position for a second. Nobody moved. Then Sinatra moved away from the stool and walked with that slow, arrogant swagger of his toward Ellison, the hard tap of Sinatra's shoes the only sound in the room. Then, looking down at Ellison with a slightly raised eyebrow and a tricky little smile, Sinatra asked: "You expecting a storm?"

Harlan Ellison moved a step to the side. "Look, is there any reason why you're talking to me?"

"I don't like the way you're dressed," Sinatra said.

"Hate to shake you up," Ellison said, "but I dress to suit myself."

Now there was some rumbling in the room, and somebody said, "Com'on, Harlan, let's get out of here," and Leo Durocher made his pool shot and said, "Yeah, com'on."

But Ellison stood his ground.

Sinatra said, "What do you do?"

"I'm a plumber," Ellison said.

"No, no, he's not," another young man quickly yelled from across the table. "He wrote *The Oscar.*"

"Oh, yeah," Sinatra said, "well I've seen it, and it's a piece of crap."

"That's strange," Ellison said, "because they haven't even released it yet."

"Well, I've seen it," Sinatra repeated, "and it's a piece of crap."

Now Brad Dexter, very anxious, very big opposite the small figure of Ellison, said, "Com'on, kid, I don't want you in this room."

"Hey," Sinatra interrupted Dexter, "can't you see I'm talking to this guy?"

Dexter was confused. Then his whole attitude changed, and his voice went soft and he said to Ellison, almost with a plea, "Why do you persist in tormenting me?"

The whole scene was becoming ridiculous, and it seemed that Sinatra was only half-serious, perhaps just reacting out of sheer boredom or inner despair; at any rate, after a few more exchanges Harlan Ellison left the room. By this time the word had gotten out to those on the dance floor about the Sinatra-Ellison exchange, and somebody went to look for the manager of the club. But somebody else said that the manager had already heard about it—and had quickly gone out the door, hopped in his car and drove home. So the assistant manager went into the poolroom.

"I don't want anybody in here without coats and ties," Sinatra snapped.

The assistant manager nodded, and walked back to his office.

It was the morning after. It was the beginning of another nervous day for Sinatra's press agent, Jim Mahoney. Mahoney had a headache, and he was worried but not over the Sinatra-Ellison incident of the night before. At the time Mahoney had been with his wife at a table in the other room, and possibly he had not even been aware of the little drama. The whole thing had lasted only about three minutes. And three minutes after it was over, Frank Sinatra had probably forgotten about it for the rest of his life—as

Ellison will probably remember it for the rest of his life: he had had, as hundreds of others before him, at an unexpected moment between darkness and dawn, a scene with Sinatra.

It was just as well that Mahoney had not been in the poolroom; he had enough on his mind today. He was worried about Sinatra's cold and worried about the controversial CBS documentary that, despite Sinatra's protests and withdrawal of permission, would be shown on television in less than two weeks. The newspapers this morning were full of hints that Sinatra might sue the network, and Mahoney's phones were ringing without pause, and now he was plugged into New York talking to the *Daily News*'s Kay Gardella, saying: ". . . that's right, Kay . . . they made a gentleman's agreement to not ask certain questions about Frank's private life, and then Cronkite went right ahead: 'Frank, tell me about those associations.' That question, Kay—out! That question should never have been asked . . ."

As he spoke, Mahoney leaned back in his leather chair, his head shaking slowly. He is a powerfully built man of thirty-seven; he has a round, ruddy face, a heavy jaw, and narrow pale eyes, and he might appear pugnacious if he did not speak with such clear, soft sincerity and if he were not so meticulous about his clothes. His suits and shoes are superbly tailored, which was one of the first things Sinatra noticed about him, and in his spacious office opposite the bar is a red-muff electrical shoe polisher and a pair of brown wooden shoulders on a stand over which Mahoney can drape his jackets. Near the bar is an autographed photograph of President Kennedy and a few pictures of Frank Sinatra, but there are none of Sinatra in any other rooms in Mahoney's public-relations agency; there once was a large photograph of him hanging in the reception room but this apparently bruised the egos of some of Mahoney's other movie-star clients and, since Sinatra never shows up at the agency anyway, the photograph was removed.

Still, Sinatra seems ever present, and if Mahoney did not have legitimate worries about Sinatra, as he did today, he could invent them—and, as worry aids, he surrounds himself with little mementos of moments in the past when he did worry. In his shaving kit there is a two-year-old box of sleeping tablets dispensed by a Reno druggist—the date on the bottle marks the kidnapping of Frank Sinatra, Jr. There is on a table in Mahoney's office a mounted wood reproduction of Frank Sinatra's ransom note written on the aforementioned occasion. One of Mahoney's mannerisms, when he is sitting at his desk worrying, is to tinker with the tiny toy train he keeps in front of him—the train is a souvenir from the Sinatra film, *Von Ryan's Express;* it is to men who are close to Sinatra what the PT-109 tie clasps are to men who were close to Kennedy—and Mahoney then proceeds to roll the little train back and forth on the six inches of track; back and forth, back and forth, click-clack-click-clack. It is his Queeg-thing.

Now Mahoney quickly put aside the little train. His secretary told him there was a very important call on the line. Mahoney picked it up, and his voice was even softer and more sincere than before. "Yes, Frank," he said. "Right . . . right . . . yes, Frank . . ."

When Mahoney put down the phone, quietly, he announced that Frank Sinatra had left in his private jet to spend the weekend at his home in Palm Springs, which is a sixteen-minute flight from his home in Los Angeles. Mahoney was now worried again. The Lear jet that Sinatra's pilot would be flying was identical, Mahoney said, to the one that had just crashed in another part of California.

On the following Monday, a cloudy and unseasonably cool California day, more than one hundred people gathered inside a white television studio, an enormous room dominated by a white stage, white walls, and with dozens of lights and lamps dangling: it rather resembled a gigantic operating room. In this room, within an hour or so, NBC was scheduled to begin taping a one-hour show that would be televised in color on the night of November 24 and would highlight, as much as it could in the limited time, the twenty-five-year career of Frank Sinatra as a public entertainer. It would not attempt to probe, as the forthcoming CBS Sinatra documentary allegedly would, that area of Sinatra's life that he regards as private. The NBC show would be mainly an hour of Sinatra singing some of the hits that carried him from Hoboken to Hollywood, a show that would be interrupted only now and then by a few film clips and commercials for Budweiser beer. Prior to his cold, Sinatra had been very excited about this show; he saw here an opportunity to appeal not only to those nostalgic, but also to communicate his talent to some rock-and-rollers—in a sense, he was battling The Beatles. The press releases being prepared by Mahoney's agency stressed this, reading: "If you happen to be tired of kid singers wearing mops of hair thick enough to hide a crate of melons . . . it should be refreshing, to consider the entertainment value of a video special titled *Sinatra—A Man and His Music* . . ."

But now in this NBC studio in Los Angeles, there was an atmosphere of anticipation and tension because of the uncertainty of the Sinatra voice. The forty-three musicians in Nelson Riddle's orchestra had already arrived and some were up on the white platform warming up. Dwight Hemion, a youthful sandy-haired director who had won praise for his television special on Barbra Streisand, was seated in the glass-enclosed control booth that overlooked the orchestra and stage. The camera crews, technical teams, security guards, Budweiser ad men were also standing between the floor lamps and cameras, waiting, as were a dozen or so ladies who worked as secretaries in other parts of the building but had sneaked away so they could watch this.

A few minutes before eleven o'clock, word spread quickly through the long corridor into the big studio that Sinatra was spotted walking through the parking lot and was on his way, and was looking fine. There seemed great relief among the group that was gathered; but when the lean, sharply dressed figure of the man got closer, and closer, they saw to their dismay that it was not Frank Sinatra. It was his double. Johnny Delgado.

Delgado walks like Sinatra, has Sinatra's build, and from certain facial angles does resemble Sinatra. But he seems a rather shy individual. Fifteen years ago, early in his acting career, Delgado applied for a role in *From Here to Eternity.* He was hired, finding out later that he was to be Sinatra's double. In Sinatra's latest film, *Assault on a Queen,* a story in which Sinatra and some fellow conspirators attempt to hijack the *Queen Mary,* Johnny Delgado doubles for Sinatra in some water scenes; and now, in this NBC studio, his job was to stand under the hot television lights marking Sinatra's spots on the stage for the camera crews.

Five minutes later, the real Frank Sinatra walked in. His face was pale, his blue eyes seemed a bit watery. He had been unable to rid himself of the cold, but he was going to try to sing anyway because the schedule was tight and thousands of dollars were involved at this moment in the assembling of the orchestra and crews and the rental of the studio. But when Sinatra, on his way to his small rehearsal room to warm up his voice, looked into the studio and saw that the stage and orchestra's platform were not close together, as he had specifically requested, his lips tightened and he was obviously very upset. A few moments later, from his rehearsal room, could be heard the pounding of his fist against the top of the piano and the voice of his accompanist, Bill Miller, saying, softly, "Try not to upset yourself, Frank."

Later Jim Mahoney and another man walked in, and there was talk of Dorothy Kilgallen's death in New York earlier that morning. She had been an ardent foe of Sinatra for years, and he became equally uncomplimentary about her in his nightclub act, and now, though she was dead, he did not compromise his feelings. "Dorothy Kilgallen's dead," he repeated, walking out of the room toward the studio. "Well, guess I got to change my whole act."

When he strolled into the studio the musicians all picked up their instruments and stiffened in their seats. Sinatra cleared his throat a few times and then, after rehearsing a few ballads with the orchestra, he sang "Don't Worry About Me" to his satisfaction and, being uncertain of how long his voice could last, suddenly became impatient.

"Why don't we tape this mother?" he called out, looking up toward the glass booth where the director, Dwight Hemion, and his staff were sitting. Their heads seemed to be down, focusing on the control board.

"Why don't we tape this mother?" Sinatra repeated.

The production stage manager, who stands near the camera wearing a headset, repeated Sinatra's words exactly into his line to the control room: "Why don't we tape this mother?"

Hemion did not answer. Possibly his switch was off. It was hard to know because of the obscuring reflections the lights made against the glass booth.

"Why don't we put on a coat and tie," said Sinatra, then wearing a high-necked yellow pullover, "and tape this . . ."

Suddenly Hemion's voice came over the sound amplifier, very calmly: "Okay, Frank, would you mind going back over . . ."

"Yes, I would mind going back," Sinatra snapped.

The silence from Hemion's end, which lasted a second or two, was then again interrupted by Sinatra saying, "When we stop doing things around here the way we did them in 1950, maybe we . . ." and Sinatra continued to tear into Hemion, condemning as well the lack of modern techniques in putting such shows together; then, possibly not wanting to use his voice unnecessarily, he stopped. And Dwight Hemion, very patient, so patient and calm that one would assume he had not heard anything that Sinatra had just said, outlined the opening part of the show. And Sinatra a few minutes later was reading his opening remarks, words that would follow "Without a Song," off the large idiot-cards being held near the camera. Then, this done, he prepared to do the same thing on camera.

"Frank Sinatra Show, Act I, Page 10, Take 1," called a man with a clapboard, jumping in front of the camera—clap—then jumping away again.

"Did you ever stop to think," Sinatra began, "what the world would be like without a song? . . . It would be a pretty dreary place . . . Gives you something to think about, doesn't it? . . ."

Sinatra stopped.

"Excuse me," he said, adding, "Boy, I need a drink."

They tried it again.

"Frank Sinatra Show, Act I, Page 10, Take 2," yelled the jumping guy with the clapboard.

"Did you ever stop to think what the world would be like without a song? . . ." Frank Sinatra read it through this time without stopping. Then he rehearsed a few more songs, once or twice interrupting the orchestra when a certain instrumental sound was not quite what he wanted. It was hard to tell how well his voice was going to hold up, for this was early in the show; up to this point, however, everybody in the room seemed pleased, particularly when he sang an old sentimental favorite written more than twenty years ago by Jimmy Van Heusen and Phil Silvers—"Nancy," inspired by the first of Sinatra's three children when she was just a few years old.

If I don't see her each day
I miss her . . .
Gee what a thrill
Each time I kiss her . . .

As Sinatra sang these words, though he has sung them hundreds and hundreds of times in the past, it was suddenly obvious to everybody in the studio that something quite special must be going on inside the man, because something quite special was coming out. He was singing now, cold or no cold, with power and warmth, he was letting himself go, the public arrogance was gone, the private side was in this song about the girl who, it is said, understands him better than anybody else, and is the only person in front of whom he can be unashamedly himself.

Nancy is twenty-five. She lives alone, her marriage to singer Tommy Sands having ended in divorce. Her home is in a Los Angeles suburb and she is now making her third film and is recording for her father's record company. She sees him every day; or, if not, he telephones, no matter if it be from Europe or Asia. When Sinatra's singing first became popular on radio, stimulating the swooners, Nancy would listen at home and cry. When Sinatra's first marriage broke up in 1951 and he left home, Nancy was the only child old enough to remember him as a father. She also saw him with Ava Gardner, Juliet Prowse, Mia Farrow, many others, has gone on double dates with him . . .

> *She takes the winter*
> *And makes it summer . . .*
> *Summer could take*
> *Some lessons from her . . .*

Nancy now also sees him visiting at home with his first wife, the former Nancy Barbato, a plasterer's daughter from Jersey City whom he married in 1939 when he was earning $25 a week singing at the Rustic Cabin near Hoboken.

The first Mrs. Sinatra, a striking woman who has never remarried ("When you've been married to Frank Sinatra . . ." she once explained to a friend), lives in a magnificent home in Los Angeles with her younger daughter, Tina, who is seventeen. There is no bitterness, only great respect and affection between Sinatra and his first wife, and he has long been welcome in her home and has even been known to wander in at odd hours, stoke the fire, lie on the sofa, and fall asleep. Frank Sinatra can fall asleep anywhere, something he learned when he used to ride bumpy roads with band buses; he also learned at that time, when sitting in a tuxedo, how to pinch the trouser creases in the back and tuck the jacket under and out, and fall asleep perfectly pressed. But he does not ride buses anymore, and his daughter Nancy, who in her younger days felt rejected when he slept on the sofa instead of giving attention to her, later realized that the sofa was one of the few places left in the world where Frank Sinatra could get any privacy, where his famous face would neither be stared at nor cause an abnormal reaction in others. She realized, too, that things normal have always eluded her father: his childhood was one of loneliness and a drive toward attention, and since attaining it he has never again been certain of solitude. Upon looking out the window of a home he once owned in Hasbrouck Heights, New Jersey, he would occasionally see the faces of teen-agers peeking in; and in 1944, after moving to California and buying a home behind a ten-foot fence on Lake Toluca, he discovered that the only way to escape the telephone and other intrusions was to board his paddle boat with a few friends, a card table and a case of beer, and stay afloat all afternoon. But he has tried, insofar as it has been possible, to be like everyone else, Nancy says. He wept on her wedding day, he is very sentimental and sensitive . . .

"What the hell are you doing up there, Dwight?"
 Silence from the control booth.
 "Got a party or something going on up there, Dwight?"
 Sinatra stood on the stage, arms folded, glaring up across the cameras toward Hemion. Sinatra had sung "Nancy" with probably all he had in his voice on this day. The next few numbers contained raspy notes, and twice his voice completely cracked. But now Hemion was in the control booth out of communication; then he was down in the studio walking over to where Sinatra stood. A few minutes later they both left the studio and were on the way up to the control booth. The tape was replayed for Sinatra. He watched only about five minutes of it before he started to shake his head. Then he said to Hemion: "Forget it, just forget it. You're wasting your time. What you got there," Sinatra said, nodding to the singing image of himself on the television screen, "is a man with a cold." Then he left the control booth, ordering that the whole day's performance be scrubbed and future taping postponed until he had recovered.

Soon the word spread like an emotional epidemic down through Sinatra's staff, then fanned out through Hollywood, then was heard across the nation in Jilly's saloon, and also on the other side of the Hudson River in the homes of Frank Sinatra's parents and his other relatives and friends in New Jersey.
 When Frank Sinatra spoke with his father on the telephone and said he was feeling awful, the elder Sinatra reported that he was also feeling awful: that his left arm and fist were so stiff with a circulatory condition he could barely use them, adding that the ailment might be the result of having thrown too many left hooks during his days as a bantamweight almost fifty years ago.
 Martin Sinatra, a ruddy and tattooed little blue-eyed Sicilian born in Catania, boxed under the name of "Marty O' Brien." In those days, in those places, with the Irish running the lower reaches of city life, it was not

uncommon for Italians to wind up with such names. Most of the Italians and Sicilians who migrated to America just prior to the 1900's were poor and uneducated, were excluded from the building-trades unions dominated by the Irish, and were somewhat intimidated by the Irish police, Irish priests, Irish politicians.

One notable exception was Frank Sinatra's mother, Dolly, a large and very ambitious woman who was brought to this country at two months of age by her mother and father, a lithographer from Genoa. In later years Dolly Sinatra, possessing a round red face and blue eyes, was often mistaken for being Irish, and surprised many at the speed with which she swung her heavy handbag at anyone uttering "Wop."

By playing skillful politics with North Jersey's Democratic machine, Dolly Sinatra was to become, in her heyday, a kind of Catherine de Medici of Hoboken's third ward. She could always be counted upon to deliver six hundred votes at election time from her Italian neighborhood, and this was her base of power. When she told one of the politicians that she wanted her husband to be appointed to the Hoboken Fire Department, and was told, "But, Dolly, we don't have an opening," she snapped, "Make an opening."

They did. Years later she requested that her husband be made a captain, and one day she got a call from one of the political bosses that began, "Dolly, congratulations!"

"For what?"

"Captain Sinatra."

"Oh, you finally made him one—thank you very much."

Then she called the Hoboken Fire Department.

"Let me speak to Captain Sinatra," she said. The fireman called Martin Sinatra to the phone, saying, "Marty, I think your wife has gone nuts." When he got on the line, Dolly greeted him:

"Congratulations, Captain Sinatra!"

Dolly's only child, christened Francis Albert Sinatra, was born and nearly died on December 12, 1915. It was a difficult birth, and during his first moment on earth he received marks he will carry till death—the scars on the left side of his neck being the result of a doctor's clumsy forceps, and Sinatra has chosen not to obscure them with surgery.

After he was six months old, he was reared mainly by his grandmother. His mother had a full-time job as a chocolate dipper with a large firm and was so proficient at it that the firm once offered to send her to the Paris office to train others. While some people in Hoboken remember Frank Sinatra as a lonely child, one who spent many hours on the porch gazing into space, Sinatra was never a slum kid, never in jail, always well-dressed. He had so many pants that some people in Hoboken called him "Slacksey O'Brien."

Dolly Sinatra was not the sort of Italian mother who could be appeased merely by a child's obedience and good appetite. She made many demands on her son, was always very strict. She dreamed of his becoming an aviation engineer. When she discovered Bing Crosby pictures hanging on his bedroom walls one evening, and learned that her son wished to become a singer too, she became infuriated and threw a shoe at him. Later, finding she could not talk him out of it—"he takes after me"—she encouraged his singing.

Many Italo-American boys of his generation were then shooting for the same star—they were strong with song, weak with words, not a big novelist among them: no O'Hara, no Bellow, no Cheever, nor Shaw; yet they could communicate bel canto. This was more in their tradition, no need for a diploma; they could, with a song, someday see their names in lights . . . Perry Como . . . Frankie Laine . . . Tony Bennett . . . Vic Damone . . . but none could see it better than Frank Sinatra.

Though he sang through much of the night at the Rustic Cabin, he was up the next day singing without a fee on New York radio to get more attention. Later he got a job singing with Harry James's band, and it was there in August of 1939 that Sinatra had his first recording hit—"All or Nothing at All." He became very fond of Harry James and the men in the band, but when he received an offer from Tommy Dorsey, who in those days had probably the best band in the country, Sinatra took it; the job paid $125 a week, and Dorsey knew how to feature a vocalist. Yet Sinatra was very depressed at leaving James's band, and the final night with them was so memorable that, twenty years later, Sinatra could recall the details to a friend: ". . . the bus pulled out with the rest of the boys at about half-past midnight. I'd said good-bye to them all, and it was snowing, I remember. There was nobody around and I stood alone with my suitcase in the snow and watched the taillights disappear. Then the tears started and I tried to run after the bus. There was such spirit and enthusiasm in that band, I hated leaving it . . ."

But he did—as he would leave other warm places, too, in search of something more, never wasting time, trying to do it all in one generation, fighting under his own name, defending underdogs, terrorizing top dogs. He threw a punch at a musician who said something anti-Semitic, espoused the Negro cause two decades before it became fashionable. He also threw a tray of glasses at Buddy Rich when he played the drums too loud.

Sinatra gave away $50,000 worth of gold cigarette lighters before he was thirty, was living an immigrant's wildest dream of America. He arrived suddenly on the scene when DiMaggio was silent, when paisanos were mournful, were quietly defensive about Hitler in their homeland. Sinatra became, in time, a kind of one-man Anti-Defamation League for Italians in America, the sort of organization that would be unlikely for them because, as the theory goes, they rarely agreed on anything, being extreme individualists: fine as soloists, but not so good in a choir; fine as heroes, but not so good in a parade.

When many Italian names were used in describing gangsters on a television show, *The Untouchables,* Sinatra was loud in his disapproval. Sinatra and many thousands of other Italo-Americans were resentful as well when a small-time hoodlum, Joseph Valachi, was brought by Bobby Kennedy into prominence as a Mafia expert, when indeed, from Valachi's testimony on television, he seemed to know less than most waiters on Mulberry Street. Many Italians in Sinatra's circle also regard Bobby Kennedy as something of an Irish cop, more dignified than those in Dolly's day, but no less intimidating. Together with Peter Lawford, Bobby Kennedy is said to have suddenly gotten "cocky" with Sinatra after John Kennedy's election, forgetting the contribution Sinatra had made in both fundraising and in influencing many anti-Irish Italian votes. Lawford and Bobby Kennedy are both suspected of having influenced the late President's decision to stay as a house guest with Bing Crosby instead of Sinatra, as originally planned, a social setback Sinatra may never forget. Peter Lawford has since been drummed out of Sinatra's "summit" in Las Vegas.

"Yes, my son is like me," Dolly Sinatra says, proudly. "You cross him, he never forgets." And while she concedes his power, she quickly points out, "He can't make his mother do anything she doesn't want to do," adding, "Even today, he wears the same brand of underwear I used to buy him."

Today Dolly Sinatra is seventy-one years old, a year or two younger than Martin, and all day long people are knocking on the back door of her large home asking her advice, seeking her influence. When she is not seeing people and not cooking in the kitchen, she is looking after her husband, a silent but stubborn man, and telling him to keep his sore left arm resting on the sponge she has placed on the armrest of a soft chair. "Oh, he went to some terrific fires, this guy did," Dolly said to a visitor, nodding with admiration toward her husband in the chair.

Though Dolly Sinatra has eighty-seven godchildren in Hoboken, and still goes to that city during political campaigns, she now lives with her husband in a beautiful sixteen-room house in Fort Lee, New Jersey. This home was a gift from their son on their fiftieth wedding anniversary three years ago. The home is tastefully furnished and is filled with a remarkable juxtaposition of the pious and the worldly—photographs of Pope John and Ava Gardner, of Pope Paul and Dean Martin; several statues of saints and holy water, a chair autographed by Sammy Davis, Jr. and bottles of bourbon. In Mrs. Sinatra's jewelry box is a magnificent strand of pearls she had just received from Ava Gardner, whom she liked tremendously as a daughter-in-law and still keeps in touch with and talks about; and hung on the wall is a letter addressed to Dolly and Martin: "The sands of time have turned to gold, yet love continues to unfold like the petals of a rose, in God's garden of life . . . may God love you thru all eternity. I thank Him, I thank you for the being of one. Your loving son, Francis . . ."

Mrs. Sinatra talks to her son on the telephone about once a week, and recently he suggested that, when visiting Manhattan, she make use of his apartment on East Seventy-second Street on the East River. This is an expensive neighborhood of New York even though there is a small factory on the block, but this latter fact was seized upon by Dolly Sinatra as a means of getting back at her son for some unflattering descriptions of his childhood in Hoboken.

"What—you want me to stay in your apartment, in that dump?" she asked. "You think I'm going to spend the night in that awful neighborhood?"

Frank Sinatra got the point, and said, "Excuse me, Mrs. Fort Lee."

After spending the week in Palm Springs, his cold much better, Frank Sinatra returned to Los Angeles, a lovely city of sun and sex, a Spanish discovery of Mexican misery, a star land of little men and little women sliding in and out of convertibles in tense tight pants.

Sinatra returned in time to see the long-awaited CBS documentary with his family. At about nine p.m. he drove to the home of his former wife, Nancy, and had dinner with her and their two daughters. Their son, whom they rarely see these days, was out of town.

Frank, Jr., who is twenty-two, was touring with a band and moving cross country toward a New York engagement at Basin Street East with The Pied Pipers, with whom Frank Sinatra sang when he was with Dorsey's band in the 1940's. Today Frank Sinatra, Jr., whom his father says he named after Franklin D. Roosevelt, lives mostly in hotels, dines each evening in his nightclub dressing room, and sings until two a.m., accepting graciously, because he has no choice, the inevitable comparisons. His voice is smooth and pleasant, and improving with work, and while he is very respectful of his father, he discusses him with objectivity and in an occasional tone of subdued cockiness.

Concurrent with his father's early fame, Frank, Jr., said, was the creation of a "press-release Sinatra" designed to "set him apart from the common man, separate him from the realities: it was suddenly Sinatra, the electric magnate, Sinatra who is supernormal, not superhuman but supernormal. And here," Frank, Jr., continued, "is the great fallacy, the great bullshit, for Frank Sinatra is normal, is the guy whom you'd meet on a street corner. But this other thing, the supernormal guise, has affected Frank Sinatra as much as anybody who watches one of his television shows, or reads a magazine article about him . . .

"Frank Sinatra's life in the beginning was so normal," he said, "that nobody would have guessed in 1934 that this little Italian kid with the curly hair would become the giant, the monster, the great living legend . . . He met my mother one summer on the beach. She was Nancy Barbato, daughter of Mike Barbato, a Jersey City plasterer. And she meets the fireman's son, Frank, one summer day on the beach at Long Branch, New Jersey. Both are Italian, both Roman Catholic, both lower-middle-class summer sweethearts—it is like a million bad movies starring Frankie Avalon. . . .

"They have three children. The first child, Nancy, was the most normal of Frank Sinatra's children. Nancy was a cheerleader, went to summer camp, drove a Chevrolet, had the easiest kind of development centered around the home and family. Next is me. My life with the family is very, very normal up until September of 1958 when, in complete contrast to the rearing of both girls, I am put into a college-preparatory school. I am now away from the inner family circle, and my position within has never been remade to this day . . . The third child, Tina. And to be dead honest, I really couldn't say what her life is like . . ."

The CBS show, narrated by Walter Cronkite, began at ten p.m. A minute before that, the Sinatra family, having finished dinner, turned their chairs around and faced the camera, united for whatever disaster might follow. Sinatra's men in other parts of town, in other parts of the nation, were doing the same thing. Sinatra's lawyer, Milton A. Rudin, smoking a cigar, was watching with a keen eye, an alert legal mind. Other sets were watched by Brad Dexter, Jim Mahoney, Ed Pucci; Sinatra's makeup man, "Shotgun" Britton; his New York representative, Henri Gine; his haberdasher, Richard Carroll; his insurance broker, John Lillie; his valet, George Jacobs, a handsome Negro who, when entertaining girls in his apartment, plays records by Ray Charles.

And like so much of Hollywood's fear, the apprehension about the CBS show all proved to be without foundation. It was a highly flattering hour that did not deeply probe, as rumors suggested it would, into Sinatra's love life, or the Mafia, or other areas of his private province. While the documentary was not authorized, wrote Jack Gould in the next day's *New York Times*, "it could have been."

Immediately after the show, the telephones began to ring throughout the Sinatra system conveying words of joy and relief—and from New York came Jilly's telegram: "WE RULE THE WORLD!"

The next day, standing in the corridor of the NBC building where he was about to resume taping his show, Sinatra was discussing the CBS show with several of his friends, and he said, "Oh, it was a gas."

"Yeah, Frank, a helluva show."

"But I think Jack Gould was right in the *Times* today," Sinatra said. "There should have been more on the man, not so much on the music . . ."

They nodded, nobody mentioning the past hysteria in the Sinatra world when it seemed CBS was zeroing in on the man; they just nodded and two of them laughed about Sinatra's apparently having gotten the word "bird" on the show—this being a favorite Sinatra word. He often inquires of his cronies, "How's your bird?"; and when he nearly drowned in Hawaii, he later explained, "Just got a little water on my bird"; and under a large photograph of him holding a whisky bottle, a photo that hangs in the home of an actor friend named Dick Bakalyan, the inscription reads: "Drink, Dickie! It's good for your bird." In the song, "Come Fly with Me," Sinatra sometimes alters the lyrics—". . . just say the words and we'll take our birds down to Acapulco Bay . . ."

Ten minutes later Sinatra, following the orchestra, walked into the NBC studio, which did not resemble in the slightest the scene here of eight days ago. On this occasion Sinatra was in fine voice, he cracked jokes between numbers, nothing could upset him. Once, while he was singing "How Can I Ignore the Girl Next Door," standing on the stage next to a tree, a television camera mounted on a vehicle came rolling in too close and plowed against the tree.

"Kee-rist!" yelled one of the technical assistants.

But Sinatra seemed hardly to notice it.

"We've had a slight accident," he said, calmly. Then he began the song all over from the beginning.

When the show was over, Sinatra watched the rerun on the monitor in the control room. He was very pleased, shaking hands with Dwight Hemion and his assistants. Then the whisky bottles were opened in Sinatra's dressing room. Pat Lawford was there, and so were Andy Williams and a dozen others. The telegrams and telephone calls continued to be received from all over the country with praise for the CBS show. There was even a call, Mahoney said, from the CBS producer, Don Hewitt, with whom Sinatra had been so angry a few days before. And Sinatra was still angry, feeling that CBS had betrayed him, though the show itself was not objectionable.

"Shall I drop a line to Hewitt?" Mahoney asked.

"Can you send a fist through the mail?" Sinatra asked.

He has everything, he cannot sleep, he gives nice gifts, he is not happy, but he would not trade, even for happiness, what he is . . .

He is a piece of our past—but only we have aged, he hasn't . . . we are dogged by domesticity, he isn't . . . we have compunctions, he doesn't . . . it is our fault, not his . . .

He controls the menus of every Italian restaurant in Los Angeles; if you want North Italian cooking, fly to Milan . . .

Men follow him, imitate him, fight to be near him . . . there is something of the locker room, the barracks about him . . . bird . . . bird . . .

He believes you must play it big, wide, expansively—the more open you are, the more you take in, your dimensions deepen, you grow, you become more what you are—bigger, richer . . .

"He is better than anybody else, or at least they think he is, and he has to live up to it."—Nancy Sinatra, Jr.

"He is calm on the outside—inwardly a million things are happening to him."—Dick Bakalyan

"He has an insatiable desire to live every moment to its fullest because, I guess, he feels that right around the corner is extinction."—Brad Dexter

"All I ever got out of any of my marriages was the two years Artie Shaw financed on an analyst's couch."—Ava Gardner

"We weren't mother and son—we were buddies."—Dolly Sinatra

"I'm for anything that gets you through the night, be it prayer, tranquilizers or a bottle of Jack Daniel."—Frank Sinatra

Frank Sinatra was tired of all the talk, the gossip, the theory—tired of reading quotes about himself, of hearing what people were saying about him all over town. It had been a tedious three weeks, he said, and now he just wanted to get away, go to Las Vegas, let off some steam. So he hopped in his jet, soared over the California hills across the Nevada flats, then over miles and miles of desert to The Sands and the Clay-Patterson fight.

On the eve of the fight he stayed up all night and slept through most of the afternoon, though his recorded voice could be heard singing in the lobby of The Sands, in the gambling casino, even in the toilets, being interrupted every few bars however by the paging public address: ". . . Telephone call for Mr. Ron Fish, Mr. Ron Fish . . . with a ribbon of gold in her hair . . . Telephone call for Mr. Herbert Rothstein, Mr. Herbert Rothstein . . . memories of a time so bright, keep me sleepless through dark endless nights . . ."

Standing around in the lobby of The Sands and other hotels up and down the strip on this afternoon before the fight were the usual prefight prophets: the gamblers, the old champs, the little cigar butts from Eighth Avenue, the sportswriters who knock the big fights all year but would never miss one, the novelists who seem always to be identifying with one boxer or another, the local prostitutes assisted by some talent in from Los Angeles, and also a young brunette in a wrinkled black cocktail dress who was at the bell captain's desk crying, "But I want to speak to Mr. Sinatra."

"He's not here," the bell captain said.

"Won't you put me through to his room?"

"There are no messages going through, Miss," he said, and then she turned, unsteadily, seeming close to tears, and walked through the lobby into the big noisy casino crowded with men interested only in money.

Shortly before seven p.m., Jack Entratter, a big grey-haired man who operates The Sands, walked into the gambling room to tell some men around the blackjack table that Sinatra was getting dressed. He also said that he'd been unable to get front-row seats for everybody, and so some of the men—including Leo Durocher, who had a date, and Joey Bishop, who was accompanied by his wife—would not be able to fit in Frank Sinatra's row but would have to take seats in the third row. When Entratter walked over to tell this to Joey Bishop, Bishop's face fell. He did not seem angry; he merely looked at Entratter with an empty silence, seeming somewhat stunned.

"Joey, I'm sorry," Entratter said when the silence persisted, "but we couldn't get more than six together in the front row."

Bishop still said nothing. But when they all appeared at the fight, Joey Bishop was in the front row, his wife in the third.

The fight, called a holy war between Muslims and Christians, was preceded by the introduction of three balding ex-champions, Rocky Marciano, Joe Louis, Sonny Liston—and then there was "The Star-Spangled Banner" sung by another man from out of the past, Eddie Fisher. It had been more than fourteen years ago, but Sinatra could still remember every detail: Eddie Fisher was then the new king of the baritones, with Billy Eckstine and Guy Mitchell right with him, and Sinatra had been long counted out. One day he remembered walking into a broadcasting studio past dozens of Eddie Fisher fans waiting outside the hall, and when they saw Sinatra they began to jeer, "Frankie, Frankie, I'm swooning, I'm swooning." This was also the time when he was selling only about 30,000 records a year, when he was dreadfully miscast as a funny man on his television show, and when he recorded such disasters as "Mama Will Bark," with Dagmar.

"I growled and barked on the record," Sinatra said, still horrified by the thought. "The only good it did me was with the dogs."

His voice and his artistic judgment were incredibly bad in 1952, but even more responsible for his decline, say his friends, was his pursuit of Ava Gardner. She was the big movie queen then, one of the most beautiful women in the world. Sinatra's daughter Nancy recalls seeing Ava swimming one day in her father's pool, then climbing out of the water with that fabulous body, walking slowly to the fire, leaning over it for a few moments, and then it suddenly seemed that her long dark hair was all dry, miraculously and effortlessly back in place.

With most women Sinatra dates, his friends say, he never knows whether they want him for what he can do for them now—or will do for them later. With Ava Gardner, it was different. He could do nothing for her later. She was on top. If Sinatra learned anything from his experience with her, he possibly learned that when a proud man is down a woman cannot help. Particularly a woman on top.

Nevertheless, despite a tired voice, some deep emotion seeped into his singing during this time. One particular song that is well remembered even now is "I'm a Fool to Want You," and a friend who was in the studio when Sinatra recorded it recalled: "Frank was really worked up that night. He did the song in one take, then turned around and walked out of the studio and that was that . . ."

Sinatra's manager at that time, a former song plugger named Hank Sanicola, said, "Ava loved Frank, but not the way he loved her. He needs a great deal of love. He wants it twenty-four hours a day, he must have people around—Frank is that kind of guy." Ava Gardner, Sanicola said, "was very insecure. She feared she could not really hold a man . . . twice he went chasing her to Africa, wasting his own career . . ."

"Ava didn't want Frank's men hanging around all the time," another friend said, "and this got him mad. With Nancy he used to be able to bring the whole band home with him, and Nancy, the good Italian wife, would never complain—she'd just make everybody a plate of spaghetti."

In 1953, after almost two years of marriage, Sinatra and Ava Gardner were divorced. Sinatra's mother reportedly arranged a reconciliation, but if Ava was willing, Frank Sinatra was not. He was seen with other women. The balance had shifted. Somewhere during this period Sinatra seemed to change from the kid singer, the boy actor in the sailor suit, to a man. Even before he had won the Oscar in 1953 for his role in *From Here to Eternity*, some flashes of his old talent were coming through—in his recording of "The Birth of the Blues," in his Riviera-nightclub appearance that jazz critics enthusiastically praised; and there was also a trend now toward L.P.'s and away from the quick three-minute deal, and Sinatra's concert style would have capitalized on this with or without an Oscar.

In 1954, totally committed to his talent once more, Frank Sinatra was selected Metronome's "Singer of the Year," and later he won the U.P.I. disc-jockey poll, unseating Eddie Fisher—who now, in Las Vegas, having sung "The Star-Spangled Banner," climbed out of the ring, and the fight began.

Floyd Patterson chased Clay around the ring in the first round, but was unable to reach him, and from then on he was Clay's toy, the bout ending in a technical knockout in the twelfth round. A half hour later, nearly everybody had forgotten about the fight and was back at the gambling tables or lining up to buy tickets for the Dean Martin–Sinatra–Bishop nightclub routine on the stage of The Sands. This routine, which includes Sammy Davis, Jr., when he is in town, consists of a few songs and much cutting up, all of it very informal, very special, and rather ethnic—Martin, a drink in hand, asking Bishop: "Did you ever see a Jew jitsu?"; and Bishop, playing a Jewish waiter, warning the two Italians to watch out "because I got my own group—the Matzia."

Then after the last show at The Sands, the Sinatra crowd, which now numbered about twenty—and included Jilly, who had flown in from New York; Jimmy Cannon, Sinatra's favorite sports columnist; Harold Gibbons, a Teamster official expected to take over if Hoffa goes to jail—all got into a line of cars and headed for another club. It was three o'clock. The night was young.

They stopped at The Sahara, taking a long table near the back, and listened to a baldheaded little comedian named Don Rickles, who is probably more caustic than any comic in the country. His humor is so rude, in such bad taste, that it offends no one—it is too offensive to be offensive. Spotting Eddie Fisher among the audience, Rickles proceeded to ridicule him as a lover, saying it was no wonder that he could not handle Elizabeth Taylor; and when two businessmen in the audience acknowledged that they were Egyptian, Rickles cut into them for their country's policy toward Israel; and he strongly suggested that the woman seated at one table with her husband was actually a hooker.

When the Sinatra crowd walked in, Don Rickles could not be more delighted. Pointing to Jilly, Rickles yelled: "How's it feel to be Frank's tractor? . . . Yeah, Jilly keeps walking in front of Frank clearing the way." Then, nodding to Durocher, Rickles said, "Stand up Leo, show Frank how you slide." Then he focused on Sinatra, not failing to mention Mia Farrow, nor that he was wearing a toupee, nor to say that Sinatra was washed up as a singer, and when Sinatra laughed, everybody laughed, and Rickles pointed toward Bishop: "Joey Bishop keeps checking with Frank to see what's funny."

Then, after Rickles told some Jewish jokes, Dean Martin stood up and yelled, "Hey, you're always talking about the Jews, never about the Italians," and Rickles cut him off with, "What do we need the Italians for—all they do is keep the flies off our fish."

Sinatra laughed, they all laughed, and Rickles went on this way for nearly an hour until Sinatra, standing up, said, "All right, com'on, get this thing over with. I gotta go."

"Shaddup and sit down!" Rickles snapped. "I've had to listen to you sing . . ."

"Who do you think you're talking to?" Sinatra yelled back.

"Dick Haymes," Rickles replied, and Sinatra laughed again, and then Dean Martin, pouring a bottle of whisky over his head, entirely drenching his tuxedo, pounded the table.

"Who would ever believe that staggering would make a star?" Rickles said, but Martin called out, "Hey, I wanna make a speech."

"Shaddup."

"No, Don, I wanna tell ya," Dean Martin persisted, "that I think you're a great performer."

"Well, thank you, Dean," Rickles said, seeming pleased.

"But don't go by me," Martin said, plopping down into his seat, "I'm drunk."

"I'll buy that," Rickles said.

By four a.m. Frank Sinatra led the group out of The Sahara, some of them carrying their glasses of whisky with them, sipping it along the sidewalk and in the cars; then, returning to The Sands, they walked into the gambling casino. It was still packed with people, the roulette wheels spinning, the crapshooters screaming in the far corner.

Frank Sinatra, holding a shot glass of bourbon in his left hand, walked through the crowd. He, unlike some of his friends, was perfectly pressed, his tuxedo tie precisely pointed, his shoes unsmudged. He never seems to lose his dignity, never lets his guard completely down no matter how much he has drunk, nor how long he has been up. He never sways when he walks, like Dean Martin, nor does he ever dance in the aisles or jump up on tables, like Sammy Davis.

A part of Sinatra, no matter where he is, is never there. There is always a part of him, though sometimes a small part, that remains Il Padrone. Even now, resting his shot glass on the blackjack table, facing the dealer, Sinatra stood a bit back from the table, not leaning against it. He reached under his tuxedo jacket into his trouser pocket and came up with a thick but clean wad of bills. Gently he peeled off a one-hundred-dollar bill and placed it on the green-felt table. The dealer dealt him two cards. Sinatra called for a third card, overbid, lost the hundred.

Without a change of expression, Sinatra put down a second hundred-dollar bill. He lost that. Then he put down a third, and lost that. Then he placed two one-hundred-dollar bills on the table and lost those. Finally, putting his sixth hundred-dollar bill on the table, and losing it, Sinatra moved away from the table, nodding to the man, and announcing, "Good dealer."

The crowd that had gathered around him now opened up to let him through. But a woman stepped in front of him, handing him a piece of paper to autograph. He signed it and then he said, "Thank you."

In the rear of The Sands' large dining room was a long table reserved for Sinatra. The dining room was fairly empty at this hour, with perhaps two dozen other people in the room, including a table of four unescorted young ladies sitting near Sinatra. On the other side of the room, at another long table, sat seven men shoulder-to-shoulder against the wall, two of them wearing dark glasses, all of them eating quietly, speaking hardly a word, just sitting and eating and missing nothing.

The Sinatra party, after getting settled and having a few more drinks, ordered something to eat. The table was about the same size as the one reserved for Sinatra whenever he is at Jilly's in New York; and the people seated around this table in Las Vegas were many of the same people who are often seen with Sinatra at Jilly's or at a restaurant in California, or in Italy, or in New Jersey, or wherever Sinatra happens to be. When Sinatra sits to dine, his trusted friends are close; and no matter where he is, no matter how elegant the place may be, there is something of the neighborhood showing because Sinatra, no matter how far he has come, is still something of the boy from the neighborhood—only now he can take his neighborhood with him.

In some ways, this quasi-family affair at a reserved table in a public place is the closest thing Sinatra now has to home life. Perhaps, having had a home and left it, this approximation is as close as he cares to come; although this does not seem precisely so because he speaks with such warmth about his family, keeps in close touch with his first wife, and insists that she make no decision without first consulting him. He is always eager to place his furniture or other mementos of himself in her home or his daughter

Nancy's, and he also is on amiable terms with Ava Gardner. When he was in Italy making *Von Ryan's Express,* they spent some time together, being pursued wherever they went by the paparazzi. It was reported then that the paparazzi had made Sinatra a collective offer of $16,000 if he would pose with Ava Gardner; Sinatra was said to have made a counter offer of $32,000 if he could break one paparazzi arm and leg.

While Sinatra is often delighted that he can be in his home completely without people, enabling him to read and think without interruption, there are occasions when he finds himself alone at night, and not by choice. He may have dialed a half-dozen women, and for one reason or another they are all unavailable. So he will call his valet, George Jacobs.

"I'll be coming home for dinner tonight, George."

"How many will there be?"

"Just myself," Sinatra will say. "I want something light, I'm not very hungry."

George Jacobs is a twice-divorced man of thirty-six who resembles Billy Eckstine. He has traveled all over the world with Sinatra and is devoted to him. Jacobs lives in a comfortable bachelor's apartment off Sunset Boulevard around the corner from Whiskey à Go Go, and he is known around town for the assortment of frisky California girls he has as friends—a few of whom, he concedes, were possibly drawn to him initially because of his closeness to Frank Sinatra.

When Sinatra arrives, Jacobs will serve him dinner in the dining room. Then Sinatra will tell Jacobs that he is free to go home. If Sinatra, on such evenings, should ask Jacobs to stay longer, or to play a few hands of poker, he would be happy to do so. But Sinatra never does.

This was his second night in Las Vegas, and Frank Sinatra sat with friends in The Sands' dining room until nearly eight a.m. He slept through much of the day, then flew back to Los Angeles, and on the following morning he was driving his little golf cart through the Paramount Pictures movie lot. He was scheduled to complete two final scenes with the sultry blonde actress, Virna Lisi, in the film *Assault on a Queen.* As he maneuvered the little vehicle up the road between the big studio buildings, he spotted Steve Rossi who, with his comedy partner Marty Allen, was making a film in an adjoining studio with Nancy Sinatra.

"Hey, Dag," he yelled to Rossi, "stop kissing Nancy."

"It's part of the film, Frank," Rossi said, turning as he walked.

"In the garage?"

"It's my Dago blood, Frank."

"Well, cool it," Sinatra said, winking, then cutting his golf cart around a corner and parking it outside a big drab building within which the scenes for *Assault* would be filmed.

"Where's the fat director?" Sinatra called out, striding into the studio that was crowded with dozens of technical assistants and actors all gathered around cameras. The director, Jack Donohue, a large man who has worked with Sinatra through twenty-two years on one production or other, has had headaches with this film. The script had been chopped, the actors seemed restless, and Sinatra had become bored. But now there were only two scenes left—a short one to be filmed in the pool, and a longer and passionate one featuring Sinatra and Virna Lisi to be shot on a simulated beach.

The pool scene, which dramatizes a situation where Sinatra and his hijackers fail in their attempt to sack the *Queen Mary*, went quickly and well. After Sinatra had been kept in the water shoulder-high for a few minutes, he said, "Let's move it, fellows—it's cold in this water, and I've just gotten over one cold."

So the camera crews moved in closer, Virna Lisi splashed next to Sinatra in the water, and Jack Donohue yelled to his assistants operating the fans, "Get the waves going," and another man gave the command, "Agitate!" and Sinatra broke out in song. "Agitate in rhythm," then quieted down just before the cameras started to roll.

Frank Sinatra was on the beach in the next situation, supposedly gazing up at the stars, and Virna Lisi was to approach him, toss one of her shoes near him to announce her presence, then sit near him and prepare for a passionate session. Just before beginning, Miss Lisi made a practice toss of her shoe toward the prone figure of Sinatra sprawled on the beach. As she tossed her shoe, Sinatra called out, "Hit me in my bird and I'm going home."

Virna Lisi, who understands little English and certainly none of Sinatra's special vocabulary, looked confused, but everybody behind the camera laughed. She threw the shoe toward him. It twirled in the air, landed on his stomach.

"Well, that's about three inches too high," he announced. She again was puzzled by the laughter behind the camera.

Then Jack Donohue had them rehearse their lines, and Sinatra, still very charged from the Las Vegas trip, and anxious to get the cameras rolling, said, "Let's try one." Donohue, not certain that Sinatra and Lisi knew their lines well enough, nevertheless said okay, and an assistant with a clapboard called, "419, Take 1," and Virna Lisi approached with the shoe, tossed it at Frank lying on the beach. It fell short of his thigh, and Sinatra's right eye raised almost imperceptibly, but the crew got the message, smiled.

"What do the stars tell you tonight?" Miss Lisi said, delivering her first line, and sitting next to Sinatra on the beach.

"The stars tell me tonight I'm an idiot," Sinatra said, "a gold-plated idiot to get mixed up in this thing . . ."

"Cut," Donohue said. There were some microphone shadows on the sand, and Virna Lisi was not sitting in the proper place near Sinatra.

"419, Take 2," the clapboard man called.

Miss Lisi again approached, threw the shoe at him, this time falling short—Sinatra exhaling only slightly—and she said, "What do the stars tell you tonight?"

"The stars tell me I'm an idiot, a gold-plated idiot to get mixed up in this thing . . ." Then, according to the script, Sinatra was to continue, ". . . do you know what we're getting into? The minute we step on the deck of the *Queen Mary*, we've just tattooed ourselves," but Sinatra, who often improvises on lines, recited them: ". . . do you know what we're getting into? The minute we step on the deck of that mother's-ass ship . . ."

"No, no," Donohue interrupted, shaking his head, "I don't think that's right."

The cameras stopped, some people laughed, and Sinatra looked up from his position in the sand as if he had been unfairly interrupted.

"I don't see why that can't work . . ." he began, but Richard Conte, standing behind the camera, yelled, "It won't play in London."

Donohue pushed his hand through his thinning grey hair and said, but not really in anger, "You know, that scene was pretty good until somebody blew the line . . ."

"Yeah," agreed the cameraman, Billy Daniels, his head popping out from around the camera, "it was a pretty good piece . . ."

"Watch your language," Sinatra cut in. Then Sinatra, who has a genius for figuring out ways of not reshooting scenes, suggested a way in which the film could be used and the "mother" line could be recorded later. This met with approval. Then the cameras were rolling again, Virna Lisi was leaning toward Sinatra in the sand, and then he pulled her down close to him. The camera now moved in for a close-up of their faces, ticking away for a few long seconds, but Sinatra and Lisi did not stop kissing, they just lay together in the sand wrapped in one another's arms, and then Virna Lisi's left leg just slightly began to rise a bit, and everybody in the studio now watched in silence, not saying anything until Donohue finally called out:

"If you ever get through, let me know. I'm running out of film."

Then Miss Lisi got up, straightened out her white dress, brushed back her blonde hair and touched her lipstick, which was smeared. Sinatra got up, a little smile on his lips, and headed for his dressing room.

Passing an older man who stood near a camera, Sinatra asked, "How's your Bell & Howell?"

The older man smiled.

"It's fine, Frank."

"Good."

In his dressing room Sinatra was met by an automobile designer who had the plans for Sinatra's new custom-built model to replace the $25,000 Ghia he has been driving for the last few years. He also was awaited by his secretary, Tom Conroy, who had a bag full of fan mail, including a letter from New York's Mayor John Lindsay; and by Bill Miller, Sinatra's pianist, who would rehearse some of the songs that would be recorded later in the evening for Sinatra's newest album, *Moonlight Sinatra*.

While Sinatra does not mind hamming it up a bit on a movie set, he is extremely serious about his recording sessions; as he explained to a British writer, Robin Douglas-Home: "Once you're on that record singing, it's you and you alone. If it's bad and gets you criticized, it's you who's to blame—no one else. If it's good, it's also you. With a film it's never like that; there are producers and scriptwriters, and hundreds of men in offices and the thing is taken right out of your hands. With a record, you're it . . ."

> *But now the days are short*
> *I'm in the autumn of the year*
> *And now I think of my life*
> *As vintage wine*
> *From fine old kegs . . .*

It no longer matters what song he is singing, or who wrote the words—
they are all his words, his sentiments, they are chapters from the lyrical
novel of his life.

> *Life is a beautiful thing*
> *As long as I hold the string . . .*

When Frank Sinatra drives to the studio, he seems to dance out of the
car across the sidewalk into the front door; then, snapping his fingers, he is
standing in front of the orchestra in an intimate, airtight room, and soon
he is dominating every man, every instrument, every sound wave. Some of
the musicians have accompanied him for twenty-five years, have gotten old
hearing him sing "You Make Me Feel So Young."

When his voice is on, as it was tonight, Sinatra is in ecstasy, the room
becomes electric, there is an excitement that spreads through the orchestra and is felt in the control booth where a dozen men, Sinatra's friends,
wave at him from behind the glass. One of the men is the Dodgers' pitcher,
Don Drysdale ("Hey, Big D," Sinatra calls out, "hey, baby!"); another is the
professional golfer Bo Wininger; there are also numbers of pretty women
standing in the booth behind the engineers, women who smile at Sinatra
and softly move their bodies to the mellow mood of his music:

> *Will this be moon love*
> *Nothing but moon love*
> *Will you be gone when the dawn*
> *Comes stealing through . . .*

After he is finished, the record is played back on tape, and Nancy Sinatra,
who has just walked in, joins her father near the front of the orchestra to
hear the playback. They listen silently, all eyes on them, the king, the princess; and when the music ends there is applause from the control booth,
Nancy smiles, and her father snaps his fingers and says, kicking a foot,
"Ooba-deeba-boobe-do!"

Then Sinatra calls to one of his men. "Hey, Sarge, think I can have a
half-a-cup of coffee?"

Sarge Weiss, who had been listening to the music, slowly gets up.

"Didn't mean to wake ya, Sarge," Sinatra says, smiling.

Then Weiss brings the coffee, and Sinatra looks at it, smells it, then announces, "I thought he'd be nice to me, but it's really coffee . . ."

There are more smiles, and then the orchestra prepares for the next number. And one hour later, it is over.

The musicians put their instruments into their cases, grab their coats, and begin to file out, saying good-night to Sinatra. He knows them all by name, knows much about them personally, from their bachelor days, through their divorces, through their ups and downs, as they know him. When a French-horn player, a short Italian named Vincent DeRosa, who has played with Sinatra since The Lucky Strike "Hit Parade" days on radio, strolled by, Sinatra reached out to hold him for a second.

"Vicenzo," Sinatra said, "how's your little girl?"

"She's fine, Frank."

"Oh, she's not a little girl anymore," Sinatra corrected himself, "she's a big girl now."

"Yes, she goes to college now. U.S.C."

"That's great."

"She's also got a little talent, I think, Frank, as a singer."

Sinatra was silent for a moment, then said, "Yes, but it's very good for her to get her education first, Vicenzo."

Vincent DeRosa nodded.

"Yes, Frank," he said, and then he said, "Well, good-night, Frank."

"Good-night, Vicenzo."

After the musicians had all gone, Sinatra left the recording room and joined his friends in the corridor. He was going to go out and do some drinking with Drysdale, Wininger, and a few other friends, but first he walked to the other end of the corridor to say good-night to Nancy, who was getting her coat and was planning to drive home in her own car.

After Sinatra had kissed her on the cheek, he hurried to join his friends at the door. But before Nancy could leave the studio, one of Sinatra's men, Al Silvani, a former prizefight manager, joined her.

"Are you ready to leave yet, Nancy?"

"Oh, thanks, Al," she said, "but I'll be all right."

"Pope's orders," Silvani said, holding his hands up, palms out.

Only after Nancy had pointed to two of her friends who would escort her home, and only after Silvani recognized them as friends, would he leave.

The rest of the month was bright and balmy. The record session had gone magnificently, the film was finished, the television shows were out of the way, and now Sinatra was in his Ghia driving out to his office to begin co-ordinating his latest projects. He had an engagement at The Sands, a new spy film called *The Naked Runner* to be shot in England, and a couple more albums to do in the immediate months ahead. And within a week he would be fifty years old . . .

> *Life is a beautiful thing*
> *As long as I hold the string*
> *I'd be a silly so-and-so*
> *If I should ever let go . . .*

Frank Sinatra stopped his car. The light was red. Pedestrians passed quickly across his windshield but, as usual, one did not. It was a girl in her twenties. She remained at the curb staring at him. Through the corner of his left eye he could see her, and he knew, because it happens almost every day, that she was thinking, It looks like him, but is it?

Just before the light turned green, Sinatra turned toward her, looked directly into her eyes waiting for the reaction he knew would come. It came and he smiled. She smiled and he was gone.

1968

Take, for example, the Internet. This year, at a computer conference in San Francisco, an engineer named Douglas Engelbart sits down at a computer whose monitor is projected onto a giant screen behind him. He clicks a mouse, moves it, highlights text, enlarges it, opens and closes windows, moves them around the screen. The audience is impressed. Such different computing elements have never been integrated before into a single system like this. But Engelbart isn't done yet. With another click of his mouse, the giant screen above him splits into two, and the monitor of a man who is typing almost thirty miles away appears over the audience alongside Engelbart's. For an hour and a half, the audience members watch both screens in awe: the two men editing each other's text, highlighting sections, cutting and pasting, and clicking on underlined phrases so that they can be transported onto whole new screens of text. "The Mother of All Demos," as this presentation has been called, doesn't really represent the invention of the Internet, but it represents instead the first public demonstration of a practical use for the Internet, of what can happen when two computers are connected to one another and allowed to share information. Today, thanks to that demonstration, we now have easy access to limitless supplies of information—of possibilities, availabilities, varieties, facts. "Life itself can only be compiled and thereby captured on a list," William Gass once wrote, "if it can be laid out anywhere at all." With so much raw data now available to us, we no longer need writers to hunt down our information. What we need is someone to help select what matters from what we have. Not to accumulate but to shape; not to report but to make.

WILLIAM GASS

In the Heart of the Heart of the Country

A Place

So I have sailed the seas and come . . .

to B . . .

a small town fastened to a field in Indiana. Twice there have been twelve hundred people here to answer to the census. The town is outstandingly neat and shady, and always puts its best side to the highway. On one lawn there's even a wood or plastic iron deer.

You can reach us by crossing a creek. In the spring the lawns are green, the forsythia is singing, and even the railroad that guts the town has straight bright rails which hum when the train is coming, and the train itself has a welcome horning sound.

Down the back streets the asphalt crumbles into gravel. There's West-brook's, with the geraniums, Horsefall's, Mott's. The sidewalk shatters. Gravel dust rises like breath behind the wagons. And I am in retirement from love.

Weather

In the Midwest, around the lower Lakes, the sky in the winter is heavy and close, and it is a rare day, a day to remark on, when the sky lifts and allows the heart up. I am keeping count, and as I write this page, it is eleven days since I have seen the sun.

My House

There's a row of headless maples behind my house, cut to free the passage of electric wires. High stumps, ten feet tall, remain, and I climb these like

665

a boy to watch the country sail away from me. They are ordinary fields, a
little more uneven than they should be, since in the spring they puddle. The
topsoil's thin, but only moderately stony. Corn is grown one year, soybeans
another. At dusk starlings darken the single tree—a larch—which stands
in the middle. When the sky moves, fields move under it. I feel, on my
perch, that I've lost my years. It's as though I were living at last in my eyes,
as I have always dreamed of doing, and I think then I know why I've come
here: to see, and so to go out against new things—oh god how easily—like
air in a breeze. It's true there are moments—foolish moments, ecstasy on a
tree stump—when I'm all but gone, scattered I like to think like seed, for
I'm the sort now in the fool's position of having love left over which I'd like
to lose; what good is it now to me, candy ungiven after Halloween?

A Person

There are vacant lots on either side of Billy Holsclaw's house. As the
weather improves, they fill with hollyhocks. From spring through fall,
Billy collects coal and wood and puts the lumps and pieces in piles near
his door, for keeping warm is his one work. I see him most often on mild
days sitting on his doorsill in the sun. I notice he's squinting a little, which
is perhaps the reason he doesn't cackle as I pass. His house is the size of a
single garage, and very old. It shed its paint with its youth, and its boards
are a warped and weathered gray. So is Billy. He wears a short lumpy faded
black coat when it's cold, otherwise he always goes about in the same loose,
grease-spotted shirt and trousers. I suspect his galluses were yellow once,
when they were new.

Wires

These wires offend me. Three trees were maimed on their account, and now
these wires deface the sky. They cross like a fence in front of me, enclos-
ing the crows with the clouds. I can't reach in, but like a stick, I throw my
feelings over. What is it that offends me? I am on my stump, I've built a
platform there and the wires prevent my going out. The cut trees, the black
wires, all the beyond birds therefore anger me. When I've wormed through
a fence to reach a meadow, do I ever feel the same about the field?

The Church

The church has a steeple like the hat of a witch, and five birds, all doves, perch in its gutters.

My House

Leaves move in the windows. I cannot tell you yet how beautiful it is, what it means. But they do move. They move in the glass.

Politics

. . . for all those not in love.

I've heard Batista described as a Mason. A farmer who'd seen him in Miami made this claim. He's as nice a fellow as you'd ever want to meet. Of Castro, of course, no one speaks.

For all those not in love there's law: to rule . . . to regulate . . . to rectify. I cannot write the poetry of such proposals, the poetry of politics, though sometimes—often—always now—I am in that uneasy peace of equal powers which makes a State; then I communicate by passing papers, proclamations, orders, through my bowels. Yet I was not a State with you, nor were we both together any Indiana. A squad of Pershing Rifles at the moment, I make myself Right Face! Legislation packs the screw of my intestines. Well, king of the classroom's king of the hill. You used to waddle when you walked because my sperm between your legs was draining to a towel. Teacher, poet, folded lover—like the politician, like those drunkards, ill, or those who faucet-off while pissing heartily to preach upon the force and fullness of that stream, or pause from vomiting to praise the purity and passion of their puke—I chant, I beg, I orate, I command, I sing—

> *Come back to Indiana—not too late!*
> *(Or will you be a ranger to the end?)*
> *Good-bye . . . Good-bye . . . oh, I shall always wait*
> *You, Larry, traveler—*
> *stranger,*
>
> *son,*
> *—my friend—*

my little girl, my poem by heart, my self, my childhood.

But I've heard Batista described as a Mason. That dries up my pity, melts my hate. Back from the garage where I have overheard it, I slap the mended fender of my car to laugh, and listen to the metal stinging tartly in my hand.

People

Their hair in curlers and their heads wrapped in loud scarves, young mothers, fattish in trousers, lounge about in the speedwash, smoking cigarettes, eating candy, drinking pop, thumbing magazines, and screaming at their children above the whir and rumble of the machines.

At the bank a young man freshly pressed is letting himself in with a key. Along the street, delicately teetering, many grandfathers move in a dream. During the murderous heat of summer, they perch on window ledges, their feet dangling just inside the narrow shelf of shade the store has made, staring steadily into the street. Where their consciousness has gone I can't say. It's not in the eyes. Perhaps it's diffuse, all temperature and skin, like an infant's, though more mild. Near the corner there are several large overalled men employed in standing. A truck turns to be weighed on the scales at the Feed and Grain. Images drift on the drugstore window. The wind has blown the smell of cattle into town. Our eyes have been driven in like the eyes of the old men. And there's no one to have mercy on us.

Vital Data

There are two restaurants here and a tearoom. two bars. one bank, three barbers, one with a green shade with which he blinds his window. two groceries. a dealer in Fords. one drug, one hardware, and one appliance store. several that sell feed, grain, and farm equipment. an antique shop. a poolroom. a laundromat. three doctors. a dentist. a plumber. a vet. a funeral home in elegant repair the color of a buttercup. numerous beauty parlors which open and shut like night-blooming plants. a tiny dime and department store of no width but several floors. a hutch, homemade, where you can order, after lying down or squirming in, furniture that's been fashioned from bent lengths of stainless tubing, glowing plastic, metallic thread, and clear shellac. an American Legion Post and a root beer stand. little agencies for this and that: cosmetics, brushes, insurance, greeting cards and garden produce—anything—sample shoes—which do their business out of hats and satchels, over coffee cups and dissolving sugar. a factory for making paper sacks and pasteboard boxes that's lodged in an old brick building bearing the legend OPERA HOUSE, still faintly golden, on its roof. a library given by Carnegie. a post office. a school. a railroad station. fire station. lumberyard. telephone company. welding shop. garage . . . and spotted through the town from one end to the other in a line along the highway, gas stations to the number five.

Education

In 1833, Colin Goodykoontz, an itinerant preacher with a name from a fairytale, summed up the situation in one Indiana town this way:

> Ignorance and her squalid brood. A universal dearth of intel-
> lect. Total abstinence from literature is very generally prac-
> ticed . . . There is not a scholar in grammar or geography,
> or a *teacher capable* of *instructing* in them, to my knowl-
> edge . . . Others are supplied a few months of the year with
> the most antiquated & unreasonable forms of teaching read-
> ing, writing & cyphering . . . Need I stop to remind you of
> the host of loathsome reptiles such a stagnant pool is fitted to
> breed! Croaking jealousy; bloated bigotry; coiling suspicion;
> wormish blindness; crocodile malice!

Things have changed since then, but in none of the respects mentioned.

Business

One side section of street is blocked off with sawhorses. Hard, thin, bit-ter men in blue jeans, cowboy boots and hats, untruck a dinky carnival. The merchants are promoting themselves. There will be free rides, raucous music, parades and coneys, pop, popcorn, candy, cones, awards and draw-ings, with all you can endure of pinch, push, bawl, shove, shout, scream, shriek, and bellow. Children pedal past on decorated bicycles, their wheels a blur of color, streaming crinkled paper and excited dogs. A little later there's a pet show for a prize—dogs, cats, birds, sheep, ponies, goats—none of which wins. The whirlabouts whirl about. The Ferris wheel climbs dizzily into the sky as far as a tall man on tiptoe might be persuaded to reach, and the irritated operators measure the height and weight of every child with sour eyes to see if they are safe for the machines. An electrical megaphone repeatedly trumpets the names of the generous sponsors. The following day they do not allow the refuse to remain long in the street.

My House, This Place and Body

I have met with some mischance, wings withering, as Plato says obscurely, and across the breadth of Ohio, like heaven on a table, I've fallen as far as the poet, to the sixth sort of body, this house in B, in Indiana, with its blue and gray bewitching windows, holy magical insides. Great thick evergreens protect its entry. And I live *in*.

Lost in the corn rows, I remember feeling just another stalk, and thus this country takes me over in the way I occupy myself when I am well . . . completely—to the edge of both my house and body. No one notices, when they walk by, that I am brimming in the doorways. My house, this place and body, I've come in mourning to be born in. To anybody else it's pretty silly: love. Why should I feel a loss? How am I bereft? She was never mine; she was a fiction, always a golden tomgirl, barefoot, with an adolescent's slouch and a boy's taste for sports and fishing, a figure out of Twain, or worse, in Riley. Age cannot be kind.

There's little hand-in-hand here . . . not in B. No one touches except in rage. Occasionally girls will twine their arms about each other and lurch along, school out, toward home and play. I dreamed my lips would drift down your back like a skiff on a river. I'd follow a vein with the point of my finger, hold your bare feet in my naked hands.

The Same Person

Billy Holsclaw lives alone—how alone it is impossible to fathom. In the post office he talks greedily to me about the weather. His head bobs on a wild flood of words, and I take this violence to be a measure of his eagerness for speech. He badly needs a shave, coal dust has layered his face, he spits when he speaks, and his fingers pick at his tatters. He wobbles out in the wind when I leave him, a paper sack mashed in the fold of his arm, the leaves blowing past him, and our encounter drives me sadly home to poetry—where there's no answer. Billy closes his door and carries coal or wood to his fire and closes his eyes, and there's simply no way of knowing how lonely and empty he is or whether he's as vacant and barren and loveless as the rest of us are—here in the heart of the country.

Weather

For we're always out of luck here. That's just how it is—for instance in the winter. The sides of the buildings, the roofs, the limbs of the trees are gray. Streets, sidewalks, faces, feelings—they are gray. Speech is gray, and the grass where it shows. Every flank and front, each top is gray. Everything is gray: hair, eyes, window glass, the hawkers' bills and touters' posters, lips, teeth, poles and metal signs—they're gray, quite gray. Cars are gray. Boots, shoes, suits, hats, gloves are gray. Horses, sheep, and cows, cats killed in the road, squirrels in the same way, sparrows, doves, and pigeons, all are gray, everything is gray, and everyone is out of luck who lives here.

A similar haze turns the summer sky milky, and the air muffles your head and shoulders like a sweater you've got caught in. In the summer light, too, the sky darkens a moment when you open your eyes. The heat is pure distraction. Steeped in our fluids, miserable in the folds of our bodies, we can scarcely think of anything but our sticky parts. Hot cyclonic winds and storms of dust crisscross the country. In many places, given an indifferent push, the wind will still coast for miles, gathering resource and edge as it goes, cunning and force. According to the season, paper, leaves, field litter, seeds, snow, fill up the fences. Sometimes I think the land is flat because the winds have leveled it, they blow so constantly. In any case, a gale can grow in a field of corn that's as hot as a draft from hell, and to receive it is one of the most dismaying experiences of this life, though the smart of the same wind in winter is more humiliating, and in that sense even worse. But in the spring it rains as well, and the trees fill with ice.

Place

Many small Midwestern towns are nothing more than rural slums, and this community could easily become one. Principally during the first decade of the century, though there were many earlier instances, well-to-do farmers moved to town and built fine homes to contain them in their retirement. Others desired a more social life, and so lived in, driving to their fields like storekeepers to their businesses. These houses are now dying like the bereaved who inhabit them; they are slowly losing their senses—deafness, blindness, forgetfulness, mumbling, an insecure gait, an uncontrollable trembling has overcome them. Some kind of Northern Snopes will occupy them next: large-familied, Catholic, Democratic, scrambling, vigorous, poor; and since the parents will work in larger, nearby towns, the children will be loosed upon themselves and upon the hapless neighbors much as the fabulous Khan loosed his legendary horde. These Snopes will undertake makeshift repairs with materials that other people have thrown away; paint halfway round their house, then quit; almost certainly maintain an ugly loud cantankerous dog and underfeed a pair of cats to keep the rodents down. They will collect piles of possibly useful junk in the back yard, park their cars in the front, live largely leaning over engines, give not a hoot for the land, the old community, the hallowed ways, the established clans. Weakening widow ladies have already begun to hire large rude youths from families such as these to rake and mow and tidy the grounds they will inherit.

People

In the cinders at the station boys sit smoking steadily in darkened cars, their arms bent out the windows, white shirts glowing behind the glass. Nine o'clock is the best time. They sit in a line facing the highway—two or three or four of them—idling their engines. As you walk by a machine may growl at you or a pair of headlights flare up briefly. In a moment one will pull out, spinning cinders behind it, to stalk impatiently up and down the dark streets or roar half a mile into the country before returning to its place in line and pulling up.

My House, My Cat, My Company

I must organize myself. I must, as they say, pull myself together, dump this cat from my lap, stir—yes, resolve, move, do. But do what? My will is like the rosy dustlike light in this room: soft, diffuse, and gently comforting.

It lets me do . . . anything . . . nothing. My ears hear what they happen to; I eat what's put before me; my eyes see what blunders into them; my thoughts are not thoughts, they are dreams. I'm empty or I'm full . . . depending; and I cannot choose. I sink my claws in Tick's fur and scratch the bones of his back until his rear rises amorously. Mr. Tick, I murmur, I must organize myself. I must pull myself together. And Mr. Tick rolls over on his belly, all ooze.

I spill Mr. Tick when I've rubbed his stomach. Shoo. He steps away slowly, his long tail rhyming with his paws. How beautifully he moves, I think; how beautifully, like you, he commands his loving, how beautifully he accepts. So I rise and wander from room to room, up and down, gazing through most of my forty-one windows. How well this house receives its loving too. Let out like Mr. Tick, my eyes sink in the shrubbery. I am not here; I've passed the glass, passed second-story spaces, flown by branches, brilliant berries, to the ground, grass high in seed and leafage every season; and it is the same as when I passed above you in my aged, ardent body; it's, in short, a kind of love; and I am learning to restore myself, my house, my body, by paying court to gardens, cats, and running water, and with neighbors keeping company.

Mrs. Desmond is my right-hand friend; she's eighty-five. A thin white mist of hair, fine and tangled, manifests the climate of her mind. She is habitually suspicious, fretful, nervous. Burglars break in at noon. Children trespass. Even now they are shaking the pear tree, stealing rhubarb, denting lawn. Flies caught in the screens and numbed by frost awake in the heat to buzz and scrape the metal cloth and frighten her, though she is deaf to me, and consequently cannot hear them. Boards creak, the wind whistles across the chimney mouth, drafts cruise like fish through the hollow rooms. It is herself she hears, her own flesh failing, for only death will preserve her from those daily chores she climbs like stairs, and all that anxious waiting. Is it now, she wonders. No? Then: is it now?

We do not converse. She visits me to talk. My task to murmur. She talks about her grandsons, her daughter who lives in Delphi, her sister or her husband—both gone—obscure friends—dead—obscurer aunts and uncles—lost—ancient neighbors, members of her church or of her clubs—passed or passing on; and in this way she brings the ends of her life together with a terrifying rush: she is a girl, a wife, a mother, widow, all at once. All at once—appalling—but I believe it; I wince in expectation of the clap. Her talk's a fence—a shade drawn, window fastened, door that's locked—for no one dies taking tea in a kitchen; and as her years compress and begin to jumble, I really believe in the brevity of life; I sweat in my wonder; death is the dog down the street, the angry gander, bedroom spider, goblin who's come to get her; and it occurs to me that in my listening posture I'm the boy who suffered the winds of my grandfather with an exactly similar politeness, that I am, right now, all my ages, out in elbows, as angular as badly stacked cards. Thus was I, when I loved you, every man I could be, youth and child—far from enough—and you, so strangely ambiguous a being, met me, heart for spade, play after play, the whole run of our suits.

Mr. Tick, you do me honor. You not only lie in my lap, but you remain alive there, coiled like a fetus. Through your deep nap, I feel you hum. You are, and are not, a machine. You are alive, alive exactly, and it means nothing to you—much to me. You are a cat—you cannot understand—you are a cat so easily. Your nature is not something you must rise to. You, not I, live in: in house, in skin, in shrubbery. Yes. I think I shall hat my head with a steeple; turn church; devour people. Mr. Tick, though, has a tail he can twitch, he need not fly his Fancy. Claws, not metrical schema, poetry his paws; while smoothing . . . smoothing . . . smoothing roughly, his tongue laps its neatness. O Mr. Tick, I know you; you are an electrical penis. Go on now, shoo. Mrs. Desmond doesn't like you. She thinks you will tangle yourself in her legs and she will fall. You murder her birds, she knows, and walk upon her roof with death in your jaws. I must gather myself together for a bound. What age is it I'm at right now, I wonder. The heart, don't they always say, keeps the true time. Mrs. Desmond is knocking. Faintly, you'd think, but she pounds. She's brought me a cucumber. I believe she believes I'm a woman. Come in, Mrs. Desmond, thank you, be my company, it looks lovely, and have tea. I'll slice it, crisp, with cream, for luncheon, each slice as thin as me.

Politics

O all ye isolate and separate powers, Sing! Sing, and sing in such a way that from a distance it will seem a harmony, a Strindberg play, a friendship ring . . . so happy—happy, happy, happy—as here we go hand in handling, up and down. Our union was a singing, though we were silent in the songs we sang like single notes are silent in a symphony. In no sense sober, we barbershopped together and never heard the discords in our music or saw ourselves as dirty, cheap, or silly. Yet cats have worn out better shoes than those thrown through our love songs at us. Hush. Be patient—prudent— politic. Still, Cleveland killed you, Mr. Crane. Were you not politic enough and fond of being beaten? Like a piece of sewage, the city shat you from its stern three hundred miles from history—beyond the loving reach of sailors. Well, I'm not a poet who puts Paris to his temple in his youth to blow himself from Idaho, or—fancy that—Missouri. My god, I said, this is my country, but must my country go so far as Terre Haute or Whiting, go so far as Gary?

When the Russians first announced the launching of their satellite, many people naturally refused to believe them. Later others were outraged that they had sent a dog around the earth. I wouldn't want to take that mutt from out that metal flying thing if he's still living when he lands, our own dog catcher said; anybody knows you shut a dog up by himself to toss around the first thing he'll be setting on to do you let him out is bite somebody.

This Midwest. A dissonance of parts and people, we are a consonance of Towns. Like a man grown fat in everything but heart, we overlabor; our outlook never really urban, never rural either, we enlarge and linger at the same time, as Alice both changed and remained in her story. You are blond. I put my hand upon your belly; feel it tremble from my trembling. We always drive large cars in my section of the country. How could you be a comfort to me now?

More Vital Data

The town is exactly fifty houses, trailers, stores, and miscellaneous buildings long, but in places no streets deep. It takes on width as you drive south, always adding to the east. Most of the dwellings are fairly spacious farm houses in the customary white, with wide wraparound porches and tall narrow windows, though there are many of the grander kind—fretted, scalloped, turreted, and decorated with clapboards set at angles or on end, with stained-glass windows at the stair landings and lots of wrought iron full of fancy curls—and a few of these look like castles in their rarer brick. Old stables serve as garages now, and the lots are large to contain them and the vegetable and flower gardens which, ultimately, widows plant and weed and then entirely disappear in. The shade is ample, the grass is good, the sky a glorious fall violet; the apple trees are heavy and red, the roads are calm and empty; corn has sifted from the chains of tractored wagons to speckle the streets with gold and with the russet fragments of the cob, and a man would be a fool who wanted, blessed with this, to live anywhere else in the world.

Education

Buses like great orange animals move through the early light to school. There the children will be taught to read and warned against Communism. By Miss Janet Jakes. That's not her name. Her name is Helen something— Scott or James. A teacher twenty years. She's now worn fine and smooth, and has a face, Wilfred says, like a mail-order ax. Her voice is hoarse, and she has a cough. For she screams abuse. The children stare, their faces blank. This is the thirteenth week. They are used to it. You will all, she shouts, you will all draw pictures of me. No. She is a Mrs.—someone's missus. And in silence they set to work while Miss Jakes jabs hairpins in her hair. Wilfred says an ax, but she has those rimless tinted glasses, graying hair, an almost dimpled chin. I must concentrate. I must stop making up things. I must give myself to life; let it mold me: that's what they say in *Wisdom's Monthly Digest* every day. Enough, enough—you've been at it long enough; and the children rise formally a row at a time to present their work to her desk. No, she wears rims; it's her chin that's dimpleless. Well, it will take more than a tablespoon of features to sweeten that face. So she grimly shuffles their sheets, examines her reflection crayoned on them. I would not dare . . . allow a child . . . to put a line around me. Though now and then she smiles like a nick in the blade, in the end these drawings depress her. I could not bear it—how can she ask?—that anyone . . . draw me. Her anger's lit. That's why she does it: flame. There go her eyes; the pink in her glasses brightens, dims. She is a pumpkin, and her rage is breathing like the candle in. No, she shouts, no—the cartoon trembling—no, John Mauck, John Stewart Mauck, this will not do. The picture flutters from her fingers. You've made me too muscular.

I work on my poetry. I remember my friends, associates, my students, by their names. Their names are Maypop, Dormouse, Upsydaisy. Their names are Gladiolus, Callow Bladder, Prince and Princess Oleo, Hieronymus,

Cardinal Mummum, Mr. Fitchew, The Silken Howdah, Spot. Sometimes you're Tom Sawyer, Huckleberry Finn; it is perpetually summer; your buttocks are my pillow; we are adrift on a raft; your back is our river. Sometimes you are Major Barbara, sometimes a goddess who kills men in battle, sometimes you are soft like a shower of water; you are bread in my mouth.

I do not work on my poetry. I forget my friends, associates, my students, and their names: Gramophone, Blowgun, Pickle, Serenade . . . Marge the Barge, Arena, Uberhaupt . . . Doctor Dildoc, The Fog Machine. For I am now in B, in Indiana: out of job and out of patience, out of love and time and money, out of bread and out of body, in a temper, Mrs. Desmond, out of tea. So shut your fist up, bitch, you bag of death; go bang another door; go die, my dearie. Die, life-deaf old lady. Spill your breath. Fall over like a frozen board. Gray hair grows from the nose of your mind. You are a skull already—*memento mori*—the foreskin retracts from your teeth. Will your plastic gums last longer than your bones, and color their grinning? And is your twot still hazel-hairy, or are you bald as a ditch? . . . bitch . . . . . . bitch . . . . bitch. I wanted to be famous, but you bring me age—my emptiness. Was it *that* which I thought would balloon me above the rest? Love? where are you? . . . love me. I want to rise so high, I said, that when I shit I won't miss anybody.

Business

For most people, business is poor. Nearby cities have siphoned off all but a neighborhood trade. Except for feed and grain and farm supplies, you stand a chance to sell only what one runs out to buy. Chevrolet has quit, and Frigidaire. A locker plant has left its afterimage. The lumberyard has been, so far, six months about its going. Gas stations change hands clumsily, a restaurant becomes available, a grocery closes. One day they came and knocked the cornices from the watch repair and pasted campaign posters on the windows. Torn across, by now, by boys, they urge you still to vote for half an orange beblazoned man who as a whole one failed two years ago to win at his election. Everywhere, in this manner, the past speaks, and it mostly speaks of failure. The empty stores, the old signs and dusty fixtures, the debris in alleys, the flaking paint and rusty gutters, the heavy locks and sagging boards: they say the same disagreeable things. What do the sightless windows see, I wonder, when the sun throws a passerby against them?

Here a stair unfolds toward the street—dark, rickety, and treacherous—and I always feel, as I pass it, that if I just went carefully up and turned the corner at the landing, I would find myself out of the world. But I've never had the courage.

That Same Person

The weeds catch up with Billy. In pursuit of the hollyhocks, they rise in coarse clumps all around the front of his house. Billy has to stamp down a circle by his door like a dog or cat does turning round to nest up, they're so thick. What particularly troubles me is that winter will find the weeds still standing stiff and tindery to take the sparks which Billy's little mortarless chimney spouts. It's true that fires are fun here. The town whistle, which otherwise only blows for noon (and there's no noon on Sunday), signals the direction of the fire by the length and number of its blasts, the volunteer firemen rush past in their cars and trucks, houses empty their owners along the street every time like an illustration in a children's book. There are many bikes, too, and barking dogs, and sometimes—halleluiah—the fire's right here in town—a vacant lot of weeds and stubble flaming up. But I'd rather it weren't Billy or Billy's lot or house. Quite selfishly I want him to remain the way he is—counting his sticks and logs, sitting on his sill in the soft early sun—though I'm not sure what his presence means to me . . . or to anyone. Nevertheless, I keep wondering whether, given time, I might not someday find a figure in our language which would serve him faithfully, and furnish his poverty and loneliness richly out.

Wires

Where sparrows sit like fists. Doves fly the steeple. In mist the wires change perspective, rise and twist. If they led to you, I would know what they were. Thoughts passing often, like the starlings who flock these fields at evening to sleep in the trees beyond, would form a family of paths like this; they'd foot down the natural height of air to just about a bird's perch. But they do not lead to you.

> *Of whose beauty it was sung*
> *She shall make the old man young.*

They fasten me.

If I walked straight on, in my present mood, I would reach the Wabash. It's not a mood in which I'd choose to conjure you. Similes dangle like baubles from me. This time of year the river is slow and shallow, the clay banks crack in the sun, weeds surprise the sandbars. The air is moist and I am sweating. It's impossible to rhyme in this dust. Everything—sky, the cornfield, stump, wild daisies, my old clothes and pressless feelings—seem fabricated for installment purchase. Yes. Christ. I am suffering a summer Christmas; and I cannot walk under the wires. The sparrows scatter like handfuls of gravel. Really, wires are voices in thin strips. They are words wound in cables. Bars of connection.

Weather

I would rather it were the weather that was to blame for what I am and what my friends and neighbors are—we who live here in the heart of the country. Better the weather, the wind, the pale dying snow . . . the snow— why not the snow? There's never much really, not around the lower Lakes anyway, not enough to boast about, not enough to be useful. My father tells how the snow in the Dakotas would sweep to the roofs of the barns in the old days, and he and his friends could sled on the crust that would form because the snow was so fiercely driven. In Bemidji trees have been known to explode. That would be something—if the trees in Davenport or Francisville or Carbondale or Niles were to go blam some winter—blam! blam! blam! all the way down the gray, cindery, snow-sick streets.

A cold fall rain is blackening the trees or the air is like lilac and full of parachuting seeds. Who cares to live in any season but his own? Still I suspect the secret's in this snow, the secret of our sickness, if we could only diagnose it, for we are all dying like the elms in Urbana. This snow—like our skin it covers the country. Later dust will do it. Right now—snow. Mud presently. But it is snow without any laughter in it, a pale gray pudding thinly spread on stiff toast, and if that seems a strange description, it's accurate all the same. Of course soot blackens everything, but apart from that, we are never sufficiently cold here. The flakes as they come, alive and burning, we cannot retain, for if our temperatures fall, they rise promptly again, just as, in the summer, they bob about in the same feckless way. Suppose though . . . suppose they were to rise some August, climb and rise, and then hang in the hundreds like a hawk through December, what a desert we could make of ourselves—from Chicago to Cairo, from Hammond to Columbus—what beautiful Death Valleys.

Place

I would rather it were the weather. It drives us in upon ourselves—an unlucky fate. Of course there is enough to stir our wonder anywhere; there's enough to love, anywhere, if one is strong enough, it one is diligent enough, if one is perceptive, patient, kind enough—whatever it takes; and surely it's better to live in the country, to live on a prairie by a drawing of rivers, in Iowa or Illinois or Indiana, say, than in any city, in any stinking fog of human beings, in any blooming orchard of machines. It ought to be. The cities are swollen and poisonous with people. It ought to be better. Man has never been a fit environment for man—for rats, maybe, rats do nicely, or for dogs or cats and the household beetle.

And how long the street is, nowadays. These endless walls are fallen to keep back the tides of earth. Brick could be beautiful but we have covered it gradually with gray industrial vomits. Age does not make concrete genial, and asphalt is always—like America—twenty-one, until it breaks up in crumbs like stale cake. The brick, the asphalt, the concrete, the dancing signs and garish posters, the feed and excrement of the automobile, the litter of its inhabitants: they compose, they decorate, they line our streets, and there is nowhere, nowadays, our streets can't reach.

A man in the city has no natural thing by which to measure himself. His parks are potted plants. Nothing can live and remain free where he resides but the pigeon, starling, sparrow, spider, cockroach, mouse, moth, fly and weed, and he laments the existence of even these and makes his plans to poison them. The zoo? There *is* the zoo. Through its bars the city man stares at the great cats and dully sucks his ice. Living, alas, among men and their marvels, the city man supposes that his happiness depends on establishing, somehow, a special kind of harmonious accord with others. The novelists of the city, of slums and crowds, they call it love—and break their pens.

Wordsworth feared the accumulation of men in cities. He foresaw their "degrading thirst after outrageous stimulation," and some of their hunger for love. Living in a city, among so many, dwelling in the heat and tumult of incessant movement, a man's affairs are touch and go—that's all. It's not surprising that the novelists of the slums, the cities, and the crowds, should find that sex is but a scratch to ease a tickle, that we're most human when we're sitting on the john, and that the justest image of our life is in full passage through the plumbing.

> *That man, immur'd in cities, still retains*
> *His inborn inextinguishable thirst*
> *Of rural scenes, compensating his loss*
> *By supplemental shifts, the best he may.*

Come into the country, then. The air nimbly and sweetly recommends itself unto our gentle senses. Here, growling tractors tear the earth. Dust roils up behind them. Drivers sit jouncing under bright umbrellas. They wear refrigerated hats and steer by looking at the tracks they've cut behind them, their transistors blaring. Close to the land, are they? good companions to the soil? Tell me: do they live in harmony with the alternating seasons?

It's a lie of old poetry. The modern husbandman uses chemicals from cylinders and sacks, spike-ball-and-claw machines, metal sheds, and cost accounting. Nature in the old sense does not matter. It does not exist. Our farmer's only mystical attachment is to parity. And if he does not realize that cows and corn are simply different kinds of chemical engine, he cannot expect to make a go of it.

It isn't necessary to suppose our cows have feelings; our neighbor hasn't as many as he used to have either; but think of it this way a moment, you can correct for the human imputations later: how would it feel to nurse those strange tentacled calves with their rubber, glass, and metal lips, their stainless eyes?

People

Aunt Pet's still able to drive her car—a high square Ford—even though she walks with difficulty and a stout stick. She has a watery gaze, a smooth plump face despite her age, and jet black hair in a bun. She has the slowest smile of anyone I ever saw, but she hates dogs, and not very long ago cracked the back of one she cornered in her garden. To prove her vigor she will tell you this, her smile breaking gently while she raises the knob of her stick to the level of your eyes.

House, My Breath and Window

My window is a grave, and all that lies within it's dead. No snow is falling. There's no haze. It is not still, not silent. Its images are not an animal that waits, for movement is no demonstration. I have seen the sea slack, life bubble through a body without a trace, its spheres impervious as soda's. Downwound, the whore at wagtag clicks and clacks. Leaves wiggle. Grass sways. A bird chirps, pecks the ground. An auto wheel in penning circles keeps its rigid spokes. These images are stones; they are memorials. Beneath this sea lies sea: god rest it . . . rest the world beyond my window, me in front of my reflection, above this page, my shade. Death is not so still, so silent, since silence implies a falling quiet, stillness a stopping, containing, holding in; for death is time in a clock, like Mr. Tick, electric . . . like wind through a windup poet. And my blear floats out to visible against the glass, befog its country and bespill myself. The mist lifts slowly from the fields in the morning. No one now would say: the Earth throws back its covers; it is rising from sleep. Why is the feeling foolish? The image is too Greek. I used to gaze at you so wantonly your body blushed. Imagine: wonder: that my eyes could cause such flowering. Ah, my friend, your face is pale, the weather cloudy; a street has been felled through your chin, bare trees do nothing, houses take root in their rectangles, a steeple stands up in your head. You speak of loving; then give me a kiss. The pane is cold. On icy mornings the fog rises to greet me (as you always did); the barns and other buildings, rather than ghostly, seem all the more substantial for looming, as if they grew in themselves while I watched (as you always did). Oh my approach, I suppose, was like breath in a rubber monkey. Nevertheless, on the road along the Wabash in the morning, though the trees are sometimes obscured by fog, their reflection floats serenely on the river, reasoning the banks, the sycamores in French rows. Magically, the world tips. I'm led to think that only those who grow down live (which will scarcely win me twenty-five from *Wisdom's Monthly Digest*), but I find I write that only those who live down grow; and what I write, I hold, whatever I really know. My every word's inverted, or reversed—or I am. I held you, too, that way. You were so utterly provisional, subject to my change. I could inflate your bosom with a kiss, disperse your skin with gentleness, enter your vagina from within, and make my love emerge like a fresh sex. The pane is cold. Honesty is cold, my inside lover. The sun looks, through the mist, like a plum on the tree of heaven, or a bruise on the slope of your belly. Which?

The grass crawls with frost. We meet on this window, the world and I, inelegantly, swimmers of the glass; and swung wrong way round to one another, the world seems in. The world—how grand, how monumental, grave and deadly, that word is: the world, my house and poetry. All poets have their inside lovers. Wee penis does not belong to me, or any of this foggery. It is *his* property which he's thrust through what's womanly of me to set down this. These wooden houses in their squares, gray streets and fallen sidewalks, standing trees, your name I've written sentimentally across my breath into the whitening air, pale birds: they exist in me now because of him. I gazed with what intensity . . . A bush in the excitement of its roses could not have bloomed so beautifully as you did then. It was a look I'd like to give this page. For that is poetry: to bring within about, to change.

Politics

Sports, politics, and religion are the three passions of the badly educated. They are the Midwest's open sores. Ugly to see, a source of constant discontent, they sap the body's strength. Appalling quantities of money, time, and energy are wasted on them. The rural mind is narrow, passionate, and reckless on these matters. Greed, however shortsighted and direct, will not alone account for it. I have known men, for instance, who for years have voted squarely against their interests. Nor have I ever noticed that their surly Christian views prevented them from urging forward the smithcreening, say, of Russia, China, Cuba, or Korea. And they tend to back their country like they back their local team: they have a fanatical desire to win; yelling is their forte; and if things go badly, they are inclined to sack the coach. All in all, then, Birch is a good name. It stands for the bigot's stick, the wild-child-tamer's cane.

Forgetfulness—is that their object?

Oh, I was new, I thought. A fresh start: new cunt, new climate, and new country—there you were, and I was pioneer, and had no history. That language hurts me, too, my dear. You'll never hear it.

Final Vital Data

The Modern Homemakers' Demonstration Club. The Prairie Home Demonstration Club. The Night-outers' Home Demonstration Club. The IOOF, FFF, VFW, WCTU, WSCS, 4-H, 40 and 8, Psi Iota Chi, and PTA. The

Boy and Girl Scouts, Rainbows, Masons, Indians and Rebekah Lodge. Also the Past Noble Grand Club of the Rebekah Lodge. As well as the Moose and the Ladies of the Moose. The Elks, the Eagles, the Jaynettes and the Eastern Star. The Women's Literary Club, the Hobby Club, the Art Club, the Sunshine Society, the Dorcas Society, the Pythian Sisters, the Pilgrim Youth Fellowship, the American Legion, the American Legion Auxiliary, the American Legion Junior Auxiliary, the Gardez Club, the Bridge for Fun Club, the What-can-you-do? Club, the Get Together Club, the Coterie Club, the Worthwhile Club, the Let's Help Our Town Club, the No Name Club, the Forget-me-not Club, the Merry-go-round Club . . .

Education

Has a quarter disappeared from Paula Frosty's pocket book? Imagine the landscape of that face: no crayon could engender it; soft wax is wrong; thin wire in trifling snips might do the trick. Paula Frosty and Christopher Roger accuse the pale and splotchy Cheryl Pipes. But Miss Jakes, I *saw* her. Miss Jakes is so extremely vexed she snaps her pencil. What else is missing? I appoint you a detective, John: search her desk. Gum, candy, paper, pencils, marble, round eraser—whose? A thief. I can't watch her all the time, I'm here to teach. Poor pale fossetted Cheryl, it's determined, can't return the money because she took it home and spent it. Cindy, Janice, John, and Pete—you four who sit around her—you will be detectives this whole term to watch her. A thief. In all my time. Miss Jakes turns, unfists, and turns again. I'll handle you, she cries. To think. A thief. In all my years. Then she writes on the blackboard the name of Cheryl Pipes and beneath that the figure twenty-five with a large sign for cents. Now Cheryl, she says, this won't be taken off until you bring that money out of home, out of home straight up to here, Miss Jakes says, tapping her desk.

Which is three days.

Another Person

I was raking leaves when Uncle Halley introduced himself to me. He said his name came from the comet, and that his mother had borne him prematurely in her fright of it. I thought of Hobbes, whom fear of the Spanish Armada had hurried into birth, and so I believed Uncle Halley to honor the philosopher, though Uncle Halley is a liar, and neither the one hundred twenty-nine nor the fifty-three he ought to be. That fall the leaves had burned themselves out on the trees, the leaf lobes had curled, and now they flocked noisily down the street and were broken in the wires of my rake. Uncle Halley was himself (like Mrs. Desmond and history generally) both deaf and implacable, and he shooed me down his basement stairs to a room set aside there for stacks of newspapers reaching to the ceiling, boxes of leaflets and letters and programs, racks of photo albums, scrapbooks, bundles of rolled-up posters and maps, flags and pennants and slanting piles of dusty magazines devoted mostly to motoring and the Christian ethic. I saw a bird cage, a tray of butterflies, a bugle, a stiff straw boater, and all kinds of tassels tied to a coat tree. He still possessed and had on display the steering lever from his first car, a linen duster, driving gloves and goggles, photographs along the wall of himself, his friends, and his various machines, a shell from the first war, a record of "Ramona" nailed through its hole to a post, walking sticks and fanciful umbrellas, shoes of all sorts (his baby shoes, their counters broken, were held in sorrow beneath my nose—they had not been bronzed, but he might have them done someday before he died, he said), countless boxes of medals, pins, beads, trinkets, toys, and keys (I scarcely saw—they flowed like jewels from his palms), pictures of downtown when it was only a path by the railroad station, a brightly colored globe of the world with a dent in Poland, antique guns, belt buckles, buttons, souvenir plates and cups and saucers (I can't remember all of it—I won't), but I recall how shamefully, how rudely, how abruptly, I fled, a good story in my mouth but death in my nostrils; and how afterward I busily, righteously, burned my leaves as if I were purging the world of its years. I still wonder if this town—its life, and mine now— isn't really a record like the one of "Ramona" that I used to crank around on my grandmother's mahogany Victrola through lonely rainy days as a kid.

The First Person

Billy's like the coal he's found: spilled, mislaid, discarded. The sky's no comfort. His house and his body are dying together. His windows are boarded. And now he's reduced to his hands. I suspect he has glaucoma. At any rate he can scarcely see, and weeds his yard of rubble on his hands and knees. Perhaps he's a surgeon cleansing a wound or an ardent and tactile lover. I watch, I must say, apprehensively. Like mine-war detectors, his hands graze in circles ahead of him. Your nipples were the color of your eyes. Pebble. Snarl of paper. Length of twine. He leans down closely, picks up something silvery, holds it near his nose. Foil? cap? coin? He has within him—what, I wonder? Does he know more now because he fingers everything and has to sniff to see? It would be romantic cruelty to think so. He bends the down on your arms like a breeze. You wrote me: something is strange when we don't understand. I write in return: I think when I loved you I fell to my death.

Billy, I could read to you from Beddoes; he's your man perhaps; he held with dying, freed his blood of its arteries; and he said that there were many wretched love-ill fools like me lying alongside the last bone of their former selves, as full of spirit and speech, nonetheless, as Mrs. Desmond, Uncle Halley and the Ferris wheel, Aunt Pet, Miss Jakes, Ramona or the megaphone; yet I reverse him finally, Billy, on no evidence but braggadocio, and I declare that though my inner organs were devoured long ago, the worm which swallowed down my parts still throbs and glows like a crystal palace.

Yes, you were younger. I was Uncle Halley, the museum man and infrequent meteor. Here is my first piece of ass. They weren't so flat in those days, had more round, more juice. And over here's the sperm I've spilled, nicely jarred and clearly labeled. Look at this tape like lengths of intestine where I've stored my spew, the endless worm of words I've written, a hundred million emissions or more: oh I was quite a man right from the start; even when unconscious in my cradle, from crotch to cranium, I was erectile tissue; though mostly, after the manner approved by Plato, I had intercourse by eye. Never mind, old Holsclaw, you are blind. We pull down darkness when we go to bed; put out like Oedipus the actually offending organ, and train our touch to lies. All cats are gray, says Mr. Tick; so under cover of glaucoma you are sack gray too, and cannot be distinguished from a stallion.

I must pull myself together, get a grip, just as they say, but I feel spilled, bewildered, quite mislaid. I did not restore my house to its youth, but to its age. Hunting, you hitch through the hollyhocks. I'm inclined to say you aren't half the cripple I am, for there is nothing left of me but mouth. However, I resist the impulse. It is another lie of poetry. My organs are all there, though it's there where I fail—at the roots of my experience. Poet of the spiritual, Rilke, weren't you? yet that's what you said. Poetry, like love, is—in and out—a physical caress. I can't tolerate any more of my sophistries about spirit, mind, and breath. Body equals being, and if your weight goes down, you are the less.

Household Apples

I knew nothing about apples. Why should I? My country came in my childhood, and I dreamed of sitting among the blooms like the bees. I failed to spray the pear tree too. I doubled up under them at first, admiring the sturdy low branches I should have pruned, and later I acclaimed the blossoms. Shortly after the fruit formed there were falls—not many— apples the size of goodish stones which made me wobble on my ankles when I walked about the yard. Sometimes a piece crushed by a heel would cling on the shoe to track the house. I gathered a few and heaved them over the wires. A slingshot would have been splendid. Hard, an unattractive green, the worms had them. Before long I realized the worms had them all. Even as the apples reddened, lit their tree, they were being swallowed. The birds preferred the pears, which were small—sugar pears I think they're called—with thick skins of graying green that ripen on toward violet. So the fruit fell, and once I made some applesauce by quartering and paring hundreds; but mostly I did nothing, left them, until suddenly, overnight it seemed, in that ugly late September heat we often have in Indiana, my problem was upon me.

My childhood came in the country. I remember, now, the flies on our snowy luncheon table. As we cleared away they would settle, fastidiously scrub themselves and stroll to the crumbs to feed where I would kill them in crowds with a swatter. It was quite a game to catch them taking off. I struck heavily since I didn't mind a few stains; they'd wash. The swatter was a square of screen bound down in red cloth. It drove no air ahead of it to give them warning. They might have thought they'd flown headlong into a summered window. The faint pink dot where they had died did not rub out as I'd supposed, and after years of use our luncheon linen would faintly, pinkly, speckle. The country became my childhood. Flies braided themselves on the flypaper in my grandmother's house. I can smell the bakery and the grocery and the stables and the dairy in that small Dakota town I knew as a kid; knew as I dreamed I'd know your body, as I've known nothing, before or since; knew as the flies knew, in the honest, unchaste sense: the burned house, hose-wet, which drew a mist of insects like the blue smoke of its smolder, and gangs of boys, moist-lipped, destructive as its burning. Flies have always impressed me; they are so persistently alive. Now they were coating the ground beneath my trees. Some were ordinary flies; there were the large blue-green ones; there were swarms of fruit flies too, and the red-spotted scavenger beetle; there were a few wasps, several sorts of bees and butterflies—checkers, sulphurs, monarchs, commas, question marks—and delicate dragonflies . . . but principally house-flies and horseflies and bottleflies, flies and more flies in clusters around the rotting fruit. They loved the pears. Inside, they fed. If you picked up a pear, they flew, and the pear became skin and stem. They were everywhere the fruit was: in the tree still—apples like a hive for them—or where the fruit littered the ground, squashing itself as you stepped . . . there was no help for it. The flies droned, feasting on the sweet juice. No one could go near the trees; I could not climb; so I determined at last to labor like Hercules. There were fruit baskets in the barn. Collecting them and kneeling under the branches, I began to gather remains. Deep in the strong rich smell of the fruit, I began to hum myself. The fruit caved in at the touch. Glistening red apples, my lifting disclosed, had families of beetles, flies, and bugs, devouring their rotten undersides. There were streams of flies; there were lakes and cataracts and rivers of flies, seas and oceans. The hum was heavier, higher, than the hum of the bees when they came to the blooms in the spring, though the bees were there, among the flies, ignoring me— ignoring everyone. As my work went on and juice covered my hands and arms, they would form a sleeve, black and moving, like knotty wool. No caress could have been more indifferently complete. Still I rose fearfully, ramming my head in the branches, apples bumping against me before falling, bursting with bugs. I'd snap my hand sharply but the flies would cling to the sweet. I could toss a whole cluster into a basket from several feet. As the pear or apple lit, they would explosively rise, like monads for a moment, windowless, certainly, with respect to one another, sugar their harmony. I had to admit, though, despite my distaste, that my arm had never been more alive, oftener or more gently kissed. Those hundreds of feet were light. In washing them off, I pretended the hose was a pump. What have I missed? Childhood is a lie of poetry.

The Church

Friday night. Girls in dark skirts and white blouses sit in ranks and scream in concert. They carry funnels loosely stuffed with orange and black paper which they shake wildly, and small megaphones through which, as drilled, they direct and magnify their shouting. Their leaders, barely pubescent girls, prance and shake and whirl their skirts above their bloomers. The young men, leaping, extend their arms and race through puddles of amber light, their bodies glistening. In a lull, though it rarely occurs, you can hear the squeak of tennis shoes against the floor. Then the yelling begins again, and then continues; fathers, mothers, neighbors joining in to form a single pulsing ululation—a cry of the whole community—for in this gymnasium each body becomes the bodies beside it, pressed as they are together, thigh to thigh, and the same shudder runs through all of them, and runs toward the same release. Only the ball moves serenely through this dazzling din. Obedient to law it scarcely speaks but caroms quietly and lives at peace.

Business

It is the week of Christmas and the stores, to accommodate the rush they hope for, are remaining open in the evening. You can see snow falling in the cones of the street lamps. The roads are filling—undisturbed. Strings of red and green lights droop over the principal highway, and the water tower wears a star. The windows of the stores have been bedizened. Shamelessly they beckon. But I am alone, leaning against a pole—no . . . there is no one in sight. They're all at home, perhaps by their instruments, tuning in on their evenings, and like Ramona, tirelessly playing and replaying themselves. There's a speaker perched in the tower, and through the boughs of falling snow and over the vacant streets, it drapes the twisted and metallic strains of a tune that can barely be distinguished—yes, I believe it's one of the jolly ones, it's "Joy to the World." There's no one to hear the music but myself, and though I'm listening, I'm no longer certain. Perhaps the record's playing something else.

1969

Here, says one writer. Let me build a bridge between the selves
that we have lost and the ones that we've become.

N. Scott Momaday

The Way to Rainy Mountain

I

You know, everything had to begin, and this is how it was: the Kiowas came one by one into the world through a hollow log. They were many more than now, but not all of them got out. There was a woman whose body was swollen up with child, and she got stuck in the log. After that, no one could get through, and that is why the Kiowas are a small tribe in number. They looked all around and saw the world. It made them glad to see so many things. They called themselves *Kwuda,* "coming out."

They called themselves Kwuda *and later* Tepda, *both of which mean "coming out." And later still they took the name* Gaigwu, *a name which can be taken to indicate something of which the two halves differ from each other in appearance. It was once a custom among Kiowa warriors that they cut their hair on the right side of the head only and on a line level with the lobe of the ear, while on the left they let the hair grow long and wore it in a thick braid wrapped in otter skin. "Kiowa" is indicated in sign language by holding the hand palm up and slightly cupped to the right side of the head and rotating it back and forth from the wrist. "Kiowa" is thought to derive from the softened Comanche form of* Gaigwu.

I remember coming out upon the northern Great Plains in the late spring. There were meadows of blue and yellow wildflowers on the slopes, and I could see the still, sunlit plain below, reaching away out of sight. At first there is no discrimination in the eye, nothing but the land itself, whole and impenetrable. But then smallest things begin to stand out of the depths— herds and rivers and groves—and each of these has perfect being in terms of distance and of silence and of age. Yes, I thought, now I see the earth as it really is; never again will I see things as I saw them yesterday or the day before.

II

They were going along, and some were hunting. An antelope was killed and quartered in the meadow. Well, one of the big chiefs came up and took the udders of that animal for himself, but another big chief wanted those udders also, and there was a great quarrel between them. Then, in anger, one of these chiefs gathered all of his followers together and went away. They are called *Azatanhop*, "the udder-angry travelers off." No one knows where they went or what happened to them.

This is one of the oldest memories of the tribe. There have been reports of people in the Northwest who speak a language that is similar to Kiowa.

In the winter of 1848–49, the buffalo ranged away from easy reach, and food was scarce. There was an antelope drive in the vicinity of Bent's Fort, Colorado. According to ancient custom, antelope medicine was made, and the Kiowas set out on foot and on horseback—men, women, and children—after game. They formed a great circle, inclosing a large area of the plain, and began to converge upon the center. By this means antelope and other animals were trapped and killed, often with clubs and even with the bare hands. By necessity were the Kiowas reminded of their ancient ways.

One morning on the high plains of Wyoming I saw several pronghorns in the distance. They were moving very slowly at an angle away from me, and they were almost invisible in the tall brown and yellow grass. They ambled along in their own wilderness dimension of time, as if no notion of flight could ever come upon them. But I remembered once having seen a frightened buck on the run, how the white rosette of its rump seemed to hang for the smallest fraction of time at the top of each frantic bound—like a succession of sunbursts against the purple hills.

III

Before there were horses the Kiowas had need of dogs. That was a long time ago, when dogs could talk. There was a man who lived alone; he had been thrown away, and he made his camp here and there on the high ground. Now it was dangerous to be alone, for there were enemies all around. The man spent his arrows hunting food. He had one arrow left, and he shot a bear; but the bear was only wounded and it ran away. The man wondered what to do. Then a dog came up to him and said that many enemies were coming; they were close by and all around. The man could think of no way to save himself. But the dog said: "You know, I have puppies. They are young and weak and they have nothing to eat. If you will take care of my puppies, I will show you how to get away." The dog led the man here and there, around and around, and they came to safety.

A hundred years ago the Comanche Ten Bears remarked upon the great number of horses which the Kiowas owned. "When we first knew you," he said, "you had nothing but dogs and sleds." It was so; the dog is primordial. Perhaps it was dreamed into being.

The principal warrior society of the Kiowas was the Ka-itsenko, *"Real Dogs," and it was made up of ten men only, the ten most brave. Each of these men wore a long ceremonial sash and carried a sacred arrow. In time of battle he must by means of this arrow impale the end of his sash to the earth and stand his ground to the death. Tradition has it that the founder of the* Ka-itsenko *had a dream in which he saw a band of warriors, outfitted after the fashion of the society, being led by a dog. The dog sang the song of the* Ka-itsenko, *then said to the dreamer: "You are a dog; make a noise like a dog and sing a dog song."*

There were always dogs about my grandmother's house. Some of them were nameless and lived a life of their own. They belonged there in a sense that the word "ownership" does not include. The old people paid them scarcely any attention, but they should have been sad, I think, to see them go.

IV

They lived at first in the mountains. They did not yet know of Tai-me, but this is what they knew: There was a man and his wife. They had a beautiful child, a little girl whom they would not allow to go out of their sight. But one day a friend of the family came and asked if she might take the child outside to play. The mother guessed that would be all right, but she told the friend to leave the child in its cradle and place the cradle in a tree. While the child was in the tree, a redbird came among the branches. It was not like any bird that you have seen; it was very beautiful, and it did not fly away. It kept still upon a limb, close to the child. After a while the child got out of its cradle and began to climb after the redbird. And at the same time the tree began to grow taller, and the child was borne up into the sky. She was then a woman, and she found herself in a strange place. Instead of a redbird, there was a young man standing before her. The man spoke to her and said: "I have been watching you for a long time, and I knew that I would find a way to bring you here. I have brought you here to be my wife." The woman looked all around; she saw that he was the only living man there. She saw that he was the sun.

There the land itself ascends into the sky. These mountains lie at the top of the continent, and they cast a long rain shadow on the sea of grasses to the east. They arise out of the last North American wilderness, and they have wilderness names: Wasatch, Bitterroot, Bighorn, Wind River.

I have walked in a mountain meadow bright with Indian paintbrush, lupine, and wild buckwheat, and I have seen high in the branches of a lodgepole pine the male pine grosbeak, round and rose-colored, its dark, striped wings nearly invisible in the soft, mottled light. And the uppermost branches of the tree seemed very slowly to ride across the blue sky.

V

After that the woman grew lonely. She thought about her people, and she wondered how they were getting on. One day she had a quarrel with the sun, and the sun went away. In her anger she dug up the root of a bush which the sun had warned her never to go near. A piece of earth fell from the root, and she could see her people far below. By that time she had given birth; she had a child—a boy by the sun. She made a rope out of sinew and took her child upon her back; she climbed down upon the rope, but when she came to the end, her people were still a long way off, and there she waited with her child on her back. It was evening; the sun came home and found his woman gone. At once he thought of the bush and went to the place where it had grown. There he saw the woman and the child, hanging by the rope half way down to the earth. He was very angry, and he took up a ring, a gaming wheel, in his hand. He told the ring to follow the rope and strike the woman dead. Then he threw the ring and it did what he told it to do; it struck the woman and killed her, and then the sun's child was all alone.

The plant is said to have been the pomme blanche, *or* pomme de prairie, *of the voyageurs, whose chronicles refer time and again to its use by the Indians. It grows on the high plains and has a farinaceous root that is turnip-like in taste and in shape. This root is a healthful food, and attempts have been made to cultivate the plant as a substitute for the potato.*

The anthropologist Mooney wrote in 1896: "Unlike the neighboring Cheyenne and Arapaho, who yet remember that they once lived east of the Missouri and cultivated corn, the Kiowa have no tradition of ever having been an agricultural people or anything but a tribe of hunters."

Even now they are meateaters; I think it is not in them to be farmers. My grandfather, Mammedaty, worked hard to make wheat and cotton grow on his land, but it came to very little in the end. Once when I was a small boy I went across the creek to the house where the old woman Keahdinekeah lived. Some men and boys came in from the pasture, where a calf had just been killed and butchered. One of the boys held the calf's liver—still warm and wet with life—in his hand, eating of it with great relish. I have heard that the old hunters of the Plains prized the raw liver and tongue of the buffalo above all other delicacies.

VI

The sun's child was big enough to walk around on the earth, and he saw a camp nearby. He made his way to it and saw that a great spider—that which is called a grandmother—lived there. The spider spoke to the sun's child, and the child was afraid. The grandmother was full of resentment; she was jealous, you see, for the child had not yet been weaned from its mother's breasts. She wondered whether the child were a boy or a girl, and therefore she made two things, a pretty ball and a bow and arrows. These things she left alone with the child all the next day. When she returned, she saw that the ball was full of arrows, and she knew then that the child was a boy and that he would be hard to raise. Time and again the grandmother tried to capture the boy, but he always ran away. Then one day she made a snare out of rope. The boy was caught up in the snare, and he cried and cried, but the grandmother sang to him and at last he fell asleep.

> *Go to sleep and do not cry.*
> *Your mother is dead, and still you feed*
> *   upon her breasts.*
> *Oo-oo-la-la-la-la, oo-oo.*

In the autumn of 1874, the Kiowas were driven southward towards the Staked Plains. Columns of troops were converging upon them from all sides, and they were bone-weary and afraid. They camped on Elk Creek, and the next day it began to rain. It rained hard all that day, and the Kiowas waited on horseback for the weather to clear. Then, as evening came on, the earth was suddenly crawling with spiders, great black tarantulas, swarming on the flood.

I know of spiders. There are dirt roads on the Plains. You see them, and you wonder where and how far they go. They seem very old and untraveled, as if they all led away to deserted houses. But creatures cross these roads: dung beetles and grasshoppers, sidewinders and tortoises. Now and then there comes a tarantula, at evening, always larger than you imagine, dull and dark brown, covered with long, dusty hairs. There is something crochety about them; they stop and go and angle away.

VII

The years went by, and the boy still had the ring which killed his mother. The grandmother spider told him never to throw the ring into the sky, but one day he threw it up, and it fell squarely on top of his head and cut him in two. He looked around, and there was another boy, just like himself, his twin. The two of them laughed and laughed, and then they went to the grandmother spider. She nearly cried aloud when she saw them, for it had been hard enough to raise the one. Even so, she cared for them well and made them fine clothes to wear.

Mammedaty owned horses. And he could remember that it was essentially good to own horses, that it was hard to be without horses. There was a day: Mammedaty got down from a horse for the last time. Of all the tribes of the Plains, the Kiowas owned the greatest number of horses per person.

On summer afternoons I went swimming in the Wasita River. The current was slow, and the warm, brown water seemed to be standing still. It was a secret place. There in the deep shade, inclosed in the dense, overhanging growth of the banks, my mind fixed on the wings of a dragonfly or the flitting motion of a water strider, the great open land beyond was all but impossible to imagine. But it was there, a stone's throw away. Once, from the limb of a tree, I saw myself in the brown water; then a frog leaped from the bank, breaking the image apart.

VIII

Now each of the twins had a ring, and the grandmother spider told them never to throw the rings into the sky. But one day they threw them up into the high wind. The rings rolled over a hill, and the twins ran after them. They ran beyond the top of the hill and fell down into the mouth of a cave. There lived a giant and his wife. The giant had killed a lot of people in the past by building fires and filling the cave with smoke, so that the people could not breathe. Then the twins remembered something that the grandmother spider had told them: "If ever you get caught in the cave, say to yourselves the word *thain-mom*, 'above my eyes.'" When the giant began to set fires around, the twins repeated the word *thain-mom* over and over to themselves, and the smoke remained above their eyes. When the giant had made three great clouds of smoke, his wife saw that the twins sat without coughing or crying, and she became frightened. "Let them go," she said, "or something bad will happen to us." The twins took up their rings and returned to the grandmother spider. She was glad to see them.

A word has power in and of itself. It comes from nothing into sound and meaning; it gives origin to all things. By means of words can a man deal with the world on equal terms. And the word is sacred. A man's name is his own; he can keep it or give it away as he likes. Until recent times, the Kiowas would not speak the name of a dead man. To do so would have been disrespectful and dishonest. The dead take their names with them out of the world.

When Aho saw or heard or thought of something bad, she said the word zei-dl-bei, "frightful." It was the one word with which she confronted evil and the incomprehensible. I liked her to say it, for she screwed up her face in a wonderful look of displeasure and clicked her tongue. It was not an exclamation so much, I think, as it was a warding off, an exertion of language upon ignorance and disorder.

IX

The next thing that happened to the twins was this: They killed a great snake which they found in their tipi. When they told the grandmother spider what they had done, she cried and cried. They had killed their grandfather, she said. And after that the grandmother spider died. The twins wrapped her in a hide and covered her with leaves by the water. The twins lived on for a long time, and they were greatly honored among the Kiowas.

In another and perhaps older version of the story, it is a porcupine and not a redbird that is the representation of the sun. In that version, too, one of the twins is said to have walked into the waters of a lake and disappeared forever, while the other at last transformed himself into ten portions of "medicine," thereby giving of his own body in eucharistic form to the Kiowas. The ten bundles of the talyi-da-i, "boy medicine," are, like the Tai-me, chief objects of religious veneration.

When he was a boy, my father went with his grandmother, Keahdinekeah, to the shrine of one of the talyi–da–i. The old woman made an offering of bright cloth, and she prayed. The shrine was a small, specially–made tipi; inside, suspended from the lashing poles, was the medicine itself. My father knew that it was very powerful, and the very sight of it filled him with wonder and regard. The holiness of such a thing can be imparted to the human spirit, I believe, for I remember that it shone in the sightless eyes of Keahdinekeah. Once I was taken to see her at the old house on the other side of Rainy Mountain Creek. The room was dark, and her old age filled it like a substance. She was white- haired and blind, and, in that strange reversion that comes upon the very old, her skin was as soft as the skin of a baby. I remember the sound of her glad weeping and the water–like touch of her hand.

X

Long ago there were bad times. The Kiowas were hungry and there was no food. There was a man who heard his children cry from hunger, and he went out to look for food. He walked four days and became very weak. On the fourth day he came to a great canyon. Suddenly there was thunder and lightning. A voice spoke to him and said, "Why are you following me? What do you want?" The man was afraid. The thing standing before him had the feet of a deer, and its body was covered with feathers. The man answered that the Kiowas were hungry. "Take me with you," the voice said, "and I will give you whatever you want." From that day Tai-me has belonged to the Kiowas.

The great central figure of the kado, *or Sun Dance, ceremony is the* taime. *This is a small image, less than 2 feet in length, representing a human figure dressed in a robe of white feathers, with a headdress consisting of a single upright feather and pendants of ermine skin, with numerous strands of blue beads around its neck, and painted upon the face, breast, and back with designs symbolic of the sun and moon. The image itself is of dark-green stone, in form rudely resembling a human head and bust, probably shaped by art like the stone festishes of the Pueblo tribes. It is preserved in a rawhide box in charge of the hereditary keeper, and is never under any circumstances exposed to view except at the annual Sun Dance, when it is fastened to a short upright stick planted within the medicine lodge, near the western side. It was last exposed in 1888.—Mooney*

Once I went with my father and grandmother to see the Tai–me bundle. It was suspended by means of a strip of ticking from the fork of a small ceremonial tree. I made an offering of bright red cloth, and my grandmother prayed aloud. It seemed a long time that we were there. I had never come into the presence of Tai–me before—nor have I since. There was a great holiness all about in the room, as if an old person had died there or a child had been born.

XI

A long time ago there were two brothers. It was winter, and the buffalo had wandered far away. Food was very scarce. The two brothers were hungry, and they wondered what to do. One of them got up in the early morning and went out, and he found a lot of fresh meat there on the ground in front of the tipi. He was very happy, and he called his brother outside. "Look," he said. "Something very good has happened, and we have plenty of food." But his brother was afraid and said: "This is too strange a thing. I believe that we had better not eat that meat." But the first brother scolded him and said that he was foolish. Then he went ahead and ate of the meat all by himself. In a little while something awful happened to him; he began to change. When it was all over, he was no longer a man; he was some kind of water beast with little short legs and a long, heavy tail. Then he spoke to his brother and said: "You were right, and you must not eat of that meat. Now I must go and live in the water, but we are brothers, and you ought to come and see me now and then." After that the man went down to the water's edge, sometimes, and called his brother out. He told him how things were with the Kiowas.

During the peyote ritual a fire is kept burning in the center of the tipi, inclosed within a crescent-shaped altar. On top of the altar there is a single, sacred peyote. After the chief priest utters the opening prayer, four peyotes are given to each celebrant, who eats them one after another. Then, in turn, each man sings four sacred songs, and all the while there is the sound of the rattle and the drum— and the fitful, many-colored glare of the fire. The songs go on all through the night, broken only by intervals of prayer, additional distributions of peyote, and, at midnight, a peculiar baptismal ceremony.

Mammedaty was a peyote man, and he was therefore distinguished by these things: a necklace of beans, a beaded staff and rattle, an eagle–bone whistle, and a fan made from the feathers of a water bird. He saw things that other men do not see. Once a heavy rain caused the Wasita River to overflow and Rainy Mountain Creek to swell and "back up." Mammedaty went to the creek, near the crossing, to swim. And while he was there, the water began strangely to move against him, slowly at first, then fast, in high, hard waves. There was some awful commotion beneath the surface, and Mammedaty got out of the water and run away. Later he went back to that place. There was a wide swath in the brush of the bank and the tracks of a huge animal, leading down to the water's edge.

1970

Or, let me try to engineer significance out of doubt.

I Remember

I remember the first time I got a letter that said "After Five Days Return To" on the envelope, and I thought that after I had kept the letter for five days I was supposed to return it to the sender.

I remember the kick I used to get going through my parents' drawers looking for rubbers. (Peacock)

I remember when polio was the worst thing in the world.

I remember pink dress shirts. And bola ties.

I remember when a kid told me that those sour clover-like leaves we used to eat (with little yellow flowers) tasted so sour because dogs peed on them. I remember that didn't stop me from eating them.

I remember the first drawing I remember doing. It was of a bride with a very long train.

I remember my first cigarette. It was a Kent. Up on a hill. In Tulsa, Oklahoma. With Ron Padgett.

I remember my first erections. I thought I had some terrible disease or something.

I remember the only time I ever saw my mother cry. I was eating apricot pie.

I remember how much I cried seeing "South Pacific" (the movie) three times.

I remember how good a glass of water can taste after a dish of ice cream.

I remember when I got a five-year pin for not missing a single morning of Sunday School for five years. (Methodist)

I remember when I went to a "come as your favorite person" party as Marilyn Monroe.

I remember one of the first things I remember. An ice box. (As opposed to a refrigerator)

I remember white margarine in a plastic bag. And a little package of orange powder. You put the orange powder in the bag with the margarine and you squeezed it all around until the margarine became yellow.

I remember how much I used to stutter.

I remember how much, in high school, I wanted to be handsome and popular.

I remember when, in high school, if you wore green and yellow on Thursday it meant that you were queer.

I remember when, in high school, I used to stuff a sock in my underwear.

I remember when I decided to be a minister. I don't remember when I decided not to be.

I remember the first time I saw television. Lucille Ball was taking ballet lessons.

I remember the day John Kennedy was shot.

I remember that for my fifth birthday all I wanted was an off-one-shoulder black satin evening gown. I got it. And I wore it to my birthday party.

I remember a dream I had recently where John Ashbery said that my Mondrian period paintings were even better than Mondrian.

I remember a dream I have had often of being able to fly. (Without an airplane)

I remember many dreams of finding gold and jewels.

I remember a little boy I used to take care of after school while his mother worked. I remember how much fun it was to punish him for being bad.

I remember a dream I used to have a lot of a beautiful red and yellow and black snake in bright green grass.

I remember St. Louis when I was very young. I remember the tattoo shop next to the bus station and the two big lions in front of the Museum of Art.

I remember an American history teacher who was always threatening to jump out of the window if we didn't quiet down. (Second floor)

I remember my first sexual experience in a subway. Some guy (I was afraid to look at him) got a hardon and was rubbing it back and forth against my arm. I got very excited and when my stop came I hurried out and home where I tried to do an oil painting using my dick as a brush.

I remember the first time I really got drunk. I painted my hands and face green with Easter egg dye and spent the night in Pat Padgett's bath tub. She was Pat Mitchell then.

I remember another early sexual experience. At the Museum of Modern Art. In the movie theater. I don't remember the movie. First there was a knee pressed to mine. Then there was a hand on my knee. Then a hand on my crotch. Then a hand inside my pants. Inside my underwear. It was very exciting but I was afraid to look at him. He left before the movie was over and I thought he would be outside waiting for me by the print exhibition but I waited around and nobody showed any interest.

I remember when I lived in a store front next door to a meat packing house on East Sixth Street. One very fat meat packer who always ate at the same diner on the corner that I ate at followed me home and asked if he could come in and see my paintings. Once inside he instantly unzipped his blood-stained white pants and pulled out an enormous dick. He asked me to touch it and I did. As repulsive as it all was, it was exciting too, and I didn't want to hurt his feelings. But then I said I had to go out and he said "Let's get together" and I said "No" but he was very insistent so I said "Yes." He was very fat and ugly and really very disgusting, so when the time came for our date I went out for a walk. But who should I run into on the street but him, all dressed up and spanking clean. I felt bad that I had to tell him that I had changed my mind. He offered me money but I said no.

I remember my parents' bridge teacher. She was very fat and very butch (cropped hair) and she was a chain smoker. She prided herself on the fact that she didn't have to carry matches around. She lit each new cigarette from the old one. She lived in a little house behind a restaurant and lived to be very old.

I remember playing "doctor" in the closet.

I remember when I painted "I HATE TED BERRIGAN" in big black letters all over my white wall.

I remember throwing my eye glasses into the ocean off the Staten Island ferry one black night in a fit of drama and depression.

I remember once when I made scratches on my face with my fingernails so people would ask me what happened, and I would say a cat did it, and, of course, they would know that a cat did not do it.

I remember the linoleum floors of my Dayton, Ohio room. A white puffy floral design on dark red.

I remember sack dresses.

I remember when a fish-tail dress I designed was published in "Katy Keen" comics.

I remember box suits.

I remember pill box hats.

I remember round cards.

I remember squaw dresses.

I remember big fat ties with fish on them.

I remember the first ball point pens. They skipped, and deposited little balls of ink that would accumulate on the point.

I remember rainbow pads.

I remember Aunt Cleora who lived in Hollywood. Every year for Christmas she sent my brother and me a joint present of one book.

I remember the first "garden painting" I ever did. It was in Providence, R.I., in 1967. It was inspired by some Japanese flower plates I gave Kenward Elmslie for Christmas.

I remember the day Frank O'Hara died. I tried to do a painting somehow especially for him. (Especially good) And it turned out awful.

I remember chenille bed spreads.

I remember canasta.

I remember "How Much Is That Doggie In The Window?"

I remember butter and sugar sandwiches.

I remember Pat Boone and "Love Letters In The Sand."

I remember Teresa Brewer and "I Don't Want No Ricochet Romance."

I remember "The Tennessee Waltz."

I remember "Sixteen Tons."

I remember "The Thing."

I remember "The Hit Parade."

I remember Dorothy Collins.

I remember Dorothy Collins' teeth.

I remember when I worked in an antique-junk shop and I sold everything cheaper than I was supposed to.

I remember when I lived in Boston reading all of Dostoevsky's novels one right after the other.

I remember my first night in Boston. I stayed at the Y.M.C.A. (Nothing happened)

I remember when I lived in Boston pan handling on the street where all the art galleries were.

I remember collecting cigarette butts from the urns in front of The Museum of Fine Arts in Boston.

I remember how small my room was in Boston.

I remember two times a night when the train would go by my window.

I remember growing a mustache.

I remember tearing page 48 out of every book I read from the Boston Public Library.

I remember living for days off nothing but "Hollywood" candy bars. It was the biggest candy bar you could buy for a nickel.

I remember the old couple who lived just below me. They drank a lot and were always fighting and yelling. He had no control over his bowels.

I remember Bickford's.

I remember the day Marilyn Monroe died.

I remember lots and lots of jerking off.

I remember that I was very close to myself in Boston.

I remember the first time I met Frank O'Hara. He was walking down Second Avenue. It was a cool early Spring evening but he was wearing only a white shirt with the sleeves rolled up to his elbows. And blue jeans. And moccasins. I remember that he seemed very sissy to me. Very theatrical. Decadent. I remember that I liked him instantly.

I remember a red car coat.

I remember going to the ballet with Edwin Denby in a red car coat.

I remember learning to play bridge so I could get to know Frank O'Hara better

I remember playing bridge with Frank O'Hara. (Mostly talk)

I remember my first lover. (Joe LeSueur) I don't think he'll mind.

I remember my grade school art teacher, Mrs. Chick, who got so mad at a boy one day she dumped a bucket of water over his head.

I remember my collection of ceramic monkeys.

I remember my brother's collection of ceramic horses.

I remember when I was a "Demolay." I wish I could remember the secret handshake so I could reveal it to you.

I remember my grandfather who didn't believe in doctors. He didn't work because he had a tumor. He played cribbage all day. And wrote poems. He had very long ugly toe nails. I avoided looking at his feet as much as I could.

I remember Moley, the local freak and notorious queer. He had a very little head that grew out of his body like a mole. No one knew him, but everyone knew who he was. He was always "around."

I remember liver.

I remember Betina Beer. (A girl) We used to go to dances together. I am sure she was a dike, tho it never would have occurred to me at the time. She cussed a lot. And she drank and smoked with her mother's approval. She didn't have a father. She wore heavy blue eye shadow and she had white spots on her arms.

I remember riding in a bus downtown one day, in Tulsa, and a boy I knew slightly from school sat down beside me and started asking questions like "Do you like girls?" He was a real creep. When we got downtown (where all the stores are) he kept following me around until finally he talked me into going with him to his bank where he said he had something to put in his safe-deposit box. I remember that I didn't know what a safe-deposit box was. When we got to the bank a bank man gave him his box and lead us into a booth with gold curtains. The boy opened up the box and pulled out a gun. He showed it to me and I tried to be impressed and then he put it back in the box and asked me if I would unzip my pants. I said no. I remember that my knees were shaking. After we left the bank I said that I had to go to Brown-Dunkin's (Tulsa's largest department store) and he said he had to go there too. To go to the bathroom. In the men's room he tried something else (I forget exactly what) and I ran out the door and that was that. It is very strange that an eleven or twelve year old boy would have a safe-deposit box. With a gun in it. He had an older sister who was known to be "loose."

I remember Liberace.

I remember "Liberace loafers" with tassels.

I remember those bright colored nylon seersucker shirts that you could see through.

I remember many first days of school. And that empty feeling.

I remember the clock from three to three-thirty.

I remember when girls wore cardigan sweaters on backwards.

I remember when girls wore lots of can-can slips. It got so bad (so noisy) that the principal had to put a limit on how many could be worn. I believe the limit was three.

I remember thin gold chains with one little pearl hanging from them.

I remember mustard seed necklaces with a mustard seed inside a little glass ball.

I remember pony tails.

I remember when hoody boys wore their blue jeans so low that the principal had to put a limit on that too. I believe it was three inches below the navel.

I remember shirt collars turned up in back.

I remember Perry Como shirts. And Perry Como sweaters.

I remember duck-tails.

I remember cherokee hair cuts.

I remember no belts.

I remember many Sunday afternoon dinners of fried chicken or pot roast.

I remember my first oil painting. It was of a chartreuse green field of grass with a little Italian village far away.

I remember when I tried out to be a cheer leader and didn't make it.

I remember many Septembers.

I remember one day in gym class when my name was called out I just couldn't say "here." I stuttered so badly that sometimes words just wouldn't come out of my mouth at all. I had to run around the field many times.

I remember a rather horsy-looking girl who tried to seduce me on a New York City roof. Although I was able to get it up, I really didn't want to do anything, so I told her that I had a headache.

I remember one football player who wore very tight faded blue jeans, and the way he filled them.

I remember when I got drafted and had to go way downtown to take my physical. It was early in the morning. I had an egg for breakfast and I could feel it sitting there in my stomach. After roll call a man looked at me and ordered me to a different line than most of the boys were lined up at. (I had very long hair which was more unusual then than it is now) The line I was sent to turned out to be the line to see the head doctor. (I was going to ask to see him anyway) The doctor asked me if I was queer and I said yes. Then he asked me what homosexual experiences I had had and I said none. (It was the truth) And he believed me. I didn't even have to take my clothes off.

I remember the night that Ted Berrigan wrote his first collage sonnet.

I remember the night that Ted Berrigan told me that I had no morals.

I remember a boy who told me a dirty pickle joke. It was the first clue I had as to what sex was all about.

I remember when my father would say "Keep your hands out from under the covers" every night as he said goodnight. But he said it in a nice way.

I remember when I thought that if you did anything bad policemen would put you in jail.

I remember one very cold and black night on the beach alone with Frank O'Hara. He ran into the ocean naked and it scared me to death.

I remember lightning.

I remember wild red poppies in Italy.

I remember selling blood every three months on Second Avenue.

I remember a boy I once made love with and after it was all over he asked me if I believed in God.

I remember when I thought that anything old was very valuable.

I remember "Black Beauty."

I remember when I thought that Betty Grable was beautiful.

I remember when I thought that I was a great artist.

I remember when I wanted to be rich and famous. (And I still do)

I remember when I had a job cleaning out an old man's apartment who had died. Among his belongings was a very old photograph of a naked young boy pinned to an old pair of young boy's underwear. For many years he was the choir director at church. He had no family or relatives.

I remember a boy who worked for an undertaker after school. He was a very good tap dancer. He invited me to spend the night with him one day. His mother was divorced and somewhat of a cheap blond in appearance. I remember that his mother caught us innocently wrestling out in the yard and she got *very* mad. She told him never to do that again. I realized that something was going on that I knew nothing about. We were ten or eleven years old. I was never invited back. Years later, in high school, he caused a big scandal when a love letter he had written to another boy was found. He then quit school and worked full time for the undertaker. One day I ran into him on the street and he started telling me about a big room with lots of beds where all the undertaker employees slept. He said that each bed had a little white tent in the morning. I excused myself and said goodbye. Several hours later I figured out what he had meant. Early morning erections.

I remember when I worked in a snack bar and how much I hated people who ordered malts.

I remember empty restaurants in Spain. (They eat late)

I remember when I worked for a department store doing fashion drawings for newspaper ads.

I remember Frank O'Hara's walk. Light and sassy. With a slight bounce and a slight twist. It was a beautiful walk. Confident. "I don't care." and sometimes "I know you are looking."

I remember four Alice Esty concerts.

I remember being Santa Claus in a school play.

I remember Beverly who had a very small cross tattooed on her arm.

I remember Mexico.

I remember Miss Peabody, my grade school librarian.

I remember Miss Fly, my grade school science teacher.

I remember a very poor boy who had to wear his sister's blouses to school.

I remember Easter suits.

I remember taffeta. And the way it sounded.

I remember my collection of Nova Scotia pamphlets and travel information.

I remember my collection of "Modess because . . ." magazine ads.

I remember my father's collection of arrow heads.

I remember a 1949 red Ford convertible we once had.

I remember *The Power of Positive Thinking* by Norman Vincent Peale.

I remember "four o'clocks." (A flower that closes at four)

I remember trying to visualize my mother and father actually fucking.

I remember a cartoon of a painter painting from a naked model (back view) and on his canvas was a picture of a parker house roll.

I remember mowing the yard once a week.

I remember dusting the Venetian blinds every Saturday.

I remember dusting baseboards every Saturday.

I remember drying dishes every night.

I remember my grandfather who lived on a farm dunking his cornbread in his buttermilk. He didn't like to talk.

I remember the outhouse and a Sears and Roebuck catalog to wipe off with.

I remember animal smells.

I remember very cold water on your face in the morning.

I remember how heavy the cornbread was.

I remember crepe paper roses. Old calendars. And cow patties.

I remember driving through the Ozarks and all the gift shops we didn't stop at.

I remember when dark green walls were popular.

I remember when in grade school you gave a valentine to every person in your class in fear that someone might give you one that you didn't have one for.

I remember home room mothers.

I remember being a safety guard and wearing a white strap.

I remember "Hazel" in *The Saturday Evening Post.*

I remember reading the complete works of Thomas Wolfe. (Under Ted Berrigan's influence)

I remember ringworm. And name tags.

I remember always losing one glove.

I remember loafers with pennies in them.

I remember Dr. Pepper. And Royal Crown Cola.

I remember those brown fur pieces with little feet and little heads and little tails.

I remember "Suave" hair cream. (Pale peach)

I remember house shoes, plaid flannel bath robes, and "Casper" the Friendly Ghost.

I remember pop beads.

I remember "come as you are" parties. Everybody cheated.

I remember game rooms in basements.

I remember milkmen. Postmen. Guest towels. "Welcome" mats. And Avon ladies.

I remember driftwood lamps.

I remember reading once about a lady who choked to death eating a piece of steak.

I remember when fiber glass was going to solve everything.

I remember rubbing my hand under restaurant table top and feeling all the gum.

I remember the chair I used to put my boogers behind.

I remember Pug and George and their only daughter Norma Jean who was very beautiful and died of cancer.

I remember Jim and Lucy. Jim sold insurance and Lucy taught school. Everytime we saw them they gave us a handful of plastic billfold calendars advertising insurance.

I remember Saturday night baths and Sunday morning comics.

I remember bacon and lettuce and tomato sandwiches and iced tea in the summer time.

I remember potato salad.

I remember salt on watermelon.

I remember strapless net formals in pastel colors that came down to the ankles. And carnation corsages on little short jackets.

I remember Christmas carols and car lots.

I remember bunk beds.

I remember rummage sales. Ice cream socials. White gravy. And Hop-along Cassidy.

I remember knitted "pants" on drinking glasses.

I remember bean bag ashtrays that would stay level on irregular surfaces.

I remember shower curtains with angel fish on them.

I remember Christmas card waste baskets.

I remember rick-rack earrings.

I remember big brass wall plates of German drinking scenes. (Made in Italy)

I remember Tab Hunter's famous pajama party.

I remember mammy cookie jars. Tomato soup. Wax fruit. And church keys.

I remember very long gloves.

I remember a purple violin bottle that hung on the wall with ivy growing out of it.

I remember very old people when I was very young. Their houses smelled funny.

I remember one old lady who, on Halloween, you had to sing or dance or do something for before she would give you anything.

I remember chalk.

I remember when green black-boards were new.

I remember a back-drop of a brick wall I painted for a play. I painted each red brick in by hand. Afterwards it occurred to me that I could have just painted the whole thing red and put in the white lines.

I remember how much I tried to like Van Gogh. And how much, finally, I did like him. And how much, now, I can't stand him.

I remember a boy. He worked in a store. I spent a fortune buying things from him I didn't want. Then one day he wasn't there anymore.

I remember how sorry I felt for my father's sister. I thought that she was always on the verge of crying, when actually, she just had hay fever.

I remember the first erection I distinctly remember having. It was by the side of a public swimming pool. I was sunning on my back on a towel. I didn't know what to do, except turn over, so I turned over. But it wouldn't go away. I got a terrible sun burn. So bad that I had to go see a doctor. I remember how much wearing a shirt hurt.

I remember the organ music from "As The World Turns."

I remember white buck shoes with thick pink rubber soles.

I remember day dreams of being a movie star.

I remember living rooms all one color.

I remember summer naps of no sleeping. And kool-aid.

I remember reading Van Gogh's letters to Theo.

I remember day dreams of dying and how unhappy everybody would be.

I remember day dreams of committing suicide and of the letter I would leave behind.

I remember day dreams of being a dancer and being able to leap higher than anyone thought was humanly possible.

I remember day dreams of being a singer all alone on a big stage with no scenery, just one spotlight on me, singing my heart out, and moving my audience to total tears of love and affection.

I remember driving in cars and doing landscape paintings in my head. (I still do that)

I remember the tiger lilies alongside the house. I found a dime among them once.

I remember a very little doll I lost under the front porch and never found.

I remember a man who came around with a pony and a cow-boy hat and a camera. For so much money he would take your picture on the pony wearing the hat.

I remember the sound of the ice cream man coming.

I remember once losing my nickel in the grass before he made it to my house.

I remember that life was just as serious then as it is now.

I remember "queers can't whistle."

I remember dust storms and yellow skies.

I remember rainy days through a window.

I remember how long summers didn't seem after they were over.

I remember salt shakers at the school cafeteria when the tops had been unscrewed.

I remember a certain all-night diner that had great hash browns.

I remember a job I once had sketching portraits of people at a coffee house. Table to table. During folk singing intermissions. By candle light.

I remember when a negro man asked me to paint a big Christmas picture to hang in his picture window at Christmas and I painted a white madonna and child.

I remember one year in school our principal was Mr. Black and my art teacher was Mrs. Black. (They were not married)

I remember a story my mother telling of an old lady who had a china cabinet filled with beautiful antique china and stuff. One day a tornado came and knocked the cabinet over and to the floor but nothing in it got broken. Many years later she died and in her will she left my father a milk glass candy dish in the shape of a fish. (It had been in the cabinet) At any rate, when the candy dish arrived it was all broken into many pieces. But my father glued it back together again.

I remember a big black rubber thing going over my mouth and nose just before I had my tonsils taken out. After my tonsils were taken out I remember how my throat felt eating vanilla ice cream.

I remember one morning the milkman handed me a camera. I never did understand exactly why. I am sure that it had something to do with a contest.

I remember my first attempts at a threesome. But it didn't come off. (Their fault)

I remember Marilyn Monroe's softness in "The Misfits."

I remember the gasoline station in the snow in "The Umbrellas of Cherbourg."

I remember when hoop skirts had a miniature revival.

I remember waking up somewhere once and there was a horse staring me in the face.

I remember sitting on top of a horse once and how high up it was.

I remember a chameleon I got at the circus that was supposed to change colors each time he was on a different color but he only changed from green to brown and from brown back to green. And it was a rather brown-green at that.

I remember never winning at bingo.

I remember a little girl who had a white rabbit coat and hat and muff. Actually, I don't remember the little girl. I remember the coat and the hat and the muff.

I remember radio ball game sounds coming from the garage on Saturday afternoons.

I remember hearing stories about why Johnny Ray was such an unhappy person but I can't remember what the stories were.

I remember the rumor that Dinah Shore was half negro but that her mother never told her and so when she had a light brown baby she sued her mother for not telling her. (That she was half negro)

I remember my father in black-face. As an end man in a minstrel show.

I remember my father in a tutu. As a ballerina dancer in a variety show at church.

I remember my first gray hair. It was white.

I remember when I first noticed hairs growing around my navel.

I remember Anne Kepler. She played the flute. I remember her straight shoulders. I remember her large eyes. Her slightly roman nose. And her full lips. I remember an oil painting I did of her playing the flute. Several years ago she died in a fire giving a flute concert at a children's home in Brookline. All the children were saved. There was something about her like white marble.

I remember people who only went to church on Easter and Christmas.

I remember cinnamon toothpicks.

I remember cherry cokes.

I remember pastel colored rocks that grew in water.

I remember drive-in onion rings.

I remember that the minister's son was wild.

I remember pearlized plastic toilet seats.

I remember a little boy whose father didn't believe in dancing and mixed swimming.

I remember when I told Kenward Elmslie that I could play tennis. He was looking for someone to play with and I wanted to get to know him better. I couldn't even hit the ball but I did get to know him better.

I remember when I didn't really believe in Santa Claus but I wanted to so badly that I did.

I remember when the Pepsi-Cola Company was on its last leg.

I remember when negroes had to sit at the back of the bus.

I remember pink lemonade.

I remember paper doll twins.

I remember puffy pastel sweaters. (Angora)

I remember drinking glasses with girls on them wearing bathing suits but when you filled them up they were naked.

I remember dark red fingernail polish almost black.

I remember that cherries were too expensive.

I remember a drunk man in a tuxedo in a bar who wanted Ron Padgett and me to go home with him but we said no and he gave us all his money.

I remember when I lived in Boston reading a lot of historical novels by ladies.

I remember how many other magazines I had to buy in order to buy one physique magazine.

I remember a climbing red rose bush all over the garage. When rose time came it was practically solid red.

I remember a little boy down the street. Sometimes I would hide one of his toys inside my underwear and make him reach in for it.

I remember how unsexy swimming naked in gym class was.

I remember that "negro men have giant cocks."

I remember that "Chinese men have little cocks."

I remember a girl in school one day who, just out of the blue, went into a long spiel all about how difficult it was to wash her brother's pants because he didn't wear underwear.

I remember slipping underwear into the washer at the last minute (wet dreams) when my mother wasn't looking.

I remember a giant gold man taller than most buildings at "The Tulsa Oil Show."

I remember trying to convince my parents that not raking leaves was good for the grass.

I remember that *I* liked dandelions all over the yard.

I remember when my mother was in the finals for "Mrs. Tulsa."

I remember that my father scratched his balls a lot.

I remember very thin belts.

I remember James Dean and his red nylon jacket.

I remember thinking how embarrassing it must be for men in Scotland to have to wear skirts.

I remember when scotch tape wasn't transparent.

I remember how little your dick is getting out of a wet bathing suit.

I remember saying "thank you" when the occasion didn't call for it.

I remember shaking big hands.

I remember saying "thank you" in reply to "thank you" and then the other person doesn't know what to say.

I remember getting erections in school and the bell rings and how handy zipper notebooks were.

I remember zipper notebooks. I remember that girls hugged them to their breasts and that boys carried them loosely at one side.

I remember trying to make a new zipper notebook look old.

I remember that I never thought that Ann Miller was beautiful.

I remember thinking that my mother and father were ugly naked.

I remember when I found a photograph of a woman naked from the waist up with very big tits and I showed it to a boy at school and he told the teacher about it and the teacher asked to see it and I showed it to her and she asked me where I got it and I said that I found it on the street. Nothing happened after that.

I remember peanut butter and banana sandwiches.

I remember jewelled sweaters with fur collars open to the waist.

I remember the Box Car Twins.

I remember not looking at crippled people.

I remember Mantovani and his (100 strings?)

I remember a woman with almost no neck. On her large feet she always wore bright colored suede platform shoes. My mother said they were very expensive.

I remember corrugated ribbon that you ran across the blade of a pair of scissors and it curled all up.

I remember that I never cried in front of other people.

I remember how embarrassed I was when other children cried.

I remember the first art award I ever won. In grade school. It was a painting of a nativity scene. I remember a very large star in the sky. It won a blue ribbon at the fair.

I remember when I started smoking I wrote my parents a letter and told them so. The letter was never mentioned and I continued to smoke.

I remember how good wet dreams were.

I remember a roller coaster that went out over a lake.

I remember visions (when in bed but not asleep yet) of very big objects becoming very small and of very small objects becoming very big.

I remember seeing colors and designs by closing my eyes very tightly.

I remember Montgomery Clift in "A Place In The Sun."

I remember a pair of bright red corduroy pants.

I remember bright colored aluminum drinking glasses.

I remember "The Swing" dance.

I remember "The Chicken."

I remember "The Bop."

I remember monkeys who did modern paintings and won prizes.

I remember "I like to be able to tell what things are."

I remember "Any little kid could do that."

I remember "Well, it may be good but I just don't understand it."

I remember "I like the colors."

I remember "You couldn't give it to me."

I remember "It's interesting."

I remember Bermuda shorts and knee length socks.

I remember the first time I saw myself in a full length mirror wearing Bermuda shorts. I never wore them again.

I remember playing doctor with Joyce Vantries. I remember her soft white belly. Her large navel. And her little slit between her legs. I remember rubbing my ear against it. I remember spreading her legs just far enough apart to see that it was mysterious inside.

I remember Lois Lane. And Della Street.

I remember jerking off to sexual fantasies of Troy Donahue with a dark tan in a white bathing suit down by the ocean. (From a movie with Sandra Dee)

I remember sexual fantasies of making it with a stranger in the woods.

I remember sexual fantasies of old faded worn and torn blue jeans and the small areas of flesh revealed. I especially remember torn back pockets with a triangle of soft white bottom showing.

I remember sexual fantasies of seducing young country boys. (But old enough) Pale and blond and eager.

I remember jerking off to sexual fantasies involving John Kerr. And Montgomery Clift.

I remember a very wet dream with J. J. Mitchell in a boat.

I remember making love with Anne Waldman in a dream.

I remember sexual dreams involving Clarice Rivers and her large breasts.

I remember sexual dreams involving Ted Berrigan.

I remember jerking off to visions of body details.

I remember navels. Torso muscles. Hands. Arms with large veins. Small feet. (I like small feet) And muscular legs.

I remember under-arms where the flesh is softer and whiter.

I remember blond heads. White teeth. Thick necks. And certain smiles.

I remember underwear. (I like underwear) And socks.

I remember good smells.

I remember the wrinkles and creases of fabric being worn.

I remember tight white t-shirts and the gather of wrinkles from under the arms.

I remember sexual fantasies in white tile shower rooms. Hard and slippery. Abstract and steamy. Wet body to wet body. Slippery, fast, and squeaky.

I remember tight pants from behind with no underwear on.

I remember eyes. Beautiful eyes. Kissing eyes. And rubbing my dick in eyes.

I remember a not very pleasant sexual dream involving Kenward Elmslie's dog Whippoorwill.

I remember green easter egg grass.

I remember never really believing in the Easter bunny. Or the sandman. Or the tooth fairy.

I remember sexual dreams involving Bill Berkson. Lewis Warsh. Pat Padgett, Scott Burton. D. D. Ryan. Fairfield Porter. And Andy Warhol. (One at a time)

I remember bright colored baby chickens. (Dyed) They died very fast. Or ran away. Or something. I just remember that shortly after easter they disappeared.

I remember farts that smell like old eggs.

I remember one very hot summer day I put ice cubes in my aquarium and all the fish died.

I remember dreams of walking down the street and suddenly realizing that I have no clothes on.

I remember a big black cat named Midnight who got so old and grouchy that my patents had him put to sleep.

I remember making a cross of two sticks for something my brother buried. It might have been a cat but I think it was a bug or something.

I remember regretting things I didn't do.

I remember wishing that I knew then what I know now.

I remember peach colored evenings just before dark.

I remember "lavender past." (He has a . . .)

I remember Greyhound buses at night.

I remember wondering what the bus driver is thinking about.

I remember empty towns. Green tinted windows. And neon signs just as they go off.

I remember (I think) lavender tinted windows on one bus.

I remember tricycles turned over on front lawns. Snow ball bushes. And plastic duck families.

I remember glimpses of activity in orange windows at night.

I remember little cows.

I remember that there is always one soldier on every bus.

I remember trees that if you painted them nobody would believe you.

I remember small ugly modern churches.

I remember that I can never remember how bathroom doors in buses open.

I remember donuts and coffee. Stools. Pasted over prices. And gray people.

I remember wondering if the person sitting across from me is queer.

I remember time. At times when it has gone very fast. And at times when it has gone very slow.

I remember rainbow colored grease spots on the pavement after a rain.

I remember undressing people (in my head) walking down the street.

I remember, in Tulsa, a red sidewalk that sparkled.

I remember being hit on the head by bird shit two times.

I remember how exciting a glimpse of a naked person in a window is even if you don't really see anything.

I remember "Autumn Leaves."

I remember a very pretty German girl who just didn't smell good.

I remember that Eskimoes kiss with their noses. (?)

I remember that the only friends my parents had who owned a swimming pool also owned a funeral parlor.

I remember laundromats at night all lit up with nobody in them.

I remember a very clean Catholic book-gift shop with practically nothing in it to buy.

I remember re-arranging boxes of candy so it would look like not so much was missing.

I remember brown and white shoes with little decorative holes cut out of them.

I remember certain group gatherings that are hard to get up and leave from.

I remember opening jars that nobody else could open.

I remember making home-made ice cream.

I remember that I liked store bought ice cream better.

I remember hospital supply store windows.

I remember stories of what hot dogs are made of.

I remember alligators and quick-sand in jungle movies. (Pretty scary)

I remember Davy Crockett hats. And Davy Crockett just about everything else.

I remember not understanding why people on the other side of the world didn't fall off.

I remember wondering why, if Jesus could cure sick people, why He didn't cure all sick people.

I remember wondering why God didn't use his powers more to end wars and stop polio. And stuff like that.

I remember "Love Me Tender."

I remember trying to realize how big the world really is.

I remember trying to figure out what it's all about.

I remember catching lightning-bugs and putting them in a jar with holes in the lid and then letting them out the next day.

I remember making clover blossom chains.

I remember in Boston a portrait of Isabella Gardiner by Whistler.

I remember in Tulsa my first one-man show of brush and ink drawings of old fashioned children. They were so intricate and fine that nobody could believe that I did them with a brush. But I did.

I remember winning a Peter Pan Coloring Contest and getting a free pass to the movies for a year.

I remember Bunny Van Valkenburg. She had a little nose. A low hairline. And two big front teeth. She was my girl friend for several years when we were very young. Later on, in high school, she turned into quite a sex-pot.

I remember Bunny Van Valkenburg's mother Betty. She was very short and dumpy and bubbly and she wore giant earrings. Once she wall papered her kitchen floor with wall paper. Then shellacked it.

I remember Bunny Van Valkenburg's father Doc. He was our family doctor. I remember him telling of a patient he had who got poison ivy inside his body. The man was in total misery but it healed very fast because there was no way that he could scratch it.

I remember that the Van Valkenburgs had more money than we did.

I remember in grade school tying a mirror to your shoe and casually slipping it between a girl's legs during conversation. Other boys did that. I didn't.

I remember eating tunnels and cities out of watermelon.

I remember how sad "The Jane Froman Story" was.

I remember George Evelyn who had a red and white face because of an explosion he was in once. And his wife Jane who wore green a lot and laughed very loud. I remember their only son George Junior who was my age. He was very fat and very wild. But I hear that he settled down, got married, and is active in church.

I remember the first time I saw Elvis Presley. It was on the Ed Sullivan Show.

I remember "Blue Suede Shoes." And I remember having a pair.

I remember felt skirts with cut-out felt poodles on them. Sometimes their collars were jeweled.

I remember bright orange canned peaches.

I remember jeweled bottle openers.

I remember the horse lady at the fair. She didn't look like a horse at all.

I remember a grape vine we had in our back yard.

I remember how sour green grapes tasted.

I remember eating too many and having a funny feeling mouth.

I remember green grape fights.

I remember pillow fights.

I remember being surprised at how yellow and how red autumn *really* is.

I remember chain letters.

I remember Peter Pan collars.

I remember mistletoe.

I remember Judy Garland singing "Have Yourself a Merry Little Christmas" (so sad) in "Meet Me In St. Louis."

I remember Judy Garland's red shoes in "The Wizard Of Oz."

I remember Christmas tree lights reflected on the ceiling.

I remember Christmas cards arriving from people my parents forgot to send Christmas cards to.

I remember the Millers who lived next door. Mrs. Miller was an Indian and Mr. Miller was a radio ham. They had five children and a very little house. There was always junk all over their yard. And inside the house too. Their living room was completely taken up by a big green ping pong table.

I remember taking out the garbage.

I remember "The Ritz" movie theater. It was full of statues and the ceiling was like a sky at night with twinkling stars.

I remember wax paper.

I remember what-not shelves of two overlapping squares. One higher than the other.

I remember ballerina figurines from Japan with real netlike tutus.

I remember wood carvings of funny doctors.

I remember the "T-zone." (Camel cigarettes)

I remember big radios.

I remember long skinny colored glass decanters from Italy.

I remember fish net.

I remember board and brick book shelves.

I remember bongo drums.

I remember chambray work shirts. And dirty tennis shoes with no socks.

I remember candles in wine bottles.

I remember one brick wall and three white walls.

I remember the first time I saw the ocean. I jumped right in and it swept me right under, down, and back to shore again.

I remember being disappointed in Europe that I didn't feel any different.

I remember when Ron Padgett and I first arrived in New York City we told the cab driver to take us to the Village. He said Where? And we said To the Village. He said But where in the Village? And we said Anywhere. He took us to Sixth Avenue and 8th Street. I was pretty disappointed. I had thought that the Village would be like a real village. Like in Europe.

I remember putting on sun tan oil and having the sun go away.

I remember Dorothy Kilgallen's face.

I remember toreador pants.

I remember a baby-blue matching skirt and sweater that Suzy Barnes always wore. She was interested in science. All over her walls were advertising match book covers hanging on rolls of string. She had a great stamp collection too. Her mother and father were both over six feet tall. They belonged to a club for people over six feet tall only.

I remember doing other things with straws besides drinking through them.

I remember an ice cream parlor in Tulsa that had a thing called a pig's dinner. It was like a very big banana split in a wooden dish made to look like a pig's trough. If you ate it all they gave you a certificate saying that you ate it all.

I remember after people are gone thinking of things I should have said but didn't.

I remember how rock and roll music can hurt. It can be so free and sexy when you are not.

I remember eating alone in restaurants a lot because of some sort of perverse pleasure I don't want to think about right now. (Because I still do it)

I remember the first escalator in Tulsa. In a bank. I remember riding up and down it. And up and down it.

I remember Royla Cochren. She lived in an attic and made long skinny people out of wax. She was married to a poet with only one arm until he died. He died, she said, from a pain in the arm that wasn't there.

I remember seeing Frank O'Hara write a poem once. We were watching a western on TV and he got up as tho to fix a drink or answer the telephone but instead he went over to the typewriter, leaned over it a bit, and typed for 4 or 5 minutes standing up. Then he pulled the piece of paper out of the typewriter and handed it to me and then lay back down to watch more TV. (The TV was in the bedroom) I don't remember the poem except that it had some cowboy dialect in it.

I remember a marshmallow fruit salad my Aunt Ruby used to make. It tasted so clean.

I remember drawing pictures in church on pledge envelopes and programs.

I remember having a casual chat with God every night and usually falling asleep before I said "amen."

I remember the great girl-love of my life. We were both the same age but she was too old and I was too young. Her name was Marilyn Mounts. She had a small and somehow very vulnerable neck. It was a long thin neck, but soft. It looked like it would break very easily. To this day I can totally recall (feel) it.

I remember sen-sen. (Little black squares that tasted like soap)

I remember that little jerk you give just before you fall asleep. Like falling.

I remember when I won a scholarship to the Dayton, Ohio Art Institute and I didn't like it but I didn't want to hurt their feelings by just quitting so I told them that my father was dying of cancer.

I remember in Dayton, Ohio the art fair in the park where they made me take down all my naked self-portraits.

I remember a middle-aged lady who ran an antique shop in the Village. She asked me to come over and fix her bathroom late at night but she wouldn't say what was wrong with it. I said yes because saying no has always been difficult for me. But the night I was to go I just didn't go. The antique shop isn't there anymore.

I remember going to bed with one of the most beautiful boys I have ever seen and it wasn't very exciting at all.

I remember jumping off the front porch head first onto the corner of a brick. I remember being able to see nothing but gushing red blood. This is one of the first things I remember. And I have a scar to prove it.

I remember white bread and tearing off the crust and rolling the middle part up into a ball and eating it.

I remember toe jams. I never ate toe jams but I remember kids that did. I do remember eating snot. It tasted pretty good.

I remember dingle berries.

I remember rings around your neck. (Dirt)

I remember thinking once that flushing away pee might be a big waste. I remember thinking that pee is probably good for something and that if one could just discover what it was good for one could make a mint.

I remember staying in the bath tub too long and having wrinkled toes and fingers.

I remember "that" feeling, cleaning out your navel.

I remember pouring out a glass of water (I was a fountain) in a front porch musical production of "Strolling Through The Park One Day."

I remember tying two bicycles together for a production number of "Bicycle Built For Two."

I remember a store we had where we bought stuff at the five and ten and then re-sold the stuff for a penny or two more than it cost. And then with the money we bought more stuff. Etc. We ended up by making several dollars clear.

I remember paying a dime and getting a red paper poppy made by people in wheel chairs.

I remember red feathers. That, I think, was the Red Cross.

I remember making tents on the front porch on rainy days.

I remember wanting to sleep out in the back yard and being kidded about how I wouldn't last the night and sleeping outside and not lasting the night.

I remember a story about my mother finding a rat walking all over my brother's face while he was sleeping. Before I was born.

I remember a story about how when I was very young I got a pair of scissors and cut all my curls off because a boy down the street told me that curls were sissy.

I remember when I was very young saying "hubba-hubba" whenever I saw a red headed lady because my father liked red heads and it was always good for a laugh.

I remember that my mother's favorite movie star was June Allyson.

I remember that my father's favorite movie star was Rita Hayworth.

I remember that my favorite movie star was Betty Grable. I think I already told you that.

I remember being Joseph in a live nativity scene (that didn't move) in a park. You just had to stand there for half an hour and then another Joseph came and you had a cup of hot chocolate until your turn came again.

I remember taking a test to see which musical instrument I would be best suited for. They said it was the clarinet so I got a clarinet and took lessons but I was terrible at it so I stopped.

I remember trying to convince Ron Padgett that I didn't believe in God anymore but he wouldn't believe me. We were in the back of a truck. I don't remember why.

I remember buying things that were too expensive because I didn't like to ask the price of things.

I remember once having an illustration in "Seventeen" magazine.

I remember having a paper route.

I remember sacking groceries in a grocery store.

I remember a spooky job I had once cleaning up a dentist's office after everyone had gone home. I had my own key. The only part I liked was straightening up the magazines in the waiting room. I saved it as the last thing to do.

I remember my first job in New York City. Making charts and graphs for business presentations.

I remember when Ted Berrigan wrote me in Boston that Andy Warhol had liked the first cover I did for "C" magazine. It was one of the biggest thrills of my life.

I remember wondering why, since I am queer, why I wouldn't rather be a girl.

I remember trying to devise something with a wet sponge in a glass to jerk off into but it didn't work out.

I remember trying to blow myself once but I couldn't quite do it.

I remember wondering how birds can fly.

I remember optical illusions when laying face down and arms folded over my head in the sun of big eyebrows (magnified) and of two overlapping noses. (Also magnified)

I remember getting rid of everything I owned on two occasions. I should do it again.

I remember wondering if my older brother is queer too.

I remember that I was a terrible coin collector because I was always spending them.

I remember gray-silver pennies. (Where did they go?)

I remember an S & M guy I once went to bed with. Not knowing what I was getting into. I think he was S (a sadist) and I am certainly no masochist. It didn't work out. But he was very nice.

I remember a guy I went to bed with who liked to come by rubbing his dick against hard stomach muscles. Fortunately I have hard stomach muscles.

I remember a guy who needed dirty words.

I remember living by candle light.

I remember when having a $1.19 steak at "Tad's" was a big treat.

I remember making it with my little sister in a dream.

I remember painting a portrait of Pat Padgett with green hair.

I remember painting a portrait of Pat Padgett with blue hair.

I remember painting many portraits of Pat Padgett with no face.

I remember "Ace" combs.

I remember "Dixie" drinking cups. And "Bond" bread.

I remember the "Breck" shampoo ladies.

I remember the skinny guy who gets sand kicked in his face in body-building advertisements.

I remember the day that Kenward Elmslie's dog Rossignol went crazy and ran off into the woods to (I assume) die.

I remember blonde women who get so much sun you can't see them.

I remember being disappointed the first time I got my teeth cleaned that they didn't turn out real white.

I remember trying to visualize what my insides look like.

I remember people who like to look you straight in the eye for a long time as though you have some sort of mutual understanding about something.

I remember almost sending away for body building courses many times.

I remember bright orange light coming into rooms in the late afternoon. Horizontally.

I remember the "$64,000 Question" scandal.

I remember "Revlon." And that ex-Miss America lady.

I remember that woman who was always opening refrigerators.

I remember the way Loretta Young entered the room each week.

I remember light blue morning glories on the fence in the morning. Morning glories always surprise me. I never really expect them to be there.

I remember getting up at a certain hour every morning to walk down the street to pass a certain boy on his way to work. One morning I finally said hello to him and from then on we always said hello to each other. But that was as far as it went.

I remember taking communion and how hard it was not to smile.

I remember smiling at bad news. (I still do sometimes) I can't help it. It just comes.

I remember that our church believed that when the Bible said wine it really meant grape juice. So at communion we had grape juice. And round paper-thin white wafers that tasted very good. Like paper. Once I found a whole jar full of them in a filing cabinet in the choir room and I ate a lot. Eating a lot was not as good as just eating one.

I remember the exact moment, during communion, that was the hardest to keep from smiling. It was when you had to stick out your tongue and the minister laid the white wafer on it.

I remember that one way to keep from smiling during communion was to think real hard about something very boring. Like how airplane engines work. Or tree trunks.

I remember movies in school about kids that drink and take drugs and then they have a car wreck and one girl gets killed.

I remember one day in psychology class the teacher asked everyone who had regular bowel movements to raise their hand. I don't remember if I had regular bowel movements or not but I do remember that I raised my hand.

I remember not being able to pronounce "mirror."

I remember changing my name to Bo Jainard for about one week.

I remember wanting to change my name to Jacques Bernard.

I remember when I used to sign my paintings "By Joe."

I remember a dream of meeting a man made out of a very soft yellow cheese and when I went to shake his hand I just pulled his whole arm off.

1971

Let me make something fabulous, fragile, and flawed enough to remind us that the things that are made by human beings are as flawed as human beings.

DONALD BARTHELME

Sentence

Or a long sentence moving at a certain pace down the page aiming for the bottom—if not the bottom of this page then some other page—where it can rest, or stop for a moment to think out the questions raised by its own (temporary) existence, which ends when the page is turned, or the sentence falls out of the mind that holds it (temporarily) in some kind of an embrace, not necessarily an ardent one, but more perhaps the kind of embrace enjoyed (or endured) by a wife who has just waked up and is on her way to the bathroom in the morning to wash her hair, and is bumped into by her husband, who has been lounging at the breakfast table reading the newspaper, and didn't see her coming out of the bedroom, but, when he bumps into her, or is bumped into by her, raises his hands to embrace her lightly, transiently, because he knows that if he gives her a real embrace so early in the morning, before she has properly shaken the dreams out of her head, and got her duds on, she won't respond, and may even become slightly angry, and say something wounding, and so the husband invests in this embrace not so much physical or emotional pressure as he might, because he doesn't want to waste anything—with this sort of feeling, then, the sentence passes through the mind more or less, and there is another way of describing the situation too, which is to say that the sentence crawls through the mind like something someone says to you while you are listening very hard to the FM radio, some rock group there, with its thrilling sound, and so, with your attention or the major part of it at least already rewarded, there is not much mind room you can give to the remark, especially considering that you have probably just quarreled with that person, the maker of the remark, over the radio being too loud, or something like that, and the view you take, of the remark, is that you'd really rather not hear it, but if you have to hear it, you want to listen to it for the smallest

747

possible length of time, and during a commercial, because immediately after the commercial they're going to play a new rock song by your favorite group, a cut that has never been aired before, and you want to hear it and respond to it in a new way, a way that accords with whatever you're feeling at the moment, or might feel, if the threat of new experience could be (temporarily) overbalanced by the promise of possible positive benefits, or what the mind construes as such, remembering that these are often, really, disguised defeats (not that such defeats are not, at times, good for your character, teaching you that it is not by success alone that one surmounts life, but that setbacks, too, contribute to that roughening of the personality that, by providing a textured surface to place against that of life, enables you to leave slight traces, or smudges, on the face of human history—your mark) and after all, benefit-seeking always has something of the smell of raw vanity about it, as if you wished to decorate your own brow with laurel, or wear your medals to a cookout, when the invitation had said nothing about them, and although the ego is always hungry (we are told) it is well to remember that ongoing success is nearly as meaningless as ongoing lack of success, which can make you sick, and that it is good to leave a few crumbs on the table for the rest of your brethren, not to sweep it all into the little beaded purse of your soul but to allow others, too, part of the gratification, and if you share in this way you will find the clouds smiling on you, and the postman bringing you letters, and bicycles available when you want to rent them, and many other signs, however guarded and limited, of the community's (temporary) approval of you, or at least of its willingness to·let you believe (temporarily) that it finds you not so lacking in commendable virtues as it had previously allowed you to think, from its scorn of your merits, as it might be put, or anyway its consistent refusal to recognize your basic humanness and its secret blackball of the project of your remaining alive, made in executive session by its ruling bodies, which, as everyone knows, carry out concealed programs of reward and punishment, under the rose, causing faint alterations of the status quo, behind your back, at various points along the periphery of community life, together with other enterprises not dissimilar in tone, such as producing films that have special qualities, or attributes, such as a film where the second half of it is a holy mystery, and girls and women are not permitted to see it, or writing novels in which the final chapter is a plastic bag filled with water, which you can touch, but not drink: in this way, or ways, the underground mental life of the collectivity is botched, or denied, or turned into something else never imagined by the planners, who, returning from the latest seminar in crisis management and being asked what they have learned, say they have learned how to throw up their hands; the sentence meanwhile, although not insensible of these considerations, has a festering conscience of its own, which persuades it to follow its star, and to move with all deliberate speed from one place to another, without losing any of the "riders" it may have picked up just being there, on the page, and turning this way and that, to see what is over there, under that oddly-shaped tree, or over there, reflected in the rain barrel of the imagination, even though it is true that in our young manhood we were taught that short, punchy sentences were best (but what did he mean? doesn't "punchy" mean punch-drunk? I think he probably intended to say "short, punching sentences," meaning sentences that lashed out at you, bloodying your brain if possible, and looking up the word just now I came across the nearby "punkah," which is a large fan suspended from the ceiling in India, operated by an attendant pulling a rope—that is what I want for my sentence, to keep it cool!) we are mature enough now to stand the shock of learning that much of what we were taught in our youth was wrong, or improperly understood by those who were teaching it, or perhaps shaded a bit, the shading resulting from the personal needs of the teachers, who as human beings had a tendency to introduce some of their heart's blood into their work, and sometimes this may not have been of the first water, this heart's blood, and even if they thought they were moving the "knowledge" out, as the Board of Education had mandated, they could have noticed that their sentences weren't having the knockdown power of the new weapons whose bullets tumble end-over-end (but it is true that we didn't have these weapons at that time) and they might have taken into account the fundamental dubiousness of their project (but all the intelligently conceived projects have been eaten up already, like the moon and the stars) leaving us, in our best clothes, with only things to do like conducting vigorous wars of attrition against our wives, who have now thoroughly come awake, and slipped into their striped bells, and pulled sweaters over their torsi, and adamantly refused to wear any bras under the sweaters, carefully explaining the political significance of this refusal to anyone who will listen, or look, but not touch, because that has nothing to do with it, so they say; leaving us, as it were, with only things to do like floating sheets of Reynolds Wrap around the room, trying to find

out how many we can keep in the air at the same time, which at least gives
us a sense of participation, as though we were the Buddha, looking down at
the mystery of your smile, which needs to be investigated, and I think I'll
do that right now, while there's still enough light, if you'll sit down over
there, in the best chair, and take off all your clothes, and put your feet in
that electric toe caddy (which prevents pneumonia) and slip into this permanent press hospital gown, to cover your nakedness—why, if you do all
that, we'll be ready to begin! after I wash my hands, because you pick up an
amazing amount of exuviae in this city, just by walking around in the open
air, and nodding to acquaintances, and speaking to friends, and copulating
with lovers, in the ordinary course (and death to our enemies! by the by)—
but I'm getting a little uptight, just about washing my hands, because I
can't find the soap, which somebody has used and not put back in the soap
dish, all of which is extremely irritating, if you have a beautiful patient
sitting in the examining room, naked inside her gown, and peering at her
moles in the mirror, with her immense brown eyes following your every
movement (when they are not watching the moles, expecting them, as in a
Disney nature film, to exfoliate) and her immense brown head wondering
what you're going to do to her, the pierced places in the head letting that
question leak out, while the therapist decides just to wash his hands in
plain water, and hang the soap! and does so, and then looks around for a
towel, but all the towels have been collected by the towel service, and are
not there, so he wipes his hands on his pants, in the back (so as to avoid
suspicious stains on the front) thinking: what must she think of me? and,
all this is very unprofessional and at-sea looking! trying to visualize the contretemps from her point of view, if she has one (but how can she? she is not
in the washroom) and then stopping, because it is finally his own point of
view that he cares about and not hers, and with this firmly in mind, and a
light, confident step, such as you might find in the works of Bulwer-Lytton,
he enters the space she occupies so prettily and, taking her by the hand,
proceeds to tear off the stiff white hospital gown (but no, we cannot have
that kind of pornographic *merde* in this majestic and high-minded sentence, which will probably end up in the Library of Congress) (that was
just something that took place inside his consciousness, as he looked at her,
and since we know that consciousness is always consciousness *of* something, she is not entirely without responsibility in the matter) so, then, taking her by the hand, he falls into the stupendous white purée of her abyss,

no, I mean rather that he asks her how long it has been since her last visit, and she says a fortnight, and he shudders, and tells her that with a condition like hers (she is an immensely popular soldier, and her troops win all their battles by pretending to be forests, the enemy discovering, at the last moment, that those trees they have eaten their lunch under have eyes and swords) (which reminds me of the performance, in 1845, of Robert-Houdin, called *The Fantastic Orange Tree,* wherein Robert-Houdin borrowed a lady's handkerchief, rubbed it between his hands and passed it into the center of an egg, after which he passed the egg into the center of a lemon, after which he passed the lemon into the center of an orange, then pressed the orange between his hands, making it smaller and smaller, until only a powder remained, whereupon he asked for a small potted orange tree and sprinkled the powder thereupon, upon which the tree burst into blossom, the blossoms turning into oranges, the oranges turning into butterflies, and the butterflies turning into beautiful young ladies, who then married members of the audience), a condition so damaging to real-time social intercourse of any kind, the best thing she can do is give up, and lay down her arms, and he will lie down in them, and together they will permit themselves a bit of the old slap and tickle, she wearing only her Mr. Christopher medal, on its silver chain, and he (for such is the latitude granted the professional classes) worrying about the sentence, about its thin wires of dramatic tension, which have been omitted, about whether we should write down some natural events occurring in the sky (birds, lightning bolts), and about a possible coup d'etat within the sentence, whereby its chief verb would be—but at this moment a messenger rushes into the sentence, bleeding from a hat of thorns he's wearing, and cries out: "You don't know what you're doing! Stop making this sentence, and begin instead to make Moholy-Nagy cocktails, for those are what we really need, on the frontiers of bad behavior!" and then he falls to the floor, and a trap door opens under him, and he falls through that, into a damp pit where a blue narwhal waits, its horn poised (but maybe the weight of the messenger, falling from such a height, will break off the horn)—thus, considering everything very carefully, in the sweet light of the ceremonial axes, in the run-mad skimble-skamble of information sickness, we must make a decision as to whether we should proceed, or go back, in the latter case enjoying the pathos of eradication, in the former case reading an erotic advertisement which begins, *How to Make Your Mouth a Blowtorch of Excitement* (but wouldn't that overtax our mouthwashes?) attempting, during the pause, while our burned mouths are being smeared with fat, to imagine a better sentence, worthier, more meaningful, like those in the Declaration of Independence, or a bank statement showing that you have seven thousand kroner more than you thought you had—a statement summing up the unreasonable demands that you make on life, and one that also asks the question, if you can imagine these demands, why are they not routinely met, tall fool? but of course it is not that query that this infected sentence has set out to answer (and hello! to our girl friend, Rosetta Stone, who has stuck by us through thick and thin) but some other query that we shall some day discover the nature of, and here comes Ludwig, the expert on sentence construction we have borrowed from the Bauhaus, who will—"Guten Tag, Ludwig!"—probably find a way to cure the sentence's sprawl, by using the improved way of thinking developed in Weimer—"I am sorry to inform you that the Bauhaus no longer exists, that all of the great masters who formerly thought there are either dead or retired, and that I myself have been reduced to constructing books on how to pass the examination for police sergeant"—and Ludwig falls through the Tugendhat House into the history of man-made objects; a disappointment, to be sure, but it reminds us that the sentence itself is a man-made object, not the one we wanted of course, but still a construction of man, a structure to be treasured for its weakness, as opposed to the strength of stones

1972

Let me *try*, in other words—even if the result of that trying is nothing more than an exhilarating attempt. "What are the ideals of form for," asked Robert Frost, "if we aren't going to be made to fear for them? All our ingenuity is lavished on getting into danger legitimately so that we may be genuinely rescued." Fifty years ago this year, Robert Frost stayed up all night in Vermont writing a long and forgettable poem about New Hampshire. In the morning, he took a walk, and within minutes of returning home he jotted down what would become one of the most famous poems in American literature. In "Stopping by Woods on a Snowy Evening," Frost assumes the role of spectator in a place that isn't his place, speculating on a life that isn't his life. It's a role essayists also know well: that of the spectatorial artist, a phrase that holds within it, of course, the phonetic redolence of *spectator*, the traditional view of the essayist as an observer of the world. But also lurking inside that phrase is the idea of a *spectre,* a ghost, a shadowy haunt that lingers over its subjects and is unable to look away, unable to tear away, unable to move beyond this world and back to where it belongs. It begins, Frost once said, "with a lump in the throat; a home-sickness or a love-sickness . . . a reaching-out toward expression; an effort to find fulfillment."

SUSAN STEINBERG

Signified

Because words are about desire and desire is about the guy who filled my two front tires when one was low. And desire is about the guy who cleaned my windshield as the other, below me, filled.

And there's the guy who pours foam onto my coffee in the shape of a heart and I, each time he pours, so slow, think, Jesus.

Because the guy who pours the foam in the shape of a heart—and I don't know how he does it—is twenty-four, and I am not twenty-four, meaning I am not thirty-four and don't think much of twenty-four except to think I must have been working through something back then, living in that railroad apartment in Baltimore, daydreaming of fame and all that came with fame.

My friends that year said, Why move, but I packed some boxes, crammed the boxes into the car, pushed the couch over the porch. My friends waved from the couch in the rearview mirror and I forgot them once I reached the highway.

Why Boston, they wanted to know.

Because why not.

Or because I imagined Boston as brick-walked and lamp-lit, and I could see myself tromping in boots through the snow.

Or because I imagined a field from a poem I'd read in school as a child.

Or because I had no good answer to, Why Baltimore.

Because I had gotten held up, a knife point pointing at my face.

All this to say that I remember those friends from then, sitting here now on my new couch, twelve years past, their tattoos I remember of gothic letters and Celtic knot work, their tangled hair. All this to say that I've made a connection, forced as it seems, of twenty-four to twenty-four. I've made a connection of couch to couch. Connections are easy when one is sitting, staring at a wall. There is no deeper meaning. There is no signified.

There is couch and there is couch.

There is the table my feet are on and the table from then. A table we sat at until the pale hum of morning.

There was no such word then as *afterparty.*

There was no such use of the word *random* then, how the kids these days use *random.*

What I mean is the guy who filled my tires looked up and said, of the lowness in one tire and not in the other, Random, and I, remembering running into a curb the night before, driving home from a bar where I sat and sat until giving up, thought, Not really.

And the guy who cleaned the windshield whistled and walked back to the garage.

And the guy who pours the foam into the shape of a heart told my friend of me, She's hot, when my friend went to the café once alone. Your friend, he said, She's hot, and my friend called later to tell me the news.

What was I doing that night. Same thing as this night. Drinking wine. Sitting on the couch, my feet up on the table. These are the clichéd years, these years. The details have been predetermined. It's a recipe I follow. Very little this, very little that.

I think I said, That's cute. Because that's what one says in this situation. One laughs and says, Cute, and one's friend says, in this situation, You should go for it. Which always seems to mean to me that I should go against something else.

I said, How old is he.

Then I said, That's cute.

Then I said, That's way too young, and my friend, exhaling smoke for emphasis, said, Exactly.

In Baltimore everyone was going for everyone else. Small town. Junkies. We were all the same age, the twenty-somethings, the fifty-somethings. When the bars closed we went to the place that stayed open until morning. Club Midnight. And we drank orange drinks until things felt unreasonable. What was the point of reason. I had no desire for reason. I had only a weak desire—in the words of my shrink from then—to fill a space, and I filled the space. There's a list, somewhere, of the drugs I did. There's a list, somewhere, of who I fucked. I wrote these lists on the backs of napkins, a night at Club Midnight, and everyone thought the lists were too short. Well that was years ago, and things have changed. And there's a list of the drugs I almost did and a list of the guys I almost fucked. And those lists. Believe me. Another story.

So I sat the other night in a bar on a snowy, lamp-lit street, until I realized he—the one I am supposed to desire—my age, a neat haircut, small hands, a tucked-in shirt, a workhorse, a perfect match—wasn't going to show. Or I realized that he would show and that I would feel disgust. So I stumbled to the car, ended up half the car on the sidewalk, no one around to see it.

I once knew better than to drive.

I mean I once considered other options.

There were no windows in Club Midnight. We knew it was morning because of sudden blue shadows under our eyes. And that shock of light, no matter how pale, when someone opened the door. And the shock of the cold. Jesus. There's no good story to tell except once I decided to wait for the bus. My friends had gone, and I was too sick from drink after drink to drive. Birds were chirping, and I wondered where from. There were no trees. There was nowhere to hide. The man with the knife had a scar on his face and I didn't want a scar on my face. I reached into my pocket, pulled out some ones, and he ran one way, I the other.

And here I am watching the blue turn darker blue behind the trees. And the color of this couch, according to the catalog, is mushroom, which means it's greenish, grayish, brownish. Which means I paid a lot for it. One must pay up when one is following a recipe, and one ingredient is a costly couch. And one is a car. And one is a man. And one is a child.

And one is not thirty-four, though feeling for that warm space in the dimming room.

The men who carried up the couch were older, no-nonsense, beer bellied and smelling of sweat, though had the room been darker, smokier, the bartender filling and filling, the music up high, well, perhaps there'd be something more to say.

The guy filling my tires, when I tried to hand him a few ones, said, No. He said, Jesus, lady, air is free.

And the guy in the café—dark curly hair, that way of dressing—his pants hanging just under his hip bones—blue eyes and so on, the thing with the foam. Well, each time I drop fifty cents into the tip jar, lift my cup, say thank you into the disintegrating heart, never looking up, though I can feel him looking down, and my friend—who always smells like smoke—did I say this—and it's comforting somehow—will say, Aw, a heart, Look, a heart.

And my friend and I will sit on the chairs on the sidewalk out front, even in cold, and a bus will pass, and the bell on the door will jingle, and the guy will come out, wiping his hands on his pants, lighting a cigarette he pulls from a pale blue box, blowing white smoke into the sky.

And I imagine he's looking at someone else.

And I remember my predestined life. My list of ingredients. And one is a man. And one is a child.

And one is a child.

And I imagine he's looking only at me.

And I imagine the bell sound comes from a horse stopped in the snow at the edge of the woods.

1973

"What is the point," asks Renata Adler, without a question mark.

> That is what must be borne in mind. Sometimes the point is really who wants what. Sometimes the point is what is right or kind. Sometimes the point is a momentum, a fact, a quality, a voice, an intimation, a thing said or unsaid. Sometimes it's who's at fault, or what will happen if you do not move at once. The point changes and goes out. You cannot be forever watching for the point, or you lose the simplest thing: being a major character in your own life.

This is the year that sees the release of Pink Floyd's *The Dark Side of the Moon,* one year after NASA's last lunar landing. It's the year in which Renata Adler writes a short piece called "Brownstone," part of a book that will eventually become a cult favorite among essayists, even though it will never be known as anything but a novel. The business of philosophy, Adler writes in the book, is to crack open metaphors which are dead. It's been almost fifteen years since I first started trying to write a new history of the essay. And all I'm really sure of now is that I still require question marks.

Brownstone

The camel, I had noticed, was passing, with great difficulty, through the eye of the needle. The Apollo flight, the four-minute mile, Venus in Scorpio, human records on land and at sea—these had been events of enormous importance. But the camel, practicing in near obscurity for almost two thousand years, was passing through. First the velvety nose, then the rest. Not many were aware. But if the lead camel and then perhaps the entire caravan could make it, the thread, the living thread of camels, would exist, could not be lost. No one could lose the thread. The prospects of the rich would be enhanced. "Ortega tells us that the business of philosophy," the professor was telling his class of indifferent freshmen, "is to crack open metaphors which are dead."

"I shouldn't have come," the Englishman said, waving his drink and breathing so heavily at me that I could feel my bangs shift. "I have a terrible cold."

"He would probably have married her," a voice across the room said, "with the exception that he died."

"Well, I am a personality that prefers not to be annoyed."

"We should all prepare ourselves for this eventuality."

A six-year-old was passing the hors d'oeuvres. The baby, not quite steady on his feet, was hurtling about the room.

"He's following me," the six-year-old said, in despair.

"Then lock yourself in the bathroom, dear," Inez replied.

"He always waits outside the door."

"He loves you, dear."

"Well, I don't like it."

"How I envy you," the minister's wife was saying to a courteous, bearded
boy, "reading *Magic Mountain* for the first time."

The homosexual across the hall from me always takes Valium and walks his
beagle. I borrow Valium from him from time to time, and when he takes
a holiday the dog is left with me. On our floor of this brownstone, we are
friends. Our landlord, Roger Somerset, was murdered last July. He was a
kind and absent-minded man, and on the night when he was stabbed there
was a sort of requiem for him in the heating system. There is a lot of music
in this building anyway. The newlyweds on the third floor play Bartok
on their stereo. The couple on the second floor play clarinet quintets; their
kids play rock. The girl on the fourth floor, who has been pining for two
months, plays Judy Collins' "Maid of Constant Sorrow" all day long. We
have a kind of orchestra in here. The ground floor is a shop. The owner of
the shop speaks of our landlord's murder still. Shaking his head, he says
that he suspects "foul play." We all agree with him. We changed our locks.
But "foul play" seems a weird expression for the case.

It is all weird. I am not always well. One block away (I often think of this),
there was ten months ago an immense crash. Water mains broke. There
were small rivers in the streets. In a great skyscraper that was being built,
something had failed. The newspapers reported the next day that by some
miracle only two people had been "slightly injured" by ten tons of falling
steel. The steel fell from the eighteenth floor. The question that preoccu-
pies me now is how, under the circumstances, slight injuries could occur.
Perhaps the two people were grazed in passing by. Perhaps some fragments
of the sidewalk ricocheted. I knew a deliverer of flowers who, at Sixty-ninth
and Lexington, was hit by a flying suicide. Situations simply do not yield to
the most likely structures of the mind. A "self-addressed envelope," if you
are inclined to brood, raises deep questions of identity. Such an envelope,
immutably itself, is always precisely where it belongs. "Self-pity" is just sadness, I think, in the pejorative. But "joking with nurses" fascinates me in
the press. Whenever someone has been quite struck down, lost faculties,
members of his family, he is said to have "joked with his nurses" quite a lot.
What a mine of humor every nurse's life must be.

I have a job, of course. I have had several jobs. I've had our paper's gossip
column since last month. It is egalitarian. I look for people who are quite

obscure, and report who is breaking up with whom and where they go and what they wear. The person who invented this new form for us is on antidepressants now. He lives in Illinois. He says there are people in southern Illinois who have not yet been covered by the press. I often write about families in Queens. Last week, I went to a dinner party on Park Avenue. After 1 a.m., something called the Alive or Dead Game was being played. Someone would mention an old character from Tammany or Hollywood. "Dead," "Dead," "Dead," everyone would guess. "No, no. Alive. I saw him walking down the street just yesterday," or "Yes. Dead. I read a little obituary notice about him last year." One of the little truths people can subtly enrage or reassure each other with is who—when you have looked away a month, a year—is still around.

The St. Bernard at the pound on Ninety-second Street was named Bonnie and would have cost five dollars. The attendant held her tightly on a leash of rope. "Hello, Bonnie," I said. Bonnie growled. "I wouldn't talk to her if was you," the attendant said. I leaned forward to pat her ear. Bonnie snarled. "I wouldn't touch her if I was you," the attendant said. I held out my hand under Bonnie's jowls. She strained against the leash, and choked and coughed. "Now cut that out, Bonnie," the attendant said. "Could I just take her for a walk around the block," I said, "before I decide?" "Are you out of your mind?" the attendant said. Aldo patted Bonnie, and we left.

DEAR TENANT:

We have reason to believe that there are impostors posing as Con Ed repairmen and inspectors circulating in this area.

Do not permit any Con Ed man to enter your premises or the building, if possible.

THE PRECINCT

The New York Chinese cabdriver lingered at every corner and at every traffic light, to read his paper. I wondered what the news was. I looked over his shoulder. The illustrations and the type were clear enough: newspaper print, pornographic fiction. I leaned back in my seat. A taxi-driver who happened to be Oriental with a sadomasochistic cast of mind was not my business. I lit a cigarette, looked at my bracelet. I caught the driver's eyes a moment in the rearview mirror. He picked up his paper. "I don't think you ought to read," I said, "while you are driving." Traffic was slow. I saw his mirrored eyes again. He stopped his reading. When we reached my address, I did not tip him. Racism and prudishness, I thought, and reading over people's shoulders.

But there are moments in this place when everything becomes a show of force. He can read what he likes at home. Tipping is still my option. Another newspaper event, in our brownstone. It was a holiday. The superintendent normally hauls the garbage down and sends the paper up, by dumbwaiter, each morning. On holidays, the garbage stays upstairs, the paper on the sidewalk. At 8 a.m., I went downstairs. A ragged man was lying across the little space that separates the inner door, which locks, from the outer door, which doesn't. I am not a news addict. I could have stepped over the sleeping man, picked up my *Times,* and gone upstairs to read it. Instead, I knocked absurdly from inside the door, and said, "Wake up. You'll have to leave now." He got up, lifted the flattened cardboard he had been sleeping on, and walked away, mumbling and reeking. It would have been kinder, certainly, to let the driver read, the wino sleep. One simply cannot bear down so hard on all these choices.

What is the point. That is what must be borne in mind. Sometimes the point is really who wants what. Sometimes the point is what is right or kind. Sometimes the point is a momentum, a fact, a quality, a voice, an intimation, a thing said or unsaid. Sometimes it's who's at fault, or what will happen if you do not move at once. The point changes and goes out. You cannot be forever watching for the point, or you lose the simplest thing: being a major character in your own life. But if you are, for any length of time, custodian of the point—in art, in court, in politics, in lives, in rooms—it turns out there are rear-guard actions everywhere. To see a thing clearly, and when your vision of it dims, or when it goes to someone else, if you have a gentle nature, keep your silence, that is lovely. Otherwise, now and then, a small foray is worthwhile. Just so that being always, complacently, thoroughly wrong does not become the safest position of them all. The point has never quite been entrusted to me.

My cousin, who was born on February 29th, became a veterinarian. Some years ago, when he was twenty-eight (seven, by our childhood birthday count), he was drafted, and sent to Malaysia. He spent most of his military service there, assigned to the zoo. He operated on one tiger, which, in the course of abdominal surgery, began to wake up and wag its tail. The anesthetist grabbed the tail, and injected more sodium pentothal. That tiger survived. But two flamingos, sent by the city of Miami to Kuala Lumpur as a token of good will, could not bear the trip or the climate and, in spite of my cousin's efforts, died. There was also a cobra—the largest anyone in Kuala Lumpur could remember having seen. An old man had brought it, in an immense sack, from somewhere in the countryside. The zoo director called my cousin at once, around dinnertime, to say that an unprecedented cobra had arrived. Something quite drastic, however, seemed wrong with its neck. My cousin, whom I have always admired—for his leap-year birthday, for his pilot's license, for his presence of mind—said that he would certainly examine the cobra in the morning but that the best thing for it after its long journey must be a good night's rest. By morning, the cobra was dead.

My cousin is well. The problem is this. Hardly anyone about whom I deeply care at all resembles anyone else I have ever met, or heard of, or read about in the literature. I know an Israeli general who, in 1967, retook the Mitla Pass but who, since his mandatory retirement from military service at fifty-five, has been trying to repopulate the Ark. He asked me, over breakfast at the Drake, whether I knew any owners of oryxes. Most of the vegetarian species he has collected have already multiplied enough, since he has found and cared for them, to be permitted to run wild. The carnivorous animals, though, must still be kept behind barbed wire—to keep them from stalking the rarer vegetarians. I know a group that studies Proust one Sunday afternoon a month, and an analyst, with that Exeter laugh (embittered mooing noises, and mirthless heaving of the shoulder blades), who has the most remarkable terrorist connections in the Middle East.

The conversation of *The Magic Mountain* and the unrequited love of six-year-olds occurred on Saturday, at brunch. "Bring someone new," Inez had said. "Not queer. Not married, maybe separated. John and I are breaking up." The invitation was not of a kind that I had heard before. Aldo, who lives with me between the times when he prefers to be alone, refused to come. He despises brunch. He detests Inez. I went, instead, with an editor who has been a distant, steady friend but who, ten years ago, when we

first came to New York, had once put three condoms on the night table beside the phone. We both had strange ideas then about New York. Aldo is a
gentle, orderly, soft-spoken man, slow to conclude. I try to be tidy when he
is here, but I have often made his cigarettes, and once his manuscript, into
the bed. Our paper's publisher is an intellectual from Baltimore. He has read
Wittgenstein; he's always making unimpeachable remarks. Our music critic
throws a tantrum every day, in print. Our book reviewer is looking for another job. He found that the packages in which all books are mailed could
not, simply could not, be opened without doing considerable damage—
through staples, tape, wire, fluttering gray stuff, recalcitrance—to the reviewer's hands. He felt it was a symptom of some kind—one of those cases
where incompetence at every stage, across the board, acquired a certain
independent force. Nothing to do with books, he thought, worked out at
all. We also do the news. For horoscopes, there are the ladies' magazines,
which tell you—earnestly—auspicious times to shave your legs. We just
cannot compete.

"All babies are natural swimmers," John said, lowering his two-year-old son
gently over the side of the rowboat, and smiling. The child thrashed and
sank. Aldo dived in and grabbed him. The baby came up coughing, not
crying, and looked with pure fear at his father. John looked with dismay at
his son. "He would have come up in a minute," John said to Aldo, who was
dripping and rowing. "You have to give nature a chance."

My late landlord was from Scarsdale. The Maid of Constant Sorrow is from
Texas. Aldo is from St. Louis. Inez's versions vary about where she's from.
I grew up in a New England mill town, where, in the early thirties, all
the insured factories burned down. It has been difficult to get fire insurance in that region ever since. The owner of a hardware store, whose property adjoined an insured factory at the time, lost everything. Afterward,
he walked all day along the railroad track, waiting for a train to run him
down. Railroad service has never been very good up there. No trains came.
His children own the town these days, for what it's worth. The two cobbled
streets where black people always lived have been torn up and turned into
a public park since a flood that occurred some years ago. Unprecedented
rains came. Retailers had to destroy their sodden products, for fear of con-
tamination. The black section was torn up and seeded over in the town's

rezoning project. No one knows where the blacks live now. But there are Negroes in the stores and schools, and on the football team. It is assumed that the park integrated the town. Those black families must be living somewhere. It is a mystery.

At the women's college where I went, we had distinguished faculty in everything, digs at Nuoro and Mycenae. We had a quality of obsession in our studies. For professors who had quarreled with their wives at breakfast, those years of bright-eyed young women, never getting any older, must have been a trial. The head of the history department once sneezed into his best student's honors thesis. He slammed it shut. It was ultimately published. When I was there, a girl called Cindy Melchior was immensely fat. She wore silk trousers and gilt mules. One day, in the overheated classroom, she laid aside her knitting and lumbered to the window, which she opened. Then she lumbered back. "Do you think," the professor asked, "you are so graceful?" He somehow meant it kindly. Cindy wept. That year, Cindy's brother Melvin phoned me. "I would have called you sooner," he said, "but I had the most terrible eczema." All the service staff on campus in those days were black. Many of them were followers of Father Divine. They took new names in the church. I remember the year when a maid called Serious Heartbreak married a janitor called Universal Dictionary. At a meeting of the faculty last fall, the college president, who is new and male, spoke of raising money. A female professor of Greek was knitting— and working on Linear B, with an abacus before her. In our time, there was a vogue for madrigals. Some of us listened, constantly, to a single record. There was a phrase we could not decipher. A professor of symbolic logic, a French Canadian, had sounds that matched but a meaning that seemed unlikely: Sheep are no angels; come upstairs. A countertenor explained it, after a local concert: She'd for no angel's comfort stay. Correct, but not so likely either.

PAUL: "Two diamonds."

INEZ: "Two hearts."

MARY: "Three clubs."

JOHN: "Four kings."

INEZ: "Darling, you know you can't just bid four kings."

JOHN: "I don't see why. I might have been bluffing."

INEZ: "No, darling. That's poker. This is bridge. And even in poker you
      can't just bid four kings."
JOHN: "No. Well, I guess we'd better deal another hand."

The host, for some reason, was taking Instamatic pictures of his guests. It
was not clear whether he was doing this in order to be able to show, at some
future time, that there had been this gathering in his house. Or whether he
thought of pictures in some voodoo sense. Or whether he found it difficult to
talk. Or whether he was bored. Two underground celebrities—one of whom
had become a sensation by never generating or exhibiting a flicker of interest in anything, the other of whom was known mainly for hanging around
the first—were taking pictures too. I was there with an actor I've known for
years. He had already been received in an enormous embrace by an Eastern
European poet, whose hair was cut too short but who was neither as awk-
wardly spontaneous nor as drunk as he cared to seem. The party was in honor
of the poet, who celebrated the occasion by insulting everyone and being
fawned upon, by distinguished and undistinguished writers alike. "This
group looks as though someone had torn up a few guest lists and floated the
pieces on the air," the actor said. The friend of the underground sensation
walked up to us and said hello. Then, in a verbal seizure of some sort, he
began muttering obscenities. The actor said a few calming things that didn't
work. He finally put his finger on the mutterer's lips. The mutterer bit that
finger extremely hard, and walked away. The actor wrapped his finger in a
paper napkin, and got himself another drink. We stayed till twelve.

When I worked, for a time, in the infirmary of a branch of an upstate university, it was becoming more difficult with each passing semester, except
in the most severe cases, to determine which students had mental or medical problems. At the clinic, young men with straggly beards and stained
blue jeans wept alongside girls in jeans and frayed sweaters—all being fitted
with contact lenses, over which they then wore granny glasses. There was
no demand for prescription granny glasses at all. For the severely depressed,
the paranoids, and the hallucinators, our young psychiatrists prescribed
"mood elevators," pills that were neither uppers nor downers but which affected the bloodstream in such a way that within three to five weeks many
sad outpatients became very cheerful, and several saints and historical figures became again Midwestern graduate students under tolerable stress.

On one, not unusual, morning, the clinic had a call from an instructor in political science. "I am in the dean's office," he said. "My health is quite perfect. They want me to have a checkup."

"Oh?" said the doctor on duty. "Perhaps you could come in on Friday."

"The problem is," the voice on the phone said, "I have always thought myself, and been thought by others, a Negro. Now, through research, I have found that my family on both sides have always been white."

"Oh," the doctor on duty said. "Perhaps you could just take a cab and come over."

Within twenty minutes, the political-science instructor appeared at the clinic. He was black. The doctor said nothing, and began a physical examination. By the time his blood pressure was taken, the patient confided that his white ancestors were, in fact, royal. The mood elevators restored him. He and the doctor became close friends besides. A few months later, the instructor took a job with the government in Washington. Two weeks after that, he was calling the clinic again. "I have found new documentation," he said. "All eight of my great-grandparents were pure-blooded Germans—seven from Prussia, one from Alsace. I thought I should tell you, dear friend." The doctor suggested he come for the weekend. By Sunday afternoon, a higher dose of the pill had had its effect. The problem has not since recurred.

The Maid of Constant Sorrow said our landlord's murder marked a turning point in her analysis. "I don't feel guilty. I feel hated," she said. It is true, for a time, we all wanted to feel somehow part—if only because violence offset the ineluctable in our lives. My grandfather said that some people have such extreme insomnia that they look at their watches every hour after midnight, to see how sorry they ought to be feeling for themselves. Aldo says he does not care what my grandfather said. My grandmother refused to concede that any member of the family died of natural causes. An uncle's cancer in middle age occurred because all the suitcases fell off the luggage rack onto him when he was in his teens, and so forth. Death was an acquired characteristic. My grandmother, too, used to put other people's ailments into the diminutive: strokelets were what her friends had. Aldo said he was bored to tearsies by my grandmother's diminutives.

The weather last Friday was terrible. The flight to Martha's Vineyard was "decisional."

"What does 'decisional' mean?" a small boy asked. "It means we might have to land in Hyannis," his mother said. It is hard to understand how anyone learns anything.

Scattered through the two cars of the Brewster–New York train last week were adults with what seemed to be a clandestine understanding. They did not look at each other. They stared out the windows. They read. "Um," sang a lady at our fourth stop on the way to Grand Central. She appeared to be reading the paper. She kept singing her "Um," as one who is getting the pitch. A young man had already been whistling "Frère Jacques" for three stops. When the "Um" lady found her pitch and began to sing the national anthem, he looked at her with rage. The conductor passed through, punching tickets in his usual fashion, not in the aisle but directly over people's laps. Every single passenger was obliged to flick the tiny punched part of the ticket from his lap onto the floor. Conductors have this process as their own little show of force. The whistler and the singer were in a dead heat when we reached the city. The people with the clandestine understanding turned out to be inmates from somewhere upstate, now on leave with their families, who met them in New York.

I don't think much of writers in whom nothing is at risk. It is possible, though, to be too literal-minded about this question. In the *Reader's Digest,* under the heading "$3,000 for First-Person Articles," for example: "An article for this series must be a true, hitherto unpublished narrative of an unusual personal experience. It may be dramatic, inspirational, or humorous, but it must have, in the opinion of the editors, a quality of narrative interest comparable to 'How I Lost My Eye' (June '72) and 'Attacked by a Killer Shark' (April '72). Contributions must be typewritten, preferably *double-spaced*..." I particularly like where the stress, the italics, goes.

When the nanny drowned in the swimming pool, the parents reacted sensibly. They had not been there for the event. They had left the nanny at poolside with their youngest child, a girl of five, and the neighbor's twins, a boy and a girl of five, and the neighbor's baby-sitter, an *au pair,* who had become the nanny's dearest friend. When they returned from their morning round of golf, they found a fire truck in the yard, the drowned body of the nanny on the tiles, the three children playing, apparently calmly, under a tree, and two disconsolate firemen trying to deal with the neighbor's baby-sitter, who was hysterical. As an ambulance pulled into the driveway, the mother was already telephoning a doctor; her husband was giving the baby-sitter a glass of water and a sedative. When her hysterics had subsided, the baby-sitter explained what she could. Neither she nor the nanny, it turned out, could really swim. They could both manage a few strokes of the breast-stroke, but they had a great fear of water over their heads. All three of what she called the "little ones" were strong and intrepid dog-paddlers. She and the nanny had always confined themselves to admonitions, and their own few stroking motions, from the shallow end. It was on account of these stroking motions that their inability really to swim had never come to any-one's attention or, for that matter, to their own. That morning, the nanny had, unaccountably, stroked a few feet out of her depth, in the direction of her charge. Then, according to the baby-sitter, who may have confused the sequence, things happened very rapidly, in the following order. Nanny's face turned blue. *Then* she swallowed water. Coughing and struggling, she reached her charge and clung to her. They both went under. Long seconds later, the little girl came up, crying and sputtering. In clear view, a few feet beyond the shallow end and beyond the grasp of the baby-sitter, who was trying to maintain her feet and her depth as she held out her hands, the nanny surfaced briefly once more, sank, and drowned.

I once met a polo-playing Argentine existential psychiatrist, who had lived for months in a London commune. He said that on days when the ordi-nary neurotics in the commune were getting on each other's nerves the few psychopaths and schizophrenics in their midst retired to their rooms and went their version of berserk, alone. On days when the neurotics got along, the psychopaths calmed down, tried to make contact, cooked. It was, he said, as though the sun came out for them. I hope that's true. Although altogether too much of life is mood. Aldo has a married friend who was in love for years with someone, also married. Her husband found out. He insisted that there be no more calls or letters. Aldo's friend called several times, reaching the husband. The girl herself would never answer. In the end, Aldo's friend—in what we regard as not his noblest gesture—sent all the girl's letters, addressed in a packet, to her husband. There was nothing more. I wonder whether the husband read those letters. If he did, I suppose he may have been a writer. In some sense. If not, he was a gentleman. There are also, on the bus, quite often ritual dancers, near-spastics who release the strap and begin a weird sequence of movements, always punctual, always the same. There are some days when everyone I see is lunatic.

I love the laconic. Clearly, I am not of their number. When animated conversations are going on, even with people interrupting one another, I have to curb an impulse to field every remark, by everybody, as though it were addressed to me. I have noticed this impulse in other people. It electrifies the room. It is resolved, sometimes, by conversations in a foreign language One thinks, it is my turn to try to say something, to make an effort. One polishes a case, a tense, a comment. The subject passes. Just as well. There are, however, people who just sit there, silent. A question is addressed to them. They do not answer. Another question. Silence. It is a position of great power. Talkative people running toward those silences are jarred, time after time, by a straight arm rebuff. A quizzical look, a beautiful face perhaps, but silence. Everyone is exhausted, drinks too much, snarls later at home, wonders about the need for aspirin. It has been that stubborn wall

I receive communications almost every day from an institution called the Center for Short-Lived Phenomena. Reporting sources all over the world and an extensive correspondence. Under the title "Type of Event: Biological," I have received postcards about the progress of the Dormouse Invasion of Formentera: "Apart from population density, the dormouse of Formentera had a peak of reproduction in 1970. All females checked were pregnant, and perhaps this fact could have been the source of the idea of an 'invasion.'" And the Northwest Atlantic Puffin Decline. I have followed the Tanzanian Army Worm Outbreak. The San Fernando Earthquake. The Green Pond Fish Kill ("Eighty percent of the numbers involved," the Center's postcard reports, "were mummichogs.") The Samar Spontaneous Oil Burn. The Hawaiian Monk Seal Disappearance. And also, the Naini Tal Sudden Sky Brightening.

Those are accounts of things that did not last long, but if you become famous for a single thing in this country, and just endure, it is certain you will recur, enlarged. Of the eighteen men who were indicted for conspiracy to murder Schwerner, Goodman, and Chaney, seven were convicted by a Mississippi jury—a surprising thing. But then a year later, a man was wounded and a woman killed in a shootout while trying to bomb the house of some Mississippi Jews. It turned out that the informer, the man who had helped the bombers, and led the F.B.I. to them, was one of the convicted seven—the one, in fact, who was alleged to have killed two of the three boys who were found in that Mississippi dam. And what's more, and what's more, the convicted conspirator, alleged double killer, was paid thirty-six thousand dollars by the F.B.I. for bringing the bombers in. Yet the wave of anti-Semitic bombings in Mississippi stopped after the shootout. I don't know what it means. I am in this brownstone.

Last year, Aldo moved out and went to Los Angeles on a story. I called him to ask whether I could come. He said, "Are you going to stay this time?" I said I wasn't sure. I flew out quite early in the morning. On the plane, there was the most banal, unendurable pickup, lasting the whole flight. A young man and a young woman—he was Italian, I think; she was German—had just met, and settled on French as their common language. They asked each other where they were from, and where they were going. They posed each other riddles. He took out a pencil and paper and sketched her portrait. She giggled. He asked her whether she had ever considered a career as a model. She said she had considered it, but she feared that all men in the field were after the same thing. He agreed. He began to tell off-color stories. She laughed and reproached him. It was like that. I wondered whether these things were always, to captive eavesdroppers, so dreary. When I arrived at Aldo's door, he met me with a smile that seemed surprised, a little sheepish. We talked awhile. Sometimes he took, sometimes I held, my suitcase. I tried, I thought, a joke. I asked whether there was already a girl there. He said there was. He met me in an hour at the corner drugstore for a cup of coffee. We talked. We returned to the apartment. We had Scotch. That afternoon, quite late, I flew home. I called him from time to time. He had his telephone removed a few days later. Now, for a while, he's here again. He's doing a political essay. It begins, "Some things cannot be said too often, and some can." That's all he's got so far.

We had people in for drinks one night last week. The cork in the wine bottle broke. Somebody pounded it into the bottle with a chisel and a hammer. We went to a bar. I have never understood the feeling men seem to have for bars they frequent. A single-story drunk told his single story. A fine musician who was with us played Mozart, Chopin, and Beethoven on the piano. It seemed a great, impromptu occasion. Then he said, we thought, "I am now going to play some Yatz." From what he played, it turned out he meant jazz. He played it badly.

We had driven in from another weekend in the country while it was still daylight. Lots of cars had their headlights on. We weren't sure whether it was for or against peace, or just for highway safety. Milly, a secretary in a brokerage office, was married in our ground-floor shop that evening. She cried hysterically. Her mother and several people from her home town and John, whose girl she had been before he married Inez, thought it was from sentiment or shyness, or for some conventional reason. Milly explained it to Aldo later. She and her husband had really married two years before—the week they met, in fact—in a chapel in Las Vegas. They hadn't wanted to tell their parents, or anybody, until he finished college. They had torn up their Las Vegas license. She had been crying out of some legal fear of being married twice, it turned out. Their best man, a Puerto Rican doctor, said his aunt had been mugged in a cemetery in San Juan by a man on horseback. She thought it was her husband, returned from the dead. She had required sedation. We laughed. My friend across the hall, who owns the beagle, looked very sad all evening. He said, abruptly, that he was cracking up, and no one would believe him. There were sirens in the street. Inez said she knew exactly what he meant: she was cracking up also. Her escort, a pale Italian jeweler, said, "I too. I too have it. The most terrible anguishes, anguishes all in the night."

Inez said she knew the most wonderful man for the problem. "He may strike you at first as a phony," she said, "but then, when you're with him, you find yourself naturally screaming. It's such a relief. And he teaches you how you can practice at home." Milly said she was not much of a screamer—had never, in fact, screamed in her life. "High time you did, then," Inez said. Our sportswriter said he had recently met a girl whose problem was stealing all the suede garments of house guests, and another, in her thirties, who cried all the time because she had not been accepted at Smith. We heard many more sirens in the streets. We all went home.

At 4 a.m., the phone rang about fifty times. I did not answer it. Aldo suggested that we remove it. I took three Valium. The whole night was sirens, then silence. The phone rang again. It is still ringing. The paper goes to press tomorrow. It is possible that I know who killed our landlord. So many things point in one direction. But too strong a case, I find, is often lost. It incurs doubts, suspicions. Perhaps I do not know. Perhaps it doesn't matter. I think it does, though. When I wonder what it is that we are doing—in this brownstone, on this block, with this paper—the truth is probably that we are fighting for our lives.

1974

The way I see it, if *fiction* means "shape" and *novel* means "new" and *poetry* means "make" and *drama* means "do," there ought to be a space that's reserved for our unknowing—that gorgeous messy practice of perpetual pursuit, the attempts that are as much about apprenticeships with knowing, as they are with failure too.

Humility

IN ANY SOCIETY BASED ON CLASS, HUMILIATION IS A POLITICAL REALITY. HUMILIATION IS ONE METHOD BY WHICH POLITICAL POWER IS TRANSFORMED INTO SOCIAL OR PERSONAL RELATIONSHIPS. THE PERSONAL INTERIORIZATION OF THE PRACTICE OF HUMILIATION IS CALLED *HUMILITY*

CAPITOL IS AN ARTIST WHO MAKES DOLLS. MAKES, DAMAGES, TRANSFORMS, SMASHES. ONE OF HER DOLLS IS A WRITER DOLL. THE WRITER DOLL ISN'T VERY LARGE AND IS ALL HAIR, HORSE-MANE HAIR, RAT FUR, DIRTY HUMAN HAIR, PUSSY.

ONE NIGHT CAPITOL GAVE THE FOLLOWING SCENARIO TO HER WRITER DOLL:

As a child in sixth grade in a North American school, won first prize in a poetry contest.

In late teens and early twenties, entered New York City poetry world. Prominent Black Mountain poets, mainly male, taught or attempted to teach her that a writer becomes a writer when and only when he finds his own voice.

CAPITOL DIDN'T MAKE ANY AVANT-GARDE POET DOLLS.

Since wanted to be a writer, tried to find her own voice. Couldn't. But still loved to write. Loved to play with language. Language was material like clay or paint. Loved to play with verbal material, build up slums and

779

mansions, demolish banks and half-rotten buildings, even buildings which she herself had constructed, into never-before-seen, even unseeable, jewels.

To her, every word wasn't only material in itself, but also sent out like beacons, other words. *Blue* sent out *heaven* and *The Virgin*. Material is rich. I didn't create language, writer thought. Later she would think about ownership and copyright. I'm constantly being given language. Since this language-world is rich and always changing, flowing, when I write, I enter a world which has complex relations and is, perhaps, illimitable. This world both represents and is human history, public memories and private memories turned public, the records and actualizations of human intentions. This world is more than life and death, for here life and death conjoin. I can't make language, but in this world, I can play and be played.

So where is 'my voice'?

Wanted to be a writer.

Since couldn't find 'her voice,' decided she'd first have to learn what a Black Mountain poet meant by 'his voice.' What did he do when he wrote?

A writer who had found his own voice presented a viewpoint. Created meaning. The writer took a certain amount of language, verbal material, forced that language to stop radiating in multiple, even unnumerable directions, to radiate in only one direction so there could be his meaning.

The writer's voice wasn't exactly this meaning. The writer's voice was a process, how he had forced the language to obey him, his will. The writer's voice is the voice of the writer-as-God.

Writer thought, don't want to be God; have never wanted to be God. All these male poets want to be the top poet, as if, since they can't be a dictator in the political realm, can be dictator of this world.

Want to play. Be left alone to play. Want to be a sailor who journeys at every edge and even into the unknown. See strange sights, see. If I can't keep on seeing wonders, I'm in prison. Claustrophobia's sister to my worst nightmare: lobotomy, the total loss of perceptual power, of seeing new. If had to force language to be uni-directional, I'd be helping my own prison to be constructed.

There are enough prisons outside, outside language.

Decided, no. Decided that to find her own voice would be negotiating against her joy. That's what the culture seemed to be trying to tell her to do.

Wanted only to write. Was writing. Would keep on writing without finding 'her own voice.' To hell with the Black Mountain poets even though they had taught her a lot.

Decided that since what she wanted to do was just to write, not to find her own voice, could and would write by using anyone's voice, anyone's text, whatever materials she wanted to use.

Had a dream while waking that was running with animals. Wild horses, leopards, red fox, kangaroos, mountain lions, wild dogs. Running over rolling hills. Was able to keep up with the animals and they accepted her.

Wildness was writing and writing was wildness.

Decision not to find this own voice but to use and be other, multiple, even innumerable, voices led to two other decisions.

There were two kinds of writing in her culture: good literature and schlock. Novels which won literary prizes were good literature; science fiction and horror novels, pornography were schlock. Good literature concerned important issues, had a high moral content, and, most important, was written according to well-established rules of taste, elegance, and conservatism. Schlock's content was sex horror violence and other aspects of human existence abhorrent to all but the lowest of the low, the socially and morally unacceptable. This trash was made as quickly as possible, either with no regard for the regulations of politeness or else with regard to the crudest, most vulgar techniques possible. Well-educated, intelligent and concerned people read good literature. Perhaps because the masses were gaining political therefore economic and social control, not only of literary production, good literature was read by an élite diminishing in size and cultural strength.

Decided to use or to write both good literature and schlock. To mix them up in terms of content and formally.

Offended everyone.

Writing in which all kinds of writing mingled seemed, not immoral, but amoral, even to the masses. Played in every playground she found; no one can do that in a class or hierarchichal society.

(In literature classes in university, had learned that anyone can say or write anything about anything if he or she does so cleverly enough. That cleverness, one of the formal rules of good literature, can be a method of social and political manipulation. Decided to use language stupidly.) In order to use and be other voices as stupidly as possible, decided to copy down simply other texts.

Copy them down while, maybe, mashing them up because wasn't going to stop playing in any playground. Because loved wildness.

Having fun with texts is having fun with everything and everyone. Since didn't have one point of view or centralized perspective, was free to find out how texts she used and was worked. In their contexts which were (parts of) culture.

Liked best of all mushing up texts.

Began constructing her first story by placing mashed-up texts by and about Henry Kissinger next to *True Romance* texts. What was the true romance of America? Changed these *True Romance* texts only by heightening the sexual crudity of their style. Into this mush, placed four pages out of Harold Robbins', one of her heroes, newest hottest bestsellers. Had first made Jacqueline Onassis the star of Robbins' text.

Twenty years later, a feminist publishing house republished the last third of the novel in which this mash occurred.

CAPITOL MADE A FEMINIST PUBLISHER DOLL EVEN THOUGH, BECAUSE SHE WASN'T STUPID, SHE KNEW THAT THE FEMINIST PUBLISHING HOUSE WAS ACTUALLY A LOT OF DOLLS. THE FEMINIST PUBLISHER DOLL AS A BEAUTIFUL WOMAN IN ST LAURENT DRESS. CAPITOL, PERHAPS OUT OF PERVERSITY, REFRAINED FROM USING HER USUAL CHEWED UP CHEWING GUM, HALF-DRIED FLECKS OF NAIL POLISH AND BITS OF HER OWN BODY THAT HAD SOMEHOW FALLEN AWAY.

Republished the text containing the Harold Robbins' mush next to a text she had written only seventeen years ago. In this second text, the only one had ever written without glopping up hacking into and rewriting other texts (appropriating), had tried to destroy literature or what she as a writer was supposed to write by making characters and a story that were so stupid as to be almost non-existent. Ostensibly, the second text was a porn book. The pornography was almost as stupid as the story. The female character had her own name.

Thought just after had finished writing this, here is a conventional novel. Perhaps, here is 'my voice.' Now I'll never again have to make up a bourgeois novel.

Didn't.

The feminist publisher informed her that this second text was her most important because here she had written a treatise on female sexuality.

Since didn't believe in arguing with people, wrote an introduction to both books in which stated that her only interest in writing was in copying down other people's texts. Didn't say liked messing them up because was trying to be polite. Like the English. Did say had no interest in sexuality or in any other content.

CAPITOL MADE A DOLL WHO WAS A JOURNALIST. CAPITOL LOVED MAKING DOLLS WHO WERE JOURNALISTS. SOMETIMES SHE MADE THEM OUT OF THE NEWSPAPERS FOUND IN TRASHCANS ON THE STREETS. SHE KNEW THAT LOTS OF CATS INHABITED TRASHCANS. THE PAPERS SAID RATS CARRY DISEASES. SHE MADE THIS JOURNALIST OUT OF THE FINGERNAILS SHE OBTAINED BY HANGING AROUND THE TRASHCANS IN THE BACK LOTS OF LONDON HOSPITALS. HAD PENETRATED THESE BACK LOTS WITH THE HOPE OF MEETING MEAN OLDER MEN BIKERS. FOUND LOTS OF OTHER THINGS THERE. SINCE, TO MAKE THE JOURNALIST, SHE MOLDED THE FINGERNAILS TOGETHER WITH SUPERGLUE AND, BEING A SLOB, LOTS OF OTHER THINGS STUCK TO THIS SUPERGLUE, THE JOURNALIST DIDN'T LOOK ANYTHING LIKE A HUMAN BEING.

A journalist who worked on a trade publishing magazine, so the story went, no one could remember whose story, was informed by another woman in her office that there was a resemblance between a section of the writer's book and Harold Robbins' work. Most of the literati of the country in which the writer was currently living were upper-middle-class and detested the writer and her writing.

CAPITOL THOUGHT ABOUT MAKING A DOLL OF THIS COUNTRY, BUT DECIDED NOT TO.

Journalist decided she had found a scoop. Phoned up the feminist publisher to enquire about plagiarism; perhaps feminist publisher said something wrong because then phoned up Harold Robbins' publisher.

'Surely all art is the result of one's having been in danger, of having gone through an experience all the way to the end, where no one can go any further. The further one goes, the more private, the more personal, the more singular an experience becomes, and the thing one is making is finally, the necessary, irrepressible, and, as nearly as possible, definitive utterance of this singularity . . . Therein lies the enormous aid the work of art brings to the life of the one who must make it . . .

'So we are most definitely called upon to test and try ourselves against the utmost, but probably we are also bound to keep silence regarding this utmost, to beware of sharing it, of parting with it in communication so long as we have not entered the work of art: for the utmost represents nothing other than that singularity in us which no one would or even should understand, and which must enter into the work as such . . .' Rilke to Cézanne.

CAPITOL MADE A PUBLISHER LOOK LIKE SAM PECKINPAH. THOUGH SHE HAD NO IDEA WHAT SAM PECKINPAH LOOKED LIKE. HAD LOOKED LIKE? SHE TOOK A HOWDY DOODY DOLL AND AN ALFRED E. NEUMAN DOLL AND MASHED THEM TOGETHER, THEN MADE THIS CONGLOMERATE INTO AN AMERICAN OFFICER IN THE MEXICAN-AMERICAN WAR. ACTUALLY SEWED, SHE HATED SEWING, OR WHEN SHE BECAME TIRED OF SEWING, GLUED TOGETHER WITH HER OWN TWO HANDS, JUST AS THE EARLY AMERICAN PATRIOT WIVES USED TO DO FOR THEIR PATRIOT HUSBANDS, A FROGGED AND BRAIDED CAVALRY JACKET, STAINED WITH THE BLOOD FROM SOME FORMER OWNERS. THEN FASHIONED A STOVEPIPE HAT OUT OF ONE SHE HAS STOLEN FROM A BUM IN AN ECSTASY OF ART. THE HAT WAS A BIT BIG FOR THE PUBLISHER. INSIDE A GOLD HEART, THERE SHOULD BE A PICTURE OF A WOMAN. SINCE CAPITOL DIDN'T HAVE A PICTURE OF A WOMAN, SHE PUT IN ONE OF HER MOTHER. SINCE SAM PECKINPAH OR HER PUBLISHER HAD SEEN TRAGEDY, AN ARROW HANGING OUT OF THE WHITE BREAST OF A SOLDIER NO OLDER THAN A CHILD, HORSES GONE MAD WALL-EYED MOUTHS FROTHING AMID DUST THICKER THAN THE SMOKE OF GUNS. SHE MADE HIS FACE FULL OF FOLDS, AN EYEPATCH OVER ONE EYE.

Harold Robbins' publisher phoned up the man who ran the company who owned the feminist publishing company. From now on, known as 'The

Boss.' The Boss told Harold Robbins' publisher that they have a plagiarist in their midst.

CAPITOL NO LONGER WANTED TO MAKE DOLLS. IN THE UNITED STATES UPON SEEING THE WORK OF THE PHOTOGRAPHER ROBERT MAPPLETHORPE, SENATOR JESSE HELMS PROPOSED AN AMENDMENT TO THE FISCAL YEAR 1990 INTERIOR AND RELATED AGENCIES BILL FOR THE PURPOSE OF PROHIBITING 'THE USE OF APPROPRIATED FUNDS FOR THE DISSEMINATION, PROMOTION, OR PRODUCTION OF OBSCENE OR INDECENT MATERIALS OR MATERIALS DENIGRATING A PARTICULAR RELIGION.' THREE SPECIFIC CATEGORIES OF UNACCEPTABLE MATERIAL FOLLOWED: '(1) OBSCENE OR INDECENT MATERIALS, INCLUDING BUT NOT LIMITED TO DEPICTIONS OF SADOMASOCHISM, [ALWAYS GET THAT ONE IN FIRST], HOMO-EROTICISM, THE EXPLOITATION OF CHILDREN, OR INDIVIDUALS ENGAGED IN SEX ACTS; OR (2) MATERIAL WHICH DENIGRATES THE OBJECTS OR BELIEFS OF THE ADHERENTS OF A PARTICULAR RELIGION OR NON-RELIGION; OR (3) MATERIAL WHICH DENIGRATES, DEBASES, OR REVILES A PERSON, GROUP, OR CLASS OF CITIZENS ON THE BASIS OF RACE, CREED, SEX, HANDICAP, AGE, OR NATIONAL ORIGIN.' IN HONOR OF JESSE HELMS, CAPITOL MADE, AS PILLOWS, A CROSS AND A VAGINA. SO THE POOR COULD HAVE SOMEWHERE TO SLEEP. SINCE SHE NO LONGER HAD TO MAKE DOLLS OR ART, BECAUSE ART IS DEAD IN THIS CULTURE, SHE SLOPPED THE PILLOWS TOGETHER WITH DEAD FLIES, WHITE FLOUR MOISTENED BY THE BLOOD SHE DREW OUT OF HER SMALLEST FINGERS WITH A PIN, AND OTHER TYPES OF GARBAGE.

Disintegration.

Feminist publisher then informed writer that the Boss and Harold Robbins' publisher had decided, due to her plagiarism, to withdraw the book from publication and to have her sign an apology to Harold Robbins which they had written. This apology would then be published in two major publishing magazines.

Ordinarily polite, told feminist publisher they could do what they wanted with their edition of her books but she wasn't going to apologize to anyone for anything, much less for twenty years of work.

Didn't have to think to herself because every square inch of her knew. For freedom. Writing must be for and must be freedom.

Feminist publisher replied that she knew writer was actually a nice sweet girl.

Asked if should tell her agent or try talking directly to Harold Robbins.

Feminist publisher replied she'd take care of everything. Writer shouldn't contact Harold Robbins because that would make everything worse.

Would, the feminist publisher asked, the writer please compose a statement for the Boss why the writer used other texts when she wrote so that the Boss wouldn't believe that she was a plagiarist.

CAPITOL MADE A DOLL WHO LOOKED EXACTLY LIKE HERSELF. IF YOU PRESSED A BUTTON ON ONE OF THE DOLL'S CUNT LIPS THE DOLL SAID, 'I AM A GOOD LITTLE GIRL AND DO EXACTLY AS I AM TOLD TO DO.'

Wrote:

> Nobody save buzzards. Lots of buzzards here. In the distance, lay flies and piles of shit. Herds of animals move against the skyline like black caravans in an unknown east. Sheep and goats. Another place, a horse is lapping the water of a pool. Lavender and grey trees behind this black water are leafless and spineless. As the day ends, the sun in the east flushes out pale lavenders and pinks, then turns blood red as it turns on itself, becoming a more definitive shape, the more definitive, the bloodier. Until it sits, totally unaware of the rest of the universe, waiting at the edge of a sky that doesn't yet know what colors it wants to be, a hawk waiting for the inevitable onset of human slaughter. The light is fleeing.

Instead, sent a letter to feminist publisher in which said that she composed her texts out of 'real' conversations, anything written down, other texts, somewhat in the ways the Cubists had worked. [Not quite true. But thought this statement understandable.] Cited, as example, her use of True Confessions stories. Such stories whose content seemed purely and narrowly sexual, composed simply for purposes of sexual titillation and economic profit, if deconstructed, viewed in terms of context and genre, became signs of political and social realities. So if the writer or critic (deconstructionist) didn't work with the actual language of these texts, the writer or critic wouldn't be able to uncover the political and social realities involved. For instance, both genre and the habitual nature of perception hide the violence of the content of many newspaper stories.

To uncover this violence is to run the risk of being accused of loving violence or all kinds of pornography. (As if the writer gives a damn about what anyone considers risks.)

Wrote, living art rather than dead art has some connection with passion. Deconstructions of newspaper stories become the living art in a culture that demands that any artistic representation of life be non-violent and non-sexual, misrepresent.

To copy down, to appropriate, to deconstruct other texts is to break down those perceptual habits the culture doesn't want to be broken.

Deconstruction demands not so much plagiarism as breaking into the copyright law.

In the Harold Robbins' text which had used, a rich white woman walks into a disco, picks up a black boy, has sex with him. In the Robbins text, this scene is soft-core porn, has as its purpose mild sexual titillation and pleasure.

[When Robbins' book had been published years ago, the writer's mother had said that Robbins had used Jacqueline Onassis as the model for the rich white woman.] Wrote, had made apparent that bit of politics while amplifying the pulp quality of the style in order to see what would happen when the underlying presuppositions or meanings of Robbins' writing became clear. Robbins as emblematic of a certain part of American culture. What happened was that the sterility of that part of American culture revealed itself. The real pornography. Clichés, especially sexual clichés, are always signs of power or political relationships.

BECAUSE SHE HAD JUST GOTTEN HER PERIOD, CAPITOL MADE A HUGE RED SATIN PILLOW CROSS THEN SMEARED HER BLOOD ALL OVER IT.

Her editor at the feminist publisher said that the Boss had found her explanation 'literary.' Later would be informed that this was a legal, not a literary, matter.

'HERE IT ALL STINKS,' CAPITOL THOUGHT. 'ART IS MAKING ACCORDING TO THE IMAGINATION. HERE, BUYING AND SELLING ARE THE RULES; THE RULES OF COMMODITY HAVE DESTROYED THE IMAGINATION. HERE, THE ONLY ART ALLOWED IS MADE BY POST-CAPITALIST RULES; ART ISN'T MADE ACCORDING TO RULES.' ANGER MAKES YOU WANT TO SUICIDE.

Journalist who broke the 'Harold Robbins story' had been phoning and leaving messages on writer's answer machine for days. Had stopped answering her phone. By chance picked it up; journalist asked her if anything to say.
'You mean about Harold Robbins?'
Silence.
'I've just given my publisher a statement. Perhaps you could read that.'
'Do you have anything to add to it?' As if she was a criminal.
A few days later writer's agent over the phone informed writer what was happening was simply horrible.

CAPITOL DIDN'T WANT TO MAKE ANY DOLLS.

How could the writer be plagiarizing Harold Robbins?
Writer didn't know.
Agent told writer if writer had phoned her immediately, agent could have straightened out everything because she was good friends with Harold Robbins' publisher. But now it was too late.
Writer asked agent if she could do anything.
Agent answered that she'd phone Harold Robbins' publisher and that the worst that could happen is that she'd have to pay a nominal quotation rights fee.
So a few days later was surprised when feminist publisher informed her that if she didn't sign the apology to Harold Robbins which they had written for her, feminist publishing company would go down a drain because

Harold Robbins or Harold Robbins' publisher would slap a half-a-million [dollar? pound?] lawsuit on the feminist publishing house.

Decided she had to take notice of this stupid affair, though her whole life wanted to notice only writing and sex.

'WHAT IS IT?' CAPITOL WROTE, 'TO BE AN ARTIST? WHERE IS THE VALUE THAT WILL KEEP THIS LIFE IN HELL GOING?'

For one of the first times in her life, was deeply scared. Was usually as wild as they come. Doing anything if it felt good. So when succumbed to fear, succumbed to reasonless, almost bottomless fear.

Panicked only because she might be forced to apologize, not to Harold Robbins, that didn't matter, but to anyone for her writing, for what seemed to be her life. Book had already been withdrawn from print. Wasn't that enough? Panicked, phoned her agent without waiting for her agent to phone her.

Agent asked writer if she knew how she stood legally.

Writer replied that as far as knew Harold Robbins had made no written charge. Feminist publisher sometime in beginning had told her they had spoken to a solicitor who had said neither she nor they 'had a leg to stand on.' Since didn't know with what she was being charged, she didn't know what that meant.

Agent replied, 'Perhaps we should talk to a solicitor. Do you know a solicitor?'

Knew the name of a tax solicitor.

Since had no money, asked her American publisher what to do, if he knew a lawyer.

WOULD MAKE NO MORE DOLLS.

American publisher informed her couldn't ask anyone's advice until she knew the charges against her, saw them in writing.

Asked the feminist publisher to send the charges against her and whatever else was in writing to her.

Received two copies of the 'Harold Robbins' text she had written twenty years ago, one copy of the apology she was supposed to sign, and a letter from Harold Robbins' publisher to the head of the feminist publishing company. Letter said they were not seeking damages beyond withdrawal of the book from publication [which had already taken place] and the apology.

Didn't know of what she was guilty.

Later would receive a copy of the letter sent to her feminist publisher from the solicitor whom the feminist publisher and then her agent had consulted. Letter stated: According to the various documents and texts which the feminist publisher had supplied, the writer should apologize to Mr Harold Robbins. First, because in her text she has used a substantial number of Mr Robbins' words. Second, because she did not use any texts other than Mr Robbins' so there could be no literary theory or praxis responsible for her plagiarism. Third, because the contract between the writer and the feminist publisher states that the writer had not infringed upon any existing copyright.

When the writer wrote, not wrote back, to the solicitor that most of the novel in question had been appropriated from other texts, that most of these texts had been in the public domain, that the writers of texts not in public domain were either writers of True Confessions stories (anonymous) or writers who knew she had reworked their texts and felt honored, except for Mr Robbins, that she had never misrepresented nor hidden her usages of other texts, her methods of composition, that there was already a body of literary criticism on her and others' methods of appropriation, and furthermore, [this was to become the major point of contention], that she would not sign the apology because she could not since there was no assurance that all possible litigation and harassment would end with the signature of guilt, guilt which anyway she didn't feel: the solicitor did not reply.

Not knowing of what she was guilty, feeling isolated and pressured to finish her new novel, writer became paranoid. Would do anything to stop the pressure from the feminist publisher and simultaneously would never apologize for her work.

Considered her American publisher her father. Told her the 'Harold Robbins affair' was a joke, she should take her phone off the hook, go to Paris for a few days.

Finish your book. That's what's important.

WOULD MAKE NO MORE DOLLS.

Paris is a beautiful city.

In Paris decided that it's stupid to live in fear. Didn't yet know what to do about isolation. All that matters is work and work must be created in and can't be created in isolation. Remembered a conversation she had had with her feminist publisher. Still trying to explain, writer said, in order to deconstruct, the deconstructionist needs to use the actual other texts. Editor had said she understood. For instance, she was sure, Peter Carey in *Oscar and Lucinda* had used other people's writings in his dialogue, but would never admit it. This writer did what every other writer did, but she is the only one who admits it. 'It's not a matter of not being able to write,' the writer replied. 'It's a matter of a certain theory which is also a literary theory. Theory and belief.' Then shut up because knew that when you have to explain and explain, nothing is understood. Language is dead.

SINCE THERE WERE NO MORE DOLLS, CAPITOL STARTED WRITING LANGUAGE.

Decided that it's stupid living in fear of being forced to be guilty without knowing why you're guilty and, more important, it's stupid caring about what has nothing to do with art. It doesn't really matter whether or not you sign the fucking apology.

Over phone asked the American publisher whether or not it mattered to her past work whether or not signed the apology.

Answered that the sole matter was her work.

Thought alike.

Wanted to ensure that there was no more sloppiness in her work or life, that from now on all her actions served only her writing. Upon return-ing to England, consulted a friend who consulted a solicitor who was his friend about her case. This solicitor advised that since she wasn't guilty of plagiarism and since the law was unclear, grey, about whether or not she had breached Harold Robbins' copyright, it could be a legal precedent, he couldn't advise whether or not she should sign the apology. But must not sign unless, upon signing, received full and final settlement.

Informed her agent that would sign if and only if received full and final settlement upon signing.

Over phone, feminist publisher asked her who had told her about full and final settlement.

A literary solicitor.

Could they, the feminist publishing house, have his name and his statement in writing?

'This is my decision,' writer said. 'That's all you need to know.'

WROTE DOWN 'PRAY FOR US THE DEAD,' THE FIRST LINE IN THE FIRST POEM BY CHARLES OLSON SHE HAD EVER READ WHEN SHE WAS A TEENAGER. ALL THE DOLLS WERE DEAD. DEAD HAIR. WHEN SHE LOOKED UP THIS POEM, ITS FIRST LINE WAS, 'WHAT DOES NOT CHANGE / IS THE WILL TO CHANGE.'

WENT TO A NEARBY CEMETERY AND WITH STICK DOWN IN SAND WROTE THE WORDS 'PRAY FOR US THE DEAD.' THOUGHT, WHO IS DEAD? THE DEAD TREES? WHO IS DEAD? WE LIVE IN SERVICE OF THE SPIRIT. MADE MASS WITH TREES DEAD AND DIRT AND UNDERNEATH HUMANS AS DEAD OR LIVING AS ANY STONE OR WOOD.

I WON'T BURY MY DEAD DOLLS, THOUGHT. I'LL STEP ON THEM AND MASH THEM UP.

For two weeks didn't hear from either her agent or feminist publisher. Could return to finishing her novel.

Thought that threats had died.

In two weeks received a letter from her agent which read something like:

On your express instructions that your publisher communicate to you through me, your publisher has informed me that they have communicated to Harold Robbins your decision that you will sign the apology which his publisher drew up only if you have his assurance that there will be no further harassment or litigation. Because you have requested such assurance, predictably, Harold Robbins is now requiring damages to be paid.

Your publisher now intends to sign and publish the apology to Harold Robbins as soon as possible whether or not you sign it.

In view of what I have discovered about the nature of your various telephone communications to me, please contact me only in writing from now on.

Signature.

Understood that she had lost. Lost more than a struggle about the appropriation of four pages, about the definition of *appropriation*. Lost her belief that there can be art in this culture. Lost spirit. All humans have to die, but they don't have to fail. Fail in all that matters.

It turned out that the whole affair was nothing.

CAPITOL REALIZED THAT SHE HAD FORGOTTEN TO BURY THE WRITER DOLL. SINCE THE SMELL OF DEATH STUNK, RETURNED TO THE CEMETERY TO BURY HER. SHE KICKED OVER A ROCK AND THREW THE DOLL INTO THE HOLE WHICH THE ROCK HAD MADE. CHANTED, 'YOU'RE NOT SELLING ENOUGH BOOKS IN CALIFORNIA. YOU'D BETTER GO THERE IMMEDIATELY. TRY TO GET INTO READING IN ANY BENEFIT YOU CAN SO FIVE MORE BOOKS WILL BE SOLD. YOU HAVE BAGS UNDER YOUR EYES.'

CAPITOL THOUGHT, DEAD DOLL.

SINCE CAPITOL WAS A ROMANTIC, SHE BELIEVED DEATH IS PREFERABLE TO A DEAD LIFE, A LIFE NOT LIVED ACCORDING TO THE DICTATES OF THE SPIRIT.

SINCE SHE WAS THE ONE WHO HAD POWER IN THE DOLL-HUMAN RELATIONSHIP, HER DOLLS WERE ROMANTICS TOO.

Towards the end of paranoia, had told her story to a friend who was secretary to a famous writer.

Informed her that famous writer's first lawyer used to work with Harold Robbins' present lawyer. First lawyer was friends with her American publisher.

Her American publisher asked the lawyer who was his friend to speak privately to Harold Robbins' lawyer.

Later the lawyer told the American publisher that Harold Robbins' lawyer advised to let the matter die quietly. This lawyer himself advised that under no circumstances should the writer sign anything.

It turned out that the whole affair was nothing.

Despite these lawyers' advice, Harold Robbins' publisher and the feminist publisher kept pressing the writer to sign the apology and eventually, as everything becomes nothing, she had to.

Knew that none of the above has anything to do with what matters, writing. Except for the failure of the spirit.

THEY'RE ALL DEAD, CAPITOL THOUGHT. THEIR DOLLS' FLESH IS NOW BECOMING PART OF THE DIRT.

CAPITOL THOUGHT, IS MATTER MOVING THROUGH FORMS DEAD OR ALIVE?

CAPITOL THOUGHT, THEY CAN'T KILL THE SPIRIT.

Elliptical

They just can't seem to . . . They should try harder to . . . They ought to be more . . . We all wish they weren't so . . . They never . . . They always . . . Sometimes they . . . Once in a while they . . . However it is obvious that they . . . Their overall tendency has been . . . The consequences of which have been . . . They don't appear to understand that . . . If only they would make an effort to . . . But we know how difficult it is for them to . . . Many of them remain unaware of . . . Some who should know better simply refuse to . . . Of course, their perspective has been limited by . . . On the other hand, they obviously feel entitled to . . . Certainly we can't forget that they . . . Nor can it be denied that they . . . We know that this has had an enormous impact on their . . . Nevertheless their behavior strikes us as . . . Our interactions unfortunately have been . . .

—Harryette Mullen

Acknowledgments

"What Else" (Part I) of *99: The New Meaning* by Walter Abish (Burning Deck, 1990). Reprinted by permission of Anyart/Burning Deck.

"Dead Doll Humility" from *The Kathy Acker Reader* reprinted by permission of SLL/ Sterling Lord Literistic, Inc. Copyright by Kathy Acker.

"Brownstone" from *Speedboat* by Renata Adler. Copyright © 1976 by Renata Adler. Reprinted by permission of Janklow & Nesbit Associates.

All best efforts have been made to secure permission to reprint "Brooklyn Is" by James Agee. The essay first appeared in the December 1968 issue of *Esquire*.

"The Fight: Patterson vs. Liston" © 1963 was originally published in *Nugget*. Copyright renewed. Collected in *The Cross of Redemption*, published by Pantheon/Vintage Books. Reprinted by arrangement with the James Baldwin Estate.

"Sentence" collected in *Forty Stories* by Donald Barthelme. Copyright © 1987 by Donald Barthelme, used by permission of The Wylie Agency LLC.

"I Remember" from *Collected Writings of Joe Brainard*, edited by Ron Padgett, with an introduction by Paul Auster (The Library of America, 2012). Reprinted by permission. All rights reserved.

"Lecture on Nothing" from *Silence* by John Cage © 1961. Published by Wesleyan University Press and used by permission.

"The Dry Salvages" from *Four Quartets* by T. S. Eliot. Copyright © 1943 by T. S. Eliot and renewed 1971 by Esme Valerie Eliot. Reprinted with the permission of Houghton Mifflin Harcourt Publishing Company.

"The Crack-Up" by F. Scott Fitzgerald, from *The Crack-Up*, copyright © 1945 by New Directions Publishing Corp. Reprinted by permission of New Directions Publishing Corp.

"In the Heart of the Heart of the Country" by William H. Gass. Copyright © 1968 by William H. Gass. Reprinted by permission of Janklow & Nesbit Associates.

"All the Numbers from Numbers" © 2015 by Kenneth Goldsmith. Used with the permission of the author.

A Note about the Title

Because if *fiction* comes from *fictio,* the Latin word for "make," then doesn't that mean that *non-fiction* can only mean "not art," prohibiting the genre from being able to do what every art medium does: *make*?

A Note about the Editor

John D'Agata teaches creative writing at the University of Iowa, where he is the director of the Nonfiction Writing Program.

A Note about the Typography

The text of these essays has been set in Adobe Garamond Pro, a typeface drawn by Robert Slimbach and based on type cut by Claude Garamond in the sixteenth century.

Book design by Wendy Holdman
Composition by Bookmobile Design & Digital Publisher Services, Minneapolis, Minnesota. Manufactured by Friesens on acid-free, 100 percent postconsumer wastepaper.